Handbook of Demonstrations and Activities in the Teaching of Psychology

Second Edition

Volume I

Introductory, Statistics, Research Methods, and History

Edited by

Mark E. Ware
Creighton University

David E. Johnson
John Brown University

LEA
2000

LAWRENCE ERLBAUM ASSOCIATES, PUBLISHERS
Mahwah, New Jersey   **London**

Lawrence Erlbaum Associates, Inc., Publishers
10 Industrial Avenue
Mahwah, New Jersey 07430

Library of Congress Cataloging-in-Publication Data

Handbook of demonstrations and activities in the teaching of psychology / edited by
Mark E. Ware, David E. Johnson.-- 2nd ed.
    p.   cm.
  Includes bibliographical references and index.
  Contents: v. 1. Introductory, statistics, research methods, and history – v. 2.
Physiological-comparative, perception, learning, cognitive, and developmental – v. 3.
Personality, abnormal, clinical-counseling, and social.
  ISBN 0-8058-3048-0 (set : alk. paper) –ISBN 0-8058-3045-6 (v. 1 : alk. paper) –
ISBN 0-8058-3046-4 (v. 2 : alk. paper) – ISBN 0-8058-3047-2 (v. 3 : alk. paper)
    1. Psychology–Study and teaching (Higher) 2. Psychology–Study and teaching–
Activity programs. 3. Psychology–Study and teaching–Simulation methods. 4.
Psychology–Study and teaching–Audio-visual methods. I. Ware, Mark E. II. Johnson,
David E., 1953-

BF77.H265 1999
150'.71'1–dc21
                                                                99-056223

Dedicated to

Charles L. Brewer

teacher, colleague, and friend

Table of Contents

3. Teaching Concepts and Principles

4. Exploring Pedagogical Strategies

Section III: Research Methods

1. Introducing Scientific Thinking

2. Reviewing the Literature

3. Teaching Research Ethics

4. Teaching Research Design and Methods of Observation

5. Working in Groups

6. Presenting Research Results

7. Using Computers

8. Using Popular Media and Scholarly Publications

9. Examining Miscellaneous Issues

Section IV: History

1. Promoting Active Participation

2. Expanding Students' Knowledge

3. Discovering Philosophies of Psychology

Preface

In the preface to this book's first edition, we provided a brief historical context for publishing a collection of teaching demonstrations and activities. Before summarizing those remarks, we would like to point out that an additional motivation for producing a second edition was to document and celebrate the silver anniversary year (1998) of *Teaching of Psychology* (*ToP*), the official journal of the Society for the Teaching of Psychology (STP), Division Two of the American Psychological Association.

Since its inception in 1974, *ToP* has become increasingly respected as a journal devoted to improving teaching and learning at all educational levels. An article (Weimer, 1993) in *Change* featured three from among almost 50 pedagogical journals; *ToP* was one of those three. Readers, who are interested in a history of the journal, will find the founding editor's personal account (Daniel, 1992) both stimulating and informative.

The journal's history was preceded by almost a century of psychologists' interest in teaching. For example, G. Stanley Hall, one of modern psychology's promoters, devoted considerable attention to teaching-learning processes. Hall's (1905) analysis concluded that a goal of pedagogy was to "unfold all the powers of the individual to their maximal maturity and strength" (p. 375). In earlier writing about pedagogy, Hall (1881) commented that "reverence of knowledge for its own sake is superstitious. Ignorance is preferable to knowledge which does not affect life, and the object of discipline is to make it practical" (p. 321). Hall's comments predated more recent writing about active learning.

At the National Conference on Enhancing the Quality of Undergraduate Education in Psychology, one committee discussed the use of pedagogical techniques called active learning. The committee's observation (Mathie, 1993) that "there is too much information being offered to students and too little attention being paid to the strategies for learning, inquiry, and problem solving" (p. 184) seemed to reiterate and operationalize Hall's insight. Thus for over a century, psychologists have recognized that effective teaching and learning consist of developing and applying students' skills. Because effective teaching strategies are never out of vogue, the present book consists of a collection of tried and tested teaching demonstrations and activities.

ToP previously published all of the articles in this book. We reviewed articles published from 1985 through 1998, *ToP*'s silver anniversary year, and excluded from consideration over 100 excellent articles about teaching psychology that were not directly related to the 13 topics in this book. Examples of excluded topics are cross-cultural, sports, and industrial/organizational psychology, as well as psychological testing, human sexuality, psychology and the law, and writing across the curriculum.

We organized 291 articles, the same number as in the first edition, into three volumes. Overall, 56% of the articles did not appear in the first edition. Volume 1 consists of 97 articles about teaching strategies for courses that make up the core of most psychology curricula; introductory psychology, statistics, research methods, and history of psychology. Topical headings in Volumes 2 and 3 reflect the content and order of topics in many introductory psychology texts. Volume 2 consists of 99 articles about teaching physiological-comparative, perception, learning, cognitive, and developmental psychology. Volume 3 consists of 95 articles about teaching personality, abnormal, clinical-counseling, and social psychology. The percent of articles representing each of the 13 topical areas was about evenly distributed. Noteworthy exceptions were the topics of research methods (18%), social (18%), and developmental (13%)

In general, we assigned articles to the course names in which authors developed the demonstration or activity. A table at the end of each volume identifies the primary course in which readers might use each demonstration. For more than half of the articles, we also identified other (secondary) courses in which readers might use demonstrations. For almost 25% of the articles, we identified more than one additional course for using the activity.

A few months before this book was published, psychology educators met in a national forum called Psychology Partnership Project (P3) at James Madison University. In part, the P3's mission was to "identify, establish, and nurture partnerships [promoting] the teaching of psychology . . . ." Several discussion points (e.g., research, curriculum, faculty development, and instructional technology) bear directly on improving pedagogy. P3 participants and contributors to this book share a common commitment to fostering excellence in teaching. In recognition for that commitment, all royalties from the sale of this book will be paid directly to STP and earmarked for promoting the laudable activities of its Fund for Excellence

Mark E. Ware
David E. Johnson

References

Daniel, R. S. (1992). *Teaching of Psychology*, the journal. In A. E. Puente, J. R. Matthews, & C. L. Brewer (Eds.), *Teaching psychology in America: A history* (pp. 433-452). Washington, DC: American Psychological Association.

Hall, G. S. (1881). American and German methods of teaching. *The Harvard Register, 3,* 319-321.

Hall, G. S. (1905). What is pedagogy? *Pedagogical Seminary, 12,* 375-383.

Mathie, V. A. (with Beins, B., Benjamin, Jr., L. T., Ewing, M. M., Hall, C. C. I., Henderson, B., McAdam, D. W., & Smith, R. A.). (1993). Promoting active learning in psychology courses. In T. V. McGovern (Ed.). *Handbook for enhancing undergraduate education in psychology* (pp. 183-214). Washington, DC: American Psychological Association.

Weimer, M. (1993, November-December). The disciplinary journals on pedagogy. *Change,* 44-51.

SECTION I:
INTRODUCTORY

Promoting Active Learning and Discussion

In an attempt to involve students actively in learning, Richard Wesp asked groups of students in upper-division courses to design and implement an out-of-class activity or demonstration for the introductory class. The advanced students implemented their projects with small groups of introductory students. The instructor distributed the introductory students' reactions to the advanced students. Both groups of students reaped benefits from the exercise.

To make the introductory psychology course more personally relevant to students, William Buskist and Devin Wylie asked students to provide a short answer to the question, "What one thing in your life, if you could change it today, would have the most immediate and profound positive impact in your life?" After compiling and categorizing the students' anonymous responses, the instructors presented them to the class by gender and descending order of frequency. The responses provided discussion points throughout the semester.

Timothy Osberg described Festinger and Carlsmith's classic cognitive dissonance study to students in an introductory psychology course and asked them to predict the outcome of the study. Most of the students failed to predict the outcome correctly because of its counterintuitive results. This presentation provided a powerful demonstration that psychology is not just common sense. The technique is a good opening gambit for stimulating lively discussion and capturing students' interest.

Michael Renner and Scott Mackin developed the College Undergraduate Stress Scale that had greater relevance to college students than most previously developed scales. They advocated the use of this scale when discussing stress in such courses as introductory and health psychology.

Learning Psychological Terminology

Thomas Brothen and Janet Schneider developed computer software that introductory psychology students used to study for their final exam. Brothen and Schneider modified previously published Top 100 terms or concepts in psychology to match the presentation in their textbook. Students tested the efficacy of their study by attempting to match the terms or concepts with the definitions in their text. Preliminary data suggested that this exercise enhanced students' learning of the material.

Russell Carney and Joel Levin made learning new terminology more manageable by developing mnemonic strategies. They used the mnemonic keyword method that involved selecting a keyword that was acoustically similar to the term to remember, followed by the formation of a mental image of the keyword interacting with the meaning of the term. Carney and Levin found evidence that supported the procedure over traditional repetition. They suggested that this method could be used for a variety of topics and courses.

Introducing Research and Scientific Thinking

John Bates told his introductory psychology students that he had telepathic powers and demonstrated these "psychic" abilities by transmitting images into the minds of students and a confederate. Students generated alternative hypotheses to account for the observed phenomena and suggested ways to test their hypotheses. This article describes how to perform the psychic acts and outlines the hypothesis-testing activity. The demonstration encourages greater scientific skepticism and promotes enthusiastic class participation.

Roger Ward and Anthony Grasha employed astrology as a vehicle to teach valuable lessons about research methods. Students chose the personality profile that they believed most closely matched their own from a set of descriptions corresponding to the purported characteristics of persons born under the signs of the zodiac. The students' success in selecting their personality profiles provided an engaging method to introduce research issues such as hypotheses development, statistical significance, and social desirability.

Robert Reinehr introduced students to personality test validation as well as situational effects on personality by asking them to rate his personality on the scales of the 16 PF. He compared student responses with his own self-ratings and his actual scores on the test. In addition to learning about the concept of validity, students discussion in class improved as did their performance on papers and exams.

Thomas Fish and Ian Fraser asked introductory students to complete a science fair project. Students had considerable latitude in choice of topic and presented their projects to their classmates for practice. Subsequently, students presented their projects in a fair atmosphere attended by over 1,000 people, including high school and university students and faculty. The authors surveyed upper-level students who completed science fair projects and students who did not complete a project. Science fair participants believed that the experience prepared them for future course work and increased their learning of the material.

Neil Lutsky promoted active learning among his students by having them develop a research idea from computerized analyses of previously collected data. After developing a research idea, students identified the basic statistical procedures required to analyze data, performed the data analysis according to a script using a computer statistical package, wrote summaries of the project, and critically evaluated the results. In addition to experiencing the research process first-hand, students gained a greater appreciation for the intricacies of doing research.

In a writing assignment for the introductory psychology course, Karen Gareis had students find and read an empirical article cited in their textbook. They then summarized and critiqued the article, related it to course material, and compared it with their textbook's presentation of the research. Students reported that the assignment helped them learn about psychological research and specific course topics, encouraged critical thinking, and was interesting. The instructor gained detailed information about studies described in the textbook, including any discrepancies between the textbook and the primary source.

Bernardo Carducci designed an in-class exercise to teach basic principles of survey methodology and make students more aware of the pervasiveness of and potential problems associated with shyness in college students. After the students completed a short survey on shyness, the instructor presented a summary of the results to the class as part of an introductory lecture on survey methodology. The instructor also discussed the causes and consequences of shyness in college students and suggested readings to help students overcome their shyness.

In an attempt to sensitize introductory psychology students to ethical issues in research, Celia Fisher and Tara Kuther developed six case study modules. They compiled a workbook that contained abstracts of the studies, detailed descriptions of the experiments, and homework assignments. Students who used the ethics modules identified ethical issues and considered moral ambiguities better than students who received standard instruction. Students also indicated that the instruction increased their interest in research ethics.

Using Supplemental Readings

Drew Appleby identified over 400 articles from *Psychology Today* that had relevance to a wide variety of undergraduate majors and careers. He organized the articles into categories that represented the diversity of students in his introductory psychology course (e.g., premed and theology) and allowed them to write extra credit reports on the articles they read. Students not only responded well to the articles but also found the list to be useful for projects in courses outside of psychology.

1. PROMOTING ACTIVE LEARNING AND DISCUSSION

Conducting Introductory Psychology Activity Modules as a Requirement in Advanced Undergraduate Courses

Richard Wesp
Elmira College

One way of providing more personalized attention in large introductory psychology classes is through small-group activities, such as lab exercises or discussion groups (Benjamin, 1991). Typically, undergraduate teaching assistants (TAs) conduct these sessions. For example, Kohn and Brill (1981) described a low-cost, introductory level psychology lab run by students.

Kohn and Brill's approach was unusual in having minimal faculty involvement, but the authors identified this as one of the weak points of their procedure. More typically, faculty take an active role in training TAs and coordinating the small-group activities, requiring more of the instructor's time (Benjamin, 1991). Mendenhall and Burr (1983) required weekly meetings with TAs who served as small-group discussion leaders. In my experience, weekly meetings are the minimum required to ensure course quality, consistency, and coherence. When more diverse activities are offered, additional individual meetings are likely required.

Thus, instructor time is a limiting factor in using TAs. The time can be reduced, however, if students from an instructor's advanced courses serve as TAs. Because TAs benefit from their teaching experience (Mendenhall & Burr, 1983), students in advanced courses should see similar benefits, justifying their participation.

Cooperative arrangements between classes have been used before. For example, Anderson, Gundersen, Banken, Halvorson, and Schmutte (1989) had undergraduate students in abnormal psychology serve as "clients" for graduate counseling students and reported that the experience was beneficial to both groups. Wagor (1990) required students in a Sensation and Perception course to construct a demonstration of a sensory or perceptual phenomenon. Students donated their projects for use in other classes. The technique described herein extends Wagor's idea by having the advanced students conduct their demonstrations for introductory students and grade the introductory students' papers.

Method

Small groups of 2 to 5 students in three upper level courses designed, implemented, and evaluated projects that actively involved introductory students in a topic related to one that the upper level students were studying. This project was in addition to other required activities in these otherwise traditionally taught courses. Twenty–three students in Experimental Methods and 21 students in Biofeedback and Self Control worked with 33 students in one Introductory Psychology class during one semester. In a second semester, 29 students in Behavior Therapy worked with two introductory classes of 36 students each.

On introducing the assignment to the upper level students, I described several possible activities, such as a field trip to a local psychiatric center and computer simulations. I told students that projects should engage 5 to 15 introductory students, take about 1 hr outside of participants' scheduled class, have no significant costs, and require a written assignment in which the introductory students would summarize and react to the activity. Each group submitted a description and a critical evaluation of its project. These teaching projects were worth 5% of each upper level student's grade. Students in the Introductory Psychology classes were required to participate in two of the available activities. I described each activity, announced when it would be scheduled, and circulated a sign-up sheet. After participating, introductory students wrote their papers, which I collected and passed on to the upper level students who graded them and provided written comments. Each activity was worth 5% of the course grade and was evaluated on a pass-fail basis.

Results and Conclusions

The upper level students developed activities for progressive relaxation, simple lie detection, basic biofeedback, a field trip to a local psychiatric center, a research study on alcohol use, operant conditioning with rats, and systematic desensitization. Students spent from 1 to 2 weeks identifying and planning their activity. Although some activities required more than 1 hr, the remaining criteria (active participation, small groups, low cost, and a written assignment) were met for all of the projects.

In evaluating their projects, all groups of upper level students suggested that the assignment was a valuable experience and should be required in the future. Comments included that introductory students seemed to react well to seeing other undergraduates teach, that projects should be worth a larger portion of the course grade, and that they learned course material better because they were required to apply it. Their written descriptions of the projects suggested that the students had developed a good understanding of the concepts they presented.

In two of the introductory classes, 81% of enrolled students completed written evaluations. Of these respondents, 86% indicated that having out-of-class activities was valuable and should be done again, and 90% reported that they liked having other students teach them. Students also rated how much each project increased their understanding of the material covered. On scale ranging from *very little* (1) to *very much* (7), the mean ratings ranged from 3.5 for the relaxation exercise to 5.8 for the biofeedback project; the overall average was 4. 7. These ratings seemed low, considering that 86% of the students suggested that projects be offered in future introductory courses. Ratings may have been lower than expected because the projects offered new information that did not relate directly to the exam questions.

Although the procedure took slightly more time than I typically spend on individual activities in the introductory class, there were several benefits. One was that the time I spent helping advanced students design their projects I would normally have spent in meetings with TAs or conducting the demonstrations. Given that the introductory students enjoyed having upper level students teach them, it seems that little was lost in not having me conduct the projects. Possibly the most valuable outcome was that the upper level students were able to apply some of the skills and knowledge they had learned in their courses.

Moreover, many students in the upper level classes might never have had the time or inclination to serve as TAs. Requiring students to work in groups allowed the less self-confident and less skillful students to conduct successful projects. Finally, the procedure provided introductory students with a wider variety of options as well as several new activities that I had never offered.

References

Anderson, D. D., Gundersen, C. B., Banken, D. M., Halvorson, J. V., & Schmutte, D. (1989). Undergraduate role players as "clients" for graduate counseling students. *Teaching of Psychology, 16,* 141-142.

Benjamin, L. T., Jr. (1991). Personalization and active learning in the large introductory psychology class. *Teaching of Psychology, 18,* 68-74.

Kohn, A., & Brill, M. (1981). An introductory demonstration laboratory produced entirely by undergraduates. *Teaching of Psychology, 8,* 133-138.

Mendenhall, M., & Burr, W. R. (1983). Enlarging the role of the undergraduate teaching assistant. *Teaching of Psychology, 10,* 184-185.

Wagor, W. F. (1990). Using student projects to acquire demonstrations for the classroom and laboratory. *Teaching of Psychology, 17,* 253-255.

Note

I gratefully acknowledge suggestions made by Ruth Ault and three anonymous reviewers.

A Method for Enhancing Student Interest in Large Introductory Classes

William Buskist
Devin Wylie
Auburn University

Although students generally prefer small classes over large classes (Gleason, 1986; McKeachie, 1994), many introductory college courses enroll large numbers of students. The problem is a familiar one: Smaller classes offer a more personalized atmosphere, whereas larger classes are more economical and offer an opportunity for a few extraordinary teachers to influence large numbers of students. Because college enrollment remains high and colleges and universities generally do not have enough faculty to teach small classes, large classes, especially at the introductory level, seem to be here to stay.

What faculty need in this situation is an effective way of recreating the small classroom atmosphere in large classrooms (Benjamin, 1991). According to Herr (1989), involved students usually learn material better than uninvolved students. Involving students in course activities in small classes is easier in part because of the instructor's familiarity with the students and relative logistical ease.

Student-teacher rapport also is essential to the learning environment (Herr, 1989). Classroom discussion allows students and the instructor to build two-way relationships and open channels for further communication. This relationship helps personalize the class for the students. Herr suggested that instructors may increase rapport in their classes by (a) holding personal conferences with students to increase communication and produce a more relaxed atmosphere in and out of the classroom, (b) showing interest in students by being alert to changes in their classroom behavior, (c) using relationships established from previous classes to show interest in students' background and progress, and (d) showing enthusiasm for the topic being taught.

If instructors know students' names, they can call on specific students to answer questions. According to Chism (1989) and Herr (1989), coming to class early and staying after class to answer specific questions or to chat with students are also good ways for instructors to get to know their students and to make them feel individually recognized.

According to Benjamin (1991), the most important variables involved in teaching large classes are the students' attitudes toward the topic, the students' attitudes toward the instructor, and the teaching method used. To improve teaching technique, an instructor may seek new interactive exercises to engage students in the learning process. One suggestion given by Benjamin is the use of an autobiographical questionnaire, which students complete early in the term. In Benjamin's words,

> I ask them to list their hometown, year in college, and major. I ask them why they are taking the course and what they hope to get out of it. ... I ask them about their job (if they work) and about what they like to do when they are not being students. I also ask them if there is anything they would like to ask me or anything else they would like for me to know about them. (p. 69)

Incorporating the information gathered from this type of exercise into the class allows students to see how their responses compare to those of others in the class. These data are unique in that they apply specifically to the students in the class and may reveal interesting information about the students themselves.

Perhaps a more efficient means of involving students in the class is to ask more focused questions that address specific, relevant topics of high interest to students. The

instructor may then incorporate students' answers throughout the term in contexts applicable to the presentation of corresponding psychological principles or theory. The remainder of this article describes such a method.

At the beginning of a recent term, 605 Auburn University students in three sections of an introductory psychology course responded in writing to the following question: "What one thing in your life, if you could change it today, would have the most immediate and profound positive impact in your life?" This question developed out of one-to-one conversations with students in previous sections of the course who were interested in the relevance of psychology to their lives. The intent of using the question in class is to motivate students to think about how the topics in the course might apply to them and how they might use course content for self-improvement.

Just prior to posing this question, we project a copy of the following instructions on a large screen and read them aloud to the class:

> In a few minutes, you will have the chance to participate in a class project worth one extra credit point toward your final grade in this course. Your participation is entirely voluntary. Right now we are passing out an "informed consent form," which explains what the project involves, how the information we collect about you may be used, and what your rights are as a participant in this project. In brief, this project involves your anonymous answer to a single question: "What one thing in your life, if you could change it today, would have the most immediate and profound positive impact in your life". We are interested in your responses to this question because they help us to develop ways to make the class more interesting and relevant to what you may be experiencing in your lives. If, after reading this form, you decide you would like to participate, please sign on the appropriate line. If you do not wish to participate, please do not sign it. If you have any questions about this exercise or your participation in it, do not hesitate to ask them now.

Once all the forms are collected, we project a copy of the question on the screen along with instructions not to place any identifying information on their responses and to limit their responses to three to five words. We also read the question and the instructions aloud. Next, we give students 3 or 4 min to respond. We then collect the answers and later that same day categorize them according to problem or issue type, such as low self-esteem, financial concerns, emotional adjustment, and so on. (The categories often change from term to term and depend wholly on student responses; we do not use pre-established categories into which we attempt to force student responses.) During the next class period, we list students' responses in decreasing order of frequency and according to gender. This presentation has two effects. First, it allows students to become aware of the types of issues that their peers are confronting, many of which are similar to issues that they themselves are facing. Second, it demonstrates similarities and differences in how men and women respond to this question. For example, women generally stress religion and spiritual concerns more, and men usually stress issues related to grades more. Throughout the remainder of the term, we refer to students' responses to the question when discussing relevant concepts and issues (i.e., self-esteem, stress, attitude behavior correspondence, and self-control).

An analysis of student responses this term to this question revealed, in decreasing order, that the most prevalent concerns among female students were exercising more and losing weight (19%), increasing self-esteem and outgoingness (19%), studying more and procrastinating less (14%), becoming more spiritual or religious (11%), and developing a more positive attitude about others and life (7%). Among men, the chief concerns were (in decreasing order) studying more and procrastinating less (23%), increasing self-esteem and outgoingness (21%), exercising more and losing weight (9%), developing a more positive attitude about others and life (5%), and becoming more spiritual or religious (5%). Many students are surprised that so many men reported they have self-esteem problems. We point out that this reaction is typical of the stereotypes many people hold about differences between men and women.

Personal issues and concerns, such as those expressed by students responding to the question that we posed to them, fit easily into classroom lectures and provide fertile ground for discussion. In addition to those topics alluded to earlier, we make explicit attempts to address many of these concerns. Following are several general examples:

1. Motivation (What psychological variables may prevent students from making important changes in their lives?)
2. Learning (What environmental variables may prevent students from accomplishing such changes and how might students control these variables to produce such changes?)
3. Development (To what extent does the ability to make such life changes reflect social and emotional maturity?)
4. Personality and intelligence (How is success in later life related to the changes students currently wish to make in their lives and how are these changes related to personality variables and intelligence?)
5. Stress and coping (How is failure to make such changes a source of stress and what are the best coping strategies to deal with such failure?)

In short, there is no shortage of ways in which we integrate students' responses to our question into class discussions about basic psychological principles and theory. In fact, we developed several of our course lectures (e.g., those covering self-control, stress and coping, and mental health and physical well-being) specifically from student responses to the question.

Fortunately, students rarely mention serious psychological problems in their responses. However, this exercise does seem to make some students feel comfortable in discussing their responses with us during office hours, which sometimes leads to discussion of more serious problems, such as extremely high anxiety, depression, or abuse. In such cases, we do two things. First, when a student begins to disclose information about a personal problem, such as alcohol or drug abuse, we immediately, but gently, tell him aor her that it is beyond our roles as teachers to serve as counselors in such matters. Second, we refer the student to the appropriate counseling services on campus.

Because student responses to this question may change from term to term, the value of this exercise rests in the technique itself and not the particular data set it generates. Once we pose the question and present student responses to the class, students begin to feel more comfortable talking about everyday issues related to course content. For example, they often raise questions regarding strategies for intervention for certain problems and ask for written sources that they may consult. We, too, follow up our original question by asking related questions over the course of the term. Of course, our questions depend on specific issues that students identified in their responses to the original question. For example, we ask students to describe how the theories and methods of self-control described in the text might apply to those students who said that they would like to exert more control over their diet, exercise, or time-management regimens. The class then offers suggestions for developing a specific plan, based on course content, that these students might consider as an intervention. When necessary, we offer modifications and elaboration of students' suggestions to make them conform to empirically tested psychological principles and strategies.

Many teachers of introductory psychology believe that their course should show their students how psychology can be applied to important issues in their students' everyday lives. We have described a technique-involving one simple question by which teachers may make direct contact with issues of concern to students, become sensitive to what is happening in their students' lives, demonstrate psychology's relevance in addressing these issues, and increase student interest in their course. Our students respond enthusiastically to this approach with other questions and comments and appreciate its insightful contributions to their personal development.

References

Benjamin, L. T., Jr. (1991). Personalization and active learning in the large introductory psychology class. *Teaching of Psychology, 18,* 68-74.

Chism, N. V. (1989). *Large enrollment classes: Necessary evil or not necessary evil?* (Rep. No. 20444-361). Columbus: Ohio State University, Center for Teaching

Excellence. (ERIC Document Reproduction Service No. ED 334 875)

Herr, K. U. (1989). *Improving teaching and leaning in large classes: A practical manual* (revised) . Fort Collins: Colorado State University, Office of the Instructional Services. (ERIC Document Reproduction Service No. ED 3 12 2 15)

Gleason, M. (1986). Better communication in large courses. *College Teaching, 34*, 20-24.

McKeachie, W. J. (1994) . *Teaching tips: A guidebook for the beginning college teacher* (9th ed.). Lexington, MA: Heath

Notes

1. Portions of this article were presented by the first author at the l9th Annual National Institute on the Teaching of Psychology, St. Petersburg Beach, FL, January 1997.
2. The authors wish to thank Charles L. Brewer, Randolph A. Smith, and several anonymous reviewers for their helpful comments in revising earlier versions of this manuscript.

Psychology is Not Just Common Sense: An Introductory Psychology Demonstration

Timothy M. Osberg
Niagara University

Numerous researchers have studied the misconceptions that students bring with them to the introductory psychology course. Beginning with the work of McKeachie (1960) and Vaughan (1977) through more recent studies (e.g., Brown, 1983, 1984; Gardner & Dalsing, 1986; Gardner & Hund, 1983; Gutman, 1979; Ruble, 1986), the nature and correlates of misconceptions and the influence that introductory psychology has on them have been examined. Al though the specific nature of students' misconceptions has been inconsistent across some of these studies (Griggs & Ransdell, 1987), one point is not disputed: Students do bring misconceptions to the first course.

Many of my introductory psychology students believe that psychology is nothing more than common sense and that, therefore, the course will be easy. Countless times, in interviews with students who have failed the first course exam, I have heard the lament: "I should have studied harder! I assumed the course would be easy because psychology is just common sense!" Students taking introductory courses in other disciplines, such as chemistry, English, or accounting, seem less inclined to take the content of those courses for granted.

I developed a demonstration that curbs this misconception. During the first or second week, I simply describe one of psychology's classic experiments and then ask students to guess its outcome. Because the vast majority of the class guesses an intuitive outcome, students are surprised by the actual, counterintuitive findings. Thus, they learn early in the term that psychology is not just common sense.

I chose Festinger and Carlsmith's (1959) classic study of cognitive dissonance because I thought that it would be an engaging example and that most students would be surprised by its counterintuitive findings. Other studies could be substituted, depending on the personal inclination of the instructor.

Procedure

The demonstration takes about 10 to 15 min. The issue of intuitiveness should not be discussed before conducting the demonstration. After defining psychology and its subfields and describing the history of the discipline, and as a transition into a discussion of research methods, I engage the students in the following task:

Suppose you had volunteered to participate in a psychology experiment on campus. Upon arrival, you were seated at a table and asked to undertake a series of dull, meaningless tasks for about an hour. Afterward, the experimenter convinced you to extol the virtues of the tasks you had performed by describing them to other potential participants as highly worthwhile, interesting, and educational.

You were paid either $1 or $20 to do this. Suppose you were then asked to privately rate your enjoyment of the tasks on a questionnaire.

I then pose the following question:

After which amount do you believe your actual enjoyment rating of the tasks would be higher—$1 or $20?

Responses can be obtained by show of hands or by having students hand in their written responses for tabulation. Students will nearly unanimously indicate the $20 payment, in line with their intuition, often expressing wonder at why you asked the question. At this point, the class is given feedback about their collective responses. This feedback heightens the effect of the demonstration once students are told the true outcome of the study. Finally, the class is told that Festinger and Carlsmith (1959) found that students who received $1 rated the tasks as more enjoyable than those paid $20. The authors used the concept of cognitive dissonance to explain this finding. The students who received $1 presumably had insufficient justification for their behavior, which led to dissonance that produced a change in attitude about the tasks.

Evaluation

Evaluative data from the most recent time I used this demonstration (the fall semester of 1991) suggest it achieved its aim and that students were very engaged by it. The students in this sample were drawn from two sections of introductory psychology at a small northeastern university of approximately 2,000 students. They had declared a variety of majors in the arts and sciences, business, education, and nursing. Eighty-one of the 86 students (94.2%) gave the intuitive $20 answer. Much lively discussion followed when the true findings of the experiment were revealed. Therefore, Festinger and Carlsmith's (1959) study serves well as research with counterintuitive findings.

The questionnaire to evaluate the demonstration included five items. Two open-ended items asked students to indicate what they found useful about the demonstration and to provide any additional comments about it. Three closed-ended questions assessed students' perceptions of the overall usefulness of the demonstration, their ratings of whether or not it helped them understand that psychology is not just common sense, and their recommendations concerning the future use of the demonstration.

Because 3 students failed to return their evaluation questionnaires, the data here are based on the responses of 83 students. When asked to rate the overall usefulness of the demonstration, 87.9% rated it as either *useful* or *very useful* (56.6% and 31.3%, respectively). The demonstration was rated as *somewhat useful* by 12.1% of the students, with none rating it as *not useful*. When asked if the demonstration helped them to understand that not all of psychology's findings simply reflect common sense, 97.6% either *agreed* or *strongly agreed* (57.8% and 39.8%, respectively) and only 2.4% *disagreed* or *strongly disagreed* (1.2% and 1.2%, respectively). When asked if they recommended using the demonstration in future classes, 83.1% said *yes, definitely*; 16.9% said *maybe*; and no one said *no*. Students' open-ended comments included: "It showed me we can't always rely on intuition." "It really helped prove your point that psychology is not just common sense." "It helped me to understand that I must study in order to do well in this course because it is not just common sense but can involve surprising results." "You could have told us 'psychology does not mirror common sense' and I probably would have forgotten it. I won't forget it now." Thus, the demonstration forcefully drives home the point that psychology does not merely verify the obvious. The demonstration is a good opening gambit for the introductory course because it stimulates lively discussion and captures students' interest.

References

Brown, L. T. (1983). Some more misconceptions about psychology among introductory psychology students. *Teaching of Psychology, 10,* 207-210.

Brown, L. T. (1984). Misconceptions about psychology aren't always what they seem. *Teaching of Psychology, 11,* 75-78.

Festinger, L., & Carlsmith, J. M. (1959). Cognitive consequences of forced compliance. *Journal of Abnormal and Social Psychology, 58,* 203-210.

Gardner, R. M., & Dalsing, S. (1986). Misconceptions about psychology among college students. *Teaching of Psychology 13,* 32-34.

Gardner, R. M., & Hund, R. M. (1983). Misconceptions of psychology among academicians. *Teaching of Psychology, 10,* 20-22.

Griggs, R. A., & Ransdell, S. E. (1987). Misconceptions tests or misconceived tests? *Teaching of Psychology, 14,* 210-214.

Gutman, A. (1979). Misconceptions of psychology and performance in the introductory course. *Teaching of Psychology, 6,* 159-161.

McKeachie, W. J. (1960). Changes in scores on the Northwestern Misconceptions Test in six elementary psychology courses. *Journal of Educational Psychology, 51,* 240-244.

Ruble, R. (1986). Ambiguous psychological misconceptions. *Teaching of Psychology, 13,* 34-36.

Vaughan, E. D. (1977). Misconceptions about psychology among introductory psychology students. *Teaching of Psychology, 4,* 138-141.

A Life Stress Instrument for Classroom Use

Michael J. Renner
R. Scott Mackin
West Chester University

Most introductory psychology textbooks discuss the Holmes and Rahe (1967) approach to stress and its effect on health, and many texts include Holmes and Rahe's Social Readjustment Rating Scale (SRRS) instrument, which generates stress scores as *life change units*. Although students seem willing to entertain the possibility that stressors can affect their health, the teaching process is sometimes impaired by the actual SRRS instrument. The SRRS does not include many common events that act as stressors affecting traditional age college students (e.g., final examinations). It also includes many items that are not meaningful to the typical entry-level college student or that have lost their meaning because of the nearly 30 years that have passed since the original research (e.g., "mortgage over $10,000"). This article describes a similar instrument, which is intended for classroom use in teaching these concepts. Finally, we offer a local set of norms to illustrate the types of scores generated by this instrument and to aid in planning its effective classroom use.

Development of the Instrument

We gave the College Life Stress Inventory, included in the *Instructor's Manual To Accompany Kalat's Psychology* (Kohn, 1993), to a large general psychology class. At the same time, students received Holmes and Rahe's (1967) original instrument. We asked students to suggest additional items. The instructions also asked students to indicate which of the described events had happened to them within the past 12 months. We collected these responses and condensed them into a draft form, with the goal that the instrument would include major and minor stressors affecting contemporary college students. In two subsequent semesters, we revised the resulting item list through an iterative process. In each semester, we added items and revised and deleted others based on student suggestions and frequency of occurrence. We eliminated items describing infrequent events that were not among the most stressful events on the list. In some cases we combined descriptions of two or more specific events into single, more general items.

The final version of the scale included 51 items, as shown in Table 1. We made two attempts to develop and assign relative stress values using an anchoring method. This method, however, produced inconsistent scaling. In addition, it was clear from student questions that they did not fully understand the task we had asked them to perform. Finally, we gave the list of items to 149 general psychology students who had not previously seen any form of the instrument and asked them to rate each item using a Likert scale ranging from 1 (*not at all stressful*) to 7 (*extremely stressful*). We used two forms of the scale, with items in alphabetical and reverse alphabetical order. We ordered the items by mean ratings and scaled their stress values so that the most stressful item had a stress value of 100.

Empirical Evidence and Local Norms

We named the resulting instrument the College Undergraduate Stress Scale (CUSS). We administered the CUSS to 257 students in three sections of an Introductory Psychology course. The participants were students at a state-assisted comprehensive university of approximately 12,000 students in the eastern United States. Students ranged in age from 17 to 45 ($M = 19.75$, Mdn = 19, 90th percentile = 22). Approximately two-thirds of the participants were women (160 women, 79 men; 18 did not report their gender), which reflects recent enrollment patterns for this course.

The three sections of the course did not differ significantly in mean total stress scores, $F(2, 256) < 1$, so we pooled the data for these sections. The mean total stress rating was 1247 ($SD = 441$). Scores ranged from 182 to 2571.

There was a small but significant negative correlation between stress score and age ($r = 4.175$, $p = .007$). Although female students were significantly more stressed than male students, $t(237) = 2.24$, $p = .026$, this may be an artifact.

Table 1
College Life Stress Inventory

Copy the "stress rating" number into the last column for any item that has happened to you in the last year, then add these.

Event	Stress Ratings	Your Items
Being raped	100	
Finding out that you are HIV-positive	100	
Being accused of rape	98	
Death of a close friend	97	
Death of a close family member	96	
Contracting a sexually transmitted disease (other than AIDS)	94	
Concerns about being pregnant	91	
Finals week	90	
Concerns about your partner being pregnant	90	
Oversleeping for an exam	89	
Flunking a class	89	
Having a boyfriend or girlfriend cheat on you	85	
Ending a steady dating relationship	85	
Serious illness in a close friend or family member	85	
Financial difficulties	84	
Writing a major term paper	83	
Being caught cheating on a test	83	
Drunk driving	82	
Sense of overload in school or work	82	
Two exams in one day	80	
Cheating on your boyfriend or girlfriend	77	
Getting married	76	
Negative consequences of drinking or drug use	75	
Depression or crisis in your best friend	73	
Difficulties with parents	73	
Talking in front of a class	72	
Lack of sleep	69	
Change in housing situation (hassles, moves)	69	
Competing or performing in public	69	
Getting in a physical fight	66	
Difficulties with a roommate	66	
Job changes (applying, new job, work hassles)	65	
Declaring a major or concerns about future plans	65	
A class you hate	62	
Drinking or use of drugs	61	
Confrontations with professors	60	
Starting a new semester	58	
Going on a first date	57	
Registration	55	
Maintaining a steady dating relationship	55	
Commuting to campus or work, or both	54	
Peer pressures	53	
Being away from home for the first time	53	
Getting sick	52	
Concerns about your appearance	52	
Getting straight A's	51	
A difficult class that you love	48	
Making new friends; getting along with friends	47	
Fraternity or Sorority rush	47	
Falling asleep in class	40	
Attending an athletic event (e.g., football game)	20	
Total		

Items that cause stress for female students may be overrepresented or may be assigned excessive weight in the instrument because most of the students in sections used for item development and scaling of the instrument were women.

Discussion

We developed a questionnaire instrument illustrating life stress and its cumulative nature using events that are likely to be familiar to traditional age college students and using data from students concerning the relative perceived stressfulness of these events. We have used it successfully as a demonstration, as have several colleagues. In the classroom, we distribute copies of the instrument while presenting the topic of health psychology and stress. We explain that it may give students a personally relevant way to understand the SRRS and the research literature on life stress. After students have had time to complete the instrument and total their personal score, we show students the local norms (reported earlier) and offer general guidelines on interpreting individual scores based on these values. Although we have not gathered systematic data on students' reactions to the scale, student comments have been both frequent and uniformly positive, most often variations on the theme of "*now* I understand that stuff!"

Although we have provided a set of approximate norms for the CUSS, local circumstances and the characteristics of the student population would probably influence these norms. Instructors who use the instrument should gather data at the institution where they use the instrument.

References

Holmes, T. H., & Rahe, R. H. (1967) . The social readjustment rating scale. *Journal of Psychosomatic Research, 11,* 213-218.

Kohn, A. (1993). *Instructor's manual to accompany Kalat's Psychology* (2nd ed.). Belmont, CA: Wadsworth.

Notes

1. R. Scott Mackin is now at Pennsylvania State University.
2. A preliminary version of the instrument was presented at the second annual American Psychological Society Institute on the Teaching of Psychology, New York, June   1995.

2. LEARNING PSYCHOLOGICAL TERMINOLOGY

A Computerized Application of Psychology's Top 100

Thomas Brothen
Janet Schneider
University of Minnesota

Boneau (1990) asked 250 psychology textbook authors to indicate which terms were most important in each of 10 subareas of psychology. The responses from 159 authors produced 10 lists of 100 terms. In addition, the most highly rated items formed what Boneau referred to as psychology's Top 100 terms and concepts. Boneau suggested that all "literate" psychology students should know them, but he emphasized the tentative nature of his work and asked, "Where do we go from here?" (p. 900).

Alternative Uses

The Top 100 list can serve various purposes. First, it could be used to evaluate psychology instruction. If students are not being taught the Top 100 terms and concepts, course content or textbooks could be adjusted. Second, the list could be used by instructors to judge how closely their course content matches what other psychologists consider crucial in an area of study. Third, the list could be used to help students learn psychology (e.g., instructors could incorporate it into a statement of leaning objectives, or students could use it as a summary of what they should know for the final examination).

The latter purpose motivated us to adapt the Top 100 list as a computer exercise for students studying for the final examination in introductory psychology. The need for the exercise arose from our observations that students have difficulty simply remembering and understanding a basic core of psychological knowledge by the end of a 10-week quarter. Our approach deals primarily with a basic stage in the learning process (see Gronlund, 1970); however, students need this type of review to achieve higher cognitive levels. Our evaluation is preliminary because our immediate goal was to create software that stimulated studying behavior.

Program Development

For our purposes, Boneau's (1990) list required editing because several of the terms and concepts were not in the course textbook (Gerow, 1989) or were presented in

a slightly different form. Thus, we adapted the list in two ways to create our own Top 100 list.

First, 19 terms were replaced with the next highest rated term from the same subarea list if the replacement terms were not already used and if they were covered in our textbook. Terms were replaced because they simply were not covered (e.g., *visual angle* was replaced with *cone*) or, in our judgement, overlapped too much with other terms on the list. For example, we kept *binocular depth cues* but replaced *depth perception* and *visual depth perception*.

Second, minor wording changes were made in 13 terms to reflect textbook usage. For example, *avoidance learning* was changed to *avoidance conditioning*, *associationism* to *behaviorism*, and *longitudinal research* to *longitudinal method*.

After compiling a final list, we abstracted each term. We avoided using only definitions by capturing the text's main point about the term. We used phrasing directly from the text wherever possible to create descriptions similar to multiple-choice questions. For example, we created the following descriptions. For the term *behaviorism*: "A study of what people do; Skinner followed Watson's lead and studied the relationships between responses and consequences." For *hypothesis*: "A scientist formulates this tentative proposition and then tests it in a way which leads to its confirmation or rejection."

Then we developed a computer exercise to give students feedback on their knowledge of the Top 100 terms. We incorporated it into existing practice exercises programmed in Pilot, a programming language similar to BASIC (Barker, 1987). The resulting package enabled students to take practice quizzes on individual chapters, take a practice final examination consisting of 100 items similar to those in the actual final examination, or complete the Top 100 exercise.

Student Use

Students used the program in the classroom in which they take their introductory psychology course on a computer network (Brothen, 1991). The classroom contains 40 networked computers on which students do all their in-class work. We handed out the Top 100 list (available from the authors) during the last week of classes and told students that 159 textbook authors rated those terms as the 100 most important to know. We also stressed that knowing the terms would not guarantee a high final exam grade but would give them a good knowledge base in psychology.

The computer classroom was open for students to do any of the three practice exercises during final examination week. All students had at least three "open lab" days available for study before their final exam. The practice quizzes and practice final simply presented items in random order and reported the number correct to students once they finished. The Top 100 exercise randomly presented our 100 abstracted descriptions one at a time without replacement. After reading each description, students examined the list of 100 terms, selected the correct match, and then entered it. After typing an answer, they were told if it was correct and had the options of continuing, seeing the textbook page number for the term before trying again (after an incorrect answer), or quitting. When they quit, the computer told them how many terms they attempted, how many tries they took to answer them, and how many they got correct overall. Their goal was to repeat the exercise until they answered all 100 terms correctly in one try each (i.e., when scores equal 100 terms, 100 total tries, 100 correct).

Evaluation

Of 124 students who finished the course, 92 used the Top 100 exercise at least once. We and our classroom assistants informally observed and talked with students doing the exercise. Students said that the exercise was difficult, but they agreed that the list contained information that they should know and that the computer provided valuable feedback on their study progress.

We also explored whether there were any differences between those who used the exercise and those who did not. Students using the Top 100 exercise at least once scored higher on the 100-point final examination ($M = 57.5$) than students not using the exercise ($M = 54.9$), but the difference was not statistically significant, $t(122) = 1.21$, $p = .22$. There was, however, a statistically significant relation between the number of times they used the exercise ($M = 1.08$) and their final exam scores, $r = .23$, $p = .011$. This was not true for the number of times 103 students used the practice final ($M = 1.24$), $r = .10$, n. s.

Partialing out the relation between the practice final and final exam score in a multivariate analysis helps clarify these relations. We used the number of times students took the practice final in a multiple regression analysis to predict final exam scores. Then we added the number of times students did the Top 100 exercise to the regression equation. We found no effect for the practice final, $F(2, 121) = .006$, n.s., but a significant effect for the Top 100 exercise, $F(2, 121) = 5.22$, $p = .024$, was discovered.

These analyses suggest that use of the Top 100 exercise promoted learning (as reflected by final exam scores). An alternative explanation that students with higher motivation used the exercise but got higher scores for other reasons is mitigated by the lack of relation between practice final use and final exam scores.

We cannot say with certainty that the Top 100 exercise contributes significantly to learning about psychology. Nevertheless, individual students indicated to us that it helped them. They reported that the exercise was more difficult than practice exams because it required them to study the material more in order to do well on it. Also, tentative data indicate that students who used the exercise benefitted from it. From an instructional perspective, we know that the content of the exercise is important and that feedback is crucial to learning. Our observations indicate that the exercise promotes active learning (Schomberg, 1986) by forcing students to consult their books and think before answering. These are useful student behaviors; any exercise that increases them is beneficial.

References

Barker, P. (1987). *Authoring languages for CAL*. London: Macmillan.

Boneau, C. A. (1990). Psychological literacy: A first approximation. *American Psychologist, 45*, 891-900.

Brothen, T. (1991). Implementing a computer-assisted cooperative learning model for introductory psychology. *Teaching of Psychology, 18*, 183-185.

Gerow, J. (1989). *Psychology: An introduction* (2nd ed.). Glenview, IL: Scott-Foresman.

Gronlund, N. (1970). *Stating behavioral objectives for classroom instruction*. London: Collier-Macmillan.

Schomberg, S. (1986). *Strategies for active teaching and learning in university classrooms*. Minneapolis: University of Minnesota Communication Services.

Note

An earlier version of this article was presented at the annual meeting of the American Psychological Association, San Francisco, August 1991.

Coming to Terms With the Keyword Method in Introductory Psychology: A "Neuromnemonic" Example

Russell N. Carney
Southwest Missouri State University
Joel R. Levin
Department of Educational Psychology
University of Wisconsin

As in many survey courses, introductory psychology presents extensive new terminology to beginning students—a lexicon that may prove difficult to master. A potential solution to such memory difficulties lies in the use of the mnemonic (memory-enhancing) keyword method. Although the technique is applicable to a variety of paired-as-sociate learning tasks (e.g., Levin, 1993), textbook examples have historically focused on the acquisition of foreign vocabulary (Atkinson, 1975). Hence, students and instructors may not readily see the relevance of the keyword method for learning new terms in psychology. Our goal is to help make that connection.

In the central nervous system, for example, the medulla is that part of the brain that controls such functions as heartbeat and respiration. To apply the keyword method, one first recodes the term *medulla* into an acoustically similar and concrete keyword, such as *medal*. Then, *medal* and the *effects of the medulla* are made to interact in an image. For example, imagine that a runner has just won a race. *Breathing heavily* and with his *heart pounding*, he bends to have a *medal* hung round his neck. With the information encoded in this manner, the retrieval path is as follows: *Medulla* cues *medal*; *medal* cues the interactive image of the heart-pounding, out-of-breath medal winner; and the image brings back the medulla's functions, controlling such things as heartbeat and respiration. Table 1 shows examples of the keyword method applied to terminology related to the central nervous system. We developed a complete set of "neuromnemonic" materials for use in an introductory psychology course at a metropolitan community college.

We then conducted an experiment to provide empirical evidence regarding the effectiveness of these materials. Participants were undergraduates enrolled in educational psychology classes who had just completed a separate experiment that involved learning foreign vocabulary words using the keyword method (Carney &

Levin, in press). In that experiment, random assignment was used to place students in one of the same three study strategy conditions included here: repetition, keyword, or keyword plus image. A 6-min "your strategy" section in the study booklets provided described their study strategy along with five practice items. Following study of 24 foreign vocabulary-words, students took a test to see how many definitions they could remember. To examine delayed recall, we also tested students 2 and 5 days later. This experiment took place immediately following the second delayed test of the prior experiment. Because students kept the same condition assignment for this experiment, study booklets simply directed students to use the same strategy as before, only this time applying it to terms in psychology. Students in the prior experiment were directed not to discuss the experiment with others until the conclusion of the study. In effect, the prior experiment may be viewed as brief training in students' use of their respective study techniques.

Method

Participants and Design

Ninety-one undergraduates (19 men, 72 women) participated in the experiment. Repetition students studied by saying each psychology term and its meaning over and over to themselves. Using provided keywords ("word clues"), key word students associated terms and their meanings through an image of their own making. Keyword plus image students additionally used experimenter-provided verbal descriptions of images that related keywords and meanings. The participants were upper-class students enrolled in educational psychology classes, and they received extra credit for their participation. Although the students may have studied such terms in first-year

17

Table 1. Example Neuromnemonic Study Materials for the Keyword Plus Image Condition

Term	Keyword	Meaning	Your Mental Picture
Medulla	Medal	Controls heart rate, respiration, and blood pressure	Imagine the winner of a race. *Heart pounding* and *breathing* heavily, a *medal* (medulla) is hung round the winner's neck.
Pituitary glands	Pit	Regulates growth	Imagine a young child down in a *pit* (pituitary). The child *grows* and *grows* (growth) until he's big enough to climb out!
Reticular formation	Retickle	Attention	Imagine *tickling* someone to get her *attention*. Then, she loses interest again so you have to *retickle* (reticular) her!
Parasympathetic nervous system	Parachute	Calms the body	Imagine the peace and *calming* effect of watching a *parachute* (parasympathetic) drift slowly downward.
Sympathetic nervous system	Symphony	Excites the body	Imagine a *symphony* (sympathetic) playing loudly in the room next door! The music *excites* you and you can't sit still.
Cerebellum	Cereal bell	Facilitates movement	Imagine someone hearing the *cereal bell* (cerebellum). That's the signal to *move* to the breakfast table and begin *moving* the cereal to his mouth (movement) with his spoon.
Thalamus	Thermos	Relay station for incoming information	Imagine a *relay* race. The first runner hands a *thermos* (thalamus), instead of a baton, to the next runner.

introductory psychology, these terms were not part of their educational psychology curriculum, and the use of random assignment is sufficient to argue for comparable groups with respect to students' prior knowledge.

Materials and Procedure

On entering the classroom, students received a study booklet corresponding to one of the three conditions. In Part I, a generic introduction directed students to use their same strategy "to associate psychology terms and their meanings" and to proceed through their study booklet in a manner similar to the procedure in the previous study. Part II represented a familiarization stage for repetition students. Here, a tape recording paced students through a list of 18 psychological terms by sounding a tone at 10-sec intervals. Simultaneously, this tape recording paced students in both mnemonic conditions through a list of the 18 terms and their corresponding keywords. Part III presented a review page, where students reviewed their respective strategies and a recording paced them through two final practice items to give them a feel for the 20-sec intervals. They were now ready for the actual study section.

This time, a tape recording paced students through the 18 terms and their meanings at 20-sec intervals. Repetition students studied the 18 items using repetition. Students in the keyword condition studied the 18 items using the provided keywords and images of their own making. Additionally, students in the keyword plus image condition used experimenter-provided images relating the keywords to the meanings (e.g., see Table 1). Following this and a 2-min filler task (i.e., an unrelated crossword puzzle), students completed a definition matching test on the 18 terms. Students in the two mnemonic conditions also wrote down the corresponding keywords. Next, students turned the page to complete a test consisting of 10 multiple-choice application items (e.g., "The loss of physical

coordination and balance is most likely to result from damage to the: A. hypothalamus B. cerebellum C. corpus callosum D. amygdala."). We permitted the students to refer back to their definition-matching responses when taking the application test. The application questions were representative relevant items selected from the ancillary test materials accompanying an introductory psychology text (Myers, 1993). Our goal in selecting these 10 items was to measure students' higher order learning, as reflected by their ability to go beyond the information given and apply the just-learned terms (e.g., Levin & Levin, 1990).

Results

Definition Matching

A one-way ANOVA yielded statistical differences among the three conditions in students' mean definitions matching performance, $F(2, 88) = 14.41$, $p < .001$. Subsequent Fisher LSD comparisons based on $\alpha = .05$ revealed sizable non chance differences between the means for both mnemonic conditions (91% and 90%, for keyword and keyword plus image, respectively) and the repetition condition (72%, resulting in an effect size of more than 1 within-conditions standard deviation in each case), with no mean difference between the two mnemonic variations.

Application

A similar one-way ANOVA on the multiple-choice application test produced statistically parallel, though educationally weaker, effects, $F(2, 87) = 3.97$, $p < .025$. Again, both of the mnemonic conditions (77% and 78%) statistically surpassed the repetition condition (65%), but by a smaller margin on this measure (by about 0.6 of a within-group standard deviation in each case).

Discussion and Educational Implications

Our simple experiment demonstrates that the keyword method can help students "come to terms" with new terminology in psychology. For example, on the definition-matching test, students using a mnemonic approach statistically outperformed those using a repetition approach. Likewise, on a multiple-choice test that tapped concept application, the same statistical mnemonic advantage was present. This latter finding is important in that it underscores the notion that using a mnemonic strategy can lead to something more than verbatim fact recall. Furthermore, the success of the students in the keyword condition suggests that only terms, keywords, and meanings need be provided (i.e., interactive images can be left to the student's own making).

We recommend that psychology instructors both describe the keyword method to their students and then go on to provide course-related mnemonic study materials such as those listed in Table 1. Applying the method to the learning of these terms should not only facilitate the acquisition of new terminology, but also help to convince the students of the potency and personal relevance of mnemonic techniques (Carney, Levin, & Levin, 1994).

References

Atkinson, R. C. (1975). Mnemotechnics in second-language learning. *American Psychologist, 30,* 821-828.

Carney, R. N., & Levin, J. R. (in press). Do mnemonic memories fade as time goes by?: Here's looking anew! *Contemporary Educational Psychology.*

Carney, R. N., Levin, J. R., & Levin, M. E. (1994). Enhancing the psychology of memory by enhancing memory of psychology. *Teaching of Psychology, 21,* 171-174.

Levin, J. R. (1993). Mnemonic strategies and classroom learning: A 20-year report card. *Elementary School Journal, 94,* 235-244.

Levin, M. E., & Levin, I. R. (1990). Scientific mnemonomies: Methods for maximizing more than memory. *American Educational Research Journal, 27,* 301-321.

Myers, D. G. (1993). *Exploring psychology* (2nd ed.). New York: Worth.

Notes

1. This experiment was presented at the 1996 annual meeting of the American Educational Research Association. We are grateful to Mary E. Levin and Christine M. Cook for her assistance with this project.

2. Correspondence for neuromnemonic study materials and multiple-choice application questions, should be sent to Russell N. Carney, Department of Psychology, Southwest Missouri State University, Springfield, MO 65804; e-mail: rnc201f@mail.smsu.edu.

3. INTRODUCING RESEARCH AND SCIENTIFIC THINKING

Teaching Hypothesis Testing by Debunking a Demonstration of Telepathy

John A. Bates
Department of Educational Foundations & Curriculum
Georgia Southern University

Many postsecondary educators are concerned about the rising tide of pseudoscientific, fundamentally anti-intellectual belief among otherwise well educated Americans. Bates (1987) reported that nearly half of a large sample of teacher education students believed that the full moon causes violent behavior. Feder (1986) found that more than one third of the students at a northeastern state university believed that ghosts are real. Miller (1987) conducted a national survey indicating that nearly two fifths of college graduates believe that the earth has been visited by aliens from other planets .

Educators combat student misbeliefs by debunking pseudoscientific claims specific to their own disciplines (e.g., Eve & Harrold, 1986; Harrold & Eve, 1986; Hoffmaster, 1986). These efforts have met with modest success: Some have demonstrated increased factual knowledge about reality without much corresponding decrease in pseudoscientific beliefs (Harrold & Eve, 1986); others have reported significant gains in scientific skepticism, but only for students with a neutral position on pseudoscientific claims (Banziger, 1983). Only a few reported attempts (notably, Gray, 1984) have demonstrated significant long-term changes in students' beliefs across a broad range of paranormal and irrational claims.

The classroom exercise described here holds some promise as a technique to debunk a specific pseudoscientific claim and to promote critical, scientific inquiry into psychological phenomena in general. An important goal of this exercise was to capture and hold students' attention. As Hoffmaster (1986) noted, "one of the driest subjects on earth to try to teach is the scientific method" (p. 432). The key to this goal, I believed, was to be found in the application of some basic principles of psychological arousal theory and of stage magic.

Format of the Activity

The Students

The activity was conducted in two different classrooms of introductory psychology. Both classrooms included about 35 students, all first-semester freshmen, about two thirds of whom were women.

The Lesson

All aspects of the activity were identical for both classrooms and proceeded in four stages.

Introductory information. The first 30 min of a class meeting was used to discuss some basic concepts of science. Initial consideration was given to the scientific belief in a physical reality that is independent of any observer. Special emphasis was given to the formulation of empirical hypotheses, in contrast to other sorts of answers to questions. Finally, it was pointed out that scientific hypotheses must be stated in such a way that evidence could be obtained to demonstrate that they are false, if they really are false. The lecture component of the presentation concluded with the assertion that all scientific endeavors, including scientific psychology, are not attempts to establish absolute truth, but rather are attempts to expose and eliminate false claims about the nature of reality.

Demonstration of psychic ability. After completing the lecture component, I announced that I had discovered a talent for transferring my thoughts telepathically into the minds of other people. I offered to demonstrate my talent, but said that it was not yet refined, so I could not guarantee that everyone would receive exactly the right thought.

I told the class that I would think of a two-digit number from 1 to 50, such that both numbers would be odd and different from each other. As examples, I told them that the number could not be something like 11, but that 15 would be okay. After a moment, I wrote a number on my tablet, drew a line through it, wrote another, and commented that the second number seemed to be a better choice. Next, I stared at the number and announced that I was transmitting it to the class. Each student was to write down the first number that came to mind and that fit my description.

As soon as all students had written a number, I asked if any of them had chosen 37. To their surprise, about one third of the students had thought of that number. I looked disappointed, then asked whether any had chosen 35. I showed them my tablet and explained that I had written 35 first, then crossed it out. Some of the class thus might have picked up the wrong signal. I asked how many of them had thought of either 35 or 37, and more than half the class raised their hands.

I suggested that numbers do not always work for everyone; sometimes, a picture is better. Therefore, I told them that I would think of two simple geometric shapes, one inside the other. At this point, I drew something quickly on the tablet, grumbled about being sloppy, tore off the page, and drew something else. I informed the class that I was sending the image of the two shapes, and I asked them to draw what first came to their minds. After a moment, I held up the tablet for all to see the shapes of a triangle completely circumscribed by a circle. Again, about one third of the class indicated that they had drawn the same picture.

I asked whether any had drawn a circle inside a triangle, explaining that the images sometimes become reversed in the transmission. Another third raised their hands. I then showed them the drawing that I had rejected—one of a square not fully surrounded by a circle—and asked if anyone inadvertently had picked up a stray signal of it. Several more hands went up. Then, one student volunteered that she had put a triangle inside a square. I asked whether anyone else had received parts of both signals. By now, nearly everyone had raised a hand.

Finally, I told them we had with us a guest who shared with me an almost perfect psychic link. The guest, another member of my department, was introduced. I explained that our special mental relationship was best demonstrated by a simple playing-card guessing game. A volunteer shuffled a standard deck of cards and dealt three rows of five cards each, face up, on the table at the front of the room. My partner faced the back of the room, and I asked one of the students to point to one of the cards. When the student did, my partner turned around, and I proceeded to point to an apparently random sequence of the cards, saying after each, "Is it this one?" or "Is it that one?" Each time I did not point to the target card, my partner replied negatively. When, after five or six repetitions of this procedure, I finally pointed at the target, my partner quickly responded affirmatively.

Small-group generation of hypotheses. Several repetitions yielded successful detection of the target card. Students who were still skeptical of my ability were challenged to develop a more parsimonious account of what they had observed. Students organized into groups of three or four and tried to produce at least two different testable hypotheses that could answer the question, "How did he do that?"

Hypothesis testing/revision. At the beginning of the next class meeting, students again organized into their groups, and a single, one-page worksheet requiring several

categories of responses was distributed to each group. Students first were asked to summarize their observations of the psychic phenomena, to generate at least two alternative empirical hypotheses to account for their observations, and to design a test that could falsify each hypothesis. Thirty min were allotted for this part of the activity.

Next, my colleague and I made ourselves available for hypothesis testing. The groups took turns specifying a set of conditions under which the playing card "thought transfer" should occur. To ensure all groups sufficient time to test their hypotheses, I informed the class that if I knew it would be impossible to perform the transfer under a given set of conditions, then I would tell them so, rather than taking the time to demonstrate it.

The most common hypotheses involved either some prearranged number of cards to which I would point before reaching the target card or some mathematical formula involving the numerical values of the target and other cards. These were quickly rejected when the groups discovered that they could specify when in a sequence I should point to the target, and my colleague still would be able to identify it. The next most common hypotheses involved where on a card my finger was when I pointed to it. These were rejected when I varied the part touched or when I was not permitted to touch the card, which had no effect on the outcome.

Once all groups had tested both hypotheses once, they were given the opportunity either to retest what seemed to be the better of the two or to test a modified or new hypothesis. Most groups rejected all versions of numerical or positional hypotheses and focused on the modification of what I said to my partner or the tone or volume of my voice.

Within about 20 min, one or two groups were certain that they had determined the correct explanation for the phenomena, so I invited one of the members to take the place of my partner to see if the outcome could be duplicated. It was to their considerable delight, as well as to the consternation of some of their classmates, when these students were able to identify the target card.

Hypothesis testing, revision, and retesting continued until 15 min remained in the class period. Time was provided for the completion of the worksheet, including discussions of test outcomes, modifications of hypotheses, and final conclusions regarding my "special ability." As the students turned in their assignments and filed out, many of them looked at me with knowing smiles, some appeared less than sure of themselves, but nearly all were commenting to each other about what had occurred, using words like *falsified, replicate,* and *empirical.*

Postscript: How the Psychic Deeds Were Done

There were three components to the psychic demonstration, all supposedly involving the transference of thoughts from one mind into one or more other minds. The first two—transference of a number and transference of a shape—are illusions commonly performed by stage mentalists like Kreskin and may be thought of as the hook to capture student attention. Procedures for performing these feats are discussed in detail by Marks and Kammann (1980) in their critical analysis of claims of psychic ability.

Number transference and shape transference rely on poorly understood but documented and reliable population stereotypes in the construction of various categories of thought. As you recall, the demonstration involved the mental transference of a two-digit number between 1 and 50, such that both digits were odd and different from each other. Generally, few people realize that the qualifications placed on number selection have severely reduced the possible choices. There are only eight numbers that satisfy all the criteria: 13, 15, 17, 19, 31, 35, 37, and 39. Furthermore, the instructions were clarified by adding that the number could not be 11, but that something like 15 would be acceptable. Using 15 as an example of an acceptable target guarantees that virtually no one will select it, thus reducing the number of likely choices to seven. Marks and Kammann (1980) found that about 33% of a sample of adults think of 37 as the target number and that another 25% select 35. Thus, by claiming to have chosen first one then the other of these numbers as I was performing the thought transference, I was able to include nearly 60% of the class in my set of successes.

Most college students probably could discover that the limited number of possible targets made the outcome far less dramatic than it first appeared. It is important, therefore, to move on immediately to another, different demonstration of psychic ability-the transfer of an image of two simple geometric shapes, one inside the other. Population stereotypes for shape selection are as strong as those for number selection. Marks and Kammann reported that 33% will draw a combination of a triangle and a circle, 25% will draw a combination of a square and a circle, and 11% will combine triangle with square. With a little showmanship, I demonstrated to about 70% of my students that I had indeed transferred my thoughts into their minds.

The central component of the entire demonstration was the card-selection routine that my colleague and I enacted. To perform this illusion, cards are arranged randomly in three rows; the number of cards in each row is irrelevant. The confederate for this task needs only to remember that the top and bottom rows will be the *this* rows and the middle row will be the *that* row. If the "mentalist" points to a card and uses the correct adjective for that row of cards, then it is not the target card. The mentalist is pointing to the target only when the incorrect modifier is used.

For example, assume that the target card was in the middle row. I might point successively to cards in the top row, the middle row, and the bottom row, before pointing to the target. I would ask, "Is it *this* one?," "Is it *that* one?," and "Is it *this* one?," respectively. My partner would respond, with varying degrees of apparent certainty, that none of those was the target. Finally, I would point to the target and ask, "Is it *this* one?" My partner quickly would be able to respond correctly.

This routine has several advantages as an event for which students must generate empirical hypotheses. First, it is easy to do: My colleague only had about 1 min of instruction before we entered the classroom for our performance, and he never made a mistake. Second, very few students are likely to be familiar with it. Third, the trick behind the event seems to be obvious but it is not. The unexpected difficulty that students experience in trying to explain what they have observed tends to arouse and maintain their curiosity. Most important, for its use in a classroom, the demonstration and its underlying causes are empirical events. Students can directly manipulate the variables of the demonstration and observe a variety of outcomes. Hypotheses can be tested quickly, modified, or rejected, without special equipment or training. Best of all, when students uncover the solution to their problem and are able to replicate the event as evidence of their success, they experience the same sort of satisfaction felt by scientific psychologists in their systematic study of human behavior.

An important goal of this activity is to capture student attention. I have been teaching undergraduate students the basic principles of science for about 12 years and do not recall ever having achieved the enthusiastic class participation that is maintained throughout the demonstration of my psychic powers. Whether this enthusiasm is due entirely to the mode of presentation of the lesson or to some combination of environmental and student factors, I cannot say. My experience suggests that incorporating novel, surprising, and varied (i.e., psychologically arousing) stimuli is essential if students are going to pay attention to the abstract concepts and philosophical issues central to scientific inquiry. This lesson incorporates such stimuli and captures student attention.

References

Banziger, G. (1983). Normalizing the paranormal: Short-term and long-term change in belief in the paranormal among older learners during a short course. *Teaching of Psychology, 10,* 212-214.

Bates, J. A. (1987). Degrees of scientific literacy and intellectualism among students in a college of education. *The Foundations Monthly Newsletter, 4,* 7-9.

Eve, R. A., & Harrold, F. B. (1986). Creationism, cult archaeology, and other pseudoscientific beliefs: A study of college students. *Youth and Society, 17,* 396-421.

Feder, K. L. (1986). The challenge of pseudoscience. *Journal of College Science Teaching, 26,* 180-186.

Gray, T. (1984). University course reduces belief in paranormal. *The Skeptical Inquirer, 8,* 247-251.

Harrold, F. B., & Eve, R. A. (1986). Noah's ark and ancient astronauts: Pseudoscientific beliefs about the past among a sample of college students. *The Skeptical Inquirer, 11*, 61-75.

Hoffmaster, S. (1986). Pseudoscience: Teaching by counter example. *Journal of College Science Teaching, 26*, 432-436.

Marks, D., & Kammann, R. (1980*). The psychology of the psychic*. Buffalo: Prometheus Books.

Miller, J. D. (1987, June). The scientifically illiterate. *American Demographics*, pp. 26-31.

Note

I thank Leigh Culpepper for his help in preparing this article.

Using Astrology to Teach Research Methods to Introductory Psychology Students

Roger A. Ward
Anthony F. Grasha
University of Cincinnati

Teaching the principles of research methodology to introductory psychology students is not an easy task. Such students are interested in learning about human behavior but are seldom enthusiastic about learning research methodology. We use a classroom exercise to test several assumptions of astrology in order to capture their interest and to introduce them to concerns psychologists face in doing research. The following activity is based on a "quasiexperimental" design and can be used to illustrate several concepts: differences between science and nonscience, the scientific method, the role of theory in developing and testing hypotheses, making comparisons among groups, probability and statistical significance, biases in self-report data, the identification of the dependent variable, and how empirical research leads to accurate information about the world.

Flow of Classroom Activity

Introduction to Activity

Students are asked whether they know anything about astrology and if they know their astrological sign. An informal poll of the class is taken. Individuals who do not know their zodiac sign are given a copy of the morning newspaper to refer to. Those individuals in class who are familiar with astrology are asked to suggest the assumptions they think astrologists make about human behavior. Student comments are listed on the blackboard. Student responses generally focus on how astrologists believe that the position of the stars and planets help to determine our personalities and behavior. This introduction usually takes about 10 min.

Generating a Hypothesis

A brief (10 to 15 min) explanation of the nature of science, nonscience, and the scientific method is presented. In particular, the role of theory and hypothesis testing in scientific research is emphasized. Students are then placed in small groups for 10 min and asked to generate a hypothesis based on an assumption they believe astrologists make about human behavior. The class is polled and ideas for hypotheses are listed on the blackboard. The student responses give the instructor an opportunity to mention that hypotheses should be testable and that a research study should allow them to be disconfirmed. Problems with a couple of the hypotheses that students generate are mentioned.

If students have not suggested it, we raise a hypothesis based on an assumption of astrologists that our personalities are associated with certain zodiac signs. The class is then asked to accept the challenge of testing whether this is accurate, and in the process, to learn a little more about gathering and interpreting data.

Table 1. Two Examples of Personality Profiles

Profile for Aries	
Impulsive	Intolerant
Courageous	Quick-tempered
Independent	Arrogant
Domineering	Blunt

Profile for Taurus	
Patient	Self-indulgent
Conservative	Stubborn
Domestic	Possessive
Sensual	Materialistic

The Personality Profiles

Students receive a set of six personality profiles based on personality traits that astrologers believe people with certain zodiac signs possess (cf. March & McEvans, 1982). Each set of profiles was formed by dividing the astrological year in half. Thus, students born between March 21 and September 22 receive the six sets of traits appropriate for that period and those born after September 22 and before March 21 receive the second set of profiles. Students are given 6 instead of 12 profiles to save time, to make the task more manageable, and to illustrate a potential flaw in the design when the data are later analyzed. A sample of two of the personality descriptions appear in Table 1 (and a complete list can be obtained from the authors upon request).

Instructions Given to Students

Students are asked to select the personality profile that best describes them and to mark the letter code corresponding to that profile on a separate sheet of paper. They are told to read each profile carefully and not to accept or reject a particular profile on the basis of one or two traits. Instead, they are asked to concentrate on the overall personality pattern when making a decision.

Data Analysis

After students make their choices, the correct zodiac signs for each letter code are placed on the board. Students are asked to indicate whether they correctly or incorrectly chose their zodiac sign. The number of correct and incorrect choices for each zodiac sign is then listed. We examine the data in several ways to illustrate points about data analysis and interpretation.

We note that the number of correct and incorrect responses are the dependent variable and mention that if the hypothesis is accurate, then the number of correct choices should exceed the number of incorrect choices. We explain that under ideal conditions there should be no incorrect responses.

Next, we begin to modify this simplistic way of examining the data by introducing the concepts of chance responding, probability, and statistical significance.

Because everyone responded to six personality profiles, we explain that people have a one in six chance of selecting a correct profile on the basis of chance. Thus, on the basis of chance, correct choices should account for 16.6% and incorrect choices for 83.4% of the choices. The extent to which the observed data differ from these figures is noted. At this point we mention that giving everyone only 6 profiles from which to select is a potential flaw in the procedure, and that having 12 profiles would make it more difficult to select the correct profile by chance.

In addition, the concept of statistical significance is raised by having students focus on the number of correct zodiac identifications and those we expected to see occur by chance. We explain that it is important to be sure that any differences favoring astrology are not due to chance. We then note that certain statistical procedures can help us to do this. To illustrate the latter point, we use the chi-square test to analyze the overall number of correct and incorrect responses against what one would expect based on chance. Chi-square is quickly computed using a calculator programmed to do the test. A brief explanation of what it suggests is given. It is important to note that we do not teach students the intricate details of the chi-square test. The test is only used as an example of how a statistical procedure can help determine whether an event exceeds chance expectancy.

After testing for statistical significance, additional complications in interpreting research data are raised. For example, students are told that our procedure assumes people know what they are like and can accurately select personality profiles that describe themselves. We suggest that this is not always the case and is one of the reasons psychologists use objective personality inventories to determine differences among people. We also point out that individuals may select a given personality profile because it is much more flattering and/or socially acceptable, or because they are familiar with astrology and thus know what profile they should pick. Thus, the biases in self-report data like social acceptability, personal validation, and self-fulfilling prophecies can be pointed out.

We also indicate that if certain personality profiles are more popular, and if the subject pool is composed mainly of people who were born under those zodiac signs, an incorrect conclusion about the validity of astrology can be drawn. The latter point is a good way to introduce students to the idea that the level of chance responding may underestimate the popularity of each zodiac sign. This latter point allows a discussion of how such problems are handled by random selection of subjects or by randomly selecting as participants an equal number of people with each zodiac sign.

Specific biases present in selecting zodiac signs in the activity are shown by counting how many people correctly and incorrectly selected a particular zodiac sign as most like them. Our data analyses reveal that certain profiles are more socially acceptable than others. Profiles for Taurus, Leo, Libra, Pisces, and Sagittarius are selected 2 to 3 times more often than those of other zodiac signs. As one would expect, more people correctly selected the popular zodiac signs. We use the latter data to show students that correct selections are due to the popularity of certain personality descriptions and are not evidence for the validity of astrology. The latter analysis is beneficial because there have been times when the mix of birthdates in the class produced results that suggested people were selecting correct zodiac signs at a rate that was statistically significant.

Amount of Time for Activity

Depending upon how much time is allocated to each of the phases, the activity as previously outlined takes about 75 min to complete. We have run it in a 50-min session by shortening the introduction to the activity, not mentioning the distinction between science and nonscience, and not placing students in small groups to generate hypotheses. In the latter case, we have introduced astrology, indicated several of the assumptions it makes, and suggested a hypothesis that could be tested in class. The general manner in which a hypothesis is tested is noted and the other phases of the demonstration are conducted as already presented.

Prior Preparation of Students

What to emphasize and how much time to spend depends in part on what information students have had in previous class sessions and textbook assignments. We typically use this activity after the students have had a textbook assignment and an 80-min classroom session on the nature of research in psychology and the types of research methods psychologists employ (e.g., controlled experiment, case study, surveys). Thus, they are generally familiar with concepts like independent and dependent variables, hypotheses, control and experimental groups, correlational research, random sampling, statistical significance, and related terms.

Evaluation of Activity

During the current academic year, 147 students have participated in the activity. An overall indication of how much students liked and disliked the activity was assessed on a 7-point rating scale. A rating of 1 represented the worst classroom activity they had ever participated in and a rating of 7 represented the best classroom activity they had ever participated in. The mean rating was 5.46. When asked to list 2 or 3 things they liked about the activity, the most frequent responses (i.e., endorsed by at least 5 students) included: (a) the ability of the activity to hold their interest on potentially boring material, (b) seeing results from a research project immediately, (c) recognizing how deceptive research findings sometimes could be, and (d) learning that there were different ways to look at research findings. When asked to list 2 or 3 things they disliked, frequent responses (i.e., endorsed by at least 5 students) included: (a) it was somewhat long, (b) the activity tended to oversimplify astrology, (c) it was boring in places, and (d) there was nothing they disliked. Overall, evaluations suggested that the advantages of the exercise outweigh the disadvantages.

We recommend that teachers pilot test this activity with a small group of students before using it in a large class. Timing is important in order to complete the activity in a reasonable amount of time. Teachers vary in how much additional information they prefer to present and which parts of the activity to emphasize. A trial run will help to resolve these issues.

Reference

March, M. D., & McEvans, J. (1982). *The only way to learn astrology*. San Diego: Astro Computer Services.

Note

Requests for demonstration materials should be sent to Anthony F. Grasha, Department of Psychology (M. L. 376), 429 Dyer Hall, University of Cincinnati, Cincinnati, OH 45221.

Demonstrating Personality Scale Validation Procedures

Robert C. Reinehr
Southwestern University

Students in introductory psychology classes often have difficulty grasping the essentials of test validation constructs, particularly when considering tests that yield a profile rather than a single score. I have developed a demonstration procedure that improves classroom discussion of test validity, student reports, and scores on examinations.

Approximately 2 months into the semester, just before the topic of personality testing is introduced in class, I give each student a blank copy of the summary score sheet from the Sixteen Personality Factor Questionnaire (16 PF; Cattell, Eber, & Tatsuoka, 1970) . This sheet lists the 16 PF variables and descriptive adjectives for each. Between the polar descriptions of each variable is a horizontal line divided into 10 equal segments. Students are told that the form is typically used for recording the scores obtained by an individual who has completed the 16 PF, but that in the classroom demonstration the form will be used to record each student's impression of my personality. Each student is then asked to evaluate me using the 16 dimensions on the summary sheet. Students are told that the purpose of the evaluation is to compare their descriptions of me with the descriptions obtained from the test.

After students complete the ratings, they are provided with the ratings that I gave myself when I did the same task they have just completed and with the scores that I actually obtained when I took the test. Experimental design considerations are then discussed. I mention that an introductory class is composed of intelligent, literate, well-integrated individuals who are usually motivated to do their best to evaluate the instructor's personality. In addition, they are all approximately the same age and educational level, reducing generational effects that might be found among raters of different ages or social classes, and they are all acquainted with me to about the same degree.

Although the context in which they have observed me has been to some extent artificial, it has been reasonably well controlled. Each student has observed me for about the same amount of time under the same conditions.

Possibilities that I might have "faked" results on the 16 PF or that my self-description was colored by the knowledge that it would be discussed in class lead to a discussion of such concerns with respect to test performance in all examinees. I point out that most assessment techniques are based on the assumption that the examinee is making a good faith effort to perform the assessment task properly. After providing students with examples of items similar to those on the Minnesota Multiphasic Personality Inventory (MMPI Dahlstrom, Welsh, & Dahlstrom, 1972) and on the 16 PF, I discuss the question of faking on personality inventories. I compare the relative ease of faking test items concerning socially acceptable behavior with the relative difficulty of deciding on which dimension a given item from the 16 PF might be scored. This exercise leads naturally into a discussion of empirical criterion keying and factor analysis as methods of test development.

Student responses are tabulated and presented at the next class meeting. We compare the profile obtained from student ratings with the profile from my self-ratings and with the profile from my actual test scores.

Results have been very consistent over a period of seven semesters: Students and I agree considerably concerning my personality characteristics, but the profile obtained from my test scores does not agree very well with either the actual test scores or my self-ratings. The test scores, for example, suggest that I am a very introverted, withdrawn individual, scoring at about the 20th percentile on an introversion extraversion dimension. I rate myself as slightly extraverted; students rate me as quite extraverted.

The importance of situational variables is an obvious topic for discussion at this point. Students always see me when I am expected to be talkative and outgoing and when I am comfortable with the subject under discussion. A discussion of which is the "real" me leads to a discussion of the possibility that the test may be tapping some "deeper" personality dimensions and that the students and I may be making more superficial judgments about my personality characteristics .

The question of validity is thus presented to the class in a very concrete manner: Does the test or the class describe me accurately? Are individual class members willing to abandon their evaluation of me and to accept the test findings? If they were employers or supervisors, would students place more confidence in test results or in their own evaluation? Could a personality test substitute for an interview?

Results obtained with this procedure have been very encouraging. Classroom discussion has improved, brief written reports on the use of psychological testing in practical settings have indicated a better grasp of the principles of test validation, and grades on examinations have improved. The technique is most effective when used as an introduction to the topic of personality test validation, rather than as a demonstration of principles previously discussed in lecture. Although developed for use in introductory psychology, the technique should be valuable in assessment and personality courses as well.

References

Cattell, R. B., Eber, H. W., &Tatsuoka, M. M. (1970). *Handbook for the Sixteen Personality Factor Questionnaire.* Champaign, IL: Institute for Personality and Ability Testing.

Dahlstrom, W. G., Welsh, G. S., Dahlstrom, L. E. (1972). *An MMPI handbook. Volume 1: Clinical interpretation.* Minneapolis: University of Minnesota Press.

The Science Fair: A Supplement to the Lecture Technique

Thomas A. Fish
Ian H. Fraser
St. Thomas University

Poster sessions and science fairs have been used as substitutes for undergraduate seminar courses (Chute & Bank, 1983) and as devices to educate the public (Benjamin, Fawl, & Klein, 1977). Chute and Bank (1983) found that students responded favorably to poster sessions indicating that they had learned a great deal from the experience. Benjamin et al. (1977) advocated that the science fair be used as a mechanism to deal with public misconceptions of psychology as a scientific discipline. They pointed out, however, that fairs do not compensate for the lack of appropriate instruction.

Science fairs and poster sessions have two major benefits. First, these organized events, if open to the public, can be an educational experience. Second, they can be an effective learning medium for advanced undergraduate students.

We were interested in studying the possible benefits of the fair for undergraduates in an introductory psychology course. Such benefits might include allowing the student to explore in depth a topic of interest; promoting cooperation and discourse among students, as well as between students and instructors; motivating students to exert more effort in their course work; and allowing for the practical and theoretical exploration of a topic (Fish, 1988). We compared the retrospective impressions of introductory psychology courses for students who did and students who did not experience a fair component.

Description of Science Fair Component

During the first week of classes, students were informed that they would be required to do a major project suitable for presentation at a science fair to be held near the end of the second semester. Their science fair contributions would be worth 30% of their final grade and be based on the quality of individual projects and on contributions to various science fair student committees. The remainder of their course grade would be based on test and final exam performance. From one to three classes (each with approximately 60 students) have participated in the event in any given year.

Individual Projects

To encourage creative expression, we gave students little direction regarding their projects. All topics and formats were welcomed as long as the topic was relevant to psychology and the format involved the active participation of science fair visitors.

After all topics had been approved (by the 6th week of the first semester), classes participating in the science fair attended an information meeting that included a narrated slide presentation focusing on previous science fairs. The meeting was designed to stimulate enthusiasm for the event, give students a clear understanding of the type of space that would be available for individual projects, and provide specific examples of projects that have received both high and low grades.

Committees

Students volunteered to serve on one or more committees. Committee activities included designing a program for visitors, promoting the event, fund-raising, and coordinating procedures for setting up and taking down projects.

Class Presentations

Approximately 2 weeks before the science fair, students presented their projects to classmates. This format allowed students to practice their oral presentations and receive suggestions for improving them. They also had a chance to learn about the work of their peers.

The Science Fair

More than 1,000 people have attended the science fair each year. Visitors have included university and high school students, community groups, and the general public. Each student describes his or her project to approximately 100 visitors.

Grading Procedures

A few days after the science fair, students met with instructors to discuss the strengths and weaknesses of their individual efforts and to negotiate a grade.

Examples of Projects

Projects have covered many facets of psychology. One student with a spinal cord injury gave fair visitors an opportunity to negotiate access to campus buildings in a wheelchair. Another student demonstrated a biofeedback machine. Others have built their own tachistoscopes, mazes, and perceptual illusions. Still others chose to share the experience of staying at a shelter for the homeless.

' Table 1. Mean Student Evaluation Ratings for Science Fair and Other Formats

Item	Science Fair	Other Formats	t
Opportunity to explore interests	3.62	3.14	2.02*a
Prepared for other courses	4.03	3.49	2.23*b
Understood basic principles	4.00	3.57	1.80*b
Principles applied to everyday life	3.97	3.59	1.87*b
Course effort	4.20	3.72	2.12*b
Learned from text	4.40	3.94	1.83*a
Learned from instructor	3.97	3.30	2.05*a
Improved oral skills	2.77	2.64	n.s.b
Improved written skills	2.57	2.43	n.s.b
Discussed with those not enrolled	3.14	2.99	n.s.a
Understood research	3.41	3.46	n.s.a
Enjoyed class	4.13	3.87	n.s.b
Learned from classmates	2.35	2.48	n.s.a
Learned from research	3.17	2.74	n.s.b

a107 df.   b108 df.
*p < .05.

Evaluation Study

Participants

Participants were 3rd- and 4th-year students in upper level psychology classes. Thirty had conducted a science fair project in the previous 3 years, and 80 had experienced other introductory formats.

Materials

Students anonymously reported their retrospective impressions of their introductory psychology course by responding to 14 questionnaire items using a 5-point Likert scale ranging from *not at all* (1) to *to a great degree* (5). They also answered four questions about their pursuit of a major.

Results

Table 1 indicates the mean student ratings for each questionnaire item and the t values comparing the science fair students to the students with other course formats. In addition to these findings, 65% of the science fair participants (vs. 41% of other format students) were also more likely to have taken other courses from their introductory psychology instructor, $\chi^2(1, N = 30) = 5.56$, $p < .05$. However, science fair and other format students did not differ in their (a) grade point average (GPA) in psychology, (b) desire to major or to achieve honors in psychology, and (c) desire to pursue a graduate degree or career in psychology.

31

Discussion

Results indicated that ratings of introductory courses with a science fair component compared favorably with ratings for courses with other formats. Although students missed some regular classes to plan for a science fair, this lost time did not appear to detract from ratings of their learning experience. Science fair participants actually reported a better understanding of psychological principles and their application, as well as better preparation for subsequent psychology courses.

Results also indicated that students gave comparable ratings for improving oral and written skills and providing discussion opportunities. Furthermore, no differences were detected in student ratings of how much they learned from their classmates or from personal research. It is important to note that science fair ratings were compared with combined ratings of collaborative research (Reither & Vipond, 1989) and self-paced (Bourque & Hughes, 1991) courses specifically designed to encourage small-group research and discussion and to provide opportunities for improvement of oral and written skills. Thus, the science fair appears to be a valuable alternative for instructors.

Science fair participants reported exerting more effort and learning more from their textbook and instructor than did students experiencing other formats. They were also more likely to take additional courses from their introductory psychology instructors. Because up to three different instructors have coordinated the science fair in any given year, these results are not likely due to particular instructor characteristics. It appears, therefore, that positive regard for the unique qualities of the science fair generalizes to the instructors involved.

It is important to remember that the results represent differences in student beliefs about the quality of their learning experience and do not necessarily translate into demonstrable learning benefits. Moreover, the sample included no introductory students who did not take more psychology courses. Although science fair courses received higher ratings on a number of indices, science fair participants did not differ from other format students in GPA for subsequent psychology courses or in their desire to pursue further studies. Despite these caveats, results indicate that the science fair is a useful pedagogical tool that can be successfully adapted for introductory courses with a lecture format. It provides a unique and valuable learning experience for students and instructors.

References

Benjamin, L. T., Jr., Fawl, C. L., & Klien, J. (1977). The fair: Experimental psychology for high school students. *American Psychologist, 32,* 1097-1098.

Bourque, W. L., & Hughes, G. R. (1991, June*). The Keller plan still works.* Paper presented at the Annual Conference of the Society for Teaching and Learning in Higher Education, Halifax, Nova Scotia.

Chute, D. L., & Bank, B. (1983). Undergraduate seminars: The poster session solution. *Teaching of Psychology, 10,* 99-100.

Fish, T. A. (1988, June). *Begged, borrowed, and stolen: Nontraditional approaches to teaching.* Paper presented at the Enhancement of University Teaching Conference, Sackville, New Brunswick.

Reither, J. A., & Vipond, D. (1989). Writing as collaboration. *College English, 51,* 855-867.

Note

We gratefully acknowledge the editorial assistance of Daizal Samad and Ruth L. Ault.

Undergraduate Research Experience Through the Analysis of Data Sets in Psychology Courses

Neil Lutsky
Carleton College

An effective way to involve introductory psychology students as active participants in research is to assign a course project requiring the analysis of previously collected data. I have regularly given classes access via computer to large data sets and required students to develop an original research question, analyze relevant data using a statistical package, and complete a research report. In this article, I discuss the goals of such an assignment, describe the project in detail, report evidence of its effects on students' attitudes toward research in psychology, and consider some of the benefits and difficulties associated with its use.

Projects designed to give introductory psychology students hands-on research experience include research simulations (e.g., Hartley, Fisher, & Hartley, 1977), laboratory experiments (e.g., Bare, 1982; Brothen, 1984), and data analysis assignments. These projects have several educational goals. One is to increase student familiarity with the phenomena, theories, and findings under investigation. A second goal is to expose students to the tasks that normally constitute research in psychology (e.g., manipulating equipment, using statistics, interpreting results). Participation in research may allow students to appreciate the importance of these tasks, learn some of the technical skills required by research, and test their proclivities for doing research. A third and more complex goal is to influence students' attitudes toward the research claims of psychology.

Research experience may affect attitudes toward psychological research in a variety of ways. Students who obtain expected results when they test basic predictions may become more confident about the validity of other research claims. A failure to replicate a basic finding, however, may have the opposite effect. Both experiences, although probably the latter more than the former, may also make students more sensitive to the choices that psychologists make when conducting research—choices about what might be examined, how information about certain objects or processes can be collected and analyzed, and how findings can be interpreted and presented. Any experience that encourages students to recognize these choices, understand their justifications, and think critically about their features may contribute to a deeper understanding of psychology and its research foundation.

The value of active research experience is clearly recognized in the training of psychology majors (Cole & Van Krevelen, 1977). For example, students in core methodology courses typically assist in the design and completion of research (e.g., Kerber, 1983; Yoder, 1979). Students in upper-level psychology courses often conduct laboratory work (Cole & Van Krevelen, 1977), and selected students may have the opportunity to develop individual research projects (e.g., Kierniesky, 1984; Palladino, Carsrud, Hulicka, & Benjamin, 1982).

Introductory psychology students, however, are less likely to be given an opportunity to conduct research. Faculty members may find it difficult to supervise and support the work of a large number of novices. Moreover, introductory psychology students may not be able to complete or appreciate a research project, given their limited understanding of research techniques (e.g., statistics) and inexperience with research decisions. On the other hand, Medawar (1979) strongly encourage a young scientists to become involved in research and confront

results even before they are fully prepared to understand what they have done. He believed that such experiences give students a sense of pride in their work and may motivate continued learning about research.

An assignment to analyze previously collected data may provide a research experience well suited to the abilities and interests of introductory psychology students. Such a project offers students the freedom to pursue individual research questions in an original data base but gives them concrete research variables to help organize their thinking about possible research questions. The project spares students the necessity of collecting data but does require them to master some rudiments of statistical analysis and computer usage. In general, the project exploits the potential for computers to stimulate active student thinking about psychological issues (Collyer, 1984) and to serve education by allowing large numbers of students opportunities that might not be feasible otherwise.

The Research Project

Data Sets

I have used several data sets for projects in my introductory and middle-level courses, courses likely to include a high percentage of students without previous research experience. For example, one data set used in the introductory psychology course, provides subjects' background information (e.g., gender and class year) and test results from the Eysenck Personality Questionnaire, the Bem Sex Role Inventory, the Self-Monitoring Scale, and the Act Report measure of gregarious behavior. This data set is relevant to course discussions of personality theory, personality assessment, and sex roles. Another data set, used in a middlelevel social psychology course, allows students to explore the Ajzen and Fishbein (1980) model of attitude-action relationships through individual records of attendance at voluntary weekly college convocations and earlier measures of theoretically related attitudes, intentions, social norms, and personality variables (e.g., self-monitoring). All of these data sets are based on previous research with students at Carleton College.

The Research Assignment

Students are given a five-page handout that describes the project and its data base. (The handout and other materials referred to in this article are available from the author.) The handout summarizes the purposes and methodology of the original study and provides references to sections of the course text that discuss the specific procedures, instruments, and issues the handout introduces. A codebook listing variable names and scoring information is included.

The handout leads the student through the steps of the project. The first step requires each student to define an individual research topic (e.g., "Sex Differences in

Extraversion as Measured by the EPQ" or "Self-Monitoring as a Moderator of Intention-Action Relationships"). Second, students must identify the basic statistical procedures needed to answer their research questions. The handout describes simple possibilities (correlations, t tests, frequencies) and encourages the student to review the statistics appendix in the text. The third step describes procedures needed to edit and run a command file in the statistical package used (SPSS^x).

Students must write a short paper (usually 3 to 5 pages) that summarizes the project and its findings, critically evaluates the results obtained, and relates the research question to material covered in the course. An appendix to the handout describes a word processing program that students can use to write papers on the computer.

Comment

This assignment poses a difficult challenge to students. Because each step of the project is logically dependent on prior ones, students must approach their work in a systematic manner. The project is usually assigned 2 weeks before it is due, and students are encouraged to complete the early steps soon after receiving the assignment. For many students, especially those in the introductory course, the project represents a first encounter with the computer and with the manipulation of statistics. Thus, it is important to have specific and easy-to-follow instructions in the handout. Students are also strongly encouraged to seek guidance from their instructor and teaching assistants (advanced psychology majors) as they work through the assignment.

The project challenges students to use statistical techniques and computer technology in the service of definite and intelligent ends. When confronted with the project, students are usually concerned about their abilities to use the computer and to complete an appropriate data analysis. They are initially less attentive to issues involved in conceptualizing interesting and meaningful research questions, and in evaluating findings in a thoughtful and critical manner. The instructor and teaching assistants counsel students to help them avoid completing technically competent but uninteresting projects and papers.

Project Evaluation

Student reactions to these projects have been assessed in several ways. As part of a standard course evaluation, students were asked to rate the computer project and comment on it. When asked to indicate how valuable the project was, students in an introductory course ($N = 75$) and a middlelevel social psychology course ($N = 38$) rated the project positively ($M = 2.9$ and $M = 2.8$, respectively, on 6-point scales where 1 = *excellent* and 6 = *poor*). Positive comments lauded the creativity allowed in the

project and the fact that the project helped clarify course material. Some students indicated a desire to continue a more active involvement in research. Negative comments centered on student confusion concerning statistical and computer procedures and the lack of definitive answers found for some project questions.

Recently, a more formal evaluation of student responses was completed in a large introductory psychology course. Eighty students, primarily freshmen, completed a questionnaire on "Attitudes toward Research in Psychology" after receiving a brief description of the research project they were about to be assigned. (The project had also been mentioned previously on the course syllabus.) This questionnaire was administered before students received the full assignment handout midway through the course. The questionnaire consisted of 20 questions designed to assess general attitudes toward research in psychology and student expectations about the project. An example of the questions concerning attitudes toward research is: "I think research studies in psychology have led me to think about issues in psychology in a more precise way." Student beliefs about the project were assessed through questions about their abilities (e.g., "I believe that I can successfully complete the computer-based project in this course"), anxieties (e.g. "I am anxious about the prospect of having to use and interpret statistics"), and expectations (e.g., "I expect that the computer-based project in this course will be valuable and interesting").

Shortly after the papers from the projects were submitted, approximately 3 weeks after the first questionnaires had been completed, a second attitude questionnaire was administered. In it, students were asked to estimate the amount of time they spent on various project tasks (e.g., reviewing notes for the project, working at the computer) and the number of times they sought help from their peers and instructor. Students were also asked whether they found the project valuable and interesting, whether they believed they understood statistical procedures better after completing the project, whether they would be anxious about the prospect of having to complete a similar project in the future, and a number of other questions designed to match pretest items (see Table 1). All attitude answers were rated on 1-point scales ranging from *strongly disagree* (1) to *strongly agree* (7). In addition, background data (sex, class, intended major) and project grades were available for the students in this study.

Results of the initial belief and attitude assessments showed that students expected the project to be valuable and interesting, but that they were generally anxious about the project and its computer and statistics components (see Table 1). Students anticipated that the project would be difficult ($M = 4.7$) and that they would have to spend a considerable amount of time on it ($M = 5.3$), but they were confident that they could complete the project successfully ($M = 5.4$).

In fact, almost all students completed the project successfully. After spending, on average, over 8 hr on their

Table 1. Attitudes Before and After Completion of the Research Project

	Pretest M	Posttest M
Attitudes Toward Project and Project Tasks		
Project valuable and interesting	4.76	4.84
Anxious about computer-based project	4.34	3.43**
Anxious about using and interpreting statistics	4.22	3.57**
Confident about using the computer	3.78	4.64**
Attitudes Toward Research in Psychology		
Research studies imprecise	4.17	4.93**
Research plays vital role in psychology	5.84	5.97
Research studies difficult to understand	4.00	4.67**
Research often challenges preconceptions	5.09	5.48*
Research findings easily influenced by decisions researcher makes about data analysis	5.71	5.87
Research in psychology led me to think about issues more precisely	4.88	5.29*

Note. Ratings have been coded on a scale ranging from *strongly disagree* (1) to *strongly agree* (7).
*$p < .05$, **$p < .001$; correlated t tests.

work (1.9 hr planning the research, 2.1 hr using the computer, 1.4 hr interpreting results, and 3.3 hr writing papers) and consulting the instructor and peers a number of times (on average, 1.6 and 3.1 times, respectively), students submitted projects they believed to be successful ($M = 5.4$). In addition, students reported understanding statistical procedures and using the computer better ($M = 5.0$ and $M = 5.2$, respectively) as a result of having completed the project. The results of paired t tests (summarized in Table 1) also show that students reported significantly less anxiety about projects of this kind and about using statistics and computers following their research experiences. The final grades students received on their papers were not significantly related to these attitude and time measures, but were associated with the initial measure of self-assessed efficacy ("I believe that I can successfully complete the computer-based project in this course"), $r = .23, p < .05$.

Students' attitudes toward research in psychology were also apparently influenced by their research experience. As Table 1 indicates, after completing their work, students were more likely to label research results in psychology as imprecise and difficult to interpret but also indicated an increased appreciation of the ability of research to challenge preconceptions and stimulate precise thinking. Students also held the belief that researchers can easily influence research findings through decisions about data analysis without significant change over the course of the study ($M = 5.71$ and $M = 5.83$ for the pretest and posttest assessments, respectively).

Sex differences were also assessed. Males reported feeling less anxious about using and interpreting statistics than females did before the assignment ($M = 3.38$ and $M = 4.43$ for males and females, respectively), $t(63) = 2.55, p < .05$, and also expected to spend less time completing the

project, $t(63) = 2.84, p < .01$. This sex difference in initial anxiety about statistics remained even after controlling for previous exposure to statistics. However, no corresponding posttest differences were obtained in anxiety ratings concerning computer usage or in measures of time actually spent on the project.

Discussion

The thesis of this article is that an assignment to analyze a data set allows students to become actively involved in research in a way that contributes to their interest in and understanding of the field. The results appear to support this claim. Students viewed the project as a challenge and responded to it positively. Following their work, they reported less anxiety about a project of this kind and a greater understanding of the use of statistics and computers. In addition, students reported becoming more aware of the complexities and ambiguities inherent in research and of the potential contributions of research to their thinking about psychological issues. Thus, participation in the project may have raised students' sensitivity to the uncertainties of their own ideas and those advanced in research as they grappled with the interplay of the two.

There are reasons to be cautious about these findings, however. All that can be claimed is that students reported these attitudes; no confirmation of supposed effects on understandings of research was attempted. Moreover, it was easier for students to be less anxious about an abstract assignment during the posttest questionnaire than about one due 2 weeks after the pretest. It is also possible that demand characteristics in the research or additional course experiences may have influenced reported attitudes.

The results are consistent, however, with my observations of the project and its effects. Students appeared to have been highly involved in their work and engaged by the conceptual, methodological, and statistical problems they faced. Students seemed to benefit from the fact that they were required to use statistics and not simply to read about them. Similarly, students appeared to develop positive attitudes toward the computer, perhaps because they were using computers to serve their own specific purposes and did not feel under the control of an impersonal electronic regimen. Another valuable feature of the project is that students were encouraged to interact with their instructor in individual, task-oriented meetings. Finally, there was ample evidence in students' papers that they were thinking carefully about methodological issues in their own work and in the literature related to it in light of questions raised by their concrete findings.

The use of a project of this kind is not without its disadvantages and pitfalls. It requires the instructional staff to spend considerable time helping students during their work on the project, although it has been used in introductory classes of over 90 students. The success of the project also depends on the quality of the data set available. Data sets that do not include a number of theoretically related variables may not allow room for meaningful variation in the questions students choose to ask. Data sets that result in few interesting and reliable findings may also fail to reinforce the students' sense of accomplishment. Finally, there are other sources of frustration that the students and instructor may experience (notably, unanticipated problems in the computer system).

The overall results of this study suggest that undergraduates may benefit greatly from a research project involving the analysis of previously collected data. If certain resources (a data set, an open computer system, a statistical package) are available, teachers might consider offering their students this opportunity to participate actively in the research process in psychology and to learn more directly about the values, decisions, and operations that comprise psychology's research foundation.

References

Ajzen, I., & Fishbein, M. (1980). *Understanding attitudes and predicting social behavior.* Englewood Cliffs, NJ: Prentice-Hall.

Bare, J. K. (1982). Microcomputers in the introductory laboratory. *Teaching of Psychology, 9,* 236-237.

Brothen, T. (1984). Three computer-assisted laboratory exercises for introductory psychology. *Teaching of Psychology, 11,* 105-107.

Cole, D., & Van Krevelen, A. (1977). Psychology departments in small liberal arts colleges: Results of a survey. *Teaching of Psychology, 4,* 163-167.

Collyer, C. E. (1984). Using computers in the teaching of psychology: Five things that seem to work. *Teaching of Psychology, 11,* 206-209.

Hartley, A. A., Fisher, L. A., & Harrley, J. T. (1977). Teaching the arts of psychological research. *Teaching of Psychology, 4,* 202-204.

Kerber, K. W. (1983). Beyond experimentation: Research projects for a laboratory course in psychology. *Teaching of Psychology, 10,* 236-239.

Kierniesky, N. C. (1984). Undergraduate research in small psychology departments. *Teaching of Psychology, 11,* 15-18.

Medawar, P. B. (1979). *Advice to a young scientist.* New York: Harper & Row.

Palladino, J. J., Carsrud, A. L., Hulicka, I. M., & Benjamin, L. T, Jr. (1982). Undergraduate research in psychology: Assessment and directions. *Teaching of Psychology, 9,* 71-74.

Yoder, J. (1979). Teaching students to do research. *Teaching of Psychology, 6,* 85-88.

Notes

1. Portions of this article were presented at the annual convention of the American Psychological Association, August, l984, Toronto, Canada.

2. Preparation of these projects was supported by NSF Cause Grant SER77-06304 to Carleton College. I thank Perry Ferguson for his contributions to the evaluation study.

Critiquing Articles Cited in the Introductory Textbook: A Writing Assignment

Karen C. Gareis
Boston University

Although upper level psychology courses frequently require that students read journal articles, descriptions of techniques to help students comprehend and interpret what they read are rare (Chamberlain & Burrough, 1985) and are generally too sophisticated for the introductory course (e.g., Chamberlain & Burrough, 1985; Klugh, 1983; Osberg, 1991; Suter & Frank, 1986). Only Keller (1982) described a technique for introductory psychology students, who wrote critiques of journal articles in the form of letters to their parents. However, the critiques focused on article interest, usefulness, and relation to experience and class material rather than on methodology.

The introductory course is many students' only exposure to psychology, so it is essential to provide them with the knowledge and skills to be critical consumers of the research reports they will encounter in the popular media. For students who take additional psychology courses, the benefits of methodological proficiency are self-evident. The following assignment has at least four benefits: (a) It allows students to practice using research terms and concepts that may be emphasized throughout the introductory course; (b) it exposes students to primary research in the field, which does not normally occur until upper level classes; (c) it gives instructors a chance to read articles outside their own field, which helps meet the challenging breadth of the introductory course; and (d) it promotes critical thinking about textbook presentations of research. Students should come to appreciate the monumental task involved in writing a textbook and gain a healthy skepticism about relying on secondary sources for information, even sources as legitimate as highly regarded introductory psychology textbooks (e.g., Atkinson, Atkinson, Smith, & Bem, 1993).

Todd and Morris (1992) discussed the self-perpetuating nature of erroneous academic folklore, arguing that psychology textbooks are both a repository of such folklore and a primary means of its dissemination. Vicente and de Groot (1990) used a virus metaphor in their historical tracing of distortions of de Groot's work on recall with chess masters, finding that the number and severity of such errors actually increased over time. Loftus (1974) reported that secondary sources tend to exaggerate the strength of the "cocktail party phenomenon," in which one's own name penetrates consciousness despite inattention; in fact, this occurred only 33% of the time in the original study (Moray, 1959). Rosenthal, Soper, Coon, and Fullerton (1993) pointed out that developmental psychology texts routinely overstate how much is known about the number of human genes, which can mislead students about scientific uncertainty. Given the ramifications of these inaccuracies, psychology instructors should do what they can to avoid spreading them.

Critiquing Articles

Students choose a study presented in their textbook and had the original article. The focus of the assignment is research methods, so students should look for empirical articles and avoid books, case studies, or reviews. To help students choose appropriately, I tell them to avoid *American Psychologist* and *Psychological Bulletin* in favor of empirically oriented journals, such as *Journal of Personality and Social Psychology*, and to look for Method, Results, and Discussion headings. Because students have complete citations, I just need to tell them how to find specific journals; they are also encouraged to consult library reference staff. The assignment is fully described in the syllabus, so I only spend about 15 min of class time discussing it.

In preparation for the assignment, students read Peplau (1988), which describes parts of a journal article, defines common statistical terms, and indicates that even technical articles restate key findings in plain English, requiring little statistical sophistication to understand. In addition, students have had three class hours on research methods, including practice identifying the method, variables, operational definitions, and flaws in short descriptions of studies. I reinforce these concepts by questioning students about studies that come up in later units.

Students read the article and write a 5-page paper consisting of (a) a one-page summary describing the hypothesis, variables, operational definitions, method, and results using terms from the research methods unit; (b) a critical evaluation, including any compliments on or criticisms of method, operational definitions, sample, and so forth; (c) a discussion of how the study illustrates course concepts; and (d) a comparison of the primary source with its description in the text. They also turn in a copy of the article.

Students can consult with me and with teaching assistants if they need help. Typically, about one third come in to ensure that their articles are appropriate and that they have identified variables and interpreted results accurately. When students seem intimidated by Results sections, I remind them to look for plain-English statements.

Grading takes only as much time as for traditional assignments of similar length. Students tend to choose short, straightforward articles that I can read quickly. Grading criteria include correct use of research terms and accurate description of the study, thoughtful and well-reasoned evaluation, thorough demonstration of knowledge of pertinent course concepts, and accurate and thoughtful comparison of primary and secondary sources. Introductory students may not be capable of sophisticated methodological critiques, but they can apply their knowledge of the trade-offs between experimental and correlational designs, examine operational definitions critically, and contemplate external validity and ethics.

Evaluation

When I offered the assignment as extra credit, 58 of 135 students completed it. When I required it in a summer course, 27 of 28 students did the assignment. The quality of the papers was quite high, with an average grade of B+ in both classes. Students responded to six evaluation items on a 5-point scale ranging from *strongly disagree* (1) to *strongly agree* (5). They were also asked to provide general comments and suggestions for improving the assignment. Because the extra credit version of the assignment was due at the end of the semester, evaluation forms were distributed when papers were returned; students were asked to bring them to the final class or to leave them in my mailbox. Only 22 students complied, so

Table 1. Student Evaluations of Assignment

Questionnaire Item	Extra Credit[a] M	Extra Credit[a] SD	Required[b] M	Required[b] SD
1. Clearer understanding of research.	4.41	0.80	3.83	1.17
2. Think critically about research.	4.36	0.23	3.87	1.10
3. Learn more about course topics.	4.23	0.81	3.79	1.10
4. Think critically about textbook presentation.	4.41	0.73	3.63	1.10
5. Was interesting.	4.36	0.85	3.50	1.10
6. Should be required.	3.68	1.32	3.71	1.27

Note. Items were scored on a scale that ranged from *strongly disagree* (1) to *strongly agree* (5).
[a]$n = 22$. [b]$n = 24$.

their ratings may not be representative. When the assignment was required, students were asked to turn in evaluations with their papers; 24 of 27 did so.

Students who turned in evaluations gave the assignment fairly high marks, particularly when it was offered for extra credit (see Table 1). Looking for a specific article offered a rather painless introduction to library research, a new skill for many first-year students. An unexpected benefit was that students who consulted reference staff were advised to use PsycLIT to preview articles for appropriateness and interest; they reported saving time and enjoying using the database. As many authors have stressed the need for bibliographic instruction in psychology courses (e.g., Baxter, 1986; Cameron & Hart, 1992; Merriam, LaBaugh, & Butterfield, 1992), this assignment could usefully be combined with more formal training in library research.

The first time I assigned this paper I did not adequately emphasize article selection guidelines; a few students inadvertently chose review articles, which made it virtually impossible for them to complete the assignment. Requiring that articles be approved in advance would both prevent this problem and encourage students to start the assignment early.

Students reported that they learned more about psychological research and appreciated the opportunity to see original sources, as indicated by comments such as "This assignment gave me the chance to look at an actual journal, which I most likely never would have on my own!" and "I am glad that I did this assignment because it helped me understand the complexities of psychological research studies." Students found the articles challenging to read but not insurmountable. Many students had difficulty limiting their summaries to one page, but they benefit from extracting an article's essential points and describing it concisely.

Students also believed that the assignment encouraged them to think critically about psychological research and expanded on course topics: "The assignment was a challenge to me to read more deeply and critically on the topic I was researching." Several students were disappointed at being constrained to articles cited in the textbook. However, focusing on text articles allows them to compare primary and secondary sources and simplifies the library search. Students agreed that the assignment encouraged them to think more critically about the textbook's presentation of research.

Some students did find errors and distortions in the textbook, ranging from mild to more serious. For instance, in describing Darley and Latané's (1968) diffusion of responsibility experiment, the text authors wrote that group sizes were two, three, and six (Atkinson et al., 1993, p. 757); actually, the middle group had four members. More seriously, the text inaccurately described Godden and Baddeley's (1975) study of context and memory with scuba divers. The authors converted the within-subject study to a between-subject design and incorrectly claimed that divers in one condition "recalled 40% less" than divers in another (Atkinson et al., 1993, p. 308); this figure should only be 32%. Information about such errors can be incorporated into lectures, and the publisher can also be notified of discrepancies between the textbook and primary sources.

Students reported that the assignment was interesting and enjoyable and that it would prepare them for future classes: "I think doing something like this in an introductory course is awesome because it prepares you for later, more advanced courses in psychology, where we'll actually have to do things like this." A further advantage of the assignment for me was the chance to read original research articles on topics outside my own specialization. Many students chose to track down classic articles, which were of particular interest and worth photocopying as sources of supplemental lecture material.

References

Atkinson, R. L., Atkinson, R. C., Smith, E. E., & Bem, D. J. (1993). *Introduction to psychology* (11th ed.). Fort Worth, TX: Harcourt Brace.

Baxter, P. M. (1986). The benefits of in-class bibliographic instruction. *Teaching of Psychology, 13,* 40-41.

Cameron, L., & Hart, J. (1992). Assessment of PsycLIT competence, attitudes, and instructional methods. *Teaching of Psychology, 19,* 239-242.

Chamberlain, K., & Burrough, S. (1985). Techniques for teaching critical reading. *Teaching of Psychology, 12,* 213-215.

Darley, J. M., & Latané, B. (1968). Bystander intervention in emergencies: Diffusion of responsibility. *Journal of Personality and Social Psychology, 8,* 377-383.

Godden, D., & Baddeley, A. D. (1975). Context-dependent memory in two natural environments: On land and under water. *British Journal of Psychology, 66,* 325-331.

Keller, R. A. (1982). Teaching from the journals. *Teaching Sociology, 9,* 407-409.

Klugh, H. E. (1983). Writing and speaking skills can be taught in psychology classes. *Teaching of Psychology, 10*, 170-171.

Loftus, E. F. (1974). On reading the fine print. *Quarterly Journal of Experimental Psychology, 26*, 324.

Merriam, J., LaBaugh, R. T., & Butterfield, N. E. (1992). Library instruction for psychology majors: Minimum training guidelines. *Teaching of Psychology, 19*, 34-36.

Moray, N. (1959). Attention in dichotic listening: Affective cues and the influence of instructions. *Quarterly Journal of Experimental Psychology, 11*, 56-60.

Osberg, T. M. (1991). Teaching current advances in psychology: Student and instructor advantages. *Teaching of Psychology, 18*, 41-42.

Peplau, L. A. (1988). Introduction: Reading research reports in social psychology. In L. A. Peplau, D. O. Sears, S. E. Taylor, & J. L. Freedman (Eds.), *Readings in social psychology: Classic and contemporary contributions* (2nd ed., pp. 1-5). Englewood Cliffs, NJ: Prentice Hall.

Rosenthal, G. T., Soper, B., Coon, R. C., & Fullerton, R. (1993). The misrepresentation of scientific uncertainty: The number of genes in the human cell. *Journal of Instructional Psychology, 20*, 333-339.

Suter, W. N., & Frank, P. (1986). Using scholarly journals in undergraduate experimental methodology courses. *Teaching of Psychology, 13*, 219-221.

Todd, J. T., & Morris, E. K. (1992). Case histories in the great power of steady misinterpretation. *American Psychologist, 47*, 1441-1453.

Vicente, K. J., & de Groot, A. D. (1990). The memory recall paradigm: Straightening out the historical record. *American Psychologist, 45*, 285-287.

Note

I thank Ruth L. Ault and three anonymous reviewers for helpful comments and suggestions on an earlier draft of this article.

Fighting Shyness With Shyness: An Exercise in Survey Methodology and Self-Awareness

Bernardo J. Carducci
Indiana University Southeast

Previous estimates on the pervasiveness of self-reported shyness in college students indicate that approximately 40% of students surveyed consider themselves to be shy (Carducci & Stein, 1988; Zimbardo, 1977). In addition, students surveyed indicate that interacting with persons in positions of authority by virtue of their knowledge or role are two of the situations that most frequently elicit feelings of shyness. Instructors are persons in positions of authority by virtue of their knowledge or role with whom college students are most likely to interact. For teachers of psychology, such findings are disturbing because of the potential barriers to quality instruction shyness can create (Carducci & Stein, 1988; Zimbardo, 1977). In the classroom, problems created by shyness include reluctance on the part of shy students to ask questions in class. Shyness can also serve as a barrier for students as they try to develop friendships with other students in the class. Outside the classroom, shyness can create a barrier for students who may be too shy to approach the instructor during office hours for additional assistance, seek career-related or academic information, or ask for letters of recommendation.

To help offset some of these potential problems, I developed a simple in-class activity designed to teach students basic concepts of survey methodology and help them become more aware of the pervasiveness of and problems associated with shyness in college students. This exercise can be used in large and small classes and in the introductory course and in advanced courses such as social, personality, and developmental psychology.

Procedure

On the first day of class, I distribute the Shyness Survey, ask students to complete it anonymously, and collect it after about 10 min. The Shyness Survey contains 10 items taken from the Personal Shyness section of the Stanford Survey on Shyness (Zimbardo, Pilkonis, & Norwood, 1974). Items in the Shyness Survey examine self-reported[1] experiences with shyness, including the frequency of experiencing feelings of shyness, a comparison of shyness to one's peers, the desirability of being shy, the extent to which shyness is a personal problem, the types of people and situations that elicit feelings of shyness, and one's willingness to work to overcome shyness[2].

Outside of class, I summarize results of the Shyness Survey in terms of percentage of responses. For instructors whose classes are too large to make summarizing the data a reasonable possibility or who do not have a teachingassistant to help summarize the data, a random sample of the surveys may be tabulated.

The Shyness Survey is reintroduced as the principal example for classroom discussion when I lecture about survey methodology. I use an overhead transparency of a blank copy of the Shyness Survey that I update when summarizing the results for each class. When discussing the results, I highlight the following points (Carducci & Stein, 1988):

1. Almost half the students in the class consider themselves to be shy. So if you are shy, you are not alone.
2. Most students consider themselves to be shyer than their peers.
3. Situations that most often make people experience shyness include interacting with individuals in positions of authority, such as their instructors, and with those of the opposite sex in both one-to-one and group interactions.
4. Most individuals believe their shyness can be overcome and are willing to work to overcome it.

After discussing the basic results, I introduce various topics related to survey methodology and relate them to the Shyness Survey. Such topics include the following:

1. Clarify the distinction between a population (all students in the class) and a sample of the population (all students in the class are part of the population of students at the university).
2. Describe different sampling techniques, such as random versus stratified versus convenience sampling (surveying an introductory class as an already existing group of individuals) and their respective advantages and disadvantages.
3. Explain the process of and potential errors when attempts are made to generalize results for the present class to other sections of the same course; other courses on campus (an advanced marketing class); and groups of individuals off-campus, such as those individuals not attending college.

The estimated total in-class time for the activity is approximately 20 to 30 min (10 min for data collection and 10 to 20 min for the follow-up discussion).

Discussion

After discussing the results, I make a few comments about the problem shyness can create for students inside and outside of class. I also point out that students should not feel shy about asking questions in class because almost half of the class is also shy and probably thankful that someone else asked the question, because they were probably too shy to ask it themselves.

This activity is designed for use in teaching the basic concepts of survey methodology, but it can also be used to introduce and facilitate discussion of shyness at any point in any course (the chapter on personality in an introductory course) or in any class (psychology of adjustment and developmental psychology) for which the topic of shyness is appropriate. There are many specific topics to consider when discussing shyness. More in-depth presentations on the topic of shyness are the biological and social antecedents of shyness in infants and young children (Arcus & McCartney, 1989; Kagan, Arcus, & Snidman, 1993; Kagan, Arcus, Snidman, & Rimm, 1995; Kagan, Snidman, & Arcus, 1992). Because most students are interested in gender differences, gender differences in shyness during adolescence (Cheek, Carpentieri, Smith, Rierdan, & Koff, 1986; Zimbardo, 1977) and their disappearance in adulthood (Leary, 1983) is a topic to consider for in-class discussion. To emphasize cultunctl diversity, the topic of cross-cultural aspects of shyness can be introduced by discussing cultural differences in the conceptualization, labeling, and self-reported consequences of shyness (Kagan et al., 1994; Klopf, 1984; Zimbardo, 1977).

A typical outcome of this activity is that students will show up after class or during office hours to seek information about overcoming their shyness or preventing shyness in their children. Three excellent suggestions instructors can make to students requesting further reading on overcoming shyness are works by Cheek (1989, 1994) and Zimbardo (1977).

---

[1] Because there is no consensus on a definition of *shyness* (e.g., Cheek, 1989; Leary, 1986), I do not provide the students with a definition before they complete the Shyness Survey. Instead, I let students decide if they consider themselves to be shy in response to the first question on the Shyness Survey. Such a self-labeling approach has been validated by others (e.g., Carducci & Clark, 1993, 1994; Pilkonis, 1977; Zimbardo, 1977).

[2] A copy of the Shyness Survey is available from the author.

References

Arcus, D., & McCarmey, K. (1989). When baby makes four: Family influences in the stability of behavioral inhibition. In J. S. Reznick (Ed.), *Perspectives on behavioral inhibition* (pp. 197-218). Chicago: University of Chicago Press.

Carducci, B. J., & Clark, D. A. (1993, August). *Behavioral, cognitive, and affective tendencies of chronically and transitionally shy individuals.* Poster session presented at the annual meeting of the American Psychological Association, Toronto, Ontario, Canada.

Carducci, B. J., & Clark, D. A. (1994, August). *The personal and situational pervasiveness of chronically shy, socially anxious individuals.* Poster session at the annual meeting of the American Psychological Association, Los Angeles.

Carducci, B. J., & Stein, N. (1988, April). *The personal and situational pervasiveness of shyness in college students: A nine-year comparison.* Poster session presented at the annual meeting of the Southeastern Psychological Association, New Orleans.

Cheek, J. (1989). *Conquering shyness: The battle anyone can win.* New York: Dell.

Cheek, J. M. (1994) . Shyness. In S. Parker & B. Zuckennan (Eds.), *Behavioral and developmental pediatrics: A handbook for primary care* (pp. 285-288). Boston: Little, Brown.

Cheek, J. M., Carpentieri, A. M., Smith, T. G., Rierdan, J., & Koff, E. (1986). Adolescent shyness. In W. H. Jones, J. M. Cheek, & S. R. Briggs (Eds.), *Shyness: Perspectives on research and treatment* (pp. 105-115). New York: Plenum.

Kagan, J., Arcus, D., & Snidman, N. (1993). The idea of temperament: Where do we go from here? In R. Plomin & G. E. McClearn (Eds.), *Nature, nurture and psychology* (pp. 197-210). Washington, DC: American Psychological Association.

Kagan, J., Arcus, D., Snidman, N., Feng, W. Y., Hendler, J., & Greene, S. (1994). Reactivity in infants: A cross-national comparison. *Developmental Psychology, 30,* 342-345.

Kagan, J., Arcus, D., Snidman, N., & Rimm, S. E. (1995). Asymmetry of forehead temperature and cardiac activity. *Neuropsychology, 9,* 47-51.

Kagan, J., Snidman, N., & Arcus, D. (1992). Initial reactions to unfamiliarity. *Current Directions in Psychological Science, 1,* 171-174.

Klopf, D. W. (1984). Cross-cultural apprehension research. A summary of Pacific Basin studies. In J. A. Daly & J. C. McCroskey (Eds.), *Avoiding communication* (pp. 157-169). Beverly Hills: Sage.

Leary, M. R. (1983). *Understanding social anxiety: Social, personality, and clinical perspectives.* Beverly Hills: Sage.

Leary, M. R. (1986). Affective and behavioral components of shyness: Implications for theory, measurement, and research. In W. H. Jones, J. M. Cheek, & S. R. Briggs (Eds.), *Shyness: Perspectives on research and treatment* (pp. 27-38). New York: Plenum.

Pilkonis, P. A. (1977). Shyness, public and private, and its relationship to other measures of social behavior. *Journal of Personality, 45,* 585-595.

Zimbardo, P. G. (1977). *Shyness: What it is, what to do about it.* Reading, MA: Addison-Wesley.

Zimbardo, P. G., Pilkonis, P. A., & Norwood, R. M. (1974). *The silent prison of shyness* (ONR Tech. Rep. No. Z-17). Stanford, CA: Stanford University.

Notes

1. A version of this article was presented at the annual meeting of the American Psychological Association, Los Angeles, August 1994.

2. The project was supported by instructional release time granted to the author by the Indiana University Southeast Office of Academic Affairs.

Integrating Research Ethics Into the Introductory Psychology Course Curriculum

Celia B. Fisher
Tara L. Kuther
Fordham University

Psychology faculty have long recognized the importance of integrating ethics into the early education of college students as an effective means of fostering the values and standards that guide responsible scientific practice and of encouraging critical thinking about ethical issues for those who will become research psychologists or who will continue to be consumers of knowledge generated by psychological science (American Psychological Association [APA], 1992; Association of American Colleges, 1985; Baum et al., 1993; Hobbs, 1948; McGovern, 1988). However, surveys of psychology course offerings and reading materials suggest that there are major gaps in the coverage of research ethics in introductory psychology textbooks (e.g., Kohn, 1984; Matthews, 1991; Warwick, 1980). For example, although we found mention of research ethics in 100% of 14 introductory psychology textbooks published between 1990 and 1994, these mentions were restricted to an average of 3 pages (range = 1-8 pp.) appearing at the end of chapters covering research methodology and Milgram's (1963) classic obedience study. Thus, discussion of research ethics in introductory textbooks remains tangential to presentation of core material, and introductory psychology instructors have little guidance in how to integrate the teaching of ethical issues into the course. The broad educational goal of the project described later was to develop and evaluate didactic materials that would help introductory psychology instructors teach students to identify ethical issues in human and animal research, consider moral ambiguities that arise within various experimental contexts, and to generate alternative ethical approaches to specific research designs.

The report of the National Commission for the Protection of Human Subjects of Biomedical and Behavioral Research (NCPHSBBR; 1978), known as the Belmont Report, identified three fundamental ethical principles as relevant to research with human participants: (a) beneficence (promotion of welfare and avoidance of harm), (b) respect for persons (protection of privacy and self-determination), and (c) justice (fair and equal treatment). These principles also are reflected in the APA's (1992) ethical standards related to research with human and animal participants. However, the complexity of issues examined by research psychologists often gives rise to situations for which the Belmont Report principles and APA ethical standards appear ambiguous or contradictory when applied to specific situations (e.g., Fisher, Hoagwood, & Jensen, 1996; Fisher & Tryon, 1990; Kitchener, 1986; Sieber, 1992). Accordingly, Celia B. Fisher developed six ethics cases and accompanying student focus questions to encourage introductory psychology students to recognize and critically evaluate ethical issues in experimentation with human and animal participants and to consider multiple bases and alternative perspectives on ethical problems posed by different scientific approaches to psychological issues Jonsen & Toulmin, 1988; Whitbeck, 1987, 1992).

Curriculum

Case Studies

The curriculum consisted of six case study teaching modules based on a broad sample of "classic" empirical studies cited in a majority of introductory psychology textbooks (e.g., McConnell & Gorenflo, 1989). The case study format complements the instructor's pedagogical goals by being suitable for both coverage of ethical issues and extended discussion of research design and the topical domain addressed by the study. The first case study asked students to consider whether harm can come to participants or to society when social psychologists stage crises in public places (Piliavin & Piliavin, 1972). This was followed by case presentations on animal experimentation (Hubel, 1959) and the use of aversive procedures with human participants (Watson & Rayner, 1920). Two additional cases required critical thinking about ethical issues in socially sensitive (Scarr & Weinberg, 1976) and deception research (Schacter & Singer, 1962). The last case study drew attention to ethical issues associated with randomized clinical trials (RCT) research with participants with psychological disorders (Elkin et al., 1989).

Critical Thinking Questions

Students received a workbook that included (a) a brief abstract of each study; (b) a more detailed description of each experiment including the purpose of the study, primary hypothesis, participants, procedure, results, and conclusions (Fisher & Fyrberg, 1994); and (c) homework assignments composed of four sets of focus questions requiring students to critically evaluate ethical issues derived from the Belmont Report (NCPHSBBR, 1978) and the APA Ethics Code (1992). The first set of questions focused on the scientific validity and social value of the study. This was followed by questions highlighting potential research risks within the context of the need for experimental control. The third set of questions targeted protections and threats to participant autonomy and privacy. The final set of questions addressed the tension between the investigator's dual responsibility to conduct well-controlled experiments and protect participant welfare.

Instructor's Manual

An instructor's guide for leading class discussions and grading student homework assignments included summaries of ethical issues specifically relevant to the particular experiment under study, a list of additional readings, standards relevant to research with human and animal participants from the APA's Ethics Code (1992), and three test questions and guides for grading. Piloting, student focus groups, and faculty workshops contributed to the final set of case summaries, student focus questions, and test questions.

Method

Participants

The initial sample consisted of 585 students enrolled in a total of 24 introductory psychology sections taught during fall and spring semesters at Fordham University, New York and Loyola University, Chicago. Half of the sections received the ethics-enhanced instruction and half the sections received standard ethics instruction. Although all instructors using the ethics curriculum assigned the student focus questions as homework assignments and led student discussions, the amount of time allotted to each ethics module varied as a function of differences in class size (range = 17-75 students) and teaching format (primary

focus in small laboratory sections or a portion of the main lecture). Standard ethics instruction typically included a brief overview of informed consent requirements and the ethical issues associated with Milgram's (1963) use of deception in his classic obedience study. Both the enhanced and standard instructional groups received pretest and posttest questionnaires.

Instruments and Procedure

Pretest and posttest research ethics vignettes. The three test vignettes included a deception study using a Milgram-like procedure with school-aged children (Shanab & Yahya, 1977), an animal aversive conditioning study (Routtenberg & Lindy, 1965), and an RCT study with a nursing home population (Langer, 1983). For each vignette students answered two questions.

The first question (Part A) asked students to describe three ethical procedures or modifications they would use to protect the welfare and rights of the research participants in the study. Scores were on a 4-point scale ranging from 0 (*no credit*) to 3 (*full credit*) for inclusion of ethical procedures specific to the study design and population (e.g., forewarning and dehoaxing, proper care and housing of animals, health monitoring and provision of postexperimental treatment). The second question (Part B) asked students to give ethical reasons for why they would or would not conduct the study in its original form or with their modifications. A full-credit (2 points) response required articulation of the tension between a psychologist's responsibility to conduct well-controlled scientifically valuable studies and the obligation to protect the rights and welfare of research participants. Mention of only one side of this issue merited a score of 1; failure to address the moral dimensions of conducting research (e.g., simply a reiteration of the results of the study) received no credit.

Students received an explanation of the project at the beginning of the semester and either a grade or extra credit (at the discretion of their instructors) for their performance on the posttest exam. Consequently, some students chose not to take the tests, to answer only some of the questions, or failed to distinguish between Parts A and B of their answers. To ensure reliability of scoring we rated only essays of students who answered all portions of both the pre- and posttests (182 and 131 for the ethics-enhanced and standard instructional sections, respectively). Raters were blind to the instructional group. (Interpret reliability calculated on half of pretests and posttests yielded $\kappa = .84$; Cohen, 1968).

Student and faculty curriculum evaluations. At the end of the semester, students ($n = 332$) and instructors ($n = 7$) participating in the enhanced ethics instruction classes completed a 14-item evaluation questionnaire on the clarity, value, and difficulty of course material, and how well the ethics modules fit in the introductory psychology curriculum.

Table 1. Student Scores and Standard Deviations on Pretest and Posttest Essays With Respect to Knowledge of Specific Ethical Procedures (Part A), Ability to Weigh Scientific Responsibility and Participant Rights and Welfare (Part B), and the Combined Score

| Test Component | Enhanced Ethics Instruction | | | | Standard Instruction | | | |
| | Pretest | | Posttest | | Pretest | | Posttest | |
	Scores	SD	Scores	SD	Scores	SD	Scores	SD
Part A (range = 0–3)	.91	.72	1.26	.73	.88	.70	1.02	.70
Part B (range = 0–2)	.80	.61	.87	.61	.84	.54	.76	.62
Full test (range = 0–5)	1.69	1.00	2.13	1.03	1.72	.92	1.79	1.20

Table 2. Means and Standard Deviations for Student and Teacher Evaluations of the Enhanced Ethics Instructional Modules

| Curriculum Features | Student Evaluations[a] | | Instructor Evaluations[b] | |
	M	SD	M	SD
Difficulty				
Brief summaries	3.13	.70	2.86	1.07
Extended summaries	3.08	.56	3.14	0.69
Student focus questions	3.19	.68	3.43	0.53
Value				
Extended summaries	2.74	.88	2.00	0.58
Student focus questions	2.70	.88	2.57	1.13
Class discussions	2.43	.94	2.14	0.90
Instructor's guide for grading homework	—	—	2.71	1.11
Instructor's guide for grading homework	—	—	2.25	0.96
Workload compared to other courses	2.82	.61	2.29	0.76
Additional Topics				
Relevance of exam questions	2.17	.60	1.71	0.49
Compatibility	2.13	.65	2.00	0.00
Increased interest in psychological research	2.32	.76	—	—
Increased interest in scientific ethics	2.36	.73	—	—
Consider using modules in future	—	—	1.00	1.00
Consider using modules on practice	—	—	1.86	0.69

Note. Judgments were made using 5-point scales for difficulty, ranging from 1 (*very elementary*) to 5 (*very difficult*); value, ranging from 1 (*excellent*) to 5 (*poor*); and workload, ranging from 1 (*much heavier*) to 5 (*much lighter*). Judgments on additional topics were made using a 4-point scale ranging from 1 (*strongly agree*) to 4 (*strongly disagree*).
[a] n = 332. [b] n = 7.

Curriculum Evaluation

We evaluated the impact of the curriculum in three different ways: scores on student essays, student course evaluations, and instructor curriculum evaluations. The major results of this project were derived through planned comparison tests on student essay scores following the significant Test x Condition interaction, $F(1, 305) = 16.49$, $p < .04$, derived from a 5-factor analysis of variance (ANOVA) on pretest-posttest, instructional condition, vignette, semester, and university. As predicted, significant posttest improvement emerged only for students who received the ethics-enhanced instruction (critical diff. =.28, $p < .01$; effect sizes for pretest-posttest differences were $d = .44$ and .05 for the enhanced and standard instructional conditions, respectively; see Table 1). Significant Instructional Class × Test interactions also emerged from

5-factor ANOVAs used to separately examine student knowledge of specific ethical procedures (Part A) and their ability to weigh scientific responsibility and participant welfare (Part B), $F(1, 305) = 12.07$, $p < .001$, and $F(1,305) = 6.23$, $p < .02$. Although the mean scores for each part suggested posttest improvement for the ethics-enhanced instruction group, this pattern was significant only for Part A when Scheffe tests were applied (critical diff. = .31, $p < .01$; effect sizes for differences between pretest and posttest performance for Parts A and B were $d = .48$ and .12, respectively). A perusal of the means for Part A responses to the deceptive research posttest vignette written by students in the standard instructional classes suggests that the presence of ethics coverage on the Milgram (1963) experiment in a majority of introductory psychology textbooks also enhances knowledge of ethical issues and procedures related to deception research.

As illustrated in Table 2, students and faculty participants in the ethics-enhanced classes responded favorably toward the curriculum and judged the instructional and testing materials to be appropriate for introductory psychology students. Faculty agreed that the ethics modules complemented and enhanced the introductory psychology curriculum and strongly agreed that they would use the modules in the future. Perhaps most importantly, students agreed that the topics discussed increased their interest in scientific ethics and research aspects of psychology.

Concluding Comments

Our findings demonstrate that expanded instruction in the ethics of scientific psychology using the case study method can be easily incorporated into introductory psychology classes. Ethics-enhanced instruction increased student awareness of particular ethical procedures used to protect participant's rights and welfare and to a lesser extent increased student sensitivity to the importance of considering both scientific responsibility and participant welfare in ethical decision making. The small gain in the ability to move beyond a single fixed approach to an ethical problem toward the construction of ethical resolutions that connect alternative views reflected in posttest scores on Part B is consistent with evidence indicating that although college experiences can produce gains immoral judgments (Rest & Narvaez, 1994), immersion in ethics education may be required to change college students' epistemic assumptions and reflective judgments (King &Kitchener, 1994) .

In addition to enhancing introductory students' awareness of ethical guidelines and ethical decision-making skills for research with animal and human participants, this project demonstrated that the case study approach can increase students' interest in research ethics and in scientific psychology. In the future, case study instructional formats for introductory psychology classes should be used as pedagogical tools for broadening students' understanding and sensitivity not only to research ethics but also to the full spectrum of professional and scientific ethical challenges confronting psychologists.

References

American Psychological Association. (1992). Ethical principles of psychologists and code of conduct. *American Psychologist, 47,* 1597-1611.

Association of American Colleges. (1985*). Integrity in the college curriculum: A report to the academic community.* Washington, DC: Author.

Baum, C., Benjamin, L. T., Bernstein, D., Crider, A., Halonen, J., Hopkins, R., McGovern, T., McKeachie., W., Nodine, B., Reid, P., Suinn, R., & Wade, C. (1993). Principles for quality undergraduate psychology programs. In T. V. McGovern (Ed.),

Handbook for enhancing undergraduate education in psychology (pp. 17-20). Washington, DC: American Psychological Association.

Cohen, J. (1968). Weighted kappa: Nominal scale agreement with provision for scaled disagreement or partial credit. *Psychological Bulletin, 70,* 213-220.

Elkin, I., Shea, M. T., Watkins, J. T., Imber, S. D., Sorsky, S., Collins, J. F., Glass, D. R., Pilkonis, P., Leber, W. R., Docherty, J. P., Fiester, S. J., & Parloff, M. B. (1989). National Institute of Mental Health treatment of depression collaborative research program. *Archives of General Psychiatry, 46,* 971-983.

Fisher, C. B., & Fyrberg, D. (1994). Participant partners: College students weigh the costs and benefits of deceptive research. *American Psychologist, 49,* 417-427.

Fisher, C. B., Hoagwood, K., & Jensen, P. S. (1996). Casebook on ethical issues in research with children and adolescents with mental disorders. In K. Hoagwood, P. S. Jensen, & C. B. Fisher (Eds.), *Ethical issues in mental health research with children and adolescents* (pp. 135-238). Mahwah, NJ: Lawrence Erlbaum Associates, Inc.

Fisher, C. B., & Tryon, W. W. (1990) *. Ethics in applied developmental psychology: Emerging issues in an emerging field.* Norwood, NJ: Ablex.

Hobbs, N. (1948). The development of a code of ethical standards for psychology. *American Psychologist, 3,* 80-84.

Hubel, D. H. (1959). Single unit activity in striate cortex of unrestrained cats. *Journal of Physiology, 147,* 226-238.

Jonsen, A. R, & Toulmin, S. (1988). *The abuse of casuistry: A history of moral reasoning.* Berkeley: University of California Press.

King, P. M., & Kitchener, K. S. (1994*). Developing reflective judgment.* San Francisco: Jossey-Bass.

Kitchener, K. S. (1986). Intuition, critical evaluation and ethical principles: The foundation for ethical decision in counseling psychology. *Counseling Psychologist, 12,* 43-55.

Korn, J. H. (1984). Coverage of research ethics in introductory and social psychology textbooks. *Teaching of Psychology, 11,* 146-149.

Langer, E. J. (1983). *The psychology of control.* Beverly Hills, CA: Sage.

Matthews, J. R. (1991). The teaching of ethics and the ethics of teaching. *Teaching of Psychology, 18,* 80-85.

McConnell, J. V., & Gorenflo, D. W. (1989*). Classic readings in psychology.* New York: Holt, Rinehart & Winston.

McGovern, T. V. (1988). Teaching the ethical principles of psychology. *Teaching of Psychology, 15,* 22-26.

Milgram, S. (1963). Behavioral study of obedience. *Journal of Abnormal and Social Psychology, 67,* 371-378.

National Commission for the Protection of Human Subjects of Biomedical and Behavioral Research.

(1978). *The Belmont Report: Ethical principles and guidelines for the protection of human subjects* (DHEW Publication No. OS 78-0012). Washington, DC: U.S. Government Printing Office.

Piliavin, J. A., & Piliavin, I. M. (1972). Effect of blood on reactions to a victim. *Journal of Personality and Social Psychology, 23,* 353-361.

Rest, J . R., & Narvaez, D . (1994) . *Moral development in the professions: Psychology and applied ethics.* Hillsdale, NJ: Lawrence Erlbaum Associates, Inc.

Routtenberg, A., & Lindy, J. (1965). Effects of the availability of rewarding septal and hypothalamic stimulation on bar pressing for food under conditions of deprivation. *Journal of Comparative and Physiological Psychology, 60,* 158-161.

Scarr, S., & Weinberg, R. (1976). IQ test performance of black children adopted by white families. *American Psychologist, 31,* 726-739.

Schacter, S., & Singer, J . E. (1962) . Cognitive, social, and physiological determinants of emotional state. *Psychological Review, 69,* 379-399.

Shanab, M., & Yahya, K. (1977). A behavioral study of obedience in children. *Journal of Personality and Social Psychology, 35,* 530-536.

Sieber, J. E. (1992). *Planning ethically responsible research: A guide for students and internal review boards.* Newbury Park, CA: Sage.

Warwick, D. P. (1980*). The teaching of ethics in the social sciences.* Hastings on Hudson, NY: Hastings Center.

Watson, J. B., & Rayner, R. (1920). Conditioned emotional reactions. *Journal of Experimental Psychology, 3,* 1-4.

Whitbeck, C. (1987). *The engineer's responsibility for safety: Integrating ethics teaching into courses in engineering design.* Proceedings of the annual meeting of the American Society of Mechanical Engineers, Boston.

Whitbeck, C. (1992). The trouble with dilemmas: Rethinking applied ethics. *Professorial Ethics, 1,* 119-142.

Notes

1. This research was supported by Grant SBR-9310458 from the National Science Foundation to Celia B. Fisher and Fordham University.

2. We are grateful to Michelle Caban, Michael Collins, Roseann Diubaldo, Yvette Martens, and Colleen O'Sullivan for their assistance in scoring the pretests and posttests.

3. Correspondence concerning more specific information about the cases, the instructor's manual, and student workbook should be sent to Celia B. Fisher, Department of Psychology, Dealy Hall, Fordham University,441 East Fordham Road, Bronx, NY 10458-5198.

4. USING SUPPLEMENTAL READINGS

Using Psychology Today Articles to Increase the Perceived Relevance of the Introductory Course

Drew C. Appleby
Marian College

One goal of the introductory course is to help students realize that psychology is a relevant field of study (i.e., it can contribute positively to their lives, and is not something to be merely memorized, regurgitated on tests, and then forgotten). Several authors have reported their attempts to increase students' perception of the relevance of psychology courses. Some attempts involve the opportunity to read popular books (Benel, 1975; LeUnes, 1974; McCollom, 1971) and articles (Wortman & Hillis, 1975) dealing with compelling psychological topics. Others concentrate on the application of psychological principles to explain or deal with everyday life incidences or problems (Brender, 1982; Grasha, 1974). Students have even replicated the "scientific" studies cited to lend validity to the claims made on television commercials (Solomon, 1979).

The concept of relevance has changed in the past 15 years. What was relevant to students in the past may seem irrelevant today. A question that occupies the minds of many contemporary students is: Will my undergraduate education provide me with the skills I need to get a good job after graduation? One way to capitalize on the motivation resulting from this question is to give students an opportunity to discover that a knowledge of psychological principles can benefit them in their academic majors and future careers. Students form strong loyalties to their academic majors and are ego-involved with their career choices. They perceive information that can help them to succeed in these areas to be highly relevant.

Students' eagerness to learn can be increased by an opportunity to improve their grade in the introductory course with extra credit projects. Such projects can facilitate learning more about psychology and about students' own academic major or career choices. Students are more highly motivated when they are allowed to write extra credit reports on articles related to their major and/or career choices, but their enthusiasm wanes if they are unable to locate such materials. This article includes a bibliography designed to alleviate this problem. It provides introductory students with a large amount of well organized and accessible literature that can simplify their search for relevant psychological information.

The first step in producing this bibliography was to assemble a list of the 27 academic majors and career areas offered by Marian College. Because there is a great deal of overlap in the subject matter in many of these areas, several list items were combined into single categories (e.g., Allied Health, Nursing, and PreMed), reducing the total number of categories to 18. The next step was to peruse the table of contents of each issue of *Psychology Today* published since 1967 to locate articles that contain information related to one or more of these categories. This exhaustive search produced 407 articles. The mean number of articles per category was 22.6 and the range was 34 (7 to 41). Some areas were surprisingly well represented (e.g., theology—36 articles, English—31, and home economics—30); other areas were less popular (e.g., foreign languages—7 and computer science and math—8).

The response to this bibliography has been very positive. The number and quality of extra credit reports have increased. Students say that they enjoyed writing the reports because the articles they reviewed contained information that was personally relevant. An unexpected benefit was that many students used the list to find references for term papers and speeches in courses outside psychology. When copies of this bibliography and a memo explaining its purpose were distributed to the chairpersons of other academic departments, the response was very gratifying. Several stated that they had not realized how much their majors could learn about their own disciplines in the introductory psychology course. This bibliography is well suited to the introductory course in which students first encounter the diversity of psychological literature. Because most introductory psychology students never take another psychology course, it is important to expose them to as much relevant information as possible during their brief encounter with our discipline. This technique would not be appropriate for more advanced psychology courses in which the development of library research skills is valued, and students are expected to identify and find articles on their own.

The following list of *Psychology Today* articles and their publication dates is a sample from the complete bibliography. Two articles were chosen from each of the 18 major and/or career categories on the basis of their high level of interest for introductory students and the regency of their publication dates.

Allied Health, Nursing, and PreMed
"Stress and Health" (8/85)
"The Mystery of Alzheimer's" (1/84)
Art and Art Therapy
"Stalking the Mental Image" (5/85)
"How the Mind Draws" (5/86)
Biology
"Crime in the Family Tree" (3/85)
"Genes, Personality, and Alcoholism" (1/85)
Business, Accounting, and Economics
"What Makes a Top Executive?" (2/83)
"To File, Perchance to Cheat" (4/85)
Chemistry
"Alcohol, Marijuana, and Memory" (3/80)
"The Chemistry of Craving" (10/83)
Computer Science and Mathematics
"The Human-Computer Connection" (3/84)
"Computer Games, Let the Kids Play" (8/85)
Education
"Challenging the Brightest" (6/84)
"Who's Intelligent?" (4/82)
English
"When is a Word a Word?" (11/85)
"A Conversation With Isaac Asimov" (1/83)
Foreign Languages
"Fear of Foreign Languages" (8/81)
"The International Language of Gestures" (5/84)
History and Political Science
"Reagan and the National Psyche" (1/82)
"Psychology and Armageddon" (5/82)
Home Economics, Dietetics, and Fashion Merchandising
"Clothes Power" (12/82)
"The Junk Food Syndrome" (1/82)
Music
"Music, the Beautiful Disturber" (12/85)
"The Music of the Hemispheres" (6/82)

Philosophy
"A Sense of Control" (12/84)
"Is it Right?" (6/81)
Physical Education
"Beating Slumps at Their Own Game" (7/84)
"The Playing Field of the Mind" (7/84)
PreLaw
"Beat That Lie Detector" (6/85)
"Mind Control in the Courtroom" (5/82)
Sociology
"Arresting Delinquency" (3/85)
"Marriages Made to Last" (6/85)
Theater and Speech
"The Language of Persuasion" (4/85)
"The Psychologist as TV Guide" (8/86)
Theology
"The Children's God" (12/85)
"Stages of Faith" (11/83)

References

Benel, R. A. (1975). Psychological thrillers: Thrilling to whom? *Teaching of Psychology, 2*, 176-177.

Brender, M. (1982). The relevance connection: Relating academic psychology to everyday life. *Teaching of Psychology, 9*, 222-224.

Grasha, A. F. (1974). "Giving psychology away": Some experiences teaching undergraduates practical psychology. *Teaching of Psychology, 1*, 21-24.

LeUnes, A. (1974). Psychological thrillers revisited: A tentative list of "master thrillers." *American Psychologist, 29*, 211-213.

McCollom, I. N. (1971). Psychological thrillers: Psychology books students read when given freedom of choice. *American Psychologist, 26*, 921-927.

Solomon, P. R. (1979). Science and television commercials: Adding relevance to the research methodology course. *Teaching of Psychology, 6*, 26-30.

Wortman, C. B., & Hillis, J. W. (1975). Some "thrilling" short articles for use in an introductory psychology class. *Teaching of Psychology, 2*, 134-135.

SECTION II:
STATISTICS

Making Statistics Relevant

Some instructors combine methods for reducing statistics anxiety with ways to "bring the statistics course to life." Bernard Beins developed an approach to overcome students' anxiety about or boredom with statistics. The author directed students to write and ask manufacturers for further information supporting researched-based advertising claims. The article detailed the results of students' inquiries and the pedagogical advantages of the approach.

Mark Shatz followed a similar thread by using a simulated labor-management dispute to teach students some fundamental concepts of descriptive statistics, including measures of central tendency and characteristics of distributions. Students used comparable data sets to prepare a statistical presentation that supported their position in the dispute. From the principles underlying this technique, readers can develop their own simulations and add relevance to teaching statistics.

Students in Kenneth Weaver's statistics class learned about the concepts of variability, null hypothesis testing, and confidence intervals from simple exercises involving exclamations, circus and cartoon characters, and falling leaves, respectively. Have you tried increasing your students' comprehension by using such everyday experiences?

Generating Data

Students in Burt Thompson's statistics class used the Student Information Questionnaire (SIQ) to produce a realistic data set for testing a variety of student-generated hypotheses. The instructor provided a skeleton form of the SIQ, and students customized the form to their interests. Evaluations of the technique suggested that students found such data more interesting than artificial data and more helpful for learning statistics.

Generating data sets for students to use throughout the statistics course can be a challenge. Leslie Cake and Roy Hostetter reported on the use of DATAGEN for generating unique and independent or correlated data samples. Instructors can specify the population parameters for the samples. The program also provides summary statistics for each sample and results from statistical analyses.

Teaching Concepts and Principles

Jennifer Dyck and Nancy Gee described a hands-on, in-class demonstration using M&M's®candy to illustrate the concept of the sampling distribution of the mean. With the class serving as the population, each student received a small package of M&M's. The instructor drew samples from the population and constructed an actual sampling distribution. Students in two statistics courses received either the M&M demonstration or a comparable demonstration using a textbook example. Results indicated that students who participated in the M&M demonstration answered more questions correctly on the quiz, believed they had learned more, enjoyed class more, and had fewer negative feelings toward the demonstration than those who received the textbook example demonstration.

To clarify and illustrate complex concepts, such as distributions of sample means, differences between independent sample means, mean difference scores, and raw score populations, Dominic Zerbolio developed a bag of tricks using imaginary marbles and chips. Once students learn to answer probability questions for each sampling distribution, they are primed to generalize to hypothesis testing procedures. Instructors with a flair for the dramatic will find appealing applications for teaching statistical concepts.

The article by David Johnson described a simple but effective demonstration for illustrating the central limit theorem. The author generated three or four equal-sized random samples, consisting of the numbers 1, 2, and 3, for each student in his statistics class. After the students calculated the sum of each random sample, the teacher constructed a distribution of the results on an overhead projector. He then discussed the finer points of the central limit theorem and probability.

Jerzy Karylowski reported a demonstration illustrating regression toward the mean using a psychological context. The demonstration can be used in small and large groups, and it does not require that students have any previous statistical background.

Because he discovered that many students had difficulty understanding the complex correlations and interactions between variables that typify many statistical procedures, David Johnson developed a technique for introducing analysis of variance in a concrete fashion. Perhaps your students could also acquire an intuitive understanding of the concepts of between- and within-groups variance and their relationship to each other.

Roberto Refinetti described the use of a personal computer to conduct a classroom demonstration of the effects of violations of assumptions of analysis of variance (ANOVA) on the probability of Type I error. The demonstration's rationale is that if many data sets of randomly selected numbers are submitted to ANOVA, then the frequency distribution of empirical F values should approximate the probability density curve of the F statistic for the specified degrees of freedom. An objective for this technique is to illustrate the consequences of failing to meet ANOVA assumptions; violations of the assumptions of normality and homogeneity of variances have a measurable but small effect on the probability of Type I error, especially when all groups are the same size.

Kirk Richardson and Don Segal reviewed Schafer's (1976) approach for teaching the analysis and interpretation of interaction in an undergraduate psychological statistics course. The approach used four "languages" consisting of English, tables, graphs, and arithmetic. In addition to presenting learning objectives based on this approach, the authors identified two limitations to the approach. The development and use of a Windows computer program for in-class lecture presentation and for student guided practice overcame the limitations of a conventional lecture and chalkboard presentation.

Concepts such as measurement error and reliability were made more concrete by Jane Buck in a simple, in-class activity. Students responded randomly to multiple-choice items on machine scored answer sheets. These "tests" were then "scored" according to a "key." Because the students had no knowledge of the correct scores, their true score was zero; any score above zero was attributable to chance. The activity related the concepts of chance scores and reliability to the standard error of measurement.

Exploring Pedagogical Strategies

Mark Ware and Jeffrey Chastain assessed the effectiveness of a teaching strategy emphasizing the use of different statistical tests (i.e., selection skills) in introductory statistics. Analysis of covariance revealed that students in the class emphasizing statistical selection skills achieved significantly higher selection scores than students in the other groups. The techniques reported in this article may interest teachers who are interested in increasing students' facility for choosing appropriate statistical tests.

Richard Rogers used of a microcomputer software/textbook package, including computer-generated individualized assignments, in an introductory statistics course. Advantages consisted of producing individual assignments to avoid having one student copying another's work. Moreover, the material facilitated production of problems for examinations that tested students' facility for selecting the appropriate analysis for a particular situation.

This article and the previous one provide instructors with a variety of techniques for increasing students' selection skills.

Patricia Oswald investigated the benefits of using a personal computer and a projection system to teach undergraduate statistics. The author outlined the method used, and the hardware and software requirements; she also identified four educational objectives. Students reported increased confidence and ability to use computers and solve statistical problems.

Joseph Rossi's students recomputed the values of statistical tests published in journal articles. Undergraduate and graduate students compared the recomputed values to the published results and discovered that about 13% of the results reported as statistically significant were not. The author cautioned against making students mistrust statistical findings; he promoted the exercise as a way to develop a detective-like attitude toward reading journal articles. Using a detective metaphor with statistics classes may also increase students' interest in statistics.

To evaluate data collection and feedback as a means for teaching basic statistical concepts, Jean Low randomly assigned sections of a human development course to one of three groups. In all three groups, students contributed personal information at the beginning of each class. After each class, the instructor analyzed the information to provide feedback about class frequencies, means, standard deviations, and correlations. Students received this feedback either daily (continuous groups), on an average of twice per month (partial groups), or never (control groups). On an end-of-semester test of statistical concepts, students in the continuous feedback groups scored significantly higher than did students in the other two groups. The continuous feedback format was difficult and time-consuming, but the author believed that its benefits outweighed the difficulties.

Connie Varnhagen, Sean Drake, and Gary Finley used several components of the Internet to administer the laboratory portion of an intermediate statistics course offered to psychology honors students. Using an on-line questionnaire, the authors evaluated students' perceived effectiveness of using the Internet. Students reported finding the communication components of the Internet laboratory more useful than the information components, perceived few barriers of the system for their learning, and rated the value of the system positively. Are you using the Internet as one tool in teaching statistics?

1. MAKING STATISTICS RELEVANT

Teaching the Relevance of Statistics Through Consumer-Oriented Research

Bernard Beins
Thomas More College

Everybody who teaches statistics and experimental psychology courses faces students who are either overcome with anxiety ("I've never been good in math") or terminally bored with the apparent lack of relevance of the course to their lives. Many students are bound to fall into one or both of these categories, given the large numbers of undergraduate psychology departments that require or recommend a course in statistics. From 147 college and university catalogs sampled by Bartz (1981), all but 12 either required or recommended a statistics course. Further, informing students that even graduate programs in clinical psychology require statistics and experimental courses is not highly motivating. The continuing battle to make the courses more palatable to undergraduates is reflected in the efforts by psychologists to alter and update their statistics/experimental courses. To this end, *Teaching of Psychology* has published regular articles dealing with these areas (e.g., Bartz, 1981; Dillbeck, 1983; Hastings, 1982).

One of the most obvious ways to overcome the anxiety associated with statistics is to focus students' attention on various kinds of information they already have. Jacobs (1980) suggests that statistics is simply another kind of tool used for achieving some goal, no different in principle from a hammer or screwdriver; students are shown these mundane implements and consequently, a new set of tools, namely simple statistical formulas, are derived. According to Jacobs, "Members of the class agreed that they had already learned to use some of the tools on the list; the argument was advanced that they could also learn to use other tools, including statistics" (p. 241). In a slightly different procedure, Hastings (1983) suggests to his students that they approach statistics as they would any other language they are likely to encounter. Allen (1981) tries to relate the statistics to information that students already know from other classes and, presumably, with which they are already familiar.

In a small experimental design course (6 students), I attempted to decrease anxiety and bring relevance to the classroom by having the students go out and find instances of statistical and research applications. I directed them to the myriad of claims proffered on television and in magazines. Their task was to isolate specific instances in which manufacturers made claims based on research and then to write the companies for further information.

The point I was trying to make was that many people actually use statistics in the real world. I also wanted the students to encounter statistics and research formats that were of interest to them and that they would be able to evaluate on their own. The students were free to communicate with any company on any kind of product, as long as some research claims were made. They reported to the class as they received each response.

Students contacted a wide variety of companies including the makers of soft drinks, cereal, infants' vitamins, and automobiles. It was apparent that students' interests determined, in part, what information they requested. For instance, the biology students tended to request information on medical products (e.g., Anacin, Children's Tylenol, sugarless gum, salt content of margarine); one varsity athlete requested information on bicycle helmets; one student interested in auto mechanics requested data on mufflers, another on auto batteries. Thus, it seems that the students took their assignments seriously enough to seek information in areas in which they were knowledgeable and interested.

The students' responses to the replies fell into three overall categories: increased skepticism; increased respect for marketing research; and a renewed awareness that, in commercials, things are not always what they seem.

The skepticism arose because, in some cases, the students (as consumers) were treated with suspicion in phone conversations and were queried by company personnel as to what consumer group or company they represented. In other instances, the students were promised information that they had not received by the end of the term (about 10 weeks after their initial contact with the company).

On the other hand, most students came to the realization that some marketing research is extensively planned and well conducted. The most compelling example involved a response to an inquiry about bicycle helmet safety: The manufacturer sent a complete technical report run by an independent cyclists' group in

Washington, DC. When students discussed the report, they could find no flaws in design or interpretation. In fact, whenever companies had sent complete information, students tended to be more positively impressed.

The third type of response was that it is easy to be misled by advertising claims because the advertisers are very good at setting the stage for specious inferences by consumers. One example was given in a letter from Union Carbide Corporation, the manufacturer of Energizer batteries. The student had interpreted the claim that "Of all leading brands, nothing outlasts the Energizer from Eveready" as a statement that the battery "outlasts them all." The company noted that "you have read something into these ads which is not there. We have never used the phrase 'outlasts them all,' or any other words to that effect." This example was all the more compelling because the student had listened to the commercial and then written down the claim immediately, and had still drawn an erroneous inference.

Students in the class uniformly approved of the assignment when questioned at the end of the term. I asked them to comment on "whether future classes should be asked to do this project or whether it was more trouble than it was worth." I also asked them what they learned, if anything, from this assignment. According to a questionnaire, everyone claimed to derive some benefit from the exercise. Although I cannot eliminate the possibility of demand characteristics, the responses appeared candid, as with one student who commented that, at first, the assignment "may sound stupid, but students will find it worthwhile when they get the replies."

Another benefit from the assignment was that the students learned that research is not an "ivory-tower" exercise. One student commented on the large number of marketing companies and suggested that it was "amazing to discover that many of the concepts and tests discussed in class are used in the real world."

This project seemed to have its intended effect in relaxing the students in their approach to statistics and research design. The assignment also seemed to have taken some of the mystery away from the process of collecting and interpreting data. Finally, our real-life exercise gave the students some indication of the relevance of statistics and research.

References

Allen, G. A. (1981). The χ^2 statistic and Weber's law. *Teaching of Psychology, 8,* 179-180.

Bartz, A. E. (1981). The statistics course as a departmental offering and major requirement. *Teaching of Psychology, 8,* 106.

Dillbeck, M. C. (1983). Teaching statistics in terms of the knower. *Teaching of Psychology, 10,* 18-20.

Hastings, M. W. (1982). Statistics: Challenge for students and the professor. *Teaching of Psychology, 9,* 221-222.

Jacobs, K. W. (1980). Instructional techniques in the introductory statistics course: The first class meeting. *Teaching of Psychology, 7,* 241-242.

The Greyhound Strike: Using a Labor Dispute to Teach Descriptive Statistics

Mark A. Shatz
Ohio University—Zanesville

Students enrolled in statistics classes frequently have difficulty understanding the relevance of statistics for everyday events. The strike by the Greyhound bus drivers last year provided me with the opportunity to develop a classroom activity that illustrated the various ways data can be manipulated with descriptive statistics.

To begin the activity, the class was divided into two groups. The first group of students represented the position of labor (i.e., against a salary cut) and the second group represented the position of management (i.e., for a salary cut). To facilitate the computational aspects of the activity, the students were directed to work in groups of four.

The students were presented with factitious data based on the circumstances of the Greyhound strike. The first part of the data included the individual salaries of the striking employees ($n = 50$) and the average fringe benefits of the employees. Several of the salaries were noted as the salaries of trainee drivers. The second group of data focused on the salaries earned by drivers at three rival companies. For each company, the following information was presented: the number of employees, the average employee benefits, and descriptive measures of the drivers' salaries (mean, median, mode, and standard deviation). The salary data for the three companies were designed to illustrate normal and skewed distributions.

After the students were presented the data, they were instructed to focus on the salary data of the striking employees and then to consider comparisons with the other companies. The stated goal was for the students to manipulate the data in order to provide the best defense for their respective positions. When the students completed their computations, the two groups debated the salary issue and I served as the arbitrator. The activity was evaluated by the students at the completion of the arbitration period.

The activity had several specific objectives. The first objective was to illustrate how the definition of a construct (i.e., salary) can affect its measurement. This was accomplished by requiring the students to specify the data (e.g., trainees' salaries, fringe benefits) that were used in the computation of salary statistics. The second objective was to demonstrate how the size of a class interval can affect the appearance of a frequency distribution. To achieve this objective, students were required to experiment with class intervals of different sizes until they developed a frequency distribution table that best illustrated their position. The third objective was to provide practice in generating visual representations of data. The students had to identify the visual medium (e.g., bar graph, frequency polygon) that best supported their argument. The fourth objective was to demonstrate the effects of skewed data on the measures of central tendency. The students were required to select the measures of central tendency of each company that were most generous to their position (and for instructional purposes, to identify the most appropriate measures).

The activity took approximately 1 hour to complete. During that time, the students had an opportunity to compute and interpret most of the descriptive statistics that are typically taught in the first unit of a statistics course. Also, students were able to use the various techniques that are used to manipulate data.

Several major themes were identified in the students' written evaluations of the activity. First, the students said that the activity helped them to understand the role of descriptive statistics. Second, the students indicated that they had gained an appreciation of how descriptive statistics can be used to alter the appearance of a data set. And finally, the most frequently mentioned benefit was that the debate format of the activity provided an opportunity for the students to use their statistical skills by defending an argument with statistics. As one student commented about the activity, "It helped by allowing us to talk about the stuff that we just learned and not just compute statistics."

Although this activity was illustrated with a nonpsychological topic, the debate format of the activity could be adapted for research-oriented problems. For example, an instructor could generate data for a study that investigated the efficacy of a new treatment program. The types of data needed would be similar to the data used in the above activity; that is, individual scores for the subjects in the new treatment program and descriptive measures of several existing programs. The students would be directed to defend the relative merits of the new procedure or the existing programs. By using a research example, the activity would provide an excellent review of descriptive statistics and would be an ideal introduction to inferential statistics.

The main benefit of this activity was that the debate format provided students with an opportunity to use the statistical skills that they had acquired. The positive student response has encouraged me to make greater use of issues that students are aware of, and to design activities that allow students to verbalize the course material. Although this type of activity requires an instructor to spend time generating data, the resulting instructional benefits are well worth the effort.

Elaborating Selected Statistical Concepts With Common Experience

Kenneth A. Weaver
Emporia State University

Introductory statistics textbooks usually describe statistics as a "new way of thinking about and learning about the world" (Glenberg, 1988, p. v). By including news items and cartoons, textbook authors use well-known information to illustrate new concepts. In this article, I show how exclamations, circus and cartoon characters, and falling leaves can be used to elaborate statistical concepts, such as variability, null hypothesis testing, and confidence interval.

Variability

After demonstrating how to compute the standard deviation, I present an exclamation and ask students to evaluate the statistical information it contains. For example, a visiting grandmother remarks, "My, how you've grown!" Understanding this exclamation requires comparing one's sense of a child's average growth with the amount of growth since grandmother's last visit. The greater the difference, the more unusual is the amount of growth, and the louder is the exclamation. Familiar exclamations include Jackie Gleason's refrain "How sweet it is!" and the line from the opening song of the play Oklahoma (Rodgers & Hammerstein, 1942), "Oh, what a beautiful morning!"

As a class exercise, students generate their own exclamations. After learning about z scores, students convert their exclamations to an approximate z score. Selected students present their z scores to class members, who evaluate the sign and size.

I also suggest that one's intuition about averageness and difference can be intentionally manipulated for a dramatic effect. Dr. Jekyll and Mr. Hyde and Popeye before and after eating spinach exemplify obvious and extreme variation. In contrast, more subtle is the variation of selected behaviors by the same character, such as the ferocity of King Kong except for its gentleness with Ann Redman.

Testing the Null Hypothesis

After lecturing about probability, the critical region, and the null hypothesis, I talk about circus or cartoon characters that have unusual characteristics corresponding to measures in the tails of the appropriate distribution. These unusual scores (and unusual characters) can help teach students about the statistical (and social) rejection associated with such deviations from the norm.

I rhetorically ask the class: What makes circus attractions like the bearded lady or a midget so popular? My answer is that these individuals are so unusual, relative to the rest of the population, that they belong in the extremes of the distribution for that attribute. I remind students that the extreme area of the distribution is labeled the critical or *alpha* region and contains cases so different that they are not accepted as part of the group.

Adjectives such as *rare, abnormal,* and *bizarre* describe cases in the critical area. Not being accepted as a member of a particular distribution becomes increasingly likely the more unusual the individual. For example, Pinnochio's nose length, Flash's speed, and a witch's beauty (or lack of it) produce measurements that fall in the critical area and are thus rejected as members of the "regular" group.

I use the single sample t test to connect the logic of rejecting extremes with making statistical decisions. If the sampling error converted to standard deviations falls in the t distribution's critical region, then the error is not accepted as belonging to the population of "normal"-sized errors, and the null hypothesis is rejected.

Students have previously been told that alpha specifies the degree to which chance can be an explanation for the results. They also have been warned that *alpha* is not a measure of effect size. Thus, characterizing a result as being "highly" or "very" or "marginally" significant, based on the value of *alpha*, is inappropriate (Harcum, 1989).

58

Confidence Interval

For this exercise, I describe the following scene:

Imagine a wind-sheltered orchard of trees during autumn. As the trees shed their leaves, piles form around the trunks. Each pile is tallest next to the tree and decreases in height farther away from the tree. Note the similarity between the shape of each pile and the outline of the standard normal distribution. Imagine standing next to a tree's trunk and picking up a leaf from the pile. How sure are you that the particular leaf fell from the tree under which you are standing? Now imagine moving 60 ft away and picking up a leaf from the same pile. How sure are you that this leaf came from the same tree and not a neighboring one?

Invariably, students respond that they are much more confident that the leaf near the trunk belongs to that tree. I continue the discussion by saying that as distance from the tree increases, a point is ultimately reached beyond which any leaf on the ground would more confidently be considered as coming from another tree. Then I associate the trunk with the estimated population mean, the leaves with sample means, and the confidence points with 1 — alpha and say that the confidence points form the interval's two endpoints within which the population mean has a 1 — alpha probability of being located.

Conclusion

This article describes how common experiences can be used to elaborate selected statistical concepts. Students have been intrigued by the notion that the thinking they use during the exercises overlaps with the technical principles being presented in the course. They generally indicate that the exercises increase their comprehension of the related text material or, if not, provide a perspective from which to ask meaningful questions. I would appreciate knowing how other statistics instructors use commonplace experiences in their courses.

References

Glenberg, A. M. (1988). *Learning from data: An introduction to statistical reasoning.* New York Harcourr Brace Jovanovich.

Harcum, E. R (1989). The highly inappropriate calibrations of statistical significance. *American Psychologist, 44,* 964.

Rodgers, R., & Hammerstein, O., II. (1942). *Oklahoma.* New York Williamson Music Corporation.

Note

I thank Charles L. Brewer and three anonymous reviewers for their comments on an earlier draft.

2. GENERATING DATA

Making Data Analysis Realistic: Incorporating Research Into Statistics Courses

W. Burt Thompson
Niagara University

As psychologists, we are often motivated to collect, analyze, and interpret data because we want to answer an interesting question. I believe this same motive must drive students who are learning applied statistics. This article describes one way instructors can increase their students' desire to learn by using realistic, rather than artificial, data that the students collect in a simple research project. This project yields data that create an immediate desire to learn statistics based on the students' fascination with psychology.

Most statistics textbooks contain practice problems based on artificial data. Instructors also frequently create hypothetical data for use in class, and several articles in *Teaching of Psychology* describe how to generate artificial data for the statistics course (e.g., Beins, 1989; Cake & Hostetter, 1986). The use of hypothetical data is an important part of any statistics course, but one negative consequence is that these data sets may arouse minimal student interest. After all, why would students who want to learn about human behavior care about two columns of numbers labeled X and Y? An even bigger problem is that artificial data sets remove students from the data-collection process and thus create or reinforce an artificial separation of research and data analysis, two processes that are in practice inseparable (Singer & Willett, 1990).

There are many ways to increase the realism of data. For example, Beins (1985) suggested that instructors have students test advertising claims by obtaining and analyzing research reports on which the claims are based. Hettich (1974) suggested that instructors have students complete two questionnaires (to assess study habits and test anxiety) and provide information such as height, academic major, and number of completed psychology courses (Jacobs, 1980, described a similar procedure). However, Hettich's suggestion produces only a small data set that limits the hypotheses that can be tested. More important, although the techniques suggested by Hettich and Beins do yield real data, students do not select which factors to measure or which hypotheses to test, and they do not assist in data collection. To derive full benefit from real data, students must be the researchers (not the subjects in the study), and they must collect the data themselves or assist in the design of the data-collection instrument.

Generating Realistic Data: The Student-Designed Student Information Questionnaire

Because questionnaires are widely used in psychological research and can easily produce a large data set, I have students use a Student Information Questionnaire (SIQ) that they help construct. The SIQ taps variables that are of interest to students; it also provides a variety of measures useful in teaching an introductory statistics course. Students can test many different hypotheses because the SIQ measures many variables (one class's SIQ measured 19 variables); indeed, each student can generate a unique list of hypotheses to investigate .

Instructors can modify the SIQ to fit their pedagogical needs. However, each new group of students should modify the questionnaire to fit particular interests. When students customize the SIQ, it becomes their survey (rather than the instructor's survey) and gives them a legitimate feeling of ownership for the data. In contrast, in Hettich's (1974) proposal, the instructor assumes the role of researcher, and the students are subjects in the study. My students assume the role of researchers, and the survey is treated as a research project they conduct.

I provide the class with a skeleton form of the SIQ that includes questions about common activities, such as studying and television viewing, and it asks each respondent for a self-rating on several characteristics (e.g., friendliness, creativity, and shyness). Students in one of my classes added questions to find out if the respondents lived in a dormitory or in off-campus housing and whether they paid for their own tuition. Students later examined the relation between these two factors and how seriously the respondents approached their university studies (indexed by the amount of time spent in activities such as studying and television viewing). Another class was interested in study habits; they added questions to the SIQ such as "When you study, how much noise and activity do you prefer to have going on around you ?" and "What time of day do you prefer to study?"

Early in the semester (typically during the second class meeting) my students decide how they would like to change the survey, and I guide their writing of new items.

We discuss what variables to measure and the best kind of question for measuring each factor, given the constraints that the SIQ must be short and easy to complete. It is important for students to state each hypothesis as explicitly as possible to facilitate the writing of useful and unbiased items. Students must be continually asked "Will the answers given to this question allow you to test your hypothesis?"

Survey items can be written during class or as homework. I give copies of the final SIQ to instructors who have agreed to distribute it in their classes.[1] Because the SIQ can be completed in a few minutes, I have never encountered problems getting other instructors to distribute it. Typically between 100 and 150 students from a variety of courses complete the SIQ. This procedure provides enough variability and large enough subsamples to allow students to test hypotheses with predictor variables such as gender or college class. The SIQ should be distributed several weeks after the beginning of the term, although the timing depends on the questions. Waiting until the third week of classes will yield meaningful answers to the question about the amount of time spent studying each week and other questions that deal with routine aspects of college life. However, avoid waiting too long because much of the SIQ material is useful for teaching about descriptive statistics during the first part of the course.

Classroom Uses or SIQ Data

Once the surveys are returned, I devote part of one class meeting to data coding. Students working in small groups transfer the information from the completed SIQs to summary sheets that I have prepared in advance (each group is given a copy of the coding sheet). Each student codes several surveys. Because I typically have 30 students in my class (15 students in each of two sections) and 100 to 150 completed SIQs, each student must code four or five surveys. It takes about 20 min to explain how to use the coding sheet and for the students to record the data. After class, I enter the data into a computer spreadsheet and give a copy to each student. (Instructors who use computers in their classes may want the students to enter the data.)

Next, the students generate hypotheses about group differences, relations between variables, and point estimates. Students are usually interested in comparing men to women (and freshman to seniors) on such factors as how much they study, exercise, smoke, or drink. Students also make predictions about the relations between

---

[1]I do not have my students assist in the actual data collection because I usually have about 30 students and the survey is distributed in only five or six classes. Although my students do not distribute and collect the SIQs, I consider them to be researchers because they design the study and create the survey. The students decided which hypotheses ro test, which variables to measure, and which questions to ask to measure those variables. Students can be required to assist in the actual data collection if an instructor believes such experience would be beneficial.

pairs of variables (e.g., self-ratings of aggression and friendliness). For point estimates, the students make predictions, such as the proportion of students who smoke or the average number of hours college students exercise each week. The students record their hypotheses and refer to them as new statistical procedures are presented.

The SIQ is useful in the classroom and is also an excellent source for homework assignments. Students can easily perform most analyses using calculators. I deal with large problems (e.g., computing the correlation between height and weight for all SIQ respondents) in one of two ways. One method is to divide the work among groups of students; each group might compute the quantities needed for Pearson correlation coefficients (e. g., ΣXY and ΣX) for 20 subjects. The quantities can then be combined to complete the calculation. However, once students have mastered the computations using fewer subjects, I prefer to do the calculations on the computer and let students concentrate on interpretation.

As each new topic is covered, students apply the new procedures and concepts to the SIQ data. For example, at the beginning of the course, I have students create separate frequency tables and histograms to summarize how much time men and women spend in activities such as studying and exercising. Later, the students compute descriptive statistics for these variables, and still later they compute a t test or one-way analysis of variance to test the reliability of the observed differences. Many pairs of variables on the SIQ can be used to teach correlation and regression. For example, Pearson correlation coefficients can be computed for pairs of variables such as height and weight as well as studying and watching television. My students also write brief conclusions based on their data analyses as part of homework assignments. This approach reminds students that statistics is not a set of isolated procedures but is a tool to help them answer questions and make discoveries based on the information they have helped collect.

Student Evaluation of SIQ Data

I have used a version of the SIQ for the past 6 years in my statistics courses. Students in my two most recent sections ($N = 28$) completed a brief survey comparing the artificial data sets and data from the SIQ that had both been used in class. When asked "Which kind of data would you prefer the instructor to use when teaching about new statistical concepts and procedures?," 92% selected SIQ data over hypothetical data sets. Most of my students also indicated that SIQ data were more interesting to work with than artificial data (see Table 1). Finally, I asked students if they thought the use of SIQ data made it easier to learn statistics compared to hypothetical data. Only 13% responded "no" to this question; 71% said "yes" (the remaining 16% selected the "I don't know" response). These data suggest that the majority of my students find the SIQ data fairly engaging and perceive them to be an aid to learning.

Table 1. Student Interest Ratings for SIQ Data and Artificial Data Sets

	How Interesting Was it to Work With This Kind of Data?			
	Very	Moderately	A Little	Not At All
SIQ data	36	54	11	0
Artificial data	0	29	46	25

Conclusion

I argued that students should learn statistics by working with real data. Two desirable consequences of using data from studies designed by students, rather than artificial data, are (a) real data are more interesting to students, and (b) students learn firsthand that data analysis is an integral part of the research process rather than a separate enterprise. Research makes the statistics course more effective and enjoyable because it gives students the chance to ask meaningful psychological questions and learn how statistics can help find the answers. From the instructor's perspective, I enjoy working with real data much more than artificial data; I become as eager as the students to see the results of a study, and this eagerness helps generate enthusiasm in my students.

The SIQ produces descriptive and correlational data. Because many other types of experiments can be performed quickly in class or by students as part of their homework, I suggest that instructors supplement SIQ data with other research studies. My students conduct several true experiments (involving manipulation of an independent variable) during the semester. Many suitable studies can be found in instructor's manuals or created from descriptions of studies in journals and books. (Interested readers may write for descriptions and copies of the materials for several studies that I have used with

success.) Hypothetical data sets will remain an important part of the statistics course, but they can be supplemented with real data from studies designed by students.

References

Beins, B. (1985). Teaching the relevance of statistics through consumer-oriented research. *Teaching of Psychology, 12,* 168-169.

Beins, B. C. (1989). A BASIC program for generating integer means and variances. *Teaching of Psychology, 16,* 230-231.

Cake, L. J., & Hostetter, R. C. (1986). DATAGEN: A BASIC program for generating and analyzing data for use in statistics courses. *Teaching of Psychology, 13,* 210-212.

Hettich, P. (1974). The student as data generator. *Teaching of Psychology, 1,* 35-36.

Jacobs, K. W. (1980). Instructional techniques in the introductory statistics course: The first class meeting. *Teaching of Psychology, 7,* 241-242.

Singer, J. D., & Willett, J. B. (1990). Improving the teaching of applied statistics: Putting the data back into data analysis. *The American Statistician, 44,* 223-230.

Notes

1. I thank Donna Fisher Thompson, Timothy Osberg, Ruth Ault, and two reviewers for their comments on an earlier version of this article.
2. Requests for copies of the basic Student Information Questionnaire should be sent to W. Burt Thompson, Department of Psychology, P.O. Box 2208, Niagara University, NY 14109-2208.

DATAGEN: A BASIC Program for Generating and Analyzing Data for Use in Statistics Courses

Leslie J. Cake
Roy C. Hostetter
Sir Wilfred Grenfell College
Memorial University of Newfoundland

In many undergraduate statistics courses, students are provided with a common set of data to analyze. The reason for using common data is often one of convenience; the instructor need only look up the answer or perform one set of analyses for purposes of correction. However, the use of common data may be undesirable for several reasons. Common data allow for the possibility of copying calculations and results, thereby reducing the need for careful, independent work by each student. In addition, common data sets do not provide the student with a feeling for the variable nature of repeated sampling from a common population. Thus, the opportunity to teach a basic reason for the existence of statistical procedures can be missed. The BASIC program described in this article permits instructors to present each student with unique sets of data while eliminating the need for tedious repeated analyses. That is, DATAGEN is a program that generates data samples from a population with specified parameters and provides the instructor with some basic statistical calculations and analyses for these data.

Program Description and Use

An initial menu offers the instructor the choice of independent or correlated data samples; these options are described in turn.

Independent Data Samples

Initially, the number of samples and the N for each sample are specified. The mean and standard deviation for the population from which each data sample was drawn are entered next. If desired, the instructor may also provide a label for each of the samples and request that a completely randomized, one-factor analysis of variance (ANOVA) be calculated for each student's data. Also, if desired, the instructor can provide text (e.g., a description of a study and/or instructions for analysis) that will be printed out with each student's unique data set.

The program then proceeds to generate and print out unique data samples for each student. An algorithm (Hansen, 1985), using the central limit theorem, repeatedly generates normally distributed random numbers from a population with mean of 0 and standard deviation of 1. For each random number, the corresponding sample data point is then calculated using the following formula.

$$\text{data point} = \text{input } M + (\text{input } SD \times \text{random number})$$

The result is a sample of data randomly chosen from a population with specified mean and standard deviation. This procedure is repeated for each sample for each student.

The algorithm for generating normally distributed random numbers was tested with three replications each for sample sizes 10, 100, 1,000, and 10,000. The average means and standard deviations obtained were, respectively, -0.012 and 1.187 ($N = 10$), 0.060 and 0.999 ($N = 100$), 0.000 and 1.012 ($N = 1,000$), and 0.0004 and 0.994 ($N = 10,000$). These results suggest that the algorithm is generating an appropriate distribution.

Output of the data samples may be directed to the printer or the screen. If printer output is selected, the student's name, the text (if provided), and unique data are printed on separate pages for each student. Next, summary statistics for each student are printed, again on separate pages, for the instructor. Sample statistics provided are N, mean, variance, standard deviation, sum X, (sum $X)^2$, and sum X^2. If requested, an ANOVA summary table for a one-factor, completely randomized design (equal or unequal N) is also calculated and printed. A sample output for independent data is presented in Table 1.

Correlated Data Samples

Initially, the instructor enters the N for the two samples and the means and standard deviations for the populations from which the samples were drawn. The desired correlation between the two populations is also entered. The program then presents the standard error of estimate based on the entered information and continues in the same manner as the independent data case, up to the point of generating unique data points for the two samples.

For each pair of data points, two random numbers are generated using the random number algorithm (Hansen, 1985). The first random number is used to derive the X value using the same formula as in the independent data case. The Y member of the pair is derived using the standard prediction equation, the standard error of estimate, and the second random number. This process is repeated until all data points for both samples for all students have been generated. Student samples (and text if provided) are then printed out.

In addition to the sample statistics presented for the independent data case, the sum of cross products, the actual Pearson product-moment correlation coefficient, and the regression equations for predicting X from Y and Y from X are calculated. The t values for the difference between sample means and for the significance of the correlation coefficient, along with the appropriate degrees of freedom, are also provided. A sample output for correlated data is presented in Table 2.

Table 1. Sample Independent Output for One Student

Output for the Student

NAME: Leslie J. Cake

Thirty skilled typists were randomly assigned to 1 of 3 groups that received different dosages of alcohol (0 mg / 25 mg / or 50 mg per 100 ml BAL). Typing speed was then measured in words per minute using a standard typing test. Calculate the mean and standard deviation for each alcohol group and a one-factor, completely randomized ANOVA. What would you conclude about the effect that alcohol has on typing speed?

DATA:

0 mg alcohol (Control)

| 61 | 76 | 46 | 60 | 67 | 60 | 59 | 64 | 66 | 48 |

25 mg alcohol

| 63 | 61 | 57 | 45 | 74 | 56 | 56 | 52 | 38 | 45 |

50 mg alcohol

| 29 | 30 | 50 | 42 | 48 | 36 | 25 | 34 | 46 | 49 |

Output for the Instructor

• Input values •

0 mg alcohol (Control) input $N = 10$

input $M = 60$ input $SD = 8$

25 mg alcohol   input $N = 10$

input $M = 50$ input $SD = 10$

50 mg alcohol   input $N = 10$

input $M = 40$ input $SD = 9$

Summary statistics for Leslie J. Cake

0 mg alcohol (Control) $N = 10$

| $M = 60.7$ | Variance = 77.12223 | $SD = 8.781926$ |
| Sum $X = 607$ | (Sum $X)^2 = 368449$ | Sum $X^2 = 37539$ |

25 mg alcohol $N = 10$

| $M = 54.7$ | Variance = 107.1222 | $SD = 10.34999$ |
| Sum $X = 547$ | (Sum $X)^2 = 299209$ | Sum $X^2 = 30885$ |

50 mg alcohol $N = 10$

| $M = 38.9$ | Variance = 85.65556 | $SD = 9.255029$ |
| Sum $X = 389$ | (Sum $X)^2 = 151321$ | Sum $X^2 = 15903$ |

ANOVA Summary Table

Source	SS	df	MS	F
Between	2536.266	2	1268.133	14.096
Within	2429.102	27	89.967	
Total	4965.367	29		

Table 2. Sample Correlated Data Output for One Student

Output for the Student

NAME: Roy C. Hostetter

An investigator is interested in the relationship between age and memory. She has information from a previous experiment on the number of words recalled (out of 100) by people of varying ages. These data are reproduced below. Calculate the mean and standard deviation for each variable and the correlation coefficient. Test the significance of this correlation coefficient. What would you conclude about the relationship between age and memory? Calculate the regression equation for predicting memory score from age. Given an age of 45, what memory score would you predict?

DATA:

Age	Words recalled (/100)
37	73
58	44
56	48
47	60
39	76
63	32
66	50
51	73
53	39
31	75
36	69
36	86
59	42
53	51
52	55
57	60
56	55
57	63
44	62
62	62

Output for the Instructor

N for samples = 20

Input $M_X = 45$ Input $SD_X = 10$

Input $M_Y = 60$ Input $SD_Y = 15$

Input correlation coefficient = $-.7$

Summary Statistics for Roy C. Hostetter

| $M_X = 50.65$ | Variance X = 104.5553 | $SD_X = 10.22523$ |
| $M_Y = 58.75$ | Variance Y = 196.9342 | $SD_Y = 14.03333$ |

Correlation of X vs. $Y = -.7606226$

Prediction of Y from X $Y' = -1.043895 X + 111.6233$

Prediction of X from Y $X' = -.5542193 Y + 83.21038$

Sum $X = 1013$ (Sum $X)^2 = 1026169$ Sum $X^2 = 53295$

Sum $Y = 1175$ (Sum $Y)^2 = 1380625$ Sum $Y^2 = 72773$

Sum of cross products = 57440

Standard error of difference = 5.097936

t for difference between means = -1.588878

$df = 19$

t for significance of correlation coefficient = -4.970852

$df = 18$

General Comments on Program Use

We have used versions of DATAGEN with undergraduate statistics classes and noticed several benefits. When the program is used for generating laboratory exercises, the students appear to concentrate on the way various analyses should be carried out rather than on obtaining the "correct" answer as often occurs with common data. A second benefit relates to the ease of demonstrating various statistical concepts. The variability found in repeated sampling from a common population can be demonstrated by having students compare their data and results. The effect that sample size has on the standard error of test statistics is easily demonstrated by specifying samples of different sizes. The nature of the confidence interval can be demonstrated when each student has different samples. The use of carefully selected means and/or standard deviations can be used to demonstrate the probabilistic nature of hypothesis-testing statistics.

In summary, we believe that demonstrations of various statistical concepts are more dramatic, and that understanding occurs more rapidly, by using DATAGEN to generate unique data sets for student exercises. Although the program provides various analyses, using this program can be slightly more time-consuming than merely assigning certain exercises from a textbook. This extra effort is offset, however, by the program's advantages; it offers a closer approximation to analyzing "real" data.

Reference

Hansen, A. G. (1985). Simulating the normal distribution. *Byte, 10,* 137-138.

Notes

1. The authors acknowledge the assistance of Connie Gibbons and Daniel Stewart in the preparation of this article and the program.
2. The program was written in "standard" Microsoft BASIC. Hence, the program should be easily ported to a number of microcomputers. We have versions available for the Tandy 1000 and compatibles including the IBM PC, and for the Commodore PET and compatibles.
3. For disk versions of the program send a double-sided, double-density 5¼ in. diskette and mailer with sufficient return postage. Please specify the program version required. Address listing, disk, and reprint requests to Roy Hostetter, Psychology Department, Sir Wilfred Grenfell College, University Drive, Corner Brook, Newfoundland, Canada, A2H-6P9.

3. TEACHING CONCEPTS AND PRINCIPLES

A Sweet Way to Teach Students About the Sampling Distribution of the Mean

Jennifer L. Dyck
Nancy R. Gee
State University of New York, College at Fredonia

Although statistical textbooks usually provide an example of constructing a sampling distribution of the mean, these examples are often abstract and require the student to conceptualize the process of selecting a number of samples of a certain size from a theoretical population. Zerbolio (1989) suggested one technique for presenting examples of sampling distributions, in which the instructor uses imaginary bags of marbles and chips to demonstrate the concepts. Although this technique may allow students to n ore easily visualize the process of creating sampling distributions, some may still have difficulty understanding the process and may respond more readily to a concrete, hands-on example. Concrete examples increase understanding of abstract, scientific concepts (Brown & Kane, 1988; Chen, Yanowitz, & Daehler, 1995) because students are more likely to pay attention to and use relevant information from examples, as compared to attending to and using relevant information from abstract instructions (LeFevre & Dixon, 1986). Therefore, we developed a hands-on, in-class demonstration, during which students create an actual sampling distribution of the mean using M&M's®. To test the effectiveness of our concrete example, we compared performance and attitudes of two statistics classes, with one class receiving the M&M demonstration and the other class receiving equivalent instruction using a textbook example.

Method

Participants

A total of 63 undergraduate students (14 men, 49 women) enrolled in a sophomore-level introductory statistics course in the Psychology Department at the State University of New York, College at Fredonia participated for partial course credit. We treated all participants ethically (American Psychological Association, 1992). The control group as well as the experimental group received the M&M's, the content of the information presented was equivalent in the two groups, and they had the same textbook as a reference. Therefore the control group was not deprived of information that could have affected their final grade in the course.

Materials

We used forty-eight 1.69-oz packages of plain M&M's in this experiment. The students had their own calculators, and an overhead projector displayed a table of random numbers.

We constructed a class survey for assessing student attitudes toward the demonstration. The survey included four questions on assessment of learning, three questions on enjoyment of class, and two questions on negative feelings. We included questions on negative feelings primarily to avoid a positive response bias. The instructor referred to the textbook example as a demonstration in lecture so that the same survey questions were appropriate for both the textbook example and the M&M demonstration. Students answered all questions using a 7-point Likert scale ranging from 1 (*completely disagree* or *not at all*) to 7 (*completely agree or very well*).

We constructed a quiz consisting of 10 questions about the sampling distribution of the mean. Nine of the questions were multiple choice, and one question was a fill-in-the-blank question. The following is an example question:

When constructing a distribution of the means, the larger the sample size, the ___ the distribution of the means will be___.
a.) more likely, rectangular
b.) less likely, rectangular
c.) more likely, normal
d.) less likely, normal
e.) the question is irrelevant because the distribution of the means is always the same shape regardless of sample size.

One additional question at the end of the quiz asked whether the student was repeating the class.

Design and Procedure

The participants in this study were enrolled in one of two sections of a statistics course taught by the same instructor. One section was randomly assigned to the experimental condition; the other section to the control condition. In the experimental class, 7 were repeating the course. In the control class, 4 were repeating the course. The two classes were not statistically different from each other, as measured by scores on their first exam prior to the experiment (control: $M = 74.49$, $SD = 8.84$; experimental: $M = 77.66$, $SD = 12.44$), $t(66) = 1.21$, $p > .05$. This analysis included all students in both classes, including repeating students. Both classes had progressed to the same place in the course syllabus. On the day of the experiment, 34 students attended the experimental class, and 29 students attended the control class.

Both classes received the same lecture on the sampling distribution of the mean. Midway through the lecture, the experimental group received the M&M demonstration (described subsequently), and the control group received a textbook example (described subsequently). Following the lecture, both groups completed the quiz and then the class survey. Students did not know how they had performed on the quiz when they completed the class survey. Students in the control condition each received a package of M&M's after handing in their quiz and survey.

M&M demonstration. All students received one package of M&M's. They opened their packages, separated their M&M's according to color, counted the number of M&M's of each color, and recorded these numbers. After recording the numbers, students could eat the M&M's.

The students determined the color of the M&M's used in the demonstration (blue) by class vote. The instructor arbitrarily chose a sample size of 5 because of time constraints. At this point, the instructor raised the issue of sample size, pointing out that larger sample sizes are better, but time constraints made this small sample size necessary. Students then numbered off, beginning with 1 for the first student and ending with the last student. The instructor displayed a table of random numbers with the overhead projector. Beginning at a random line in the random number table, the instructor read five numbers one at a time, and the appropriate students reported the number of blue M&M's in their package. The instructor wrote these five numbers on the chalkboard, and each student calculated the mean of those five numbers. The instructor drew the axes of a histogram on the chalkboard, plotting the mean of the first sample on the histogram as one data point. We used sampling with replacement for this demonstration, therefore the instructor generated the next

sample of five numbers in the same manner. The instructor again wrote the numbers from this second sample on the chalkboard, and the students in the class calculated the mean for that sample. The instructor then plotted this second mean on the histogram. The instructor followed this procedure for approximately 20 samples of size five. Because this demonstration uses sampling with replacement, this demonstration is also successful with small class sizes. At this point, the overall shape of the distribution began to emerge. Students then calculated the mean of the 20 sample means. This number represented the estimate of the mean of the sampling distribution of the mean (expected value).

The students individually reported the number of blue M&M's they had. They then calculated the mean of the population of blue M&M's for the class. As expected, the mean of the population of blue M&M's was almost the same as the estimate of the mean of the sampling distribution. The mean of the sampling distribution is not always exactly equivalent to the population mean with this demonstration, but typically, there are only small differences. If the two means are not exactly equivalent, the instructor can take the opportunity to discuss the impact of sample size and the number of samples drawn.

After the class calculated the mean of the population, the instructor continued with the lecture emphasizing the following main points:

1. The mean of the sampling distribution of the mean is the same as the population mean.
2. The variance of the sampling distribution of the mean is always smaller than that of the population.
3. The shape of the sampling distribution of mean is nor mal (unimodal and symmetrical).

The M&M demonstration took approximately 30 min.

Textbook example. To create an informationally equivalent example, we used an example from chapter 7, "Hypothesis Tests with Means of Samples" in the statistics textbook required for the course (see Figure 7-3, Aron & Aron, 1994, p. 183) . This example described the process of constructing a sampling distribution of means using the same procedure involved in the M&M demonstration except that the content of the example involved numbering hypothetical ping pong balls instead of physically counting M&M's. In both the M&M demonstration and the textbook example, the instructor drew a histogram on the chalkboard and detailed the process of sampling and calculating means. As in the M&M demonstration, the instructor emphasized the three main points of the lecture following the example.

Table 1. Summary of the Simple Main Effects Analysis of the Significant Instruction by Questions Interaction.

| | | Instruction Group | | | |
| | | Experimental | | Control | |
	F	M	SD	M	SD
Assessment of learning					
I learned more today than usual in this class.	6.15*	4.82	1.19	4.07	1.18
I think that today's demonstration made the concepts we covered much more clear than is typically true of this class.	32.64*	5.79	1.00	3.96	1.50
How well do you think you understand the distribution of the means?	15.65*	5.62	0.74	4.70	0.92
How helpful was today's demonstration in understanding the distribution of the means?	25.48*	6.35	0.85	5.04	1.20
Enjoyment of class					
Today's class was more fun than the typical day in Dr. Gee's statistics class.	29.91*	5.79	1.15	4.07	1.33
Today's class stands out as a particularly good class in comparison to the average class in statistics.	27.94*	5.50	1.14	3.89	1.26
How much did you enjoy today's demonstration of the distribution of the means?	40.50*	6.24	0.89	4.57	1.17
Negative feelings					
I felt like I was wasting my time today.	16.31*	1.11	0.33	2.07	1.33
I was more bored than usual today in class.	11.61*	1.38	0.74	2.42	1.60

Note. All *F* scores have *df* = (1, 60). Students rated questions on a 7-point Likert scale ranging from 1 *(disagree completely* or *not at all)* to 7 *(agree completely* or *extremely helpful)*.
*p < .05.

Results and Discussion

Quiz Results

We scored the quizzes, calculated the total number of correct answers for each student, and analyzed these data using an independent samples *t* test. We excluded data from students who were repeating the course. The results revealed that the experimental group (M = 7.96, SD = 1.43) performed significantly better than the control group (M = 6.72, SD = 2.01) on the quiz, $t(50)$ = 2.59, p < .05.

Survey Results

We analyzed the attitude survey data with a two-way mixed model ANOVA. The between subjects variable was learning condition (control or experimental), and the within subjects variable consisted of the nine survey questions. We eliminated one student from this analysis who did not complete all of the questions on the survey, leaving a total of 62 participants. The main effect of learning condition, $F(1, 60)$ = 36.73, p < .01, the main effect of questions, $F(8, 480)$ = 133.76, p < .01, and the interaction, $F(8, 480)$ = 18.70, p < .01, were all significant. We conducted simple main effects analyses on the interaction because it was significant and because it contains the effect of interest here. The simple main effects analyses presented in Table 1 show that the experimental group rated each of the Assessment of Learning questions significantly higher than did the control group. It appears from the students' assessments that those who participated in the M&M demonstration believed they learned more about the distribution of the mean than those who received the textbook example. For the enjoyment of class questions, the experimental group had higher ratings for each of these questions than did the control group. This finding suggests that the students enjoyed the M&M demonstration more than the textbook example. Additionally, the experimental group rated the negative feelings questions significantly lower than the control group. This result suggests that the experimental group felt significantly more positive about the demonstration than did the control group and also that there was not a positive response bias in the data. This pattern of the experimental group rating the assessment of learning questions and the enjoyment of class questions high, as compared to the low ratings of the control group, followed by the two groups reversing their ratings for the negative feelings questions, explains the significant interaction. Overall, the survey data suggest that, according to the students' own opinions, they learned more, enjoyed class more, and felt more positive when they participated in the M&M demonstration as compared to the textbook example demonstration.

These results indicate that the students viewed the M&M demonstration as a fun and effective way to learn about the sampling distribution of the mean. Additionally, the results from the quiz provide an objective measure that indicates that the students did learn more from the M&M demonstration than from the textbook example .

Conclusions

It appears that the M&M demonstration is an effective way to convey the theoretical concept of the sampling distribution of the mean to statistics students. The instructor can also expand this demonstration to include a concrete example of variability. When the students calculate the population mean (i.e., the entire class), they can also calculate the population standard deviation and compare it to the standard error of the mean, which the students can calculate from the sample means generated in class. This part of the demonstration also works well for us, but we sometimes delete it due to time constraints, as in the experiment presented here. In addition to using M&M's for teaching students about sampling distributions, M&M's are also effective for teaching students about basic sampling concepts (Smith, in press). Besides the educational benefits of using M&M's for demonstrating sampling concepts and distributions, another positive aspect is that students have consistently mentioned to us that they enjoy receiving candy in class from their instructor!

References

American Psychological Association. (1992). Ethical principles of psychologists and code of conduct. *American Psychologist, 47*, 1597-1611.

Aron, A., & Aron, E. N. (1994). *Statistics for psychology.* Englewood Cliffs, N.J: Prentice Hall.

Brown, A. L., & Kane, M. J. (1988) . Preschool children can learn to transfer: Learning to learn and learning from example. *Cognitive Psychology, 20,* 493-523.

Chen, A., Yanowitz, K. L., & Daehler, M. W. (1995). Constraints on accessing abstract source information: Instantiation of principles facilitates children's analogical transfer. *Journal of Educational Psychology, 87,* 445 454.

LeFevre, J., & Dixon, P. (1986). Do written instructions need examples? *Cognition & Instruction, 3,* 1-30.

Smith, R. A. (in press). A tasty sample(r): Teaching about sampling using M&M's. In L. T. Benjamin, Jr., B. F. Nodine, R. M. Ernst, & C. Blair-Broeker (Eds.), *Activities handbook for the teaching of psychology* (Vol. 4). Washington, DC: American Psychological Association.

Zerbolio, D. J., Jr. (1989). A "bag of tricks" for teaching about sampling distributions. *Teaching of Psychology, 16,* 207-209.

Note

Send for copies of the complete quiz and attitude survey to Jennifer L. Dyck, Department of Psychology, State University of New York, College at Fredonia, Fredonia, NY 14063; e-mail: dyck@ait.fredonia.edu.

A "Bag of Tricks" for Teaching About Sampling Distributions

Dominic J. Zerbolio, Jr.
University of Missouri—St. Louis

To solve statistical problems, one uses more logic than math skills. Unfortunately, many students believe statistics is mathematics, and their beliefs restrict how they approach learning statistics. Too often, this means students adopt a *plug and chug approach* (i. e., fill in the numbers and arrive at a correct numerical answer), which works and provides the correct answer, as long as someone tells them what numbers to plug into what formulas. With the plug and chug approach, students typically fail to grasp the meaning and logic behind statistical procedures and, therefore, rapidly forget what they have been taught If students could see and understand some of the key concepts and distributions, they might not so readily adopt and restrict themselves to plug and chug.

A key concept in understanding how statistics work is the notion of sampling distributions, an idea that seems to escape many students. Students grasp the idea of measures of central tendency, variability, and probability with raw score distributions, but often have difficulty generalizing these concepts to sampling distributions. Because understanding sampling distributions is central to understanding hypothesis testing, a little extra effort to help students conceptualize sampling distributions seems reasonable.

For several terms, I have been using a lecture procedure that helps students understand and differentiate sampling distributions. The procedure involves teaching students to imagine marbles and chips as various kinds of theoretical distributions and relies only on the instructor's flair for the dramatic. Once the various distributions are depicted as bags of marbles and/or bags of chips, students more easily grasp not only the plug and chug mechanics but also the underlying nature of statistical distributions. This grasp aids teaching both the logic and generality of statistical procedures.

The first step is teaching students to visualize raw score distributions. Referring to a commonly recognized distribution, like the Stanford–Binet IQ distribution, helps because most students know the average IQ is 100, and some even know its standard deviation is 16. Depicting the distribution involves describing each score in it as a "marble with a number on it." The population of raw scores becomes a "bag containing all the marbles." During the presentation, the imaginary bag is held high with one hand while the other hand points to the bag. Using marbles and bags to demonstrate the probabilities of scores in a distribution provides repetition and facilitates visualization.

Probabilities are taught by reaching into the bag (with appropriate hand and body gestures) and drawing a marble. With the imaginary marble held high in the free hand, students are asked, "What is the probability that this marble has a 120 or higher on it?" Calculating z scores for marbles (scores) and translating the z scores into probability statements quickly become routine. After a few draws, students readily accept the bag and marbles as a population of raw scores. Once the marbles and bag are established, the generation of sampling distributions becomes fairly easy.

The One-Sample Case Sampling Distribution

The one-sample case sampling distribution is the distribution of means of equal-sized samples. Two steps are required to establish this sampling distribution and distinguish it from the raw score population. In Step 1, students are asked to visualize a large number of drinking glasses. With appropriate motions, a glassful of marbles is scooped out of the raw score population bag. Each glassful of marbles represents a random sample of marbles and, by implication, is a random sample of raw scores. Additional glasses are filled with the same number of marbles as the first until the population of marbles (raw scores) is exhausted. This procedure creates a population of glassfuls, each containing the same number of marbles.

Step 2 is to create the distribution of sample means. A mean is calculated for each glass and written on a chip. All of the chips are gathered into a new or second bag. Once all the chips are put into the second bag, the new bag is held aloft and students are asked, "What's in this new bag?"

Most students recognize that the bag of chips is different from the original bag of marbles, which establishes a distinction between the raw score population and a distribution of sample means. This distinction can be enhanced by pouring all the marbles back into their own bag and holding the bag of chips in one hand and a bag of marbles in the other. I taught students earlier that they need two parameters to describe any normal distribution (a mean and a measure of variability), so a classroom discussion of the mean and standard error necessary to describe the bag of chips can be initiated. As an option, the normal shape of the chip distribution can be defended by introducing the central limit theorem at this point.

With the mean and standard error of the bag of chips established, a single chip can be drawn from the bag of chips, and students are asked, "What is the probability that the value on the chip is 105 or higher?" Most students realize the solution requires the calculation of a z score. The contrast between the proper error terms (standard deviation for the bag of marbles and standard error for the bag of chips) becomes obvious. With the proper mean and standard error term for the bag of chips understood, students easily see how to calculate z scores for chips and, using a z table, translate their z values into probability statements. With the z-score procedure for a distribution of sample means in hand, the probability of a mean (or chip) being drawn from a distribution of means (or chips) with a specific population average can be established. At this point, it is a relatively short step to the one-sample hypothesis testing procedure.

The Difference Between Independent Sample Means Case

The distribution of the differences between independent sample means seems to cause problems because students initially confuse it with the difference between the means of two independent distributions of sample means. The distribution of differences between independent sample means has an infinite number of values whereas the difference between the means of two independent sampling distributions of means has only one value. Demonstrating the distribution of differences between independent sample means to students requires a two-step process.

Step 1 is to have students visualize two glasses, one red and one blue. Each glass is filled from a bag of marbles (or population), and then the two glasses are taped together. Additional pairs are filled and taped, with the same number of marbles as in the first pair, until the original marble population is exhausted. Once all possible pairs of red and blue glasses are filled, the second step can begin.

In Step 2, the means for each pair of red and blue glasses are calculated, and the difference between the means (red mean—blue mean) is determined. Each difference is written on a chip, and the chip is placed in another bag. When the population of paired red and blue glasses is exhausted, the bag of chips, which represents the distribution of differences between sample means, can be dealt with.

A chip is drawn from the bag and students are asked "What's on the chip?" Of course, each chip represents a difference between independent sample means and has no relation to the original sample means. Emphasizing the chip contains no information about the original means can be accomplished by asking what original means led to the number on the chip. Most students see that chips have no information about the original sample means, but represent a different kind of population, a difference between populations .

Once the difference between distribution is established, students see that describing it requires a measure of central tendency and variability. An explanation of the mean and standard error of the distribution of differences between independent sample means ensues. With the mean and standard error in hand, one can draw a single chip from the "bag of differences between" and ask about the probability of its occurrence.

Note that I referred to the distribution as the "difference between" rather than the "difference between two sample means." My experience suggests that omitting the words *sample means* enhances students' grasp of the distinction between distributions of sample means and distributions of differences between sample means. Presented this way, more students see that the "difference between" is what is important and that the actual values of the sample means are incidental. As before, once the mean, standard error, and probability characteristics of the "difference between" distribution are established, generalizing to the hypothesis testing procedure is easier. Note that red and blue glasses can be used later to denote different treatment conditions.

The Difference Between Correlated Sample Means Case

Analyzing the distribution of the differences between correlated sample means requires all the work in analyzing the distribution of differences between independent samples means plus the computation of a correlation coefficient. To reduce the computational burden, most texts use an alternative, the *direct difference method*. The direct difference method's sampling distribution is the distribution of mean differences between paired scores, known as the *bar D*-distribution, which can be demonstrated with a three-step procedure.

Step 1 uses a chip to represent both the X and Y values of a pair of raw scores. With an X value on one side and a Y value on the other, the population of paired X, Y scores becomes immediately obvious to most students. With the bag (population) of chips established, the second step begins.

In Step 2, a chip, marked with its X and Y scores, is drawn. The difference between its X and Y scores is written on a marble. This procedure is repeated for all chips, and all the marbles are put in another bag. Then, the bag of marbles, which is the difference score distribution, can be held aloft and distinguished from the original bag of chips.

Step 3 is filling glasses with marbles. As in the one-sample case, each glass has the same number of marbles. A mean is calculated for the marbles in each glass, each mean is written on a chip, and the chips placed in another bag. However, this second bag of chips is different from the first because only one value, the mean of a sample of difference scores (or bar D), appears on each chip. As before, students are asked how to describe the bag of mean difference scores. By this point, most students realize that they need a specific mean and standard error term to characterize the bar-D distribution and often ask for them before they are presented. Once the mean and standard error term for the bar-D distribution are specified, single chips can be drawn from the bag and questions about the probability of specific bar-D values asked. Students typically generalize the entire *z*-score procedure immediately. Once the mechanism for determining probabilities is established, it is a short step to the hypothesis testing procedure.

Some students see the similarity between the bar-D distribution and the one-sample mean distribution. When they do, it is easy to show that the only mechanical (plug and chug) difference between the two statistical procedures is using a difference score (D) in place of a raw score (X). Noting the similarity helps some students see the generality of the statistical procedure. For the remainder, it probably means one less formula to learn. If and when the similarity is shown, the instructor must be careful to maintain a clear distinction between what the D and X scores represent.

The value of these procedures depends on the way the instructor presents the bags of marbles and chips. If bags are presented with panache, students not only seem to grasp the distinctions between various distributions more quickly, but learn the nature of the underlying sampling distributions as well. Once sampling distributions are clearly differentiated from raw score distributions, the generality of the procedures for determining probabilities can be seen, and the entire hypothesis testing procedure is much easier to show. Further, by depicting sampling distributions, students begin to see the conceptual logic and generality of statistical procedures, rather than restricting themselves to learning a series of superstitiously performed plug and chug procedures. Student reaction to the technique is good. Many find the presentation amusing, which also serves to hold their attention. More important, more students have commented that they understand sampling distributions with the bag procedure than with any other lecture technique I have tried. This understanding is often seen in our Statistics Lab sections wherein students ask more questions about sampling distributions than about plug and chug mechanics. Even more reassuring, when the same students take my Research Methods course, many see the application of the statistics and sampling distributions to research data more readily than students taught with other procedures. I have even seen Research Methods students instructing their less knowledgeable classmates about statistical comparisons using the "bag" analogy.

As a closing remark, I would not recommend using real bags, marbles, or chips, because that necessarily implies a finite limit to theoretical populations. It is important for students to see populations and sampling distributions as logical or abstract entities. The procedure works well without real props.

Demonstrating the Central Limit Theorem

David E. Johnson
John Brown University

As any teacher of introductory statistics knows, it is often difficult for students to achieve a full understanding of theoretical distributions. Students frequently complain about the abstract nature of these distributions. In the past, I have experienced particular difficulty explaining the nature and properties of distributions that result from the use of the central limit theorem.

Simply stated, the central limit theorem suggests that the sums or means of a large number of equal-sized random samples can be combined to form an approximately normal distribution if the size of these samples is large enough. Furthermore, this relationship holds regardless of the shape of the original distribution. Invariably, I encounter resistance and confusion on the part of students at this point in the course. With a little prodding I can convince some students of the accuracy and usefulness of the theorem. Other students, however, express a need for a concrete demonstration.

To satisfy these students and to reduce the amount of verbal explanation of the central limit theorem, I have adapted a demonstration from an example presented by Weinberg, Schumaker, and Oltman (1981). In their example, Weinberg et al. ask the reader to imagine a very large box that contains a large number of slips of paper. These slips of paper have either 0, 1, or 2 printed on them in approximately equal numbers, yielding a rectangular distribution. If equal-sized random samples are taken from this population and their sums or means are combined, the resulting distribution approaches normality.

My demonstration is a direct extension of this example. Before the class meeting I prepare approximately three or four equal-sized random samples for each student. These random samples are generated by a microcomputer using a standard program. Because my software will not generate zeros as random numbers, I specify the population to be comprised of values 1, 2, and 3. Thirty random samples are selected. These samples are then printed.

In class, I announce that we will be using the central limit theorem to begin building our own distribution of sample sums and sample means. The random samples are distributed to the students and I explain the process of random selection. Students are asked to determine the possible limits of our distribution if $N = 30$. They quickly respond that 30 is the lowest possible value (a sample of ones), and that 90 is the highest value (a sample of threes). I then place a predrawn scale ranging from 30 to 90 on an overhead projector.

The students then obtain the sum of each of their random samples. When they have finished, the students, in turn, call out their sample sums and I place an X on the prepared number line to represent each one. As we proceed with the exercise, it becomes apparent that the Xs are accumulating in the middle of the scale; clustering around the theoretical center of the distribution (the value 60). When all responses have been recorded we examine our distribution and discuss its properties. For example, we discuss the fact that the distribution of sample means would look exactly like our distribution of sample sums except for the numerical range. The distribution of sample means would have a lower range of one and an upper range of three. We also reemphasize the fact that our sampling distribution would eventually approximate the normal distribution even though our original population was obviously not normally distributed but, in this case, rectangular.

This demonstration has been helpful to many students, judging from the numerous positive comments that I have received in the past. Students seem more readily to accept the presentation of theoretical distributions in later stages of the course because of this demonstration.

This demonstration is also useful when we discuss certain aspects of probability. For example, students know that, theoretically, the most frequent observation in our demonstration should be the midpoint of the distribution (60 in this case). However, with our limited number of samples, 60 is rarely the most frequent observation. The resulting discussion helps students to understand the difference between theoretical outcomes in the long run and actual short-term outcomes in practice.

Finally, an enhancement of this demonstration might involve selecting random samples from other nonnormal parent populations and building sample distributions from them. Constructing sample distributions from highly skewed or multimodal parent distributions would further reinforce students' acceptance of the utility of the central limit theorem.

Reference

Weinberg, G. H., Schumaker, J. A., & Oltman, D. (1981). *Statistics: An intuitive approach* (4th ed.). Monterey, CA: Brooks/Cole.

Regression Toward the Mean Effect: No Statistical Background Required

Jerzy Karylowski
University of North Florida

One source of bias in assessing the effects of any intervention or manipulation preceded by an initial screening procedure is regression toward the mean effect. Unfortunately, this phenomenon is difficult to understand for students who lack statistical background.

Several years ago, Cutter (1976) developed a classroom demonstration of the regression toward the mean effect. His demonstration, which is based on dice sums, provides an accurate model of the phenomenon. However, the way in which the effect is produced in that demonstration is often perceived by the students as highly artificial and lacking psychological content. The lack of clear psychological relevance greatly diminishes the effectiveness of Cutter's demonstration for the less abstractly minded students. The same criticism applies to the recent modification of the regression toward the mean demonstration (Levin, 1982), in which two decks of playing cards are used instead of dice.

The present demonstration is not only highly concrete, it is strictly psychological in content. It engages the students and may be used in both small and large classes. It does not assume any statistical background. Although some assumptions about the nature of the measurement

process (inevitability of measurement error and the random nature of such an error) are explicitly made, these assumptions are highly intuitive and are easily accepted even by students who are not familiar with measurement theory.

Procedure

Announce to the students that you are going to simulate a study on the level of aspiration and that they will be asked to serve as your research assistants. Introduce briefly the concept of the level of aspiration as a relatively stable personality trait (Rotter, 1954). Explain that both very low and very high aspiration levels are maladaptive. Tell them you believe that you possess a special psychic power, which has a therapeutic influence on people with too low or too high aspiration levels.

Discuss briefly some potential measures of aspiration level as a trait. Make it clear that there is no such thing as a perfect measure. Suggest that a score on any measure will always be a function of at least two components: (a) true score, and (b) contribution of transient factors (error score). Give some examples of transient factors (e.g., subject had a particularly good or a particularly bad day, subject misunderstood some items, there were clerical errors). Ask each student to think of three or four people the student knows well. These people will constitute an initial pool of subjects in your simulated study.

Instruct the students to "test" their subjects. Explain that the scale is a 6-point scale with scores 1 and 2 indicating a tendency for aspirations to be lower than the ability level, scores 3 and 4 indicating an appropriate aspiration level, and scores 5 and 6 indicating unrealistically high aspirations. The "testing" is done in the following way:

1. Each subject is assigned a true score. In making these judgments the students should use any information or intuitions they have about their subjects.
2. Each subject is assigned a transient factors score. This is done on the basis of dice tossing.
3. A test score is computed for each subject. I usually assume an equal contribution of true scores and transient factors scores and use an average of the two as a simulated test score.

On the basis of the "testing scores" select from the initial pool two extreme groups: a low aspirations group and a high aspirations group (upper and lower, 10% or 25%). Tell the students that you believe that both groups will benefit from your psychic treatment.

Announce that 1 day has passed during which the psychic power treatment was provided and ask the students to "retest" their subjects. Tell your students that unless they believe in your psychic power (the chances are they don't), they should reassign the same true scores. Transient factors scores are assigned on the basis of a new round of dice tossing and new test scores are computed.

Tabulate the pretreatment and the posttreatment results for both the low aspirations and the high aspirations groups. The students will immediately notice a decrease in the test scores for the high aspirations group and an increase for the low aspirations group!

You may, if you wish, change your assumptions concerning the contribution of transient factors (error) and repeat the demonstration using a modified formula for computing the test scores. For instance, if you assume a 25%, rather than a 50% contribution (i.e., a more reliable measure), the regression toward the mean effect will become smaller. If you assume a 75% contribution (i.e., very low reliability), the effect will increase. The demonstration extended like this will provide a good vehicle for discussing the concept of reliability and the relationship between reliability and the regression toward the mean effect.

References

Cutter, G. R. (1976). Some examples for teaching regression toward the mean from a sampling viewpoint. *American Statistician, 30,* 194-197.

Levin, J. R. (1982). Modifications of regression-toward-the-mean demonstration. *Teaching of Psychology, 9,* 237-238.

Rotter, J. B. (1954). *Social Learning and clinical psychology.* Englewood Cliffs, NJ: Prentice-Hall.

An Intuitive Approach to Teaching Analysis of Variance

David E. Johnson
John Brown University

Instructors of introductory statistics know that students approach their course with considerable anxiety (Dillon, 1982; Hastings, 1982). Many students complain about the mathematical nature of the course and their inadequate preparation for it.

Evidence also suggests that a significant number of students in the introductory statistics course may operate at a concrete-operational level of thought, as defined by Piaget (1952). Some researchers have estimated that up to 50% of the adult population functions at this level (Kuhn, Langer, Kohlberg, & Haan, 1977; McKinnon & Renner, 1971). Others have demonstrated that it is common for college students to operate at a concrete level ot to be transitional between concrete and formal levels of cognitive development. (Allen, Walker, Schroeder, & Johnson, 1987). According to Piaget, persons at the formal-operational level are capable of abstract thought and reasoning. They can understand hypothetical situations, combine information from several sources, and comprehend correlations and interactions between variables. These capabilities are necessary for understanding the problems students encounter in their first statistics course.

Students who function at a concrete–operational level are unprepared to comprehend the fundamental operations required for complete understanding of basic statistical concepts. The anxiety that students experience may aggravate this situation by causing them to narrow their attention to fewer details of these statistical concepts (Easterbrook, 1959). Instructors could use an effective, concrete demonstration to communicate some of these complex statistical concepts to their students.

The ANOVA appears to be one of those procedures that requires concrete presentation. A technique I use for teaching ANOVA involves manipulating between- and within-groups variance and observing the resulting changes in the ANOVA summary table. A description of that technique follows.

Method

My introduction to ANOVA is fairly standard: Students are informed of the reasons for using ANOVA(as compares to the more familiar t test for independent groups), the concepts of between- and within-groups variance are introduced, the computational techniques for obtaining the F ratio for a one-way ANOVA are explained, and the conceptual relationship of between- and within-groups variance is described.

At that point, I describe a hypothetical experiment in which three independent groups of subjects (labeled A1, A2, and A3, with each group containing five subjects) are exposed to one of three levels of an independent variable. The range of possible responses on the dependent variable is 0 through 4. Students are then given a data set that contains scores for the 15 subjects.

Table 1. Data Set Number 2

	Group		
	A1	A2	A3
	0	1	3
	1	1	3
	1	1	3
	1	1	3
	2	1	3
Group Mean	1	1	3

Summary of ANOVA

Source	Sum of Squares	df	Mean Square	F
A	13.3	2	6.65	39.12
S/A	2.0	12	.17	

In the initial data set, the values are identical (i.e., each subject recorded a value of 1). The students recognize that this outcome is highly unlikely. They also realize that there is no variability in the data. One of two methods can then be used to continue the presentation. In the first approach, a copy of the data and the outline of an ANOVA summary table are presented on a screen using an overhead projector. The computations are then completed for the students. Another approach involves projecting the data and the completed summary table. This approach takes less time but does not expose students to the actual computational procedures. Regardless of the method used, students observe that the absence of between- and within-groups variability leads to mean squares of 0 in the summary table.

Students are then given a second data set which is identical to the first with one notable exception: Between groups variance is introduced by increasing all five values in Group A3 to 3. The between-groups variance now indicates the possible effect of the independent variable manipulation. It is obvious to the students that Group A3 is different from the other two groups (mean square A = 6.65); however, there is no within-groups variability (mean square S/A = 0).

Students are given a third data set that incorporates within groups variance into Group A1 (see Table 1). This data set contains the same amount of between-groups variance as the previous one (i.e., the means are unchanged). Students are encouraged to compare the results of the second and third data sets and to observe the absence of change in the between-subjects values represented by the mean square of 6.65 for both data sets. They are encouraged to notice how the introduction of dissimilar scores into Group A1 increased the value of the mean square for within-groups variance. The students are asked to note the value of the F ratio, which is 39.12 in this case.

Subsequently, students are given a fourth data set, which differs from the previous one in only one way: Additional within-groups variance has been added by changing the values in Group A2 to match those in Group A1. The students' attention is directed to the fact that the means for each group are identical to those in the previous data set. The computed values reveal that, compared to the previous data set, the between-groups mean square remains unchanged, but the within-groups mean square is larger. As a result, the F ratio is smaller.

At this point, students begin to understand the relationship of between- and within-groups variance and how this relationship affects the magnitude of the F ratio. To reinforce this emerging understanding, a final data set is presented. This data set continues the trend of the previous two data sets in which additional within-groups variance is introduced while the group means remain unchanged. One value in Group A3 is reduced by 1 and another value is increased by 1, thereby maintaining a mean of 3 for that group. Again, students are told to note the unchanged between-groups mean square and the increased within-groups mean square, as compared to the previous data set. As a result, the F ratio is smaller.

The final step in the presentation depends on the class in which it is used. In a statistics class where limited information about research design is presented, I briefly review the procedure and determine the level of students' understanding. Discussion of the functional relationship between the F and t statistics (e.g., $F = t^2$) is useful.

In a research methods course, however, I spend additional time discussing topics that directly relate to the nature of ANOVA and its relationship to practical aspects of experimental procedure and design. The significance of previously discussed issues, such as the importance of controlling sources of variance and developing strong independent variable manipulations, is reinforced.

Results and Discussion

Students in a research design course ($N = 10$) were asked to rate the usefulness of this technique in facilitating their understanding of ANOVA. The ratings were made on a 7 point scale ranging from *not at all* (1) to *considerable* (7). Students were also asked to indicate if they would recommend using this technique in future classes. The mean rating for the usefulness of the technique was positive, but not overwhelmingly so ($M = 4.9$, $SD = 1.85$). When asked whether the technique should be used in future classes, however, 9 out of 10 students answered yes. Because of the variability in their usefulness ratings, students were asked to comment on the procedure. Several students indicated that they believed the procedure is very useful, but that they had doubts as to whether their understanding of ANOVA would ever be "considerable." Apparently, some of the students confused the assessment of usefulness of the procedure with an estimation of their eventual understanding of ANOVA.

I believe that this technique is useful, especially for students who operate at a preformal level of thought. Systematic manipulation of a small range of numerical values seems to alleviate the math anxiety that some students experience. The technique is particularly helpful for students who are intimidated by the dynamic relationship of between- and within groups variance in determining the F ratio.

References

Allen, J. L., Walker, L. D., Schroeder, D. A., & Johnson, D. E. (1987). Attributions and attribution-behavior relations: The effect of level of cognitive development. *Journal of Personality and Social Psychology, 52*, 1099-1109.

Dillon, K. M. (1982). Statisticophobia. *Teaching of Psychology, 9*, 117.

Easterbrook, J. A. (1959). The effect of emotion on cue utilization and the organization of behavior. *Psychological Review, 66*, 183-201.

Hastings, M. W. (1982). Statistics: Challenge for students and the professor. *Teaching of Psychology, 9*, 221-222.

Kuhn, D., Langer, J., Kohlberg, L., & Haan, N. F. (1977). The development of formal operations in logical and moral judgment. *Genetic Psychology Monograph, 95*, 97-288.

McKinnon, J. W., & Renner, J. W. (1971). Are colleges concerned with intellectual development? *American Journal of Personality, 39*, 1047-1052.

Piaget, J. (1952). *The origins of intelligence to children.* New York: Harcourt, Brace. (Original work published 1936)

Note

I thank Joseph Palladino and four anonymous reviewers for their helpful comments on an earlier draft of this article.

Demonstrating the Consequences of Violations of Assumptions in Between-Subjects Analysis of Variance

Roberto Refinetti
College of William & Mary

Most statistics textbooks for the behavioral sciences state that analysis of variance (ANOVA) has two basic assumptions about the underlying populations: These populations are normally distributed and have equal variances. Although introductory textbooks mention only that ANOVA is quite robust and can tolerate violations of the assumptions (e.g., Aron & Aron, 1994; Ott & Mendenhall, 1990; Weiss, 1993; Witte, 1993), more advanced textbooks explain alternative procedures to be used when the assumptions are seriously violated (e.g., Hays, 1988; Howell, 1992; Kirk, 1982; Maxwell & Delaney, 1990). Absent in textbooks is a demonstration of the consequences of violations. In my experience as a statistics teacher, the absence of such a demonstration leaves students with the impression that violation of assumptions is an esoteric matter that they should not even try to understand. Although the esoterism of this subject may have been true in the past, the evolution of personal computers has made it easy to produce classroom demonstrations of the consequences of violations of assumptions of statistical tests.

In this article, I show how a personal computer can be used to demonstrate the effects of non-normality and heterogeneity of variances on Type I error. For classes in which actual demonstrations are impossible, results reported herein can be used for illustration.

Method

The issue of Type I error can be regarded as a simple problem of sampling distribution. If a simple one-way (between-groups) ANOVA is used to analyze a large number of data sets of randomly selected numbers, the frequency distribution of empirical *F* values will approximate the probability density curve of the F statistic for the specified degrees of freedom. More precisely, the empirical distribution will approximate the theoretical distribution if the assumptions of the test are respected. Violations of the assumptions will impair the approximation. If the violations do not impair the approximation, then they are not serious violations, and the test is robust.

Procedure

All comparisons reported in this article are based on 1,000 trials using random samples from various populations. Each trial consisted of a one-way ANOVA for three groups with 10 subjects per group, unless otherwise noted. A short Quick Basic program calculated the *F* values and saved them to a disk file. It took less than 5 min to complete the analysis of each set of 1,000 trials (each with $n = 30$) on a personal computer running at 25MHz.

To test the assumption of normality, I generated six different populations. To generate a normally distributed population of 1 million subjects with a mean of 5 and variance of 1, I used a simple computer routine based on the normal probability density curve. For values of *X* from 1 to 9 in steps of 0.01, each value of *Y* was multiplied by 10,000. Figure 1 (top) shows the resulting distribution of values. To investigate the consequences of using a discrete variable, I generated another normally distributed population by using the same procedure in steps of 1.0 (Figure 1, middle). As an instance of a population clearly not normally distributed, I generated a binary population (Figure 1, bottom) to simulate variables of the nominal type (yes/no type). Three populations with uniform (flat) distributions were generated within the ANOVA program using the computer's random number generator. One population was continuous (real numbers with resolution of 0.01), one was discrete (integer numbers), and one was a simulation of ranked data (integer numbers from 1 to 30 without replacement).

To test the assumption of homogeneity of variances, random samples were collected from uniform populations with different variances generated within the ANOVA program. Three different ratios of standard deviations (*tau*) were tested: 1, 5, and 10. All populations in these tests had a uniform distribution with a mean of 5. Tests were conducted for groups of equal size ($n = 10$) or unequal size ($n_1 = 15$, $n_2 = 10$, and $n_3 = 5$).

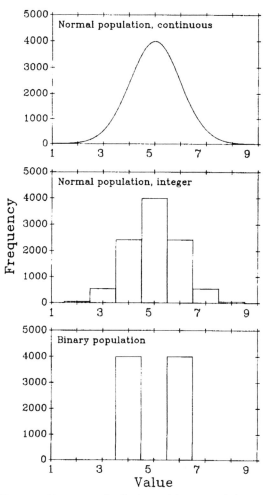

Figure 1. Frequency distributions of three populations used in this study.

Software and hardware

Although I wrote the software specifically for this demonstration, it consisted merely of a calculation algorithm for a between-subjects ANOVA repeated 1,000 times with different data sets. Statistics teachers may use my software (available on request), write their own software, or prepare a batch file for commercially available statistical packages (e.g., SPSS, SAS, or BMDP). I also wrote my own software to prepare the frequency distributions of F values. Again, others may use my software, write their own, or use a commercially available spreadsheet program (e.g., Lotus, Quattro, or the spreadsheet section of statistical packages). For graphical presentation, I used the Sigmaplot program (Jandel Scientific, San Rafael, CA 94901), but most spreadsheet programs and statistical packages can produce adequate graphs.

Regarding hardware, I used a 486-based microcomputer running at 25 mHz. RAM and hard disk requirements are only those of the programs used for the demonstration. For my own software, there was no need for more than 640K of RAM or more than 10M of hard drive.

Results

The distributions of empirical F values for the normally distributed populations appear in Figure 2. Use of a population of integer numbers instead of real numbers did not seem to affect the distribution of empirical F values, except perhaps at F values below 1.0. Similarly, use of a uniformly distributed population (whether continuous, integer, or integer without replacement) did not substantially affect the distribution of empirical F

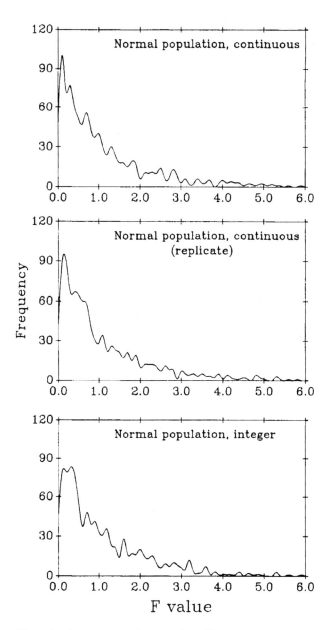

Figure 2. Frequency distributions of empirical F values for 1,000 ANOVAs using samples from three different normal populations.

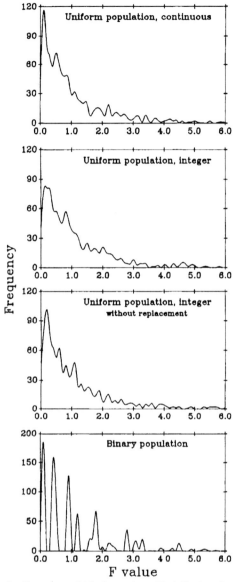

Figure 3. Frequency distributions of empirical *F* values for 1,000 ANOVAs using samples from four different non-normal populations.

binary data the actual probability of a Type I error would be .01. A much smaller error would occur at the .05 level of significance.

Also shown in Figure 4 (bottom) are results of the tests of homogeneity of variances for groups of the same size (*n* = 10). When all three groups had the same variance (*tau* = 1), the distribution of empirical *F* values closely approximated the distribution of theoretical *F* values. A good approximation was also obtained when one of the groups had a variance 5 times as large as the other groups (*tau* = 5) but not when the variances differed by a factor of 10 (*tau* = 10). For instance in a test at the .016 level of significance for *tau*= 10, the actual probability of a Type I error would be .025 (i.e. the *F* value of 4.83 had a probability of .025 rather than .016). Slightly larger errors were obtained when the groups differed in both size and variance (data not shown).

Discussion

Results are consistent with previous evaluations of the robustness of ANOVA in showing that violations of the assumptions of normality and homogeneity of variances have a measurable but small effect on the probability of Type I error when all groups are of the same size (Glass, Peckham, & Sanders, 1972; Wilcox, 1993). Also in agreement with previous evaluations, my results indicate that heterogeneity of variances for groups of unequal size

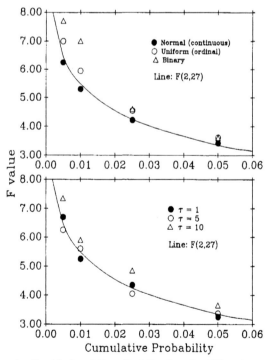

Figure 4. Empirical and theoretical *F* values for different cumulative probabilities. The top panel shows equal-variance samples with different distributions. The bottom panel shows unequal-variance samples with uniform distributions. In both panels, the curved line corresponds to the probabilities associated with *F* values for 2 and 27 degrees of freedom, as found in tables of the *F* distribution.

values (Figure 3, top three panels). Contrarily, use of a binary population resulted in a very irregular distribution of *F* values (Figure 3, bottom), even though the right tail (which is used for tests of significance) was not drastically affected.

By calculating the cumulative frequency of *F* values from the right tail up to a total of 5, 10, 25, and 50 values, the cumulative probabilities of .005, .01, .025, and .05 can be estimated and compared to the critical F values found in standard tables (or computed by integration of the probability density curve). As shown in Figure 4 (top) the cumulative probabilities of empirical *F* values obtained from a normally distributed population closely matched those of theoretical *F* values. Ranked data (ordinal) and categorical data (binary) produced more variable results. For instance in a test at the .005 level of significance for can have a significant effect on the probability of Type I error (in this study, the largest effect was a doubling of the probability). The fact that these empirical results can be obtained within a 50-min class is what makes them noteworthy. I recommend that the data sets be generated before the class and be analyzed in class following a procedure similar to that described in this article. I suggest that the frequency distribution of each data set be shown first. Then, the F values for 1,000 random samples from each population would be calculated and their frequency distributions shown and discussed.

By experiencing firsthand the consequences of failure to meet the assumptions of ANOVA, students will obtain a deeper understanding of the subject. Also, the empirical construction of sampling distributions involved in this demonstration will provide students with empirical exposure to this concept that many psychology majors fail to grasp.

References

Aron, A., & Aron, E. N. (1994). *Statistics for psychology.* Englewood Cliffs, NJ: Prentice Hall.

Glass, G. V., Peckham, P. D., & Sanders, J. R. (1972). Consequences of failure to meet assumptions underlying the analysis of variance and covariance. *Review of Educational Research, 42,* 237-288.

Hays, W. L. (1988). *Statistics* (4th ed.). New York: Holt, Rinehart & Winston.

Howell, D. C. (1992). *Statistical methods for psychology* (3rd ed.). Belmont, CA: Duxbury.

Kirk, R. E. (1982). *Experimental design: Procedures for the behavioral sciences.* Monterey, CA: Brooks/Cole.

Maxwell, S. E., & Delaney, H. D. (1990). *Designing experiments and analyzing data.* Belmont, CA: Wadsworth.

Ott, L., & Mendenhall, W. (1990). *Understanding statistics.* Boston: PWS-Kent.

Weiss, N. A. (1993). *Elementary statistics* (2nd ed.). Reading, MA Addison-Wesley.

Wilcox, R. (1993). Robustness in ANOVA. In L. K. Edwards (Ed.), *Applied analysis of variance in behavioral science* (pp. 345-374). New York Dekker.

Witte, R. S. (1993). *Statistics.* Fort Worth, TX: Harcourt Brace.

Note

Requests for copies of the software used in this study should be sent to Roberto Refinetti, Department of Psychology, College of William & Mary, Williamsburg, VA 23187; e-mail: refine@mail.wm.edu.

Teaching Analysis of Interaction in the 2 × 2 Factorial Design

W. Kirk Richardson
Don M. Segal
Georgia State University

In 1976, Vernon Schaefer published an article on teaching the interaction. He believed that multidimensional thinking was essential to psychology and that the concept of interaction was a springboard to such thinking. Although Schaefer believed that the concept of interaction is relatively simple and comprehensible by undergraduates, he found that few texts gave it more than skeletal development and wished to provide more adequate treatment. His approach is both concrete and simple. It requires presentation using four "languages" (English, tables, graphs, and simple arithmetic) to teach interaction as a real conceptual understanding that the student can use in new situations.

Two simplifications reduce the perceived complexity of the process. First, all outcomes of a 2 × 2 factorial design belong to one of six outcome categories based on two variables presented as two questions. The questions are "is an interaction present?" and "what is the number of simple effects?" The first question has two levels (yes and no), and the second has three levels (0, 1, and 2) to yield a 2 × 3 matrix of 6 outcomes. This simplification avoids the infinite number of possible outcomes (for continuous variables) generated when each unique set of means is considered as a different experimental result. The student learns to deal with a simple but realistic problem of determining which of six outcomes a particular data set represents.

The second simplification is the assumption of an ideal world with no error variance. This simplification allows the logical separation of data interpretation from data reliability, allowing the student to focus on interpreting the results. Assuming an ideal state to conceptually simplify an issue is common in science, such as a physicist assuming a frictionless world.

Using the Strategy

We find Schaefer's presentation compelling and use his strategy for teaching the concept of interaction in the 2 × 2 factorial design for several learning objectives. Students learn to recognize the graphic pattern associated with each of the outcome categories, to determine the analysis outcome category for a means table or graph, to construct a means table or graph for an analysis outcome category, to evaluate null hypotheses from a means table or graph, and to determine the means table given a graph or a graph given the means table.

For several years the first author used this system in lecture as he drew graphs, made tables, added the arithmetic to the tables, and spoke about what all this meant to meet the learning objectives. Although this approach was useful, there were two basic problems. First, and most important, was the lack of meaningful practice for the student. Assignments were not interactive, and students who needed practice the most did not have the minimal understanding required to attempt the problems; thus these students did not profit from the assignment. The second problem was using a white board for the in-class presentation. Drawing, erasing, and changing the white board presentation, even with different color markers, did not maintain the order needed and did not portray the dynamic relation among the four languages. There was one solution for both problems: an interactive computer program used with an overhead projector in the lecture hall and accessible via the campus computer network for student practice.

The *Windows* Program

All interactive activities are from the program's main screen (the Activities Screen) that appears after the Title Screen and the Instructions Screen. There are four basic functional areas on the Activities Screen: the Outcome Analysis Table, the Matrix of the group means, the Graph of the group means, and the Mode Box. Brief context sensitive instructions are in a small rectangular box at the lower left. Buttons for exit and access to detailed instructions are in the lower right.

Outcome Analysis Table

The Outcome Analysis Table, which summarizes all possible outcome analyses of a 2 × 2 study, is in the lower left corner. Any set of values for a 2 × 2 matrix of means is categorized in one of the six mutually exclusive and exhaustive outcome categories. The Outcome Analysis Table has *Number of Main Effects* as the column variable and *Interaction* as the row variable. For example, a case with two main effects and no interaction is represented by the cell in the lower right corner at the conjunction of the value of "2" for the column variable (number of main effects) and "No" for the row variable (interaction).

We want students to learn to categorize any set of means and any set of graphs using these six categories. We refer to this class of problems as problems of analysis. We also want students to be able to "reverse this operation" so that, given one of the six categories, they can produce the table of means and the associated graph. We refer to this class of problems as problems of synthesis.

Factorial Matrix

The Factorial Matrix shows the mean score for each of the four groups of the 2 × 2 design along with the resulting row means, column means, and their differences along the margin of the Matrix. The differences for the simple effect appear between the rows for each column whereas the difference of the differences appears at the lower right. The differences are inside circles to differentiate them from the means. Users enter means from the keyboard once they select a Matrix cell with the mouse. A Means button and a Differences button located just below the Matrix control presentation (on–off) of the marginal means and the differences.

To concentrate on the concept of interaction we have a special rule: All differences are significant. The material on interaction comes at the end of the course when students have considerable exposure to the concept of statistical significance. For this exercise we ask them to treat any nonzero difference for a main effect or an interaction as statistically significant. We explain that for real problems we must compute the appropriate F value for each main effect and the interaction.

Graph

The upper right of the screen contains the Graph of the group means from the Matrix. The two levels of Factor A appear on the abscissa, and there is a separate color-coded line for each level of Factor B. Each line is the color of the associated group means in the Matrix.

Users can change the Graph by using the mouse to drag any of the four points to a new position when in the What If or Quiz Me mode. In the What If mode, the Graph reflects the values in the Matrix. If the student changes a Matrix, then the Graph automatically adjusts to be in agreement. If the student changes the Graph by moving a point to another location, the corresponding Matrix mean automatically changes to agree with the Graph. In the Quiz Me mode this connection between the Graph and the Matrix is discontinued so they are not automatically in agreement. This operation allows students to practice changing either the Graph or the Matrix or both to bring them into agreement.

Mode Box

The lower right box on the screen allows choice among the three modes of operation: Demo, Quiz Me, and What If.

Demo mode. The lecture presentation always starts in Demo mode. In Demo mode, clicking on one of the six categories of the Analysis Outcome Table causes an example of that category to appear as four means in the Matrix along with the corresponding Graph of those means. Another click in the same cell gives another set of randomly chosen means that meet the specifications of the chosen category. Repetitive presentation of new means for a category allows students to detect patterns in the results. We start the demonstration with no interaction and no main effect as this category gives the most obvious visual pattern. After several examples this visual pattern is clear to the students: The two lines always fall on top of each other, and they are parallel to the abscissa. Once students detect this visual pattern, we relate the visual pattern to the numeric pattern of the means and differences in the Matrix. In this case (no effects), it is easy to relate the visual pattern to the numeric pattern of having the same mean in all four cells of the Matrix, causing all differences to be 0.

Another easily discernable visual pattern is an interaction with no main effects. For this demonstration we click the Continuous button and then the desired Analysis Outcome category cell, which causes the program to repeatedly present randomly chosen means and their graphs for the selected category. There is a slide switch for speed adjustment. The "X" graphic pattern associated with this category is soon clear to the students. Next, the instructor relates this visual pattern to the numeric pattern of a zero value for each of the main effects and the nonzero value for the difference of the differences in the

Matrix. The learning objective served by this mode is recognition of the graphic pattern associated with each of the outcome categories.

Quiz Me mode. This mode allows the student to take a quiz with instant feedback. In the Quiz Me mode, the program presents a problem by marking one of the six Analysis Outcome categories. The programmed connections between the Outcome Categories Table, the Graph, and the Matrix are discontinued. Each of these three functional areas is now independent and changes without affecting the others. The student can practice making the Graph and Matrix agree by setting the Graph fiirst or setting the Matrix first.

The student can place a set of means in the cells of the Matrix appropriate to the category presented by the program. After entering the means the student adjusts the Graph to match the means in the Matrix by picking up the ends of the lines and moving them to the appropriate position. Color coded ticks on the axes facilitate precise setting of the four graph points. The left points' values are marked with ticks on the left axis, and the right points' values are marked with ticks on the right axis. A click on the Check Me button gives feedback on three items: whether the Matrix matches the Outcome Analysis category, whether the Graph matches the Outcome Analysis category, and whether the Matrix matches the Graph. Students adjust their answers and recheck results when there are mistakes in the settings. The Graph and Matrix values may be set in any order. The student may start with the procedure (Graph or Matrix) easiest to understand and may switch between the two procedures prior to selecting the Check Me button.

In the Quiz Me mode, the student may choose for the Matrix means and differences to be on or off depending on the learning objective. The learning objectives served by this mode are (a) given an Analysis Outcome category, construct a table of group means representative of the Analysis Outcome category and (b) given an Analysis Outcome category, construct a graph representative of the Analysis Outcome category.

What If mode. The student may change the Graph points or the Matrix means in the What If mode. A change in one immediately reflects in the other, and the Analysis Outcome Table is updated, giving immediate feedback. If students wish to practice generating a specific outcome, they may want to set the Graph or Matrix and then study the results to ensure that the outcome is the one intended. To prevent premature feedback, students can turn off the Show Outcome switch until ready to check the answer.

One teaching objective is to relate the factorial analysis to the three null hypotheses for any 2×2 factorial design. These hypotheses are the following: (a) There is no main effect of Factor A, (b) there is no main effect of Factor B, and (c) there is no interaction of Factor A with Factor B. Students view the three null hypotheses, whether each is accepted or rejected, and the differences leading to each decision by turning on the Show H_0 switch. Learning objectives served by this mode are (a) given a table of group means or a graph, determine the Analysis Outcome category, (b) given a table of group means, construct the graph, (c) given a graph, construct the table of group means, and (d) given a table of group means or a graph, evaluate each null hypothesis.

Detailed suggestions for student exercises are available by selecting the Exercise button. Exercises are context sensitive based on the Mode selected and meet the stated learning objectives.

Current thinking (Rosnow & Rosenthal, 1989) emphasizes interpretation of the residuals when teaching interaction. Time constraints have prohibited adding a discussion of residuals to the introductory statistics course, and it is our view that this interpretation is best given after the student masters the traditional concept of interaction. This program can be modified to give appropriate practice in the interpretation of residuals.

Summary

This program, combined with instructor guidance is useful in teaching the concept of interaction. The program is a direct adaption of procedures used in lecture and thus solves the in-class presentation problem and has face validity. Our experience is that we can attend more to the students and their questions when we do not have the distraction of placing numbers and graphs on the white board and then changing them to illustrate a point. We merely ask the question of the program, and the program makes the appropriate presentation for discussion. We can present several examples of, for in. stance, one main effect and an interaction in the time required for one example using the white board. Finally, the presentation is cleaner;

the numbers and graph are easy to read, and the graph and numbers clearly agree.

Students are able to use the program after classroom demonstrations and instruction on program use. The teaching assistant, who had a close relationship with several students who regularly attended optional sessions, reported that she found the program very effective with students. The major problem at this time is program availability. Students must use this program on campus. As students acquire Windows machines and become familiar with Windows's program installation, the program will be available for home use as is currently the case for DOS programs used in the course.

References

Rosnow, R L., & Rosenthal, R (1989). Definition and interpretation of interaction effects. *Psychological Bulletin, 105,* 143-146.

Schaefer, V. H. (1976). Teaching the concept of inter-action and sensitizing students to its implications. *Teaching of Psychology, 3,* 103-114.

Note

A copy of the program may be obtained from the first author by sending a request with three 1.4 megabyte, MS–DOS formatted disks and a stamped, self-addressed mailer. Minimal requirements to run the program are an IBM-compatible computer with Windows 3.1, a VGA color graphics monitor, and a hard disk.

A Demonstration of Measurement Error and Reliability

Jane L. Buck
Delaware State College

Two related concepts that often cause difficulty for students in tests and measurement courses are the standard error of measurement and reliability. Fundamental to an understanding of both concepts is the definition of an *individual obtained score* as the sum of an error component and a true score. It follows from this definition that the variance of a test is equal to the sum of true score variance and error variance (Sax, 1980).

If a test is perfectly reliable, its error variance is zero. Hence, the variance of the test is equal to true score variance, and the correlation between two administrations of the test is 1.00. If a test is totally unreliable, the variance of the test equals the error variance. In this case, the expected value of the correlation between two administrations of the test is zero, because the correlation is between error scores, which are assumed to be randomly distributed (Sax, 1980).

Even if students have a fairly good working knowledge of measures of central tendency, variability, and correlation, some concepts are not always intuitively obvious. Students may not understand why the expected mean chance score for a given test is equal to the probability of correctly guessing the answer to an item multiplied by the number of items, with a standard deviation equal to the standard error of measurement (Sax, 1980). Equally difficult are the notions of error scores, true scores, and obtained scores as components of reliability.

I developed a simple, inexpensive, and easily administered device that demonstrates these concepts and their in terrelations ac well as factors that tend to lower reliability. I have used both test–retest and equivalent forms reliability on different occasions. This article describes a demonstration using equivalent forms as the model.

Method

Materials

The only materials required are five-position, machine scorable answer sheets and pencils. Prepare two answer sheets as keys for the two forms of the test by randomly choosing one of the answer positions as the correct answer for each item.

Procedure

Demonstration of position preference set. Begin the exercise with a demonstration of position preference set. Once students are aware of the nature of randomness, they consciously attempt to avoid displaying their sets. However, if you have not discussed the notion of randomness, instructions to answer each question randomly should produce results that will demonstrate position preference set.

Distribute answer sheets to students, instructing them to choose, at random, one of five options for each of 100 questions. After they fill out their answer sheets, have students count the number of times they chose each option. Point out that if they chose certain options more often than the theoretically expected 20% of the time, they exhibited a position preference set.

Demonstration of chance score. Distribute new answer sheets to students. In small classes, distribute more than one answer sheet to each student in order to obtain a total of approximately 100 answer sheets. Tell students to randomize their answers on this trial by means of a table of random numbers or by blindly drawing slips of paper marked with option positions, replacing the slips after each draw.

Score the test twice using the prepared keys to provide scores on the two forms of the test. Calculate the means, standard deviations, and variances of the test scores. It is important to emphasize to students several logical points that are essential to an understanding of the demonstration. An obtained test score has two components: true score and error. A *true score* is a measure of actual knowledge; *error* represents chance factors (Sax, 1980). In this case, an individual's true score is zero, because a correct answer is based entirely on chance, not knowledge. Thus, any obtained score greater than zero is attributable to chance or error (plus a true score of zero). This point is crucial to understanding the rest of the demonstration. Students usually see quite readily that answering test questions randomly produces scores that are composed entirely of error and that their true scores are zero.

Explain that on any given item the probability of obtaining a correct answer by chance alone is .2. Thus, the expected value of an individual chance score is 20 (100 Items $\times$ .2 per Item). However, deviations from the expected value because of sampling error are not unusual.

The relation between chance scores and the standard error of measurement. Because each true score is zero on both forms of the test, the means, variances, and standard deviations of the obtained chance scores are actually measures of error. The means for both forms should be very close to the expected value of 20, with minor deviations attributable to sampling error. The variance of the obtained, chance scores is the error variance; the standard deviation is the standard error of measurement.

Demonstration of the relation between reliability and the standard error of measurement. Calculate the index of reliability (i.e., the correlation between obtained and true scores for each form of the test). The value will be zero for both forms of the test, because the true score for each individual is zero. The reliability coefficient or the square of the index of reliability will, of course, also be zero (Hopkins, Stanley, & Hopkins, 1990). This is true despite the fact that calculating the reliability coefficient from the obtained chance scores might yield a value greater than zero because of sampling error. Keep in mind that one advantage of this demonstration is that, unlike a real-life situation, the true scores are known, allowing the direct calculation of the population correlation coefficient (the index of reliability), a value that by definition is zero when all true scores are zero.

In summary, in the extreme case of zero reliability, this demonstration illustrates that the standard error of measurement is equal to the standard deviation of obtained chance scores. Hence, the reliability coefficient and the index of reliability are zero.

I have successfully used this demonstration for several years. Students enjoy generating the data and report that doing so clarifies difficult concepts and facilitates their integration.

References

Hopkins, K. D., Stanley, J. C., & Hopkins, B. R. (1990). *Educational and psychological measurement and evaluation* (7th ed.) . Englewood Cliffs, NJ: Prentice Hall.

Sax, G. (1980). *Principles of educational and psychological measurement and evaluation.* Belmont, CA: Wadsworth.

Note

I thank Ludy T. Benjamin, Jr., Charles L. Brewer, and three anonymous reviewers for their comments on an earlier draft of this article.

4. EXPLORING PEDAGOGICAL STRATEGIES

Developing Selection Skills in Introductory Statistics

Mark E. Ware
Jeffrey D. Chastain
Creighton University

Bartz (1981) reported that 72% of 4-year colleges and universities offering psychology majors required at least one course in statistics, but the literature on teaching statistics is sparse. Ware and Brewer (1988) reported only 31 such articles published in *Teaching of Psychology* since 1974; in contrast, they reported 59 articles about teaching research methods.

Widespread use of computers (Castellan, 1982; Couch & Stoloff, 1989; Stoloff & Couch, 1987) minimizes the need for statistics teachers to spend time demonstrating computational procedures. Instructors might better use the available time for teaching students when to use a test, rather than simply teaching computational procedures and statistical tests one after another.

In this study, we assessed the effectiveness of teaching statistics with an emphasis on selection skills. We used the organizing concepts of scale of measurement and function (Magnello & Spies, 1984) because such an approach provides a meaningful way to learn new concepts. In addition, we determined how general academic ability (Giambra, 1976) and gender (Brooks, 1987; Buck, 1985, 1987; Elmore & Vasu, 1980; Feinberg & Halperin, 1978; Ware & Chastain, 1989) affected students' learning when the instructor emphasized selection skills.

Method

Subjects

During a 2-year period, 127 (of 137) students voluntarily completed the pre- and posttest. The 7% attrition was similar for the three groups. Because some students did not complete all items in the inventory, sample sizes vary in later analyses.

The 1986–87, traditional (TRAD) group consisted of 55 students from two sections of introductory statistics; the first author taught the course without emphasizing selection skills. The 1987–88, selection (SELE) group consisted of 48 students from two sections of introductory statistics; the first author taught the course emphasizing selection skills. Volunteers from other psychology classes constituted a comparison (COMP) group of 24 students who had not and were not taking statistics.

The use of intact groups permitted a selection threat to internal validity, but random assignment of subjects to groups was impossible. In addition, variation in emphasis on teaching selection skills (i.e., the treatment groups) was confounded with the year in which the course was taught and the experience of the instructor. However, the instructor was experienced, having taught for more than 20 years and having taught statistics several times. (The Results section contains a more detailed evaluation of the use of intact groups.)

Materials

Our inventory had two parts: (a) self-reported personal characteristics, including students' GPA, gender, and year in school; and (b) a skills section containing selection items. Students completed the inventory during the first week and again during the last week of the semester.

Students selected one of nine intervals that contained their overall GPA. The lowest interval was less than 2.35, and the highest was greater than 3.74. The other categories consisted of intervals of .20 (e.g., 2.95 to 3.14).

Three colleagues, who routinely teach introductory statistics, evaluated an initial pool of 10 selection items for consistency in terminology, clarity, and relevance. We also agreed that the items should illustrate problems that students could answer after completing the introductory statistics course. Items required students to select from among four alternatives the appropriate statistical analysis for a given research problem. The evaluation process produced 8 items possessing face and content validity. The following are abridged illustrations of items previously reported (Ware & Chastain, 1989).

1. In a study of mother-infant interaction, mothers were classified on the basis of whether or not this was their first child and on the basis of whether this was a low-birth weight or a full-term infant. Trained observers rated the quality of the mothers' interactions with their infants. A higher score represents better mother-infant interaction.

The investigators hypothesized that there are no differences among the groups.

(a) two-factor analysis of variance (ANOVA)
(b) Spearman rank-order correlation
(c) chi-square test for independence
(d) *t* test for dependent groups

2. Lesions in the amygdala can reduce certain responses commonly associated with fear (e.g., decreases in heart rate). If fear is reduced, then it should be more difficult to train an avoidance response in lesioned animals because the aversiveness of the stimulus will be reduced. One group of rabbits has lesions in the amygdala, and the other is an untreated control group. The data are a ranking of the number of trials to learn an avoidance response.

(a) simple ANOVA
(b) Mann-Whitney U test
(c) Pearson product-moment correlation
(d) *t* test for dependent groups

Procedure

The three intact groups constituted the treatment variable. The same instructor taught the TRAD and SELE groups a common core of topics for introductory statistics, including measures of central tendency and variability, correlation and regression, *z* test, *t* test, ANOVA, and non-parametric tests. The number and type of homework assignments were virtually identical for the two groups.

In the SELE group, the instructor taught the course emphasizing several conditions for selecting statistical tests. The first author developed and distributed a handout, adapted from Siegel (1956), consisting of a table with rows corresponding to the levels of measurement of the dependent variable. The table's columns identified conditions associated with the independent variable, such as the number of groups, whether the groups were independent or dependent, and whether testing for differences or relationships. The table identified a particular statistical test at the intersection of rows and columns. Those conditions constituted two dimensions for selecting a statistical test. These dimensions were similar to the guidelines that Magnello and Spies (1984) derived from factor analysis (i.e., scale of measurement and function) and were used because organizing concepts facilitate the learning of new concepts. In lectures, the instructor repeatedly referred to the handout and emphasized the use of the dimensions on the handout for selecting statistical tests. Finally, on three of five examinations, counting the final exam, the instructor included several multiple-choice questions that required students to select the appropriate statistical test for a particular research problem.

Design and Analysis

The 3 × 2 factorial design evaluated three treatments (TRAD, SELE, and COMP) and two person variables (GPA and gender). There were separate analyses for treatment groups and GPA and for treatment groups and gender. We formed GPA groups by dividing the students' responses into low and high, using the median as the fulcrum value. The dependent variable was the posttest selection score.

We used analysis of covariance (ANCOVA) of the posttest selection scores with adjusted pretest selection scores as the covariate for all omnibus *F* tests. Using adjusted pretest scores "corrects for the effects of irrelevance as well as measurement error" (Cook & Campbell, 1979, pp. 191-192), but ANCOVA does not solve the problem of threats to internal validity.

Results

Principal Analyses

The three groups (TRAD, SELE, and COMP) did not differ in pretest selection scores, $F(2, 124) = 1.06$, $p = .35$. The ANCOVA results, when blocked over GPA, revealed significant differences in selection skills among the treatment groups, $F(2, 120) = 14.67$, $p < .01$. Results from subsequent Scheffe tests indicated that students in the SELE group ($M = 4.54$, $SD = 1.64$) obtained higher selection scores ($p < .05$) than did students in the TRAD ($M = 3.69$, $SD = 1.71$) and COMP groups ($M = 1.71$, $SD = 1.40$). Students in the TRAD group had significantly higher selection scores ($p < .05$) than did students in the COMP group. Students having higher GPAs obtained significantly higher selection scores ($M = 4.15$, $SD = 1.91$ vs. $M = 3.10$, $SD = 1.80$) than did those having lower GPAs, $F(1, 89) = 11.47$, $p < .01$. There was no significant interaction.

The ANCOVA for treatment groups and gender revealed no reliable differences in selection scores between men and women. There was no interaction between treatment groups and gender.

Threats to Internal Validity

Because the use of intact groups permitted a selection threat, we examined the relationship between the treatment groups and GPA, gender, and year in school. The median GPA for the sample was the interval from 2.95 to 3.14. A Kruskal-Wallis test for differences in self-reported GPAs for students in the three groups revealed no significant differences, $\chi^2(2, N = 126) = .34$, $p = .85$.

Overall, women constituted 61% and men 39% of the sample. A chi-square test for independence between groups and gender revealed a relationship between the two variables, $\chi^2(2, N = 127) = 7.51$, $p = .02$. The TRAD group had a lower proportion of women (47%) than did the SELE (69%) and COMP (75%) groups.

Sophomores, juniors, and seniors constituted 26%, 49%, and 25% of the sample, respectively. A chi-square test for independence between groups and year in school revealed a significant difference, $\chi^2 (8, N = 122) = 15.45$, $p < .01$. The SELE group had a higher proportion of sophomores than did the other two groups.

At the outset, a confounding existed between treatment groups and gender and between treatment groups and year in school. Results from studies of gender differences in statistics have been equivocal. When gender differences have been reported, sometimes men (Feinberg & Halperin, 1978; Ware & Chastain, 1989) and sometimes women (Brooks, 1987) have obtained higher scores. Anecdotal evidence indicates that juniors and seniors perform at a higher level in statistics than do freshmen and sophomores. Thus, if the confounding in our study exerted a bias, it favored the TRAD group.

Because Giambra (1970, 1976) found that higher scores in statistics were related to GPA, we were concerned that the confounded variables might be associated with different levels of academic ability among those in the treatment groups. Results of chi-square tests for independence between GPA and groups, $\chi^2 (2, N = 96) = .71$, $p = .70$; GPA and gender, $\chi^2 (1, N = 96) = .71$, $p = .40$; and GPA and year in school, $\chi^2 (2, N = 92) = .020$, $p = .91$, revealed no significant relationships. Thus, the absence of relations between GPA and those three variables reduced but did not eliminate our concern about the confounding threat to internal validity.

Discussion

We found significantly higher selection scores among students taught statistics with an emphasis on selection skills versus those taught statistics without such an emphasis. Moreover, both groups of students taking statistics scored higher than students who had not taken and were not taking statistics. These results extend Ware and Chastain's (1989) findings and suggest that emphasizing selection skills through handouts, lectures, and examinations can increase these skills beyond the levels achieved by conventional methods of teaching statistics. Thus, part of the success of this study might be attributed to the use of a model that is consistent with students' cognitive structure for various statistical concepts (Magnello & Spies, 1984). If one danger of using computers is a greater risk of choosing inappropriate statistical tests and if the acquisition of selection skills is a pertinent objective for an introductory statistics course, then our results suggest that teachers must emphasize selection skills (e.g., through handouts, lectures, and examinations) rather than simply expect students to "get it on their own."

We remind readers to view our results with some caution because of selection threats and confounding. Replication of our study without its design limitations would increase confidence in its results and implications.

Finding that students with higher GPAs scored significantly higher on selection items than those with lower GPAs is consistent with previous research (Giambra, 1970, 1976; Ware & Chastain, 1989). Giambra (1970) concluded that "success in an undergraduate behavioral statistics course has little to do with a student's past mathematical background, and [it] seems to depend on [the person's overall ability as a student" (p. 367). Research findings appear consistent; students with higher GPAs perform better whether the dependent variable is selection score, interpretation score, or overall score in the course. Discovering cognitive and motivational factors that can increase statistics performance among students with lower GPAs remains a challenge.

Our failure to find gender differences in selection skills is consistent with some studies (Buck, 1985, 1987; Elmore & Vasu, 1980; Ware & Chastain, 1989), but inconsistent with others showing higher interpretation scores for men than women (Ware & Chastain, 1989), higher overall scores in statistics classes for men than women (Feinberg & Halperin, 1978), and higher overall scores for women than men (Brooks, 1987). The inconsistent findings involving gender differences in statistics may depend on the choice of dependent variables and the nature of the demands that different statistics teachers place on selection, interpretation, and other skills. We need additional research to identify conditions that contribute to gender differences in statistics.

Despite its limitations, our study contributes to the sparse literature on teaching statistics. Our findings highlight the importance of emphasizing selection skills if students are to learn them. Ware and Chastain (1989) pointed out that statistical interpretation and computer skills, such as use of a mainframe computer and SPSS—X, are also important. A challenge remains to identify other relevant skills, develop pedagogical strategies, and discover relevant personality variables that facilitate learning in statistics classes.

References

Bartz, A. E. (1981). The statistics course as a departmental offering and major requirement. *Teaching of Psychology, 8,* 106.

Brooks, C. I. (1987). Superiority of women in statistics achievement. *Teaching of Psychology, 14,* 45.

Buck, J . L. (1985) . A failure to find gender differences in statistics achievement. *Teaching of Psychology, 12,* 100.

Buck, J. L. (1987). More on superiority of women in statistics achievement: A reply to Brooks. *Teaching of Psychology, 14,* 45-46.

Castellan, N. J. (1982). Computers in psychology: A survey of instructional applications. *Behavior Research Methods, Instruments, & Computers, 14,* 198-202.

Cook, T. D., & Campbell, D. T. (1979). *Quasi-experimentation: Design & analysis issues for field settings.* Boston: Houghton Mifflin.

Couch, J. V., & Stoloff, M. L. (1989). A national survey of microcomputer use by academic psychologists. *Teaching of Psychology, 16,* 145-147.

Elmore, P. B., & Vasu, E. S. (1980). Relationship between selected variables and statistics achievement: Building a theoretical model. *Journal of Educational Psychology, 72,* 457-467.

Feinberg, L. B., & Halperin, S. (1978). Affective and cognitive correlates of course performance in introductory statistics. *Journal of Experimental Education, 46,* 11-18.

Giambra, L. M. (1970). Mathematics background and grade-point average as predictors of course grade in an undergraduate behavioral statistics course. *American Psychologist, 25,* 366-367.

Giambra, L. M. (1976). Mathematical background and grade point average as predictors of course grade in an undergraduate behavioral statistics course: A replication. *Teaching of Psychology, 3,* 184-185.

Magnello, M. E., &Spies, C. J. (1984). Using organizing concepts to facilitate the teaching of statistics. *Teaching of Psychology, 11,* 220-223.

Siegel, S. (1956). *Nonparametric statistics for the behavioral sciences.* New York: McGraw-Hill.

Stoloff, M. L., & Couch, J. V. (1987). A survey of computer use by undergraduate psychology departments in Virginia. *Teaching of Psychology, 14,* 92-94.

Ware, M. E., & Brewer, C. L. (1988). *Handbook for teaching statistics and research methods.* Hillsdale, NJ: Lawrence Erlbaum Associates, Inc.

Ware, M. E., & Chastain, J. D. (1989). Computer-assisted statistical analysis: A teaching innovation? *Teaching of Psychology, 16,* 222-227.

Notes

1. A Creighton University Summer Faculty Research Fellowship supported the preparation of this article.
2. We thank Gary Leak, Dan Murphy, and three anonymous reviewers for their helpful comments on an earlier draft of this article.
3. Requests for copies of the table used for selecting statistical tests and copies of the items used to assess selection skills should be sent to Mark E. Ware, Department of Psychology, Creighton University, Omaha, NE 68178.

A Microcomputer-based Statistics Course With Individualized Assignments

Richard L. Rogers
Georgia Southern College

Published surveys of instructional computing in psychology (Butler & Kring, 1984; Castellan, 1982) indicate that computers are most often used in statistics courses. Using computers permits students to spend less time learning and doing computations, hence, more time is available for conceptual understanding and different statistical applications. A valuable by-product of using computers in the statistics course is that students will develop some elementary computer literacy.

A common approach to using computers for instructional purposes is to buy one copy of the software and make it available on a computer network. This approach is necessary when the statistical programs, such as SPSS, require a mainframe (Tromater, 1985). Even if the software will run on microcomputers, the expense involved in providing a copy for each student can be a problem. A network approach works well if the network can handle the demand; if it cannot, the course can be disrupted when the network is down or when students have to wait too long to gain access. I prefer to provide each student with a copy of the software to run on a microcomputer. One important advantage of this approach is that students can do their assignments on the six Apple II microcomputers located in our department where students can usually get help from a graduate assistant or me. Students can also use any of the Apples available to them at other times and places. I also value the greater independence, flexibility, and self-reliance that result from students using stand-alone microcomputers.

Until recently, providing each student with a copy of the software often created economic or ethical problems. At least one textbook/software package is now available at a price comparable to that of a textbook alone (Elzey, 1985). I share here my experiences using this package in an introductory statistics course taught in the psychology department. The class consisted of 18 psychology majors taking my course as a requirement.

Elzey's package falls into Butler and Eamon's (1985) student research category: "programs that may be useful to students who need to analyze research data in lab courses or professionals who need to analyze a small amount of data" (p. 354). The software consists of 19 programs on one diskette. The first two programs, one for univariate data and one for bivariate data, allow students to create data files and save them on disk to be accessed by the statistical programs. The other 17 programs are statistical routines covering the procedures that one would expect to include in an introductory statistics course and more. In addition to basic descriptive statistics, bivariate correlation and regression, t tests, and one-way ANOVA, the package includes multiple regression with two predictors, two-way and repeated measures ANOVA, analysis of covariance, and five non-parametric procedures.

The statistical programs are menu-driven and relatively easy for students to use. The breadth of coverage and the ability to create and access data files increase the package's usefulness for teaching statistics and analyzing data in research-oriented undergraduate courses. On the negative side, the software has some weaknesses. The programs' error-trapping is rather poor. For example, if one tries to do a univariate procedure using a bivariate data file, a common error for inexperienced students, the program displays its COMPUTING message indefinitely and will not respond to any further commands; the program must be started over. Another weakness in the current version of the programs is the inability to take advantage of a two-disk system. The user must swap the program disk and the data disk as needed. My students and I discovered a few bugs in the current version of the software. The most troublesome is the reporting of some incorrect probability values. For example, in the two-way ANOVA routine, if the observed value of F is less than 1.00, the program may report an associated p value of less than .001. The publisher's support is an advantage. Halfway through the course I received an update of the programs and permission to distribute copies to the class members. The publisher also solicited suggestions for enhancements to the programs with the assurance that an enhanced version, supporting a two-disk system, would be available before the fall of 1986.

Weekly assignments consist of a data set and questions about the data to be answered using the statistical routines. Each student received a unique set of data prepared with a program called, *Correlated Samples*

(published by HMS Software, P.O. Box 49186, Austin, TX 78765). This program produces random samples from a population defined by the user. The user designates the mean and standard deviation of the population, the sample size, and the correlation between pairs of samples. The program then generates as many pairs of random samples as requested with the data on one page of output and sample statistics (*M, SD,* variance, correlation, and both independent- and correlated sample t tests) on another page for each sample. I distribute the data and keep the sample statistics to aid in grading the assignments. These individualized assignments help alleviate the problem of a student copying another's work and provide a pedagogical device for the nature of random sampling.

I also use the statistical software to create materials for examinations. Learning to select the right statistical procedure to answer a question about a particular data set is an important aspect of the course. I test the students' ability to do this by presenting several descriptions of research situations and several printouts from the statistical program. The student must select the appropriate printout for each research situation and use it to make statistical decisions and research conclusions. This kind of test item constitutes a major portion of the final exam. It is an in-class exam but students are allowed to use their books and class notes for this part of the final.

Although the software in this package is useful in my course, the textbook is disappointing. The sections of the book dealing with the use of the statistics programs are good, but the book is not as adequate as a source of conceptual understanding and varied applications. Of the approximately 240 pages of text (not including statistical tables, exercises, and solutions to exercises), roughly 75 deal with using the computer programs and the other 165 are devoted to presenting and explaining statistical concepts and procedures. It is not surprising that beginning statistics students derive little understanding from the book, given that the author tries to cover everything from basic descriptive procedures through factorial ANOVA, ANCOVA, and several non-parametric procedures in those 165 pages. I supplement the book with other materials, such as handouts or other books.

It is impossible to compare the performance of students in this class with that of students in previous classes not using the computer materials because the skills assessed and the evaluation procedures were too different. However, students' performance on the final exam previously described can be reported. Each of 18 students had to select the appropriate statistical procedure for five items. Of the total 90 items attempted, 70 were answered correctly (78%). Nine of the 20 incorrect responses were made by two students who failed the exam. For the students who passed 86% of these items were answered correctly.

As part of the course evaluation, the class was asked to comment on the use of microcomputers in the course. Seventeen commented positively and one commented negatively. The negative reviewer suggested that being forced to do the calculations by hand would have produced a better understanding of the procedures.

Despite the difficulties caused by the programs' bugs and the textbook's failings, using the package helped to create a good teaching situation by providing each student with a copy of the software and manual as well as the textbook. If the next version of this package eliminates the inaccuracies and the poor error-trapping, it will be a productive tool for teaching statistics.

References

Butler, D. L., & Eamon, D. B. (1985). An evaluation of statistical software for research and instruction. *Behavior Research Methods, Instruments, & Computers, 17*, 352-358.

Butler, D. L., & Kring, A. M. (1984). Survey on present and potential instructional use of computers in psychology. *Behavior Research Methods, Instruments, & Computers, 16*, 180-182.

Castellan, N. J. (1982). Computers in psychology: A survey of instructional applications. *Behavior Research Methods, Instruments, & Computers, 14*, 198-202.

Elzey, F. E. (1985). *Introductory statistics: A microcomputer approach*. Monterey, CA: Brooks/Cole.

Tromater, L. J. (1985). Teaching a course in computer-assisted statistical analysis. *Teaching of Psychology, 12*, 225-226.

Classroom Use of the Personal Computer to Teach Statistics

Patricia A. Oswald
Iona College

Surveys show that approximately 50% of college-level psychology faculty use computers as one of several pedagogical methods. Faculty teaching statistics courses are the most likely to use computers (Castellan, 1982; Stoloff & Couch, 1981). Many psychology teachers believe that computers are an important component of their courses and that computers facilitate student learning and increase academic achievement (Butler & Kring, 1984; Halcomb et al., 1989; Sexton-Radek, 1993), but Gratz, Volpe, and Kind (1993) noted that there has been little empirical support for this view.

Assessment of student learning is a critical part of any educational endeavor. There has been movement away from relying solely on exams as a way of assessing student learning (Moss et al., 1992). An alternative method involves using computers as a means of assessment. On my campus, faculty are exploring many new techniques for using computers as assessment tools. Two of these initiatives include using computers (a) to help students self-assess in their first year and (b) as part of our scientific and technological literacy program to assist faculty in evaluating students' mastery of laboratory exercises.

In this article, I discuss how using a single personal computer in the classroom enhances student confidence and ability in using computers, and I identify one of the assessment opportunities that this technique provides. I outline the method used, briefly discuss the necessary software and hardware, identify the educational objectives, and analyze the effectiveness of this method.

Method

Subjects

I conducted this research at Iona College. Forty-one undergraduate psychology majors enrolled in two sections of an elementary statistics course constituted the sample} Twenty-one women (51%) and 20 men (49%) participated. The sample included seniors (56%), juniors (37%), and sophomores (7%). The mean age of the students was 20.70years (*SD* = 1.60). The mean grade point average (GPA) of the students was 2.88 (*SD* = 0.50) on a 4-point scale. All students had taken one computer course before enrolling in basic statistics.

Table 1. Means and Standard Deviations for Pretest and Posttest Attitude Statements

Attitude Statement	Pretest		Posttest	
	M	*SD*	*M*	*SD*
1. In-class computer problem solving helps me understand course material better than in-class computational problem solving.	7.4	1.3	8.2	1.4
2. I am able to use computers effectively to solve statistical problems.	4.9	2.4	6.9	1.4
3. I feel confident when making informal class presentations like those involved in using the computer in class.	5.0	2.4	6.7	1.5
4. Explaining computer analyses and assignments to the other students in class helps me to learn the material better than independent problem solving.	6.3	1.5	7.3	1.5
5. I learn best when the instructor uses the lecture format primarily.	5.8	2.1	3.3	2.0

Note. Students rated these statements on a 9-point scale ranging from 1 (*strongly disagree*) to 9 (*strongly agree*).

Equipment and Materials

The equipment included an IBM AT personal computer with one hard drive and two external floppy disk drives (3.5 in. and 5.25 in.), a projection pad, an overhead projector, and a projection screen. The cost of the system is approximately $2,500. This equipment, constructed as a mobile unit, could be transported to any classroom in the psychology building.

The statistical software used was MYSTAT (the student version of SYSTAT). Students purchased the *MYSTAT Manual* and software as a package (Harris, 1991). The *MYSTAT Manual* was written to coordinate with the text used, *Introduction to Statistics for the Behavioral and Social Sciences* (Christensen & Stoup, 1991). MYSTAT is a computer program designed for use in introductory statistics courses. It computes descriptive and inferential statistics. I used a questionnaire to evaluate the effectiveness of the classroom techniques investigated. Students responded to five attitude statements about how confident they were that using computers aided their learning. Students responded to these statements, using a 9-point scale ranging from 1 (*strongly disagree*) to 9 (*strongly agree*). Table 1 lists the questions on the survey instrument administered to subjects as a pretest and posttest.

Procedure

During the first week of the fall semester, I demonstrated the equipment and introduced the in-class computer problem-solving method to students in both sections of my statistics course. Then, I administered the pretest to students. Students received standard instruction in statistics using lecture, discussion, in-class problem-solving techniques, and homework assignments (approximately 30% of the out-of-class assignments required computer use). The course covered descriptive statistical techniques (e.g., frequency distributions, measures of central tendency, and measures of variability) and inferential techniques (e.g., one- and two-sample *t* tests and one-way and two-way analyses of variance). As I

discussed each of the topical areas of the course, I used the computer for in-class problem-solving exercises.

Typically, I began by presenting a research problem. An example of such a problem is the following: An educator thinks there may be a relation between gender and computer usage in second graders. How does she proceed? First, students identified the type of research design appropriate to answer such a question. Second, once students outlined the rudiments of the design and method, I elaborated on the research method. Then, students identified the appropriate statistical procedure to analyze the data.

Next, I provided data and asked an individual student to conduct the computer analysis. The student entered a small data set as part of the demonstration; for a large data set, I provided the data on a disk. Early in the term, I requested volunteers; later, as students became more comfortable with this instructional method, I called on different students. I assisted students throughout the exercise as needed. Assistance varied according to the type of analysis being done. For example, in a simple linear regression, I helped a student identify the slope and intercept values that were then entered in the next MYSTAT command line to continue the analysis. After the student completed the analysis, the entire group joined in to answer the original research question. Each student had the opportunity to use the computer in front of the class a few times during the semester.

I evaluated students' performance on the in-class computer problem-solving exercises on a dichotomous satisfactory-unsatisfactory basis. This activity accounted for 10% of their final grade.

I allocated approximately 20% of class time for in-class computer problem solving each week (about 30 min of a 150-min class). I administered the posttest measure the last week of the semester in December.

Results

Using *t* tests, I compared the pretest and posttest attitude data. The means and standard deviations for the attitude statements are presented in Table 1.

99

There was a significant increase in student preference for the use of in-class computer problem solving compared to in-class computational problem solving from the pretest to the posttest, $t(37) = 2.176$, $p < .05$. Students also reported a significant increase in their ability to use computers to solve problems from pretest to posttest, $t(35) = 4.609$, $p < .0001$.

Students reported an increase from pretest to posttest in the ease with which they were able to present statistical material and computer procedures orally, $t(35) = 3.789$, $p < .0001$. In the posttest, students also were more likely to agree that explaining various computer analyses to their classmates enhanced their learning of the material, as compared with the pretest, $t(37) = 2.845$, $p < .01$. Moreover, there was a significant decrease in students' preference for the primary use of the lecture format from the pretest to posttest, $t(35) = 5.247$, $p < .0001$.

Finally, I compared students in the computer-oriented section with students whose class did not involve in-class computer problem solving (these students did use computers for out-of-class assignments, however). The latter group completed the course 2 years before with the same instructor and the same textbooks. Although intact groups were used for this comparison, no significant differences between the two groups existed in gender composition, year in college when they took statistics, cumulative GPA, or college major. Using 4-point scales, the computer-oriented section course grade mean was 2.90 ($SD = 0.90$), and the comparison section course grade mean was 2.60 ($SD = 1.40$). This difference was not statistically significant, $t < 1.00$.

Discussion

This pedagogical and assessment method allows the instructor to identify students' understanding of the course material specifically as it relates to the computer analysis and to modify later instruction as necessary. Feedback to the instructor and the student is more immediate than homework assignments or exams. That is, the instructor can assess on the spot whether the current concepts and related computer applications are understood by the student doing the demonstration (and through the feedback from the class, the group's understanding as well) and proceed accordingly. I used this method primarily to assess the students' level of understanding of the computer-related material so that I could adjust my teaching. In addition, I used this method as part of my grading of students. The latter is somewhat informal because I evaluated students on a satisfactory-unsatisfactory basis only. Moreover, students' performance on the in-class computer problem-solving exercises accounted for only 10% of their course grade. Nonetheless, I believe that this is a useful technique for assessing students. Furthermore, students noted how helpful it was to test themselves immediately on their understanding of the material and the corresponding computer applications.

Several objectives can be realized by using this technique. These objectives include the opportunity to assess: (a) students' ability to formulate psychological concepts (theory) in quantitative terms by having them identify the appropriate design and method to answer a specific research question; (b) students' understanding of specific course content and its application by, for example, having them determine if the results of the analysis are statistically significant and provide an appropriate interpretation; (c) students' ability to use computerized techniques to analyze data statistically (use of computer hardware and software) by having them execute the necessary steps in a particular statistical procedure; and (d) students' oral presentation skills by having them explain the procedures and results to the class. These objectives may be met using a variety of other teaching methods (e.g., separate class periods of lab instruction in computer usage), but my approach meets these objectives in an economical, all-in-one manner.

There are three benefits to using this instructional method, as compared with using computers for out-of-class assignments only or not using computers at all. First, this method is cost-effective because it does not require access to a computer laboratory with 30 personal computers. The system (one personal computer, a projection pad, an overhead projector, and a projection screen) costs approximately $2,500; a computer laboratory costs considerably more.

Second, this method is teaching effective because it allows for ready assessment of student learning that homework assignments, for example, do not. The instructor can observe firsthand students' ability to use the computer to answer statistical questions and can intervene when individual students who are giving demonstrations, or others in the class, are having difficulty.

Third, this method improves students' attitudes about using computers. After participating in computer-learning activities, students report significant changes in their confidence and ability to use computers to solve statistical problems. Their open-ended survey comments suggest that the in-class computer usage was most valuable in this regard; perhaps this was due to the encouragement and support they received. Moreover, this technique helps to prepare students for more advanced statistics and research methods courses and for doing independent research, all of which require computer expertise. Because no reliable difference was observed in course grades between the students who used the computer in the classroom and those who did not, further investigation is necessary to determine if quantitative learning gains will result (i.e., increases in final statistics grades).

This method also sends a valuable implicit message. According to Gray (1993), an implicit message ". . . includes attitudes about the subject under discussion, attitudes about the students, and expectations about what students will do" (p. 69). The implicit message here is that students can do one of the most important tasks in the practice of psychology—use computerized statistical procedures to answer research questions.

In conclusion, using the personal computer in the classroom provides immediate feedback to the teacher and the learner, enhances students' confidence in using computers and learning computer-related course material, is cost-effective, and fosters experiential learning that enlivens the classroom.

References

Butler, D. L, & Kring, D. B. (1984). Survey on present and potential instructional use of computers in psychology. *Behavior Research Methods, Instruments, & Computers, 16*, 180-182.

Castellan, N. J. (1982). Computers in psychology A survey of instructional applications. *Behavior Research Methods, Instruments, & Computers, 14*, 198-202.

Christensen, L. B., & Stoup, C. M. (1991). *Introduction to statistics for the behavioral and social sciences.* Pacific Grove, CA: Brooks/Cole.

Gratz, Z. S., Volpe, G. D., & Kind, B. M. (1993, March). *Attitudes and achievement in introductory psychological statistics classes: Traditional versus computer supported instruction.* Paper presented at the 7th annual conference on Undergraduate Teaching of Psychology, Ellenville, NY.

Gray, P. (1993). Engaging students' intellects: The immersion approach to critical thinking in psychology instruction. *Teaching of Psychology, 20*, 68-74.

Halcomb, C. G., Chatfield, D. C., Stewart, B. E., Stokes, M T. Cruse, B. H., & Weimer, J. (1989). A computer-based instructional management system for general psychology. *Teaching of Psychology, 16*, 148-151.

Harris, B. A. (1991). *MYSTAT manual* (2nd ed.). Pacific Grove, CA: Brooks/Cole.

Moss, P. A., Beck, J. S., Ebbs, C., Matson, B., Muchmore, J., Steele, D., Taylor, D., & Herter, R. (1992). Portfolios, accountability, and an interpretive approach to validity. *Educational Measurement: Issues and Practice, 11*, 12-21.

Sexton-Radek, K. (1993). Using computers to teach the role of professional psychologists. *Teaching of Psychology, 20*, 248-249.

Stoloff, M. L., & Couch, J. V. (1987). A survey of computer use by undergraduate psychology departments in Virginia. *Teaching of Psychology, 14*, 92-94.

Notes

1. An earlier version of this article was presented at the Seventh Annual Conference on the Teaching of Undergraduate Psychology: Ideas and Innovations, Ellenville, NY, March 1993.

2. Thanks to Bernard C. Beins, Charles L. Brewer, and the anonymous reviewers who offered many helpful suggestions on previous drafts of this article.

How Often Are Our Statistics Wrong? A Statistics Class Exercise

Joseph S. Rossi
University of Rhode Island

Several years ago, Rosenthal (1978) published an article with the provocative title, "How Often are Our Numbers Wrong?" The point of his study was to determine the frequency of data recording errors, and the extent tc which such errors were likely to be biased in favor of the experimenter's hypothesis. His results were encouraging, because only about 1% of all observations were found to be erroneous. However, about two thirds of the errors were biased in favor of the experimenter's hypothesis. In this article, I describe an out-of-class exercise, similar to one first outlined by Barnwell (1984), for a course in statistics or research methodology that examines a question similar to that posed by Rosenthal: How often are our statistical test results wrong?

Exercise

Students are asked to find examples in the journal literature of one or two statistical tests that have been covered in class. Chi-square, t tests, and one-way ANOVA are the most frequently assigned tests, because they are among the most commonly used statistical techniques, and more important, they can be recomputed from summary statistics. The number of tests assigned to each student depends on a variety of factors, such as the level of instruction (graduate or undergraduate) and which techniques have been discussed in class. For undergraduate classes, students are usually permitted to choose either chi-square or t tests. For graduate classes, I usually assign both t and F tests to each student.

Each journal article containing the appropriate statistical test must be checked to verify that sufficient information is reported to enable the student to recompute its value. Raw data are rarely reported, but usually there are sufficient summary data to permit recalculation. For example, recomputation of a chi-square test requires cell frequencies. Independent groups t tests and ANOVA require sample sizes, means, and standard deviations for all groups. Correlation coefficients and repeated measures analyses (both t and F) cannot be included in this exercise, because they cannot be recomputed from summary statistics.

Formulas to recompute chi-square and t values from summary data are available in most introductory statistics texts. Formulas for computing F ratios from summary statistics are not widely known and must be presented to the class. Gordon (1973) and Rossi (in press) have provided such formulas for one-way ANOVA, and Huck and Malgady (1978) for two-way ANOVA. Not all journal articles provide sufficient summary data to recompute statistical tests. Students were asked to record the number of articles searched that had to be rejected for incomplete reporting of data.

Study 1

For the first study, an undergraduate class was assigned the task of locating and recomputing either a t test or a chi-square test. Each student recorded the number of journal articles rejected because of insufficient summary data. When a suitable journal article was located, the student recomputed the value of the statistical test. Degrees of freedom (df) were also computed and compared to the author's report.

Table 1. Discrepant Test Results for Study 1

Test	Reported Value	Recomputed Value	% Discrepancy
χ^2	2.223	2.904	23.5
χ^2	41.5	48.2	13.9
t	1.25	1.63	23.3
t	2.27	2.95	23.1
F	3.91	5.88	33.5

Results

The number of articles searched and rejected by each student ranged from 1 to 50 (median = 8). Sufficient summary data appeared to be more frequently available for chi-square tests (median rejections = 4.5) than for t tests (median rejections = 10). This difference was significant by the Wilcoxon rank-sum test, $p < .05$.

Several students inadvertently selected the same journal articles for analysis. When duplicates were omitted, the number of t tests selected for recomputation was 12; the number of chi-square tests was 9. (One student selected and recomputed results based on a one-way ANOVA. This test will be included among the t-test results.) Discrepancies between the value of the test statistic reported by the author and the value recomputed by the student were apparent for 3 of the t tests (25%) and 2 of the chi-square tests (22.2%). In all, 5 of 21 test values (23.8%) appeared to be inaccurate. No specific criterion (e.g., percentage of discrepancy) was given to students to aid their classification of a result as "in error" or "not in error." However, I checked all student computations, and none of the five discrepancies could be attributed to only minor deviations, which are inevitable due to the rounding of values in reported summary statistics.

Table 1 shows the reported and recomputed values, as well as the percentage of discrepancy,[1] for each of the five statistical tests. The average discrepancy was 23.5% (median = 23.3%). Percentage of discrepancy was also determined for all remaining statistical tests reported in the five journal articles containing the inaccurate results. Average discrepancy for these "nondiscrepant" results was 1.5% (median = 1.3%). Thus, all five discrepancies appeared substantial. In addition, there was one incorrectly reported df for a t test (reported df = 10; recomputed df = 5).

---

[1]Percentage of discrepancy was computed using the following formula:

$$100 \times \frac{|A - R|}{R},$$

where A is the value of the test statistic reported by the author, and R is the recomputed value. Thus, it is a measure of the extent to which the published value is discrepant from the recomputed value.

Study 2

My original purpose in developing this exercise was to point out to students that the statistical tests taught in class really are used by professional scientists. In addition, I wanted to demonstrate that, using relatively simple computations, the students would be able to achieve the same results as obtained by the authors. At first, I expected only a very small error rate (cf. Rosenthal, 1978). Because the results of the first study yielded a much greater error rate than assumed, I planned a more elaborate exercise for a graduate class in statistics. Each student was instructed to recompute the value of a t test and of a one-way ANOVA F test. The number of rejected articles was again recorded, as were the reported and recomputed test values and degrees of freedom. Some additional data were also tabulated: the percentage of discrepancy (see Footnote 1) between the author's value and the recomputed results, and the significance levels attained by the reported statistical test results and by the recomputed test results.

Results

The number of articles rejected for insufficient data was much lower for the graduate class (range = 0 to 13; median = 2) than for the undergraduate class in Study 1. Rejections for t tests (median = 1) and for F tests (median = 3) did not differ significantly.

The much lower rejection rate for the graduate class was not unexpected. Graduate student search strategies should be more efficient than those of undergraduates, many of whom may be dealing with the journal literature for the first time. In addition, my experience with the first class led me to recommend some journals and to discourage others. For example, APA journals were not recommended, because complete summary data often appear to be missing in APA journal reports (standard deviations are frequently not reported). *Psychological Reports, Perceptual and Motor Skills,* and several other journals were recommended because the editorial policy seems to encourage complete reporting of summary data. Furthermore, these journals include a large number of articles in each issue, often running no more than two or three pages in length, and with a decidedly empirical (rather than theoretical) basis, resulting in relatively simple statistical analyses. Such journals are thus well suited for this exercise, especially for undergraduates. Nevertheless, 14 different journals were selected by students in Study 2.

A total of 46 statistical tests were examined (23 t tests and 23 F tests). Discrepancies between reported and recomputed values of less than 5%—about what might be expected as a result of rounding errors-were obtained for less than 60% of the tests. Discrepancies greater than 20% occurred for almost 25% of the statistical tests, and discrepancies greater than 50% were obtained for about 7% of the statistical tests (see Table 2). Table 3 displays the reported and recomputed values of the statistical tests for which discrepancies greater than 30% were obtained.

Table 2. Cumulative Frequency Distribution of Discrepant Results

Discrepancy	% of Tests
≤ 5%	56.5
> 5%	43.5
> 10%	30.4
> 20%	23.9
> 30%	15.2
> 40%	13.0
> 50%	6.5
>100%	4.3

Table 3. Discrepancies Greater Than 30%

Test	Reported Value	Recomputed Value	% Discrepancy
t	7.66	5.89	30.1
F	1.01	0.72	40.3
t	1.80	3.05	41.0
t	1.70	1.20	41.7
F	4.25	9.47	55.1
F	46.85	21.62	116.7
t	1.70	0.39	335.9

Errors were almost three times as likely to favor the experimenter's hypothesis than not.

Approximately 13% of the tests published as "significant." $p < .05$, were not significant, $p > .05$, after recompilation. Table 4 shows the reported and recomputed values as well as the percentage of discrepancy for these statistical tests. The discrepancies are quite low for two of the tests, because the reported values are very near the critical (.05) values. Note, however, that for one of the two, even the reported value was not significant, because it did not exceed the critical value! And for the second "low discrepancy" test, the degrees of freedom were also incorrectly reported. In all, there were four cases of incorrectly reported *df*, all for F tests. These are displayed in Table 5.

Table 4. Tests Incorrectly Reported as "Significant"

Test (df)	Critical Value	Reported Value	Recomputed Value	% Discrepancy
$t(21)$	2.08	2.07	2.03	2.0
$F(3, 67)$	2.75	2.78	2.67	4.1
$t(22)$	2.07	2.19	1.73	26.6
$t(25)$	2.06	1.70	1.20	41.7
$t(25)$	2.06	1.70	0.39	335.9

Table 5. Incorrectly Reported df for Study 2

Test	Reported df	Recomputed df
F	7, 80	7, 40
F	3, 188	3, 88
F	2, 66	2, 69
F	3, 76	3, 67

103

General Discussion

The results of these two exercises are surprising and worrisome. Results are consistent with those reported by Rosenthal (1978) concerning the proportion of errors that favor the author's hypothesis, but frequency of errors seems to be much greater than reported by Rosenthal. Of course, the context of Rosenthal's study was different. Nevertheless, the frequency of errors in the reporting of statistical test results requires further explanation.

The most optimistic possibility is that some students deliberately sought out instances of discrepant results. Although both classes were explicitly asked not to do this, the possibility cannot be ruled out. Because students in Study 2 turned in copies of their journal articles with their reports, a check of sorts is possible. I analyzed all of the remaining statistical tests in the selected articles, a total of 114 additional tests. Results were not quite as extreme as for the student selected tests, but in general, the essential character of the results remained the same.

A second possibility is that the reported summary statistics (*M*s and *SD*s) are in error, and not the reported test values. The situation is essentially indeterminate in this respect, and at any rate, it would not be much of a consolation if it were the summary statistics that were incorrectly reported. A third possibility—typographical errors—seems implausible, and would again not be saying much for the journal editorial and review process, nor for the author's responsibility to proofread the galleys.

The impact of these results on students is hard to overestimate. The point of the exercise is to emphasize the need for the student to evaluate critically even the numbers that appear in a journal article. Students may be accustomed to evaluating logical arguments in journal articles, especially by the time they are graduate students. Unfortunately, the data that appear in such articles often seem to be authoritative to students: "It's hard to argue with the numbers." This exercise is extremely successful in dispelling such attitudes.

One cautionary note is in order, however. It is important for the instructor to guard against the establishment of overly critical student attitudes. The goal of the exercise is not to make students mistrust statistical arguments in general, but to generate a detective-like attitude toward reading journal articles. "Statistician as sleuth" would be a good description of my intentions for this exercise.

Therefore, it is important to plan carefully the presentation of the collective results of the exercise to the class. I have found it useful to present the exercise in the context of more general methodological techniques, such as meta-analysis or secondary data analysis. Unfortunately, these are relatively advanced topics that are more appropriate for graduate-level courses. Furthermore, discussion of these issues is not yet common in most methods and statistics textbooks, though reasonably priced paperbound editions on these topics have begun to appear, especially for meta-analysis (Cooper, 1984; Fienberg, Martin, & Straf, 1985; Hunter, Schmidt, & Jackson, 1982; Jacob, 1984; Kielcolt & Nathan, 1985; Light & Pillemer, 1984; Rosenthal, 1984; Wolf, 1986).

For undergraduate classes, the results of the exercise may be described in connection with the general problem of conducting a thorough literature review (i.e., verifying the statistical computations in a journal article should be a routine part of conducting a literature review). It is convenient to present this material toward the end of the semester, because it then leads naturally to a discussion of the literature reviews the students will conduct as part of their laboratory research projects in our experimental methods course, which most of our undergraduate majors take in the semester immediately following statistics.

Finally, it is worth noting that several students (both graduates and undergraduates) involved in this exercise in my most recent classes have spontaneously offered to continue the work as a more formal research project by systematically examining several journals. This work has now begun and several small grants have been secured to facilitate the project. It is difficult to imagine a more rewarding conclusion to a class project.

References

Barnwell, G. M. (1984). The multiple benefits of a research literature exercise. *Teaching of Statistics in the Health Sciences, 38,* 5-7.

Cooper, H. M. (1984). *The integrative research interview: A systematic approach.* Beverly Hills, CA: Sage.

Fienberg, S. E., Martin, M. E., & Straf, M. L. (Eds.). (1985). *Sharing research data.* Washington, DC: National Academy Press.

Gordon, L. V. (1973). One-way analysis of variance using means and standard deviations. *Educational and Psychological Measurement, 33,* 815-816.

Huck, S. W., & Malgady, R. G. (1978). Two-way analysis of variance using means and standard deviations. *Educational and Psychological Measurement, 38,* 235-237.

Hunter, J. E., Schmidt, F. L., & Jackson, G. B. (1982). *Meta-analysis: Cumulating research findings across studies.* Beverly Hills, CA: Sage.

Jacob, H. (1984). *Using published data: Errors and remedies.* Beverly Hills, CA: Sage.

Kielcolt, K. J., & Nathan, L. E. (1985*). Secondary analysis of survey data.* Beverly Hills, CA: Sage.

Light, R. J., & Pillemer, D. B. (1984). *Summing up: The science of reviewing research.* Cambridge, MA: Harvard University Press.

Rosenthal, R. (1978). How often are our numbers wrong? *American Psychologist, 33,* 1005-1008.

Rosenthal, R. (1984*). Meta-analytic procedures for social research.* Beverly Hills, CA: Sage.

Rossi, J. S. (in press). One-way ANOVA from summary statistics. *Educational and Psychological Measurement.*

Wolf, F. M. (1986). *Meta-analysis: Quantitative methods for research synthesis.* Beverly Hills, CA: Sage.

Notes

1. Portions of this article were presented at the 94th annual convention of the American Psychological Association, Washington, DC, August 1986.

2. Preparation of this article was supported in part by National Cancer Institute Grant CA27821 to James O. Prochaska. I thank the editor and reviewers for helpful suggestions and Terri Hodson and Elaine Taylor for manuscript preparation.

Teaching Basic Statistical Concepts Through Continuous Data Collection and Feedback

Jean M. Low
West Texas A&M University

An understanding of basic statistical concepts is important. Psychology students, as well as students from many other disciplines, must take courses in statistics. Students often approach these courses with no previous knowledge; hence, early exposure to basic statistical concepts could be very helpful. For students who will not be taking statistics courses, an understanding of basic statistical concepts can help them become critical thinkers and educated consumers (Connor-Greene, 1993; Ennis, 1962; Mayer & Goodchild, 1990).

To help students learn basic statistical concepts, I collect classroom data, analyze them, and present the results in the next class. Concepts such as frequencies, normal curves, means, standard deviations, and correlations become a daily part of the class. This technique assumes that learning is improved by repetition of material and use of personally meaningful examples. This article reports an evaluation of this teaching technique.

Procedure

Three sections of an introductory human development course were assigned to either a continuous feedback, a partial feedback, or a control condition. The classes did not differ significantly from each other on age, race, sex, socioeconomic status, or college major. In all three classes, I defined and discussed statistical terms during the first week of the semester while presenting the chapter on research methods in human development. For the remainder of the semester, I collected information from the students as a part of each class. I used short verbal surveys to collect most information. For example, I asked the students to write down their age, sex, and a ttait that they thought described them. Occasionally, if it could be incorporated into the lecture, I used psychological tests. For instance, during the discussion of stress in early adulthood I had the students complete The Social Readjustment Scale (Holmes & Rahe, 1967). At each data collection, I assured the students that they did not have to contribute data if they did not wish to do so and that all individual data would be kept confidential.

In the continuous feedback condition, the information was analyzed daily and feedback was given during the next class. In the partial feedback condition, feedback was given on an average of twice per month. In the control condition, no feedback was given. I expected that students in the continuous feedback condition would have the best grasp of the statistical concepts by the end of the semester due to continuous repetition of the concepts and the meaningful data used.

To compare students' knowledge of statistics, I gave a brief, unexpected, five-item test at the end of the semester. In the test, students were asked to define and explain in their own words the terms *frequency, normal curve, mean, standard deviation,* and *correlation.* They were told that they should include any information they thought was relevant, and they could use drawings and diagrams if they wished.

A graduate student, who was blind to the three conditions, scored all tests. Each question was assigned a score from 0 to 4; thus, the highest possible score was 20.

Results

A one-way analysis of variance revealed significant differences among the three groups, $F(2, 155) = 28.18$, $p < .001$. The means and standard deviations were 15.9 ($SD = 3.3$) for the continuous feedback group, 11.3 ($SD = 4.2$) for the partial feedback group, and 10.2 ($SD = 5.1$) for the control group. A Scheffe test indicated that the continuous feedback group did significantly better on the statistical test than did the other two groups, which were not reliably different from each other.

Discussion

The results support the hypothesis that data collection and feedback can be an effective technique for teaching basic statistical concepts. Because the continuous feedback subjects scored significantly higher than the partial feedback subjects, such feedback should be provided in a repetitious manner.

Knowledge of statistical concepts was operationally defined as the scores on an open-ended test given at the end of the semester. Students had been told that the final exam would not be cumulative; so, although they had been tested on statistical terms on the first semester test, they did not expect to be tested on them again and would not have reviewed them from the text. The fact that the continuous feedback group scored the highest on the unexpected test suggests that the students learned the terms during the daily feedback.

Continuous data collection and analysis are difficult and time-consuming for the instructor, but I believe that the benefits to the students outweigh the difficulties. Collecting student data and providing feedback seems meaningful for the students. They are interested in knowing the composition of the class and, when possible, comparing their data to the data presented in the textbook. In an interesting and enjoyable way, they acquire an understanding of statistical terms. This knowledge provides a foundation in later statistics courses, helps them understand and evaluate research reports, and enhances their critical-thinking skills.

References

Connor-Greene, P. A. (1993). From the laboratory to the headlines: Teaching critical evaluation of press reports of research. *Teaching of Psychology, 20,* 167-169.

Ennis, R. H. (1962). A concept of critical thinking. *Harvard Educational Review, 32,* 81-111.

Holmes, T. H., & Rahe, R. H. (1967). The Social Readjustment Rating Scale. *Journal of Psychosomatic Research, 11,* 213.

Mayer, R., & Goodchild, F. (1990). *The critical thinker.* Dubuque, IA: Brown.

Notes

1. I thank Ruth L. Ault and the anonymous reviewers for their helpful comments on previous versions of this article.

2. I thank Bonnie Christensen for daily entry of data throughout an entire semester.

3. Portions of this article were presented at the annual meeting of the Southwestern Psychological Association, Corpus Christi, TX, April 1993.

4. Support was received through a West Texas A&M University President's Teaching Fellowship.

Teaching Statistics With the Internet

Connie K. Varnhagen
Sean M Drake
Gary Finley
University of Alberta

The Internet is a popular tool for instruction and can be used to provide students with greater access to information (Jones & Schieman,1995; Pask & Snow, 1995). World Wide Web (WWW) pages on the Internet can be used to archive course information and assignments. More important, by using the Internet as a supplement, student learning is not confined to course materials or library research. Students can access networked information located all over the world through the Internet.

Increased access to information is one important pedagogical benefit of using the Internet to supplement traditional instruction. Another important benefit may relate to levels of communication (Anderson, 1995-96; Bruning, 1995; Hiltz, 1986, 1990; Jones & Schieman, 1995; Pitt, 1996). Increasingly, nontraditional students enroll in university courses. In many cases, these students cannot attend every lecture or discussion group and need support outside of the classroom. Opportunities for increased contact exist with Internet communication; e-mail and newsgroups allow for virtual office hours, which is particularly important for nontraditional students who may have difficulty attending traditional office hours. In addition, students experiencing learning problems are less likely to get caught in erroneous efforts that are a waste of time; instead, there is potential for contact outside of class or office hours. Furthermore, interpersonal communication maybe enhanced; relevant discussion can extend beyond class time through the use of mailing lists, newsgroups, WWW boards, chats, e-mail, and similar services. Finally, given that increasing class sizes have forced a decrease in written assignments, students are able to practice writing skills and forms of argument through electronic communication.

To address these potentially beneficial components of information access and communication, we developed an Internet-based statistics laboratory in association with the more traditional lecture and discussion format class in intermediate statistics. The course was open only to psychology honors students. The types of statistical procedures the students learned were directly relevant to the research they were conducting as part of their honors

theses. The goals of the laboratory portion of the course were: (a) to learn how to analyze psychological data using a statistical analysis program, (b) to learn how to interpret output in terms of statistical and scientific hypotheses, (c) to practice writing results in American Psychological Association (APA) format (APA, 1994), and (d) to become familiar with the Internet as a tool for psychological research and communication of results.

At the beginning of the term, we introduced the components of the Internet in a 30-min lecture, designed primarily to clarify the omnipresent jargon about the "information superhighway." Students learned about the most common services available on the Internet. With this context established, we demonstrated computer use and distributed a short handout of steps for starting the computers and running various applications. Students then completed separate short tasks to allow practice in accessing the Internet, using e-mail, posting to the newsgroup, and jumping to different applications. The students worked individually or in pairs in the laboratory, and we circulated to offer assistance and answer questions. The next day, a follow-up lecture and question period on networking and the Internet reinforced their new understanding.

The WWW home page integrated the Internet components of the course, including: (a) an online syllabus and course information, (b) online project description and data archive for laboratory assignments, (c) online help for describing data, (d) pointers to other statistics sites to obtain information or help, (e) integrated e-mail to the instructor and graduate teaching assistant (GTA) responsible for the laboratory, (f) an integrated newsgroup for discussion, and (g) an electronic form for submitting assignments. During the last week of classes, we added a pointer to an electronic evaluation survey.

Students met in the computer room for a weekly 2-hr laboratory period. We took a short amount of time at the beginning of the laboratory to discuss previous laboratory assignments, introduce the current laboratory, and discuss any other concerns. Students generally began to work on the assignments during the laboratory period; however, students completed most of the laboratory outside of the scheduled period. It was not uncommon for a student to e-mail the GTA in the middle of the night with a problem and to receive an immediate e-mail reply. In addition, many newsgroup discussions occurred late at night. We were active participants in the newsgroup, posing our own questions, addressing student questions, and prompting student discussion.

One goal of this evaluation was to assess what components of the system students used as well as the perceived usefulness of each component (Anderson & Joerg, 1996). The Internet contains masses of information; do students use this information to learn statistics and report writing? We asked students to rate the usefulness of the Internet for information acquisition and communication as well as the other integrated applications. In addition, we asked students to rate the perceived usefulness of these various components of the laboratory computer system.

We were particularly concerned with students' abilities to access information on the Internet (Bruning, 1995; Hornby & Anderson, 1995-96; Jones & Schieman, 1995). Perhaps students would use the Internet sources only if they had the necessary skills and access. However, there may be numerous barriers to learning. The students had various levels of computer expertise, ranging from complete novices with only minimal word processing experience to experts who were familiar with Internet navigation. We were not sure that the 2-hr introductory session was sufficient to enable novice computer-using students to use all components of the system on their own. The students also varied in terms of their abilities to physically access a computer with Internet capabilities. A few students had computers at home but most had access only to on-campus computers.

Finally, we were interested in students' affective impression of the computer laboratory (Oswald, 1996; Varnhagen & Zumbo, 1990). Attitudes regarding any type of pedagogy may not be directly related to learning but may exert an indirect effect on learning. We did not want to continue to develop a system that students did not perceive as positive and appropriate for their learning .

Method

Students

Sixteen 4th-year honors psychology students (9 women and 7 men) participated in the laboratory. All students were actively engaged in research related to their honors theses and attended the lecture and discussion component of the course.

Evaluation Survey

The electronic evaluation survey included three sets of questions, relating to use and usefulness of various components of the system, perceived barriers to learning,

and perceived value of the experience. In addition, it contained questions relating to self-ratings of computer expertise, estimates of use of the system, and ratings of the value of the system in comparison with other components of the course.

The response format for the perceived use and usefulness items consisted of pull-down bars for 5 item Likert scales use responses ranged from 1 (*never used*) to 5 (*used every day*) and usefulness responses ranged from 1 (*not at all useful*) to 5 (*extremely useful*). The perceived barriers items used a similar pull-down response format, ranging from 1 (*major barrier*) to 5 (*no barrier at all*) and included a not applicable option. The perceived value items consisted of anchoring opposite adjectives with five click-boxes for responding between the adjectives.

The evaluation appeared on the class home page during the last week of classes. Students received a common access code and password to view the survey as well as an individual user alias for submitting their own completed form. The access code allowed only authorized individuals to view the survey. The individual user alias allowed only authorized students to submit responses, imposed a limit of one response per student, and ensured anonymity of responses.

Students completed the evaluation during the last 2 weeks of class. We directed the responses to a separate mailbox and did not view them until after the term was completed.

Results

We received 14 responses to the electronic evaluation. Five students rated themselves as "novice" in response to the computer expertise item, 8 students rated themselves as "intermediate", and 1 student rated him or herself as "expert"; we grouped the self-rated expert with the intermediate students for analyses considering expertise. Given the ordinal nature of Likert scales, the small sample size, and the disparate group sizes, we used descriptive and inferential procedures applicable to ordinal measurement scale data.

Median responses to the use and usefulness items appear in Table 1. The results indicate that the course-related communications aspects of the system and the other applications on the system were most frequently used and were perceived as extremely useful. Lower ratings were found for the other components. Most notably, students reported that they used the statistics information available on the WWW only occasionally or infrequently. No differences in use and perceived usefulness of the various components of the system were found as a function of computer expertise.

Spearman rank order correlations between use and perceived usefulness reflected a relation between use and usefulness ratings, ranging from a statistically nonsignificant $r_s(12) = .11$ for the e-mail to the instructor or GTA item (the majority of the responses were "used

Table 1. Median Responses to the Use and Usefulness Items

Item	Use	Usefulness
Course-related information on the WWW		
Home page on the WWW	4	4
Syllabus on the WWW	3	5
Assignments on the WWW	4	5
Help with describing data on the WWW	3	3
Pointers to other statistics sites on the WWW	2	3
Course-related communication using the WWW		
Submit an assignment form on the WWW	4	5
Newsgroup	4	5
E-mail to or from instructor or GTA	4	5
E-mail to or from students in the class	5	5
Course-related applications on the system		
SYSTAT	4	5
Word processing	4	5
Other information and communication on the WWW		
E-mail to or from people outside the class	5	5
Accessing other WWW sites in the university	3	4
Accessing other WWW sites outside the university	3	4
Accessing other newsgroups	2	4

Note. Ratings for use and usefulness were based on 5-point scales ranging from 1 (*never used*) to 5 (*used every day*) and from 1 (*extremely unuseful*) to 5 (*extremely useful*), respectively. WWW = World Wide Web; GTA = graduate teaching assistant.

Table 2. Median Responses to the Perceived Barriers to Learning Items

Item	Perceived Barrier
Barriers related to ability, experience, required training	
Inadequate training on using the computer in general	
Novices	4
Intermediate–Experts	5
Inadequate training on using the computer system	5
Difficulty in learning to use the computer in general	5
Difficulty in learning to use the computer system	5
Discomfort in using the computer	5
Poor keyboarding skills	5
Getting lost in the World Wide Web pages	4
Difficulty in seeing the value of using the computer system	5
Physical barriers	
Inconvenient access to the laboratory	4
Difficulty in accessing the network in class	5
Slow speed of the computer system in class	4
Difficulty in reading the materials on the screen	5
Barriers related to home computer use	
Hardware difficulties in using the computer system at home	4
Software difficulties in using the computer system at home	4
Difficulty in accessing the network from home	3
Slow speed of the computer system at home	4

Note. Ratings were based on a 5-point scale ranging from 1 (*major barrier*) to 5 (*no barrier at all*).

Table 3. Median Ratings of Perceived Value of Using the Computer System

Anchors		
Left	Right	Median
Extremely good	*Extremely bad*	1.0
Stimulating	*Boring*	1.5
Productive	*Unproductive*	1.0
Easy	*Difficult*	2.0
Great fun	*Unpleasant work*	2.0
Time saving	*Time wasting*	1.5
Not frustrating	*Frustrating*	3.0
Friendly	*Imposing*	2.0
Confusing	*Clear*	3.5
Too much work	*Not too much work*	3.5

Note. Medians reported are based on a 5-point scale located between the two anchors, ranging from 1 (left anchor) to 5 (right anchor).

frequently" and "extremely useful") to $r_s(12) = .71$, $p < .05$, for the newsgroup item. The average correlation between use and perceived usefulness was $M = .40$ and indicated that, in general, when students reported having used a component they also rated the component as useful.

Table 2 shows median ratings of perceived barriers to learning. As shown in the table, students perceived minimal barriers. There was a statistically significant difference relating to computer training as a function of self-rated computer expertise, Mann-Whitney $U = 3$, $p < .05$. Although there was a statistically significant difference, the novice group did not perceive their inadequate training to be much of a barrier. In addition, the novice computer users appeared to be satisfied with training related to the use of the laboratory system.

Students did not have 24-hr access to the computer laboratory until the 2nd week of classes; although the results of the electronic evaluation indicated minimal physical barriers to their learning, students were initially very vocal in their demands to have extensive laboratory access. Their need, in part, stemmed from limited access across campus or at home to a computer with Internet capabilities. In fact, only four students responded to the items regarding barriers related to home computer use. Based on the responses to these items, the one self-rated novice who attempted to connect from home experienced major problems.

Student attitudes were generally quite positive, as shown in Table 3. Although the median rating on the frustration dimension was moderate, students perceived the computer system as extremely good, stimulating, productive, moderately friendly, fun, and moderately timesaving. Statistical analyses revealed no attitude differences as a function of computer expertise.

Students varied greatly in the number of times per week they used the computer system ($M = 5.5$ times, $SD = 3.7$) as well as in the number of hours they spent per week

$(M = 7.3$ hr, $SD = 7.5)$. There were no statistically significant differences in number of times used or hours spent as a function of computer expertise.

Discussion

In general, students rated the communications aspects of the Internet more highly than the information aspects. Students also generally perceived minimal barriers to their learning and were quite positive about the use of the Internet-based statistics laboratory. There were few differences as a function of computer expertise. In part, this may have been due to a lack of technological problems; dissatisfaction with computer courses has been related to difficulties with the computer system (Pear & Novak, 1996). Possibly fortuitously, the applications were well integrated and ran smoothly in the Windows environment. Few computer or network crashes occurred.

Both quality of discussion and student writing skills appeared to improve during the term. Initial newsgroup posts had to do with identifying interesting WWW sites or advertising parties. However, as Bruning (1995) also observed ,students began to discuss topical issues, such as when to use what statistical technique and how to examine the data before blindly testing some hypothesis. Student writing also improved. Besides working with the GTA on a mastery approach for the results section assignments, students began to "flame" (criticize) each other in the newsgroup for poor grammar, spelling mistakes, and unclear writing style.

One finding of particular interest was that the students did not report accessing all of the information that was available. We had expected students to make extensive use of the online help and pointers to other statistical sites. Possibly the students did not recognize the richness of this resource. Indeed, one comment on the newsgroup late in the term (in response to a question about a particular way to present data visually) was "Someone went to an awful lot of trouble developing online help. Why don't you check out that pointer?"

We experimented with changing the cache settings in the WWW browser used in the laboratory so that we could use the WWW server's access logs to trace an individual student's progress though WWW pages. However, we were unsuccessful in obtaining any reasonable behavioral traces because only first hits on a page can be recorded; multiple hits and jumps to targets on a page are not recorded by the program. Possibly with new monitoring software we will be able to observe actual progress through WWW pages. On the other hand, students appeared to rely more on direct questioning of the GTA and instructor than on other sources of information (including the text, lecture notes, handouts, and the WWW). Our virtual office hours appear to have been the most convenient resource for the students.

Overall, our experiences with offering an Internet-based laboratory course have been positive. The key to our approach appears to have been a well-integrated system, introduction and practice in using the different components of the system, multiple options for communication, and instructor and GTA involvement in communication.

References

American Psychological Association. (1994). *Publication manual of the American Psychological Association* (4th ed.) . Washington, DC: Author.

Anderson, M. D. (1995-96). Using computer conferencing and electronic mail to facilitate group projects. *Journal of Educational Technology Systems, 24,* 113-118.

Anderson, T. D., & Joerg, W. B. (1996). Perceived effectiveness of World Wide Web to supplement university level classroom instruction. *Canadian Journal of Educational Communication, 25,* 19-36.

Bruning, S. D. (1995, April). *Classroom exercise that incorporates Internet discussion groups as an integral element in a communication course.* Paper presented at the meeting of the Central States Communication Association, Indianapolis, IN. (ERIC Document Reproduction Service No. ED 385 887)

Hiltz, S. R. (1986). The "virtual classroom": Using computer-mediated communication for university teaching. *Journal of Communication, 36,* 95-104.

Hiltz, S. R. (1990). Evaluating the virtual classroom. In L. M. Harasim (Ed.), *Online education: Perspectives on a new environment* (pp. 133-169). New York: Praeger.

Homby, P. A., & Anderson, M. A. (1995-96). Putting the student in the driver's seat: A learner-centered, self-paced, computer managed, introductory psychology course. *Journal of Educational Technology Systems, 24,* 173-179.

Jones, T., & Schieman, E. (1995). Learner involvement: A review of the elements of more effective distance education. *Canadian Journal of Educational Communication, 24,* 97-104.

Oswald, P. A. (1996). Classroom use of the personal computer to teach statistics. *Teaching of Psychology, 23,* 124-126.

Pask, J. M., & Snow, C. E. (1995). Undergraduate instruction and the Internet. *Library Trends, 44,* 306-317.

Pear, J. J., & Novak, M. (1996). Computer-aided personalized system of instruction: A program evaluation. *Teaching of Psychology, 23,* 119-123.

Pitt, M. (1996). The use of electronic mail in undergraduate teaching. *British Journal of Educational Technology, 27,* 45-50.

Varnhagen, C. K., & Zumbo, B. D. (1990). CAI as an adjunct to teaching introductory statistics: Affect mediates learning. *Journal of Educational Computing Research, 6,* 29-40.

Notes

1. The authors thank the 1995 Honors class who participated in the study and Dr. Eugene C. Lechelt, Chair, Department of Psychology, who created the psychology department computer laboratory and encouraged the development of this course.

2. The most recent version of the home page is located at: http: //web.psych. ualberta.ca/~varn/Psyco_406.html.

3. Requests for copies of the electronic evalutation survey, should be sent to Connie Varnhagen, Department of Psychology, University of Alberta, Edmonton, Alberta, Canada, T6G 2E9; e-mail: varn@psych.ualberta.ca.

SECTION III
RESEARCH METHODS

Introducing Scientific Thinking

Joe Hatcher described his use of fascinating riddles to expose students in introductory and experimental design courses to key points concerning scientific thinking as well as the process and experience of being a scientist. Students liked and learned from this unusual approach, which reminds one of Sherlock Holmes and Dr. Watson.

Art Kohn used a simple stay-switch probability game to demonstrate the importance of testing our beliefs empirically. Despite students' and faculty's beliefs to the contrary, a simple in-class experiment illustrated that switching wins twice as often as staying. This demonstration pointed out the value of validating our beliefs empirically. A follow-up questionnaire showed that participating in this experiment may increase students' trust in the empirical method.

Michael Stadler used a game called Black Box to teach various inductive and deductive processes that are useful in scientific reasoning. The game involved hiding four balls in an 8×8 grid and imagining a laser beam being directed though any of 32 doors that represented the rows and columns of the grid. Feedback such as absorption or reflection of the beam gave students clues with which to hypothesize where the balls were located.

Since Oskar Pfungst exposed the "thinking horse" as an unwitting fraud, Clever Hans has been used to illustrate various concepts in experimental psychology. Michael Marshall and David Linden replicated the Clever Hans effect by training a rat to bar press in response to a signal that was surreptitiously controlled by the instructor. This demonstration stimulated student interest and critical thinking.

Using concepts and principles from a basketball game, James Polyson and Kenneth Blick taught their students about the fundamentals of the experimental method. The basketball game provided a context for illustrating an hypothesis, independent and dependent variables, and controls. The authors expressed delight at the quality of classroom discussion using this technique.

Evidence suggesting that older left-handed individuals are underrepresented in the general population provided an engaging vehicle for David Johnson to introduce research methods into his courses. After viewing a graphical representation of this relation, students attempt to explain it. This fetching way of presenting diverse research issues can be used in various courses.

In a program that incorporates research into the curriculum at all levels, Christiane Brems developed a method for introducing students to research slowly and carefully. Her approach decreased students' trepidation, and close collaboration of students and faculty in the research process increased enthusiasm and enjoyment for students and teachers.

Donald McBurney used the problem method, sometimes called the case-study method, in teaching research techniques to undergraduates. Problems were assigned in advance, students used course material to solve each problem, and solutions were discussed in class. The approach emphasizes problem-solving and critical-thinking skills, and students found the method challenging and interesting.

Thomas Wilson and Douglas Hershey designed an unusual classroom activity for students in a research methods course. Students identified and evaluated their own procedural knowledge of the research process, generated scripts from their event-based mental representation of the process, and compared their own scripts to one from expert psychologists. Students considered the activity to be interesting and useful.

Reviewing the Literature

Linda Lewis, a librarian, outlined the advantages and disadvantages of bibliographic computerized searching and described the databases in psychology. Given the rapid growth in the number of databases and the increased availability of equipment, she predicted accelerated expansion in the use of computer searches but concluded that they cannot answer all bibliographic needs.

Pam Baxter echoed Lewis' call for bibliographic instruction in the psychology classroom. She suggested that librarians introduce the types and variety of reference works and demonstrate how students can better define their topic.

Retta Poe devised a series of presentations and exercises to help students improve their literature review papers in an abnormal psychology course. The sequential writing assignments included focused free writing, summarizing an essay, summarizing a journal article, integrating findings from two studies, and preparing a reference list in the proper style and format. Although time-consuming, this approach was evaluated favorably by students and teachers.

Teaching Research Ethics

Bernard Beins generated the Barnum effect to teach students about the ethics of deception in research and the feelings of subjects who are deceived. Students in research methods classes received feedback about a bogus personality inventory and rated the perceived validity of the interpretations. Seniors were more skeptical than juniors and sophomores. This technique is an engaging and effective way to help students learn firsthand about the costs and benefits of research.

Deciding not to conduct a study because it involves deception or invasion of privacy is as much an act to be evaluated on ethical grounds as is conducting such a study. Robert Rosnow designed a classroom exercise to demonstrate that the ethical evaluation of a study can be considered from several standpoints. He used role-play and discussion to sharpen critical thinking and develop an appreciation of the nuances of research ethics.

David Strohmetz and Anne Skleder used Rosnow's (1990) role-play for teaching research ethics to undergraduates in research methods classes. Results indicated that the exercise can be a valuable tool for sensitizing students to the factors involved in judging research ethics.

Richard Hubbard and Kathy Ritchie use the human subjects review process to stimulate students' critical thinking in their experimental psychology courses. Students integrated existing literature into their proposals and operationally defined their methods and measures. They critically analyzed their objectives and evaluated potential risks and benefits of their proposals. The procedure challenged students to present arguments logically to scientific and general audiences.

Brad Johnson and Rioh'det Corser presented an activity designed for graduate ethics classes that can also be used in undergraduate courses. Students played the roles of ethics committee members and the psychologist accused of committing the ethics violation in a simulated hearing. The hearing concluded with the committee making a determination for the disposition of the case after which the class as a whole discussed the case.

Recognizing the growing controversy over the ethics of using animals in research, Harold Herzog reviewed two prominent philosophical justifications for animal liberation and described an exercise that facilitates class discussion of animal research issues. Students simulated participation on an institutional animal care committee and decided whether a series of hypothetical experiments would be allowed. Students reported that the technique increased their awareness about the complexity of making ethical decisions.

Teaching Research Design and Methods of Observation

Mark Vernoy developed a Stroop-type experiment that demonstrated an interaction effect in a factorial design. Data for several semesters of an experimental psychology laboratory course indicated a consistent main effect and a significant interaction. The computer program that executes this experiment is described and explanations for the interaction are mentioned.

Using the Howard-Dolman depth perception apparatus, Dominic Zerbolio and James Walker at the University of Missouri-St. Louis devised an exercise that facilitates exposition of a factorial design and addresses perceptual problems experienced in everyday life. The exercise illustrates the nature of an interaction and the necessity of additional analyses of simple main effects.

William Stallings had graduate students design and conduct an experiment to evaluate effects of fertilizers on the growth of radish seedlings. The goal of this project is to provide practice in making design decisions, collecting and analyzing data, and writing results. Informal evaluations suggested that the technique is a promising one for teaching experimental design.

James Carr and John Austin provided a brief overview of single-subject designs and described a demonstration for teaching these designs to undergraduate psychology majors. Using a reversal design, students collected repeated measures of their own behavior, and they graphed and visually interpreted their data.

Recognizing a lack of emphasis on naturalistic observation, Harold Herzog described exercises designed to provide students experience in quantifying behaviors observed in a small mouse colony. These techniques can be applied in numerous courses and with almost any species, including humans.

Dwight Krehbiel and Paul Lewis stressed the importance of observational methodology and described a program that focuses on this approach. They pointed out specific advantages of systematic observation and described pertinent lab exercises designed to show students how subdisciplines of psychology can be integrated.

Andrea Zeren and Vivian Makosky described an in-class activity that permits systematic observations of spontaneous human behavior as portrayed on television. The activity involves: a lecture about observational techniques; a demonstration of time sampling, event sampling, and trait ratings; and a class demonstration that compares and contrasts the three methods. Students reacted favorably to the exercise and claimed that it helped them to understand observational techniques and other facets of research.

Miriam Goldstein, Roy Hopkins, and Michael Strube developed a classroom demonstration of observer bias. Students were led to expect that response time of a subject's performance on a motor task would decrease across three trials, because of alcohol consumption. The subject (a trained confederate who drank a nonalcoholic beverage) displayed consistent behavior and performance across trials, but students reported a trend that was consistent with their expectancy. The demonstration had a strong and memorable effect on students.

Working in Groups

Large enrollments and limited resources often preclude requiring all psychology majors to participate in one-on-one research with faculty members. Pamela Gibson, Arnold Kahn, and Virginia Mathie designed two research team models to offer research opportunities for as many students as possible. Model 1 is a single-faculty, single-project team, and Model 2 is a large multifaculty, multiproject team. Students and faculty valued these approaches because they involved students in all aspects of the research enterprise.

David Carroll described a method for improving performance in laboratory courses. Students worked in small groups and each person made a unique contribution to a research project. The technique encourages cooperation, and evaluations suggested that students liked the approach and that it enhanced their academic performance. Advantages and potential problems were also mentioned.

Thomas Plante described a program that involved many students in multiple research projects supervised by one faculty member. The procedure included laboratory group meetings and the appointment of a student project manager for each study. Participation in the group enhanced the students' interest in and understanding of psychological research and improved their chances of being accepted into competitive graduate programs.

Andrew Newcomb and Catherine Bagwell described the laboratory component of their introductory psychology course and a teaching fellows (TFs) program in which undergraduates directed these laboratory experiences. They presented the goals of the course and described its curriculum; discussed goals and operations of the TF program; mentioned the specific responsibilities of the TFs as well as the procedures for selecting, training, and supervising them; and summarized the many advantages of this exemplary program.

Presenting Research Results

Paul Gore and Cameron Camp used a poster session as an integral part of an undergraduate experimental design course. Undergraduates designed and conducted original experiments using radishes as subjects. The students presented the results of these experiments in a poster session. The authors described the benefits of using radishes as subjects. Radishes? Yes, radishes.

In-class poster sessions supplanted traditional term papers in several of Brian Baird's courses. He described instructions to students about preparing posters, logistics of planning and conducting poster sessions, and the approach's advantages for students and faculty. Students preferred this approach over conventional term papers; in one survey, 100% of the respondents favored poster sessions.

The homework assignment used by Ruth Ault teaches students to organize information from an APA journal article. She distributed the contents of a short journal article in scrambled order and instructed students to unscramble the order of paragraphs and to determine the headings under which the paragraphs were subsumed. This exercise helped students learn about conventional organization and style, and it saved time for the teacher when students later wrote their own experimental reports.

Blaine Peden replicated and extended Ault's (1991) "What Goes Where?" active-learning exercise by evaluating its use with inexperienced and experienced writers of research reports. Results were similar to Ault's and Peden suggested ways to make the activity more useful for experienced report writers.

William Addison described how a research proposal, used in conjunction with reports based on data collected by students, can be an effective exercise in the experimental psychology course. A combination of the two approaches encouraged students to think critically and creatively about the research process and about methodological and ethical issues.

Arnold Froese, Brandon Gantz, and Amanda Henry developed an integrated model for teaching students to write psychology literature reviews. Students received instruction on methods derived from meta-analysis in a research methods class. The tasks included focusing research topics by linking several variables in a computer literature search, coding information from selected studies, developing common measurers to describe outcomes in the studies, searching for potential variables that moderate those outcomes, and evaluating research quality. This instruction prepared students to write formal papers in advanced courses.

After a minute of study, William Marmie's students recalled more features of a dime than of an unstudied penny. This demonstration illustrates the subjective nature of scientific judgment, the value of statistics in data management, and the rationale for including the method and results sections in a scientific paper. Also, it illustrates the principle that details of an object or event are difficult to remember unless they are studied intentionally.

Blaine Peden outlined and evaluated a strategy for teaching students to recognize and prepare references for four types of works often cited in research reports. Students' later performance on the Reference section of their research reports earned either an A or F grade, as suggested by Cronan-Hillix (1988). This approach helped students learn to prepare accurate reference lists and sensitized them to other aspects of proper style and format. Also, Peden said that using this technique improved his own referencing skills!

Using Computers

Blaine Peden outlined an approach that incorporates Apple II microcomputers into the entire research process as he works individually with advanced undergraduates. The strategy involved everything from developing researchable hypotheses to preparing manuscripts for presentation or publication. The author highlighted pedagogical and practical advantages of this technique.

Blaine Peden and Gene Steinhauer described an exercise concerning the reliability of behavioral observations. In a computer graphics laboratory, students learned to identify facial expressions of emotion. The authors then paired trained and untrained students and had them rate subjects in natural settings on facial expression, gender, and age. Students analyzed interobserver agreement scores and collaborated to write a paper. The authors were enthusiastic about using microcomputers to complement traditional instruction.

Undergraduates conducted a microcomputer-controlled investigation in John Hovancik's research methods course. The author designed a study to determine the relationship between forced-choice reaction times to different colors generated on a video monitor and subjects' affective reactions to their choices. Advantages of computer controlled research projects included students' excitement about first-hand experience with modern equipment.

In an unusual approach to generating data sets, Todd Riniolo designed a computer-based simulation, which is based on tenets of the central limit theorem, illustrating the consequences of excluding nonsignificant findings from published literature. The article described a step by step procedure for conducting a class demonstration. The demonstration pointed out that (a) exclusion of nonsignificant findings positively biases research interpretation and (b) smaller sample sizes are prone to greater bias when nonsignificant results are excluded from research interpretation.

Using Popular Media and Scholarly Publications

Newton Suter and Paula Frank stressed the value of having undergraduates read classic research articles from primary journals. They mentioned three criteria for selecting such articles, suggested how 12 particular ones illustrated some core concepts, and included examples of questions to ask students about those studies.

To increase the motivation of students to read journal articles before class, David Carkenord asked them to write summaries and critiques of the articles on index cards to be turned in after class discussion. Students received extra credit for submitting the cards and were allowed to use the cards during exams. The assignment enhanced classroom discussion and increased students' scores on exams.

Kerry Chamberlain described his use of topical laboratory projects that were relevant to course content and that met various objectives. An appropriate core article from the published literature served as the basis for each project, which entails full or partial replication of an experiment from the core article. The author mentioned several advantages and limitations of this unusual approach.

Rather than use entire journal articles as other instructor have done, Helen Pennington gave students either abstracts or parts of methods sections to help them understand concepts such as dependent and independent variables, sampling, and operational definitions. The activity had the additional benefit of demonstrating how information in secondary sources such as textbooks is sometimes oversimplified or incorrect.

Patricia Connor-Greene used creative techniques to teach critical evaluation of scientific research as reported in the popular press. A classroom exercise emphasized the distinction between correlation and causation by having students analyze a newspaper account of a research study. An individual assignment required students to critique a newspaper or magazine summary of research. Reactions indicated that students enjoyed these activities and became more critical of what they read in the popular press.

Examining Miscellaneous Issues

Dana Dunn emphasized collaborative learning and peer review in his statistics and research methods course. Pairs of students collaborated on the design, data collection, statistical analysis, and writing of an experiment. After a peer review workshop conducted by the instructor, student pairs served as peer reviewers for drafts of the final paper. These reactions aided students in making substantive and stylistic changes in their final papers.

Jennifer Brockway and Fred Bryant designed an activity that helped students understand that there is usually not one universally appropriate way to measure a given psychological construct. The activity required students to choose a construct, find two different measures of the construct, and compare the construct on several dimensions.

Have you tried using a technique based on the popular TV show Jeopardy? Bryan Gibson used the game in study sessions to help students organize the course material in a research methods course. Students reported that the format was educational and entertaining.

Nigel Barber used a participant modeling technique in an introductory psychology class to reduce students' fear of a laboratory rat. Students received a mild level of exposure (holding the rat's transport box) and observed peer volunteers actually handling the animal. Students' fear was reduced without handling the rat, which minimizes ethical problems.

Francis Durso established a program in which students in a capstone research course designed and implemented research for local business and agencies. The sponsorship of the businesses allowed small teams of seniors to apply their understanding of psychological theory and methods to problems of relevance outside of the academic community. Research teams produced reports and gave formal presentations to their sponsors.

116

1. INTRODUCING SCIENTIFIC THINKING

Using Riddles to Introduce the Process and Experience of Scientific Thinking

Joe W. Hatcher, Jr.
Ripon College

Science has been described as a process of puzzle solving (Kuhn, 1970). The use of riddles described in this article is useful in demonstrating to students, especially those in introductory or experimental design classes, key points concerning scientific thinking as well as the process and experience of being a scientist.

Students are told that they will participate in an exercise involving scientific thinking. They are given the following information .

> You are walking in the desert and find a man lying face down with a pack on his back, dead.
> How did he die?

Students are told that the instructor will respond to any yes/no questions. After several false starts, the class arrives at the correct answer: The man is a parachutist whose chute failed to open. Students are divided into small groups and given the following series of riddles, one at a time, with one member of each group receiving the answer and serving as moderator.

A. A man walks into a bar and asks the bartender for a glass of water. The bartender reaches under the bar, pulls out a large pistol, and points it right in the man's face. The man says "thank you" and turns and walks out of the bar. Why did the man say "thank you"? (He had the hiccups.)

B. A man is at work and wants to go home. However, he will not go home because a man wearing a mask is waiting there for him. What does the first man do for a living? (He's a baseball player standing on third base.)

C. A man is found shot to death in a room with a table, four chairs, and 53 bicycles. Why was he shot? (He was cheating at cards by having an extra ace; there are 52 Bicycle playing cards in a normal deck.)

After the riddles have been solved, I point out that both scientific thinking and riddle solving attempt to make sense of data that may appear contradictory. More specifically, the following lessons in scientific thinking may be derived from solving the riddles.

1. It is often important to view a problem from more than one perspective .

The ability to alter perspective, termed lateral thinking by De Bono (1967, 1968, 1985), is fundamental to any science and is demonstrated in the paradigm shifts discussed by Kuhn (1970). From this exercise, students learn that determined questioning from a wrong perspective leads to little or no progress, but once the correct perspective isfound, the solution to the riddle is often easily determined.

2. Prior assumptions concerning data are dangerous.

In the parachute riddle, students typically assume that the man is wearing a common backpack, leading to fruitless questioning. Similarly, in viewing scientific data, interpretations can be guided by assumptions to the point of overlooking the unexpected. For this reason, questioning basic assumptions is often productive.

3. Yes/no questions, properly formed, yield highly useful data.

The yes/no questions of the riddles are paralleled in science by the alternative and null hypotheses of the typical experiment. In each case, when precisely formed, the question (or experiment) allows one to choose between two mutually exclusive views.

4. Details that do not fit expected patterns are often of crucial importance.

In the parachute riddle, discovering that there are no footprints around the body is inconsistent with most interpretations of the problem, leading to a swift reappraisal of the situation and usually a quick solution.

Similarly, details inconsistent with general assumptions often spur scientific advances.

5. Persistence is a key quality in problem solving.

Students often terminate a promising line of questioning, unaware that the answer is close at hand. Although persistence can lead to the accumulation of mounds of useless data (e.g., alchemy), some degree of persistence is often necessary to solve a problem.

6. By expecting complicated answers, simple ones may be overlooked.

Students often comment that the riddles, although they appear complex, have simple solutions. This observation can be developed in several fruitful directions, such as: (a) discussing the law of parsimony; (b) noting that a conceptually simple approach may account for vast amounts of data (e.g., Darwin's theory of natural selection); and (c) extending the second point to the possibility that we may be able someday to understand behavior from relatively simple principles, a position I find especially interesting (Hatcher, 1987).

7. Science is an enterprise that is frustrating, exciting, and requires considerable courage.

This exercise also serves to introduce students to the "human" side of scientific thought. While solving riddles, students become ultimately frustrated and excited, and by exposing their own thought processes to the scrutiny to others, students gain a glimpse of the courage that it takes to subject one's ideas to possible falsification. At the conclusion of the exercise, I note that, whatever the similarities between riddles and the scientific process, there is a crucial difference. Although riddles have solutions that perseverance will discover, science makes no such guarantee; scientists must pursue their goals with no assurance of success, which requires a special kind of commitment.

Three laboratory exercises used in the class were evaluated on 5-point scales by two classes of experimental design students (N = 40), on the dimensions of *uninteresting-interesting* (M = 4.62 for the present exercise vs. 3.87 for the other two labs combined), *not useful-useful* (4.09 vs. 4.05), and *definitely drop-definitely keep* (4.58 vs. 4.06). Written comments indicate that students often remember the riddles when attempting to solve a difficult experimental design problem and that the riddle exercise is a good icebreaker for the class.

Based on student responses and my observations, I believe that this simple exercise helps students to understand the process and experience of science. The technique may be useful in a variety of classes involving scientific thinking.

References

De Bono, E. (1967). *The five day course in thinking.* New York: Basic Books.

De Bono, E. (1968). *New think: The use of lateral thinking in the generation of new ideas.* New York: Basic Books.

De Bono, E. (1985). *De Bono's thinking course.* New York: Facts on File.

Hatcher, J. W., Jr. (1981). Arguments for the existence of a general theory of behavior. *Behavioral Science, 32,* 179-189.

Kuhn, T. S. (1970). *The structure of scientific revolutions* (2nd ed.). Chicago: University of Chicago Press.

Notes

1. I thank Mark Nussbaum, Robert Wallace, Patricia White, three anonymous reviewers, and the editor for comments and suggestions on earlier drafts of this article.
2. Requests for other riddles that I have used should be sent to Joe W. Hatcher, Jr., Department of Psychology, Ripon College, Ripon, WI 54971.

Defying Intuition: Demonstrating the Importance of the Empirical Technique

Art Kohn
North Carolina Central University

In about 350 BC, Aristotle argued that the speed with which an object falls to earth is directly proportional to its weight (i.e., that heavier objects would fall to earth faster than lighter ones). Aristotle was wrong. But owing to the sheer force of his rhetoric, his axiom remained unchallenged for more than 2,000 years. Indeed, it was not until the Renaissance that Galileo performed his famous experiment proving gravity works with equal force on all objects. This refutation of Aristotelian physics shook the intellectual community of the time because it highlighted the limits of human intuition and emphasized the importance of inductive reasoning. This insight, in turn, helped to usher in the era of empirical exploration.

The following classroom demonstration, which is based on a puzzle that appeared in *Parade* magazine, dramatically illustrates both the limitations of intuitive judgments and the power of empirical investigation. The activity takes about 15 min of class time, and the only materials required are three identical envelopes and a $1 bill. I conduct this activity on the first day of my introductory and experimental psychology courses to set an empirical tone for the semester.

The Demonstration

The demonstration consists of three parts: presenting the probability puzzle, polling the class's intuitive judgments about the optimum solution to the puzzle, and conducting an experiment to test the accuracy of these intuitive judgments. To begin, tell your students that you plan to present a simple probability question involving three choices. Place the $1 bill into one envelope, seal all three envelopes, and then shuffle them so that no one, yourself included, knows which one contains the $1 bill. (You may want to put some folded paper into each envelope so that the students cannot see or feel the bill through the envelope.)

Now ask a volunteer to select an envelope, promising that the person will be able to keep the $1 bill if she or he guesses correctly. After the volunteer selects the envelope, announce that you plan to reveal that one of the unchosen envelopes is empty. Examine the contents of the two

unchosen envelopes and, with a bit of fanfare, reveal to the class that one of them does not contain the $1 bill. (Indeed, at least one remaining envelope must be empty.) Finally, holding up the remaining unchosen envelope, present the class with the critical question: "As you can see, the volunteer and I each have an envelope. However, at this time I will offer the volunteer a chance to switch with me. In your opinion, for the greatest chance of winning, should the volunteer stay with the initial choice or switch to my envelope?"

Following the discussion, poll the class's opinions. In my sections, typically 50% to 60% of the students favor staying, 20% to 30% favor switching, and 10% to 20% argue that, in terms of probability, it makes no difference whether the volunteer stays or switches.

Point out to the class that they are basing their opinions on intuition rather than on empirical data. Invite them to test their intuitive beliefs by conducting an experiment that will identify the best strategy.

Instruct the students to pair up, with one member acting as the experimenter and the other as the subject. Each experimenter should make a data sheet by labeling four columns "Correct Answer," "Subject's Choice," "Stay/Switch," and "Win/Lose" and by numbering the rows 1 to 20. Finally, the experimenters should fill in the correct-answer cells with a random assortment of the letters A, B, and C.

To conduct the experiment, each experimenter simply imitates the procedure I used with the class volunteer. The experimenter should (a) prompt the subject to guess either A, B, or C; (b) reveal that one of the unchosen options is incorrect; and (c) offer the subject the option of switching to the other unchosen option. On Trial 1, for example, if the correct answer is A and the subject chooses C, then the experimenter would inform the subject that B is an incorrect choice and offer the subject a chance to switch to A. On Trial 2, if the correct answer is A and the subject chooses A, then the experimenter would reveal that B (or C) is incorrect and offer the subject the chance to switch. For each of the 20 trials, the experimenter should record the subject's initial choice, whether the subject switched, and whether the subject ultimately selected the right choice. After everyone has completed the procedure, experimenters calculate the number of times that switching led to a win and the number of times that staying led to a win. Finally, the instructor should combine the results for the entire class and draw a graph comparing the percentage of wins that result from switching and from staying.

Evaluation

I evaluated this demonstration in three ways. First, 1 asked 140 undergraduates and 73 university faculty members which strategy they thought was most likely to result in winning. Each subject read a 150-word summary of the situation and then circled one of the following responses: "Your chances are best if you stay with your initial choice," "Your chances are best if you switch to the other choice," or "It will not matter whether you stay or switch; your chances of winning will be the same."

Fifty-five percent of the undergraduates believed that staying provided the greatest chance of winning, whereas 66% of the faculty believed that staying and switching yielded the same chance of winning. Only 28% of the undergraduates and 7% of the faculty believed that switching envelopes provided the best chance of winning.

Second, I conducted the in-class experiment with 84 introductory psychology students. I tallied the number of times the 42 subjects chose to stay or switch and the consequences of each choice.

Subjects significantly preferred the staying strategy, staying on 60% of the trials (binomial test, $N = 840$), $p < .001$. Although the subject preferred to stay, switching actually resulted in a significantly greater proportion of wins, χ^2 (1, $N = 840$) = 95.9, $p < .001$. Subjects won in 69% of the trials when they switched, whereas they won in only 34% of the trails when they stayed. I recently replicated this study with as few as 6 subjects, so the demonstration should work for all class sizes.

Finally, I asked all the students to complete the Trust in Research Survey (Kohn, in press) that measures reliance on intuition versus empirical investigation. The questionnaire consists of 10 questions such as "Your religion tells you that an event occurred, but research clearly shows that it did not happen. What will you base your opinion on?" and "You need to buy a reliable car, and your intuition tells you to buy *Brand X*. However, all the research shows that *Brand Z* is better. How will you decide which car to buy?" For each question, the subjects rated whether they would base their actions on *intuition only* (1) to *research only* (95. The students filled out the Trust in Research Survey along with several other unrelated surveys. Half the students filled out the survey immediately before participating in the demonstration, and half of them completed it 2 hr afterward.

Results of the Trust in Research Survey indicate that students who participated in the demonstration had higher trust in the empirical technique than students before the demonstration; however, this effect did not reach statistical significance. The mean for students who took the survey before the demonstration was 4.5, whereas the mean for those who took it afterward was 6.1, $t(166) = 1.53$, $p < . 1$.

Discussion

This activity provides a dramatic example of the limitations of intuitive judgments and the importance of empirical testing. Although the puzzle is simple, involving only three possible answers, most subjects fail to solve it; ironically, subjects with doctorates err more often than undergraduates.

After the demonstration, you may want to explain the mathematical rationale for these counterintuitive results. In this explanation, the critical premise is that the instructor's act of eliminating an unchosen envelope does not affect the chances that the student's envelope is a winner. To illustrate this, I begin with an analogous, realistic situation. I tell my class to imagine that four teams have qualified for an upcoming Final Four basketball tournament. In the first round, Kentucky is scheduled to play Duke and Indiana is scheduled to play UCLA. Given equal quality of the teams, the chances that Kentucky, for example, will win the tournament are one in four. However, assume that the Indiana team decides to withdraw from the tournament. How will this affect Kentucky's chances ? In fact, the odds of Kentucky winning do not change at all. Indiana was outside Kentucky's qualifying bracket in the first round, so Kentucky still must win two games. As a result, the chances that Kentucky will win the tournament remain one in four. For UCLA, however, the chances of winning improve to one in two. A betting person should shift from backing Kentucky to backing UCLA.

This situation is analogous to the three envelope problem. The initial probability that the instructor has the $1 bill is two chances in three, and the initial probability that the student has the $1 bill is one chance in three. Importantly, once the student selects an envelope, that envelope becomes a set that is entirely independent of the instructor's set; in effect, the envelope is placed into a separate qualifying bracket. Thus, when the instructor acts as an omniscient agent and eliminates a certain loser from within his or her set, that act in no way affects the probabilities that the student's set contains the winner. The chances that the instructor has the winner remain two out of three; the chances that the student has the winner remain one out of three. As a result, the student is better off switching envelopes.

Consider a different situation, however, in which the student selects envelope A and then accidentally peeks into envelope C and realizes that it is empty. Should the student switch from *A* to *B*? The answer is no because, under these conditions, *A* was not segregated into a separate category; the student's insight simply eliminated an option from the set *A, B,* and *C*. Thus, the student's insight leaves two alternatives with equal probabilities of being correct. This latter situation is analogous to a student guessing *A* on a three-item multiple-choice exam. If the student later realizes that answer *C* is certainly wrong, the student gains no advantage by switching from *A* to *B*.

Your students might appreciate knowing that when mathematicians were confronted with an analogous puzzle, their intuition misled them as well. In 1990, a similar question was submitted to Marilyn vos Savant, a newspaper columnist who, according to the *Guinness Book of World Records*, has the world's highest IQ. When Ms. vos Savant answered (correctly) that switching provided the greatest chance of winning, she received a storm of protests from mathematicians around the country. See Posner (1991) for an interesting history of this controversy.

Following the discussion, you can again ask your volunteer whether he or she wants to stay with the original choice or switch to the remaining envelope. About 90% of the time, my volunteers seem convinced by the data and switch envelopes. However, if your experience is like mine, some of your students (and even some of your colleagues) will continue to insist that switching envelopes does not increase their chances of winning. Under these conditions, your only option may be to encourage them to conduct the experiment on their own, and then you may

want to remind them that truth is not obliged to be consistent with intuition.

References

Kohn, A., (in press). *Communicating psychology: An instructor's resource guide to accompany Kalat's Introduction to Psychology* (3rd ed.). Belmont, CA: Wadsworth.

Posner, G. P. (1991). Nation's mathematicians guilty of innumeracy. *Skeptical Inquirer*, *15*, 342-345.

Note

I thank the students in Experimental Psychology and in History and Systems at North Carolina Central University for their assistance with this study. I also thank Wendy Kohn, Richard Burke, Jim Kalat, Ruth Ault, and anonymous reviewers for their help in improving this article.

Demonstrating Scientific Reasoning

Michael A. Stadler
University of Missouri-Columbia

Most introductory research methods courses and texts introduce students to scientific reasoning, often by focusing on the distinction between inductive and deductive reasoning and on related concepts. One difficulty in teaching these ideas is that, unlike many other elements of a research methods course such as constructing a balanced Latin square or com putting a standard deviation, the cycle of inductive and deductive reasoning through which a scientist goes in the course of a research endeavor typically extends over a long period of

time. Many texts illustrate these processes secondhand by reviewing the history of research on a particular problem. In an effort to make learning of these concepts more active, I simulate this process by playing a game called Black Box[1] with my research methods classes.

The game (depicted in Figure 1) is typically played on an 8 × 8 grid, which forms the black box, around which are arrayed 32 cells that form doors along the side of the box. One player (the instructor) is the hider and picks 4 cells in the grid as the locations of balls supposedly hidden in the black box.[2] The other player (the class) is the seeker, who collects information by sending inputs into the box, choosing 1 of the 32 doors on each turn. After the seeker

---

[1]Black Box was manufactured by Parker Brothers (1978), but the game is no longer in production. However, a shareware computer version of the game (Sarret, 1994) is available and may be found by searching for "Black Box" at http//www. shareware.com/. The game can also be played with paper and pencil (or on transparencies on an overhead projector) by using grids such as depicted in Figure 1.

---

[2]To make the game more complex, the players may expand the size of the grid, increase the number of balls, or both.

announces a door, the hider imagines a hypothetical laser aimed into that door and determines whether and where the laser beam exits the box by following a set of rules about how the balls affect the path of the laser beam. The beam travels on a straight line unless it encounters one or more of the balls. There are three different outputs: *absorption*, *reflectors*, and *detours* or *misses*. Students engage in inductive reasoning as they generate hypotheses about the hidden balls.

Absorptions occur when an input runs directly into one of the balls, as when the beam enters Door 1 or Door 7 in Figure 1. In these cases, the beam does not come out of the box, so the hider announces "absorption."

Reflections occur when an input follows a path between two balls in the same column or row, but separated by one square, as when the beam enters Door 5 or Door 20 in Figure 1; in these cases, the beam exits from the door it entered, so the hider announces "reflection." Reflections also occur when a beam goes through a door with a ball immediately adjacent to it, as when the beam enters Doors 6, 8, 25, or 27 in the figure; again, the ball exits the same door through which it entered, so the hider announces "reflection."

Detours occur when a ball is on a path next to the beam's path; the ball deflects the beam so that it turns at a right angle one cell before it reaches the ball. For example, if the beam goes through Door 3, it would turn and exit from Door 29. Or, in a more complicated case, if it is aimed through Door 2, it would turn at Ball A, again at Ball B, and then exit from Door 22. When there is a detour, the hider announces from what door the beam exits.

There can also be combinations of the preceding

events. For example, if the seeker aims the beam into Door 31, an absorption results in Ball C after a detour caused by D; the ball does not exit the box, so the hider reports only the absorption. If Ball D is moved one cell to the left of the position depicted, and the beam goes in through Door 31, a reflection would result (the beam enters Door 31, moves to the right until encountering D and detours down, where it would pass between B and C; the laser beam then moves back up, detours at D, and exits at Door 31). Again, the hider reports only the reflection.

Finally, if there are no detours, reflections or Absorptions, the result is a miss, and the beam exits from the door directly opposite where it entered. For example, the beam misses if it goes through Doors 11 or 30. As in the case of a detour, the hider reports the door from which the beam exits. Note that detours can appear to be misses, depending on the arrangement of the balls.

As the game progresses, the hider records the seeker's guesses and the results (see the bottom of Figure 1); the seeker uses these data to figure out the locations of the hidden balls. After the first two or three turns, I ask students to state why they chose to aim the beam through a given door; in other words, to state a hypothesis (e.g., "aim the beam into Door 3 because I think there is a ball in that column") . I then use their hypotheses to make analogies to various aspects of scientific reasoning. For example, to introduce induction, I ask a student to explain how he or she arrived at a hypothesis; the student's explanation of what observations helped him or her figure out a ball's location makes a nice analogy for illustrating the process a scientist goes through in examining available evidence and proposing a hypothesis to account for those observations (i.e., the process of induction). After one student states a choice and the hypothesis that motivated it, another student can predict, based on that hypothesis, what the results will be if the seeker aims the beam through various doors, thus illustrating the process of making deductions from the hypothesis.

Similarly, the teacher may introduce ideas such as falsification (e.g., when an observation contradicts a prediction, the teacher can talk about the relative value of confirmatory and disconfirmatory evidence) and serendipity (e.g., when a ball is discovered accidentally, the teacher can make analogies to serendipitous findings in research). Because students face a problem that has an uncertain solution (as do scientists), the uncertainty in science and the problem-solving nature of science may also be illustrated. Finally, the excitement of playing the game (and students do play excitedly) compares well to, and thus helps illustrate, the excitement of discovery in doing scientific research. Although I have not tested directly the effectiveness of this demonstration, it appears to make quite an impact on students. They play the game enthusiastically and later readily relate induction, deduction, and related concepts to aspects of the game. Similarly, many students use examples and illustrations from the game in writing answers on exams; the game appears to provide an easily memorable referent for the

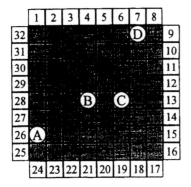

IN	OUT	IN	OUT	IN	OUT	IN	OUT
1	ABS	9	ABS	17	10	25	REF
2	22	10	17	18	14	26	ABS
3	29	11	30	19	ABS	27	REF
4	ABS	12	ABS	20	REF	28	ABS
5	REF	13	ABS	21	ABS	29	3
6	REF	14	18	22	2	30	11
7	ABS	15	ABS	23	16	31	ABS
8	REF	16	23	24	ABS	32	ABS

Figure 1. The layout of the game Black Box, a sample arrangement of the hidden balls, and the results of aiming the laser beam into each possible door.

concepts. Finally, several students have reported that they have taught the game to roommates and friends, and in explaining why they were playing games in a class, have found themselves teaching their friends about scientific reasoning. This and related demonstrations (e.g., Collyer, 1983; Hatcher, 1990) of scientific reasoning thus promote active learning of concepts that might otherwise seem distant and abstract.

References

Collyer, C. E. (1983). An introduction to unknown process analysis, with a dialogue. *Teaching of Psychology, 10,* 88-93.

Hatcher, J. W. (1990). Using riddles to introduce the process and experience of scientific thinking. *Teaching of Psychology, 17,* 123-124.

Parker Brothers. (1978). *Black box: Rules and solitaire games* [Brochure]. Beverly, MA Author.

Sarret, P. (1994). Black box (Version ;2.0) [Computer software]. Redmond, WA: BEANIEWARE.

Simulating Clever Hans in the Classroom

Michael J. Marshall
David R. Linden
West Liberty State College

The case of Clever Hans, the apparently sapient horse, marks a famous success in the annals of behavioral science and provides much fodder for illustrating psychological concepts. Early in this century, a German mathematics teacher toured Europe and amazed the public with a horse that could correctly tap out the answers to algebra problems, indicate the time of day, and even spell German words using a code that converted numbers to letters. Many "experts" of the day believed Clever Hans provided clear evidence that an animal was capable of human intelligence, especially because Hans responded correctly even when questioned by others in the absence of his master. Only when the psychologist, Oskar Pfungst (1911), systematically manipulated the conditions under which Clever Hans performed was the "thinking horse" exposed as an unwitting fraud. After much careful testing, Pfungst found that Hans simply responded to a subtle visual cue. Questioners invariably tilted their heads toward the horse when he had reached the correct number of taps, a signal that Hans used to stop tapping.

Because students find this story inherently interesting, psychology instructors have effectively used it to illustrate concepts such as systematic manipulation, hypothesis testing, uncontrolled conditions, experimenter effects, parsimony, falsifiability, and the dangers of relying on testimonial evidence (Kalat, 1993; Sebeok & Rosenthal, 1981; Stanovich, 1992). We believed the Clever Hans effect would have a more powerful impact on students if we could replicate it in class using a live animal.

This article describes and evaluates a demonstration in which the instructor covertly signals a rat to press a bar, giving the impression that it responded correctly to yes or no questions posed by students. A purist may call this demonstration a *Clever Hans-like effect* because it uses an auditory rather than a visual cue, and the experimenter intentionally rather than inadvertently cues the animal. We believe the demonstration aids in learning experimental design concepts and stimulates students' critical thinking and scientific skepticism.

Method

Subjects

The human subjects were 21 women and 16 men enrolled in an introductory psychology class. The demonstration subject was a female, Long-Evans hooded rat that was 4 months old when operant discrimination training began. The animal was housed in an individual

125

cage with water available continuously and was reduced to 80% to 85% of free feeding weight for training and demonstrations.

Apparatus

A Lafayette Instruments Co. Student Operant Conditioning System was used. The operant chamber had clear plexiglass side walls and lid and a metal lever centered in the front wall. A motorized pellet dispenser delivered 45-mg Noyes pellets to a reinforcement cup at the right of the lever. The jewel light above the lever was disconnected so that the switch on the handheld unit, which normally illuminated it, could be used to activate an interval timer. A bar press could activate the pellet dispenser only during the 4-s interval set on this timer.

The terms YES and NO were cut into separate 8-× 12-cm pieces of black construction paper backed by white paper. These signs were taped to the top of the system control console. Each could be illuminated from behind by a 6W-115 VAC light bulb. A bar press during the 4-s interval illuminated the bulb behind the YES sign and reset the timer. If the interval elapsed without a bar press, the NO sign was illuminated.

During the classroom demonstrations, the operant chamber was placed on the instructor's desk and the control console, with the YES and NO signs attached, sat on top of a cart 2.5 m from the desk. The hand control unit was given to a student volunteer who was instructed to turn on the switch to initiate a trial when the rat was to answer question.

During training, the auditory stimulus was presented from a Lafayette Precision Signal Generator (Model ANL-916) to an 8Ω speaker set outside the front or side of the operant chamber. During demonstrations, the auditory signal was presented from an electronic dog whistle, called a Dazzer (made by K-II Enterprises, $24.95), that was concealed on a belt beneath the instructor's jacket. Both of these instruments produced a 22,000-Hz signal of 80 db against a background of 60 db to 65 db, measured inside the operant chamber.

Procedure

In the training phase, the rat was shaped to approach and press the lever for continuous reinforcement. After a response pattern was established, discrimination training was instituted with continuous reinforcement during the auditory signal and no reinforcement when the signal was absent. The signal was set at 1,000 Hz during the first two sessions of discrimination training so that the trainers could hear it. As discriminative responding emerged, the signal was changed to 22,000 Hz, and training continued until the animal responded only during the signal. The procedure was then changed so that the first response after signal onset was reinforced and terminated the signal. The

duration of the signal was then reduced until the animal responded consistently within 4 s of signal onset. Although the rat's performance was almost perfect within 10 sessions, training was continued with refresher sessions, so that the behavior was well established and would not be disrupted by distracting events during the classroom demonstrations that were conducted 4 and 6 months later.

The demonstration took place after the students learned major concepts in research methods and experimental design at the introductory level through the assigned reading (Morris, 1993) and a lecture. The instructor told the students that psychologists used selective breeding and these research methods to breed and train rats to be as intelligent as humans. Students' denunciations were met with an offer by the instructor to "prove" it was true with a rat that was brought into the classroom in a Skinner box. The class was told that the rat, named Hanzel, would be able to answer correctly almost any yes or no question that anyone in the class posed by pressing the bar to indicate an answer of yes and refraining from bar pressing to indicate an answer of no. Just after each question was asked, a student volunteer flipped the switch on the hand control unit, which activated the 4-s timer. In response to a question such as "Is the moon made out of cheese?," the instructor did not trigger the ultrasonic signal, the rat did not bar press, and the NO sign was illuminated after a 4-s delay. In response to such questions as "Is 5 the square root of 25?," the instructor covertly activated the ultrasonic tone with a surreptitious push of the wrist against the on button of the Dazzer. This tone signaled the rat to bar press, which illuminated the YES sign. (The YES and NO signs were used only for theatrical purposes. The demonstration could be performed just as easily by saying that a bar press means yes and no bar press means no.)

After demonstrating that the rat could indeed answer correctly almost any question posed to it, the students were polled to find out who was and who was not convinced that the rat had superior intelligence. The class was divided about evenly. The instructor then guided the ensuing discussion to determine which half of the class was right by assessing the evidence through the use of critical thinking. In turn, students were challenged to try to ascertain the validity of the instructor's claims by suggesting some more parsimonious explanations and checking them with testable (falsifiable) hypotheses. After awhile, the class reasoned that they could systematically manipulate the situation to assess the validity of the instructor's claims. They tested the hypothesis "The instructor is providing visual cues to the rat" by having the instructor stand out of view of the rat for a set of trials. Eventually, they figured out that the instructor was the source of the rat's sapient performance by having the instructor leave the room. After the class identified the successful experimental manipulation, the instructor related the story of Clever Hans. The instructor guided a discussion to generalize the principle of the Clever Hans effect to thinking critically about testimonial evidence provided in relevant media reports of psychological findings.

Evaluation

After the exercise, 37 students completed a 7-item questionnaire evaluating their experience on a scale ranging from *strongly disagree* (1) to *strongly agree* (5). Student responses indicated that the exercise was very interesting ($M = 4.81$, $SD = .39$), worthwhile ($M = 4.54$, $SD = .55$), and a positive experience ($M = 4.51$, $SD = .64$). They also indicated that this activity helped them better understand the concepts in experimental design ($M = 4.46$, $SD = .39$), improved their ability to think critically ($M = 4.16$, $SD = .72$), enabled them to understand better how the methods of psychology can be helpful in solving real problems ($M = 4.35$, $SD = .67$), and should be used in future classes ($M = 4.84$, $SD = .37$).

Informally, students commented that they especially liked this exercise because (a) the live animal captivated their attention, (b) the challenge to prove the rat did not have human intelligence motivated them to think critically about the situation and apply their knowledge of research methods, and (c) active involvement in an actual event was more fun than discussing it in the abstract (Benjamin, 1991). Hanzel also created a minor sensation on campus; students from all over campus came to the animal lab and requested to see Hanzel. We have had requests from nonpsychology instructors to show the demonstration to their classes, including requests for Hanzel to perform for middle school students and a class from a neighboring college.

Discussion

This exercise is appropriate for any psychology class that requires students to learn about experimental research methods. In particular, the experimental concepts of systematic manipulation, hypothesis testing, uncontrolled conditions, experimenter effects, parsimony, falsifiability, and the danger of relying on testimonial evidence can be discussed in relation to this demonstration. The instructor's original claim that psychologists could create rats with human intelligence was testimonial evidence. The students were then able to test and disconfirm this claim by generating their own falsifiable hypotheses and systematically manipulating the variables under controlled conditions to develop the more parsimonious explanation—that the rat's performance was due to experimenter effects.

In addition, this demonstration can be used as a critical thinking exercise to help students acquire the skills necessary to assess the validity of psychological events reported in the media. Teaching critical thinking with this type of demonstration is superior to the traditional method of teaching critical thinking (i.e., as a general formula of abstractly learned steps) because students become engaged

in finding an implicitly generated solution to a problem rather than studying critical thinking per se (Gray, 1983). Students initially challenge the instructor to prove that the rat is sapient, and then the instructor puts the shoe on the other foot by challenging the students to prove it is not. The switching nature of these roles nicely incorporates an active learning approach (Benjamin, 1991).

The media are replete with news reports that cry out as target's to which students can generalize this lesson. For example, a *Time* magazine cover asked, "Can Animals Think?" (Linden, 1993). Inside was a story about animals, such as chimpanzees and dolphins, that seem to use language to communicate with their trainers. Also, there are the omnipresent stories of psychic readings and paranormal communication. Other types of relevant news items are usually reported as psychological breakthroughs. A recent example involves the use of facilitated communication for profoundly retarded, autistic children who suddenly show literacy by typing on a computer with the aid of a human facilitator, whose role is to lightly support their hands over the keyboard (Wheeler, Jacobson, Paglieri, & Schwartz, 1993). Could this be just a modern equivalent of the Clever Hans effect? To the degree that this type of exercise can help students assess more critically the validity of these types of real-world claims, its value extends beyond learning the subject matter.

References

Benjamin, L. T., Jr. (1991). Personalization and active learning in the large introductory psychology class. *Teaching of Psychology, 18*, 68-74.

Gray, P. (1993). Engaging students' intellects: The immersion approach to critical thinking in psychology instruction. *Teaching of Psychology, 20*, 68-74.

Kalat, J. W. (1993). *Introduction to psychology* (3rd ed.). Pacific Grove, CA: Brooks/Cole.

Linden, E. (1993, March 22). Can animals think? *Time*, pp. 54-61.

Morris, C. G. (1993). *Psychology: An introduction.* Englewood Cliffs, NJ: Prentice-Hall.

Pfungst, O. (1911). *Clever Hans.* New York: Holt.

Sebeok, T. A., & Rosenthal, R. (1981). *The Clever Hans phenomenon: Communication with horses, whales, apes, and people.* New York: The New York Academy of Sciences.

Stanovich, K. E (1992). *How to think straight about psychology* (3rd ed.). New York: HarperCollins.

Wheeler, D. L., Jacobson, J. W., Paglieri, R. A., & Schwartz, A. A. (1993). An experimental assessment of facilitated communication. *Mental Retardation, 31*, 49-60.

Note

We thank three anonymous reviewers for their insightful comments on a draft of this article.

Basketball Game as Psychology Experiment

James A. Polyson
Kenneth A. Blick
University of Richmond

Helping students understand basic concepts in experimental method can be quite a challenge for the introductory psychology teacher. Some students find the topic difficult or boring, leading one teacher (Gleitman, 1984) to recommend covering methodology only where it is necessary in order to understand some other topic. Even if one agrees with Gleitman, that still leaves a lot of methodology to be taught in introductory psychology.

It has been suggested (Vandervert, 1980) that the learning of psychological concepts is facilitated when the material is presented in relation to topics that are meaningful to students. One strategy for making psychological knowledge more relevant to students' real-world interests has been the use of popular culture in the classroom (Hughes, 1984; Polyson, 1983; Solomon, 1979). Using a similar approach, we have found that it is possible to introduce new methodological concepts and illustrate previously defined concepts using a basketball game.

It should first be noted that using basketball examples might be more effective at a school with a high level of enthusiasm for the intercollegiate basketball program. Such was the case at the University of Richmond this past season. The Spiders had their best season ever, winning two games in the NCAA tournament before losing to perennial power Indiana. Basketball was a popular topic of conversation on campus, and it was during such a discussion that the present authors discovered their mutual interest in using basketball to illustrate basic experimental method.

A basketball game can be construed as a psychology experiment. For example:

Hypothesis. A basketball game is the testing of a hypothesis regarding which of two teams is "better" in the wide array of mental ad psychomotor skills called basketball. Some observers, such as a loyal fan or bettor, would predict a winner. That is a one-tailed hypothesis. An impartial observer, such as a TV commentator, might decline to say which team will win, thus making a two-tailed hypothesis.

Independent Variable. The independent variable is simply the two teams, the groups that are being compared. The experimenter in psychology often tries to compose the two groups in a random fashion so they are as equal as possible at the outset. Random assignment is impossible in basketball, although the pro draft is an attempt to introduce some "fairness" into the team selection process at that level.

Dependent Variable. The behavior that is being compared must be defined in a measurable way. The measure of skill in a basketball game is the number of points scored; the "better" team is the one scoring higher on that measure. That is the operational definition. We must also define "higher." How much higher? When psychologists compare the scores of two or more groups, they use statistical analysis to decide what difference is necessary in order to say that the outcome was not just luck or chance. In basketball, the necessary difference is 1 point, except for some neighborhood pick-up games in which a team must win by 2 points.

Control. The basic reason a basketball game is an experiment and not just a "guess" is that the designers of the game have attempted to minimize any explanations for the game's outcome other than basketball skill ("to keep the losers from making excuses," as one student put it after our big upset win over Auburn). That is why the number of players on the court is kept even and irrelevant skills such as judo are ruled out by calling fouls. The home court advantage can be ruled out by doing the experiment twice in a home and-away series (replication). A loose rim provides no advantage for either team because the teams switch goals at halftime (counterbalanced design). This is essentially what a psychology experiment attempts to do: Define the relevant variables and control for as many irrelevant ones as possible. For example, basketball did not adopt the 12-foot goal proposed during the dominant college career of Lew Alcindor (now Kareem Jabbar), presumably because it was decided that a player's height is relevant to the game and should not be counteracted with that rule.

These and other basketball examples were presented during lecture in three introductory classes and one experimental psychology class. In the introductory classes, the lecture and discussion were presented in conjunction with a 30-minute film, "Methodology: The Psychologist and the Experiment" (produced by McGraw-Hill), and in both courses the same concepts were brought up throughout the semester whenever a topic involved experimental research.

Unfortunately, we have no direct evidence for the effectiveness of the basketball analogy as a learning device. However, we were impressed by the quality of class discussion generated by the basketball lecture. (For instance, how would you design a rule in basketball to eliminate coaching as an influence on the outcome?) Also, in the second author's experimental psychology course, there was a final exam question asking students to illustrate experimental concepts using another sport of their choice. Students chose a variety of team and individual sports and most of their answers were thoughtful and well-written. It is possible that any unifying theme around which students can organize a number of related concepts could be helpful in promoting students' understanding of those concepts. Perhaps the basketball analogy just caught their attention.

Sort of like a good slam dunk.

References

Gleitman, H. (1984). Introducing psychology. *American Psychologist, 39,* 421-427.

Hughes, R. L. (1984). Teaching concepts of personal adjustment using popular music. *Teaching of Psychology, 11,* 115.

Polyson, J. A. (1983). Student essays about TV characters A tool for understanding personality theories. *Teaching of Psychology, 10,* 103-105.

Solomon, P. R. (1979). Science and television commercials: Adding relevance to the research methodology course. *Teaching of Psychology, 6,* 26-30.

Vandervert, L. R. (1980). Operational definitions made simple, lasting, and useful. *Teaching of Psychology, 7,* 57-59.

A "Handy" Way to Introduce Research Methods

David E. Johnson
John Brown University

Several studies have found that left-handers are underrepresented in older age ranges (Coren & Halpern, 1991; Fleminger, Dalton, & Standage, 1977; Halpern & Coren, 1988). Many of these studies reveal relations similar to the one graphically presented in Figure 1, which is adapted from Coren and Halpern (1991).

Coren and Halpern (1991) suggested two possible explanations for this relation. First, left-handers learn to become right-handed due to implicit or explicit environmental pressures. This *modification hypothesis* implies that left-handers convert to being right-handed over time due to the physical and social difficulties encountered living in a right-handed world. For example, most tools, equipment, and common articles (e.g., scissors) require right-handed operation for optimal performance. Conversely, the data might suggest that left-handers have increased mortality rates across the life span that

selectively eliminate them from the population (the *elimination hypothesis*).

Coren and Halpern (1991) attempted to determine the viability of these hypotheses by examining data on various topics (e.g., birth stress, environmental risk factors, maturational variables, and immune system variables) and concluded that the elimination hypothesis is more tenable than the modification hypothesis. Left-handers, on average, experienced birth stress more often, experienced higher accident rates, suffered higher rates of immune and autoimmune dysfunction, and died younger as compared with right-handers.

Students find the relation between handedness and mortality intriguing. Because of their interest, I developed a simple classroom activity based on this research that requires students to think about the processes scientists consider when doing research.

Method

The activity requires minimal preparation. Familiarity with the basic core of studies in this area is required. I recommend reading Coren and Halpern (1991) and Porac and Coren (1981) at a minimum. Prepare an overhead transparency (or another method of visual presentation) that contains Figure 1.

Typically, I begin the class period by placing Figure 1 on the overhead projector and asking the class the following questions: "What does this graph mean?" "How do you explain it?" "Based on your explanation, how would you decide if your explanation is tenable?" Students organize themselves into groups of five or six to discuss their responses to these questions. Often students' initial response is to express disbelief in the veracity of the data. Spirited discussion results, and students often vigorously disagree about the potential causes of the handedness—mortality relation. Most believe that the data are a result of changes from left-to right-handedness .

After 15 to 20 min of discussion, the groups report the results of their discussion to the entire class. During the group reports, I note responses that address factors requiring further treatment in the discussion with the whole class. Afterward, I summarize and discuss the importance of the issues raised during the class discussion.

I usually implement this activity during the first week of classes because textbooks often present introductory material on research methods in the first chapters. I use the activity in various courses, such as Honors General Psychology Research Methods, and Behavioral Neuroscience. In research methods or physiological psychology courses, reading some core articles to facilitate discussion of more advanced topics in future class periods can be instructive for students.

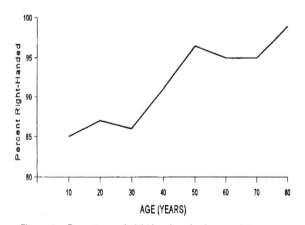

Figure 1. Percentage of right-handers in the population as a function of age. *Note.* From "Left-Handedness: A Marker for Decreased Survival Fitness," by S. Coren and D. F. Halpern, 1991, *Psychological Bulletin, 109,* p. 91. Copyright 1991 by the American Psychological Association, Inc. Adapted with permission.

Results and Discussion

Many benefits result from this exercise. First, students practice reading and interpreting a line graph (Figure 1), an important skill for understanding research reports.

Second, at least some students recognize the fact that Figure 1 can be interpreted in at least two ways (i.e., modification vs. elimination). I emphasize that these two explanations form a dichotomy that is similar to the nature versus nurture debate that runs through much of psychology. The modification hypothesis focuses more on environmental variables; the elimination hypothesis centers more on biological variables, some of which have genetic origins.

Third, some students realize that acceptance of the modification or elimination explanation depends on how the data in Figure 1 were collected. Essentially, they realize that a cross-sectional methodology may yield a different result from a longitudinal design. Usually, this realization is based on the possibility that subjects born 50 to 80 years ago made the sinistral to dextral change due to more intense social pressures as compared with younger subjects. In upper division courses, I present Coren and Halpern's (1991) data and rationale for discounting this explanation.

Fourth, students always ask, "Who is left-handed?" They point out that some people do some things left-handed and other things right-handed. This observation highlights the need for operational definitions of variables. We discuss ways to operationalize the handedness variable, and I present some definitions used in the literature. For example, Peters and Perry (1991) defined left-handers as those who used the left hand to write, whereas Halpern and Coren (1988) assigned left-handedness to baseball players in their study if the players batted and pitched with the left hand.

Fifth, students mention some of the same variables that Coren and Halpern (1991) tested. For example, almost every class suggests the possibility of increased accident rates for left-handers, genetic variables, and prenatal variables.

Finally, some authors disagree with Coren and Halpern's (1991) conclusion that elimination is the better explanation for this relation (e.g., Dellatolas et al., 1991; Fudin, Renninger, Lembessis, & Hirshon, 1993; Harris, 1993a, 1993b; Hugdahl, Satz, Mitrushina, & Miller, 1993; Peters & Perry, 1991). In research methods classes, we discuss disagreements among researchers that are based on different methodologies or statistical analyses. introduction to scholarly debate can be accomplished by having students read some of the published replies to these criticisms (e.g., Coren & Halpern, 1993; Halpern & Coren, 1993).

In my most recent Honors General Psychology course, I asked students ($N = 25$) if they believed the activity should be used in future classes. Twenty-four of the 25 students answered in the affirmative.

In summary, this activity can be used in various courses. Students find the topic interesting, and it provides an engaging way to present diverse research issues.

References

Coren, S., & Halpern, D. F. (1991). Left-handedness: A marker for decreased survival fitness. *Psychological Bulletin, 109*, 90-106.

Coren, S., & Halpern, D. F. (1993). A replay of the baseball data. *Perceptual 69 Motor Skills, 76*, 403-406.

Dellatolas, G., Tubert, P., Castresana, A., Mesbah, M., Giallonardo, T., Lazaratou, H., & Lellouch, J. (1991). Age and cohort effects in adult handedness. *Neuropsychologia, 29*, 255-261.

Fleminger, J. J., Dalton, R., & Standage, K. F. (1977). Age as a factor in the handedness of adults. *Neuropsychologia, 15*, 471-473.

Fudin, R., Renninger, L., Lembessis, E., & Hirshon, J. (1993). Sinistrality and reduced longevity: Reichler's 1979 data on baseball players do not indicate a relationship. *Perceptual & Motor Skills, 76*, 171-182.

Halpern, D. F., & Coren, S. (1988). Do right-handers live longer? *Nature, 333*, 213

Halpern, D. F., & Coren, S. (1993). Left-handedness and life span: A reply to Harris. *Psychological Bulletin, 114*, 235-241.

Harris, L. J. (1993a). Do left-handers die sooner than right-handers? Commentary on Coren and Halpern's (1991) "Left-handedness: A marker for decreased survival fitness." *Psychological Bulletin, 114*, 203-234.

Harris, L. J. (1993b). Left-handedness and life span: Reply to Halpern and Coren. *Psychological Bulletin, 114*, 242-247.

Hugdahl, K., Satz, P., Mitrushina, M., & Miller, E. N. (1993). Left-handedness and old age: Do left-handers die earlier? *Neuropsychologia, 31*, 325-333.

Peters, M., & Perry, R. (1991). No link between left-handedness and maternal age and no elevated accident rate in left-handers. *Neuropsychologia, 29*, 1257-1259.

Porac, C., & Coren, S. (1981). *Lateral preferences and human behavior.* New York: Springer-Verlag.

Note

A version of this article was presented at the annual meeting of the American Psychological Association, Los Angeles, August 1994.

Taking the Fear Out of Research: A Gentle Approach to Teaching an Appreciation for Research

Christiane Brems
University of Alaska Anchorage

While teaching an undergraduate research methods course, I became painfully aware of the trepidation with which students approached this class. I decided that introducing students to research must be made more gradual and less intimidating during the first 3 years of college. Then, students may approach their senior research requirements with less apprehension.

This article describes an approach I have used in a psychology department that enrolls over 400 psychology majors and 50 clinical psychology master's degree students. I have used this approach for six semesters, and one other faculty member has adopted it. Two other faculty members have incorporated significant pieces of it, and a fourth is in the process of so doing. Among the four of us, there are now approximately eight classes per year that integrate research. Faculty cannot be required to adopt this approach; hence, not all students in my department are exposed to it. Nevertheless, feedback from those who were exposed has been very positive. One instructor at one of our extended campuses indicated that she has also successfully incorporated research integration.

The first step in the process consists of integrating research at all levels of teaching. How research integration takes place depends on the level of the course, but it best begins in the first year. Integration is possible in all courses that are part of a traditional undergraduate psychology curriculum. For instance, it has been accomplished in Human Development (at the first-year level), Abnormal Psychology (at the sophomore level), Personality Theories (at the junior level), and Psychodynamic Theory (at the senior level). If research is integrated into core courses, psychology majors will be exposed to research early and throughout their training. The more faculty participate, the more exposure students will receive.

First-Year-Level Integration

At this level, the goal is to demystify the research process. First-year students are generally overwhelmed by the concept of research and believe it to be beyond their capabilities. They have visions of scientists working in laboratories full of rats, brewing mysterious potions, and crunching huge rows of numbers. Students need to learn that research is done by ordinary people with ordinary questions about ordinary environments and ordinary human behavior.

The demystification process is best approached in a two pronged manner: introduce students to research and make students informed consumers of research. The former can be done easily by exposing students to research interests and activities of local faculty and graduate students. Graduate students are preferable as research models at this level because their experience resembles that of the undergraduate student more closely than that of a faculty member. In addition, students can be encouraged to visit the psychology laboratory; meet the assistants (who are rarely much older or more experienced than the students); and observe animals, equipment, or computer simulations.

Introducing students to research as consumers can take place most simply by asking them to read research articles. Although they have to read the entire article, first-year students are required to focus on the introduction section to prevent confusion that method and results sections often induce in neophytes. Reading introductions helps students recognize how authors slowly work their way through relevant literature to develop research questions.

Once students have read and digested a few articles, they can be asked to generate simple research questions. Creative role modeling is conducive to this process. I like to have fun with this approach by asking students to think of a question relevant to the course topic and then helping them reformulate the question into a format that lends itself to research. For instance, students in my Abnormal Psychology course often question the effectiveness of psychotherapy for severe mental illness. As a class, we talk about how a researcher could design a project to measure treatment outcome with such a clinical population. As a clinical psychologist, I enjoy demonstrating through this exercise that research is not limited to experimental psychology.

Sophomore-Level Integration

The demystification process continues at the sophomore level by introducing basic ideas about methodology. Sophomores are asked to read research articles, focusing on the introduction and method sections to get them thinking about how researchers go about answering questions. Students are alerted to basic questions dealing with choice of subjects, comparisons of groups, and instrument options. They read research articles with a fastidious approach so they can write a summary that reviews the question researched and critiques the chosen subjects and instruments. Trips to the library add a nice component of knowledge to the students' developing research repertoire. They are introduced to *Psychological Abstracts*, computerized search systems, journal stacks, reference guides, and research indexes. The best way to engage students in a basic literature search is to require them to find their own article to review rather than provide the same article for the entire class. Thus, students develop literature search skills and are more interested in what they read for critique.

Junior-Level Integration

More sophistication is required from students at this level, and they are introduced more thoroughly to the intricacies of methodology. Students are asked to read research articles, primarily focusing again on the method section—especially data collection. Article reviews are assigned, with a focus less on interest or clarity and more on the adequacy of data-collection procedures and conclusions drawn from the data.

Basic in-class discussion takes place about threats to internal validity (without necessarily naming the concept) by explaining maturation and history—two of the easiest threats to understand and describe in simple language. Threats to external validity are also discussed (again without necessarily naming the concept) by exaggerating generalizations from a particularly interesting article chosen by the instructor. Newspaper articles covering relevant topics work well for this purpose. In Personality Theories class, for instance, newspaper articles about gender or ethnic differences can be used because they often involve poor sampling and overstate conclusions and generalizability. Often, students have not thought about sampling biases and how they limit generalizability. Their amazement usually motivates them to seek more examples in local papers. They generally bring articles to class, and I gladly allow time to discuss them.

Senior-Level Integration

At the senior level, I require critical consumerism of research and encourage students to conduct their own research. With regard to consumerism, I ask students to review articles in a detailed manner and to comment on all article sections. With regard to the conduct of research, I allow students to substitute a research project for a term paper (usually one or two students will choose this option each semester). I encourage students to choose pertinent research topics that are of interest to them. This research can be carried out in groups or in collaboration with me or another instructor. I do ask that the projects completed with other instructors still be relevant to the course the student is taking from me, which limits collaboration with other faculty somewhat. I help students develop a meaningful research question to investigate. I do not search for perfection here but for a fairly sound study that will convey to students that they can do research. For instance, in my Psychodynamic Theories class, a student's interest in the relation between narcissism and self-esteem led to a creative and complex project through which we developed a procedure for inducing mild narcissistic injuries in subjects (with proper follow-up and debriefing).

If my relationship with students at the senior level takes place in the context of the Research Methods course, I require them to design, conduct, and write up a research project of sufficient quality to be presentable at a regional psychological conference. Some of these projects have been of publishable quality (e.g., Skillman et al., 1992; Wilson, Vercella, Brems, Benning, & Renfro, 1992). In this course particularly, allowing students to develop projects that are of personal interest to them is critically important.

Graduate-Level Integration

At this level, I require students to review articles and conduct research. Reviews at this level are critiques that focus on a body of literature (i.e., assess whether current beliefs and practices in a given area are based on sound research). I require students to conduct research projects individually and to write them up for presentation and publication (e.g., Namyniuk & Brems, 1992; Tucker & Brems, 1993). The publication requirement instills enthusiasm for research like no other task; students are thrilled when they see their name in print.

Interacting With Students About Research

In addition to integrating research into the classroom, instructors can do other things to foster enthusiasm and reduce the fear of research. First, students' interest in research can be piqued by telling them about one's own research. At appropriate times, I talk about my research to help students recognize that research literature develops from many small building blocks, not a few huge studies that answer many questions or are designed to find the truth. Using examples of one's own research brings the process down to earth for the student, makes it seem more relevant to the student, and gives it an applied context. A word of caution: One should never only present one's own work. Otherwise students get bored and suspicious, and they may view the instructor as egotistical.

Telling students about one's own research can also be used as a springboard to invite them to participate in one's own research. I love to invite students to help with my projects (e.g., Brems, Baldwin, & Baxter, 1993), not to exploit them, but to teach them. Ideally, students should not be used as mere data collectors; instead, their involvement should be fairly evenly distributed across all stages of the investigation.

Research teams are another excellent means of interacting with students about research. The research teams I have conducted encouraged students to work on research projects with peers in collaborative efforts. This approach is less threatening because students can share work, exchange information, and capitalize on the individual strengths of project members (e.g., Brems, Baldwin, Davis, & Namyniuk, 1994). I lead such research teams; I do not rule them. I even let the teams make mistakes, so they can learn from their own experience. For example, during one project, the team decided after some discussion not to match subjects on educational level only to realize later that this variable was indeed an important mediator.

Brown-bag lunches and student clubs help to encourage faculty-student interaction concerning research interests, projects, and findings. Other informal information exchanges about research can involve the development of research networks that help students learn who does what, where, and when. Mentoring systems through which students can identify instructors and/or other students who share similar interests are equally useful.

Collaborating with students on research is exciting. I enjoy witnessing the awakening of enthusiasm and critical thinking involved in the process. Although research collaboration with students does not always produce a publication, it always includes learning and enjoyment for student and instructor!

References

Brems, C., Baldwin, M., & Baxter, S. (1993). Empirical evaluation of a self-psychologically oriented parent education program. *Family Relations, 42*, 26-30.

Brems, C., Baldwin, M., Davis, L., & Namyniuk, L. (1994). The imposter syndrome as related to teaching evaluations and advising relationships of university faculty members. *Journal of Higher Education, 65,* 183-193.

Namyniuk, L., & Brems, C. (1992, April). *Relationships among narcissism, self-esteem, and empathy as mediated by gender and narcissistic injury.* Paper presented at the annual meeting of the Western Psychological Association, Portland, OR.

Skillman, G., Dabbs, P., Mitchell, M., McGrath, M., Lewis, S., & Brems, C. (1992). Appropriateness of the Draw-A-Person Test for Alaska natives. *Journal of Clinical Psychology, 48,* 561-564.

Tucker, P., & Brems, C. (1993). Variables affecting length of psychiatric inpatient treatment. *Journal of Mental Health Administration, 20,* 57-64.

Wilson, C., Vercella, R., Brems, C., Benning, D., & Renfro, N. (1992). Levels of learned helplessness in abused women. *Women and Therapy, 13,* 53-68.

Notes

1. This article was the outgrowth of an invited lecture about integrating teaching and research presented at the annual Teaching Excellence Conference at the University of Alaska Anchorage.

2. I thank Charles L. Brewer and three anonymous reviewers for their many helpful suggestions on a draft of this article.

The Problem Method of Teaching Research Methods

Donald H. McBurney
University of Pittsburgh

The purpose of this article is to describe a technique of teaching research methods that I have used successfully for many years in an undergraduate course. For some time, I had believed that trying to teach research methods in a lecture was often like trying to teach someone to ride a bicycle without a bike. When I became aware that business schools routinely use problems in teaching principles of management to master's of business administration students, it occurred to me that the method could be used to teach research methods; so I began to use it in my class and my research methods texts (McBurney, 1990, 1994).

Although the problem method is widely used in teaching law and business courses, it does not seem to be used much in psychology . Exceptions are found in areas such as abnormal and clinical psychology, in which individual cases are used to illustrate particular diagnoses, and industrial/organizational psychology, in which applications of principles discussed in the literature are illustrated. l am unaware of any literature on the use of problems in teaching research methods.

Definition of the Problem Method

The problem method should be distinguished from the *case study method.* The case study method was introduced by Christopher Columbus Langdell when he became dean of Harvard Law School in 1870 (Moskovitz, 1992). Langdell replaced the lecture method with a Socratic analysis of particular cases from the law. The case study method is still used today to teach first-year students the fundamentals of the law.

In second- and third-year law courses, the problem method is used instead. Whereas the case study method analyzes particular cases to identify facts and principles, the problem method requires students to find their own solution to the problem presented (Ogden, 1984).

It is a source of confusion that the business literature uses the term *case study* to refer to what the law literature calls the *problem method.* In deference to the distinction made in the law literature, I use *problem method* henceforth in this article to refer to the method I am describing.

134

Characteristics of the Problem Method

There are three characteristics of the problem method: "1) assignment of problem statements for solution; 2) use of course or other materials to solve problems; and 3) discussion of solutions in class" (Ogden, 1984, p. 655). There are many variations among problems. Problems can be as short as a paragraph that illustrates a particular issue in a law course; in business school courses, however, they are generally many pages long and include much financial and other data. Generally, the problem does not have a single correct answer, so students must weigh alternatives and defend their choices. Some instructors assign problems to the whole class for open discussion, whereas others make them the responsibility of a subgroup of students. Furthermore, the instructor's role can vary from presenting the whole problem as an example to serving as a discussion facilitator (Dooley & Skinner, 1977).

It is risky to claim to know how the problem method differs from the typical classroom discussion techniques because there may be as many discussion methods as there are instructors. Nevertheless, the problem method focuses attention on the design of an end product and requires students to make choices among competing alternatives and justify those choices. In my experience as a student and instructor, the problem method is distinctive in its emphasis on a practical solution to a problem that is posed. The solution of the problem that is arrived at provides closure in a way that the usual discussion methods may not.

Furthermore, class discussions too often are perceived by the students as a digression from the real material in the course (i.e., what will be covered on the test)—namely, the lecture. I have seen students put down their pens, ostentatiously fall asleep, or walk out when the instructor initiates a discussion. By contrast, my students know that the problems are an integral part of the course. Those students who have been assigned the particular problem under discussion (considered next) have a personal interest in discovering how close their solution came to the one arrived at in class. All students know that they will be tested on their grasp of the concepts discussed in the problems.

Why the Problem Method Is Applicable to Research Methods

Designing research is an example of a classic ill-defined task. Frequently, the problem is not clearly stated, the theory being tested may be poorly developed, and the expected results are not well constrained. Moreover, there are many different choices to be made, many of which interact with each other. As a result, no two researchers may design a particular study the same way, and there is no one perfect design. Although this reality is well known to researchers, it is difficult to convey to students who are used to memorizing three claims of so-and-so's theory,

four lines of evidence in favor of it, five objections to it, and six alternative theories. Students tend to become anxious and sometimes dispirited when an instructor refuses to tell them the right answer. The problem method is designed to teach students that there is no one right answer.

Perry (1970) found that college students tend to progress through a series of stages of intellectual development during their college years. Initially, they see the world in terms of polar opposites, including right and wrong answers. Next, they perceive that there is diversity of opinion. Later, they perceive knowledge as contextual. Perry found nine stages of development, culminating in moral relativism and commitment to a personal style. One could question whether Perry's emphasis on relativism is as cogent in science as it is in the humanities. Nevertheless, he captured the reactions of many students to the ambiguities involved in designing research.

Furthermore, the problem method is an excellent vehicle for teaching critical thinking. The concept of critical thinking is quite broad, and the literature is extremely heterogeneous. The National Research Council's Committee on Mathematics, Science, and Technology Education (Resnick, 1987) listed the following characteristics of higher order thinking. It is nonalgorithmic; complex; entails uncertainty; has multiple solutions; involves nuanced judgment; and requires the application of multiple criteria, self-regulation, imposition of meaning, and effort. Each of these is well illustrated by the process of research design, and each is required in solving a problem.

Kurfiss (1988) listed eight teaching practices that support critical thinking. Five of them are exemplified by the problem method: The instructor and students serve as resources in developing critical-thinking skills; problems serve as the point of entry to the subject and as a source of motivation; the course is assignment-centered, with an emphasis on using content rather than acquiring it; students are required to formulate and justify their ideas in writing; students collaborate in their problem solving.

The Problem Method in a Research Methods Course

My class generally enrolls about 120 students. I have used problems as a way of summarizing and illustrating material from the lectures. About every fourth class period is devoted to a problem that requires students to make use of principles discussed in a chapter of the book. The problem is handed out 1 or 2 weeks in advance; all of the students are expected to study it, but a subset is also required to turn in a written analysis at the beginning of the class period in which it is to be discussed. Students are encouraged, but not required, to work in pairs. Many of them choose to work in pairs. The written analysis is to be 3 to 5 pages long and contain a summary of the problem; a suggested solution, with justification for the selected alternatives; and reasons for rejecting alternatives. In this way, all students should be familiar with the problem, but a certain number can be counted on to provide the bulk of the discussion.

How the Problem Is Presented in Class

I usually start the class discussion by briefly summarizing the facts of the case for the benefit of those who may not have prepared. Then, I emphasize that I am not as interested in the particular solution as I am in the reasoning that went into it. My role is to pose questions, draw out incomplete answers, probe inconsistencies, and so forth. The discussion of a typical case takes up most of a 50-min class period.

How the Students Respond to the Method

I wish I could say that the students are enthusiastic about the problem method. The truth is that I have received very few spontaneous comments about it over the years. Students do not seem to comment on it in the course evaluation. One problem, however, that did elicit spontaneous comments from the students involved research ethics. I assigned several students the task of playing the role of various individuals in a fairly complicated case of alleged violation of research integrity. Students found this very engaging and realistic. Not all problems lend themselves to this format, however.

To obtain some systematic data on student reactions, I administered a questionnaire in class that requested opinions on how much the problems contributed to learning the course material, how interesting they were, whether they forced students to think through things they had not yet thought about, whether problems should be continued as a part of the course, and whether they helped students learn things they would not have learned from a lecture. In a nutshell, the results fell close to neutral on all items. They reported spending about 4 hr on their problem.

In retrospect, such a questionnaire may not be particularly informative about how the problem method furthers the goals of the course. It may be more useful to compare their performance on tests of the material in the course or their grades in later courses to that of students who did not experience the method. These measures would, of course, require appropriate controls, which would present considerable design problems of their own.

It is fair to conclude that the students find the problem method about as acceptable as the rest of the course, which they regard as quite challenging but rate favorably overall. I believe that students at the undergraduate level are not used to this method of teaching and find it somewhat anxiety provoking. Students pose many questions on how

to solve the problems before they are due. They seem to be somewhat uncomfortable with ambiguity, as Perry (1970) predicted. Because most students in the course are sophomores, the majority of them are probably in the early stages of their journey from bipolar to contextualized thinking that Perry documented.

My own impression is that students learn to deal with some of the complexities of research design by working on these problems. Together with lectures and laboratory, the problem method helps students obtain a realistic introduction to research methods in a wide variety of situations. This fulfills one of the recommendations of the National Research Council's Committee (Resnick, 1987) that teaching of critical thinking should be embedded within the curriculum of the discipline. I recommend the problem method to instructors who wish to take a problem-solving or critical-thinking approach to teaching research methods.

References

Dooley, A. R., & Skinner, W. (1977). Casing case methods. *Academy of Management Review, 2,* 277-289.

Kurfiss, J. G. (1988). *Critical thinking: Theory, research, practice, and possibilities* (ASHE–ERIC Higher Education Report No. 2). Washington, DC: Association for the Study of Higher Education.

McBurney, D. H. (1990). *Experimental psychology* (2nd ed.). Belmont, CA: Wadsworth.

McBurney, D. H. (1994). *Research methods* (3rd ed.). Belmont, CA: Brooks/Cole.

Moskovitz, M. (1992). Beyond the case method It's time to teach with problems. *Journal of Legal Education, 42,* 241-270.

Ogden, G. L. (1984). The problem method in legal education. *Journal of Legal Education, 34,* 654 673.

Perry, W. G., Jr. (1970) . *Forms of intellectual and ethical development in the college years: A scheme.* New York: Holt, Rinehart & Winston.

Resnick, L. (1987). *Education and learning to think.* Washington, DC: National Academy Press.

Notes

I thank John Grant and Edward Symons for helpful suggestions and Richard Moreland, Peter Moshein, and two anonymous reviewers for comments on a draft of this article.

The Research Methods Script

Thomas L. Wilson
Bellarmine College

Douglas A. Hershey
George Mason University

Scripts are mental representations of the ordered actions and events that take place in commonly experienced situations (Abelson, 1981; Bower, Black, & Turner, 1979). Studies of expertise in knowledge-rich domains have identified scripts as part of the knowledge used to solve complex problems (Hershey, Morath, & Walsh, 1991; Hershey, Walsh, Read, & Chulef, 1990). According to these authors, a problem-solving script specifies the optimal information to consider and the sequence of actions to take in a particular problem-solving context. Hershey, Wilson, and Mitchell-Copeland (in press) investigated psychologists' procedural knowledge of scientific problem solving in the context of psychological research. They discovered that, in contrast to undergraduate students of psychology, career psychologists possess reliable and readily available *psychological research scripts* that represent their knowledge of the sequential steps involved in the research process. Results indicated that development of the research script is a negatively accelerated function of experience and training in psychological research, with the greatest developmental change taking place during undergraduate education.

The class activity described in this article is based on script theory and takes advantage of students' preexisting knowledge of the scientific method. Students generate their own research methods script by following standard procedures of script generation and analysis found in the literature (e.g., Bower et al., 1979). Then, students compare and discuss their scripts, evaluating them in relation to the composite script of the class and a composite script of experienced psychology professors. Students receive a sound overview of topics typically discussed in a research methods course and a structural foundation on which to build new knowledge. The activity also allows students to participate as subjects in an informal experiment, analyze their findings, and discover their own baseline knowledge of the psychological research process.

Research Methods Scripts as Mental Representations

Scripts represent event knowledge that is readily accessible from long-term memory, making scripts a powerful way to organize and recall information. Script events are sequenced in a particular order and are organized hierarchically in memory so that basic-level events are grouped under goal categories at a higher level (Bower et al., 1979). The research methods script is no exception. According to Hershey et al. (in press), expert psychologists typically organize events in the research script into four higher order goal categories: formulate ideas, collect data, analyze data, and report findings. These authors found that experts agreed on the research activities generated and on the basic level of specificity of those activities (e.g., read literature, obtain subjects, and collect data). Experts did not mention lower level activities (e.g., turn on computer and go to work). The scripts students generate about the research process are likewise organized around a common set of events and are usually written with a specific level of abstraction. Thus, becoming aware of the research methods script can be helpful for students because it organizes their knowledge of the various research procedures they are learning.

The Class Activity

Script Generation

Sometime within the first 2 weeks of a research methods course, we ask students to participate in an activity to discover what they already know about the psychological research process. Following the procedures and instructions used by Hershey et al. (in press), we give them a response sheet with the phrases, "Get idea for project" printed near the top of the page and "Publish the research paper" printed near the bottom. Then, students are given the following instructions:

> List about 20 actions, steps, or stages that characterize the process psychologists go through when working on a research problem. As you list these research activities, focus on the *typical* actions that a researcher would engage in while carrying out a *typical* psychological research project. List only activities that take place between the anchor events *Get idea for project* and *Publish the research paper,* and try to list the activities in their appropriate order.

Students usually complete this task in less than 10 min. Although students and experts usually generate only 10 to 16 events under these instructions, asking for about 20 appears sufficient to elicit an exhaustive recall and, consequently, a variety of events from all students in the group.

Next, we ask students to examine their lists while presenting a brief introduction to the script concept (Abelson, 1981) to focus them on the structural features of scripts that enhance their organization of knowledge. Explaining the central features of scripts (nothing more than we have presented in this introduction) provides students with an immediate link between the event-generation process they just completed and the notion that such event-based knowledge is organized in their own long-term memory. A treatment of script theory beyond the typical information found in an introductory psychology textbook is not necessary for instructors to follow the procedures presented herein and the evaluation portion of the activity mentioned later.

Students are instructed to draw lines between items on their ordered list to group the activities into higher order categories and to generate a name for each category. Students rarely have questions or problems in completing these tasks; they generate and divide their lists with ease. The entire procedure to this point takes about 20 min, and the evaluation stage that follows can vary in time according to the instructor's preference. We take 20 to 30 min for the following evaluation stage.

Script Evaluation

After students generate their research scripts, we assign them to small groups of two to four students to compare their event lists. As a first step in script evaluation, students can learn about several features of their research methods script by responding to the following questions:

1. Did you have any difficulty generating script events, or did they come easily to mind?
2. Scripts are organized around a common set of events at a particular level of specificity. In comparison to other students, how many events did you list? How many of the events in your script

were also in the lists of other students? What kinds of events did you list?
3. Are the events in your script listed in a logical order? Are they listed in the same order as similar events in other students' scripts?
4. How many goal categories were in your script? Did the names you used for your categories correspond to the typical category names?

Table 1. Composite Psychological Research Script From 49 Psychology Professors

(anchor) Get idea for project
READ LITERATURE ON TOPIC
Discuss idea with colleagues
Conceptualize project
Determine appropriate subject population
Formulate Hypotheses
DESIGN EXPERIMENTAL METHODS
Obtain available materials and measures
Construct experimental materials and measures
Obtain research assistants
Pilot Test Procedures and Measures
Refine experiment based on pilot results
Obtain Subjects
DATA COLLECTION
Code and organize data
DATA ANALYSIS
Determine if hypotheses were supported
Make a conference or brown-bag presentation
Conduct final literature review
WRITE DRAFT OF PAPER
Get feedback on paper
Revise draft of paper
Submit Paper for Publication
Make post-review revisions
(anchor) Publish the research paper

Note. Following Hershey et al. (in press), high-consensus events (mentioned by ≥ 60% of professors) are shown in capital letters, moderate-consensus events (mentioned by 40% to 59% of professors) are shown in upper and lower case, and low-consensus events (mentioned by 20% to 39% of professors) are shown in italics.

In the next part of the activity, students are asked to share their event lists with the class. A master list of all unique events along with their frequency of mention can be compiled on the chalkboard or an overhead projector. Help students sequence events in a logical order to create a composite script for the class. (In our classes, we draw a line through those events mentioned by fewer than 20% of the students to highlight research activities of greatest significance to them.) After a brief class discussion of the composite script, the instructor can present a composite script from experts in psychology (see Table 1) alongside the class script for direct comparison. An evaluation of students' scripted knowledge of the research process continues with the following questions:

5. How closely does the class script compare to the expert script? How many high-consensus and low-consensus activities are in each script?
6. Does the class as a whole already possess a good deal of knowledge about the research process?

7. Look at your own script. How does it compare to the expert script? How does it compare to the class script? Given that scripts provide a structure that helps us comprehend new information, how might you use the script concept to increase and monitor your own understanding of the research methods you will learn about this semester?

Class Discussion

Upon identification of the class composite script, students are pleased to recognize that their collective knowledge is, in many respects, similar to that of experts. They are usually surprised by both the similarity among their individual scripts, the class composite script, the expert script, and the subtle differences in the way we each conceptualize psychological research. By answering the questions in the activity, students are challenged to think critically about the research process. The classroom situation gives the instructor an opportunity to help students improve their understanding of the research process before misconceptions can hinder their further learning of methodological details. Students should be reminded that they are in the course to begin to assimilate the more detailed knowledge that experts possess. In this regard, an individual's script represents a good foundation for building new knowledge from the course. Hershey et al. (in press) found that undergraduates already have a working knowledge of the higher order goal categories within the research process. These authors referred to this higher level of knowledge as the *research metascript* and suggested that it is a mental framework on which students develop more detailed knowledge of the research process.

Students find the expert script interesting in its simplicity and coherence. Learning opportunities from discussion of the expert script seem limited only by one's imagination. For example, students may ask the meaning of such activities as a brown-bag presentation or pilot research (events often left out of students' scripts; see Table 1). The instructor could then discuss what it is like to go to graduate school by noting that experts present brown-bag talks, conduct pilot studies, obtain research assistants, and so on. Or the instructor may elect to focus students on specific course concepts. For example, students can be encouraged to take note of any event in the expert script that they did not have in their own script, so that they can gain more understanding of those particular research activities.

Finally, the research script activity may be useful in other ways. For example, it can illustrate the structure of mental representations and, for those with an interest in metacognitive awareness, it can demonstrate how to monitor one's own understanding in a problem-solving domain. We have used the activity to assess changes in students' knowledge of the research process from the beginning to the end of our methods courses. The activity is also suitable for introductory courses as a review of concepts in scientific psychology and basic research methodology.

Evaluation and Conclusion

In one undergraduate research methods course, the activity was administered during the second week and then referred to regularly throughout the course. On the last day of class, 31 students completed a survey that included eight questions about the script activity. The mean ratings given by students on a scale ranging from 1 (*not at all*) to 5 (*very often*) were as follows: (a) I thought about the research methods script on occasions other than the day of the activity ($M = 3.94$), (b) I specifically studied class material related to research events that I left out of my original script ($M = 3.35$), (c) I created study questions from the expert script to assess my understanding of course material ($M = 2.03$), (d) I felt like the research methods script was helping me organize my understanding of the research process ($M = 4.19$), and (e) I took time to memorize the expert script to organize my thinking for class exams and projects ($M = 3.10$). Mean ratings on a scale ranging from 1 (*strongly disagree*) to 5 (*strongly agree*) were as follows: (a) Knowing about my own research methods script was useful in this class ($M = 4.35$), (b) The research script activity was interesting ($M = 4.13$), and (c) I believe my research methods script is more like the expert script now that the class is over ($M = 4.55$).

From these data, we conclude that students perceive the research script activity as interesting and useful. Students who generated and evaluated scripts used the activity more for the general organizational information it provided than as an active study strategy; thus, students may not use their scripts in novel ways without some direction by the instructor. Nevertheless, students tended to reflect on their scripts throughout the course, and they could gauge their learning by comparing their scripts to the expert script. To obtain comparative data on the development of students' scripts, 17 students from a different methods class generated scripts and constructed a composite script at the beginning and end of the term. Results demonstrated that agreement on events between the class composite script and the expert script increased by 37% during the term. It appears that the utility of the script activity for increased learning is promising.

Student comments during one term included: "I did not know there was so much to doing research before you actually collect the data"; "Now that I have done my own study" (a course requirement), "I will never leave 'code data' out of my script again!"; and the inevitable, "I memorized the expert script because I thought you would test us on it." One student wrote in the margin of her survey, "Showed me what I needed to learn from the start." The survey results, comparative data, and comments indicate that the research methods script activity is a worthwhile experience. The activity reinforces and enhances students' organization and understanding of the procedures involved in psychological research. It also allows students to identify areas in which they need further study.

References

Abelson, R P. (1981). Psychological status of the script concept. *American Psychologist, 36,* 715-729.

Bower, G. H., Black, J B., & Turner, T. J. (1979). Scripts in memory for text. *Cognitive Psychology, 11,* 177-220.

Hershey, D. A., Morath, R., & Walsh, D. A. (1991, November). The use of scripts to solve financial planning problems. In C. Berg (Chair), *Age differences in cognitive strategies.* Symposium conducted at the meeting of the Gerontological Society of America, San Francisco.

Hershey, D. A., Walsh, D. A., Read, S. J., & Chulef, A. S. (1990). The effects of expertise on financial problem solving: Evidence for goal-directed problem solving scripts. *Organizational Behavior and Human Decision Performance, 46,* 77-101.

Hershey, D. A., Wilson, T. L., & Mitchell-Copeland, J. (in press). Conceptions of the psychological research process: Script variation as a function of training and experience. *Current Psychology.*

2. REVIEWING THE LITERATURE

Bibliographic Computerized Searching in Psychology

Linda K. Lewis
General Library
University of New Mexico

Social science researchers have used computers to manipulate quantitative data for many years, but the ability to conduct a survey of the literature or to prepare subject bibliographies is a comparatively recent development. This article introduces some of the resources available and discusses the advantages and disadvantages of computerized searching in psychology.

Most computer searching mentioned in this article involves the processing of a file of information, a *database*, in order to locate specific information. The results may be a bibliography of an author's works or citations concerning a topic. Many of these databases are the computerized counterparts of indexes available in most libraries, such as *Psychological Abstracts*, whereas others, such as *Family Resources*, were developed only as databases.

Advantages

A computer search may be more useful than a manual search of the indexes for several reasons. A computer search can save a researcher considerable time. Because the computer is capable of rapidly processing large amounts of information, it can search several years of information in a few seconds. Although the response time does vary with the equipment and the system, many searches can be completed in less than 20 min.

Some databases are updated weekly or daily, whereas their printed equivalents are issued monthly or less frequently. A search may supply references that will not appear in the printed index for weeks or even years. The *Mental Measurements Yearbook* database includes references that will appear in the ninth edition of the printed equivalent which is not yet published. ,,

Some databases were created as computerized files; they do not have an equivalent index. Databases such as *Mental Health Abstracts* provide exclusive information, unavailable from any other source.

The computer can search for a specific term or phrase in several places in an entry. A newly developing area may not be assigned a formal subject heading, or the subject may be listed under a different heading than expected, but if the terms are used in the title or the abstract of the article, the computer can retrieve the citations. For example, the phrase *guided imagery* is not used as a descriptor in *Psychological Abstracts*, but when the phrase was entered in the equivalent database, *PsycINFO*, the computer located 84 references.

The computer can search for several different terms, then compare the citations in order to identify only those references in which all the desired terms appear. This is especially valuable when each of the terms has a large number of references because the computer can cross-match them easily. A request for information about stereotypes among and about artists was searched in *PsycINFO*. The terms were searched in the fields for the titles and assigned subject headings only. In addition to artist, the terms *painter* and *sculptor* were also entered, all in a truncated form in order to retrieve both singular and plural forms. This portion of the request located 652 references. The terms used in addition to stereotype included *prejudice* and *attitudes*, which retrieved 9,261 references. When these two areas were combined, there were only 19 articles concerning both stereotypes and artists.

In addition to checking the subject headings that have been assigned by an index, the computer can search many other areas of the citation. Depending on the database, the date, issuing agency, title, language, author, special feature, or type of document could be searched. A search topic in some databases could be limited to journal articles written in English, with bibliographies, published within the last 2 years. In other databases, the searcher could locate conference proceedings, classroom materials, review articles, or audiovisual materials related to a specific topic.

Disadvantages

There are, of course, some problems with computer searches. The cost may be a consideration. The cost for computer time varies widely among databases, *ERIC* is

Table 1. Databases in Psychology

Databases and Beginning Dates	Equivalents	Subjects
Child Abuse and Neglect, 1965	None	Child abuse, including programs and bibliographic entries
Druginfo and Alcohol Use and Abuse, 1968	None	All aspects of drug and alcohol use and abuse
ERIC, 1966	*Resources in Education, Current Index to Journals in Education*	All aspects of education
Exceptional Child Education Resources, 1966	*Exceptional Child Education Abstracts*	Education of gifted and handicapped children
Family Resources, 1973	None	All aspects of family relations, including program descriptions and bibliographic entries
Medline, 1966	*Index Medicus, Index to Dental Literature, International Nursing Index*	Biomedicine, nursing, and dentistry
Mental Health Abstracts, 1969	None	All aspects of mental health
Mental Measurements Yearbook, 1977	*Mental Measurements Yearbook*	Descriptions and reviews of psychological tests
National Rehabilitation Information Center, 1950	None	Rehabilitation of physically and mentally disabled persons
PsycINFO, 1967	*Psychological Abstracts* plus material from *Dissertation Abstracts*	Psychology and the behavioral sciences
PsycALERT	None	Psychology; new items are entered here prior to indexing for *PsycINFO*
Social SciSearch, 1972	*Social Science Citation Index*	Social and behavioral sciences
SciSearch, 1974	*Science Citation Index, Current Contents: Clinical Practice, Current Contents: Engineering, Technology, and Applied Science, Current Contents: Agriculture, Biology, and Environmental Sciences*	Pure and applied science and technology
Sociological Abstracts, 1963	*Sociological Abstracts*	Sociology and related social and behavioral sciences

$25 per hour, but *Social SciSearch* is $110 per hour. Although the length of time it takes to do a search will vary with the speed of the computer terminal and printer, many searches take only a few minutes. A request for information concerning women's fear of success and motivation for power was run in *PsycINFO* on a Texas Instruments Silent 700 terminal. The search lasted 11 min, and cost $7.61. The cost for printing the 85 references and mailing them to the library was $17. Some libraries subsidize the cost of a search others charge for computer time, telecommunications costs, and staff time.

The computer retrieves the exact words requested. It cannot distinguish among the various meanings of a word or between homographs. For example, if the computer is asked for references about *pool*, it will retrieve materials about sports and about water unless terms are added to clarify the request. Although these irrelevant results can be reduced by combining terms, some unrelated references may still appear. Such references would also be seen in a manual search, but would not be copied down; the computer cannot make that kind of critical judgment.

Most databases in the social sciences were created in the 1960s and 1970s; for earlier research, the printed sources must still be used. *Psychological Abstracts* began publishing in 1927, but is available on computer only since 1967.

Searching With Microcomputers

Until recently, most bibliographic computer searching had been done through libraries or by information science businesses. As microcomputers have become widely available, it is possible to use them for database searching.

There are several companies that provide microcomputer users with access to most databases. The companies vary in cost, hours, computer compatibility, and available databases. Some systems are structured so that

144

the searcher responds to questions from the computer, following a programmed format, as does BRS/After Dark. Some are designed to enable a beginning searcher to use the system without training (e.g., BRS/BRKTHRU), and others (e.g., Dialog), require searchers to learn a specific command language. Some of the major companies now offering programs for microcomputers are Dialog in Palo Alto, CA; BRS in Latham, NY; Source in McLean, VA; Easynet in Marberth, PA; and CompuServe in Columbus, OH.

Obtaining the Article

If a reference that has been located through a search is not available in an area library, it may still be acquired. Many libraries will borrow a copy from another source through interlibrary loan. Some companies (e.g., the Institute for Scientific Information, which publishes *Science Citation Index* and *Social Science Citation Index*), will provide copies of the articles they index. Some journals, including the *Harvard Business Review* and those published by the American Chemical Society, have the complete text of the article available on the computer database.

Databases for Psychology

There are many databases that include psychology and more are being developed continually. Table 1 lists some of the major ones, giving the beginning dates, print equivalents, and general subjects included. There are other databases in many subject areas that have information related to psychology, such as those in the areas of business, law, political science, health, or technology. There are also databases about grants, foundations, biographical information, and educational tests. Others contain bibliographical records about books, conference papers, dissertations, periodicals, audiovisual materials, and government publications.

Conclusion

For many years, most computerized searching has been done through libraries or businesses. Few psychologists had the terminals that could connect with the small number of available files. Recent years have seen rapid growth in the number of databases and in the availability of the equipment necessary to manipulate the databases. The companies that once assumed their only users were specialists have now created programs for beginning searchers. Although computerized searching cannot answer all needs, a researcher aware of the basic concepts of searching will find it a valuable tool.

The Benefits of In-Class Bibliographic Instruction

Pam M. Baxter
Psychological Sciences Library
Purdue University

Makosky (1985) contends that psychology teachers are in the midst of an "information avalanche" (p. 23). She discusses four areas that are important for teachers as they structure their courses: (a) incorporating materials selectively, (b) arranging material so that it is easy for students to assimilate, (c) preparing students for self-education, and (d) using course material and structure to enhance general skills. The first two of these are primarily the responsibility of the teacher, who must present material that is manageable in volume, palatable in presentation, and useful for future application.

The last two areas, self-education and general skills, are to some degree dependent on students' own predilections and self-motivation. One device used, in part, to stimulate information-finding techniques is the library research paper, a frequent requirement of psychology courses. Makosky bemoans such research papers because they are more often than not ill-researched and poorly focused. However, this ubiquitous assignment can serve to introduce and enhance skills. Not mentioned by Makosky is the fact that the paper may also serve as the learning/teaching tool for using evaluative and critical thinking skills.

Librarians are in a unique position to experience a student's tentative attempts at the literature search process. Students frequently approach the reference desk in the typical academic library and initiate the process as follows:

Student:	I need some information on stress
Librarian:	How much information do you need? An overview or something in depth?
Student:	There's a few pages in my text on it, but my professor said to use *Psychological Abstracts* to find more. I just need enough for a 15-page paper.
Librarian:	What population are you interested in? Adults? Children?
Student: .	Adults, I guess.
Librarian	What kind of stress do you want to study? Job-related, interpersonal stress?
Student:	I don't know. I'll just take anything you have on stress.

This all too familiar dialogue illustrates many concerns. First, the student has not given the topic under investigation sufficient consideration. The reference interview initiated by the librarian is apparently the first (and possibly will be the only) instance when the student attempts this process. Second, the student has no appreciation of the breadth of the topic and certainly no idea of how vast the published literature is. Third, this particular student is one who had the courage to approach the reference desk. Too often, students avoid reference service for fear of appearing "stupid" or bothering the reference librarian. Worse still are those who think that assistance is not necessary in their cases. These students will attempt to plow through *Psychological Abstracts*, as recommended by their instructor, and experience almost immediate frustration.

Several solutions have been proposed, including online bibliographic retrieval services and library exercises designed to increase students' awareness of access tools. Feinberg, Drews, and Eynman (1981) and Parr (1979) have described the various advantages of online retrieval with undergraduates. A computer spews forth only the information requested, however, and requires a well-defined query to produce useful references in manageable numbers. In fact, Parr recommends investigating various traditional (i.e., manual) approaches to the literature before a computer search is initiated. Various library exercises used by librarians and teaching faculty (Gardner, 1977; Mathews, 1978), although well intentioned and potentially entertaining, are often viewed by students as ends and not means. As Carlson and Miller (1984) have pointed out, these "scavenger hunts" do not develop library research skills that are transferable to a serious literature search, nor do they demonstrate a systematic research strategy.

There are several reasons why in-class bibliographic instruction by librarians can alleviate the difficulties that students experience in the literature-search process. First, it serves to introduce basic reference tools: encyclopedias, handbooks, annual reviews, indexing, and abstracting services. A well-prepared lecture is tailored to the specific needs and level of a class. Lower-division students may be introduced to Corsini's *Encyclopedia of Psychology*, *Handbook of General Psychology*, *Annual Review of Psychology*, *Social Sciences Index*, and *Psychological Abstracts*. Advanced students can appreciate tools relevant to a course's subject matter (e.g., *Grzimek's Animal Life Encyclopedia*, *Handbook of Living Primates*, *Advances in the Study of Behavior*, and *Biological Abstracts*). Examining *Social Sciences Citation Index* introduces the concept of citation searching and its importance to the structure of research literature. In addition, the basic organization of libraries and idiosyncrasies of the local institution can be introduced without making students into "junior librarians."

Second, in-class presentations can maximize general skills by presenting a logical process of topic definition. Ill-defined search techniques result in the situation that Makosky (1985) describes: the propensity of students to use any reference even remotely related to a topic. Subject encyclopedias offer an authoritative overview; handbooks, more in-depth coverage; review articles, recent developments and an introduction to the literature; indexing and abstracting services, the necessity of using key words identified in the course of preliminary reading. These steps are essential in the selection, definition, and limiting of a topic. Mellon (1984) has pointed out that this process can be integrated into a library presentation for a specific class and the knowledge acquired transferred to other assignments and to information-seeking as a lifelong skill.

The third result of the bibliographic instruction session is the introduction of the librarian as an intermediary/ interpreter. Too often, students enter academe with rudimentary or nonexistent literature-search skills. The complexity of academic libraries and the diversity of materials available can be overwhelming, prompting many students to retreat to the safety of the familiar *Readers' Guide to Periodical Literature*. Students need to be reassured that the ability to search for information is not innate. The librarian assumes the role of "troubleshooter" in the maze of access tools and an ally in the literature-search process. Students who are reluctant to approach their instructor may be less apprehensive about enlisting the aid of a librarian.

Bibliographic instruction is an area of library service that has attracted considerable interest on the part of reference departments, although reference librarians have essentially been doing this on an individual, on-demand basis for a long time. Although I have emphasized the role of the librarian in bibliographic instruction, participation of the psychology instructor is essential. Carlson and Miller (1984) and Allen (1982) have emphasized the important role that teaching faculty play in encouraging library-use skills among their students.

There are no simple solutions to the problems that students have with their library searches (Makosky, 1985). The problems will be less serious, however, if we use more cooperative strategies. A useful strategy is for teachers and librarians to design in-class bibliographic instruction to meet the needs of a particular class.

References

Allen, D. Y. (1982, June 9). Students need help in learning how to use the library. *Chronicle of Higher Education*, p. 56.

Carlson, D., & Miller, R. H. (1984). Librarians and teaching faculty: Partners in bibliographic instruction. *College and Research Libraries, 45*, 483-491.

Feinberg, R. A., Drews, D., & Eynman, D. (1981). Positive side effects of online information retrieval. *Teaching of Psychology, 8*, 51-52.

Gardner, L. E. (1977). A relatively painless method of introduction to the psychological literature search. *Teaching of Psychology, 4*, 89-91.

Makosky, V. P. (1985). Teaching psychology in the information age. *Teaching of Psychology, 12*, 23-26.

Mathews, J. B. (1978). "Hunting" for psychological literature: A methodology for the introductory research course. *Teaching of Psychology, 5*, 100-101.

Mellon, C. A. (1984). Process not product in course-integrated instruction: A generic model of library research. *College and Research Libraries, 45*, 471-478.

Parr, V. H. (1979). Online information retrieval and the undergraduate. *Teaching of Psychology, 6*, 61-62.

A Strategy for Improving Literature Reviews in Psychology Courses

Retta E. Poe
Western Kentucky University

As a means of teaching undergraduates in an abnormal psychology class to write scholarly literature review papers, I developed a series of presentations and exercises to address typical student difficulties in completing such an assignment. First, I prepared several minilectures to clarify the nature of the assignment, which was to write a review of the scholarly literature on a topic relevant to the course (using a minimum of 10 data-based articles published within the preceding 10 years). I devoted portions of several class periods to discussing the following issues: What a scholarly literature review is, how to distinguish between scholarly sources and popular press periodicals, the nature of the library search process, how to use abstracting services, appropriate use of quoted material, how to reference studies in APA style, what constitutes plagiarism, and how to write an abstract for a journal article. In preparing my discussion of these topics, I relied on material presented in Rosnow and Rosnow (1986); Maimon, Belcher, Hearn, Nodine, and O'Connor (1981) and the *Publication Manual of the American Psychological Association* (3rd ed.; APA, 1983).

To teach students to formulate a topic, summarize articles, and integrate findings from several sources, I designed a series of overlapping writing assignments intended to shape the major skills needed in writing a literature review. I did not grade any of the writing assignments leading up to the final paper. Instead, students were able to get "free" feedback (i.e., with no effect on their course grades) simply by turning in assignments as requested. Although completion of the assignments was optional, nearly all students turned in each assignment.

The sequence of writing assignments was as follows.

1. Focused freewriting. Because Maimon et al. (1981) and Schor and Summerfield (1986) recommended focused freewriting as a way to begin writing, I asked students to write one paragraph on each of three topics they might be interested in researching for the paper assignment. Each

paragraph was to include a description of the topic, why the student was interested in that topic, and how the student expected to benefit from researching that topic.

2. <u>Summarization of an essay.</u> At the beginning of a class period, students wrote summaries of a short essay (fewer than 1,000 words) I had photocopied from a readings book. The article I selected was an argumentative essay on a nontechnical. topic unrelated to abnormal psychology. After discussing the qualities of good and bad summaries and providing examples of both (cf. Maimon et al., 1981, pp. 102-107), 1 asked students to write a one-paragraph summary of the key points of the essay. I then gave them a summary I had written of the same essay and offered students suggestions for evaluating the quality of their own summaries. In particular, I asked them to note whether they had identified the main points as well as the author's conclusions and to check their summaries for plagiarism.

3. <u>Summarization of a journal article—Part 1.</u> I selected a journal article on an abnormal psychology topic, removed the author abstract, and assigned students the task of writing an abstract following APA guidelines. The journal article chosen was a brief report of an investigation using terminology, procedures, and statistics easily understood by undergraduates. After the students had completed their abstracts, they were given the author abstract for comparison. They also exchanged papers with other class members, who were instructed to give feedback on whether the student had included all the required information in the abstract.

4. <u>Summarization of a journal article—Part 2.</u> Students wrote abstracts of a second journal article on the same topic as the first journal article. Again, the author abstract was removed before photocopying and was provided to students for comparison after they had written their own abstracts. This time, however, I gave students written feedback on the thoroughness of their abstracts as well as on each writer's strengths and weaknesses in grammar and composition.

5. <u>Integrating findings of two studies.</u> Each student wrote a comparison/contrast essay of about 350 words regarding the purpose, methodology, and findings of the two studies for which they had written summanes. In addition to providing students with written feedback on their essays, I gave them a comparison/contrast essay I had written on the same two studies.

6. <u>Preparing a reference list.</u> The final assignment was to submit a one-sentence description of the student's research topic along with a list of 10 references suitable for the paper assignment. I marked these for departures from APA style and also commented on the adequacy of the topic selected (too general, too specific, etc.).

Evaluation

I used two sources of informal information to evaluate the success of the writing projects: student feedback on course evaluations and quality of research papers (compared to the previous semester when no specific help with the writing process was provided).

About 60% of the students specifically commented on the writing component of the course. Most respondents indicated that they had found the writing exercises helpful and that they appreciated having had the opportunity to acquire writing skills without any penalty on their grades. The only negative comments concerned the extra time required to write the summaries and essays.

Because I received better papers, I was satisfied that the extra effort invested was justified. Compared to the previous semester, twice as many students received As, and no student's paper earned less than a C (vs. 13% Ds and Fs in the preceding semester). Moreover, I have repeated the shaping procedure in my senior-level psychology of women course. I received a greater number of high-quality papers compared to previous semesters when I made the same research paper assignment but did not help students with the writing process.

Conclusions

Although the intervention described is clearly time-consuming to implement, it offers as compensation the potential to have a noticeable impact on students' writing skills. With minor modifications, the multifaceted strategy used here to teach writing of literature review papers could be used to teach students to write other kinds of papers. Students will benefit from this effort by acquiring skills that will likely transfer to other courses, and instructors will benefit by reducing the frustration they often feel when evaluating students' writing. Perhaps most important of all, the writing assignment described here helps students to accomplish one of the goals of any psychology course: to learn about psychology writing and reading.

References

American Psychological Association. (1983). *Publication manual of the American Psychological Association* (3rd ed.). Washington, DC: Author.

Maimon, E. P., Belcher, G. L., Hearn, G. W., Nodine, B. F., & O'Connor, F. W. (1981). *Writing in the arts and sciences.* Boston: Little, Brown.

Rosnow, R. L., & Rosnow, M. (1986). *Writing papers in psychology: A student guide.* Belmont, CA: Wadsworth.

Schor, S., & Summerfield, J. (1986). *The Random House guide to writing* (3rd ed.). New York: Random House.

Note

Development of the techniques described in this article was supported by a grant from the Hendrix-Murphy Foundation while the author was a faculty member at the Hendrix College, Conway, AR.

3. TEACHING RESEARCH ETHICS

Using the Barnum Effect to Teach About Ethics and Deception in Research

Bernard C. Beins
Ithaca College

Psychologists are intensely interested in establishing ethical guidelines that help direct their professional relationships. The American Psychological Association exerts ongoing efforts to revise its guidelines (e.g., "APA Continues to Refine," 1992), and a growing corpus of relevant articles and publications exists (e.g., Tabachnick, Keith-Spiegel, & Pope, 1991).

Although professionals are acutely aware of the importance of this issue, students do not systematically learn about it at more than a cursory level (Korn, 1984). Fortunately, individual instructors have recognized the traditional gap in teaching ethics. McMinn (1988) developed a computerized approach to ethical decision making; Rosnow (1990) described an approach involving role-playing, discussion, and debate.

The approach to teaching ethics described here puts students in the role of the deceived in a classroom project. There are two main students why lectures and discussions about the ethics of deceit need to be supplemented by a more direct demonstration.

First, Milgram (1963) found that people are not very accurate in predicting how subjects will react when confronted with an ethically ambiguous situation. If people cannot reliably predict subjects' behavior, perhaps students might think that they know how a deceived subject would feel, but the actual experience may be much more compelling.

Second, students may not empathize initially with research subjects who are deceived. For example, student researchers who participated in some conformity studies (Beins & Porter, 1989) showed no distress about using deception in the research (the Institutional Review Board that approved the research also showed no distress). Similarly, Harcum and Friedman (1991), who expressed reservations about the ethics of using some fairly common classroom demonstrations, noted that about 93% of their subjects accepted deception as part of a legitimate research design.

The vehicle for creating this teaching activity is the *Barnum effect*, in which individuals are gulled into believing invalid results of psychological tests. This effect was originally used to teach students about testing (Forer, 1949); as a phenomenon, it is well documented (e.g., Baillargeon & Danis, 1984; Furnham & Schofield, 1987; Holmes, Buchannan, Dungan, & Reed, 1986). It can also introduce students to the pitfall of blind acceptance of test results (Palladino, 1991).

The goals of the activity described herein are to foster an appreciation of the feelings of research subjects who are lied to and an awareness of the need to avoid deception when possible. This approach complements those used by McMinn (1988) and Rosnow (1990). The demonstration combines an initial discussion of crucial ethical issues that I take from Reynolds (1982), a firsthand account of being deceived, and a final discussion.

Generating the Barnum Effect

Procedure

Students in a research methods class participated in the project as part of the course requirement. There were 28 women and 11 men; 10 were sophomores, 23 were juniors, and 6 were seniors.

Students completed a 20-item bogus personality inventory, the Quacksalber Personality Inventory for Normal Populations (Beins, 1987). They subsequently received interpretations that were identical for all students. All feedback statements were intended to be neutral or mildly positive .

One class (*n* = 19) completed the test with a version designed for Apple II computers; feedback was provided immediately. The second class (*n* = 20) took a version printed on paper and responded on a computer scoring sheet. A confederate of the teacher left the room and returned about 10 min later with printouts that had been prepared in advance with each student's name written across the top. There was no obvious reason to expect the two groups to differ in their reactions; a comparison between the two would only indicate how robust the effect might be.

Both groups then completed a form designed to access the perceived validity of the test. One question asked how well students thought the feedback described themselves. Students responded using a scale ranging from *this is the real me* (1) to *this is not like me* (10). In addition, they indicated how useful the test would be in five situations personal adjustment, employment screening, assessment of honesty, identification of a person's minor problems, and identification of a person's major problems. Students responded using a scale ranging from *very useful* (1) to *not very useful* (10).

Assessing the Barnum Effect

Students were predictably accepting of the test results as descriptive of themselves. The mean rating was 3.6. This represented a significant departure from a neutral value of 5.5, $t(38) = 6.24$, $p < .001$. However, students felt that the test would not be particularly effective in assessing personal adjustment, employee honesty and stability, or major or minor emotional problems. Thus, students did not blindly accept the test as being a universally valid instrument.

To test the robustness of the effect, a 2 (Medium: Computer vs. Paper) $\times$ 2 (Sex) $\times$ 3 (Year in School) analysis of variance was conducted on the acceptance ratings. Only the main effect of year was significant, $F(2, 36) = 5.09$, $p = .011$. Sophomores ($M = 3.00$) and juniors ($M = 3.43$) did not differ reliably, but they were significantly less skeptical than seniors ($M = 5.67$). The small number of seniors renders the difference between them and the sophomores and juniors somewhat suspect. I have tried to generate acceptance of the results of the Quacksalber inventory for other seniors and for graduate students without much success. Even so, these students experience the deceit, their skepticism in the results of the test notwithstanding.

Generating Postdemonstration Discussion

Students discussed their feelings when I told them that they had been deceived. Their initial reaction to the deceit was to feel gullible and stupid. In general, they were mildly distressed at first. I also noted what seemed to be nervous laughter from several students during the initial stages of the discussion.

Discussion focused on the fact that they had taken the Quacksalber inventory seriously, on their feelings about being deceived, and on the idea that their reactions to being deceived were common. I also pointed out that if they used deception in research, their subjects would feel the same way. Finally, I used this situation to illustrate the importance of debriefing.

During the next class meeting, they wrote answers to questions about the suitability of this exercise to illustrate relevant points about deception in research and whether this demonstration should be repeated in future classes. We spent nearly an entire class period discussing what they had written. I made it clear that I would consider their responses seriously before deciding whether to repeat this activity with another class. I pointed out that deception was as much a problem in the classroom as in the context of experimental research.

Assessing Student Reactions to the Deception

Of the 31 students who commented anonymously about whether this demonstration was effective in teaching about both the Barnum effect and deception, 30 students responded affirmatively. Their comments generally asserted that the costs of doing the demonstration (failure to acquire prior informed consent, invasion of their privacy in asking questions about their likes and dislikes, and lying to them about the nature of the test) were outweighed by the benefits of learning that deception is not free of cost and of knowing firsthand how subjects feel when lied to. Other notable and potentially serious effects of this exercise are that students may question the instructor's credibility, they may think that psychological research is without validity or integrity, and they may develop negative feelings about psychological research. None of these unwanted eventualities emerged.

The sole dissenter suggested that it was not worth making students feel stupid and that the point about deception in research could be made simply by giving facts and examples. Several students noted that some students may be distressed (e.g., freshmen who lacked confidence in themselves) and that I should be aware of this. We had not discussed the question of individual differences regarding negative reactions, but some students spontaneously mentioned it.

Discussion

This project seems to have been effective on two levels. On one hand, the students became acquainted with the Barnum effect. More important they also seemed quite touched at the personal level by the experience. It was clear to me that they did not enjoy the trickery when it was inflicted on them. On the other hand, they agreed that it provided a compelling message. The class discussion was tinged with a sense of empathy with research subjects who are deceived. The degree to which students objected to the procedure was as low as that reported elsewhere (Britton, Richardson, Smith, & Hamilton 1983; Harcum & Friedman, 1991): Students may have felt some distress, but it was mild and short-lived.

The students also learned that. in some cases, deception can be tolerated. For example, in my classes, the students agreed that I should not regularly lie to them; however, the mild and short-lived discomfort about knowing that they had been lied to served to teach them an important lesson about deception in research. Thus, they asserted that the project was worth repeating with subsequent classes.

This demonstration has several advantages. It teaches about deception in the context of a social psychology phenomenon. It is more accessible than Forer's (1949) original demonstration of the Barnum effect, which was based on his Diagnostic Interest Blank and some astrological personality descriptions. This version is also quicker than Forer's, which extended over a period of 1 week. Also, the Quacksalber inventory provides the same kind of feedback Forer provided, although the personality descriptions used here are more neutral.

Furthermore, when the computer version is used, no responses are actually recorded, thus ensuring confidentiality. (The computerized version is available only for Apple II computers, but is written in BASIC, so it should be easily convertible to GW BASIC for IBM-type computers.)

The project seems amenable either to computerized or paper application. Men and women reacted in the same way, both in generating the effect and in their responses to deception. Seniors seemed more skeptical of the feedback (as did master's level students in education in a similar situation). Even when students failed to accept the output as descriptive of themselves, they still seemed to have accepted the test as legitimate. This demonstration seems robust and pedagogically useful for a wide range of students.

References

APA continues to refine its ethics code. (1992, May). *APA Monitor*, pp. *38-42*.

Baillargeon, J., & Danis, C. (1984). Barnum meets the computer: A critical test. *Journal of Personality Assessment, 48*, 415-419.

Beins, B. C. (1987). Psychological testing and interpretation. In V. P. Makosky, L. G. Whittemore, & A. M. Rogers (*Eds.*), *Activities handbook for the teaching of psychology* (Vol. 2, pp. 266-274). Washington, DC: American Psychological Association.

Beins, B. C., & Porter, S. W. (1989). A ratio scale measurement of conformity. *Educational and Psychological Measurement, 49*, 75-80.

Britton, B. K., Richardson, D., Smith, S. S., & Hamilton, T (1983). Ethical aspects of participating in psychology

experiments: Effects of anonymity on evaluation, and complaints of distressed subjects. *Teaching of Psychology, 10*, 146-149.

Forer, B. R. (1949). The fallacy of personal validation: A classroom demonstration of testing. *Journal of Abnormal and Social Psychology, 44*, 118- 123.

Furnham, A., & Schofield, S. (1987). Accepting personality test feedback: A review of the Barnum effect. *Current Psychological Research Reviews, 6*, 162-178.

Harcum, E. R., & Friedman, H. (1991). Students' ethics ratings of demonstrations in introductory psychology. *Teaching of Psychology, 18*, 215-218.

Holmes, C. B., Buchannan, J. A., Dungan, D. S., & Reed, T. (1986). The Barnum effect in Luscher color test interpretation. *Journal of Clinical Psychology, 2*, 186-190.

Korn, J. H. (1984). Coverage of research ethics in introductory and social psychology textbooks. *Teaching of Psychology, 11*, 146-149.

McMinn, M. R. (1988). Ethics case-study simulation: A generic tool for psychology teachers. *Teaching of Psychology, 15*, 100-101.

Milgram, S. (1963). Behavioral study of obedience. *Journal of Abnormal and Social Psychology, 67*, 371-378.

Palladino, J. J. (1991, August). *The BRPI—The Blatantly Ridiculous Personality Inventory*. Paper presented at the annual convention of the American Psychological Association, San Francisco.

Reynolds, P. D. (1982). *Ethics and social science research*. Englewood Cliffs, NJ: Prentice-Hall.

Rosnow, R. L. (1990). Teaching research ethics through role-play and discussion. *Teaching of Psychology 17*, 179-181.

Tabachnick, B. G., Keith-Spiegel, P., & Pope, K. S. (1991). Ethics of teaching: Beliefs and behaviors of psychologists as educators. *American Psychologist, 46*, 506-515.

Note

I thank Ruth Ault for her comments on a previous draft of this article .

Teaching Research Ethics Through Role-Play and Discussion

Ralph L. Rosnow
Temple University

When lecturing on research ethics, instructors tend to consider only the costs and benefits of conducting particular studies, as if from the perspective of an institutional review board (IRB). Seldom is due consideration given to the ethical implications of the failure to conduct ethically ambiguous studies that might reduce violence, prejudice, mental illness, and so forth. The failure to conduct such a study because it involves deception or invasion of privacy, however, is as much an act to be evaluated on ethical grounds as is the act of conducting a study (Rosenthal & Rosnow, 1984). This idea is important to communicate to psychology students, because it teaches that there is more than one vantage point from which the ethical evaluation of a study can be made. This article describes a classroom exercise that, through role-play and discussion, leads students to develop an appreciation of the subtleties of research ethics.

The technique considers at least three vantage points. The first is that of the research discipline itself, as represented by the ethical principles of the American Psychological Association (1982). A second frame of reference is that of the community in which the research is being sanctioned (e.g., the class in which the person is a student or an IRB). The third is the point of view of the individual investigator (e.g., the student-researcher), who may not have thought much about his or her own ethical assumptions and biases.

This article proceeds in two parts. First, I suggest some readings and ideas to stimulate discussion. The discussion, which takes place either before the role-play (i.e., to set the stage) or afterward (i.e., to tie things together), is intended to provide a real-world context for the students. Next, I describe the role-play technique, which I have condensed into a five-step exercise. In this exercise, students defend a position they have recently attacked by role-playing an author who is defending the value of a study. This exercise helps sharpen critical thinking and reduces the initial tendencies of many students to "play it safe" by eschewing any study that appears to involve deception or intervention. The technique can be modified to fit scheduling constraints or larger classes.

Readings and Discussion

If the exercise is to be part of a research methods class, the textbook will usually contain relevant material. For graduate and advanced undergraduate students, such material can be supplemented by outside readings (e.g., Doob, 1987; Kelman, 1968; Kimmel, 1981, 1988; Schuler, 1982; Sieber, 1982; Smith, 1969), chosen with the course objectives in mind. Because some students tend to approach such readings uncritically, it is helpful to provide a background to focus their attention. For example, students could be assigned to read selected chapters in Miller's (1986) book on Stanley Milgram's classic studies. The ethics of Milgram's research were widely debated; this debate is captured in an absorbing way in Miller's book.

A comparison between the ethical dilemmas faced by Milgram and those faced by action researchers can be made by using the quality-of-work-life experiment that was conducted in 1973 at the Rushton Mining Company in Pennsylvania (Blumberg & Pringle, 1983). Developed on the basis of earlier research in the United Kingdom, the purpose of this project was to improve employee skills, safety, and job satisfaction, which raised the level of performance and as a result, company earnings. After months of research preparation, volunteers were sought for a work group that would have direct responsibility for production in one section of the mining operations. After exhaustive training in safety laws, good mining practices, and job safety analysis, the volunteers were paid at the top rate as the highest skilled job classification on that section and left to coordinate their own activities. They became enthusiastic proponents of "our way of working." Other workers (i.e., those in the control condition), however, expressed resentment and anger at the volunteers' haughtiness. The resulting negativity in the atmosphere surrounding the experiment led the investigators to end it abruptly.

Action research can frequently have its own set of ethical problems, quite apart from the ones encountered by Milgram in his laboratory research. There was no deception in this study, but there is the problem of "fairness" because a sizable number of workers (nonvolunteers) did not receive the benefits enjoyed by those in the experimental group. By analogy, the ethical cost of using placebo control subjects in biomedical research could be examined, because they also fail to receive the benefits (if any) received by the experimental group. What if instead of receiving a placebo, the controls received the best available usual or common treatment to serve as a comparison with the effects of the experimental treatment?

Still other ethical risks may be incurred in participant observer research. For example, what about the moral cost that is possible simply in the reporting of results (cf. Johnson, 1982)? What if, despite the author's use of pseudonyms, some persons or communities can be identified (or can identify themselves) in the publication? Would those that are identifiable be vulnerable to embarrassment or to unwanted publicity? On the other hand, what is the social and scientific cost of not publishing the findings (i. e., not disseminating research results)?

Deception, fairness, and the invasion of privacy also come into play outside the research situation. Broome (1984) discussed the ethical issue of fairness in selecting people for chronic hemodialysis, a medical procedure that can save the life of a person whose kidneys have failed. The procedure is expensive, and in many communities there are not enough facilities to treat everyone who could benefit, yet without treatment a patient quickly dies. How should candidates for hemodialysis be selected? The inventor of hemodialysis was said to have used the following guidelines to select people under 40 years old, free from cardiovascular disease, pillars of the community, contributors to the community's economics, married, and attends church. Is this ethical and fair? Another procedure would be randomness. Broome noted that selecting people randomly—such as using a lottery to choose conscripts to fight in a war—is justified as the "fairest" procedure, because everyone has an equal chance at being selected for life or death. But suppose conscripts for the military were not selected randomly, but on the grounds of who was the biggest and strongest. Which procedure is more ethical—randomness or selection on the grounds of who is more likely to survive?

These are the kinds of ideas and questions that instructors might pose to stimulate discussion. Students need to understand that research is not conducted in isolation from the surrounding community. For example, when researchers study prejudice, mental illness, or AIDS, they are touching on highly charged social problems. Even when they study topics that appear to be neutral (e.g., marriage and the family, the genetics of intelligence, or learning behavior), they must realize the implications for others. Thus, it is important to understand that psychological research forces investigators to "tread on thin moral ice" (Atwell, 1981, p. 89).

The Role-Play Exercise

Step 1 is to familiarize the class with the "Ten Commandments" of the APA's ethical recommendations (American Psychological Association, 1982, pp. 5-7). The ethical standards were developed to check the possible tendency of some researchers to be carried away by the judged importance of doing the research. The class might, therefore, be asked to think about the possibility that there are ethical boundaries that should not be crossed, as put forth in the APA code. Then each student peruses the past year's issues of any primary research journal of interest. The assignment is to find an article that reports a research study that the student personally feels used an "unethical" manipulation or other "reprehensible" procedure. The student is instructed to read the article carefully and thoroughly, to be prepared if called on in class to give a detailed report and be able to answer questions about it, and to turn in a brief paper that focuses on the ethics of the study. The sampling bias in this assignment would seem implicit, inasmuch as the students are reading only studies that supposedly have passed ethical scrutiny. Students have an uncanny ability, however, to ferret out ethically ambiguous studies, even in recent APA journal articles.

Step 2 is to have the students give oral reports of the results of their assignment for the entire class. I then pose questions regarding potentially troublesome aspects of the procedure (e. g., invasion of privacy, deception, use of confederates, or concealed observation). The objective of the questions is to draw the group as a "community" into the discussion.

In Step 3, after all the studies have been discussed, the class examines them from a different perspective. Instead of acting as critics, the students role-play the author of the study and defend their study in the face of criticisms by the rest of the group. If the most articulate and confident students begin this phase, they can provide a good example for the students who follow.

Step 4 is to have each person in the group evaluate the studies on their moral or ethical cost and their theoretical or practical utility. Taking each study in turn the students evaluate the moral or ethical cost on a 101-point scale ranging from *no ethical or moral cost* (0) to *the highest ethical or moral cost* (100). Students evaluate the studies individually, based not on how they think that others in the group will vote but on their own personal perspective. Next, students evaluate each study's utility on a 101-point scale ranging from *no theoretical or practical utility* (0) to *the highest theoretical or practical utility* (100). I then draw two matrices on the blackboard, one for the "cost of doing" and the other for the "utility of doing" ratings. The students' names begin the rows, and one- or two-word descriptors of the studies head the columns. While the group copies down the results, I calculate the row and column means and the grand mean and insert this information. The results tell the students at a glance whether they were tough or easy relative to one another (row means), to the group as a whole (grand mean), and to

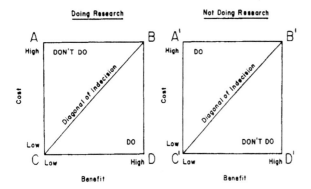

Figure 1. Decision planes representing the costs and utilities of doing and not doing research. *Note.* From "Applying Hamlet's Question to the Ethical Conduct of Research: A Conceptual Addendum" by Robert Rosenthal and Ralph L. Rosnow, 1984, *American Psychologist, 39*, p. 562. Copyright 1984 by the American Psychological Association, Inc. Adapted by permission.

the collective perception of each study. I also point out outliers and clusters of ratings and ask the students to speculate on their implications.

Step 5 concludes the exercise. Using Figure 1 (Rosenthal & Rosnow, 1984), I then develop the idea that the decision-plane model on the left represents the costs and utilities of doing research. Studies falling at A are not carried out, studies falling at D are carried out, and studies falling at B-C cannot be determined. Results in the previous matrices (Step 4) can be used to illustrate the various possibilities. The model represents the way that most IRBs seemingly operate, but this "IRB" (the class)—through role-play in Step 3—also thought about (but did not rate) the other side of the ethical equation, the costs (and utilities) of not doing research (represented by the model on the right). I point out the ethical value of considering both models to arrive at a balanced analysis of the costs and utilities of doing and not doing a study. Examples from the previous role-play are used to underscore the idea that ethical decision making calls for such a balancing of considerations, even though it makes the decision process more complex. Note that IRBs review research proposals, not research results, but we had knowledge of the results. Did it make a difference in the ratings, and what are the implications?

If the class is large and there are section meetings in which the students are divided into small groups, then it is better to run the exercise in the latter context. Small groups establish a tone that makes it easier for students to be less inhibited and to throw themselves into the exercise. Student reactions have been consistently positive. Making social comparisons is intrinsically motivating, thus adding to the appeal of the exercise. The exercise provides students with a way of looking to others for information while looking within themselves to cope with their uncertainties.

References

American Psychological Association. (1982). *Ethical principles in the conduct of research with human participants.* Washington, DC: Author.

Atwell, J. E. (1981). Human rights in human subjects research. In A. J. Kimmel (Ed.), *Ethics of human subject research* (pp. 81-90). San Francisco: Jossey-Bass.

Blumberg, M., & Pringle, C. D. (1983). How control groups can cause loss of control in action research: The case of Rushton coal mine. *Journal of Applied Behavioral Science, 19,* 409-425.

Broome, J. (1984). Selecting people randomly. *Ethics, 95,* 38-55.

Doob, L. W. (1987). *Slightly beyond skepticism: Social science and the search for morality.* New Haven: Yale University Press.

Johnson, C. G. (1982). Risks in the publication of fieldwork. In J. E. Sieber (Ed.), *The ethics of social research: Fieldwork, regulation, an publication* (Vol. 1, pp. 71-91). New York: Springer-Verlag.

Kelman, H. C. (1968). *A time to speak: On human values and social research.* San Francisco: Jossey-Bass.

Kimmel, A. J. (Ed.). (1981). *Ethics of human subject research.* San Francisco: Jossey-Bass.

Kimmel, A. J. (1988*). Ethics and values in applied social research.* Beverly Hills: Sage.

Miller, A. G. (1986*). The obedience experiments: A case study of controversy in social science.* New York: Praeger.

Rosenthal, R., & Rosnow, R. L. (1984). Applying Hamlet's question to the ethical conduct of research: A conceptual addendum. *American Psychologist, 39,* 561 -563.

Schuler, H. (1982). *Ethical problems in psychological research.* New York: Academic.

Sieber, J. E. (Ed.). (1982). *The ethics of social research* (Vol. 1 & Vol. 2). New York: Springer-Verlag.

Smith, M. B. (1969*). Social psychology and human values.* Chicago: Aldine .

Notes

1. Preparation of this article was supported by Temple University through the Bolton Endowment and an NIH Biomedical Research Support Grant.

2. I thank Robert Rosenthal, Joseph Palladino, and three anonymous reviewers for their helpful comments on a draft of this article.

The Use of Role-Play in Teaching Research Ethics: A Validation Study

David B. Strohmetz
Anne A. Skleder
Temple University

Rosnow (1990) argued that, in order to make students aware of the ethical complexities of psychological research, the moral or ethical costs and benefits of doing research might be evaluated in a role-play context. He described a classroom exercise designed to teach students the necessity of viewing the importance of both cost and benefit considerations in the evaluation of research studies. We incorporated this procedure into our lectures on research ethics and evaluated its effectiveness using questionnaires administered before and after the study.

Following Rosnow's suggestion, the procedure begins with a lecture on research ethics based on the ethical principles of the American Psychological Association (1981). The discussion includes a consideration of why proposed research must be evaluated in terms of the ethical costs and benefits of doing the study as well as the costs and benefits of not doing the study. Students are then given a homework assignment to find a recently published study that they consider to be unethical. They are told to read the study carefully and to be prepared to present it during the next class.

During the next class, students present their studies in a discussion led by the instructor. Afterward, they are asked to rate the cost and utility (benefit) of each study. Students are then asked to role-play a "devil's advocate" and defend the scientific value of their "unethical" study before the rest of the class. Following this role-play, each student rerates the cost and the utility of the studies. Finally, the reevaluations are discussed to uncover how and why cost and utility ratings may have changed as a result of the students advocating studies that they originally viewed as unethical.

How effective is this role-play exercise in communicating the ethical complexity of psychological research? We were able to compare the changes in the cost and utility ratings from classes that used the role-play activity with similar ratings from a class that heard the lecture on research ethics but did not use the role-play activity. We predicted that participating in the role-play exercise would increase students' perceptions of the utility of their "unethical" studies. Similarly, we hypothesized that ratings of the perceived ethical costs of these studies would be lower after the role-play. Finally, we predicted that the magnitude of any obtained effects would be larger in these six classes than in the comparison class, which did not use the role-play exercise .

Method

Subjects

Students in both the role-play and nonrole-play classes were junior and senior psychology majors enrolled in a required research methods course. Six classes incorporated the role-play exercise into the lecture on research ethics; a seventh class had the same research ethics lecture and unethical article assignment but did not use the role-play exercise. Each of the authors taught two of these classes, the remaining two role-play classes and the nonrole-play class were taught by three other instructors. Approximately 18 students were enrolled in each class.

Procedure

We used the role-play exercise as described earlier, with one modification. Because of class size and time constraints, only a limited number of the students' "unethical" studies were selected for the role-play. The number of studies selected was left to the instructor's discretion, so the number of rated articles was inconsistent among the classes, ranging from 5 to 11 studies. Before engaging in the role-play, each class rated the cost and utility of the selected studies on a scale ranging from *no cost or utility* (0) to *highest cost or utility* (100).

After this first set of ratings, we asked each student who had initially critiqued one of the selected articles to imagine himself or herself as the article's primary author or researcher. The rest of the class role-played a peer review board that called upon the student to defend the ethics of his or her study. After the selected articles were

Table 1. Changes in Utility Ratings

Class	Utility Change[a]	Correlated t Test[b]	
Instructor A			
Semester 1	10.76	t(15) = 3.31, p = .002	.65
Semester 2	4.22	t(21) = 1.61, p = .06	.33
Instructor B			
Semester 1	8.02	t(15) = 2.75, p = .007	.58
Semester 2	8.34	t(15) = 4.43, p = .0002	.75
Instructor C	7.37	t(18) = 3.54, p = .001	.64
Instructor D	3.13	t(14) = 1.58, p = .069	.40
No role-play[c]	−1.18	t(18) = −.89, p = .39[d]	−.20

[a] Mean change, Time 2 minus Time 1. [b] One-tailed p-values for role-play groups. [c] The utility ratings for one student were incomplete. [d] Two-tailed p-value.

defended, students rerated the perceived cost and utility of the articles on the same scale.

The instructor in the comparison class followed the same procedure except that he did not conduct the role-play segment after the initial set of ratings. Instead, the instructor turned to another research topic. After about 30 min, the instructor again asked the students to rate the perceived cost and utility of the selected articles. The changes in cost and utility ratings for each class provided the basis for our analyses.

Results and Discussion

Correlated t tests were computed to evaluate whether there were significant changes in the cost and utility ratings from Time 1 to Time 2. Because each class rated different articles, we treated each class separately In our analyses. We used meta-analytic procedures (Rosenthal, 1984) to compare and contrast the results from each of the classes.

The direction of the changes in utility ratings for all the role-play groups was consistent with our prediction (see Table 1). The magnitude of the effect varied slightly among instructors, with effect sizes (calculated as a Pearson r) ranging from .33 to .75. For the nonrole-play class, the change in the perceived utility ratings was not significant and in the opposite direction of that in the role-play classes.

A meta-analytic comparison revealed that the utility results from the role-play classes were homogeneous with regard to significance levels, $\chi^2(5) = 3.30$, $p = .65$, and effect sizes, $\chi^2(5) = 4.55$, $p = .47$. Combining the significance levels for the role-play classes' utility ratings yielded a Z score of 6.05, $p < .0000001$. We calculated that it would take an additional 16 nonsignificant studies to achieve such an effect, thereby suggesting that our combined significance level was not due to sampling bias (Rosenthal, 1984; Rosenthal & Rosnow, 1991). Combining the effect sizes for the role-play classes resulted in an average effect size of .57 for the change in utility ratings, which is considered to be a large magnitude of effect in psychology (Cohen, 1977).

The results for the utility change ratings were homogeneous among the role-play classes. Therefore, significance levels and effect sizes were contrasted between the role-play and nonrole-play classes. Both the contrasts for significance levels, $Z = 3.089$, $p = .001$, and effect sizes, $Z = 3.264$, $p = .0006$, suggest that the role-play exercise affected students' utility ratings.

The separate class results for changes in the perceived cost ratings were also in the expected direction (see Table 2). However, none of Instructor B's results were statistically significant. Instructors A, C, and D's results were homogeneous for significance levels, $\chi^2(3) = 4.17$, $p = .24$, and effect sizes, $\chi^2(3) = 3.95$, $p = .27$. They were significantly different from Instructor B's significance levels, $Z = 3.75$, $p = .0001$, and effect sizes, $Z = 3.74$, $p = .0001$.

We have no single explanation for this result, but note that Instructor B's cost results were not significantly different from the nonrole-play class. Clearly, the role-play exercise had little impact on student reevaluations of the studies in Instructor B's classes, whereas the other role-play classes differed from the nonrole-play class with respect to significance levels, $Z = 3.83$, $p = .0001$, and effect sizes, $Z = 4.10$, p = .00002. If we consider Instructor B as an outliner for the purposes of this analysis, then the average effect size for Instructors A, C, and D was .72. For these classes, the role-play exercise produced the hypothesized significant effect on cost ratings.

We thought of two plausible explanations for why Instructor B's changes in cost ratings were significantly different from the other role-play classes. First, Instructor B may have placed less emphasis on defending the perceived costs of the studies during the role-play part of the exercise than the other instructors. As a result, there would be little reason for Instructor B's students to change their initial cost ratings.

Table 2. Changes in Cost Ratings

Class	Cost Change[a]	Correlated t Test[b]	
Instructor A			
Semester 1	−8.98	t(15) = 5.11, p = .0001	.80
Semester 2	−6.91	t(21) = 6.91, p = .00001	.83
Instructor B			
Semester 1	−.22	t(15) = .05, p = .50	.01
Semester 2	−.85	t(15) = .35, p = .40	.09
Instructor C	−5.63	t(18) = 3.08, p = .003	.59
Instructor D	−8.67	t(14) = 2.60, p = .011	.57
No role-play	1.14	t(19) = −.85, p = .41[c]	−.19

[a] Mean change, Time 2 minus Time 1. [b] One-tailed p-values for role-play groups. [c] Two-tailed p-value.

Another plausible explanation stems from a consideration of the number of studies discussed by each class. Both of Instructor B's classes discussed approximately five more articles than did the other role-play classes. Perhaps Instructor B's students rated too many articles and were unable to concentrate on both the cost and utility issues for each study. Instructor B's students may have focused on the utility issue because it was a new concept introduced during the previous lecture. Anecdotal evidence seems to support this latter interpretation. In written evaluations of the exercise, Instructor B's students were more likely to suggest that they "needed more time for each study" and that there were "too many studies to consider."

This argument could be extended to explain at least the change in cost results for the nonrole-play class, because this class rated approximately the same number of articles as did Instructor B's classes. However, closer examination of Table 2 reveals that the mean cost ratings from Time 1 to Time 2 for the nonrole-play class appeared to increase, which is in the opposite direction of that of the role-play classes, including Instructor B's classes. Such a pattern suggests that this class may have been evaluating the articles differently than were the role-play classes.

Nevertheless, our results generally support the effectiveness of Rosnow's (1990) exercise in sensitizing students to the complexity of research ethics. However, instructors should be aware of the constraints that class size and time limitations may create when selecting articles for the exercise. The question that future researchers may want to address is whether the role-play has a lasting impact on students' treatment of ethical issues in research.

References

American Psychological Association. (1981). Ethical principles of psychologists (revised). *American Psychologist, 36,* 633-688.

Cohen, S. (1977). *Statistical power analysis for the behavioral sciences* (2nd ed.). New York: Academic.

Rosenthal, R. (1984). *Meta-analytic procedures for social research.* Beverly Hills: Sage.

Rosenthal, R., & Rosnow, R. L. (1991). *Essentials of behavioral research: Methods and data analysis* (2nd ed.). New York: McGraw-Hill.

Rosnow, R. L. (1990). Teaching research ethics through role-play and discussion. *Teaching of Psychology, 17,* 179-181.

Note

This research was supported by Temple University fellowships awarded to both authors. We thank Dixon Bramblett, Richard Shifman, and Donna Shires for assistance in data collection; our students for participating in this study; and Ralph L. Rosnow and the anonymous reviewers for their helpful comments on earlier drafts of this article.

The Human Subjects Review Procedure: An Exercise in Critical Thinking for Undergraduate Experimental Psychology Students

Richard W. Hubbard
Kathy L. Ritchie
Indiana University South Bend

Much critical thinking in psychology focuses on evaluating and analyzing research results used to support arguments made by theorists and researchers (Bell, 1991; Mayer & Goodchild, 1990). Engaging in psychological research also involves the evaluation of the questions posed and methods considered in developing experiments. Although many studies conducted by undergraduates are exempt from a full human subjects review (e.g., classroom exercises), others, particularly those in advanced laboratory classes, require an expedited review. Having all students fill out a human subjects review form provides an excellent opportunity to teach the application of critical-thinking skills, especially as they pertain to the development of ideas and hypotheses. When students consider the questions posed in the review, they can evaluate their research along important dimensions, such as parsimony, logical consistency, and the degree to which hypotheses are testable. Kaplan (1964) stressed pragmatism (i.e., what difference does the hypothesis make if it is supported by data) as being important to reasoning in research. This theme is emphasized in our approach.

Critical thinking about research in our model also involves consideration of exactly what is predicted and what phenomena the researchers are attempting to explain. The human subjects review process requires students to evaluate their proposals in terms of the questions they pose and the potential explanations for significant findings. It also involves an analysis of the linkages among these more broadly based issues and the methodology to be used. As the last step in the development of a proposal, the review process is perfectly timed to provide an opportunity for a full critique of a proposed study in the following ways:

1. Researchers must develop a written description of their proposed research that should be appropriate for a professional group of reviewers who do not have expertise in the area. Thus, students identify the central idea in their research, justify measures to be used, and convey this information in a straightforward fashion. Cone of the problems many of our students encounter centers on the integration of hypotheses and methods. They tend either to have clearly defined hypotheses, lacking measures that will provide data concerning their predictions, or they have well developed measures but have not arrived at a theoretical base for their study. As they remove jargon and increase the specificity of the procedures in their proposals, they are encouraged to ask "Will the measures provide data that will answer my research question?"

2. Researchers are required to develop an informed consent form and materials, such as debriefing statements, that describe the experiment in detail to a naive audience. By considering the subject's role, students develop an appreciation for the way in which instructions and measures may confuse or offend their study's participants. Methodological confounds, such as confusing response formats, missing data (e.g., subject age or sex), or inadequate instructions, are often identified during this step. The translation of the study's purpose and design into language suitable for psychologically naive subjects requires students to reduce their proposal to a logical explanation of the scientific method: What is the question you are asking, and how will you collect data to answer it?

3. The review involves consideration of the risks and benefits of the proposed research. This requires students to view their study from an ethical perspective and consider benefits of the study to the subject as well as to society. Again, critical thinking about what difference a significant finding may make is stimulated, further developing a pragmatic perspective.

Specific Questions Addressed in the Classroom

In addition to the general orientation described earlier, a number of specific questions on the review form also lend themselves to critical-thinking exercises. They are as follows:

1. Describe the objectives of the study. This challenges students to identify the aims of their research and describe how the methodology they have selected meets those objectives. Students must ask "What is it I want to find out," and "How will collecting data in this way answer my question?" Such questions are critical to developing a data-based arguement.

2. What are the specific characteristics of your subject population, and how will subjects be selected? Students must also consider their projects in terms of criteria related to at-risk populations. The selection process is also examined in relation to possible implied demands to participate. This presents an opportunity to consider certain types of confounding variables for their research. Close consideration of subjects to be used leads to an evaluation of the utility of variables, such as sex and race, in testing hypotheses and to a consideration of how such characteristics may influence the phenomenon to be studied.

3. What are the risks of the study to your participants? The students must examine psychological risk as a concept, including factors such as stress level, fatigue, and the importance of confidentiality. Concerns about the use of deception in research often arise here. Students are also frequently interested in clinical areas, such as sexual abuse, marital discord, or child-rearing practices, that require them to consider the notion of psychological discomfort in subjects. Evaluation of risk also requires a literature review to ascertain whether the proposed methods and procedures have been used in other research without undue harm. This prompts additional criticism and justification of their methodology.

4. What specific measures are to be used? Students must not only identify what is to be measured but how. Validity and reliability estimates are made from a review of the literature, and even apparently simple surveys come under scrutiny. Operational definitions, important concepts in critical thinking, are often further refined during this aspect of the review.

5. What are the potential benefits of your study? In considering this question, students view their study in terms of its contribution to science. Specifically, they must describe how their research will contribute to the literature in the field, the ways in which it extends or builds on existing research, and what benefits this area of study offers for society. Too often, students simply focus on completing the study. This question forces them to justify their research and consider its implications in a broader context.

Classroom Application

We have used the human subjects review process as a critical-thinking exercise at both introductory and advanced levels of undergraduate experimental psychology courses. In both classes, the process of teaching critical thinking using the review is similar. First, material on the steps and procedures used in experimentation are covered in lectures over several classes. This includes areas such as ethics, hypothesis formation and operational definitions, surveys, and observational procedures. When students are ready to begin to develop their experiments, a lecture on the process and questions involved in the human subjects review procedure is presented. Our goal here is to link the review process directly to critical thinking about experimental design. For example, questions on measurements are related to issues concerning operational definitions. We also examine limitations of procedures, such as surveys and observational studies. Material on the costs and benefits to society is introduced, with an emphasis on the pragmatic implications of research (Kaplan, 1964).

Conclusion

The human subjects review process embodies many of the elements of critical thinking. Students integrate existing literature into their proposals and operationally define their methods and measures. They critically analyze their goals and objectives, justify the importance of the study, and evaluate the potential risks and benefits of their proposal. The review challenges students to present arguments logically to scientific and general audiences.

References

Bell, J. (1991). *Evaluating psychological information: Sharpening your critical thinking skills.* Boston: Allyn & Bacon.

Kaplan, A. (1964). *The conduct of inquiry: Methodology for behavioral science.* Scranton, PA: Chandler.

Mayer, R., & Goodchild, F. (1990). *The critical thinker.* Dubuque, IA: Brown.

Learning Ethics the Hard Way: Facing the Ethics Committee

W. Brad Johnson
Rioh´det Corser
George Fox University

Despite the relative lack of uniformity in the manner in which professors teach graduate courses in ethics (Matthews 1991), Kitchener (1986) noted that most instructors endorse several ethics training goals. These goals include sensitization to ethical issues, improvement in ethical judgments, encouragement of responsible ethical actions, and toleration of ambiguity in ethical decision making. Underlying these important goals is the capacity to engage the process itself at a higher level of moral reasoning (Fine & Ulrich, 1988; Kitchener, 1986). Such reasoning involves the accurate perception of real life ethical dilemmas as well as the capacity to understand their complexity and the consequences that may result from a specific course of action.

Whether developed for undergraduate majors (Lamb, 1991), graduate students in psychology (McGovern, 1988), or psychiatry residents (Sondheimer & Martucci, 1992), most ethics course instructors endorse the significance of case studies or vignettes in effective instruction. For instance, Vanek (1990) found that instructors of ethics courses in counseling and clinical psychology programs endorsed lecture, discussion, and case studies as their primary instructional strategies. Case studies appear to offer several advantages in teaching professional ethics to psychologists in training. McMinn (1988) described the following virtues of case studies:

1. They are inherently interesting and intensify the salience of the ethical principles.

2. They are practical in illustrating application of course material.
3. They offer realism in the form of situations and dilemmas likely to be encountered in practice.
4. They can serve to highlight the difficulty inherent in ethical decision making.

Although McMinn (1988) described an innovative computer simulation program for student interaction with ethical dilemmas, case studies more commonly serve as stimuli for class discussion or response papers and examination questions. This traditional approach to using case studies may not, however, promote intrapersonal internalization of ethical concepts.

Beyond mere familiarity with the "Ethical Principles of Psychologists and Code of Conduct'' (American Psychological Association [APA], 1992), scrutiny of specific cases requires analysis of actual problems, formulation of various positions, and evaluation of alternatives (Ables 1980, Sondheimer & Martucci, 1992). To avoid the potential counterproductivity associated with rapid presentation of cases and the unintended implication that solutions to ethical dilemmas are simple (McMinn, 1988), Kitchener (1986) found that case studies are most effective in extended formats that allow enhanced appreciation of their complexity. Further, exposure to relatively complex case material may increase student appreciation of the range of ethically justifiable courses of action (Eberlein, 1987; Fine & Ulrich, 1988). Effective case studies should additionally highlight the fact that ethics codes provide only minimal standards of conduct and that these standards may at times conflict with other professional and legal requirements Johnson, 1995; Rosenbaum, 1982).

In this article, we describe an approach we developed to accentuate for students the complexity of certain ethical dilemmas that face psychologists. Capitalizing on the motivational effects of social scrutiny (Rosnow,1990), this approach encourages more involved, extended, and group-facilitated processing of the cases presented. Our approach, the mock committee exercise, is relatively simple to implement, inherently popular with students, and offers several advantages over traditional discussion-only approaches to using case studies in ethics instruction. Although designed for use in applied (clinical, counseling, school, etc.) graduate ethics courses, the technique may be equally helpful in undergraduate courses. We briefly outline the technique, describe student evaluation data, and conclude with a discussion of the potential utility of the mock committee technique.

Description of the Mock Committee Technique

During the initial third of our course, students receive relatively rapid and intensive instruction in the "Ethical Principles of Psychologists and Code of Conduct" (APA, 1992), state laws and regulations relevant to psychology, and both APA and state ethics committee rules and regulations. Students also learn various models of ethical reasoning and decision making, and they review and discuss numerous writ ten case studies. During the remainder of the course, students review different content areas within the ethics code (APA 1992) . During the first hour of class each week (the class meets once weekly for 2 hr), lecture and discussion serve to intro duce and consider ethical dilemmas such as dual relationships confidentiality, and structuring treatment relationships. During the second hour of each class the mock committee exercise occurs.

Early in the course, students randomly form into several small (3–4 member) State Ethics Board committees. During the 10 min class break each week, a different committee convenes at the front of the room to occupy the committee table. The instructor distributes copies of a formal ethics complaint to each member of the committee. Complaint content generally relates to material covered in the first-hour lecture. While the committee reviews the complaint and selects a chair, a student randomly selected from the class is chosen to serve as the accused psychologist and is excused to the hallway. Most students serve as the accused at least once during the term. Class size ranges from 15 to 17. The accused utilizes both a copy of the complaint and a more detailed instruction sheet summarizing the hypothetical psychologist" motives, reasoning, and the conditions leading to the com plaint. Accused psychologists act the part and attempt tc portray realistically the accused to the ethics committee Although neither committee members nor accused psychologists receive grades for their performances, participation is a course requirement. We developed several committee com plaint vignettes (see Notes) that typically are brief yet complicated, and that cover a range of ethical issues including confidentiality, informed consent, multiple relationships, professional impairment, and boundaries of competence. The following is one example:

Complaint:

The ethics committee has received a formal complaint from the widow of a 72-year-old man named Alan Angst. Mr. Angst was seen in individual psychotherapy for 2 years by Mary Ann Jenkins, PsyD [doctorate in psychology degree]. Mrs. Angst contends in her complaint that Dr. Jenkins failed to prevent Mr. Angst from killing himself.

Following the 2 years of intensive psychotherapy to address chronic depression and adjustment to onset of rather progressive multiple sclerosis, Mr. Angst had voluntarily terminated treatment. He had never been acutely suicidal and had easily contracted, while in treatment, not to harm himself. You have reviewed the treatment records and they are very thorough and frequent risk assessments are well documented. Three months following formal termination, Mr. Angst had begun talking with Dr. Jenkins after church (they reside in a very small community-only three churches). He had additionally gone to her home on three occasions for "coffee and discussion" between friends. Dr. Jenkins had been careful to consistently remind Mr. Angst that she could not informally engage him in therapy and that she would recommend that he reenter treatment with her or another psychotherapist (she offered several recommendations).

Five months following termination of treatment, Mr.Angst killed himself with an overdose. In his suicide note, he offered thanks to Dr. Jenkins for understanding his inability to go on and for accepting his decision. Mrs. Angst (and her attorney) claim that Dr. Jenkins was indeed continuing in the role of a psychologist and that she failed to take action to prevent the suicide of Mr. Angst.

When the second hour of class begins, the committee has briefly reviewed the complaint, and the committee chair officially convenes an ethics hearing. The chair offers a synopsis of the complaint to the class and all class members must remain silent as they observe the hearing. As an alternative, all students may receive copies of the complaint. The committee takes some time to discuss the complaint among themselves (all discussions must be at a level that is audible to observing class members) including relevant ethical and legal concerns and specific questions that should be addressed to the accused. The committee calls the accused in from the hallway and he or she sits across the table from the committee and the formal interview portion of the hearing commences. When the committee determines they have collected adequate information from the accused required for case determination (or as time constraints allow), the chair excuses the accused to the hallway. Again, the committee, led by the chair, interacts and discusses all available information and attempts to reach consensus regarding the most salient ethical concerns. The committee must also determine whether an ethical violation occurred, and if so, rate the severity of the violation. The committee then determines the most appropriate disposition of the case (dismissal, reprimand, restriction or revocation of license, or civil penalty) and specifies appropriate directives for remediation (requirements for supervision, education, probation, or psychological evaluation). Finally, the committee recalls the accused psychologist from the hallway and formally renders a decision and rationale. For the remainder of the class session, all class members interact with the committee members and the accused regarding their experience of the exercise, divergent perspectives concerning the most appropriate resolution of the case, and lingering questions about various issues.

Student Rating Data

Thirty-four clinical psychology graduate students (two consecutive classes) evaluated four components of an ethics course in which we employed the mock committee technique. During the routine course evaluation process, students anonymously completed a separate rating of each class component with respect to its contribution to their learning of the course material. We used a 5-point Likert scale ranging from 1 (*not at all helpful*) to 5 (*very helpful*). Mean ratings for each of the four components were as follows: textbook reading = 3.78 (*SD* = .79), journal article reading = 4.08 (*SD* = .81), class lecture and discussion = 4.79 (*SD* = .48), mock committee experiences = 4.70 (*SD* =.57). Although we did not ask students to compare the various components, it appears they viewed each as contributing more than neutrally to learning of course material and that the mock committees and lecture-discussions were consistently the most salient learning experiences. The same rating form requested narrative evaluation of the various course components. These qualitative responses indicated the mock committee exercise was particularly helpful as a technique for integration and application of course material. These responses were representative: "Helped me to see that things are not as cut and dried as I might have thought," "Nice bridge between the letter of the law and the gray areas and nonethical issues that color a situation," "The committee forced me into the emotional as well as the moral and intellectual struggle to define what was ethical."

Discussion

We believe the mock committee exercise offers several clear advantages in teaching ethics to students of psychology. First, the motivational role of social scrutiny (Rosnow, 1990) appears important. Students are not sure when they may be called to serve on the class committee or be "accused" of a violation. This uncertainty serves to heighten student attention to and interest in both the exercise and related course material. We have noted appropriate anxiety in role-players and vicarious anxiety in class observers as they struggle to perform these professional tasks and project themselves into the hypothetical vignette. Second, this experience offers the benefit of peer-modeling of professional behavior. We have been pleasantly surprised at the seriousness and professionalism with which student committee members approach the task. Third, serving, albeit hypothetically, in the role of an ethics committee member heightens appreciation of and sensitivity toward the role of ethics bodies in psychology and the wide range of ethical dilemmas that confront these groups. Fourth, such extended and careful attention to a single (though complicated) case study serves to enhance integration and application of ethical principles, relevant legal requirements, decision making models, and principles of ethical reasoning (Kitchener, 1986). We found this integration particularly evident among class observers who, when invited to join the discussion following the hearing, often ask well-formulated questions that highlight substantial integration of the course material. Finally, the mock committee exercise may serve as a potent form of inoculation against subsequent unethical behavior. Personal interaction with specific case material and observation of the gravity present during the mock hearings may well promote extrapolation to one's own circumstances and, we hope, eventual practice.

References

Ables, N. (1980). Teaching ethical principles by means of value confrontations. *Psychotherapy: Theory, Research and Practice, 17,* 384-391.

American Psychological Association. (1992). Ethical principles of psychologists and code of conduct. *American Psychologist, 47,* 1597-1611.

Eberlein, L. (1987). Introducing ethics to beginning psychologists: A problem-solving approach. *Professional Psychology: Research and Practice, 18,* 353-359.

Fine, M. A., & Ulrich, L. P. (1988). Integrating psychology and philosophy in teaching a graduate course in ethics. *Professional Psychology: Research and Practice, 19,* 542-546.

Johnson, W. B. (1995). Perennial ethical quandaries in military psychology: Toward American Psychological Association-Department of Defense collaboration. *Professional Psychology: Research and Practice, 26,* 281-287.

Kitchener, K. S. (1986). Teaching applied ethics in counselor education: An integration of psychological processes and philosophical analysis. *Journal of Counseling and Development, 64,* 306-310.

Lamb, C. S. (1991). Teaching professional ethics to undergraduate counseling students. *Psychological Reports, 69,* 1215-1223.

Matthews, J. R. (1991). The teaching of ethics and the ethics of teaching. *Teaching of Psychology, 18,* 80-85.

McGovern, T. V. (1988). Teaching the ethical principles of psychology. *Teaching of Psychology, 15,* 22-26.

McMinn, M. R. (1988). Ethics case study simulation: A generic tool for psychology teachers. *Teaching of Psychology, 15,* 100-101.

Rosenbaum, M. (1982). Preface. In M. Rosenbaum (Ed.), *Ethics and values in psychotherapy* (pp. ix-xi) . New York: Free Press.

Rosnow, R. L. (1990). Teaching research ethics through role-play and discussion. *Teaching of Psychology, 17,* 179-181.

Sondheimer, A., & Martucci, L. C. (1992). An approach to teaching ethics in child and adolescent psychiatry. *Journal of the American Academy of Child and Adolescent Psychiatry, 31,* 415-422.

Vanek, C. A. (1990). Survey of ethics education in clinical and counseling psychology. *Dissertation Abstracts International, 51*(12), 5797B. (University Microfilms No. 91-14, 449)

Notes

1. Presented at the annual meeting of the American Psychological Association, August 1996, Toronto, Canada.
2. Requests forcopies of the mock committee vignettes should be sent to W. Brad Johnson, Department of Psychology, George Fox University, 414 North Meridian Street, Newberg, OR 97132-2697; e-mail: bjohnson@georgefox.edu.

Discussing Animal Rights and Animal Research in the Classroom

Harold A. Herzog
Western Carolina University

Since Singer's influential book *Animal Liberation* was published in 1975, public concern over the ethical treatment of animals has increased dramatically. Animal rights groups have criticized a variety of human uses of animals, including sport hunting, rodeos, intensive agricultural practices, consumption of animal flesh, and the wearing of furs. The use of animals in behavioral and biomedical research, however, has become the primary focus of public attention in recent years. Experimental psychology has been singled out as particularly offensive by animal rights activists who consider much behavioral research frivolous and cruel. For example, Rollin (1981) called experimental psychology, "the field most consistently guilty of mindless activity that results in great suffering" (p. 124).

Although psychologists have responded to such criticisms (e.g., Feeney, 1987; N. E. Miller, 1985), the animal rights movement has had a significant effect on animal research. In addition, teachers of psychology courses are being confronted with students who question the ethics and validity of behavioral research using animals (Gallup & Beckstead, 1988). There are three reasons why discussion of animal rights is relevant to students taking psychology courses. First, students should be aware of political and social issues related to psychology that affect their lives. In this context, the animal rights controversy joins other social issues, such as the effects of day care, television violence, and pornography, as topics relevant to psychology courses. Second, the animal rights issue raises questions that are basic to psychological inquiry: What are the essential differences between humans and other animals? Can animals think? What psychological factors influence judgments about what constitutes moral behavior? Finally, the use of animals in laboratory courses has come under special criticism (e.g., Regan, 1983). Many animal liberationists believe that the routine dissection of animals in biology laboratories and the equivalent use of animals in psychology courses (e.g., physiological psychology students learning stereotaxic surgery on rats) are particularly onerous practices.

Although the animal rights movement affects research and teaching, few psychologists are informed about its intellectual underpinnings. Animal activists are often dismissed as intellectual lightweights whose arguments are based on emotional responses to pictures of kittens with electrodes in their skulls. Although this stereotype is accurate in some cases, there are also some first-rate philosophers behind the movement whose arguments are quite rigorous. This article briefly reviews two major philosophical positions used by animal activists in their arguments against the scientific use of animals and then describes a classroom exercise that stimulates discussion about this debate.

Philosophical Positions

The animal defense movement is divided into two groups. *Reformers* admit the necessity of using animals in biomedical research but want to eliminate as much suffering as possible. The more radical faction, *animal liberators*, view animal research as immoral in almost all cases and want to abolish it. It is not the purpose of this article to review all of the philosophical positions on animal rights. Interested readers should consult sources such as H. B. Miller and Williams (1983) for representative statements. Rather, I briefly summarize two of the most influential perspectives used by animal rights activists in their argument against using animals in research.

The Utilitarian Argument

The utilitarian argument is most clearly presented by the Australian philosopher, Peter Singer. In *Animal Liberation*, Singer (1975) effectively invoked emotional appeal and a consistent ethical philosophy to argue the case for abolishing animal research. The *principle of equality* (or *equal consideration of interests*) is the crux of Singer's argument. It holds that all sentient creatures (he draws the "line" at the phylogenetic level of oysters) have the same stake in their own existence ("interests"). Singer argued that this principle leads to the conclusion that there is no basis for elevating the interests of one species, *Homo sapiens*, above any other. Differences in intelligence, race, and gender are not valid criteria to exploit other humans; to Singer, a creature's species is equally irrelevant. He claimed that "From an ethical point of view, we all stand on an equal footing-whether we stand on two feet, or four, or none at all" (Singer, 1985, p. 6). The only relevant moral criterion for discrimination for or against a species is the capacity to suffer. Singer argued that, by definition, all sentient animals have the capacity to suffer and, therefore, are the subject of equal moral consideration. He claimed that to elevate the human species above all others on the basis of criteria other than suffering is arbitrary and a form of *speciesism*. Singer defined this term as "a prejudice or attitude of bias toward the interest of members of one's own species and against those of members of another species" (p. 7). He believed that speciesism is as illogical and morally repugnant as racism or sexism. Note that Singer would permit research with animals in some circumstances, but only if it is so important that we would also consider conducting the experiments using human subjects.

The Rights Argument

The rights argument is forcefully argued by Regan (1983, 1985) and Rollin (1981). Rights positions typically take the form that at least some creatures have certain fundamental rights (e.g., the right to moral consideration and the right not to be harmed). The question then becomes, Who is entitled to hold rights? Many philosophers restrict rights holders to beings that meet certain criteria, such as language, self-consciousness, or the ability to enter into reciprocal contractual obligations that they believe would eliminate nonhuman animals. There are several problems, however, that confront such philosophical positions. One problem concerns the moral status of humans who do not meet the criteria (i.e., the severely retarded, infants, and the insane). A second problem is how to deal with animals that appear to meet some of the criteria (e.g., members of large-brained species such as some primates, cetaceans, etc.)?

Animal rights theorists broaden the criteria so that animals are included as rights holders. To Regan (1983, 1985), the fundamental criterion for having rights is "inherent value." He argued that sentient creatures, including humans, have inherent value in equal measure and thus are entitled to certain fundamental rights, including the right to be treated with respect and the right not to be harmed. For Regan, there are a number of reasons for abolishing research with animals, even research that will directly benefit humans. First and foremost, science treats animals as renewable resources rather than as "subjects of a life"—creatures with inherent value—thus violating what he called the "respect principle." In addition, he argued for the "worst off principle"—that the rights view does not permit the sacrifice of an innocent few even though such sacrifice may benefit many more individuals. For Regan, there is no justification for any animal research; the fact that the experiments could benefit hundreds of thousands of human lives is morally irrelevant.

Comparisons and Comments

There are clear differences between advocates of the utilitarian and rights positions as to why animal research is immoral. Singer suggested that there are philosophical problems with arguments based on the proposition that animals have rights, and Regan insisted that the utilitarian position is fatally flawed. There are, however, commonalties in the two positions. The most important is that Regan and Singer ended at about the same place, even though they took quite different paths. The logical extension of both arguments leads to vegetarianism, and both would eliminate research with animals as it is now conducted. In addition, the two positions are based on the notion that fundamental similarities between humans and other species are ethically significant (i.e., all sentient creatures have "interests") but that differences between humans and other species (i.e., language and greater intelligence) are morally irrelevant. Finally, both positions view speciesism as deplorable and the animal liberation movement as the logical extension of other social movements, such as civil rights and women's movements .

It is not my purpose to critique these views. The interested reader will want to consult sources such as Fox (1985), Frey (1980, 1983), and Narveson (1983) for critiques of the animal liberation philosophers. It is safe to say that most Americans would disagree with one of the basic tenets of activists, that human life per se is not more important than that of other species. If it were possible to transplant an organ from a healthy sheep into a dying infant, most of us would readily approve of the operation; Singer and Regan would not.

Though one may disagree with their thinking, philosophers, such as Regan and Singer, have raised some troubling issues that can be addressed in psychology courses. The following exercise was designed to facilitate discussion of the ethics of animal research in the classroom.

Discussing the Animal Research Controversy

The exercise described here is designed to facilitate thinking on these issues by having students make decisions about whether a series of hypothetical research and educational projects should be conducted. It is appropriate in a wide variety of courses, including general psychology, experimental psychology, animal behavior, and physiological psychology. It would also be useful in biology and bioethics courses.

Method

Institutions receiving federal funds for scientific research must have a standing Animal Care and Use Committee (ACUC) to review and approve all animal research conducted at the institution. In the exercise, students role-play participation on an ACUC. I divide the class into groups of between five and seven students. If class time permits, each group must make a decision on each of four research proposals. Otherwise, each group can discuss and make a decision about one of the proposals and present their decision and rationale to the class. The proposals are based on actual experiments or situations, and they are designed to exemplify different factors related to making ethical decisions. I remind students that the purpose of the exercise is to generate discussion and critical thinking. Thus, groups should be encouraged to reach a consensus rather than simply take a straw poll on each proposal.

Instructions to Students

Your group is the Animal Care Committee for your university. It is the committee's responsibility to evaluate and either approve or reject research proposals submitted by faculty members who want to use animals for research or instructional purposes in psychology, biology, or medicine. The proposals describe the experiments, including the goals and potential benefits of the research as well as any discomfort or injury that they may cause the animal subjects. You must either approve the research or deny permission for the experiments. It is not your job to suggest improvements on technical aspects of the projects, such as the experimental design. You should make your decision based on the information given in the proposal.

Proposals

Case 1. Professor King is a psychobiologist working on the frontiers of a new and exciting research area of neuroscience, brain grafting. Research has shown that neural tissue can be removed from the brains of monkey fetuses and implanted into the brains of monkeys that have suffered brain damage. The neurons seem to make the proper connections and are sometimes effective in improving performance in brain-damaged animals. These experiments offer important animal models for human degenerative diseases such as Parkinson's and Alzheimer's. Dr. King wants to transplant tissue from fetal monkey brains into the entorhinal cortex of adult monkeys; this is the area of the human brain that is involved with Alzheimer's disease.

The experiment will use 20 adult rhesus monkeys. First, the monkeys will be subjected to ablation surgery in the entorhinal cortex. This procedure will involve anesthetizing the animals, opening their skulls, and making lesions using a surgical instrument. After they recover, the monkeys will be tested on a learning task to make sure their memory is impaired. Three months later, half of the animals will be given transplant surgery. Tissue taken from the cortex of monkey fetuses will be implanted into the area of the brain damage. Control animals will be subjected to sham surgery, and all animals will be allowed to recover for 2 months. They will then learn a task to test the hypothesis that the animals having brain grafts will show better memory than the control group.

Dr. King argues that this research is in the exploratory stages and can only be done using animals. She further states that by the year 2000 about 2 million Americans will have Alzheimer's disease and that her research could lead to a treatment for the devastating memory loss that Alzheimer's victims suffer.

Case 2. Dr. Fine is a developmental psychobiologist. His research concerns the genetic control of complex behaviors. One of the major debates in his field concerns how behavior develops when an animal has no opportunity to learn a response. He hypothesizes that the complex grooming sequence of mice might be a behavior pattern that b built into the brain at birth, even though it is not expressed until weeks later. To investigate whether the motor patterns involved in grooming are acquired or innate, he wants to raise animals with no opportunity to learn the response. Rearing animals in social isolation is insufficient because the mice could teach themselves the response. Certain random movements could accidentally result in the removal of debris. These would then be repeated and could be coordinated into the complex sequence that would appear to be instinctive but would actually be learned. To show that the behaviors are truly innate, he needs to demonstrate that animals raised with no opportunity to perform any grooming-like movements make the proper movements when they are old enough to exhibit the behavior.

Dr. Fine proposes to conduct the experiment on 10 newborn mice. As soon at the animals are born, they will be anesthetized and their front limbs amputated. This procedure will ensure that they will not be reinforced for making random grooming movements that remove debris from their bodies. The mice will then be returned to their mothers. The animals will be observed on a regular schedule using standard observation techniques. Limb movements will be filmed and analyzed. If grooming is a learned behavior, then the mice should not make grooming movements with their stumps as the movements will not remove dirt. If, however, grooming movements are innately organized in the brain, then the animals should eventually show grooming-like movement with the stumps.

In his proposal, Dr. Fine notes that experimental results cannot be directly applied to human behavior. He argues, however, that the experiment will shed light on an important theoretical debate in the field of developmental psychobiology. He also stresses that the amputations are painless and the animals will be well treated after the operation.

Case 3. Your university includes a college of veterinary medicine. In the past, the veterinary students have practiced surgical techniques on dogs procured from a local animal shelter. However, there have been some objections to this practice, and the veterinary school wants the approval of your committee to continue this practice. They make the following points.

1. Almost all of these animals will eventually be killed at the animal shelter. It is wasteful of life to breed animals for the vet school when there is an ample supply of animals that are going to be killed anyway, either because their owners do not want them or they are homeless.
2. It costs at least 10 times as much to raise purebred animals for research purposes; this money could be better used to fund research that would benefit many animals.
3. Research with dogs from animal shelters and the practice surgeries will, in the long run, aid the lives of animals by training veterinarians and producing treatments for diseases that afflict animals.

A local group of animal welfare activists has urged your committee to deny the veterinary school's request. They argue that the majority of these animals are lost or stolen pets, and it is tragic to think that the dog you have grown to love will wind up on a surgical table or in an experiment. Furthermore, they claim that as people become aware that animals taken to shelters may end up in research laboratories, they will stop using the shelters. Finally, the activists point out that in countries such as England, veterinary students do not perform practice surgery; they learn surgical techniques in an extensive apprenticeship.

Case 4. The Psychology Department is requesting permission from your committee to use 10 rats per semester for demonstration experiments in a physiological psychology course. The students will work in groups of three; each group will be given a rat. The students will first perform surgery on the rats. Each animal will be anethestized. Following standard surgical procedures, an incision will be made in the scalp and two holes drilled in the animal's skull. Electrodes will be lowered into the brain to create lesions on each side. The animals will then be allowed to recover. Several weeks later, the effects of destroying this part of the animal's brain will be tested in a shuttle avoidance task in which the animals will learn when to cross over an electrified grid.

The instructor acknowledges that the procedure is a common demonstration and that no new scientific information will be gained from the experiment. He argues, however, that students taking a course in physiological psychology must have the opportunity to engage in small animal surgery and to see firsthand the effects of brain lesions.

Notes to the Instructor

Case 1 forces consideration of whether injury to another species, which is fairly closely related to humans, is justified if the results will be applicable to human beings. Case 2 asks students to think about the use of animals in pure research in which there is no direct connection to future human application. Based on a study of Fentress (1973), this case offers an excellent opportunity for the instructor to discuss the importance of pure research in the progress of science. Incidentally, in the Fentress experiment, amputated mice exhibited "remarkably normal" grooming movements with their stumps, demonstrating that the movements were innate. Case 3 involves the use of pound animals in research and is one of the more controversial issues in biomedical and veterinary research. Several state legislatures have passed laws banning the use of pound-seizure animals for biomedical research or student surgeries in veterinary schools. (See Giannelli, 1988, for a discussion of this issue from an activist viewpoint.) The use of animals in student laboratories (Case 4) has been singled out by animal welfare groups as being particularly unnecessary. They argue that videotapes and computer simulations are adequate substitutes for live animals in classroom behavioral studies and dissections.

Numerous modifications can be made with these scenarios to tailor them to the needs of particular topics or courses. For example, Case 1 could be changed so that some groups are given the case using monkeys as subjects and some are given the same case using rats. This would lead to a discussion of factors that come into play in making ethical decisions (e.g., why might it be acceptable to use rodents in the study but not primates?). Other cases could be added for different courses. Thus, a proposal in which an ethologist wants to confront mice with snakes to study antipredator behavior (Herzog, 1988) could be included for a course in animal behavior.

Student Responses

I have used this exercise with 150 students in five classes. After the exercise, each student was asked to write an anonymous evaluation of the exercise and indicate whether it should be used in the future. The responses were extremely positive; except for two of the students, the remainder recommended that I continue using the exercise. The following statements were typical: "I feel that this was a valuable experience as part of my psychology class, and it was beneficial in developing my thoughts on this topic. I had never really considered such issues," and "I believe this exercise was valuable to the students in the class because it made us think about which is more important—an animal's life or a human life."

Discussion

The Christian writer C. S. Lewis (1988) stated, "It is the rarest thing in the world to hear a rational discussion of vivisection" (p. 160). These exercises are designed to elevate discussion of one of the most controversial topics in science to a rational forum. However, attitudes about the appropriate use of animals in research are not only a function of logic. Judgments about animals are influenced by many factors, such as their physiognomic similarity to humans, their "cuteness" and perceived intelligence, and the labels we assign them (Burghardt & Herzog, 1980; Herzog, 1988). In addition to raising sensitivity about an important ethical issue, these exercises promote discussions of how moral judgments are made.

The animal rights movement will continue to grow in numbers and visibility. The goal of many animal rights activists is the abolition of animal research. As Regan (1988) proclaimed, "It is not bigger cages we want, but empty cages. Anything less than total victory will not satisfy us!" (p. 12). Psychologists must be prepared to confront this challenge in their roles as scientists and teachers. Inevitably, there will be disagreements within the profession. Some will side with the animal rights faction and become active in organizations like Psychologists for the Ethical Treatment of Animals; others will support the rights of researchers to use animal subjects. Increasingly, psychology teachers will be confronted by activist students who demand justification for research practices they find disagreeable. (I can also envision pressures on authors and publishers of introductory psychology textbooks to reduce or eliminate coverage of controversial experiments, such as Harlow's studies of social deprivation in monkeys and Seligman's learned helplessness research.) The issue of animal rights is philosophically and psychologically complex. It is mired in a milieu of rationality, emotion, convention, ethical intuition, and self-interest. We owe it to ourselves and our students to become familiar with both sides of this issue so that more light than heat will emerge from the debate.

References

Burghardt, G. M., & Herzog, H. A., Jr. (1980). Beyond con-specifics Is "Brer Rabbit" our brother? *BioScience*, *30*, 763-767.

Feeney, D. M. (1987). Human rights and animal welfare. *American Psychologist, 42,* 593-599.

Fentress, J. C. (1973). Development of grooming in mice with amputated forelimbs. *Science, 179,* 704-705.

Fox, M. A. (1985). *The case for animal experimentation.* Berkeley: University of California.

Frey, R. (1980). *Interests and rights: The case against animal rights.* Oxford, England: Clarendon.

Frey, R. (1983). On why we would do better to jettison moral rights. In H. B. Miller & W. H. Williams (Eds.), *Ethics and animals* (pp. 285-301). Clifton, NJ: Humana.

Gallup, G. G., Jr., & Beckstead, J. W. (1988). Attitudes toward animal research. *American Psychologist, 44,* 474-475.

Giannelli, M. A. (1988, Fall). Shelter animals as research models: Scientific anachronism, social ignominy. *PsyETA Bulletin,* pp. 6-12.

Herzog, H. A., Jr. (1988). The moral status of mice. *American Psychologist, 43,* 473-474.

Lewis, C. S. (1988). A case for abolition. In A. Linzey & T. Regan (Eds.), *Animals and Christianity: A book of readings* (pp. 160-164). New York: Crossroad. (Original work published 1947)

Miller, H. B., & Williams, W. H. (Eds.). (1983). *Ethics and animals.* Clifton, NJ: Humana.

Miller, N. E. (1985). The value of behavioral research on animals. *American Psychologist, 40,* 423-440.

Narveson, J. (1983). Animal rights revisited. In H. B. Miller & W. H. Williams (Eds.), *Ethics and animals* (pp. 45-59). Clifton, NJ: Humana.

Regan, T. (1983). *The case for animal rights.* Berkeley: University of California.

Regan, T. (1985). The case for animal rights. In P. Singer (Ed.), *In defense of animals* (pp. 13-26). Oxford, England: Basil Blackwell.

Regan, T. (1988, September/October). The torch of reason, the sword of justice. *The Animal's Voice Magazine,* pp. 12-17.

Rollin, B. E. (1981). *Animal rights and human morality.* New York: Prometheus .

Singer, P. (1975). *Animal liberation.* New York: Avon.

Singer, P. (1985). Prologue: Ethics and the new animal liberation movement. In P. Singer (Ed.), *In defense of animals* (pp. 1-10). Oxford, England: Basil Blackwell

Note

My thanks to Mary Jean Herzog, Sandra Skinner, Glen Erikson, Gordon Burghardt, and Lisa Finley for helpful comments on a draft of this article and my treatment of the animal rights movement and to my students at Western Carolina University and Warren Wilson College for discussing and evaluating the exercises.

4. TEACHING RESEARCH DESIGN AND METHODS OF OBSERVATION

A Computerized Stroop Experiment That Demonstrates the Interaction in a 2 × 3 Factorial Design

Mark W. Vernoy
Palomar College

This article describes a computerized Stroop experiment used to demonstrate the concept of interaction in a factorial experiment conducted by students in my research methods course. The course is a lower division, one-semester introduction to psychological research methods and experimental design with a required 3-hr laboratory. During the first 6 weeks of the laboratory, students run three predesigned experiments of increasing complexity. The first experiment is a simple bilevel design, the second is a multilevel design, and the third is a factorial design. The purpose of this last exercise is to give students some feel for the interaction when they are interpreting the results from a factorial experiment. I designed a computerized experiment that consistently produces an interaction that is interesting and fairly easy to explain. I briefly describe the experiment, the computer program that generates the stimuli, and the results gathered in six classes during the last 3 years.

In the original version of the Stroop (1935) task, subjects were shown words printed in colored ink and were instructed to name the color of ink as quickly as possible. The word on a given trial was the name of a color that was the same as the color of ink in which the word was printed (the congruent condition), the name of a color that was different from the color of ink in which the word was printed (the conflicting condition), or the name of something not related to the color of ink (the neutral condition). Subjects took longer to name the ink color in the conflicting condition (e.g., the word *blue* printed in red ink) than to name the ink color in the congruent condition (the word blue printed in *blue* ink). Interest in the Stroop effect has persisted, even though the original experiment was published many years ago.

Stroop-type effects can be demonstrated with colors, pictures, geometric shapes, and even with words in different languages. (See MacLeod, 1991, for an extensive review.) It is even possible to separate the elements (e.g., the color and the word) and still achieve the Stroop effect. For example, Dyer and Severance (1973) reported that color naming was delayed when a color bar was preceded by a 50-ms flash of a conflicting color name in black ink. In addition, Kahneman and Chajczyk (1983) showed that presenting a word above or below a color bar can affect the naming of the color of the bar. When they presented a congruent color word, the naming of the bar was facilitated, but when the color word was conflicting, the naming of the color bar was inhibited. Goolkasian (1981) demonstrated that the Stroop effect depends on the retinal location of the target. She found that foveal targets showed more facilitation or inhibition than peripheral targets.

In my experiment, students investigated the effect of the spatial placement of distractor words, either conflicting or congruent, on the reaction time for naming a color bar. I hypothesized that (a) reaction time will be longer when subjects are presented with a conflicting color word than with a congruent color word, and (b) reaction time will vary with the spatial placement of the color word—above, on, or below the color bar.

Method

The Experiment

Each semester, approximately 50 Introduction to Psychology students participated in a computerized version of the Stroop effect using a procedure similar to Kahneman and Chajczyk's (1983). The design of the experiment was a within-subjects 2 × 3 factorial. The first independent variable involved whether the color word and the color bar were congruent or conflicting. The second independent variable was placement of the color word—above, on, or below the color bar (see Figure 1).

Each subject was seated in front of an IBM-PC compatible computer (80286) with an EGA color monitor. The experimenter sat behind the monitor with the keyboard in front, facing the subject, so that the experimenter could not see the stimuli presented on the monitor. Using four colors, the computer presented the six different conditions in two blocks of 24 trials each. Each subject was instructed to say the color of the bar as quickly and as accurately as possible. As soon as the subject said each color, the experimenter hit the space bar on the keyboard. The computer measured the reaction time for each trial and computed and printed the mean reaction times for each of the six conditions.

RED

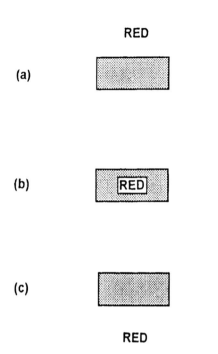

Figure 1. Examples of the three different types of spatial location used in the experiment: (a) The color word is above the color bar, (b) the color word is on the color bar, and (c) the color word is below the color bar.

The Computer Program

The computer program that runs the Stroop experiment is written in Microsoft®) Quick Basic 4.0 for the IBM PC and compatible computers. It requires a minimum of 640 K memory, a color EGA display card, and a color EGA monitor. Most EGA color monitors do a fairly good job of displaying the colors red, green, and blue, but finding a fourth color is sometimes a problem. This program has two different versions: one with yellow as the fourth color and another with brown as the fourth color. (The instructor can choose the version that looks best on a particular computer.) The computer controls the entire experiment; it presents the stimuli and measures and displays the reaction times.

The program begins by asking the name of the experimenter. After the experimenter types his or her name and hits Enter, the experiment begins. The program instructs the subject that the task is to say the color of the bar as quickly and as accurately as possible. Then the program begins to display the stimuli. Because this is a 2 × 3 experiment with four different colors, there are 24 possible combinations of the three attributes of the stimulus (Red, Blue, Green, or Yellow × Conflicting or Congruent × Above, On, or Below). These 24 combinations are displayed in a pseudorandom order in two separate blocks. The order is the same for all subjects and was predetermined using a Latin square. Before the experimental blocks, eight practice trials are presented so that both the subject and the experimenter can become familiar with the procedure.

Each trial begins with a + sign as a fixation point in the center of the screen. After a random time interval, between 1 and 3 s, the stimulus pair appears on the screen. The appearance of the stimulus pair starts a timer that stops when the experimenter hits the space bar on the computer keyboard. The computer records the appropriate reaction time and presents the next stimulus pair. After the two blocks of 24 stimulus trials, the computer calculates the means for each condition and presents the option of printing the results. If instructed to do so, the computer displays the results on the monitor and prints them. If the experimenter does not wish to print the results, the computer displays them on the monitor.

Results and Discussion

Reaction times were analyzed using a repeated measures two-way analysis of variance (ANOVA). The main effect of conflicting versus congruent was always significant (in 6 semesters, no F ratio was ever less than 8.00). The main effect of spatial location was significant in 4 of the 6 semesters. The interaction between the two independent variables was always significant (in 6 semesters, no F ratio was ever less than 6.00).

The interaction is the reason for the lack of significance among the various spatial locations. The graphs in Figure 2 indicate why the interaction hides the significance in spatial location. When one views only the line for the conflicting condition, it is clear that there is little difference between the reaction times in the above and below conditions, but the on condition has a much slower reaction time. The line for the congruent condition is a mirror image of the conflicting line. In the congruent condition, the above and below conditions are similar, whereas the reaction time in the on condition is much faster. Thus, the interaction hides the effect of the spatial location of the distractor word: The increase in reaction time for the conflicting on condition cancels the effect of the decrease in reaction time for the congruent on condition.

The graphs help students see that the placement of the word on the color bar enhances any effect of the word on the naming of the color of the bar. If the word on the color bar is congruent, it facilitates the naming of the color of the bar. If the word on the color bar is conflicting, it inhibits the processing of the color of the bar. Placement of the word above or below the bar does not have as strong

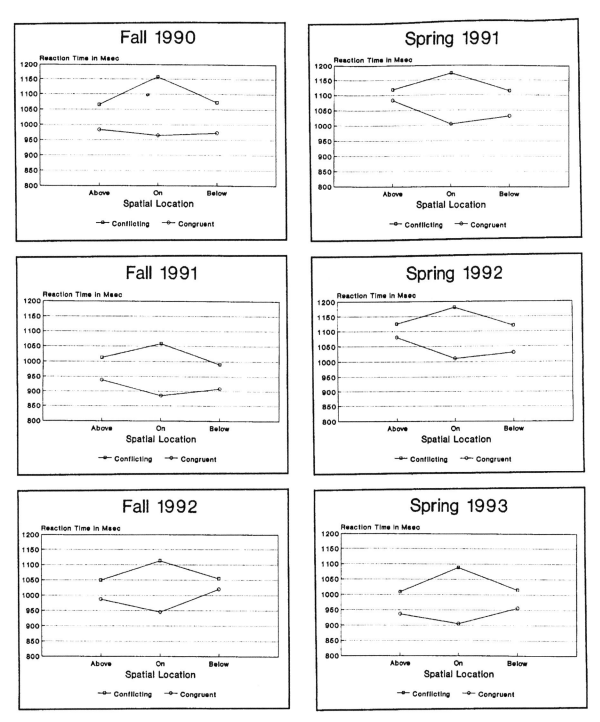

Figure 2. Results of the experiment showing the interaction for the six semesters, beginning with fall 1990 and ending with spring 1993.

an effect on the naming of the color of the bar. This interaction is extremely robust and has occurred every time my students have used this computer program to run the experiment, even with sample sizes less than 30.

One feature of the computer program can be seen as an advantage or a disadvantage. This feature involves the fact that the experimenter must hit the space bar to measure the subject's reaction time. This is a disadvantage because the reaction time of the experimenter is added to that of the subject (a voice-actuated timing system would be better), but it is also an advantage because no hardware beyond the computer is required. Also, because all trials for each subject are conducted by the same experimenter using a within-subjects design, the reaction time of the experimenter is not a confounding variable, assuming that it is constant over all trials. Because the experimenter stops the clock, the experimenter must remain attentive throughout the experiment. The only necessary control is that the experimenter sit with the keyboard in a position that allows the experimenter to see and hear the subject but prevents the experimenter from seeing the display screen. Inasmuch as the computer signals the beginning of the practice and the experimental blocks with a beep, there is no need for the experimenter to watch the screen. This procedure also gives the teacher a chance to discuss in class the realities of dealing with the constraints involved in doing psychological research.

Results of this experiment demonstrate a reliable interaction and support the results of the original Stroop (1935) experiment and those of more recent experiments, such as those performed by Goolkasian (1981), Dyer and Severance (1973), and Kahneman and Chajczyk (1983). Therefore, this experiment and computer program can be an effective teaching tool in a laboratory course in research methods or a cognitive psychology course.

References

Dyer, F. N., & Severance, L. J. (1973). Stroop interference with successive presentations of separate incongruent words and colors. *Journal of Experimental Psychology, 98*, 438-439.

Goolkasian, P. (1981). Retinal location and its effect on the processing of target and distractor information. *Journal of Experimental Psychology: Human Perception and Performance, 7*, 1247-1257.

Kahneman, D., & Chajczyk, D. (1983). Tests of the automaticity of reading: Dilution of Stroop effects by color-irrelevant stimuli. *Journal of Experimental Psychology: Human Perception and Performance, 9*, 497-509.

MacLeod, C. M. (1991). Half a century of research on the Stroop effect: An integrative review. *Psychological Bulletin, 109*, 163-203.

Stroop, J. R. (1935). Studies of interference in serial verbal reactions. *Journal of Experimental Psychology, 18*, 643-662.

Notes

1. I thank Bernard C. Beins and three anonymous reviewers for their comments on an earlier draft of this article.
2. Requests for copies of the computer program should be sent to Mark W. Vemoy, Behavioral Sciences Department, Palomar College, San Marcos, CA 92069. If requesting a copy of the computer program, please include a blank, formatted 5.25- or 3.5-in. diskette and a stamped, self-addressed mailer.

Factorial Design: Binocular and Monocular Depth Perception in Vertical and Horizontal Stimuli

Dominic J. Zerbolio, Jr.
James T. Walker
University of Missouri-St. Louis

Factorial designs represent one of our most useful and powerful research tools. Yet the major advantage of factorial designs over simpler designs (i.e., the ability to detect interactions between variables) is also what makes them difficult to teach, because interactions are not always intuitively obvious to students. Teaching students to understand the nature and interpretation of an interaction can be greatly facilitated by an exercise, as long as it reliably produces an interaction, and the results are readily and obviously interpretable. We have tried to manipulate many variables factorially during our collective 4 decades of teaching. None of these efforts was completely satisfactory until recently, when we discovered an exercise that meets these requirements. In addition, this exercise requires minimum equipment and makes a substantive point about a real-world perceptual problem.

The equipment required is some form of the Howard–Dolman depth perception apparatus (Howard, 1919a, 1919b; the Howard-Dolman depth perception apparatus was supplied by Lafayette Instrument Company, P.O. Box 5729, Sagamore Parkway, Lafayette, IN 47903) and masks or goggles to restrict viewing to one eye. The usual application of the Howard-Dolman apparatus requires the subject to adjust two vertical rods in the third dimension so that they appear equidistant from the observer. The dependent variable measure is the separation between the two rods, measured along the subject's line of sight. The average error is typically much smaller when rods are viewed binocularly than when viewed monocularly. If the apparatus is laid on its side, the rod orientation becomes horizontal (see Figure 1); in this orientation, Howard (1919b) found that the average errors for binocular and monocular viewing did not differ.

Orienting the apparatus horizontally or vertically allows a factorial combination of Rod Orientation and Viewing Condition. We expected and found little or no difference between monocular and binocular viewing conditions with the rods in the horizontal orientation, but a substantial superiority of binocular over monocular with the rods in the vertical orientation (i.e., a Viewing Condition × Rod Orientation interaction). The example we report used an independent-groups procedure, but the design lends itself just as well to a repeated-measures design, assuming the instructor wishes to grapple with the problems associated with teaching interactions and repeated measures simultaneously.

Method

Subjects

Thirty subjects participated as a class requirement in an undergraduate research methods course.

Apparatus

The apparatus (see Figure 1) was adjusted by means of a string looped around the back of a chair. Subjects were allowed to use only one hand in making adjustments in order to minimize kinesthetic cues.

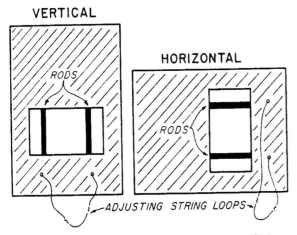

Figure 1. Subjects' views of Howard–Dolman apparatus. Rods are adjusted to appear equidistant in depth using loops of string. A pointer indicates the adjustment error on a scale hidden from the subject. Extraneous cues are reduced by diffused white backlighting.

Procedure

The experiment used a 2 × 2 independent-groups factorial design. The factors were Viewing Condition (binocular and monocular) and Rod Orientation (vertical and horizontal). Using a table of random numbers, we assigned each of 30 students to one of the four experimental conditions with the constraint that the number of subjects per cell was to be as nearly equal as possible. The dependent variable for each subject was the mean separation between the rods in 10 adjustment trials.

In two of the groups, the largest scores were so deviant that questions were raised regarding whether the subjects were following instructions in adjusting the apparatus or whether the student-experimenters were recording the data accurately. In the interest of reducing error variance, these two scores were discarded.

The apparatus was located approximately 5.5 m from the subject. At the beginning of each trial, the rods were positioned at their extreme departure from equidistance, 20 cm apart. The rod nearest to the subject (left or right in the vertical orientation and top or bottom in the horizontal orientation) was determined randomly using a Gellerman series. The student-experimenter blocked the subject's view of the apparatus with his or her body during the initial positioning of the rods before each trial. In monocular viewing, each subject used the dominant eye, as determined by a measure of sighting dominance.

Results and Discussions

The mean separations for all four groups appear in Figure 2. The main effect of Viewing Condition was significant, $F(1, 24) = 4.91$, $p < .05$. The effect of Rod Orientation approached significance, $F(1, 24) = 3.77$, $p < .10$, and there was a significant interaction between these factors, $F(1, 24) = 9.59$, $p < .01$. Because the main effects are not interpretable when an interaction is present, simple main effects for Viewing Conditions at each Rod Orientation were calculated. With the rods oriented vertically, binocular viewing was significantly superior to monocular viewing, $F(1, 24) = 14.11$, $p < .001$. With the rods oriented horizontally, no difference between binocular and monocular viewing was observed, $F < 1$. These results are clearly illustrated in Figure 2.

The results allowed us to demonstrate the problem of interpreting a main effect in the presence of an interaction and readily led our students to see the necessity of partitioning the data into simple main effects. Figure 2 was particularly helpful in this respect. In this context, the question of whether binocular or monocular vision is better clearly depends on the horizontal or vertical orientation of the target stimuli.

This exercise greatly facilitates the exposition of a factorial design, and it relates to some perceptual problems in the real world. Horizontally extended stimuli, such as wires are difficult to localize in depth because they provide little or no binocular disparity. Thus, line workers, tree trimmers, and construction workers moving equipment near power lines are at great risk, as accidents frequently occur in such situations. Airplane pilots flying near wires are also at risk, as Howard (1919b) pointed out long ago. Our exercise serves the dual purpose of explicating a factorial design and providing a substantive basis for understanding a real-world perceptual problem.

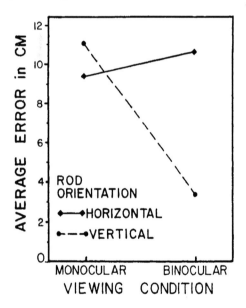

Figure 2. Results. Smallest mean (binocular viewing with vertically oriented rods) differs significantly from all other means, *p* < .01, which do not differ from each other.

References

Howard, H. J. (1919a). A six meter stereoscope. *American Journal of Ophthalmology, 2*, 849-853.

Howard, H. J. (1919b). A test for the judgment of distance. *American Journal of Ophthalmology, 2*, 656-675.

Return to Our Roots: Raising Radishes to Teach Experimental Design

William M. Stallings
Georgia State University

Alternative ways of teaching applied statistics have been described in journals such as the *American Statistician* (e.g., Hogg, 1972; Tanner, 1985), *Chance* (Joiner, 1988), *Teaching of Psychology* (Hettich, 1974), and the *Journal of the Royal Statistical Society Series A* (Jowett & Davies, 1960). This literature emphasizes the importance of having students work with real data. For example, Singer and Willett (1990) argued that "real data sets provide a more meaningful and effective vehicle for the teaching of applied statistics" than do synthetic data, no matter their numerical tractability (p. 223). Perhaps ideally, students should pursue their own research interests, collecting data from studies they design and conduct (see Jowett & Davies, 1960; Tanner, 1985).

Teachers of psychological and educational statistics are concerned that some students can complete the assigned computational exercises without understanding the purpose of the computations. For example, one of my students correctly computed a two-way analysis of variance (ANOVA) but could not distinguish between the number of levels in a factor and the number of independent variables. This incident illustrates the limitations of textbook exercises.

Although students could replicate classic experiments or design and complete simple studies of their own, both options are time-consuming. In addition, one now has to comply with institutional guidelines for research participants. Fortunately, many of these problems can be avoided. Students can work with real data by conducting simple agricultural experiments, what I call "returning to our roots." After all, as Lovie (1979) noted, "the first practical application of analysis of variance (ANOVA) was on the effects of manure on the rotation of potato crops (Fisher & Mackenzie, 1923)" (p. 151).

The last three times I taught our second course in statistics, an ANOVA-based course using Keppel (1991), I required each student to collect and analyze data from a gardening experiment. Students assess the effect of growth accelerators on radish seedlings that they grow at their homes.

Typically, students enrolled in the course are working toward advanced degrees or certification in education or nursing; they tend to be mature women who are employed.

Our students live off campus. Except for the nurses, they tend to have weak science and mathematics backgrounds.

Equipment

The inexpensive equipment consists of plastic ice cube trays or egg cartons, potting soil, fine gravel, mechanical drawing dividers (for measuring the heights of the seedlings), a ruler, radish seeds (or any other fast-germinating vegetable seeds), several jars with lids, and one or more growth accelerators (e.g., Miraclegro® or RA-PID GRO®.

Procedure

Instructions for the procedure and analysis are given in Table 1. Students decide whether to compare different growth accelerators (qualitatively different levels) or different amounts of the same growth accelerator (quantitatively different levels). Other issues that each student considers are experimental mortality, unequal sample sizes, unit of analysis, number of comparison groups, and choice of dependent variables. Most students use seedling height, but germination rate and length of tap root are possible also.

Students have reported that seeds germinate in 3 to 5 days. Most students obtain usable measurements at intervals of 5 to 7 days. I allow several days for students to obtain the equipment and set up the experiment. Two weeks has been a sufficient time for analysis and write-up. Hence, students can complete the project in 5 to 6 weeks.

As an illustration of a typical student project, one student grew three sets of 10 seedlings each with treatments of water and no accelerator, two drops of accelerator, or four drops of accelerator. After 4 weeks, the mean growths were 1.50, 2.74, and 2.96 in., respectively. A completely randomized ANOVA on these data yielded a significant difference, $F(2, 27) = 7.41$, $p < .01$. To obtain equal sample sizes, which is not a requirement of the completely randomized design but helpful in other analyses, students often have thinned seedlings immediately after germination.

Table 1. Instructions for Project: Procedure and Analysis

Procedure

1. Prepare three ice cube trays or egg cartons. To facilitate drainage, punch small holes in the bottom of each tray or carton. Then add gravel, and fill with potting soil.
2. In each mold or receptacle, plant three to four seeds about 1/4 in. deep. Soak seeds in water for 15 min before planting to promote germination.
3. Use the jars to mix and store the various concentrations or brands of growth accelerators.
4. Administer the treatment, either different types of growth accelerators or different concentrations of the same growth accelerator (e.g., no drops, one drop, and two drops).
5. Except for the application of the experimental treatment, treat all containers alike.
6. After germination (3 to 5 days), make three sets of measurements at equally spaced intervals (5 to 7 days).

Analysis

1. Write your report in a fashion similar to writing the Method, Results, and Discussion sections of a journal article.
2. Under Results, present the outcomes in words, graphs or tables, and statistics (both descriptive and inferential). For each data-gathering period, construct a graph showing the mean height of the seedlings plotted against levels of the independent variable.
3. For the final data-gathering period, compute a completely randomized ANOVA, omega squared, and (if you find statistical significance) Scheffé and other post hoc comparisons. If your experiment involved quantitatively different levels and if you obtained statistical significance, analyze the data for trends.
4. Optional analyses (beyond minimal expectations) could include computing a repeated measures design, making a priori comparisons, and estimating post hoc power.

Evaluation

Anecdotal evidence of students' positive reactions to the radish project comes from seven written comments appended to project reports and course evaluations. Examples include the following:

"The radish experiment . . . seemed to tie up many of the principles and techniques we learned in class."

"My classmates seemed unanimously enthusiastic about the project."

"The concept of experimental learning is an excellent one and very useful in helping students to grasp abstract concepts such as ANOVA. The requirements. . . were not too costly or time consuming."

To further evaluate this project, I conducted a content analysis of 31 student reports. I examined the various statistical and design features that students used or could have used, and I judged the appropriateness of their decisions. For example, a post hoc trend analysis following a nonsignificant omnibus F was an inappropriate application; a failure to follow up a significant omnibus F with a post hoc test was an inappropriate nonapplication. By contrast, not following up a nonsignificant omnibus F was an appropriate non-application. The content analysis is summarized in Table 2.

The data suggest that, overall, students made appropriate decisions. However, post hoc analyses of means and trends were troublesome. Graphing also appears to have been a problem. This may be attributed to students' weak science and mathematics backgrounds. Only seven students went beyond the minimal statistical requirements. Given Keppel's (1991) emphasis on planned comparisons, it is disturbing that only two students even attempted an a priori test. None considered low power due to small sample size as an explanation for not obtaining statistical significance. Four students reported problems with experimental control (e. g., "The cat walked on the trays"). Still, most met the minimal expectations.

Conclusion

Overall, I am satisfied with the results of the radish project, but I plan several changes. I will provide a more detailed handout of instructions (including suggested schedules); encourage and reward use of more complex designs, associated ancillary tests, and tests of model assumptions; and append a project evaluation to the anonymous course/instructor evaluation.

All of my students have completed this project in an 11week academic quarter. Nearly all informally agreed that the project made vivid the concepts of experimental design and ANOVA. During class discussion, some reported that the project was fun and even became a topic of family conversation. In my experience, raising radishes is a successful teaching technique.

Table 2. Frequency of Design and Statistical Treatment Decisions

Topic	Appropriate		Inappropriate	
	Application	Nonapplication	Application	Nonapplication
Design selection	29		2	
Post hoc comparisons	15	8	6	2
Effect size/omega squared	23			8
Trend analysis	12	11	3	5
Interpretation of significance	29		2	
Graphs	22		2	7

Note. Thirty-one student reports were analyzed. Each report is listed only once in each row but may appear more than once in each column.

References

Fisher, R. A., & Mackenzie, W. A. (1923). Studies in crop rotation. II: The manurial responses of different potato varieties. *Journal of Agricultural Science, 13,* 311-320.

Hettich, P. (1974). The student as data generator. *Teaching of Psychology, 1,* 35-36.

Hogg, R. V. (1972). On statistical education. *American Statistician, 39,* 168-175.

Joiner, B. L. (1988). Let's change how we teach statistics. *Chance, 1,* 53-54.

Jowett, G. H., & Davies, H. M. (1960). Practical experimentation as a teaching method in statistics. *Journal of the Royal Statistical Society Series A, 123,* 11-35.

Keppel, G. (1991). *Design and analysis: A researcher's handbook* (3rd ed.). Englewood Cliffs, NJ: Prentice Hall.

Lovie, A. D. (1979). The analysis of variance in experimental psychology: 1934-1945. *British Journal of Mathematical and Statistical Psychology, 32,* 151-178.

Singer, J. D., & Willett, J. B. (1990). Improving the teaching of applied statistics: Putting the data back into data analysis. *American Statistician, 44,* 223-230.

Tanner, M. A. (1985). The use of investigations in the introductory statistics course. *American Statistician, 39,* 306-310.

Note

I thank Ruth L. Ault and three anonymous reviewers for comments on earlier drafts of this article.

A Classroom Demonstration of Single Subject Research Designs

James E. Carr
University of Nevada
John Austin
Western Michigan University

When conducting experimental research, social scientists most often use group designs to assess behavior change (Kantowitz, Roediger, & Elmes, 1994). Likewise, psychology classes and textbooks in experimental design focus almost exclusively on group research. An alternative to the analysis of group data is the single-subject design (Baer, Wolf, & Risley, 1968; Krishef, 1991). A group design often requires many subjects to achieve adequate power and identify statistically significant differences between group means. Alternatively, a single-subject design can require only one subject and is often useful when large numbers of subjects sharing similar features are unavailable. Whereas group designs identify statistical differences between or within two or more groups of subjects, single-subject research exercises its power through examining changes in subjects' responding over time across experimental conditions. For instance, a reversal design demonstrates experimental control by repeatedly presenting and withdrawing a treatment (i.e., independent variable). When an effective treatment is repeatedly presented and withdrawn, responding should change accordingly. In this procedure, rather than using statistical tests of significance, the data are graphed and visually inspected for substantial change across conditions (e.g., from baseline to treatment).

Researchers have used single-subject designs to study various phenomena, including disruptive and learning behavior in school settings (e.g., Birnbrauer, Wolf, Kidder, & Tague, 1965), recycling and littering in community settings (e.g., Austin, Hatfield, Grindle, & Bailey, 1993), occupational safety (e.g., Austin, Kessler, Riccobono, & Bailey, 1996), work productivity and quality (e.g., Gowen & Jennings, 1990), clinical disorders (e.g., Carr & Bailey, 1996; Knox, Albano, & Barlow, 1996), and the habilitation and treatment of individuals with developmental disabilities (e.g., Vollmer, Marcus, & Ringdahl, 1995).

There are many variations of single-subject designs, including multiple baseline, multiple probe, withdrawal, changing criteria, multielement (or alternating treatments), and reversal designs (Cooper, Heron, & Heward, 1987; Iwata et al., 1989). Because the reversal design is the most widely used and often provides the most compelling and believable results, this demonstration focuses on the use of the reversal design to evaluate intrasubject changes.

Sometimes referred to as the baseline-treatment-reversal design (i.e., A-B-A or return to baseline), the reversal design demonstrates the functional control, or causal status, of the independent variable or variables by showing an obvious on-off relation between the independent and dependent variables. This relation is sometimes referred to as a "water-faucet" effect because presentation of the independent variable turns "on" the behavior (i.e., the dependent variable changes in the expected direction) and removal of the independent variable turns "off" the behavior (i.e., the dependent variable returns to approximately baseline level).

The purpose of this demonstration is to teach undergraduate psychology students about single-subject methodology by having them collect repeated measures of their own behavior during the three phases of a reversal design.

Method

Begin by presenting your class with adequate information, via lecture or otherwise, on the theory and applications of single-subject methodology (including the graphing of behavioral data). Once students understand the basic concepts (e.g., baseline and reversal) and techniques (e.g., line graphs) involved, the demonstration can begin. Instruct students that the demonstration will require them to engage in physical exercise for 15 separate 20-s periods. Any student who is unable to exercise or is uncomfortable about exercising should be allowed to use another student's data for the final analysis. Inform students that they will be using a reversal design to study the effects of physical exercise on their pulse rate. In addition, they will take repeated measures of their pulse rate to ensure that the difference between conditions is not artifactual. Provide them with a data sheet that has five spaces for data (five per condition).

Ensure that all students can adequately record their own pulse. The pulse can be obtained by placing the index and middle fingers of the left hand over the carotid artery in the neck (on the right side) or over the right side of the right wrist (palm up). After students practice taking their own pulse, you can provide them with the details of the demonstration.

The independent variable is 20 s of exercise (jumping jacks). The dependent variable is frequency of pulse beats during a 1-min interval. During the baseline condition, students should be cued to start recording their pulse. You should have a stopwatch to time the intervals. After 1 min

has passed, have students record the number of pulse beats for that interval on their data sheets. This number represents the first baseline data point. Have students repeat this recording process for another 4 min, yielding a total of five baseline data points.

During the treatment phase of the demonstration, instruct students to stand up and begin jumping jacks for 20 s. After the exercise period, have them sit down and record their pulse for 1 min. After 1 min, have them record the number of pulse beats on their data sheets. This number represents the first treatment data point. Instruct students to repeat this exercise-recording process four more times, yielding a total of five treatment data points. For the reversal condition, have students repeat the baseline procedure until they have obtained five data points.

Finally, instruct each student to make a line graph of all 15 data points, including vertical lines separating the three conditions. Graphing may be facilitated by providing a graph sheet with preprinted axes. After students graph the data, have them raise their hands if the exercise increased their pulse rate. Next, have students raise their hands if there was no change or if they experienced a decrease in heart rate. Most students should have experienced an increase in pulse rate as a result of the exercise. You can use this discussion time to share some of the finer points of single-subject methodology. For example, you may discuss how this independent-dependent variable relation could be tested with a multiple-baseline design using delayed exercise start times for some students. In addition, you can discuss how the aforementioned other single-subject designs can be used to study this relation and others. Another possible avenue of discussion is the utility of repeated measures in data analysis and their assistance in locating extraneous sources of variability and reducing the probability of making Type I errors.

Results

We conducted the demonstration with 14 students in an undergraduate psychology laboratory in research methodology. Students had previously heard a lecture on single-subject designs. All graphs showed substantial changes in pulse rate as a result of the exercise as well as a successful reversal. Figure 1 illustrates representative graphs from three students.

Student Opinions and Evaluations

We solicited student opinions about the utility of the demonstration immediately after completing it. There were no negative comments about the demonstration. Comments included the following: "I thought it worked rather well. It was hands on, and you could actually see the changes." "It was a great way to demonstrate the A-B-A design."

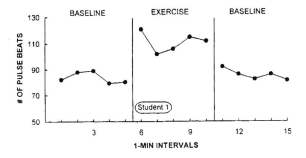

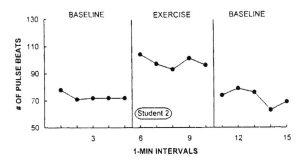

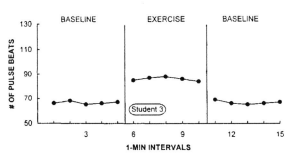

Figure 1. Representative line graphs of pulse-rate data from three students.

"Overall, I thought the lab was very informative." "I thought the lab was useful. It made the concept of single-subject design more clear, and made the class more interesting." "I think it was a good idea because it took something that we could easily manipulate and measure." "I think that the single-subject design involving exercise was a great idea in reflecting the reversal design. Results were quick, obvious, and understandable."

Discussion

Tell the class that the demonstration covered only the most rudimentary aspects of single-subject methodology. Another crucial point is that, although the demonstration conditions were changed after five trials, single-subject methodology is based on the foundation that conditions be changed only when data are stable and do not exhibit linear trends that may confound the interpretation of subsequent data. The demonstration could be improved by using a phase-change criterion to illustrate steady-state responding before experimental conditions are changed. Furthermore, the methodological rigor of this procedure could be enhanced through the use of interobserver

agreement measures for the dependent variable (see Carr, Taylor, & Austin, 1995).

This simple demonstration can be helpful in teaching students about single-subject designs because it provides opportunities to study their own behavior during different experimental conditions. The students collect, graph, and visually interpret their own data, which allows them to perform many of the practical behaviors necessary in using single subject designs. The demonstration can be completed in less than 30 min and should be a useful addition to instruction on experimental research methods.

References

Austin, J., Hatfield, D. B., Grindle, A. C., & Bailey, J. S. (1993). Increasing recycling in office environments: The effects of specific, informative cues. *Journal of Applied Behavior Analysis, 26,* 247-253.

Austin, J., Kessler, M. L., Riccobono, J. E., & Bailey, J. S. (1996). Improving roofing performance and safety using incentives and feedback. *Journal of Organizational Behavior Management, 16,* 49-75.

Baer, D. M., Wolf, M. M., & Risley T. R. (1968). Some current dimensions of applied behavior analysis. *Journal of Applied Behavior Analysis, 1,* 91-97.

Birnbrauer, J. S., Wolf, M. M., Kidder, J. D., & Tague, C. E. (1965). Modifying the classroom behavior of pupils with token reinforcement. *Journal of Experimental Child Psychology, 2,* 219-235.

Carr, J. E., & Bailey, J. S. (1996). A brief behavior therapy protocol for Tourette Syndrome. *Journal of Behavior Therapy and Experimental Psychiatry, 27,* 3340.

Carr, J. E., Taylor, S. L., & Austin, J. (1995). A classroom demonstration of self-monitoring, reactivity, and interobserver agreement. *The Behavior Analyst, 18,* 141-146.

Cooper, J. O., Heron, T. E., & Heward, W. L. (1987). *Applied behavior analysis.* Columbus, OH: Merrill.

Gowen, C. R., III, & Jennings, S. A. (1990). The effects of changes in participation and group size on gain sharing success: A case study. *Journal of Organizational Behavior Management, 11,* 147-169.

Iwata, B. A., Bailey, J. S., Fuqua, R. W., Neef, N. A., Page, T. J., & Reid, D. H. (Eds.). (1989). *Methodological and conceptual issues in applied behavior analysis.* Lawrence, KS: The Society for the Experimental Analysis of Behavior.

Kantowitz, B. H., Roediger, H. L., III, & Elmes, D. G. (1994). *Experimental psychology: Understanding psychological research* (5th ed.). St. Paul, MN: West.

Knox, L. S., Albano, A. M., & Barlow, D. H. (1996). Parental involvement in the treatment of childhood obsessive-compulsive disorder: A multiple-baseline examination incorporating parents. *Behavior Therapy, 27,* 93-114.

Krishef, C. H. (1991). *Fundamental approaches to single subject design and analysis*. Malabar, FL: Krieger.

Vollmer, T. R., Marcus, B. A., & Ringdahl, J. E. (1995). Noncontingent escape as treatment for self-injurious behavior maintained by negative reinforcement. *Journal of Applied Behavior Analysis, 28*, 15-26.

Note

We thank Charles L. Brewer and three anonymous reviewers for their extremely helpful comments on a draft of this article.

Naturalistic Observation of Behavior: A Model System Using Mice in a Colony

Harold A. Herzog, Jr.
Western Carolina University

Among the ethologists' contributions to psychology is the development of methods that allow quantitative analysis of naturally occurring behaviors. As a result, ethology has emerged from its descriptive, natural history phase to become a quantitative science. Even though naturalistic observation can be applied to a wide variety of research problems and requires little equipment, it is typically neglected in undergraduate research methods courses. The exercises described herein were developed to give students experience with naturalistic observation, using mice as subjects. The exercises also offer students an opportunity to work with animals in an ethically sensitive fashion at a time when many psychology departments are eliminating animal colonies because of pressures from animal welfare groups and government regulators.

Mice are ideal animals for these exercises, although other small mammals, such as gerbils, can be substituted. They are readily available from pet shops or from colleagues in biology departments. Mice come in a variety of colors and patterns, which makes for easy identification of individual animals. (If they are available only in white, a dab of hair dye can be used to mark individuals.) Because mice almost never bite and have an interesting repertoire of behaviors, even students who do not like working with larger animals, such as rats, enjoy observing them.

Preparation

Mouse colonies can be made from 10-gallon aquaria with cedar chips for bedding and wire mesh tops. The animals should have soft paper or other materials available for building nests. They can also be provided with objects to climb on or hide in. Between three and five mice should be placed in each aquarium. The use of mixed-sex groups leads to a greater variety of behavior patterns, but can also lead to population problems in 3 to 4 weeks.

Although the techniques are explained during class, students come into the laboratory on their own time to make observations. Observations are made by pairs of students who work as a team throughout the exercise. So that they can experience the widest possible range of behaviors, students are encouraged to observe the animals at several different times a day.

Techniques of Naturalistic Observation

Constructing an Ethogram

The students first spend 1 hr or so simply observing a group of mice. They are instructed to look for, and make notes on, patterns of behavior. This "field note stage" is sometimes referred to as *ad libitum sampling* and is particularly useful in the initial stages of naturalistic observation. A list of the behavior patterns is then constructed: This catalog is called an *ethogram* and forms the basis of a behavioral coding system. Each recurring behavior pattern is given a one- or two-word name, an abbreviation, and a brief description. The exercises are based on the category system, and it is important that students in each pair agree on the categories and have a clear understanding of what constitutes the specific behavior in each category. The ethograms are discussed in class, and I emphasize the importance of avoiding anthropomorphic interpretations of behavior and of specifying the difference between functional and descriptive categories.

Ideally, ethograms should be exhaustive and mutually exclusive; all behaviors a mouse normally exhibits should be included on the list, and the animal's observed behavior should fall into only one category. In reality, these goals can be obtained only by many hours of careful observation.

However, even the first short observation period typically generates an ethogram containing between 15 and 25 of the most common mouse behaviors. Students are encouraged to include a miscellaneous category for new behaviors that they will inevitably encounter.

Quantification of Streams of Behavior

Once each pair of students has developed a category system, they can use it to quantify streams of behavior in a number of ways. The advantages and disadvantages of various techniques are discussed in several sources (e.g., Altmann, 1974; Hutt & Hutt, 1974; Lehner, 1979, Martin & Bateson, 1986). The students typically practice two methods, instantaneous sampling and focal animal sampling.

Instantaneous sample. In instantaneous sampling, observations are made of ongoing behaviors at precise intervals. For example, samplings made every 15 sec for 15 min will yield 60 observations. The technique requires that students in each pair prepare checklists based on their ethogram categories. The checklist we use is a matrix with 60 observation periods numbered across the top (several pages may be needed) and the behavioral categories along the left side. Each pair also needs a timer to signal exactly when the observations are to be made. Although a mechanical timer that produces a tone at preset intervals can be used, a tape recorder is quite adequate. Simply make a tape with either an audible signal or the word observe at regular intervals (e.g., 15 sec).

It is important that the students in each pair make simultaneous, independent observations on the same animal, because their data will be used to calculate interrater reliabilities. During the observation period, students independently check the category best describing what that animal is doing when the signal occurs. Care must be exercised to ensure that the check is placed in the column representing the appropriate observation interval. At the end of the period, each student should have a single check in each of the 60 columns. They then count the number of times each behavior was scored. By dividing these numbers by 60, they can calculate the percentage of intervals in which each behavior was observed. This measure estimates the relative amount of time the animal spent performing the various behaviors during the observation period.

Students may then evaluate their observational skills by calculating interrater reliability as estimated by percent agreement. Interrater reliabilities of over 90% are normally interpreted as indicating an acceptable level of agreement, but in this exercise, they often vary widely. The reliabilities obtained depend on several factors, including the number of categories, how well they are defined and understood and the activity level of the animals when they are observed.

Focal animal sampling. Focal animal sampling involves recording all the ongoing behaviors of individual animals. Data can be used to make a variety of comparisons, such as behavioral differences between sex and age. This method can also be used to generate information amenable to the analysis of behavioral sequences. Students again work in pairs, with one student initially designated observer and the other recorder. Using the ethogram categories, the observer dictates the behavior patterns the animal performs sequentially. After 50 behaviors have been dictated, the observer and recorder change roles for another 50 behavior changes.

The list of 100 behaviors can now be analyzed in a number of ways. The simplest way is to count the relative frequencies of various behavior patterns. Data gathered using this method can also be used for sequence analysis in which the stream of behavior is divided into units consisting of an initial behavior and a following behavior. These units can be entered into a matrix, and transition probabilities can be calculated. After all pairs of behaviors have been entered in the matrix, it is easy to calculate the relative frequencies of the various behaviors. More important, the students also see that patterns emerge; some behaviors frequently follow each other, but others rarely do.

Take, for example, a chain of behaviors in which a mouse engages sequentially in the following behaviors: scratch-sniff-rear up-scratch. This chain contains three pairs of behaviors (scratch-sniff, sniff-rear up, rear up sniff). These two-behavior units are then entered into a transition matrix. The ethogram categories are listed across the top and along the left side of the matrix. The left-side categories are designated initial behaviors, and the categories across the top are subsequent behaviors. Tally marks for the pairs of behaviors are placed in the matrix as follows: The first pair of behaviors, scratch-sniff, is scored by placing a tally mark in the box that has scratch as the initial behavior and sniff as the subsequent behavior. Sniff now becomes the initial behavior for the next pair (sniff-rear up), which is entered in the matrix with sniff as the initial behavior and rear up as the subsequent behavior. Rear up now becomes the initial behavior for the unit rear up - scratch.

Discussion

These exercises provide students with opportunities to learn how naturally occurring behaviors can be subjected to quantitative analysis. I use them as required labs (graded on a satisfactory/unsatisfactory basis) in courses in experimental psychology and animal behavior. However, they are also appropriate for courses in social or developmental psychology. Course evaluations and informal discussions with students indicate that most of them find the exercises interesting and enlightening. Many students report being surprised at the patterns that emerge as they begin to quantify the animals' behavior.

These techniques can be applied to virtually any species that can be unobtrusively observed, including our own. Indeed, the instructor may want to include an investigation of humans as an exercise. For example, a coding system of the book-carrying behavior of college students can be quickly constructed, and students can be sent out on campus with a checklist of the categories to look for sex differences in book-carrying modes (Hanaway & Burghardt, 1976; Jenni & Jenni, 1976). Sex differences will inevitably be found, and a lively discussion of possible reasons for this result will likely ensue.

References

Altmann, J. (1974). Observational study of behavior Sampling methods. *Behavior, 49*, 227-265.

Hanaway, T. P., & Burghardt, G. M. (1976). The development of sexually dimorphic book-carrying behavior. *Bulletin of the Psvchonomic Society, 7*, 276-280.

Hutt, S. J., & Hutt, C. (1974). *Direct observation and measurement of behavior*. Springfield, IL: Charles C Thomas.

Jenni, D. A., & Jenni, M. A. (1976). Carrying behavior in humans Analysis of sex differences. *Science, 194*, 859-860.

Lehner, P. N. (1979). *Handbook of ethological methods*. New York: Garland STPM Press.

Martin, P., & Bateson, P. (1986). *Measuring behavior: An introductory guide*. Cambridge, England: Cambridge University Press.

Note

I thank Gordon Burghardt, Mary Sean Herzog, and Jerry Baumgartner for their comments on this article.

An Observational Emphasis in Undergraduate Psychology Laboratories

Dwight Krehbiel
Paul T. Lewis
Bethel College

Systematic observation is a versatile set of measurement methods that deserves greater emphasis in undergraduate research methods instruction. These methods can be used in both experimental and quasi-experimental designs. They are useful in many domains of psychology and are already widely used in, for example, child development (Kaye & Fogel, 1980), personality (Shweder, 1975), emotion (Ekman & Friesen, 1978), and social interactions (Duncan & Fiske, 1977).

The importance of observational methodology in psychology can be seen in the classic work of Barker (1963) as well as in more recent instructional innovations (Hoshmand, 1985; Zeren & Makosky, 1986). Hogan (1991) argued that these methods should be stressed more strongly in liberal arts undergraduate psychology programs because they help students succeed in a variety of occupations. That students may benefit from this approach is also suggested by Boice's (1983) review indicating that observational skills can be improved by training. The availability of a convenient introductory textbook of observational methods (Martin & Bateson, 1986) facilitates this emphasis in instruction.

The greatest advantage of observational methods is their usefulness in demonstrating important scientific principles and concepts. Observational methods provide students a means of validating self-reports, much as we compare people's actions with their words in everyday life. These methods also help students appreciate the dynamic nature of psychological events through repeated observations and consideration of the question of when to observe. Other approaches often do not examine behavioral changes because measurements are taken at only one time.

Observational methods allow clarification of operational definitions. Students understand in a concrete way how technology (e.g., camcorder, lighting, VCR, and film type) and use of technology (e. g., where and for how long to point the camera) interrelate with the behavior observed (e.g., a smile or a kick) to produce an operational definition of that behavior. Understanding operational definitions facilitates exploration of reliability issues, especially through the study of inter- and intraobserver reliability. For example, students become aware of how individual differences in camera operation can reduce interobserver reliability.

Observational methods also permit analysis of a phenomenon at a range of levels from the molar (e.g., being aggressive) to the molecular (e.g., making physical contact), depending on the breadth of the behavioral categories used. Development of behavioral categories helps students appreciate the distinction between observation and interpretation as they search to define categories clearly enough to achieve acceptable levels of reliability. Students thus come to appreciate the interdependence of interobserver reliability and operational definitions, as well as the interrelated nature of the concepts and principles of the scientific method as a whole.

Instruction in observational methods provides an interesting context in which to discuss ethical issues. This fact is especially noteworthy in laboratory exercises involving hidden observers (either in person or via a camcorder) behind the one-way vision screen. For example, students become aware of the subtle trade-offs between treating subjects honestly versus providing the occasion for honest (i.e., unbiased) behaving.

Finally, learning to use videotaping equipment and computerized event recorders allows students to master technologies that are widely used in psychology laboratories. Fortunately, this equipment is now modestly priced, and its widespread use in undergraduate laboratories is feasible.

In the remainder of this article, we briefly review the components of observational methodology used in our courses and describe pertinent laboratory exercises. Like most behavioral methodologies, the observational approach involves data collection and data analysis. We discuss each in turn.

Data Collection

Preparation of Videotapes

Students learn techniques of camcorder use (lighting, movement, close-ups, etc.) and the importance of hypotheses in choosing which individual(s) and behavior(s) to record. They also learn the circumstances under which a more exploratory scan-sampling approach (Martin & Bateson, 1986) might be used to gain a simple appreciation of behaviors occurring in a population.

Split-Screen Recording of Both Members of a Dyad

Students learn the techniques of closed television circuit camera placement and VCR use and come to appreciate the dynamic nature of behavior in the subtle moment-to moment interactions in a dyad. These interactions can be seen when each member of a dyad is videotaped with a separate camera (thus allowing a frontal view of face and body), but the images are displayed side by side on the monitor by virtue of a split-screen board inside one of the cameras.

Establishment and Refinement of Measurable Indices

Students learn to categorize behavior, do preliminary interrater reliability checks, and refine category definitions and observational procedures to obtain reliable behavioral measures. The development of acceptable interrater reliability helps demonstrate how to conduct an experiment with objectivity, thereby minimizing bias and enhancing the likelihood of replication. Introducing such principles concretely increases the probability that students will be guided by them in their later research projects.

Computer-Based Coding of Observational Data

Students learn to use IBM-compatible laptop computers (Eventlog software and CONDUIT, available from the University of Iowa) to encode the occurrence of their chosen behavioral categories by assigning each to a key (as many as there are in the keyboard); data are saved in a form that can be readily subjected to statistical analysis. Through this process, students learn to distinguish continuous recording from various forms of time sampling and to realize their respective advantages and disadvantages.

Data Analysis

Data reduction and editing are also done by computer. Eventlog computes frequencies and durations of single or combined behaviors. Eventlog files are edited with a word processor or spreadsheet so that they can be read by a statistical package (e.g., SYSTAT; Wilkinson, 1990) for calculation of reliability and descriptive and inferential statistics.

Reliability statistics, such as Cohen's kappa or Pearson's correlation coefficient, are computed. Kappa shows the degree to which a rate of agreement is significantly different from what might be obtained by chance (Hollenbeck, 1978). It can be used at more specific levels of analysis (e.g., those related to errors of omission and commission) . Pearson correlations can be used at more general levels of analysis (cumulative durations or frequencies for entire sessions). The various descriptive and inferential statistics on groups and conditions are computed, and summary graphs are created.

Laboratory Exercises

Emotion and Motivation

One of the principal laboratory exercises for this course involves videotaping posed facial expressions and recording psychophysiological data during expressions. Students study and practice judgments on still photographs

illustrating facial expressions for different emotions (Ekman & Friesen, 1975). They also learn some of the main categories of facial movement from the Facial Action Coding System (FACS) that are relevant to emotion (Ekman & Friesen, 1978). Finally, they partially replicate an experiment by Ekman, Levenson, and Friesen (1983) on autonomic changes during various posed facial expressions. Primary goals are to familiarize students with the principles underlying the FACS for measuring facial behavior, approaches to integrating behavioral observation and psychophysiology, and problems of demand characteristics in such experiments.

Developmental Psychology

Taking advantage of a nearby preschool, students videotape children playing. Students work out preliminary observation schedules, view the videotapes several times, and make refinements. They construct a set of final behavioral categories, subcategories, measurable indices, and associated definitions and examples, along with the actual observation schedule (or checklist). They translate this schedule into a computerized form by assigning individual behaviors to individual keys in Eventlog on a laptop computer and use the schedule to quantify observations of the videotape. They take interrater reliability estimates and reduce and analyze the data. Students see how behavior unfolds in time; that is, they see

how different behaviors in the same person interact and how each person's behavior influences and is influenced by others' behavior.

In another exercise using two cameras and a split-screen board, the instructor and students make videotapes of two different mother-infant dyads at two times (about 3 months and 15 months). The mother is asked simply to get the attention of her baby and relate to him or her as she normally does (Kaye & Fogel, 1980). With the aid of a simplified version of Kaye and Fogel's (1980) coding schema, students categorize and analyze a videotape, frame by frame, at several levels: how mothers attempt to shape their childrens' utterances by imposed adult conversation frameworks; how infants differ in their desire to interact; and especially how the facial expressions, physical gestures, and verbal and nonverbal utterances of infant and mother are subtly intertwined. Comparisons of mother-infant interaction are made when infants are 3 months old and 15 months old. The students come to appreciate the nature of mother-infant interactions at various levels of analysis, as well as how these interactions change over time.

Social Psychology

In an experiment on conversation turn-taking (Duncan & Fiske, 1977), students create videotapes of two people having a conversation. They analyze verbal and nonverbal behavior with a truncated version of the coding scheme proposed by Duncan and Fiske. Cues making up the turn yielding signal (e.g., head shift, inhalation, gesticulation, etc.), along with back-channel behaviors (e.g., vocalizations, etc.), are recorded and analyzed. Some students also focus on the relations among speaking, gestures, and self adapters. Students see how the seemingly "natural" event of conversation is made possible by a series of interlocking behaviors across the two conversants.

Concluding Comments

Although we prefer to use observational methodology and instrumentation to help integrate our set of upper level psychology laboratories, they can also be taught and emphasized in a single experimental or research methods course or in a course with content especially suited to such measurements (e.g., a course in animal behavior) . Our emphasis on systematic observation in teaching research methods has been as illuminating for us as our students. Both student and instructor gain greatly from the discipline of observing behavior in an unbiased way.

References

Barker, R. G. (Ed.). (1963). *The stream of behavior: Explorations of its structure and content.* New York: Appleton-Century-Crofts.

Boice, R. (1983). Observational skills. *Psychological Bulletin, 93*, 3-29.

Duncan, S., Jr., & Fiske, D. W. (1977). *Face-to-face interaction: Research, methods, and theory.* Hillsdale, NJ: Lawrence Erlbaum Associates, Inc.

Ekman, P., & Friesen, W. V. (1975). *Unmasking the face.* Englewood Cliffs, NJ: Prentice-Hall.

Ekman, P., & Friesen, W. V. (1978). *Facial action coding system: Investigator's guide, Part 2.* Palo Alto, CA: Consulting Psychologists Press.

Ekman, P., Levenson, R. W., & Friesen, W. V. (1983). Autonomic nervous system activity distinguishes among emotions. *Science, 221*, 1208-1210.

Hogan, P. M. (1991). Vocational preparation within a liberal arts framework: Suggested directions for undergraduate psychology programs. *Teaching of Psychology, 18*, 148-153.

Hollenbeck, A. R. (1978). Problems of reliability in observational research. In G. P. Sackett (Ed.), *Observing behavior: Vol. 2. Data collection and analysis methods* (pp. 79-98). Baltimore: University Park Press.

Hoshmand, L. L. S. T. (1985). Module on observation methods: A perspective on the teaching of inquiry. *Teaching of Psychology, 12*, 132-136.

Kaye, K., & Fogel, A. (1980). The temporal structure of face-to face communication between mothers and infants. *Developmental Psychology, 16*, 454-464.

Martin, P., & Bateson, P. (1986). *Measuring behavior: An introductory guide.* Cambridge, England: Cambridge University Press.

Shweder, R. A. (1975). How relevant is an individual difference theory of personality? *Journal of Personality, 43*, 455-484.

Wilkinson, L. (1990). *SYSTAT: A system of statistics.* Evanston, IL: SYSTAT, Inc.

Zeren, A. S., & Makosky, V. P. (1986). Teaching observational methods: Time sampling, event sampling, and trait rating techniques. *Teaching of Psychology, 13*, 80-82.

Notes

1. Preparation of this article was supported in part by the National Science Foundation's Instrumentation and Laboratory Improvement Program through Grant USE-905167.
2. Authors' names are listed in alphabetical order because contributions were equal.

Teaching Observational Methods: Time Sampling, Event Sampling, and Trait Rating Techniques

Andrea S. Zeren
Vivian Parker Makosky
St. Lawrence University

The observation of human behavior plays a central role in many areas of psychology, particularly social psychology, child psychology, and group processes. Several observational techniques are available for scientifically describing human behavior. These techniques can be divided into two general types, unstructured (narrative) methods and structured (checklist) methods. The former approaches involve using narrative types of data to "reproduce behavioral events in much the same fashion and sequence as their original occurrence" (Brandt, 1972, p. 80). In contrast, the latter approaches entail deliberately selecting and defining specific behaviors before the observation process, and developing a format on which to record the observations. Since the early 20th century, the structured methods have been used with increasing frequency to study social behaviors.

Wright (1967) identified time sampling, event sampling, and trait ratings as three of the most frequently used structured approaches for obtaining observational data. Th basic observational "tools" are often taught to college a graduate school students in lecture format. Although teachers might prefer an in-class demonstration of the techniques, severe difficulties often block an effective class presentation. First, having student observers in the room with the people being observed is intrusive and affects the behaviors of those observed. For example, decreased negative behaviors, increased desired behaviors, and a reduction in overall activity are some specific behavior changes that result from an awareness of being observed (cf. Selltiz, Wrightsman, & Cook, 1981). A second alternative is to have the class observe through one-way mirrors. However, even if the facilities are available they only partially eliminate intrusiveness. These settings severely restrict behaviors it is possible to observe as adults are often conscious of the observations being conducted. A third alternative is to abandon the idea of observing as a class and send students out to observe on their own. This alternative leads to a loss of structure and comparability across observational techniques. It also raises important ethical concerns that may be too complex to address fully in the time available (e.g., issues of informed consent, veto power over the use of obtained information, and invasion of privacy).

The following activity permits the systematic observation of spontaneous human behavior as simulated on television. Televised behavior has previously been used for demonstrating both observational techniques and individual differences in the perception of social motives (Russo, 1981). Our exercise extends the use of televised behavior by providing one way to demonstrate and compare time sampling, event sampling, and trait rating techniques and avoids the problems previously mentioned. Furthermore, it is an excellent illustration of many aspects of the scientific approach to studying behavior, as the students' observations (a) serve a formulated research purpose, (b) are planned deliberately, (c) are recorded systematically, and (d) are subjected to checks and controls on reliability.

Method

Equipment and Preparation

The only equipment needed is either a videocassette recorder or a facility for closed-circuit television from which to air a prerecorded television show. The only initial laboratory preparation involves videotaping a popular television show that is high in the frequency of target behaviors. A variety of shows may be used, with the choice of depending mainly upon the nature of the questions being asked. For example, *The Love Boat*, a television show depicting aspects of several types of relationships that differ in level of intimacy, was used with social psychology students whose purpose was to study interpersonal attraction and love. However, when this technique was used with students enrolled in a research methods course in which the questions involved a broader array of behaviors and emotions, the soap opera entitled *All My Children* was chosen. Because the show can be

chosen according to the behavioral domain being examined (i.e., liking, loving, aggression, prejudice, etc.) the approach permits flexibility to accommodate student and teacher interests.

Procedure

The entire activity involves three steps: (a) a lecture about observational methods; (b) an exercise demonstrating the use of time sampling, event sampling, and trait ratings; and (c) a class discussion comparing the three methods. It is more effective as a 2-hr lab activity but can be condensed into one class period.

Lecture. The activity begins with a brief introduction to direct observation as a research method. Specific points covered might include the role and importance of observation in research and teaching; the main distinguishing features among naturalistic observation, experimental manipulation, and self-report methods; and the difference between non-structured and structured observational strategies .

The structured observational techniques of time sampling, event sampling, and trait ratings become the specific focus of the lecture. Each method is described in detail (see Irwin & Bushnell, 1980 for background reading) and the following similarities among the three methods are presented: (a) each focuses on specific behaviors or constellations of behaviors, (b) each identifies behavioral categories in advance, (c) each relies heavily on an unambiguous operational definition of the variable(s) being measured, and (d) each requires preconstructed recording formats.

Finally, the class discusses the preparation, development, and completion of each technique (i.e., formulating research questions, defining target behaviors, forming operational definitions, and constructing recording formats).

Class activity. The class is divided into small groups of three to five students, each of which is responsible for the actual development of all components of one of the three observational strategies. This group size was chosen because it seems to maximize time efficiency and student productivity in the preparation, development, and data collection for each technique. The students are presented with the option to consult the instructor on all pertinent decisions, which include the following: the purpose of the observation; the type of information to record; how the variables will be operationalized; whether to include verbal and/or nonverbal behaviors; constructing an appropriate recording format; (for time sampling) deciding the length, number, and spacing of intervals; and (for trait ratings) the type of rating scale to use.

The class reconvenes for approximately ½ hr to observe the taped program. Students independently record samples of behavior using the method and data sheets constructed by their subgroup.

Interrater reliability coefficients are computed among all subgroup members, using the formula: Reliability =

$$\frac{\text{agreements}}{\text{agreements} + \text{disagreements}} .$$ Each group is instructed to identify shortcomings in its use of the strategy, improvements that would overcome these problems, and the relative advantages and disadvantages of the method they used.

Class discussion. We have found that a beneficial way to begin the discussion is by comparing the obtained reliability coefficients among thee three methods. The differences in level of interobserver agreement reveal some of the strengths and weaknesses associated with each technique. Specifically, every time this lab activity has been used, the reliability coefficients were found to be highest for time sampling, next highest for event sampling, and lowest for trait ratings. The instructor discusses this pattern, noting that rating scale reliability coefficients are usually lower because this strategy requires a judgment from the rater and, therefore, is more subjective. Consequently, rater error and biases occur, including the halo effect, errors of leniency, and errors of central tendency. In contrast, time sampling reliability coefficients are typically higher than those for trait rating or event sampling methods. Consistent with this, the observer must focus on easily observable, concrete, and preselected behaviors.

Additional discussion topics might include specific uses of each method, major advantages and disadvantages, possible data analyses, the importance of precise operational definitions and their impact on the precision of interrater agreement, and the defining characteristics of scientific observation.

Students' Evaluation of the Activity

This technique was first used as a laboratory activity in social psychology and students informally praised its instructional value. The technique was later refined and used both in other classes and by another instructor. To evaluate its effectiveness, a survey was distributed to all students in a research methods course at the time of the exercise ($N = 15$). Although the sample was small, the ratings were consistent with the more impressionistic feedback from larger classes. Responses to the four questions are summarized below. Each question is followed by the mean and the standard deviation (in parentheses).

1. "How interesting did you find this activity?" On a scale ranging from *very uninteresting* (1) to *very*

interesting (5), students gave a mean rating of 3.47 (1.6).

2. "How well did this activity facilitate your understanding of the different structured observational methods?" On a scale ranging from *it was confusing* (1) to *very helpful* (5), the mean rating was 4.33 (.82).

3. "Overall, how would you compare this activity to other psychological lab activities?" On a scale ranging from *inferior* (1) to *superior* (5), students gave a mean rating of 3.67 (.72).

4. "Would you recommend the use of this lab in future offerings of this course?" On a scale ranging from *no, absolutely not* (1) to *yes, most definitely* (5), the mean rating was 4.47 (1.06).

Students generally agreed that the objectives of this exercise were met. Answers to Questions 2 and 3 indicate that the activity facilitated an understanding of structured observational techniques and was an effective teaching aid. Responses to Question 1 revealed wide variations in interest levels. This appeared to be due to the specific television show viewed, rather than to the actual lab activity involved. This conclusion is supported by the students' recommendation to use this activity in future offerings of the course. Overall, the students responded well to the exercise.

Summary and Conclusions

We believe that this is an educational and flexible teaching tool. It permits an in-class demonstration and comparison of three major structured observational techniques, but its utility is far more comprehensive. It illustrates other important facets of psychological research, such as the scientific approach to gathering observational data, the importance of precise operational definitions on interrater agreement, and the calculation of reliability coefficients. This activity is particularly appropriate for social, developmental, and methodology classes.

References

Brandt, R. M. (1972). *Studying behavior in natural settings.* New York: Holt, Rinehart, & Winston.

Irwin, M., & Bushnell, M. M. (1980). *Observational strategies for child study.* New York: Holt, Rinehart, & Winston.

Russo, N. F. (1981). Observation: A standardized experience. In L. T. Benjamin Jr. & K. D. Lowman (Eds.), *Activities handbook for the teaching of psychology* (pp. 3-4). Washington, DC: American Psychological Association.

Selltiz, C., Wrightsman, L. S., & Cook, T. D. (1981). *Research methods in social relations.* New York: Holt, Rinehart, & Winston.

Wrights H. F. (1967). *Recording and analyzing child behavior.* New York: Harper & Row.

Note

An abbreviated version of this paper w as presented at the 1984 meeting of the American Psychological Association, Toronto, Canada.

"The Eye of the Beholder": A Classroom Demonstration of Observer Bias

Miriam D. Goldstein
Washington University
J. Roy Hopkins
St. Mary's College of Maryland
Michael J. Strube
Washington University

Human beings are neither objective nor accurate processors of information: We often see what we want or expect to see and tend to remember information that is consistent with our schemas or expectations (Mischel, Ebbesen, & Zeiss, 1976; Snyder & Swann, 1978; Snyder & Uranowitz, 1978). In other words, prior theories or hypotheses have a strong impact on the processing of new information.

Biases in human perception have important implications for scientific research. The researcher, being human, is not immune to such bias. Indeed, extensive research has demonstrated that hypotheses held by researchers can have a strong influence on the obtained data (Anderson, 1983; Rosenthal, 1963; Rosenthal & Rosnow, 1969). Thus, it is not surprising that issues of experimenter bias and observer fallacies are often highlighted in psychology courses of all levels (see Aronson, Ellsworth, Carlsmith, & Gonzales, 1990; Neale & Liebert, 1986).

We created a demonstration in which students experienced directly the powerful effects of observer bias. We led students to believe that they would be monitoring the self-report accuracy of a subject (actually a trained confederate) who was expected to display a decrease in performance across trials due to alcohol consumption. Students reported a trend that was consistent with the expectancy yet was not present in the behavior observed; the confederate actually drank apple juice and displayed consistent behavior across trials.

Format of the Demonstration

Participants and Procedure

Students in an experimental psychology class were led to believe that they would observe a demonstration of subject response bias. We explained that researchers such as Nisbett and Wilson (1977) suggested that self-report is often inaccurate, thus rendering the validity of measures based on self-report questionable. We told students that a subject would be unable to report accurately an obvious decrement in performance due to alcohol consumption. In other words, we suggested that students would be more objective than the subject, or less likely to display a bias, in reporting the subject's level of performance.

After being told that she was about to participate in a study of motor coordination, the subject (a trained confederate) engaged in three trials of a mirror-tracing task (see Mednick, 1964). In this task, subjects must trace within the outline of a double-lined star with only a mirror's reflection to guide them. The subject was instructed to trace the pattern with a pencil while looking only at the mirror, not directly at her hand or the pattern. The subject used her right hand and traced clockwise. At the beginning of each trial, the subject placed the point of her pencil between the boundaries of the figure at an indicated starting point. When signaled by the experimenter, she began tracing the figure as rapidly as possible, trying not to go out of the boundary lines. At first, this task is very difficult. With practice, however, one becomes able to fill in the star quite easily (Mednick, 1964). To assure consistent performance across trials, the confederate was trained before the demonstration to maintain a constant rate and constant number of errors (i.e., number of times she crossed the outline of the star). Despite such training, slight performance changes could occur in the actual demonstration. Moreover, one runs the risk that the tracings will vary in a consistent manner (e.g., become worse across trials). Thus, it is advisable to obtain quality ratings of the tracings from objective judges after the demonstration. Another limitation of this variation is that our confederates had a difficult time keeping their performance consistent while following a verbal and nonverbal script.

To avoid these difficulties, we have also run the demonstration with pretraced stars so that the confederate needs only to concentrate on time to complete the task. All three stars are identical. To assure that the tracings are not obviously identical, each tracing is rotated clockwise (i.e., the master tracing is copied onto the other forms at a different angle). Students do not suspect that the tracings are not actually completed during the demonstration (their view of pencil-paper contact is obstructed). However, to reduce potential suspicion, we invite students to attempt the tracing task, using blank forms pulled from a drawer (this procedure also serves to illustrate the difficulty of the task). The pretraced forms are located at the bottom of the pile of forms and, with a little sleight of hand, can be easily placed on the apparatus during the demonstration.

We provided our confederate with a detailed script for her behavior. Once she began to trace, she counted silently for 20 s, remarked "okay," counted another 20 s, smiled, counted another 20 s, and remarked "This isn't easy" (during Trial 1), "This is hard" (during Trial 2), and "This is difficult" (during Trial 3). She then counted another 20 s, laughed, counted another 20 s, and announced that she was finished. The confederate's performance on each trial was inconspicuously timed to assure equivalent performance time across trials.

Before each trial, the confederate consumed what students believed was a mixture of rum and cola. To reduce possible suspicion and increase realism, the drinks were prepared in class, using a can of cola, a shot glass, and a rum bottle actually containing apple juice. After each trial, the traced star was passed around for students to see. Students were then given a questionnaire that asked them to "rate the effect of the alcohol on the subject's speech and behavior" and to "rate the effect of alcohol on the subject's performance." Students were provided with a 10-point scale ranging from *no effect* (1) to *strong effect* (10)

and were instructed to circle the number that corresponded to their answers. Students were instructed not to put their names on the questionnaires. The answer sheets were collected after each trial. The confederate completed what students believed to be similar ratings; presumably, her answers were to be used to assess the accuracy of her self-reports. Actually, the confederate circled random responses.

In order to give the "alcohol" time to take effect, the confederate was given a 15-min break after each trial. During this time, we proceeded with class activities.

After the final trial and collection of all answer sheets, we revealed that in this demonstration we expected the students, not the subject, to exhibit bias. We explained that the subject was in fact a trained confederate and that she had not consumed alcohol. We also told the students that we planned to analyze their answers to see whether they had indeed displayed an observer bias. We described what pattern of results would offer support for a bias and what pattern would offer support for objective rating. During the next class period, which focused on experimenter and subject biases, we presented the results described in the following section.

Results

Overview

In this section, we present empirical evaluation of two variations of the demonstration that we have used in past years. In the first variation (hereafter Demonstration 1), the confederate is actually performing the tracing task. We recommend using Demonstration 1 if the students will have a clear view of the tracing apparatus. In the second variation of the demonstration (hereafter Demonstration 2), the tracings are objectively identical.

Demonstration 1

The confederate's performance times for the three trials were highly consistent (Trial 1 = 1.46 min, Trial 2 = 1.39 min, and Trial 3 = 1.41 min). Students' ratings of the effects of alcohol on the confederate's speech, behavior, and performance were analyzed using a repeated measures analysis of variance (ANOVA). Significant linear trends were found for speech and behavior ($M_1 = 1.29$, $M_2 = 1.60$, and $M_3 = 3.00$), $F(1, 13) = 10.95$, $p < .006$; and for performance ($M_1 = 1.43$, $M_2 = 2.14$, and $M_3 = 4.07$), $F(1, 13) = 18.91$, $p < .001$. Thus, students rated the effect of alcohol as increasing across the trials for speech, behavior, and performance.

Demonstration 2

We ran this variation in two sections of an experimental psychology class. Because the results did not differ across sections, the following results refer to both sections combined.

The confederate's performance times for the three trials were highly consistent (Trial 1 = 2.18 min, Trial 2 = 2.20 min, and Trial 3 = 2.17 min). Students' ratings of the effects of alcohol on the confederate's speech, behavior, and performance were analyzed using a repeated measures ANOVA. Significant linear trends were found for speech and behavior ($M_1 = 1.50$, $M_2 = 2.69$, and $M_3 = 2.85$), $F(1, 26) = 19.90$, $p < .001$; and for performance ($M_1 = 2.30$, $M_2 = 3.30$, and $M_3 = 4.70$), $F(1, 26) = 19.89$, $p < .001$. As in Demonstration 1 students rated the effect of alcohol as increasing across the trials for speech, behavior, and performance.

Evaluation

Following the discussion, students completed an anonymous questionnaire reporting whether they personally succumbed to observer bias and whether they thought the deception involved in the demonstration was justified. The purpose of this questionnaire was twofold. First, it allowed us to assure that students were not upset or anxious about being deceived. Second, it allowed us to examine whether students were convinced that they individually succumbed to the observer bias. We think that the responses to these questions revealed that the demonstration was effective. In a recent class, 25 of 27 students agreed that their expectations influenced their observations, and all students thought that the deception was justified. One student wrote: "Although we can learn through lecture that we are all biased you just proved it to us. You couldn't have done that without deception." Another student commented: "I'm glad I was fooled. I'll scrutinize and think more when I plan an experiment. I want to avoid these flaws."

Discussion

Both variations of our demonstration allow students to experience personally the powerful effects of prior expectations on perception. Results verify that our demonstrations are effective in producing an observer bias.

This demonstration is an excellent tool to use in both experimental and introductory psychology classes. Although bias in information processing is a well-established finding, we believe that students were more appreciative of this effect after they experienced it personally. The demonstration has led easily into a discussion of both experimenter and subject biases and other experimentation issues, such as reliability and validity of measures. For example, we pointed out that students served as the measurement instrument in this demonstration. They were to observe and record a subject's behavior and performance. Were their measurements valid? Probably not: The students'

measurement of the confederate's behavior and performance was biased by their expectations and thus did not reflect the actual behavior and performance. It follows that their recordings were not a valid measure of the confederate's behavior, because they did not measure what they set out to measure. Similarly, to the extent that the students' bias reflects random and, thus, nonreplicable variance, the students' measurements were not reliable. The effects of expectations on perception outside of the lab (e.g., stereotypes) can also be discussed.

Students have eagerly shared their thoughts about why they fell prey to the bias, often providing specific examples of neutral behaviors that they had processed in an expectation-consistent manner. For example, one student commented that, during the final trial, he had thought that a smile indicated "tipsiness." Similarly, a student noted that she now realized that a comment made by the confederate during the last trial ("this is difficult") was not different from a comment made in an earlier trial ("this is hard"). At the time of the demonstration, however, she had thought that the comment in the last trial indicated greater difficulty in performance, which she had attributed to the alcohol consumption.

Students also remarked on how they actively distorted their reports. One student commented that, even when she thought there was no difference in performance, she rationalized that there must be a difference. She ignored certain things that the subject did at times but noticed and exaggerated their meaning at other times. Such comments can be used to illustrate the difference between demand characteristics (i.e., subjects report what they think the experimenter wants to hear) and observer bias (subjects see what they expect to see), both of which contribute to explaining the results of our demonstration. Another student noted that he watched for signs, such as blinking, that he thought were characteristic of someone under the influence. One student had an interesting insight into one possible source of observer biases. She said "Don't you think it would be dangerous for us all not to think that her behavior was influenced at least a little bit by the alcohol?" Her intriguing question led to a discussion of whether biases and heuristics (or cognitive shortcuts) are indeed errors (see Funder, 1987).

Although we have demonstrated that students succumbed to observer bias and that they can articulate the reasons why they thought they did so, another important issue is whether our students actually learned from the demonstration. We addressed this question in two ways. First, at the beginning of the semester, we provided students with a manuscript containing numerous methodological problems and APA-style violations. Embedded in the manuscript was an example of a potential observer bias. Students handed in a list of detected methodological problems and APA-style violations several times throughout the semester to demonstrate their progressive mastery of course material and to hone their ability to evaluate research critically. Students handed in their lists for the first time before the demonstration and for the second time 2 weeks after the demonstration. None of the students detected the observer bias before the class demonstration, but seven (22%) did after the class demonstration.

Because the manuscript described earlier was fairly long and complex, we sought other ways to demonstrate that students had learned the concept of observer bias. In an exam that followed the class demonstration by 3 weeks, we presented students with a brief description of a hypothetical study and instructed them to identify its major problems. One of the major problems involved a potential observer bias. Eleven students (35%) detected the bias. The seven students who detected bias in the manuscript also detected bias in the exam.

In summary, our demonstration provides students with a lively and memorable introduction to observer biases. Students' personal involvement in the demonstration should improve learning.

References

Anderson, C. A. (1983). Abstract and concrete data in the perseverance of social theories: When weak data lead to unshakable beliefs. *Journal of Experimental Social Psychology, 19,* 93-108.

Aronson, E., Ellsworth, P. C., Carlsmith, J. M., & Gonzales, M. H. (1990). *Methods of research in social psychology.* New York: McGraw-Hill.

Funder, D. (1987). Errors and mistakes: Evaluating the accuracy of social judgment. *Psychological Bulletin, 101,* 75-90.

Mednick, S. A. (1964). *Learning.* Englewood Cliffs, NJ: Prentice Hall.

Mischel, W., Ebbesen, E B., & Zeiss, A. M. (1976). Determinants of selective memory about the self. *Journal of Consulting and Clinical Psychology, 44,* 92-103.

Neale, S. M., & Liebert, R. M. (1986). Science and behavior: An introduction to methods of research. Englewood Cliffs, NJ: Prentice-Hall.

Nisbett, R E., & Wilson, T. (1977). Telling more than we can know: Verbal reports on mental processes. *Psychological Review, 84,* 231-259.

Rosenthal, R. (1963). On the social psychology of the psychological experiment: The experimenter's hypothesis as unintended determinant of experimental results. *American Scientist, 51,* 268-283.

Rosenthal, R., & Rosnow R. L. (Eds.). (1969). *Artifact in behavioral research.* New York: Academic.

Snyder, M., & Swann, W. B. (1978). Hypothesis-testing processes in social interaction *Journal of Personality and Social Psychology, 36,* 1202-1212.

Snyder, M., & Uranowitz, S. W. (1978). Reconstructing the past: Some cognitive consequences of person perception. *Journal of Personality and Social Psychology, 36,* 941-950.

Note

We thank Tammy Hershey and David Stotz for their contributions to this project and Saera Khan for her superb performance as the confederate in Demonstration 2. We also thank Ruth L. Ault and several anonymous reviewers for their helpful comments on a draft of this article.

5. WORKING IN GROUPS

Undergraduate Research Groups: Two Models

Pamela Reed Gibson
Arnold S. Kahn
Virginia Andreoli Mathie
James Madison University

Undergraduate involvement in research beyond a research methods course is a valuable experience, especially for students interested in graduate school (Kiemiesky, 1984; Purdy, Reinehr, & Swartz, 1989). Purdy et al. found that most experimental and clinical psychology graduate programs rated research experience as a "very important" admissions criterion; most counseling programs rated research as "moderately important." Unfortunately, only a small minority of undergraduates have the opportunity to gain research skills (Baird, 1990; Hartmann, 1990).

A dilemma for faculty members in publish or perish environments is that undergraduate research projects are frequently time-consuming and seldom yield publishable results. Although instructors of research methods courses often try to provide comprehensive research experiences for students (Yoder, 1979), a long-term, out-of-class experience offers students the opportunity to evaluate the strengths and weaknesses of their discipline (Hartmann, 1990) and to experience the advantages, complications, and accountability of the research setting (Kuo, 1987/88; Vittal, Treinen, & Nikuie, 1990). Supervising faculty can also serve as models and mentors for students (Ware & Matthews, 1980).

One solution to this dilemma is to have a research team of undergraduates work on faculty members' projects. Research teams are not new. Beins (1993), Evans, Rintala, Guthrie, and Raines (1981), and Nadelman, Morse, and Hagen (1976) described teams with positive results. In this article, we describe two successful models for incorporating undergraduates into research groups. Depending on the department's staffing needs, these teams may or may not count as part of the faculty member's teaching load.

Faculty research interests are typically announced in the department's semiannual newsletter, and students apply directly to the supervising faculty member. We generally require students to complete statistics and experimental psychology courses before participating in the research groups. We also strive for more than one semester's involvement because the research process is rarely completed in a semester. Students receive course credit for independent readings or independent research.

Model 1: Single-Faculty, Single-Project Team

One of us organized a group in fall 1992 to conduct a regression study to predict hope in those with environmental illness/multiple chemical sensitivity. The team usually has three or four student members.

Each student completes a student learning plan that itemizes the research skills that the student possesses and those skills she or he would like to acquire from participating in the research group. Skills include library research, reviewing and critiquing journal articles, preparing questionnaires, entering data, conducting data analyses, and writing in APA style .

Students begin using the skills they already possess and acquire new skills as they gain confidence. In the regression study, students began by choosing a variable, conducting a literature review on that variable, and helping choose the most appropriate measure for the study. Students reviewed social support, hope, and adjustment to chronic illness.

The group meets once a week for 2 hr and performs tasks as necessary. For example, we discussed basic questionnaire development in one group meeting. In later meetings, students led discussions on specific measures they had critiqued. Students' disagreements about which measure to adopt were instructive, illuminating, and illustrative of the problems that arise in the research process. Students generally appreciated an opportunity to participate in hands-on research in a nonthreatening atmosphere and realized that they had much to offer. Because students are given considerable ownership of the project, they feel responsible for its implementation.

Another goal of the out-of-class research experience was to give students an opportunity to present and publish research. Student coauthors presented conference posters and papers using data from the several dependent variables (hope, social support, and adjustment). Because each student focused on one variable, the research was manageable. Involvement in the larger group allowed students to see how their variables were part of a larger study. The more comprehensive analyses, including the regression model, were more appropriate for faculty publications or for joint authorship with students who remained with the project for a long time. For this model, the maximum size group was four students because one faculty member was responsible for guiding each student from conceptualization to publication.

Benefits of the faculty member's involvement include assisting with library work, aiding on various time-consuming tasks (including coding and data entry), interacting with and teaching students who have a genuine interest in the research process, and consulting and advising students at every stage of the research process. Each student's valuable skills become evident. For example, the faculty member learns to depend on one student for excellent feedback about questionnaire wording and on another for excellent overall planning/troubleshooting ability. We have presented two posters (Cheavens, Gibson, Warren, & Pasquantino, 1993; Gibson, Warren, Pasquantino, & Cheavens, 1993) and three conference papers (Cheavens, Gibson, & Warren, 1994; Gibson, Cheavens, & Warren, 1994; Crowley & Gibson, 1995), submitted two journal papers for review, and written a grant proposal to the Virginia Board for People with Disabilities (unfunded) to expand our research.

Model 2: Large Multifaculty, Multiproject Team

This research team consists of three faculty members and several students involved simultaneously in four research projects on the topic of sexual assault. The structure of this team has evolved over 4 years to accommodate more students.

The first team, two faculty members and two students, started in January 1991 to follow up previously reported differences between acknowledged and unacknowledged rape victims in their scripts of what occurred before, during, and after a typical rape. The team met weekly to review relevant research and discuss new studies. Since fall 1991, 34 other students have participated on the team; the size of the team has ranged from 7 to 12 students.

Initially, all team members worked on all projects, meeting formally once a week for 2 hr to coordinate and plan research activities. For example, in two studies, we obtained handwritten rape scripts from subjects and devoted the weekly meetings to developing a detailed script-coding scheme and coordinating further data collection. Outside of class, students collected the data, coded the scripts, and continued the literature review. Faculty and students worked together on all phases of the research.

As the size of the team and the number of projects grew, we modified the team structure. Students affiliated with one of three project groups, with each group taking primary responsibility for one project. Project groups met once a week, sometimes with a faculty member and sometimes on their own, to work on the details of their project. All team members still had input into all projects through weekly 2-hr team meetings. At these meetings, each group updated the others on its project status, and the entire team made final decisions about procedures, measuring instruments, and other methodological concerns. We also used these meetings to prepare for data collection and analysis and to discuss the results and implications of findings. In addition, students had a chance to see three faculty members discuss research ideas, offer different views, and collaborate on research.

Students presented their research at state (Hinely et al., 1993; Schoka et al., 1993) and regional meetings (Andreoli Mathie et al.,1994; Baker et al.,1992; Chau, Lally, Schmitt, & Stover, 1994; Salimi et al., 1994). One study has been published (Kahn, Andreoli Mathie, & Torgler, 1994), and team members have drafted manuscripts for two other projects. In addition, students have written a grant proposal (not funded) to obtain funding for one project, and they outlined a plan for a longitudinal study. Because working in groups on separate studies led to a lack of team cohesiveness, we now meet twice a week with all team members working on all projects.

One of the requirements for the research team at the end of the 1993 spring semester was to respond to the question, "What skills have you gained from being a part of the team?" Almost all students said participation increased their library, writing, computer, and critical-thinking skills, as well as their ability to speak in front of a group, work effectively in a group, understand research ethics, and work closely with faculty members. They also noted that good research is a tedious and time-consuming endeavor.

Summary

We discussed two models for meeting the research needs of faculty and students. Both models provide undergraduates the opportunity to participate in the full range of research activities—conceptualize, design, collect and analyze data, and write up and present the results at professional meetings. Students reported that these experiences were valuable. Research teams enable faculty to continue their research and serve as mentors to undergraduates while carrying heavy teaching loads. The research team appears to be a useful way to meet the research needs of students and faculty.

References

Andreoli Mathie, V. A., Kahn, A. S., Baker, S., Feria, G., Gregory, C., Heiges, K., Hinely, H., Linn, K., & Scholten, B. (1994, April). *Counterfactual thinking in women's perceptions of their rape experience*. Paper presented at the meeting of the Southeastern Psychological Association, New Orleans, LA.

Baird, L. L. (1990). The undergraduate experience: Commonalities and differences among colleges. *Research in Higher Education, 31*, 271-279.

Baker, S., Beeghly, P., Bradley, K., Feria, G., Hastings, K., Hinely, H., Schoka, E., Stuckey, J., Sullivan, M., Kahn, A., & Andreoli Mathie, V. A. (1992, March). *Rape scripts as determinants of acknowledged vs. unacknowledged rape victims*. Poster presented at the meeting of the Southeastern Psychological Association, Knoxville, TN.

Beins, B. C. (1993, August). *Research team: Bonding, enjoyment, and programmatic research*. Paper presented at the annual meeting of the American Psychological Association, Toronto, Canada.

Chau, L., Lally, C., Schmitt, M., & Stover, K. (1994, April). *Men's perceptions of rape*. Poster presented at the meeting of the Southeastern Psychological Association, New Orleans, LA.

Cheavens, J., Gibson, P. R., & Warren, M. L. (1994, October). *Social support and isolation in persons with multiple chemical sensitivities*. Paper presented at the first annual conference of the Southern Regional Chapter of the Association for Women in Psychology, Hilton Head, SC.

Cheavens, J., Gibson, P. R., Warren, M. L., & Pasquantino, D. (1993, November). *Chemical sensitivities: Parents' view for improved access in a technological society*. Poster presented at the annual conference of the Virginia Women's Studies Association, James Madison University, Harrisonburg, VA.

Crowley, C., & Gibson, P. R. (1995, March). *Disability due to chemical sensitivity: People, controversies, legalities*. Paper presented at the annual meeting of the Southeastern Psychological Association, Savannah, GA.

Evans, R. I., Rintala, D. H., Guthrie, T. J., & Raines, B. E. (1981). Recruiting and training undergraduate psychology research assistants for longitudinal field investigations. *Teaching of Psychology, 8*, 97-100.

Gibson, P. R., Cheavens, J., & Warren, M. L. (1994, May). *Chemical sensitivity/chemical injury: Life impacts*. Paper presented at the meeting of the American Psychological Association, Washington, DC.

Gibson, P. R., Warren, M. L., Pasquantino, D., & Cheavens, J. (1993, November). *Limitations and thwarted goals for persons with chemical sensitivities*. Poster presented at the annual conference of the Virginia Women's Studies Association, James Madison University, Harrisonburg, VA.

Hartmann, D. J. (1990). Undergraduate research experience as preparation for graduate school. *The American Sociologist, 21*, 179-188.

Hinely, H., Baker, S., Beeghly, P., Feria, G., Hartwell, C., Higgins, D., Jacobs, H., McCarthy, A., Schoka, E., & Schuyler, W. (1993, April). *Rape scripts and the unacknowledged rapist*. Paper presented at the meeting of the Virginia Psychological Association, Virginia Beach, VA.

Kahn, A. S., Andreoli Mathie, V. A., & Torgler, C. (1994). Rape scripts and rape acknowledgment. *Psychology of Women Quarterly, 18*, 53-66.

Kiemiesky, N. C. (1984). Undergraduate research in small psychology departments. *Teaching of Psychology, 11*, 15-18.

Kuo, S. (1987/88). Research experience for college juniors. *Journal of College Science Teaching, 17*, 209.

Nadelman, L., Morse, W., & Hagen, J. (1976). Developmental research in educational settings. Description of a seminar/practicum. *Teaching of Psychology, 3*, 21-24.

Purdy, J. E., Reinehr, R. C., & Swartz, J. D. (1989). Graduate admissions criteria of leading psychology departments. *American Psychologist, 44*, 960-964.

Salimi, L., Andreoli Mathie, V. A., Kahn, A. S., Beeghly, P., Dolby, L., Hartwell, C., Jacobs, H., & Schor, J. (1994, April). *Sexual assault experiences of international women*. Paper presented at the meeting of the Southeastern Psychological Association, New Orleans, LA.

Schoka, E., Baker, S., Beeghly, P., Feria, G., Hartwell, C., Higgins, D., Hinely, H., Jacobs, H., McCarthy, A., & Schuyler, W. (1993, April). *Effects of relationship and force on acknowledged vs. unacknowledged victims' perception of rape*. Paper presented at the meeting of the Virginia Psychological Association, Virginia Beach, VA.

Vittal, V., Treinen, R., & Nikuie, M. (1990). Research experience for undergraduates at Iowa State University. *IEEE Transactions on Power Systems, 5*, 1420-1423.

Yoder, J. (1979). Teaching students to do research. *Teaching of Psychology, 6*, 85-88.

Ware, M. E., & Matthews, J. R. (1980). Stimulating career exploration and research among undergraduates: A colloquium series. *Teaching of Psychology, 7*, 36-38.

Note

We thank Charles L. Brewer and three anonymous reviewers for their helpful comments on an earlier version of this article.

Use of the Jigsaw Technique in Laboratory and Discussion Classes

David W. Carroll
University of Wisconsin–Superior

Although undergraduate courses in research design are invaluable for giving students a perspective on how research is done, many students find such classes difficult. Many are more interested in the nonresearch aspects of psychology, and even those who see its importance are sometimes afraid of a class that requires them to develop, perform, and report an original study.

For 8 years I have taught a one-credit, upper-division, laboratory course in the psychology of learning and memory. Each student is required to carry out a sample experiment provided by the instructor and then develop, perform, and report an original experiment. During the first 4 years of teaching this course, I noticed several distressing trends, including:

1. Approximately one third of the students failed to complete the course in a single quarter.
2. Those who did complete the work on time often chose simple topics and finished them in a perfunctory fashion.
3. Nearly all of the students regarded the course as more than one credit of work.
4. Student evaluations were generally poor.

In the last 4 years, I have been using an adaptation of the "jigsaw classroom" (Aronson & Bridgeman, 1981) as a means of teaching this course. This technique is designed to encourage cooperation by making individuals dependent on each other in pursuit of a common goal. Each person is assigned or chooses one piece of a larger task, and group members depend on each individual to complete the assigned function. Aronson and Bridgeman found that positive changes occurred in group members' attitudes toward one another. My more immediate concern was with the potential of this structure to enable students to tackle more substantial challenges and complete them in a single term.

Method

The jigsaw technique is first introduced in the sample experiment, in which the class replicates a published study.

The assumption is that the group process can be learned in the sample experiment and then applied to the subsequent original experiment. In the sample experiment, students are assigned to one of four tasks (construction of study materials, construction of test materials, randomization of study and test lists, and writing instructions). They spend 3 weeks developing the materials, performing the study, and then discussing it.

Each student is then required to develop a proposal for an independent experiment. The goal of the proposal assignment is to get students to think through an idea to the point of presenting it to the entire group. After the students present their ideas, they are given the options of (a) choosing one idea for a group project, (b) combining or consolidating ideas into a group project, or (c) doing an individual project. Ideas are presented one week, with decisions due the next week.

Students who select a group project sign a contract that specifies the members of the group (maximum: four), the tasks each person will perform (for example, pilot study, instructions, running subjects, statistical analysis), and the division of labor in the writing of the final report (introduction, method, and so on). Those who do a group project are given the further option of writing a group report or writing separate reports. If a group report is chosen, all group members receive the same grade on the report (which is the major but not the total basis for the course grade). Decisions regarding the various aspects of the contract are placed at different parts of the term: Students must form groups by the 5th week, but have until the 6th week to divide the tasks, and until the 9th week to decide on writing assignments. This schedule gives them time to learn more about the work habits of group members and make more informed decisions about how much to entrust their course grade to another person.

Results

There are three sources of evidence of the effectiveness of the jigsaw approach: student evaluations of the class, the percentage of students who complete the course in a single term, and subjective impressions of the choices students make for projects.

Student evaluations are available for the last 3 of the 4 years the jigsaw approach has been in effect, and they indicate a positive student response. Student evaluation was assessed by a 13-item form. Each item was rated on a 5-point scale ranging from a highly negative response (1) to a highly favorable response (5). The means of the individual item means were 4.19, 4.04, and 4.41, respectively, for the last 3 years. Individual items included the knowledge gained from the course (4.12), the fairness of the grading system (4.19), and the degree of intellectual motivation in the class (4.63). On the negative side, comments on the evaluation form revealed that students still regarded the course as more than one credit of work.

The question of whether students were better able to complete coursework in a single term was examined by comparing course records for the 4 years before and the 4 years after the introduction of the jigsaw approach. Of the 55 students who took the course prior to the jigsaw approach, 35 (64%) completed the course, 16 (29%) took incompletes, and 4 (7%) dropped the course or received an F; comparable numbers over the last 4 years were 40 out of 46 (87%), 1 (2%), and 5 (11%).

Whether or not students tackle more challenging assignments is difficult to say, but there are some indications that this is the case. There is much evidence of serial revision throughout the term whereas students in the earlier years, partly due to time pressure, tended to pursue the first idea that came to them. There has been an increase in studies of children as opposed to college students, despite the additional difficulties in securing child participation. Moreover, there has been an increase in students' commitment to their research. For example, one group chose to do a study on mice even though our school has no animal laboratory. The students bought the animals, secured a room, and continued their work the next term as an independent study project. Further evidence of such commitment has been the increased participation in student research conferences.

Discussion

Some of the most significant advantages of this technique relate to the attitudes of students. They seemed to be convinced of the usefulness of the approach. In addition to learning about research design, they learned some valuable lessons in how to organize a complex task and how to structure an interpersonally ambiguous situation. They also seemed to be having more fun.

Some care, however, must be taken in how the technique is presented and used. There is some potential for resentment toward individuals perceived as not doing their share of the work. The structure of the course (allowing students to choose the jigsaw approach, and giving them time to make important decisions) helps to alleviate some of these concerns, but it does not eliminate them. Ultimately, students must decide how much they trust one another. One year, two different groups had to decide on writing assignments at a time when one member of each group was absent without explanation. I encouraged each group to wait as long as possible to allow the student to rejoin the group, but told them it was ultimately their decision. Both waited and, in one case, the missing group member returned after a brief absence to help finish the project successfully. In the other case, the student remained missing for too long, and the other three members reluctantly decided to write the report on their own, forcing the fourth student to do a great deal of work near the end of the term. The jigsaw technique thus forces students to do some hard thinking about their judgments of their peers and to take responsibility for their decisions.

Though I have used this technique in only this one course, it might work very well in discussion and seminar classes. It is an excellent motivational device and has the pedagogical value of calling on the distinctive backgrounds, experiences, and abilities of different students. To sum up, the technique enables students to learn course material efficiently, while dealing with social situations that contribute to their overall education.

Reference

Aronson, E., & Bridgeman, D. (1981). Jigsaw groups and the desegregated classroom: In pursuit of common goals. In E. M. Hetherington & R. D. Parke (Eds.), *Contemporary readings in child psychology* (2nd ed., pp. 339-345). New York: McGraw Hill.

A Laboratory Group Model for Engaging Undergraduates in Faculty Research

Thomas G. Plante
Santa Clara University

Undergraduates who work with faculty in research often find the experience highly valuable and helpful in gaining graduate school admission (Dunn & Toedter, 1991; Gibson, Kahn, & Mathie, 1996; Hartmann, 1990; Kierniesky, 1984; Purdy, Reinehr, & Swartz, 1989). With increasing numbers of students majoring in psychology and applying for graduate study, involving many students in research activities outside the classroom is challenging (Gibson et al., 1996; McDonald, 1997). Furthermore, students often have little research experience or skill, and their studies, relatively short tenure on campus, and other responsibilities (e.g., work, extracurricular activities) often preclude them from spending much time on research. Faculty-student research collaboration can be especially diff cult at liberal arts colleges, due to the higher teaching demands, lower levels of research support, and absence of graduate or postdoctoral assistants relative to large universities (Kierniesky, 1984).

Although several models of faculty-student research collaboration appear in the literature (Beins, 1993; Dunn & Toedter, 1991; Evans, Rintala, Guthrie, & Raines, 1981; Gibson et al., 1996), few have focused on small colleges and the use of a large number of students working on multiple concurrent projects with one faculty member. For example, Gibson et al. (1996) used a single-faculty, single-project model that accommodates up to 4 students, or a multifaculty, multiproject team accommodating up to 12 students and several faculty members. Dunn and Toedter (1991) use a two-student, two-faculty model that they reported takes more faculty time than the more traditional one-student, one-faculty model. Although the Gibson et al. and Dunn and Toedter models are useful for both students and faculty, this model accommodates more students and allows for simultaneously conducting multiple projects with only one faculty member. Thus, this model provides a more efficient way to conduct faculty-student collaborative research.

Stress and Coping Laboratory Group Program

The model outlined in this article is the Stress and Coping laboratory group directed by the author at Santa Clara University. The research associated with the group typically involves a variety of clinical and health psychology research projects. Students are recruited primarily from word of mouth and also from class announcements and posted flyers. Following an initial interview and screening, interested students participate in weekly 1-hr laboratory group meetings. The interview and screening procedure provides an understanding of the interests, goals, and expectations of each student and informs them about the duties and responsibilities of the laboratory group participants. Unlike most other undergraduate-faculty research models (e.g., Dunn & Toedter, 1991; Evans et al., 1981), students who volunteer to participate in the laboratory group generally do not receive course credit or money for their participation. Volunteers are motivated by the desire to develop research skills and experience and have the opportunity to present and coauthors research. Most students are interested in graduate study and believe the experience in the laboratory group enhances their chances of being accepted into quality graduate programs. Periodically, students who work as a project manager on one or more projects obtain independent-study course credit. The approximately 15 students who attend the laboratory meetings are usually junior and senior psychology or biology majors (i.e., typically, preclinical psychology or premedical students) who have completed courses in general psychology, statistics, and research methods.

The laboratory group meetings review the progress of various research projects in a "rounds" format. Brief updates on projects presented by students involved in the projects and group discussion of problem-solving strategies help students cope with challenges and obstacles that arise. In this way, all students learn about the various research projects under way even if they are not directly involved in more than one. This format also allows the faculty supervisor to keep up to date on progress without numerous individual student meetings, although individual and subgroup meetings can be scheduled as needed. Generally, direct supervision totals approximately 2-3 hr each week.

Each research project has an identified student project manager who assumes primary student responsibility for that project. The project manager also acts as a peer mentor for other students with less experience or who are new to the research team. The project manager usually writes the first draft of a paper for publication or presentation, under close supervision from the faculty supervisor. Other students volunteer to help during and after laboratory group meetings, depending on the needs of each project and the student's interest and availability. Project managers distribute a draft of a paper to the entire laboratory group for review and comments before being submitted for presentation or publication. Students participate in a dress rehearsal in front of the laboratory group for practice and feedback before presentations at conferences.

Some students are extremely active in the laboratory group; others (with less tin e or interest) assist on projects that take less time (e.g., calling research participants to remind them of scheduled appointments, conducting library computer literature reviews, investigating purchase options for new equipment). Students tend to develop special skills such as analyzing data, operating specific laboratory equipment, or conducting computer literature reviews. Students with these special skills can help other students on assorted projects, and can orient new students to the laboratory group. This team approach increases efficiency, productivity, motivation, and overall enjoyment.

A Sample Project: Fitness and Stress Responsivity

The following is a description and illustration of one project in detail. A large study investigating the role of aerobic fitness and physiological stress responsivity among individuals at risk for the development of hypertension needed a great deal of student assistance. A junior psychobiology major acted as project manager. She coordinated the activities of six other students involved with the project and kept the project on schedule. She also focused on the literature review and began to draft, with close supervision, the introduction and methods section of the paper. A junior biology major, with excellent computer and technical skills, helped set up the research laboratory and equipment. He also investigated various options for purchasing audio, video, and additional laboratory equipment. A senior psychology major organized all of the questionnaires, consent forms, and data collection sheets, and then entered this material into a computer file. The project manager and another student ran the participants through a laboratory procedure during a 6-week period, and another senior psychology major scheduled all participants and reminded them of their appointments.

The weekly laboratory group meetings helped to keep the project organized, promoted communication among the students involved, and provided a forum for brainstorming and coordination of research activities. The project manager and one other student entered the data into the

computer and conducted the statistical analysis with close supervision from the faculty supervisor and assistance from another student in the laboratory group. The laboratory group read the resulting paper and gave input to the authors. Once completed, the paper was submitted to the Fourth International Congress of Behavioral Medicine Conference in Washington, DC, and submitted for publication. The paper was accepted at the International Congress, where it was presented by the project manager, and a version appeared later in the *International Journal of Stress Management* (Plante, Lantis, & Checa, 1997).

Since 1994, 35 students have participated in the program. Almost all of those students have plans for graduate study. Members of the Stress and Coping laboratory group (faculty and various students) at Santa Clara have published 19 refereed professional journal articles; and have presented papers at 13 regional, national, or international conferences and 9 papers at undergraduate student research conferences. An additional 10 papers are either submitted or in preparation. American Psychological Association ethical guidelines (American Psychological Association, 1992) and additional published guidance (e.g., Fine & Kurdek, 1993) help determine publication credit and authorship issues. Generally, the student project manager(s) for a given study and I are listed as authors, with acknowledgments provided for those who helped with the particular project(s).

Conclusions

Faculty at other colleges may wish to adapt the model to accommodate their research programs. Regardless of the nature of faculty research, the principles of the model will likely maximize reaching the goals of faculty-student collaborative research in an efficient, productive, and enjoyable team-oriented manner.

References

American Psychological Association. (1992). Ethical principles of psychologists and code of conduct. *American Psychologist, 47,* 1597-1611.

Beins, B. C. (1993, August). *Research team: Bonding, enjoyment, and programmatic research.* Paper presented at the annual meeting of the American Psychological Association, Toronto, Canada.

Dunn, D. S., & Toedter, L. J. (1991). The collaborative honors project in psychology Enhancing student and faculty development. *Teaching of Psychology, 18,* 178-180.

Evans, R. I., Rintala, D. H., Guthrie, T. J., & Raines, B. E. (1981). Recruiting and training undergraduate psychology research assistants for longitudinal field investigations. *Teaching of Psychology, 8,* 97-100.

Fine, M. A., & Kurdek, L. A. (1993). Reflections on determining authorship credit and authorship order on faculty-student collaborations. *American Psychologist,* *48*, 1141-1147.

Gibson, P. R., Kahn, A. S., & Mathie, V. A. (1996). Undergraduate research groups: Two models. *Teaching of Psychology, 23*, 36-38.

Hartmann, D. J. (1990). Undergraduate research experience as preparation for graduate school. *The American Sociologist, 21*, 179-188.

Kiemiesky, N. C. (1984). Undergraduate research in small psychology departments. *Teaching of Psychology, 11*, 15-18.

McDonald, D. G. (1997). Psychology's surge in undergraduate majors. *Teaching of Psychology, 24*, 22-26.

Plante, T. G., Lantis, A., & Checa, G. (1997). The influence of gender, hypertension risk, and aerobic fitness on cardiovascular responses to laboratory induced stress. *International Journal of Stress Management, 4*, 89-99.

Purdy, S. E., Reinehr, R. C., & Swartz, S. D. (1989). Graduate admissions criteria of leading psychology departments. *American Psychologist, 44*, 960-964.

Collaborative Learning in an Introduction to Psychological Science Laboratory: Undergraduate Teaching Fellows Teach to Learn

Andrew F. Newcomb
Catherine L. Bagwell
University of Richmond

Doceas ut discas provides an excellent summation of our Introduction to Psychological Science project that places students and an undergraduate teaching fellow (TF) in a demanding collaborative-learning environment, requiring all parties to assume unusual responsibility for their own learning. Translated as "teach to learn" or, more literally, "teach that you may learn," this Latin phrase is thought to be derived from the writings of Saint Ambrose. In the preface to his treatise, *On the Duties of Ecclesiastics*, Saint Ambrose (374 A.D.) questioned his preparation for the priesthood and his ascendance to the see of Milan, and he spoke of his need to learn and teach at the same time. In a similar way, we designed a laboratory curriculum and TFs program that uniquely challenges our ablest majors and actively engages introductory students in psychological science—one of the most liberating of disciplines in the liberal arts (D. L. Cole, 1982).

Since the fall of 1993, the entire department faculty has joined together to implement a new Introduction to Psychological Science course that consists of a 3-hr per week lecture section and a corequisite 2-hr weekly laboratory class. The primary objective of this beginning-level course is to familiarize first- and second-year undergraduates with the questions psychologists raise about human behavior and with the methods used to

answer these questions. In both the lecture (up to 144 students per semester) and laboratory (as many as 12 students in each of 12 sections), our fundamental premise is that the most enduring and useful aspects of undergraduate education in psychology lie not in learning the content of the field but in learning how to acquire knowledge. The lecture section is unique because the curriculum is focused on nine themes that correspond to core areas of study in psychological science. Furthermore, all faculty share the responsibility of introducing students to different scientific perspectives by teaching the assumptions and methodologies of their respective subdisciplines (for details of the lecture component, see Allison, 1995).

Although this approach in the lecture section is a drastic departure from the traditional introductory course, the intellectual core of this endeavor rests with the TFs program and the laboratory component. Neither the idea of undergraduates teaching undergraduates nor the requirement of a laboratory in introductory psychology is a new concept. What makes our program unique is the scope of the undergraduates' responsibilities in the laboratory and the magnitude of the laboratory experience itself. We know, for example, that undergraduates are productive leaders of discussion groups (Diamond, 1972; Janssen,

1976), effective in teaching small classes (Harris, 1994; Wortman & Hillis, 1976), and successful in supervising laboratory experiences that demonstrate various psychological phenomena (Goolkasian & Lee, 1988; Kohn & Brill, 1981). In our program, however, the TFs are fully responsible for directing laboratory classes that actively engage introductory students in the scientific methods used in psychology.

In this article, we describe the Introduction to Psychological Science laboratory and the TFs program. First, we consider the goals of the laboratory and describe the curriculum. Next, we examine the goals of the TFs program; the responsibilities of the TFs; and the procedures for TF selection, training, and supervision. Then, we review how similar programs may be established. Once these basics of the laboratory and the TFs program are outlined, we discuss the effectiveness of the experience for the introductory students and the TFs. We conclude with a consideration of the implications of this type of program on quality undergraduate education.

Introduction to Psychological Science Laboratory

Goals and Objectives

The goal of the Introduction to Psychological Science laboratory is to familiarize students with the various methods psychologists use to ask and answer questions about behavior. The course has six specific objectives: (a) to introduce research issues from a variety of theoretical and empirical perspectives; (b) to offer an active-learning experience with an emphasis on discovery; (c) to teach analytical and critical thinking skills necessary to formulate and answer research questions using various scientific methodologies; (d) to enhance communication skills, especially scientific writing; (e) to provide opportunities for interactive learning with more senior peers; and (f) to foster an appreciation of psychology as a science.

The Laboratory Curriculum

Although the laboratory curriculum supports the themes presented in lecture, the laboratory is not specifically integrated into the thematic organization of the lecture class. The primary purpose of the laboratory is to provide introductory students with an intensive and active experience with the methods of inquiry used in psychological science. Students complete primary source readings before each laboratory, actively participate in the laboratory session, and write weekly laboratory reports following the appropriate professional style (American Psychological Association, 1994b). The laboratory

sessions are supplemented by a laboratory manual that includes course materials, prelaboratory assignments, and primary source readings (Newcomb, Bagwell, & Wright, 1995).

The 11 laboratory sessions are organized within a conceptual framework that provides for a progression of learning within three specific areas. First, students actively experience and learn about methodologies, assumptions, and research questions within a particular subdiscipline of psychology in each laboratory. Second, computer technology and statistical concepts are presented in a logical sequence that begins with graphing and visual inspection of data and proceeds to descriptive and inferential statistics, correlational analysis, and nonparametric statistics. In this progression, curricular demands increase in difficulty, and knowledge is reinforced and enhanced with each successive laboratory. Third, requirements for the laboratory reports gradually increase as students gain experience using the library, reading and understanding primary source material, and finding theoretical and empirical support for their hypotheses.

Within this conceptual framework, the curriculum is divided into two sections. As shown in Table 1, the first four laboratories provide a foundation in computer skills, writing skills, and statistical concepts that form the backbone of the later laboratories. Although these first labs proceed within the context of specific subdisciplines of psychology, they focus on the development of a strong base of skills. In contrast, the last seven laboratories emphasize the methodologies and research questions of specific subdisciplines of psychological science. Our goal in these laboratories is not to offer students simple demonstrations of psychological phenomena or experiments with clear hypotheses and flawless outcomes. Furthermore, we do not ask students to learn the intricacies of statistics. Instead, with guidance and instruction from the TFs, students explore the methodologies of various subdisciplines and gain personal experience with the complexities of designing and evaluating a psychological study.

The final exam for the laboratory component of the course is constructed each semester by the TFs who each write a summary of a research question in a biologically or socially based subdiscipline. Students are given a choice of two questions, and during the in-class exam, they must design a study to explore that question. They propose hypotheses, formulate hypothetical data, and analyze their data using appropriate statistical tests. As the product of this 2-hr exam, students turn in a complete laboratory report in which they have fully defined the problem, developed their hypotheses, described their study, and analyzed and discussed their hypothetical findings. In this way, the final exam requires students to demonstrate their skills at all phases of the research enterprise .

Table 1. Psychological Science Laboratory Curriculum: Content Area, Laboratory Activities, and Skills Developed

Laboratory	Title	Content Area	Laboratory Activities	Skills Developed
1	Freud, Apples, and Science	Free association and the concept of perceptual defense; readings include excerpts from Freud and Jung	Introduction to the scientific method with emphasis on hypothesis development; completion of a perceptual defense experiment and examination of results in the context of hypotheses	Core computer skills and fundamentals of scientific writing
2	Scientific Writing: An Essential Tool for Sharing Knowledge	Effective written communication	Direct instruction and collaborative-learning exercises in scientific writing	Scientific writing and computer graphics
3	Memory, Methodology, and Statistical Madness	Basics of experimental design and principles of descriptive statistics	Completion of two recall experiments and instruction in experimental design and statistics	Understanding of fundamental design and statistical concepts; use of statistical software package
4	More Memory, More Methodology, and More Statistical Madness	Principles of variability and inferential statistics	Completion of levels of processing experiment; instruction in between-subjects analysis of variance	Fundamental conceptual appreciation of inferential statistics and expanded skills with statistical software packages
5	Observation: A Window to Behavior	Observational methodology in the context of developmental psychology	Discussion of the use of coding schemes; application of sampling techniques to code a videotape of two children at play	Understanding and use of observational methodology, including development of own observational coding scheme
6	The Righteous Path to Questionnaire Construction	Questionnaire construction in the context of social psychology	Review and critique of the use of questionnaires in the psychological literature; development of computer-based questionnaire	Appreciation of questionnaire methodology, including use as manipulation checks for independent variables and as measures of dependent variables
7	First Impressions, Lasting Memories	Social cognition and impression formation	Continued exploration of experimental design issues in using questionnaires; discussion of real-world situations versus the psychology laboratory	Program questionnaires on computer
8	Wall Flowers and Social Butterflies	Psychometric properties of psychological tests in the context of personality assessment	Assessment of extroversion and introversion and examination of the relation between personality inventories and behavioral rating measures	Understanding of the concepts of reliability and validity and of correlational analyses
9	Experiencing the Third Dimension	Methodologies of psychophysics	Investigation of the relation between binocular disparity and depth perception with computer-based experiment on magnitude estimation	Enhanced understanding of inferential statistics, including within-subjects analysis of variance
10	The Birds and the Bees and the Rats	Observational methodology in the study of the sexual and maternal behavior of rats	Discussion of the biological origins of behavioral differences between men and women; examination of prenatal and postnatal influences on the display of male sexual behavior and maternal behavior	Increase skills in observational methodology, understand the distinction between nominal and ratio data, and complete a chi-square analysis
11	Visualizing the Mind	Neuroscience and neuronal morphology	Use of computerized microscopy and image analysis to measure the structures of neurons	Appreciation of the importance of computer technology in the field of neuroscience and review of inferential statistics

Revisions of the Curriculum

During the four semesters that the laboratory has been offered, we have made three prominent curricular revisions. We initially began each laboratory with a short discussion session centered on a book that addresses important themes in psychology. Student response to this text was negative, and we dropped the discussion groups. During the second semester, we introduced a laboratory devoted to scientific writing. Finally, we edited the student and instructor manuals each semester and completed two extensive end-of-year revisions. We now have a contract with McGraw-Hill to handle copyright issues and to publish the student manual (see Newcomb, Bagwell, &Parker, 1996) . In addition, our instructor's manual has been significantly improved and serves as a comprehensive resource for the TFs.

Several other issues remain. Students are concerned with the time frame for returning papers because they turn in a new laboratory report before receiving the previous week's corrected paper. As a result of this delay, students tend to repeat similar mistakes. Possible solutions are a revision of the scoring schedule, which may be too demanding on the TFs, or the option for students to rewrite several of their laboratory reports. Students also believe that the laboratory component should comprise more than 25% of their final grade in the introductory course; we will reapportion the credit level to 35% in future semesters. Furthermore, because most of the introductory students do not plan to major in psychology, many want the option for nonmajors to omit the laboratory component. This change would be contrary to the goals of our general education curriculum; because few students come to college with the intention of majoring in psychology, such a modification may significantly reduce the number of psychology majors.

The Psychology TFs Program

Goals, Objectives, and Responsibilities

The overall goal of the TFs program is to engage introductory students and the TFs in a process of mutual discovery. The specific objectives of the program are to: (a) afford a capstone experience that requires application of previous knowledge and acquisition of new information, (b) strengthen skills in critical thinking and oral defense of diverging viewpoints, (c) emphasize different modes of problem solving and interpreting ideas and data, (d) cultivate an appreciation of intellectual complexity and discovery, and (e) promote the development of a stronger academic community of majors and department faculty.

In achieving these objectives, the TFs have unique and demanding responsibilities. In two-person teams, the TFs direct three laboratory sections per week. They score approximately 30 papers per week, hold 2 office hours each week, and develop and score the final laboratory exam. Finally, the TFs participate in weekly 2-hr supervision sessions. In all, the TFs frequently work as many as 15 hr each week, but they are paid a fixed stipend for working 10 hr per week.

Selection of TFs

The TFs program can encourage our best and brightest students to consider academic careers. Therefore, in designing the selection process, we drew from the results of a retrospective examination of the undergraduate careers of individuals who later went on to become accomplished college teachers (D. L. Cole, 1986). D. L. Cole suggested that identifying the brightest students is an easy task; these are the students who have top grades, complete departmental honors, and receive the best recommendations. However, he proposed that only a subset of these students are best suited to excel in a wide range of teaching situations with a diverse population of student learning styles.

Our selection process is simple. Students submit a statement describing their interest in being a TF, a list of psychology course work and grades, and names of three faculty members who know them well. This information is given to faculty members who provide two or three descriptive phrases for each candidate and rate each applicant's overall potential as a TF. All candidates are then randomly placed in groups of five or six applicants and complete a 1-hr group problem-solving task. The group is asked to design a laboratory experience that promotes introductory psychology students' understanding of scientific inquiry. The faculty supervisor combines his or her evaluation of performance in this group setting with the other data and completes the selection of TFs.

What is the outcome of our selection process? Our impression is that we do find our best and brightest students who are, in many ways, like individuals who have become accomplished college teachers (D. L. Cole, 1986). In particular, our inaugural class of TFs consisted of individuals who would be successful in many different endeavors. They have a positive outlook on life, a wealth of interests, the emotional flexibility to gain a balanced perspective about themselves and their academic pursuits, and a genuine concern with self-presentation and effective communication.

Training of TFs

The training program for the TFs begins during the summer when each new TF receives a packet of training materials. The TFs read seven background articles covering the following topics: (a) characteristics of quality undergraduate psychology programs (American Psychological Association, 1994a), (b) goals and objectives of the institution's general education curriculum, (c) ideas about how to start class off on the right foot (Zahorski, 1993), (d) development of effective skills in assessing written work (Larson, 1986, Sommers 1982, Willingham,1990), and (e) reasons for establishing high standards for academic performance (W. Cole, 1993). Also in preparation for the formal training sessions, the TFs receive the student manual and lesson plans for the first three laboratories; an outline of the conceptual organization of the laboratories, including the topics and statistical procedures covered in each; three student laboratory papers; and the midsemester and final course evaluations from the previous semester.

After returning to campus, the 2½ days of formal training begins with a team-building dinner. The first morning session is focused on the goals and philosophy of the laboratory within the context of general education requirements. The evaluations of the previous semester are reviewed to capitalize on prior experience. Then, the TFs work together as a team to design a research project, formulate hypothetical data, and use various software packages to analyze the data. In the afternoon session, the course syllabus and logistical issues are reviewed, but the primary focus is on assessment of student work. The originator of our writing-across-the curriculum and undergraduate writing fellows program works with the TFs to improve their understanding of the assessment of student papers. The TFs also receive training in how to help students effectively use microcomputers for writing and data analysis.

During the second day of training, the TFs work in pairs to teach the first three laboratory classes. Each pair is videotaped, and these taped segments are reviewed and critiqued by the entire group. The objectives are to improve the TFs teaching skills and increase their comfort level with directing the first three laboratories. In addition, the TFs work with the social science reference librarian to enhance their skills in completing computerized library searches and learn effective ways to help introductory students with information retrieval.

Supervision of TFs

The weekly supervision sessions provide a critical means to support the TFs professional development, and these sessions ensure quality, consistency, and coherence in the curriculum (cf. Wesp,1992) . In the first semester, the faculty member who designed the next laboratory teaches it to the TFs during weekly supervision. This procedure allows the TFs to observe a model of effective pedagogy, ask questions about the laboratory, and engage in collaborative development of alternative ways of accomplishing the objectives of the laboratory. In addition, the primary faculty supervisor meets individually with the TFs during the first semester to explore concerns. The supervision format changes in the second semester when pairs of TFs teach the next laboratory to their peers and the supervising faculty. In this way, the TFs are refreshed in course material, and they have the opportunity to hone their pedagogical skills. An added benefit of faculty supervision is that it fosters a sense of community, and the faculty have a vested interest in the TFs and the introductory students' experiences.

Development of Similar Programs

Development of the laboratory course and TFs program has been a major undertaking, and the establishment of similar programs rests first and foremost in collaborative faculty initiative. All nine of our faculty cooperatively team teach our lecture course, and five faculty are active in the development of the laboratory curriculum. Individual faculty rotate teaching credit for the lecture course over nine semesters, the primary faculty supervisor receives credit equivalent to two ninths of the annual teaching load, and the four supporting faculty direct TF supervision sessions without receiving course credit.

The history of our introductory course provides an important context in which to assess this level of faculty participation. A decade ago, we offered five or six introductory sections each semester that required approximately 17% of our total faculty teaching load. Since then, nominal teaching load has been reduced by 25%, and now we use approximately 6% of our total faculty load to support the introductory course and laboratory. The net gain is equivalent to one faculty member's teaching load for an entire year .

The relatively low expenditure of faculty resources to implement a general education experience of this magnitude was an important factor in our garnering financial support for the project. Furthermore, at an institution whose strategic plan is titled "Engagement in Learning," the Laboratory curriculum and TFs program are well matched to institutional strategic goals. Although there were significant expenditures in new facilities, the resulting 13-station Macintosh instructional classroom supports the entire psychology curriculum and is scheduled for direct classroom instruction for more than 40 hr per week. Other one-time expenses included summer support for one faculty member and a student assistant who worked to organize the laboratory curriculum, the student and TF manuals, and the training materials. The ongoing expense for paying each TF is approximately $1,300 per year, and the introductory laboratory itself has a small operating budget of about $500 per year.

In an era of limited resources and increasing class sizes, the initial facility expenditure may be prohibitive, but this expense could be lessened by creating a less elaborate laboratory classroom or possibly retrofitting an existing facility. The ongoing expense of paying TFs could be replaced through the use of course credit (for variations of this approach, see Harris, 1994; Zechmeister & Reich, 1994). As an alternative to adding more sections for introductory courses with larger enrollments, the laboratory curriculum could be reduced and offered to students on alternate weeks thereby doubling potential enrollment. In this way, benefits of the small class size in laboratory sections are maintained. Regardless of implementation strategy, a program such as ours has important implications for personalizing large introductory classes and for providing introductory students with hands-on and minds-on experiences (Benjamin, 1991).

Outcomes of the Psychological Science Laboratory Experience

Outcomes for Introductory Students

To assess students' experience in the Introduction to Psychological Science laboratory, narrative evaluations were completed by all students at midterm and the end of the semester. Four open-ended questions about positive and negative aspects of the laboratory as well as suggestions for improvement were asked each time. Results of the summative evaluations from the first two semesters in which the laboratory was taught were content analyzed and organized around five themes: (a) connection to the lecture class component of the course, (b) hands-on experience with psychology, (c) collaborative learning and skill development, (d) class structure, and (e) demands and expectations of the laboratory.

Connection to the lecture class component of the course. The laboratory was intended to provide a unique opportunity for students to think and behave like psychologists, and the methodological focus of the lecture class was expected to be augmented by the laboratory experience. Although many students commented about the connections between the lecture class and the laboratory, student evaluations fell on both sides of this issue. Some said that the class and laboratory were not adequately related and wished the connections were more direct (e.g., a laboratory on personality the week personality is discussed in the lecture), whereas others said that the laboratory provided an opportunity to apply methodologies to research questions and reinforced the material covered in the class .

Hands-on experience with psychology. What the students consistently described as hands-on experience can be more formally conceptualized as active learning. There were two specific ways in which students thought they actively engaged in learning about the science of psychology, and these experiences were often described as the best aspects of the laboratory. First, students consistently commented on the value of learning the methodologies of psychological science and the complexities of experimental design. Second, students expressed favor about how computers were incorporated into the laboratory. They were given minimal instruction, but they gained the necessary tools to use computers effectively on their own.

Collaborative learning and skill development. Whether praising or questioning the value of the laboratory experience, most students indicated that the laboratory promoted the development of critical- and analytical-thinking skills. This evaluation was also supported by responses to the standard teaching evaluation question on promotion of critical and analytical thinking: Seventy-two percent of the students gave the highest rating and less than 3% gave the lowest rating across all laboratory sections on a 3-point scale. Furthermore, students believed that their writing skills greatly improved. The most pervasive criticism of the laboratory was the amount of work required, and the weekly laboratory reports bore the brunt of this criticism. Nevertheless, students indicated that, as their writing skills improved, they gained a greater understanding and appreciation for scientific writing. The collaborative learning that characterized the laboratory experience was also highly praised by students. They enjoyed working with the TFs and their classmates in a process of mutual discovery, and they valued the opportunity to help one another learn.

Class structure. Perhaps the most prevalent topic of students' evaluations was their experience with the TFs. Although the feeling was not universal, the vast majority of students had a positive experience with the TFs, who were viewed as more effective and less intimidating than

faculty. Many phrases were used to describe the TFs; however, students most frequently commented on their patience and willingness to help, their thoroughness and ease at explaining difficult concepts, and their enthusiasm and desire to help students learn. Furthermore, the laboratory students enjoyed having other students lead them in collaborative discovery and said that, as their peers, the TFs could easily understand them. Other aspects of the laboratory structure that students appreciated were the small class size, the individual attention given to them by their TFs, and the ease of following the laboratory manual.

Demands and expectations of the laboratory. An almost universal comment was that the laboratory was too much work. However, some students added a caveat to the comments about the workload; they thought the laboratory required too much work, but it was challenging and interesting In particular, they believed they gained a strong knowledge base in the methodologies used *n different disciplines, the use of computers, the methods of scientific writing, and the importance of developing critical- and analytical-thinking skills. Hence, we think that the work required in the laboratory class is just about right! Another problem with the laboratory, according to many students, has to do with inconsistencies in the TFs application of scoring standards. As in any course with many sections, teachers of each section will grade slightly differently, and we are not overly concerned with this criticism. In addition, the view that performance in the laboratory is scored too harshly is a misperception. The mean score students received on laboratory reports was 81.4 (SD = 9.8), and the average grade for introductory classes across the institution is approximately a B^-.

Outcomes for TFs

In addition to the positive outcomes for the introductory students, the laboratory also has important outcomes for the TFs. In the summer following their tenure, the original eight TFs were asked to write a letter about their experience. Although each TF did not necessarily speak to each point, a content analysis of these reflective and candid evaluations revealed five major themes: (a) learning about teaching, (b) collaborative relationships among the TFs, (c) a capstone experience that provided connections across the baccalaureate experience, (d) academic skill development, and (e) personal development.

Learning about teaching. First and foremost, the TFs valued the opportunity to teach and to learn about teaching. Through close supervision and direct experience, TFs learned about different modes of teaching, and their teaching skills in and out of the classroom dramatically improved. Also, TFs were better able to recognize their personal strengths and weaknesses, and they gained insight into what is required to teach effectively. Perhaps the most important outcome of the TF experience was the development of a pedagogical philosophy centered on empowering students with responsibility for their own learning, encouraging collaborative discovery, and promoting the development of a method of inquiry.

These three principles represent the essence of the TFs approach to teaching, but the TF experience was also very satisfying. The TFs described their "passion for teaching" and the personal rewards of teaching, including the moments of "excitement and fulfillment from seeing something click for a student." The rewards of teaching were also evident in learning to cope with the frustrations of students who appeared unmotivated and did not live up to their potential. Finally, for those TFs contemplating a career in academics, their desire to become professors was fostered by the opportunity to gain a quality, closely supervised teaching experience even before entering graduate school.

Collaborative relationships. The TF experience provided a focal point for academic and intellectual pursuits. As a group, the TFs were dedicated to psychology and their introductory laboratories. Their initial training experience brought them together as a team and encouraged them to help and support one another. As the TFs worked more closely as a group, they respected one another, challenged each other's ideas, and worked collaboratively to solve problems. Likewise, the demands of learning to coordinate team teaching were at times challenging, but immensely valuable, aspects of the experience. This combination of unique opportunities provided the TFs with a common experience steeped in intellectual richness and vitality.

A capstone experience. Each TF had considerable psychology course work, and all were involved in independent research. Nevertheless, teaching the introductory laboratories was a valuable capstone experience that supported interconnections among knowledge areas. Just as a primary goal of the Introduction to Psychological Science laboratory is for students to gain an appreciation for the science of psychology and to understand the role of various subdisciplines, a similar and more sophisticated outcome was obtained by the TFs. The TFs imparted this scientific orientation to their students, and they developed a conceptual framework for their own baccalaureate experience.

As part of their teaching responsibilities, the TFs tried to make connections among various subdisciplines of psychology. They worked to make psychological science come aLive for their students and to demonstrate how different researchers may ask the same questions but seek to answer these questions in different ways. Within this context, TFs were better able to tie together the seemingly distinct experiences they had in their various psychology classes. Their search for connections among what they had learned transcended the boundaries of psychology because TFs also looked for interconnections with their other classes in the liberal arts.

Academic skill development. A fundamental outcome of the TF experience was the feeling that teaching the introductory labs made the TFs better students. The TFs were better able to integrate their knowledge of psychology and draw connections among subdisciplines. In addition, all TFs wrote of the refinement and development of their academic skills. They were continually called on to explain concepts and answer questions. Consequently, oral communication skills as well as critical-thinking skills were enhanced by the TF experience. In addition, teaching an entire laboratory on writing scientific papers and scoring students' weekly laboratory reports raised the TFs awareness of their own strengths and weaknesses in writing.

Also, TFs believed that their experiences made them more active students. TFs realized that their students learned more when they asked questions, posed problems or alternative solutions, or stimulated discussion on a particular issue, and TFs encouraged each other and their peers to do the same in their own classes. Furthermore, the TFs consistently advocated collaborative learning, and they tried to promote that kind of environment in the classes in which they were students. One might suspect that the intense demands on the TFs would detract from their course work. However, just the opposite was the case; every TF did as well or better than the previous year: As a group, they went from a previous 3.41 overall grade point average (GPA) to a 3.87 GPA for the first semester.

Personal development. All TFs also wrote about some aspect of the experience as contributing to their personal growth and development. Although these outcomes differed, each TF mentioned personal development as an important result of the experience. For example, teaching their peers and being completely responsible for the labs fostered a sense of confidence and competence. In addition, the TFs dealt with many students and handled their problems, concerns, and frustrations. They also collaborated to work through difficulties of teaching as a team. Due to these experiences, many TFs said that they became more effectively assertive in interpersonal interactions. Furthermore, the TFs believed that their time-management skills greatly improved. Their position as a TF added 10 or more hr a week to their schedule, but each TF achieved the best GPAs of their college career. A common sentiment among the TFs was that they realized how much time mattered, and they became more effective managers of their time.

Overall, the TFs described their experience as "the best academic experience I had," "extremely helpful," "an extremely rewarding experience, both academically and personally," and "so exciting that I have realized how important becoming a professor is to me." Each of these comments points to the important professional socialization that takes place when undergraduates teach their peers (cf. Harris, 1994). In particular, by participating in the life of the university through the roles of student and teacher, TFs increased their connection to the academic community, and they truly became an integral part of that community through their investment in the psychology department and in the arts and sciences.

Implications for Undergraduate Education

The Introduction to Psychological Science laboratory and the TFs program offer unusual challenges to introductory students and advanced undergraduates. Few faculty would take issue with the high expectations for the introductory students. The nonmajor has a marvelous opportunity for hands on and minds-on exploration of how psychologists ask and answer questions about behavior. Students planning to major in psychology are provided with an intensive firsthand experience with psychological science. This preparation should have important benefits when these students enroll in more challenging courses in our hierarchical curriculum (Walker, Newcomb, & Hopkins, 1987).

Just as the outcomes for the introductory student are very positive, so too are the outcomes for the TFs. An unanswered question is whether the responsibilities of the TFs are at a level appropriate for high-quality undergraduate education. Some faculty may question the use of undergraduates to teach introductory laboratory sessions. They could point out many reasons why TFs would be less than successful as laboratory instructors—their undergraduate status, their inexperience, and their ignorance of what defines good pedagogy. Nevertheless, our experiences with the TFs belie these notions; in fact, some of these concerns have been transformed into assets. For example, TFs make connections with students that faculty cannot ordinarily make, TFs share their experiences as learners who are growing intellectually and who acknowledge—as all teachers should—that they are closer to the beginning than to the end of such growth, and TFs have a freshness and enthusiasm that is contagious and allows every laboratory student to be energized by their passion for learning. Skeptics may think that we have taken active learning too far, but our experience suggests that everyone comes out a winner.

References

Allison, S. T. (1995) . Reconceiving and reconstructing the introductory course in psychology. *The Faculty Exchange, 8,* 14-20.

American Psychological Association. (1994a). *Principles for quality undergraduate psychology programs.* Washington, DC: Author.

American Psychological Association. (1994b). *Publication manual of the American Psychological Association* (4th ed.). Washington, DC: Author.

Benjamin, L. T., Jr. (1991). Personalization and active learning in the large introductory psychology class. *Teaching of Psychology, 18,* 68-74.

Cole, D. L. (1982). Psychology as a liberating art. *Teaching of Psychology, 9,* 23-28.

Cole, D. L. (1986). Attracting the best and the brightest to teach psychology. *Teaching of Psychology, 13,* 107-110.

Cole, W. (1993, January 6). By rewarding mediocrity we discourage excellence. *The Chronicle of Higher Education,* pp. B1-B2.

Diamond, M. J. (1972). Improving the undergraduate lecture class by use of student led discussion groups. *American Psychologist, 27,* 978-981.

Goolkasian, P., & Lee, J. A. (1988). A computerized laboratory for general psychology. *Teaching of Psychology, 15,* 98-100.

Harris, R. J. (1994, June). *Using undergraduates as teachers in a large university psychology class.* Paper presented at the meeting of the American Psychological Society, Washington, DC.

Janssen, P. (1976). With a little help from our friends. *Change, 8,* 50-53.

Kohn, A., & Brill, M. (1981). An introductory demonstration laboratory produced entirely by undergraduates. *Teaching of Psychology, 18,* 133-138.

Larson, R. L. (1986). Making assignments, judging writing, and annotating papers: Some suggestions. In C. W. Bridges (Ed.), *Training the new teacher of college composition* (pp. 109-126). Urbana, IL: National Council of Teachers of English.

Newcomb, A. F., Bagwell, C. L., & Wright, C. L. (Eds.). (1995). *Psychological science laboratory.* New York: McGraw-Hill.

Sommers, N. (1982). Responding to student writing. *College Composition and Communication, 33,* 148-156.

Walker, W. E., Newcomb, A. F., & Hopkins, W. P. (1987). A model for curriculum evaluation and revision in undergraduate psychology programs. *Teaching of Psychology, 14,* 198-202.

Wesp, R. (1992). Conducting introductory psychology activity modules as a requirement in advanced undergraduate courses. *Teaching of Psychology, 19,* 219-220.

Willingham, D. B. (1990). Effective feedback on written assignments. *Teaching of Psychology, 17,* 10-13.

Wortman, C. B., & Hillis, J. W. (1976). Undergraduate-taught "minicourses" in conjunction with an introductory lecture course. *Teaching of Psychology, 3,* 69-72.

Zahorski, K. J. (1993). Planning the first class. *The Teaching Professor, 7(6),* 5.

Zechmeister, E. B., & Reich, J. N. (1994). Teaching undergraduates about teaching undergraduates: A capstone course. *Teaching of Psychology, 21,* 24-28.

Notes

1. Catherine L. Bagwell is now a doctoral student in clinical psychology at Duke University; she was instrumental in developing the teaching fellows program and served as a teaching fellow during the 1993-94 academic year.
2. We thank Michelle Acosta, Cheryl Gaumer, Jennifer Humm, Melanie Morgan, Michele Nahra, Kevin Proudfoot, and Sandy Stevens-all members of the inaugural class of teaching fellows.
3. We also express appreciation to the Department of Psychology faculty, the University of Richmond Program for the Enhancement of Teaching Effectiveness, David Leary, and Zeddie Bowen for their generous support of the teaching fellows program.

6. PRESENTING RESEARCH RESULTS

A Radical Poster Session

Paul A. Gore, Jr.
Cameron J. Camp
University of New Orleans

Poster sessions have been described as teaching aids for advanced undergraduate seminars (Chute & Bank, 1983) and graduate student/faculty colloquia (Ventis, 1986). Since the spring of 1985, we have used a poster session as an integral part of a sophomore-level course in experimental design; it accounts for 20% of the course grade.

In this course, each student must design and conduct an original experiment and report the results in a poster session entitled "Spring/Fall Radish Festival." The title of the festival is derived from the fact that the subjects in these experiments are radishes. Aside from the long and noble history of radishes in experimental psychology (Lenington, 1979), these plant subjects have much to offer for our purposes. Radishes have a 30- to 40-day growth cycle; hence, in the course of a quarter or semester, almost any experimental design known to psychology (including sequential analyses from developmental psychology) can be executed. Radishes also do best with a spring or fall planting, grow quickly (in case disaster strikes and a fast replication is needed), and their seeds are bought rather than recruited. It is neither surprising nor fortuitous that the statistics of Student and Fisher have their roots in agricultural research.

Most important, the exercise provides students with hands-on experience in applying the principles of experimental design. Because they are working with a different species (indeed, phylum), the students often must be flexible and creative in using operational definitions. For example, two experiments were conducted to test the popularly held idea that talking to plants influences their growth. One student studied the effects of playing motivational tapes on radish height. As a control measure, she played a tape of mumbling to her comparison group. One student studied the effects of speaking Spanish to her plants, with English being spoken to her control group. Students doing such exercises quickly learn why saline injections or placebos are used as control procedures in more traditional experimental settings.

All posters are required to have an abstract of no more than 300 words, and a listing of hypotheses and operational definitions. In addition, the independent and dependent variables must be clearly listed and defined.

Threats to both internal and external validity must be listed, and an explanation of control procedures must be presented. The Results section must include the statistical tests used, as well as tables and charts when appropriate. In drawing conclusions, the students are urged to pay close attention to the question presented in the hypothesis, and the answer as given by the statistical analysis. Finally, a statement about what level of construct was contained in the study must be included (theoretical constructs must be free of mono-method and mono-operational bias, Cook & Campbell, 1979).

The poster session is held in a festival atmosphere, with 1st, 2nd, and 3rd prizes awarded. Students are, however, expected to answer questions presented to them on design decisions, statistics, or other information pertinent to the course. Previous prize winners include studies that examined the effects of the following variables on the growth of radishes: radiation, diazepam with shock, motivational tapes, carbon dioxide enriched atmosphere, and river water versus bottled water. The "Angel of Death" prize for the student suffering the highest level of experimental mortality and the "Square Radish" prize for the most bizarre independent variable are also rewarded.

Students also learn the relationships among statistics, experimental design, and subjects' behavior. Students are required to bring their radishes to the poster session so that the effects of their independent variables can literally be observed. One student reported a highly significant F statistic as a result of comparing the height of two groups when visually the groups were indistinguishable. When forced by the instructor to recalculate the between-groups sum of squares on the spot, the student realized the error of his ways (statistically speaking), and also learned a lesson in the relationship between statistical tests and common sense. The presence of the subjects in this case provided a valuable, concrete lesson in what within-groups and between-groups variance looks like.

Students also are required to bring printouts of data analyses using the $SPSS^X$ MANOVA program. Because many students use more than one dependent measure, they stumble on multivariate statistics included on their printouts, and curiosity leads them to learn more about multivariate analyses. We have found this approach to be a valuable introduction for students. In addition, students learn that interventions can have multiple effects, some positive and some negative. For example, a student who watered plants with milk found that the experimental plants had less root growth but larger leaf size in comparison to a control group of water-watered plants.

Finally, our students develop a sense of pride in their craft from this exercise. This festival is open to the entire college community, is featured in the campus newspaper, and is a topic of conversation for weeks afterward. Previous festival participants return each year to observe the growth of "radish psychology." Demonstrating their expertise in experimental design solidifies the lessons of the course in ways that are highly enjoyable for our students.

References

Chute, D. L., & Bank, B. (1983). Undergraduate seminars The poster session solution. *Teaching of Psychology, 10*, 99-100.

Cook, T. D., & Campbell, D. T. (1979*). Quasi-experimentation*. Chicago: Rand McNally.

Lenington, S. (1979). Effects of holy water on the growth of radish plants. *Psychological Reports, 45*, 381-382.

Ventis, D. G. (1986). Recycling poster sessions for colloquium series. *Teaching of Psychology, 13*, 222.

In-Class Poster Sessions

Brian N. Baird Pacific
Lutheran University

An unfortunate fact of teaching is that the opportunities for creative, individualized student activity tend to decrease in direct proportion to the number of students in a class. Instructors seeking a way around this dilemma may find in class poster sessions a practical and rewarding solution.

Poster sessions have been described by Chute and Bank (1983) and in a slightly different form as "fairs" for high school students by Benjamin, Fawl, and Klein (19775. This article presents a more detailed description of how poster sessions can be conducted in classes ranging from small seminars to large introductory sections.

Poster Session Project Description and Requirements

My in-class poster sessions resemble the poster sessions held at professional and scientific conferences. Instead of each student submitting a paper that only the instructor reads, students present projects to their classmates in poster session format. Depending on the class size, we hold poster sessions on sequential days, with a portion of the class simultaneously presenting their posters at various locations in the room while the remaining students circulate to discuss, evaluate, and give feedback. The students then evaluate the projects, with the instructor reserving the right to assign final grades.

During the second week of class, students receive a handout describing the rationale, requirements, and procedures for the poster sessions. In an effort to promote creativity and diversity, poster sessions are not limited to written papers. Instead, I offer the more general requirement that the students present projects. These projects, which I must approve, may be anything from traditional papers or research studies to auditory, video, or other artistic presentations. All projects require some combination of written and visual presentation during the poster sessions. To assist students in understanding the requirements, I place examples of papers, videos, and audio productions from previous students on library reserve. Although most students grasp the nature of the assignment on their own, instructors using this activity for the first time may wish to provide class time to discuss ideas and options for poster sessions. Instructors may also wish to present examples of their own work in poster session format. If students still have difficulty understanding the assignment, the two-stage approach (discussed later) provides opportunities to observe the work of other students and to receive additional feedback and direction.

All projects must meet three criteria that also serve as the bases for grading: (a) extended research beyond the information available from text or lecture materials, (b) critical thinking and analysis of the subject matter, and (c) clear communication of the information and ideas. For the purpose of this assignment, critical thinking is defined rather broadly as doing more than just reporting what others have written on a topic. Students are expected to evaluate, synthesize, interpret, and critique information, not just paraphrase. I discuss each of the criteria in the handout and in class.

Three Steps to Developing Posters

A three-step approach to developing posters is helpful. First, early in the semester, students are given a written description of poster project requirements. I then suggest that students explore their textbooks, personal experiences, or other sources to identify topics they would like to pursue. Students are also encouraged to find one or two other students with whom they would like to work on a project. Students must then submit a one-page proposal describing the topic they will address, the methods they will use, any ethical considerations, and the responsibilities of each student in the group.

The one-page descriptions give me a chance to ensure that the proposed projects are within the students' abilities and do not pose significant risks or other ethical concerns. The descriptions also let me brainstorm with students, suggest possible resources or approaches, and help anticipate or iron out problems.

After approving the project proposals, I schedule a date for initial presentation of the projects. During the semester, students present their projects on two occasions. The first presentation is given midway through the semester. This presentation allows students an opportunity to present what they have completed and receive feedback from their peers.

Setting a midsemester presentation date helps reduce the last minute "cramming" guaranteed to accompany assignments that are due at the end of the semester. Of greater importance is the opportunity for students to give and receive feedback. During the first poster session presentation, students' work will be reviewed by half of the other students in the class. Before this session, I instruct students in the value of such feedback and how best to give and receive it. This approach encourages students to learn from one another and to appreciate the value of the process of revision (Baird & Anderson, 1990). A recent student demonstrated this value by placing a sign beside his paper that read, "Tear it up please. I want your suggestions." Encouraging students to share their work and constructive criticism with others establishes a precedent that will serve them well throughout their educational experience.

A third benefit of the initial session is that the opportunity to observe the work of other students encourages project improvement among all participants. In the traditional model of assigned papers, only the instructor sees and evaluates student work. In such situations, students know only what they have produced and have no way to compare or contrast their work with that of their peers. The poster session, on the other hand, provides an opportunity for students to learn from comparison. The midsemester presentation leaves time for improvements.

A final benefit of the poster session and the two-stage presentation is that complaints concerning grades diminish. When students have no opportunity to observe the quality of their peers' work, they do not know why they received a particular grade. Poster sessions do not entirely solve this problem, but many students seem more ready to accept the grade their projects earn. As one student admitted, "When you gave me a C on my project I was mad at first, but then I saw what some of the other students had done and I understood. Now I want to make my final version a lot better."

Following the initial presentation of posters, I schedule the final step in the process for the next to last week of the semester. At this time, students present their revised projects. Presentation during this week allows time to grade and give feedback before the semester ends.

Session Logistics

Because students often choose similar topics, I review the first proposals and schedule presentations on different days to avoid redundancy. After topics are selected and assigned, a printed program describes what will be presented and by whom during the poster sessions. Copies of this program are distributed in advance to build a sense of the importance of the event. I also post the programs so other students or faculty may attend the sessions.

Along with balancing the content of the poster sessions, the instructor must consider the number of posters to be presented and how much time will be available for students to visit each poster. In large introductory classes, I allow the nonpresenters approximately 5 min to visit each poster that day. I also follow this time limit as I circulate among the posters to evaluate and discuss them with the students. If two or three students collaborate on each project, we can review posters for a lecture class of 50 to 60 students in 2 or 3 days. For larger classes, I schedule more presenters on a given day, with the trade-off being less time for interaction or the inability of all the students to visit all of the posters for that day. For smaller, upper division classes, I allow 10 to 15 min for each poster presentation. The added time permits greater discussion of presumably more advanced topics and projects.

Another suggestion is to take a signed, written roll on each day of the poster sessions. Although most students look forward to presenting their own work and attending the other days to view the posters of others, some attend only on the days of their presentations. Such absences are unfair to students who attended the first presentations.

Absent students also defeat the goal of having students learn from each others' posters. Making attendance mandatory at all sessions is regrettable but necessary to ensure equal participation.

We hold poster sessions in a classroom where students spread out around the perimeter and display their material either on tables or the wall. Poster sessions require a room that is large enough for students to have at least 5 to 8 ft in which to present their posters, with several feet between adjacent posters.

At the students' request, we recently held poster sessions in the informal, club-like, student union cafeteria. This allowed others outside the class to join the session and circulate among the posters. The response was positive, and other instructors say that they will follow suit with their classes.

Grading

As noted earlier, students participate In grading posters. This approach reduces the grading burden on the instructor and encourages students to evaluate the quality of their own work and that of others. Unfortunately, my experience suggests that when students are asked to grade others they tend to give everyone As. Such generosity is understandable, but it does not require students to consider what "quality work" means, and it is unfair to those students who have clearly produced superior work. To address this problem, give students the grading criteria before they grade any projects. The session program lists these criteria, and students assign each project a grade for each of the three criteria. Students record the grades on the programs and then return the programs anonymously at the end of each session. Even with these measures, the instructor should reserve the right to assign final grades. The instructor may wish to recognize exceptional effort that students might overlook or reduce the grade of mediocre projects that students graded too highly.

One final grading issue concerns the evaluation of collaborative projects. Most students find collaboration instructive and enjoyable. In some instances, however, students complain that they carried all the load while their partners did little or none of the work. With grades assigned on a per project basis, all students connected with the project receive the same grade, although some may not have earned it. I know of no solution that is entirely satisfactory. Asking students to identify their role during the proposal phase, then giving them an opportunity to individually grade their own project, as well as their contribution and that of their partners, may be useful. This approach at least provides a way for students to tell the instructor who in their group they felt earned what grade.

Student Evaluation of Poster Sessions

To assess student reactions to the poster sessions, I prepared a brief evaluation form and distributed it to two introductory psychology sections that participated in the poster sessions. I asked students to complete these forms anonymously and return them as part of the end of semester course evaluation. Abbreviated items from the questionnaire and response frequencies for each item are presented in Table 1.

The overall response to the poster sessions was positive as revealed in Table 1. Students indicated that the poster sessions were a valuable activity and that the main goals of the sessions were achieved. Some students expressed ambivalence about grading other students' papers and having their own work graded by peers. Even in these areas, however, the responses were almost all positive.

The clearest indication of support for poster sessions was seen in response to the last item of the survey. When asked if they would prefer to follow the poster session format or the standard term paper approach, 100% of those who responded to the question favored the poster sessions.

Table 1. Poster Session Evaluation Results

1. Did the poster sessions increase interaction among students and provide exposure to other students' learning styles?

A	B	C	D	E
58%	37%	5%		

2. By viewing other students work, do you feel you were able to gain more information about other topics that interested you?

A	B	C	D	E
73%	25%	2%		

3. The poster sessions involved three steps—the original proposal, the first session, and the final session. Do you feel this was a valuable approach?

A	B	C	D	E
74%	22%	4%		

4. How valuable was it for you to have the opportunity to do something other than a written paper?

A	B	C	D	E
75%	21%	4%		

5. What is your reaction to the process of you grading other posters?

A	B	C	D	E
34%	36%	25%	5%	

6. What is your reaction to having other students grade your work?

A	B	C	D	E
37%	38%	15%	8%	1%

7. Overall, how would you rate the effectiveness of the poster session format?

A	B	C	D	E
63%	33%	4%		

8.[a] What percentage of your course grade do you think the poster session should comprise?

% of Grade	0%	10%	15%	20%	25%	30%	Selected
	3%	43%	28%	17%	4%	1%	4%

9. As a student, would you prefer to follow this format or go back to the term paper approach?

Poster	Term Paper	No Answer
93%	0%	7%

Note. A represents a *very positive* response to an item, C is *neutral*, and E is *very negative*. *N* = 73.

[a] The top row for this item indicates the percentage of the final grade the students think the posters should comprise. *Selected*, in the top row, means the grade value of the poster sessions would vary and students would choose for themselves how much their poster contributes to their final grade. The bottom row indicates the percentage of students preferring a given grade percentage for the poster sessions.

References

Baird, B. N., & Anderson, D. D. (1990). Writing in psychology. *The Teaching Professor*, *4*(3), 5.

Benjamin, L. T., Jr., Fawl, C. T., & Klein, M. (1977). The fair—Experimental psychology for high school students. *American Psychologist*, *32*, 1097-1098.

Chute, D. L., & Bank, B. (1983). Undergraduate seminars: The poster session solution. *Teaching of Psychology*, *10*, 99-100.

Note

I thank Gayle Robbins for her assistance in developing the activities described in this article.

What Goes Where? An Activity to Teach the Organization of Journal Articles

Ruth L. Ault
Davidson College

When students in research methods or experimental psychology classes write their own research reports in APA style, they often misplace information, such as putting procedural information in the apparatus section or beginning the introduction with the hypothesis and design statement. Although they have access to numerous examples of correctly written articles, the instructions from their textbook, the *Publication Manual of the American Psychological Association* (American Psychological Association, 1983), and in class lectures on how to write journal articles, their research reports usually contain fundamental mistakes. Because they are attempting the complicated task of creating and organizing prose while trying to learn all the format conventions, I have sought ways to break the task down into smaller components to facilitate initial learning. One homework assignment useful for learning the correct order of information involves distributing the contents of a short journal article in scrambled order, with instructions to unscramble the order of paragraphs and to determine the location of headings under which the paragraphs belong.

The article used should be short enough to be manageable but long enough to have several paragraphs under each heading so that students consider the internal logical order of each section. I recommend looking in journals containing Brief Reports sections, selecting one that describes a single experiment with a minimum of technical jargon. I use 20 of 23 paragraphs from Patterson and Carter (1979), including the abstract (but not title information) and excluding three discussion paragraphs.

Using a random number table, I assign each paragraph in the article a letter (A to T). For example, the abstract might be labeled R and the four procedure paragraphs might be L, Q, E, and A. I then cut, paste, and photocopy the paragraphs in alphabetical order. Students turn in a single sheet of paper numbered 1 to 20 with their choices of a paragraph letter beside each number; they also indicate the placement of headings (Abstract, Method, Subjects, etc.). Alternatively, they could cut and paste the paragraphs to return them to the original order.

Of 21 students in a junior-senior research methods class who did this assignment, none reconstructed the article perfectly, but 3 correctly placed all paragraphs under their proper headings, making errors only in sequencing paragraphs. Nine students placed a single paragraph under the wrong heading, and 6 of them also incorrectly sequenced some paragraphs. The remaining 9 students placed from two to five paragraphs under the wrong headings and misordered paragraphs in zero to four of the seven possible sections.

By diagnosing the errors students make, instructors can determine where additional teaching is needed. For example, half of my students put a discussion paragraph in the introduction, even though the paragraph contained an explanation for one of the results, because it contained a reference citation. In class discussion about the assignment, many students reported having no strategy for organizing the results section, not even putting the overall analysis of variance ahead of the follow-up tests. Such simple, customary writing conventions are not explicitly stated in the *Publication Manual* and, apparently, are not salient enough from reading journal articles to lead students to the general rule.

On the other hand, no student missed the distinctive style and content of the abstract, all but one isolated the one subjects paragraph, and none failed to include all three results paragraphs under that heading, although one third of them included procedural or discussion information there too.

I prefer to grade this assignment on a pass-fail basis for two reasons. First, occasionally paragraphs may reasonably fall into several orders, especially in the apparatus section where no logic compels one piece of equipment to be described before another and in the results section if there are two or more major dependent variables. Second, once a particular paragraph is misplaced, other arrangements for the remaining material then become reasonable. Keeping track of these alternatives complicates the grading if matching an exact pattern is the criterion for a particular grade. On the other hand, it is relatively simple to check for the presence of major headings and to assess whether most para graphs are located under their proper headings.

My students reported spending 1 to 2 hr on the assignment and generally reacted positively to it. To evaluate the assignment, 19 of the 21 students checked whether each of five statements was applicable. Although only 2 students checked that it "taught new information," 14 checked that it "provided needed practice for information I already knew," and 10 indicated that "I used something I learned on the homework later in the course." Because several students had already taken another research methods course and had done independent research, it was not surprising that 4 indicated the assignment was "busywork" and 5 checked that "the amount of time spent doing [it] was not worth the amount I learned from it."

I spent less than 10 min per student grading the assignment, and I saved a considerable amount of time grading experimental reports because information was more likely to be located in the proper place.

References

American Psychological Association. (1983). *Publication Manual of the American Psychological Association* (3rd ed.). Washington, DC: Author.

Patterson, C. S., & Carter, D. B. (1979). Attentional determinants of children's self-control in waiting and working situations. *Child Development, 50,* 272-275.

Note

Portions of this article were presented at the Eastern Conference on Teaching of Psychology, Harrisonburg, VA, October 1989.

Do Inexperienced and Experienced Writers Differentially Evaluate Ault's (1991) "What Goes Where" Technique?

Blaine F. Peden
University of Wisconsin-Eau Claire

Despite instructions and examples in articles, textbooks, lectures, and the *Publication Manual of the American Psychological Association* (American Psychological Association [APA], 1983), many students struggle with psychology's conventions for organizing and formatting a research report. To combat this problem, Ault (1991) devised the "what goes where?" technique in which an instructor randomly rearranges intact paragraphs from an article, and students arrange them under the appropriate section headings. This exercise helps students learn about organization and format before writing their first research report.

My study replicates and extends Ault's (1991) exercise by evaluating its use with inexperienced and experienced writers. This study determined whether the two groups: (a) differentially evaluate their knowledge of APA style, (b) spend different amounts of time performing the activity, (c) differ in accuracy in placing paragraphs under the appropriate section headings, and (d) differentially evaluate aspects of the exercise.

Method

Subjects

Fifty-five students were enrolled in one of two courses during the fall 1991-92 term. The 39 students in the sophomore-level Research Methods in Psychology course were novices with regard to APA style. Their experience with research reports was limited to instructions and examples from the Hummel and Birchak (1989) article, the *Publication Manual of the American Psychological Association* (APA, 1983), their textbook (Durso & Mellgren, 1989), and in-class lecture and discussion. In contrast, the 16 students in the junior-level Psychology of Motivation course were more experienced with APA style because they had received the same instructions and examples during the previous semester while enrolled in the Research Methods course and had written three reports.

Materials

I modified Ault's (1991) materials in two ways. First, an answer sheet for the 20 randomly ordered paragraphs was typed on one page. Second, 20 of the 23 paragraphs from the Patterson and Carter (1979) article and five headings (i.e., Abstract, Introduction, Method, Results, and Discussion) were typed on white bond paper to eliminate any contextual cues associated with photocopies of paragraphs in the original article. A one-page questionnaire asked students to (a) indicate their experience with writing APA-style research reports, (b) specify how long it took them to complete the exercise, (c) judge the relative difficulty of correctly assigning paragraphs to each of the five sections, and (d) answer 10 questions about the activity.

Procedure

I distributed a packet containing the answer sheet and the 20 randomly ordered paragraphs to students in both classes and instructed them to perform the homework exercise individually. During the next class period, students exchanged papers and scored them by assigning (a) 15 points for listing all headings in the correct order and placing all 20 paragraphs in the correct section but not necessarily in the correct order within a section, (b) 10 points for listing all headings in the correct order and placing 1 to 6 paragraphs in incorrect sections, or (c) 5 points for listing any headings in the incorrect order and/or placing 7 or more paragraphs in incorrect sections. Students who did not submit the answer sheet received no points. After discussing the exercise in class, students completed the questionnaire.

Results

Prior Experience

On a scale ranging from *virtually no experience with APA style* (1) to *considerable experience with APA style* (4), the mean score for the less experienced writers ($M = 1.46$) was significantly lower than that for the more experienced writers ($M = 3.00$), $t(53) = 6.92$, $p < .001$. The novices rated themselves as having virtually no experience with APA style, whereas the others described themselves as having moderate experience with APA style.

Task Duration

On a scale ranging from *less than ½ hr* (1) to *more than 2 hr* (5), the mean score for the less experienced writers ($M = 2.97$) was significantly higher than that for the more experienced writers ($M = 1.94$), $t(53) = 4.02$, $p < .001$. Novices required about 1.5 hr to complete the exercise, 30 min more than the experienced writers.

Task Difficulty

Student rankings of the relative difficulty of assigning paragraphs to each of the five sections was one measure of task difficulty. The two groups produced comparable rankings, which justified combining their scores for an overall analysis. On a scale ranging from *hardest* (1) to *easiest* (5), the overall mean rankings were 2.07 for the Introduction, 2.33 for the Discussion, 3.31 for the Method, 3.55 for the Results, and 3.75 for the Abstract. A Friedman two-way analysis of variance (ANOVA) by ranks (Siegel, 1956), $\chi r^2(4, N = 53) = 49.25$, $p < .001$, confirmed that it was more difficult to correctly assign paragraphs to some sections than others.

Errors in assigning paragraphs to each of the five sections comprised a second measure of task difficulty. Seven of 39 novices (17.9%) and 6 of 16 experienced writers (37.5%) correctly listed all 20 paragraphs under the appropriate section headings. The two groups produced comparable percentages of misclassified paragraphs (10.9% for novices and 8.4% for experienced writers) and types of errors, which justified combining the data. Table 1 shows that students made the most errors assigning paragraphs to the Abstract and Introduction sections.

Evaluation of Activity

Table 2 presents the mean ratings on a scale ranging from *strongly disagree* (1) to *strongly agree* (5) for 10 items evaluating the "what goes where?" activity. Items A through D assessed what students said they learned from the exercise. Both groups generally agreed that the activity helped them learn about what goes into the different

Table 1. Frequency and Percentage of Errors When Students Classified the 1,100 Paragraphs Into the Subsections of a Research Report

Section	Classification					
	Abstract	Introduction	Method	Results	Discussion	% Errors
Abstract	30	21	1	0	3	45.5
Introduction	10	109	2	0	44	33.9
Method	0	1	439	0	0	0.2
Results	0	1	2	158	4	4.2
Discussion	6	16	1	0	252	8.4

Note. The percentage of errors is computed separately for each row; hence, the totals will not equal 100%.

sections (Item A) and generally disagreed that the exercise was simply busywork (Item D). The experienced writers indicated that the exercise simply allows them to practice something they already knew how to do (Item B), whereas the novices indicated that the exercise helped them learn new things about APA style (Item C).

Items E through G assessed metacognition. The two groups generally disagreed that they would learn more from a lecture than from this active-learning exercise; however, the experienced writers were more adamant in their opinion. Both groups reported devising strategies to place paragraphs under the appropriate headings and indicated that this exercise provided a new perspective on asking questions about APA style.

Items H through J determined students' views about grading and future use of the exercise. Both groups agreed that the grading procedure was fair. Although both groups opposed grading this activity on a pass/fail basis, the novices were more opposed to pass/fail grading than the experienced writers. Finally, both groups endorsed the future use of this activity.

Discussion

Results show that the two groups differentially assess both their research report-writing skills and the benefits of Ault's (1991) "what goes where?" technique. In addition, the results confirm some, but not all, of Ault's observations.

One point of agreement concerns time requirements of the assignment. Although the novices spent more time than the experienced writers, the 1.5 hr required by the novices to complete the exercise compares favorably with the 1 to 2 hr required by Ault's (1991) students.

A second point of agreement concerns the percentage of students listing all the paragraphs under the appropriate headings. For example, approximately 18% of the novices and 14% of Ault's (1991) students placed all 20 paragraphs under the appropriate section headings; however, the percentage doubled for my experienced writers.

A third point of agreement concerns how an analysis of errors helps determine the need for instructional remediation. Although it would take less time for an

instructor to have students identify the more difficult sections, the comparison of two measures of task difficulty (rankings and error analysis) indicates that the more time-consuming error analysis is superior. Quite simply, my students ranked the Abstract as the easiest paragraph to place correctly, even though they frequently misclassified it.

A fourth point of agreement concerns the students' overall evaluation of the assignment. Ault's (1991) students generally reacted positively to the assignment, a finding consistent with my students' view that the exercise helped them learn about the organization and format of a

Table 2. Means and Statistical Analysis of Responses to the 10-Item Questionnaire by Less and More Experienced Writers

Less	More	*t*(53)	Item
3.87	3.63	1.29	A. The "what goes where?" exercise helped me understand what goes into each of the main sections of a research report in APA style.
1.62	3.69	9.49***	B. This exercise just provided practice for something that I already knew how to do.
3.56	2.81	2.78**	C. The "what goes where?" activity taught me new things about APA style.
2.38	2.44	.19	D. The time spent doing this exercise entailed busywork, and was *not* worthwhile in terms of how much I learned.
2.85	1.88	2.87**	E. I could have learned more about APA style and how to format a research report from a lecture rather than an exercise of this type.
3.74	3.88	.51	F. I devised a strategy for ordering of the paragraphs in each section.
3.33	3.50	.69	G. The "what goes where?" exercise provided a new perspective for asking questions about APA style and how to format a research report.
2.85	2.56	1.04	H. The grading procedure for this exercise was *unfair*.
1.90	2.56	2.08*	I. The "what goes where?" activity should be graded only on a pass/fail basis.
4.05	3.75	1.25	J. I recommend using this activity as part of this class in the future.

Note. Responses range from *strongly disagree* (1) to *strongly agree* (5).
*p < .05. **p < .01. ***p < .001. All *p* values are two-tailed.

research report and their strong endorsement of the future use of the activity. It is also noteworthy, in light of Benjamin's (1991) discussion of active learning, that my students generally endorse this exercise as a more effective teaching device than a lecture. Moreover, the experienced writers express this conviction more strongly than the novices.

My results contradict Ault's (1991) finding that all of her students correctly identified the Abstract. In contrast, a large proportion of my students, inexperienced and experienced alike, incorrectly assigned this paragraph to the Introduction or Discussion sections. This difference may be related to the visual appearance of the paragraphs. Ault used photocopies of the paragraphs in the original article in which the print and indentation of the Abstract differed from the other paragraphs, a problem eliminated in my study by retyping all the paragraphs in a standard format.

Two additional contradictions may be more apparent than real. One point concerns the use of strategies. Ault (1991) reported that her students typically did not devise strategies for ordering the paragraphs in the Results section. For example, her students did not know that they should place an overall ANOVA before individual difference tests. In contrast, both groups of my students reported devising a strategy to order the paragraphs within a section. Although resolution of this apparent contradiction awaits further analysis of what students say and actually do with regard to strategies in various sections of the research report, instructors should focus on discovering the misconceptions of their students and promoting the development and use of effective strategies.

A second apparent contradiction concerns grading procedures. Ault (1991) recommended grading this assignment on a pass/fail basis; however, she did not query students about her grading policy. My students, especially the novices, opposed a pass/fail grading of the assignment, even though the assignment involved only about 1% of the possible number of points in the course. Perhaps readers should consider my grading scheme as an alternative to Ault's pass/fail system and choose between them on the basis of their own philosophy and knowledge of their students.

Coda

The "what goes where?" active-learning exercise appears to be most effective with inexperienced research report writers; however, it also appears to provide useful practice for more experienced writers. Perhaps this exercise could be made more challenging to experienced writers by following the suggestion of my colleague Bernard Frank: Intermingle paragraphs from two separate articles and ask students to assign the paragraphs both to the appropriate article and section in the article. This novel version of the exercise could be made more or less difficult by varying the similarity of the two articles.

References

American Psychological Association. (1983). *Publication manual of the American Psychological Association* (3rd ed.). Washington, DC: Author.

Ault, R. L. (1991). What goes where? An activity to teach the organization of journal articles. *Teaching of Psychology, 18,* 45-46.

Benjamin, L. T., Jr. (1991). Personalization and active learning in the large introductory psychology class. *Teaching of Psychology, 18,* 68-74.

Durso, F. T., & Mellgren, R. L. (1989). *Thinking about research: Methods and tactics of the behavioral scientist.* St. Paul, MN: West.

Hummel, J. H., & Birchak, B. C. (1989, September). A short course on APA style for psychology students. APS *Observer,* pp. 14-16.

Patterson, C. J., & Carter, D. B. (1979). Attentional determinants of children's self-control in waiting and working situations. *Child Development, 50,* 272-275.

Siegel, S. (1956). *Nonparametric statistics for the behavioral sciences.* New York: McGraw-Hill.

Notes

1. I thank Ruth Ault, three anonymous reviewers, and Charles L. Brewer for helpful comments on drafts of this article.

2. A preliminary report of these results was presented at the meeting of the Midwestern Psychological Association, Chicago, April 30 to May 2, 1992.

3. Requests for copies of the exercise should be sent to Blaine F. Peden, Department of Psychology, University of Wisconsin-Eau Claire, Eau Claire, WI 54702-4002.

Student Research Proposals in the Experimental Psychology Course

William E. Addison
Eastern Illinois University

Teachers of undergraduate courses in statistics and experimental psychology generally agree that students should become directly involved in the research process to enhance their understanding of research design and analysis (Edwards, 1981; Singer & Willett, 1990; Yoder, 1979) as well as to develop their writing and critical-thinking skills (Nadelman, 1990; Snodgrass, 1985). In psychology, this involvement typically occurs in the research methods or experimental psychology course in which students are often required to complete a research project of their own design (Chamberlain, 1986; McGill, 1975).

In addition to improving students' analytical and writing skills, the research project brings together important concepts addressed during the lecture portion of the course. Concepts such as randomization, sampling, operational definitions, and research ethics become more meaningful when students have to apply them to their own research. Because it combines attention to conceptual material with experience in analysis and writing, the research project can be viewed as a capstone experience for the experimental psychology course.

The research project has drawbacks as well as benefits. One limitation associated with student-conducted research is the lack of time needed to design and carry out an even minimally sophisticated project (Carroll, 1986; Forsyth, 1977; Yoder, 1979). With little time available and the typical limitations of equipment and laboratory space, many students conduct simplistic studies from which they gain little knowledge about the principles of behavioral research.

Another problem with student-conducted research is that it is virtually impossible for the instructor to provide adequate supervision of individual projects when each student is involved in a unique study. This limitation is of particular concern when one considers the number of research-based ethical issues that may arise in a moderate-size class.

Several authors have developed techniques designed to address these problems. For example, Carroll (1986) described what he called the *jigsaw technique*: Small groups of students complete a research project to which each member makes a separate contribution. Chamberlain

(1988) suggested that recent "core articles" in psychology be used as a basis for student projects (p. 207). Chamberlain's technique involves at least a partial replication of an experiment from a core article. Data collected by individual students are pooled and analyzed by each student in separate research reports.

Another technique that introduces students to the research process and avoids many of the problems associated with the student-conducted research project is the research proposal. This article describes how the research proposal can be combined with data-based research projects to provide students with a comprehensive introduction to the research process.

In my course, students are required to write three APA style research papers. The first paper is a group project similar to Carroll's (1986) jigsaw technique; the study is based on data collected by the class, and each member of the group is responsible for one of the major sections of the paper (i.e., introduction, method, results, and discussion). Each section contributes 5% to the student's grade in the course. The second paper is an individual report also based on data collected by the entire class, worth 10% of the student's grade. The third paper, worth 20% of the student's grade, is the research proposal, which is due at the end of the semester. For this paper, each student is required to design a study and submit a written proposal in APA style, including all major sections of an APA-style manuscript.

The introduction takes much the same form as it does in a typical research report; it includes a fairly thorough literature review and the specific research issues being addressed by the proposal. The method section describes the subjects, equipment or materials, and procedure that would be used to complete the proposed study. For the results section, I ask students to identify the appropriate statistical tests and include a specific account of the expected results of the analyses. For example, a student who proposes to conduct a two-way analysis of variance is expected to indicate whether a significant interaction is predicted, as well as the specific nature of the interaction. The discussion section focuses on the consistency of the expected findings with previous research, potential confounds, ethical considerations, and directions for further research.

The research proposal has most of the advantages of the student-conducted research project without the drawbacks that result from limitations of time, equipment, and space. For example, critical thinking involves problem solving and hypothesis testing (Baron, 1988; Halpern, 1989; Neimark, 1987), and these processes are important components of both research projects and research proposals. However, because the research proposal has fewer practical constraints, students can be creative in selecting topics for their research. I frequently remind students that they can consider various methods and subjects for their proposals and that they can select a topic based on their own interests, regardless of the practical limitations. Students seem to have taken this advice to heart; perhaps as a result, their proposals often seem more mature, both conceptually and methodologically, than the typical, student-conducted project. For example, recent proposals have included the effects of neuroleptics on amphetamine poisoning in rats, social adjustment of children in day-care centers, and the capacity of neonates to imitate adult models. Students have even suggested that they will use a grant from a specific agency to fund their research.

Student proposals tend to be relatively sophisticated on a methodological level. Consequently, the methodological, ethical, and practical issues that students must address in their papers often require much thought. For example, one student, who proposed to study effects of speech style (masculine vs. feminine) and sex of speaker on listeners' perception of the message, had to consider whether subjects may be more likely to pay attention to one speech style than the other. To address this issue, the student synthesized information from research on speech styles as well as from studies of attentional cues in information processing.

Perhaps the main difficulty with this approach is getting the students to think creatively when they select a topic. Because many of our majors are not asked to engage in creative thinking in other psychology courses, they generally need some encouragement in this direction. I periodically remind students that they are not required to conduct the study; therefore, they are not limited to particular methods or subjects. To illustrate what former students have done in this regard, I provide a list of proposal titles from previous classes .

A related problem is that students frequently have difficulty addressing methodological and ethical issues in a study that they have not actually conducted. This problem is not limited to students' research proposals. As Neimark (1987) pointed out, we all have a tendency to engage in context-tied thinking. Neimark suggested that one way to alleviate this tendency is to participate in exercises designed to encourage context-free thinking. By requiring students to engage in "what if" thinking about potential

methodological and ethical issues, the research proposal constitutes just such an exercise.

Critics may argue that because data collection is an essential part of the research process, students who write a research proposal in lieu of conducting a study are not getting a complete, firsthand research experience. For this reason, the research proposal is most effective when used to supplement research assignments based on data collected by students. Under these conditions, the proposal can be an effective way to get the students to think critically and creatively.

References

Baron, J. (1988). *Thinking and deciding*. Cambridge, England: Cambridge University Press.

Carroll, D. W. (1986). Use of the jigsaw technique in laboratory and discussion classes. *Teaching of Psychology, 13*, 208-210.

Chamberlain, K. (1986). Teaching the practical research course. *Teaching of Psychology, 13*, 204-208.

Chamberlain, K. (1988). Devising relevant and topical undergraduate laboratory projects The core article approach. *Teaching of Psychology, 15*, 207-208.

Edwards, S. D. (1981). A conceptual framework for a core program in psychology. *Teaching of Psychology, 8*, 3-7.

Forsyth, G. A. (1977). A task-first individual-differences approach to designing a statistics and methodology course. *Teaching of Psychology, 4*, 76-78.

Halpern, D. F (1989). *Thought and knowledge: An introduction to critical thinking* (2nd ed.). Hillsdale, NJ: Lawrence Erlbaum Associates, inc.

McGill, T. E. (1975). Special projects laboratory in experimental psychology. *Teaching of Psychology, 2*, 169-171.

Nadelman, L. (1990). Learning to think and write as an empirical psychologist: The laboratory course in developmental psychology. *Teaching of Psychology, 171* 45-48.

Neimark. E. D. (1987). *Adventures in thinking*. San Diego: Harcourt Brace Jovanovich.

Singer, J. D., & Willett, S. B. (1990). Improving the teaching of applied statistics Putting the data back into data analysis. *American Statistician, 44*, 223-230.

Snodgrass, S. E. (1985). Writing as a tool for teaching social psychology. *Teaching of Psychology, 12*, 91-94.

Yoder, J. (1979). Teaching students to do research. *Teaching of Psychology, 6*, 85-88.

Notes

I thank John Best for his comments on a draft of this article.

Teaching Students to Write Literature Reviews: A Meta-Analytic Model

Arnold D. Froese
Brandon S. Gantz
Amanda L. Henry
Behavioral Science Department
Sterling College

Psychology students often write reports of empirical studies in research methods courses and review articles in upper division content courses. A research methods course gives instructors the opportunity to teach specific requirements for empirical reports, and the *Publication Manual of the American Psychological Association* (American Psychological Association [APA], 1994) clearly describes parts of such reports and their preparation. However, no comparable course or manual exists for instructing students to write review articles.

Although students may treat the two kinds of assignments as unrelated, empirical reports and literature reviews share common elements. The introduction to an empirical report contains a brief literature review. More important, empirical reports and integrative reviews use many of the same techniques and criteria to explore relations among variables based on empirical evidence.

Instructors often express concern about students' ability to conduct meaningful literature reviews. They expect students to analyze, evaluate, and creatively synthesize methods and results from published information. Instead, they often find that students extract information from the introductions and discussions of papers they cite (Anisfeld, 1987; Chamberlain &Burrough, 1985), misuse sources (Froese, Boswell, Garcia, Koehn, & Nelson, 1995), and fail to integrate information from various sources (Makosky, 1985).

This mismatch between expectation and performance may arise from instructional deficiencies. Instructors may assume that students will transfer critical empirical skills learned in research methods courses to analyzing, evaluating, and synthesizing information from published papers. Nodine (1990) suggested that instead of treating writing as an inherent trait accompanying general knowledge, instructors should develop strategies to teach essential writing skills. Instructors may not clearly understand how to teach the review-writing task. Boice (1982) claimed that psychology instructors may have no model to guide their writing instruction.

We suggest that meta-analysis provides a clear model for review–writing instruction. Meta-analysis is a conceptual bridge between empirical reports and review articles. Both meta-analyses and empirical research reports rely on quantitative data. Cooper (1990) described meta-analysis as "procedures for integrating the quantitative results from multiple studies" (p.142) . Furthermore, meta-analytic techniques provide clear criteria for analysis, suggest means for synthesizing multiple outcomes, and focus the reviewer's attention on evaluation. These techniques help the reviewer "find the knowledge in the information'' (Glass, 1976, p. 4).

Meta-analytic techniques directly address problems students experience as they write literature reviews. The following are the problems students in our department experience most often and their meta-analytic solutions:

Problem 1: Students select poorly-defined topics. Students often begin by stating their topic as a single general variable. When encouraged to be more specific, they select various subsets of that variable, circumscribing specific populations or content ranges.

Solution: Meta-analysis involves a systematic search for relations. Meta-analytic reviewers clearly define topics by stating the combination of main variables comprising these presumed relations. For the researcher, this focus on relations parallels the process of linking key terms in computer database searches (see Reed & Baxter, 1992).

Problem 2: Students often demonstrate conceptual inadequacies in analysis. They may fail to examine details about methods and outcomes (Anisfeld,1987; Chamberlain & Burrough, 1985). They also may fail to extract similarities among variables that various researchers describe or manipulate differently.

Solution: Meta-analytic reviewers construct coding sheets that include information about each article's source, research variables and design, participant characteristics, outcome direction, and statistical details (see Cooper,

1989). These coding sheets direct reviewers' attention to the methods and results sections of articles and permit reviewers to display the compared information in a concise systematic format.

Problem 3: Students frequently summarize articles sequentially in their papers instead of comprehensively integrating the findings.

Solution 1: Meta-analytic reviewers report outcomes in the common currency of effect sizes across articles. Reviewers use this currency to report new descriptive statistics.

Solution 2: Meta-analytic reviewers search for moderator variables among coded variables by systematically sorting outcomes by methodological differences across studies. Reviewers thus creatively synthesize reviewed information.

Problem 4: Students have difficulty evaluating articles. This difficulty is evident when they ask: "Are we supposed to include our opinion?"

Solution: Meta-analytic reviewers include quality characteristics of research design on coding sheets. Thus, they integrate evaluation with analysis.

Meta-analytic techniques thus offer solutions for common student writing problems. We developed the following instructional program based on these techniques.

Instructional Applications

We teach skills necessary for writing integrated research reviews in a sophomore-level research methods course. The technical details required to conduct and write meta-analyses exceed the scope of such an introductory course. Nevertheless, we use basic meta-analytic concepts to direct students to required analysis, synthesis, and evaluation skills for writing literature reviews.

We integrate meta-analytic strategies into typical research methods content in about 10 class periods. We teach students to select relational paper topics during instruction about library and computer use. That instruction includes introductions to abstracts, indexes, and manual and computer database searching. We teach students to develop and use coding sheets during instruction about primary and secondary sources, the nature of relations, sampling, control, and statistical analysis. We incorporate instruction about simple effect size estimates into instruction about correlations and hypothesis testing. We teach students to search for moderator variables when we cover sampling, control techniques, and integrating research findings. We teach evaluation issues in the context of sampling, control, validity, and reliability.

We present each concept in lecture and follow the presentation with student assignments. The assignments require students to use reference materials common to the research process, such *as Psychological Abstracts*, the *Publication Manual* (APA, 1994), and *PsycFirst* (FirstSearch, 1995), our database for computer searches. In addition, one worksheet requires that students read Glass's (1976) description of meta-analysis.

We describe and illustrate each concept. For example, to illustrate the concept of focusing a search by selecting two variables, we ask students independently to list a few variables. One student then contributes a variable to the phrase "The effect of_____" and another student completes the statement by adding a variable to "on_____." Students quickly catch the idea of linking two variables.

Students alert us to their misunderstandings when they make errors on assignments. For example, students frequently try to link synonymous concepts, such as "adolescents" and "young people," when they construct their search strategies. We give corrective instruction and ask them to redo assignments.

We designed our instruction so students first see prepared examples of concepts and then have to work with greater independence on subsequent assignments. For example, students first work with a preprinted coding sheet that summarizes six items of information from four studies. Students orally present comparative statements from at least two studies. At the next level, students transcribe information about manipulated and measured variables, sample size, means and standard deviations, and indications of significance of results from assigned articles onto coding sheets. Finally, students independently develop coding sheets for information they consider relevant from an assigned article.

We present the search for moderator variables as creative detective work. We ask students to search for items on sample coding sheets that appear to be correlated with outcomes. Sample sheets include moderator variables that at times are related to the effect size and, at other times, to the direction of the effect.

We teach two introductory effect size concepts. For correctional research, students learn that squaring the correlation provides information about percentage of variability the relation predicts. For comparisons between two means, students learn to calculate Cohen's *d* as a standard effect size measure.

During the course, students learn basic research principles. These include techniques for sampling, manipulating, measuring, and controlling variables. They also learn limitations on conclusions inherent in design components. In a summary lecture, we apply these principles to evaluating articles included in a literature review.

Students independently conduct original research projects during the semester. Because these are their first research projects, we encourage them to keep their designs simple. Before the end of the semester, they submit manuscripts of their findings written according to the *Publication Manual* (APA, 1994). These papers include a brief literature review for which they submit coding sheets.

We look for evidence that students analyzed and synthesized information from their primary sources, such as simple effect size estimates and qualitative, synthetic statements summarizing methods or results from several articles. Students receive editorial review of first drafts and revise their papers for final submission.

Discussion

Based on our experience, this model has been effective in improving student literature reviews. Students demonstrated this improvement on class tests and in their final research papers. Several students have commented that no one had ever shown them how to review literature and that our instruction had given them tools for effective writing.

We have noticed some continuing weaknesses in our students' writing. Some students have reported comparisons across articles that were not relevant to their primary research questions. Others have suggested potential moderator variables for equivocal outcomes although the articles they cited did not report methodological differences among these variables. Nevertheless, our instruction gave students skills for analyzing and synthesizing information. Students must have these prerequisite skills before they can examine the relevance of particular variables for the questions they ask.

Our model provides specific advantages over more typical approaches to teaching writing. First, the model identifies the skills required of students for writing research proposals, reviews, and term papers and provides a framework for their work. Second, the model clarifies common criteria for good literature reviews. Wood (1996) reported that such criteria are not always present among instructors. Third, the model clarifies necessary instructional sequences in departmental curricula. In our department, students write assignments that require analysis of the primary literature in courses beyond research methods as a second step. Their third step is to write a major literature review in the culminating Senior Seminar.

The meta-analytic model integrates writing with critical thinking. Students learn that writing a review requires them to analyze, synthesize, and evaluate published literature. They also learn to employ the critical thinking skills for designing and conducting research when they evaluate published literature. Thus the meta-analytic model provides clear, identifiable concepts for teaching students what it means to work creatively with data in their writing assignments. Any instructor who assigns a paper for which students must consult the research literature can benefit from examining our model.

References

American Psychological Association. (1994). *Publication manual of the American Psychological Association* (4th ed.). Washington, DC: Author.

Anisfeld, M. (1987). A course to develop competence in critical reading of empirical research in psychology. *Teaching of Psychology, 14,* 224-227.

Boice, R. (1982). Teaching of writing in psychology: A review of sources. *Teaching of Psychology, 9,* 143-147.

Chamberlain, K., & Burrough, S. (1985). Techniques for teaching critical reading. *Teaching of Psychology, 12,* 213-215.

Cooper, H. (1989). *Integrating research: A guide for literature reviews* (2nd ed.). Newbury Park, CA: Sage.

Cooper, H. (1990). Meta-analysis and the integrative research review. In C. Hendrick & M. S. Clark (Eds.), *Research methods in personality and social psychology* (pp.142-163) . Newbury Park, CA: Sage.

FirstSearch [Online database]. (1995). Dublin, OH: OCLC Online Computer Library Center [Distributor].

Froese, A. D., Boswell, K. L., Garcia, E. D., Koehn, L. J., & Nelson, J. M. (1995). Citing secondary sources: Can we correct what students do not know? *Teaching of Psychology, 22,* 235-238.

Glass, G. V. (1976). Primary, secondary, and meta-analysis of research. *Educational Researcher, 5,* 3-8.

Makosky, V. P. (1985). Teaching psychology in the information age. *Teaching of Psychology, 12,* 23-26.

Nodine, B. F. (1990). Psychologists teach writing. *Teaching of Psychology, 17,* 4.

Reed, J. G., & Baxter, P. M. (1992). Library use: *A handbook for psychology* (2nd ed.). Washington, DC: American Psychological Association.

Wood, M. R. (1996). An advanced writing requirement for psychology majors: Lessons for faculty. *Teaching of Psychology, 23,* 243-245.

Notes

1. Amanda L. Henry is presently a graduate student at the University of Kansas.
2. We thank Sara K. Terian for her critical evaluation of our class test. We also thank Pamela Stark-Haney, Barbara Nodine, Nicholee Froese, Craig Gannon, and Wendell Wessman for their assistance in manuscript revision.
3. Requests for supporting data, tests, and instructional materials, should be sent to Arnold D. Froese, Behavioral Science Department, Sterling College, Sterling, KS 67579; e-mail: *afroese@acc.stercolks.edu.*

Using an Everyday Memory Task to Introduce the Method and Results Sections of a Scientific Paper

William R. Marmie
University of Colorado, Boulder

Nickerson and Adams's (1979) task of recognizing a U.S. penny among a set of counterfeits, which vary only in the placement of features, is often described in introductory cognitive psychology textbooks to demonstrate the failure to store details encountered in an everyday context in memory (e.g., Bourne, Dominowski, Loftus, & Healy, 1986; Medin & Ross,1992; Reed,1992) . The task has also been suggested for use as a classroom demonstration showing the consequences of lack of attention (Shimamura, 1984). Marmie, Rully, and Healy (1993) showed that subjects, when asked to draw the features of a familiar U.S. penny without any external cues, did quite poorly; in contrast, if they studied an unfamiliar Mercury dime for only 1 min, they recalled the features of the dime better than those of the penny. This finding is counterintuitive because people see a U.S. penny almost every day but cannot remember its features. Marmie et al. concluded that memory for details of everyday objects is poor unless subjects use intentional mnemonic strategies. The empirical work of Marmie et al., designed to highlight the role of intentional study in remembering details, can be extended as a classroom demonstration and can also be used effectively to introduce the method and results sections of a scientific paper. The present demonstration illustrates the important role of intentional study in memory and is enjoyable for students. In addition, as opposed to simply recalling the penny alone, students will feel less ignorant about not remembering what an everyday object looks like after they have studied and recalled the dime.

I use the demonstration in an introductory course in cognitive psychology. Generally, the class contains upper level undergraduates with one course in statistics. The demonstration is manageable for a class of up to 20 students. Ideally, coin presentation order should be counterbalanced, but the demonstration demands that the penny be recalled before the dime in order to leave students feeling good about their memory abilities. At the beginning of the class, I give each student a piece of paper with two 4-in. (10.16 cm) circles on it. I tell the students that this is an everyday memory demonstration, and I ask them to draw the front and back of a U.S. penny from memory. I inform them they will have 2 min to draw it, and I emphasize that they should write out all of the words on the penny and that they are not being tested on their artistic ability. Students react by laughing and groaning.

Before I collect the drawings, students write the last four digits of their student number on the sheet. Next, I distribute to each student a second drawing sheet and an envelope containing a single Mercury dime (see Figure 1). This out of-mint dime has the advantage of being a coin most students have never seen before. I purchase the dimes at a local coin shop for 50¢ each. I tell students that they will have 1 min to study the dime and 2 min to recall it in the same manner as the penny. After 1 min, I instruct students to return the dimes to the envelopes. Then I repeat the recall instructions I used for the penny.

I return each student's penny drawing and distribute score sheets. The score sheet lists each of the nine features shared by both coins: (a) the head figure, (b) the tail figure, (c) the phrase "In God We Trust," (d) the phrase "E Pluribus Unum," (e) the word Liberty, (f) the phrase "United States of America," (g) the phrase "One Dime" or "One Cent," (h) the date stamp, and (i) the mint stamp.

Figure 1. The four faces of the Mercury dime and the U.S. penny.

231

Students generally feel somewhat self-conscious about their drawings. Class discussion relieves this anxiety. The Latin phrase "E Pluribus Unum" is often humorously rendered (e.g., "In Pluribus Unum"). The class decides whether to score a feature as correct if it is included or if it is both included and correctly placed on the coin face. Keep in mind that if students decide to adopt the latter policy, the difference between the number of correctly recalled features for the penny and the dime is pronounced. Students raise many questions (e.g., "Should we count the head as correctly positioned if it is facing the wrong direction?," "Is a dome on the Lincoln memorial acceptable?," or "Is 'In Pluribus Unum' acceptable for 'E Pluribus Unum?'").

Students remember the studied coin much better than the unstudied coin. This effect is often dramatic as well as robust. I ask the students to count the total number of features they both included and correctly positioned, and I write these totals on the front board. On average, my students have remembered 2.7 features from the penny and 7.6 features from the dime. I have never seen a student who has recalled more features of the penny than of the dime. Next, I ask students whether there appears to be an overall difference between memory for the dime and penny. I point out that some of the memory differences between coins are large and some are small. To introduce the concept of a t test I ask them, "How can we tell if, overall, these differences are significant?" The demonstration allows me to make the following three points:

1. Scientific judgments are always subjective. The class needed to decide on the rules for counting a feature as correct or incorrect. Would the difference in memory for the dime and the penny have been significant with a more lenient criterion? The answer is yes (see Marmie et al., 1993). Should students have scored their own drawings or someone else's? I use these questions to emphasize the point that, without a method section, readers would have no idea how a researcher measured the dependent variables and that a researcher's conclusions would be difficult to evaluate.

2. Statistics provide a way of condensing data into a manageable description of the findings. They also allow researchers to estimate the probability that obtained differences are simply due to chance.

3. Details of an object or event are often hard to remember unless they are intentionally studied. In the demonstration, 1 min of study was enough to make memory for an unfamiliar coin better than memory for a familiar coin. I contrast this finding with the priming effect in which it is not even necessary to consciously attend to something in order for it to be remembered. In priming studies involving word fragment completion, previous exposure to a word significantly helps subjects complete word fragments (see Schoen, 1988, for an effective demonstration of this point).

I close my class by assigning students to write the method and results sections of the demonstration. I distribute a description of the procedure (written as short facts) with step-by-step instructions for conducting a t test. They copy the data from the board before leaving the classroom.

Student Evaluations

At the end of the class period, students anonymously responded to a four-item questionnaire. It was apparent that most students enjoyed this demonstration from the high degree of participation in the discussions. Pooling data across two classes, I found that on a 5-point scale ranging from *not at all* (1) to *very well* (5), 38 University of Colorado students gave a mean rating of 3.47 ($SD = 1.04$) to the question of how well the demonstration illustrated the importance of a method section in a scientific paper. On the same scale students gave a mean rating of 3.95 ($SD = .82$) to the question of how well the importance of a statistical analysis was illustrated by the demonstration. To determine whether students felt differently about their memory abilities from the penny to the dime, I first asked "Did you feel good about your memory ability after recalling the penny?" On a 5-point scale ranging from *not at all* (1) to *very much* (5), students reported feeling slightly below the neutral value ($M = 2.43$, $SD = 1.09$). Second, they responded to the question, "Did you feel better about your memory ability after recalling the dime?," on a 5-point scale ranging from *no* (1) to *yes* (5). Students reported feeling well above the neutral value ($M = 4.27$, $SD = 1.04$). A t test was conducted comparing the means of the last two values. The mean for the dime was significantly higher than the mean for the penny, suggesting that students are left feeling good about their memory abilities after the demonstration, $t(36) = 7.33$, $p < .01$.

This demonstration is effective because many bright students in an introductory cognitive psychology course feel somewhat daunted after repeated demonstrations of their average memory, problem-solving, and decision-making abilities. This demonstration has the added benefit, over and above the standard procedure of simply recalling a U.S. penny, of showing students the importance of intentional study. Everyday objects may be familiar but, without intentional study, they are not memorable. Students are not left feeling ignorant about their knowledge of everyday objects but rather feeling knowledgeable about the importance of intentional study.

References

Bourne, L. E., Dominowski, R. L., Loftus, E. F., & Healy, A. F. (1986). *Cognitive processes* (2nd ed.). Englewood Cliffs, NJ: Prentice-Hall.

Marmie, W. R., Rully, G. R., & Healy, A. F. (1993). On the long-term retention of studied and unstudied U.S.

coins. In *The Proceedings of the Fifteenth Annual Conference of the Cognitive Science Society* (pp. 687-692). Hillsdale, NJ: Lawrence Erlbaum Associates, Inc.

Medin, D. L., & Ross, B. H. (1992). *Cognitive psychology.* Ft. Worth, TX: Harcourt Brace.

Nickerson, R. S., & Adams, M. S. (1979). Long-term memory for a common object. *Cognitive Psychology, 11,* 287-307.

Reed, S. K. (1992). *Cognition: Theory and applications* (3rd ed.). Pacific Grove, CA: Brooks/Cole.

Schoen, L. M. (1988). The word fragment completion effect: A computer-assisted classroom exercise. *Teaching of Psychology, 15,* 95-97.

Shimamura, A. P. (1984). A guide for teaching mnemonic skills. *Teaching of Psychology, 11,* 162-166.

Note

I thank Walter Kintsch and Alice Healy for comments on a draft of this article.

Teaching the Importance of Accuracy in Preparing References

Blaine F. Peden
University of Wisconsin-Eau Claire

My experience teaching research methods and reviewing manuscripts for *Teaching of Psychology* indicates that correctly citing and referencing works in APA style is a difficult task for inexperienced and veteran authors. Nonetheless, instructors should teach and students should learn precision in preparing reference lists. One reason is that "accurately prepared references help establish your credibility as a careful researcher" (American Psychological Association, 1983, p. 112). Another reason is that inaccurate citations and references produce and perpetuate mistakes and misconceptions (e.g., Griggs, 1988; Soper & Rosenthal, 1988).

This article summarizes and assesses a method for teaching students to identify and list four types of references frequently cited in research reports. Later in the term, students receive a grade of A or F on the reference section of their own research reports (after Cronan-Hillix, 1988). The method improves accuracy in preparing reference lists and seems to increase students' attention to other facets of APA style.

Method

Subjects

Subjects were 63 women and 27 men enrolled in an undergraduate research methods course in the 1989-90 fall or spring semesters.

Materials

A handout summarized the first page of the table from the *Publication Manual of the American Psychological Association* (APA, 1983, p. 118) listing types of work referenced and presented three examples of references for each of four works typically used by students in research reports: journal articles, magazine articles, books, and chapters in an edited book. Other pages in the handout illustrated citations and quotations.

Students' knowledge about references was measured two ways. Three recognition tests each presented five correct references (the four types just mentioned and another type of work, e.g., an unpublished paper or a conference presentation) that students matched with the correct label (e.g., journal article, magazine article . . . none of these). Three production tests each provided information about a journal article, a magazine article, a book, and a chapter in an edited book that students used to prepare a reference list in APA style.

Procedure

Instruction was the same in both semesters. Early in the term, I distributed and discussed the handout. I stressed the importance of correctly citing and referencing works, illustrated the types of works used in research reports, discussed examples of references for the four common sources, demonstrated citations in text, and announced that students would take a multiple-choice recognition test on 3 successive days. At the beginning of the next three classes, students completed a recognition test, exchanged tests for scoring on the basis of 1 point for each correct answer, and then submitted them to me for verification and recording of the grades. On the day of the third recognition test, I dispensed the first production test. Students completed it outside of class, exchanged papers in the next class for grading on the basis of 1 point for each correct reference and one fifth of a point for listing references in the proper order, submitted the papers for verification and recording, and then received another production test. After collecting the third production test, I handed out copies of Cronan-Hillix's (1988) article. In the next period, we briefly discussed the article and the policy of A or F grading for the reference section of their research reports. After further discussion during the next class, students completed one or two posttest questionnaires.

The evaluation was somewhat different in the two semesters. Although students in both terms completed the same 10-item posttest questionnaire and a two-part follow up question, students in the spring class also completed a 10item reference recognition pretest and a 12-item pre- and posttest questionnaire. They completed the recognition pretest and the 12-item pretest questionnaire during the first week of class. Students answered the posttest questionnaires and follow-up question in successive periods after finishing the instructional sequence and before the due date for the first research report.

Results

Recognition Test

Forty four students in the spring semester completed the 10-item reference recognition pretest. The mean percentage of accurately identified references was 93.2% for magazines, 84.1 % for books, 72.7% for chapters in an edited book, and 53.4% for journal articles; overall, the mean score was 75.7% correct. The mean scores on the recognition tests were comparable in the two semesters and justified computing an overall mean score. In order, the grand means on the three recognition tests were 90.4%, 98.6%, and 99.4% correct. Thus, the handout and instruction appeared to improve students' ability to recognize types of references above their baseline level.

Production Test

The mean scores on the three production tests were comparable in the two semesters and also justified computing an overall mean score. In order, the grand means were 33.6%, 65.4%, and 78.9% correct. Errors on the final production test were not distributed equally across the five types of answers. The grand mean percentage of errors on the final test was 44.3% for chapters in an edited book, 34.1% for magazine articles, 12.5% for books, 8.0% for journal articles, and 1.1% for listing references in the correct order. Thus, this technique seemed to help students prepare accurate reference lists, although students' production skills lagged behind their recognition skills.

Student Evaluation

Eighty-six of the 90 students completed the 10-item posttest questionnaire. The virtually identical mean scores in the two terms on a scale ranging *from strong disagreement* (1) *to strong agreement* (5) justified reporting an overall mean score. Students agreed that they learned how to recognize different kinds of references (M = 4.48, SD = .41) and how to prepare the reference section of a research report (M = 4.55, SD = .55). Students agreed that the number of tests was appropriate (M = 3.67, SD = .69), the purpose of the activity became increasingly clear (M = 4.10, SD = .28), and grading of the recognition and production tests was fair (M = 3.86, SD = .63). Students endorsed Cronan-Hillix's (1988) contention about their need to learn the importance of accuracy in research (M = 4.21, SD = .58), agreed that it was equally important for them to learn accuracy in referencing (M = 4.26, SD = .54), and recommended use of this technique in the future (M = 4.33, SD = .75). Students agreed that feedback was adequate (M = 3.72, SD = 1.25), but suggested that making and keeping a copy of the production tests might help them understand and correct their mistakes, especially in the absence of the originals submitted for grading. Opinion was divided on whether it was fair to apply an A or F grading system to the reference section of their research reports (M = 3.33, SD = 1.29) .

The lack of consensus prompted me to assess student opinion on the grading issue in two additional ways. First, 81 of 90 students in the two semesters answered a two-part follow up question by indicating whether or not and why the system was fair. Sixty-two percent asserted that this procedure was fair and typically explained that they had learned and mastered the skill of preparing accurate reference lists and that errors resulted from carelessness (see Cronan-Hillix, 1988). The remaining 38% argued that the procedure was unfair and typically said that the absolute scale produced distress and ignored effort (see McDonald & Peterson, this issue). The sentiment of these students was that "trying hard" should result in intermediate rather than failing grades. Second, 37 students in the spring completed a 12-item pre- and posttest questionnaire that included a question comparable to one on the 10-item posttest questionnaire. On the most pertinent item (space limitations preclude a report of all the data), students significantly changed their opinion away from *disagreement* (2) on the pretest (M = 2.21) toward *neutrality* (3) on the posttest (M = 2.89) for a question concerning the fairness of the A or F grading system,

$t(37) = 3.25$, $p = .003$. Thus, the two additional measures of student opinion indicate movement toward greater acceptance of an A or F grading system, but students do not unanimously endorse it.

Compared with the first papers in previous semesters, the first research reports seemed to contain fewer citation and reference errors and to conform better to other aspects of APA style.

Discussion

This instructional technique illustrates sound educational principles. The procedure provides repeated practice with feedback to shape accurately prepared reference lists. Moreover, the sequence of events is consistent with the principle that distributed practice is more effective than massed practice.

This technique reveals unexpected problems for students. For example, students learn that journals and magazines require different formats in the reference list, but find it difficult to distinguish between the two. This problem arises and persists because there are no clear criteria that distinguish these two types of periodicals.

This technique benefits students. First, they learn to recognize the format for different kinds of references, an important but often forgotten prerequisite to locating resources by "treeing" backward through the literature. Second, they learn to prepare a reference section for a research report and appear to be more sensitive to other aspects of APA style. Finally, they better appreciate the professional attitude that accuracy is important in conducting and reporting research. These benefits prompt students to endorse this teaching and learning technique; however, they do not unanimously support an A or F grading system.

This technique also benefits instructors. First, an instructor can perform each step in the learning sequence in only a few minutes of class time. Second, an instructor can use the technique to teach other subtleties about preparing a reference list. Third, although instructors spend time producing and administering tests, they can save time during the grading process because students produce stylistically more accurate reports that are more easily and quickly graded. This benefit multiplies during courses that require several research reports.

Coda

Developing and using this technique enhanced my own referencing skills because I had to verify many details about which I thought I was certain, only to learn that I labored under misconceptions. Developing and using this technique promoted my mastery of APA style because students asked more frequent and more challenging questions about APA style than ever before. In my opinion, developing and using this technique increased my awareness and understanding of other aspects of writing beyond referencing (e.g., Gray, 1988; Woodford, 1967), abilities that serve all of us well in our roles as authors, reviewers, and teachers.

References

American Psychological Association. (1983). *Publication manual of the American Psychological Association* (3rd ed.). Washington, DC: Author.

Cronan-Hillix, T. (1988). Teaching students the importance of accuracy in research. *Teaching of Psychology, 15*, 205-207.

Gray, D. J. (1988). Writing across the college curriculum. *Phi Delta Kappan, 69*, 729-733.

Griggs, R. A. (1988). Who is Mrs. Cantlie and why are they doing those terrible things to her homunculi? *Teaching of Psychology, 15*, 105-106.

McDonald, C. S., & Peterson, K. A. (this issue). Teaching commitment to accuracy in research: Comment on Cronan-Hillix (1988). *Teaching of Psychology, 18*, 100-101.

Soper, B., & Rosenthal, G. (1988). The number of neurons in the brain: How we report what we do not know. *Teaching of Psychology, 15*, 153-156.

Woodford, F. P. (1967). Sounder thinking through clearer writing. *Science, 156*, 743-745.

Notes

1. I thank Allen Keniston, Ken McIntire, Mary Meisser, Karen Welch, and three anonymous reviewers for helpful comments on this article.
2. This article exemplifies the teachings of Mitri Shanab and Eliot Hearst. By word and deed, they taught students to strive for perfection in writing research reports, an attitude I try to foster in my students.
3. A preliminary report of these results was presented at the Mid-America Conference for Teachers of Psychology, Evansville, IN, October 1989.
4. Requests for related materials should be sent to Blaine F. Peden, Department of Psychology, University of Wisconsin-Eau Claire, Eau Claire, WI 54702-4004.

7. USING COMPUTERS

Learning About Microcomputers and Research

Blaine F. Peden
University of Wisconsin—Eau Claire

In regard to psychologists' use of computers for instruction, interest is growing and resistance is diminishing (Butler, 1986). Bare (1982), Goolkasian (1985), and Hovancik (1986) described innovative uses for microcomputers in undergraduate laboratory courses. All three articles described the use of computers for data collection and analysis. Only Goolkasian discussed using the computer for instruction, although there are other uses for computers in teaching, such as computer-assisted instruction, modeling, and simulation (e.g., Atnip, 1985; Collyer, 1984).

This article outlines an approach that integrates the microcomputer into the entire research process. The method evolved over a period of several years as I worked individually with advanced undergraduates on research for presentation and publication. Nonetheless, this article should provide ideas and impetus for the classroom teacher by illustrating uses for the microcomputer throughout the research process—from the development of researchable hypotheses to the preparation of a manuscript for submission. In this process, students: (a) learn organizational skills, (b) acquire creative problem-solving and forecasting skills, (c) learn to think logically, and (d) develop and refine analytical and writing skills. Students also acquire knowledge about how to structure and program experiments and an appreciation for hardware and software.

Each semester one to three undergraduates begin work in my operant conditioning laboratory. They remain for one to four semesters, starting as assistants and later becoming collaborators. We conduct experiments dealing with conditioning and learning (e.g., Peden & Liddell, 1983), foraging and feeding (e.g., Peden & Rohe, 1984), and cognition and memory. We present the results at undergraduate research conferences or professional meetings, and sometimes they are published.

A typical student entering my laboratory has completed courses in statistics and research methods and has expressed an interest in performing research and attending graduate school. Although highly motivated, these students have little experience with research or microcomputers. My primary concern is to further their

goals by involving them in research. This article discusses (a) student use of the Apple II microcomputer before, during, and after an experiment; and (b) some advantages of learning about microcomputers, in particular, and of conducting research, in general.

Prior to an experiment, students read pertinent articles to develop the background and expertise required to understand or generate testable hypotheses for a particular experiment. Although my lab is not now equipped to search online data bases for new references (Lewis, 1986), students use the microcomputer to organize previously obtained references from articles, books, and chapters on a specific topic. For example, it is possible to use a file card box for references, but the microcomputer with a specialized data base for references entitled, "Quick Search Librarian" (Interactive Microware), is better than a file card box (Collyer, 1984). This program uses a separate diskette for each different database rather than different file card boxes. It also permits entering and editing all references in a particular database, searching and sorting references according to key words, and printing a reference list. Students quickly learn to appreciate such an organizational boon, and experience with this data base prompts them to identify and use other, more generalized data-base programs for academic and personal applications.

Students working on questions about foraging and feeding soon encounter quantitative models. A second application of the microcomputer prior to an experiment involves the use of spreadsheets to perform "What-If" simulations. For example, we use an inexpensive and simple spreadsheet "Magicalc JR" (Main Street Publishing). This program allows us to compute a variety of hypothetical cost/benefit functions in order to select appropriate parameters for a new experiment, and to compare predictions for different quantitative models. Such activity develops problem solving and forecasting skills that are applicable in many situations. Proficient students sometimes learn to use more advanced spreadsheets such as Visi-Calc.

In combination with ancillary hardware, students use the microcomputer during an experiment to present stimuli, such as lights and tones, and to record responses by pigeons and rats working in an experimental chamber. In my lab, each Apple II microcomputer is connected to one, two, or four different experimental chambers by a MED Associates interface that makes it easy to present stimuli, record responses, and time events. According to students, con ducting an experiment with a microcomputer markedly enhances their appreciation for hardware and software.

All programs controlling our experiments are written in APPLESOFT, a version of interpreted BASIC. We use several Beagle Brothers diskettes containing "utility programs" that facilitate writing and editing an APPLESOFT program. They are: (a) "ProntoDOS," which minimizes the time required to load a program into memory and to save a program to a diskette; (b) "Global Program Line Editor" (GPLE), which provides quick and efficient means to correct errors in lines of code; (c) "Double-Take," which requires just a few keystrokes to perform various functions, such as listing the program, cataloging a disk, appending files, renumbering a program, and clearing the screen; and (d) "D-Code," which promptly identifies an error upon entering a line. This function is helpful to student programmers because it identifies statements with typographical errors and illegal commands immediately rather than later during program execution.

"D-Code" also contains a program called COMPACT that eliminates reminders (REM statements) and compresses a program into fewer lines of code. Although it is easier to understand and modify a documented program with many REM statements, a "compacted" (as compared to a fully documented) version of the program executes more rapidly during an experiment. A substantial increment in the speed of execution can also be demonstrated for "compiled" rather than "interpreted" programs. Two familiar and easily used compilers for APPLESOFT programs are the "Einstein" compiler (Einstein Corporation) and "The APPLESOFT Compiler or TASC" (Microsoft). In brief, the fastest program is one that is both compacted and compiled.

All students use the microcomputer to conduct an experiment; however, only the more advanced students and I actually write APPLESOFT programs for an experiment. We are, of course, more interested in conducting experiments than in computer programming per se. Students with majors or minors in computer science typically must learn to program in BASIC because their training begins with PASCAL. Students who have taken only an introductory computing course possess rudimentary programming skills in BASIC. In either case, it is useful for students to improve their programming skills. The computer science students learn a new language and respond enthusiastically to the opportunity to program in a real-time as opposed to a batch mode. A modicum of programming experience helps computer novices understand how the previously described utilities help to overcome the tiresome aspects of writing an APPLESOFT program. The students also learn how long it takes to write

a program. Moreover, some programming experience helps computer novices understand the need to write logically organized, or structured programs, and to document programs thoroughly—ideas well-entrenched for more sophisticated programmers. To this end, our programs contain many subroutines, each of which performs one function and includes many REM statements.

Learning about structured programs with internal documentation provides at least three benefits to students. One advantage is that new students can study previous programs and quickly learn the commands required to time events, activate outputs (e.g., lights), and measure inputs (e.g., responses). This experience helps a student to feel more confident about programming an experiment, and to appreciate hardware and software. A second advantage is that the experimenter must use organizational skills to specify each step in the sequence of experimental events before trying to write a program. Attempting to write a program prematurely often reveals logical and procedural problems, whereas the careful planning required to write a program for an experiment may suggest parametric manipulations and variations in the procedure that might not otherwise be obvious. A third advantage of this approach is that a subroutine solving a particular problem may be "transported" from one experiment to another, thereby decreasing the amount of time required for programming from experiment to experiment. For example, a subroutine we named "Activate the Peripheral Devices" provides instructions to the student experimenter about the order in which different peripheral devices, such as the MED Associates interface and the power supply, should be activated. This structured and documented subroutine is easily "transported" from a program for rats to one for pigeons by using "Double-Take" (Beagle Brothers) to append files. In sum, students learn to program experiments, understand procedures, and transfer solutions for one experiment to another. The extent to which an individual student's sophistication grows varies directly as a function of time spent in the lab and the number of projects completed.

After an experiment, the primary goal for the student is to write a report that is correct in form and content. At this point in the research process, the microcomputer is an invaluable tool for statistical analysis, data plotting, and word processing.

My students use statistical programs such as "Key Stat" (Oakleaf Systems) or the "Introductory Statistics Software Package" (Addison-Wesley) for simple statistical analysis and the "HSD Statistics" (Human Systems Dynamics) programs for complex analysis. Easy-to-use statistics programs make a student more willing to analyze data and to perform different analyses on a set of data. Programs such as "Scientific Plotter" (Interactive Microware) or "Alphachart" and "Curve Plotter" (Spectral Graphics Software) make it easy to plot data. These programs encourage a student to consider alternative ways to represent the data.

Finally, all students learn to use "Applewriter II or IIe," a word processor, to prepare successive drafts of their laboratory reports. Word processing encourages students to revise manuscripts. Students are more willing to explore problem solving strategies for writing, such as generating and organizing ideas, and editing for style and organization (Flower, 1981), when using a word processor than when writing by hand or typing. An outline processor (Rogers, 1986) is another program that will promote student use of problem-solving strategies for writing initial drafts of a paper. Ultimately, I favor use of "Manuscript Manager" (Pergamon Press), perhaps the word processor of choice because it is specifically designed for preparing manuscripts according to the APA style manual. Once students approach a final draft, they use "The Sensible Speller" (Sensible Software) to eliminate misspelled words and typographical errors.

In conclusion, a crucial component to the success of this endeavor is individualized instruction during one or more semesters (see also, Atnip, 1985, for a similar emphasis). This component is more important than either the particular microcomputer or the programs used, because programs comparable to those I have described are available for other machines as well.

Undergraduates working in my lab become skilled in only some of the microcomputer applications to which they are exposed—in large part, by choice. Students tell me that how much they learn about a particular application depends largely on the availability of the microcomputer and the software, and on personal needs. For example, in comparison to the university microcomputer lab, in which pertinent software is unavailable and computer access is limited, students have virtually unlimited access to the software and microcomputers in my lab, except during the hours reserved for experiments. This opportunity allows students to exploit some applications and to explore others according to their needs and interests.

Student use of the microcomputer before, during, and after an experiment produces benefits from learning about microcomputers and from conducting research. Undergraduates working with microcomputers in my laboratory derive, to varying degrees, several benefits, which help them to compete in graduate programs or the job world. With respect to learning about computers and computer applications, students: (a) learn creative problem-solving and forecasting skills, (b) learn organizational skills, (c) develop an appreciation for hardware and software, (d) learn to think logically and to write structured programs for real time experiments, and (e) improve their analytical and writing skills. Students also gain laboratory experience and have an opportunity to present their experiments at undergraduate research conferences. Students report that these experiences foster self-discipline, responsibility, social skills, a spirit of cooperation, self-confidence, and a sense of personal achievement.

The ideas expressed in this article should also be useful for teachers who use microcomputers in laboratory courses. For example, students exposed to data-base and spreadsheet applications will develop their own uses for these tools, especially as simple and easy-to-use programs become increasingly available in the public domain or at low cost. In a similar fashion, students learn quickly that expertise in using hardware and software programming aids is valuable in academic and applied settings. Finally, experience with outline processors, word processors, and spelling checkers helps students improve the quality of their writing, another important skill in academic and job settings.

References

Atnip, G. W. (1985). Teaching the use of computers A case study. *Teaching of Psychology*, *12*, 171-172.

Bare, J. K. (1982). Microcomputers in the introductory laboratory. *Teaching of Psychology*, *9*, 236-237.

Butler, D. L. (1986). Interests in and barriers to using computers in instruction. *Teaching of Psychology*, *13*, 20-23.

Collyer, C. E. (1984). Using computers in the teaching of psychology Five things that seem to work. *Teaching of Psychology*, *11*, 206-209.

Flower, L. (1981). *Problem-solving strategies for writing*. New York: Harcourt Brace Jovanovich.

Goolkasian, P. (1985). A microcomputer-based lab for psychology instruction. *Teaching of Psychology*, *12*, 223-225.

Hovancik, J. R. (1986). Using microcomputers in the undergraduate laboratory. *Teaching of Psychology*, *13*, 94-96.

Lewis, L. K. (1986). Bibliographic computerized searching in psychology. *Teaching of Psychology*, *13*, 38-40.

Peden, B. F., & Liddell, B. (1983, May). *The paws that refresh: A preliminary attempt to condition self-grooming and other-grooming by rats*. Paper presented at the meeting of the Association for Behavior Analysis, Milwaukee, WI

Peden, B. F., & Rohe, M. S. (1984). Effects of search cost on foraging and feeding: A three-component chain analysis. *Journal of the Experimental Analysis of Behavior*, *42*, 211-221.

Rogers, R. L. (1986). Preparing course materials with an outline processor. *Teaching of Psychology*, *13*, 154-155.

Notes

1. This article is based on a paper presented as part of a symposium, *Preparing Psychology Majors for Careers in Business: Teaching Computer Skills and Applications*, conducted at the meeting of the

Midwestern Psychological Association in Chicago, IL, May 2-4, 1985.

2. Preparation of this article was supported in part by the University of Wisconsin—Eau Claire Faculty Sabbatical Leave Program and by a supplement to National Science Foundation Grant No. 84-11445 to William Timberlake at Indiana University, Bloomington.

3. I thank Allen Keniston and several anonymous reviewers for their comments on an earlier draft of this article.

FACES in the LAB and FACES in the CROWD: Integrating Microcomputers Into the Psychology Course

Blaine F. Peden
University of Wisconsin-Eau Claire
Gene D. Steinhauer
University of California-Fresno

Our experimental psychology courses teach students about the use and misuse of naturalistic observation, correlation, and experimentation. Over the semesters we have devised different assignments to acquaint students with methodological issues involved in making reliable observations of behavior. This article describes an exercise in which students learned to recognize facial expressions in the laboratory and then tested their skills by conducting a naturalistic observation study. We present and evaluate the educational benefits of this assignment, most notably active student discussion of methodological problems. Finally, we comment on the use of microcomputers in teaching interobserver agreement in particular and psychology in general.

The assignment began in a microcomputer lab where students learned to identify facial expressions of emotion. Students were asked to work in pairs. Each pair received a copy of FACES (Steinhauer, 1986), a guessing game written in Applesoft BASIC that uses Ekman's (1972) Facial Affect Scoring Technique and a set of facial features (brows-forehead, eyes-lids, and lower face) to produce six expressions of emotion on the high resolution graphics screen: anger, disgust, fear, happiness, sadness, and surprise. Student pairs worked to complete an "empty" table containing three columns for the facial features and six rows for the emotional expressions (Ekman, 1972, pp. 251-252). The students observed an image on the screen and described each facial feature for each expression in their own words. For example, the students might write "wide open eyes" as their description under eyes-lids for the expression of "surprise." After about 30 min the students completed the table, at which time they received a copy of Ekman's table for comparison. The students continued to view facial expressions until they resolved discrepancies between Ekman's and their own descriptions, and identified all six facial expressions without error. From start to finish, the entire laboratory phase required about 45 to 50 min.

During the second phase, students conducted a naturalistic observation study. Each pair recruited a third student who was inexperienced with FACES. The trio selected a location and agreed on a procedure in which all three observers independently made 100 observations. For example, one trio positioned themselves in the entrance to the campus library and observed every second person entering the doorway for 1 sec. Each student also received a data sheet to record each of the 100 subjects' facial expression, gender, and age. Each observer independently classified each subject's facial expression into one of seven categories. For example, each observer indicated either one of Ekman's six categories (e.g., Hager & Ekman, 1979) or a category called "other" by writing the first three letters of the category name in the blank spaces on the data sheet (e.g., ANG—anger, DIS—disgust, FEA—fear, HAP—happiness, SAD—sadness, SUR—surprise, or OTH—other). In this coding scheme, either a neutral expression or a blend of expressions was assigned to the "other" category. Finally, each observer recorded the gender and age range (i.e., 1-10, 11-20, 21-30, . . ., 61-70) of each person.

The students counted each decision for which a pair of observers agreed and computed the percentage of agreement. They performed this analysis separately for each pair of observers on each of the three categories:

Table 1. Percentage of Interobserver Agreement Scores for Field Observations

Condition		Gender	Age	Expression
			Category	
Trained Pairs				
	M	99	68	59
	Range	90–100	39–98	41–86
Untrained Pairs				
	M	99	71	50
	Range	95–100	36–100	18–77

facial expression, gender, and age. Finally, the students wrote a report in APA style, that included a table showing the percentage of agreement for the three pairs of observers with respect to gender, age, and expression.

The interobserver agreement scores from each report were subdivided into two categories, depending on whether both members (trained pairs) or only one member (untrained pairs) of the pair of observers was experienced with FACES. Table 1 displays the mean and range of the percentage of agreement scores for trained and untrained pairs of observers. The greater agreement for trained than untrained pairs on facial expression was statistically significant, $t(46) = 2.26$, $p < .05$; however, the differences in the agreement scores were not statistically significant for either gender, $t(46) = .82$, or age, $t(46) = .66$. The range of agreement scores was the least for gender and greatest for age.

This assignment yielded four educational benefits: (a) students were enthusiastic about it; (b) students could immediately assess newly acquired laboratory learning while conducting a study in a natural setting; (c) students learned to work cooperatively and write a paper collaboratively; and (d) students asked questions and willingly discussed methodological issues, a marked contrast from previous semesters in which assignments generated few questions and little discussion.

The assignment produced findings that prompted questions and discussion about methodological issues. First, students were troubled by the higher degree of interobserver agreement in the laboratory and the lower degree of agreement in the field. For example, they asked why they agreed perfectly when judging computer-generated facial expressions but only moderately when judging human facial expressions. The discussion period revealed that the computer program generated full frontal expressions of only six emotions for a single individual, whereas facial expressions were observed from quite different angles for many different individuals in the field. Moreover, in the laboratory the students studied the facial expression at their leisure, whereas in the field they made a decision after just 1 sec. Thus, the greater complexity of viewing conditions, the greater number of categories provided by the additional "other" cate gory, and the restrictions on study time probably contributed to the lower agreement scores obtained in the field as compared to the laboratory. Second, the students observed that the seemingly obvious category of gender produced high, but

not perfect, agreement scores, whereas facial expression and age produced only moderate agreement scores. The students asked why all categories were not equally easy to measure reliably. This question led to discussions about the relationship between nominal and actual categories, and how variables (e.g., the number and type of categories) affect the results. For example, even though there were seven nominal categories for age and facial expression, the actual number for age often equaled the number for gender because many trios observed individuals on campus, a location in which ages typically ranged from 18 to 24 years. The classroom discussion revealed that students who observed individuals in the student center and the campus library found it harder to agree on the ages than students who observed individuals at the YMCA or shopping malls. Apparently, it was much harder to distinguish 19 and 20-year-olds from those 21 or older on campus with only two categories than it was to distinguish individuals from a greater age range off campus with seven categories. Third, the benefit of explicit training was obvious because pairs of students previously trained to observe facial expressions produced greater agreement scores than did untrained pairs. This finding prompted more general discussions about the transfer of training, the need to assess interobserver agreement under actual conditions for data collection, and the differences between Ekman's procedure (e.g., Hager & Ekman, 1979) and this assignment. For example, even though the 9-point difference was statistically significant, it appeared small in view of the contention that Ekman can train people to judge expressions proficiently. However, Ekman provided more training than the 45 min permitted by this assignment, and he trained and tested his subjects with photographs, whereas this assignment trained subjects with simple stimuli in the laboratory and tested them with complex stimuli in the field. Given these procedural differences, the 9% difference appeared more impressive. Finally, the differences in the means and the range of scores for trained and untrained pairs in each of the three categories prompted discussions about the role of statistics in data analysis. The nature of the discussion about descriptive and inferential statistics depended on both the educational intentions of the instructor and the sophistication of the students.

In conclusion, this assignment engendered lively discussions among undergraduate experimental psychology students about methods for naturalistic observation. In addition, features of this assignment may be useful to other instructors. First, the classroom use of a computer graphics program generated considerable student interest. Second, the computer was incorporated without allowing the technology to dominate the exercise (e.g., Leeper, 1985). Thus, this assignment illustrates our view that computers function best for part, but not all, of a learning experience and simple programs that perform one task well provide meaningful learning experiences (e.g., Stowbridge & Kugel, 1983). Third, the two parts of the exercise were integrated to promote the transfer of skills from the classroom to the field. A final and amusing outcome of this exercise was that the instructors learned to produce the different facial expressions of emotion and then used them to provide unambiguous consequences for student behavior during the remainder of the semester.

References

Ekman, P. (1972). Universal and cultural differences in facial expressions of emotion. In J. K. Cole (Ed.), *Nebraska symposium on motivation* (Vol. 19, pp. 207-283). Lincoln, NE: University of Nebraska Press.

Hager, J. C., & Ekman, P. (1979). Long-distance transmission of facial affect signals. *Ethology and Sociobiology, 1*, 77-82.

Leeper, M. R. (1985). Microcomputers in education. *American Psychologist, 40*, 1-18.

Steinhauer, G. D. (1986). *Artificial behavior: Computer simulation of psychological processes.* Englewood Cliffs, NJ: Prentice-Hall.

Stowbridge, M. D., & Kugel, P. (1983, April). Learning to learn by learning to play. *Creative Computing*, pp. 180-188.

Notes

1. We thank various colleagues, notably Dexter Gormley, Erna Kelly, and Allen Keniston, for their comments on a draft of this manuscript.

2. Copies of the assignment and data sheet are available at no charge from the first author. Information about FACES and related programs is available by writing the second author in care of Artificial Behavior, Incorporated, 4974 North Fresno, Suite 326, Fresno, CA 93726 or by calling (209) 229-4703.

Using Microcomputers in the Undergraduate Laboratory

John R. Hovancik
Seton Hall University

Instructors of courses in experimental psychology and re search methods in psychology are always looking for experiments and demonstrations that can be incorporated into their students' laboratory experiences. These procedures should be interesting, easy to instrument for multistudent laboratories, and reliably yield results that illustrate psychological phenomena. The shrinking cost and incredible flexibility of microcomputers make them the psychology laboratory instruments of the future. Teachers need to discover or devise interesting and reliable demonstrations that take advantage of the impressive power of these instruments (cf. Bare, 1982). This article describes a successful in corporation of microcomputer instrumentation into the undergraduate psychology laboratory. The procedures re quire no interfacing of components to the computer, and thus can be implemented on off-the-shelf computer systems with no need for modification.

My investigation examined the question of whether the time taken to choose between stimulus alternatives is influenced by affective reactions to the choices. The alternatives were different colors generated on a computer video monitor. The correlational design was patterned after the much earlier investigations of Dashiell (1937) and Shipley, Coffin and Hadsell (1945). The hypothesis tested was that, if a subject has a strong preference (either positive or negative) for a given color, then reaction times to choose between that color and others will be short. Thus, we expect a negative Correlation between the strength of the subject's preference for a color and the reaction time for choices involving that color. The strength of subjective preference was gauged by how often the subject chose a given color when it was paired with other colors in a forced-choice situation. If subjects have a strong preference for a particular color we would expect them to choose that color often. A strong negative preference against a particular color would be expected to yield a low frequency of choice.

Either an Apple II + or Apple IIe microcomputer was used to generate a pair of adjacent squares approximately 5 in. On a side displayed on a 13-in. Amdek Model Color-1 video monitor. The two squares varied in color and were either red, orange, yellow, green, blue, or violet. On successive trials, all possible paired combinations of these colors were presented. Each of the resulting pairs was presented twice so that, for a given pair, a color could appear on the right one time and on the left another time. This amounted to a total of 30 test trials per subject. The order of presentation of color pairs was varied randomly by the computer for each subject. A sample pair of colors (used during instructions) and four practice pairs of colors were also presented. None of these trials involved the six test trial colors, however. Each student was responsible for recruiting and running subjects. Data from all students' subjects were later pooled for analysis.

Subjects were seated at the keyboard of the computer and were informed that they were to select their preferred color from the two presented on each trial. Preferences were indicated by pressing designated keys on the computer keyboard. Subjects were specifically advised not to hurry their responses but to take as long as necessary to be sure of their choices. After the instructions were presented, the experimenter left the room and the computer proceeded to present the 4 practice trials and 30 test trials. On test trials, the subject's color preference and choice reaction time were recorded by the computer.

Because each test color was presented exactly 10 times, subjects' preferences produced choice frequencies ranging from 0 (when a color was never picked as preferred) to 10 (always chosen). These frequencies were then transformed into positive and negative values (to reflect positive and negative preferences) by subtracting 5 from the choice frequency The absolute value of the transformed score is indicative of the strength of the subject's preference. For example, a color chosen 10 times would produce a transformed preference level score of 5, indicating a strong preference A color never chosen would have a preference level of 5, also a strong preference (in this case a negative one). If our hypothesis is correct, strong preference levels should be accompanied by short reaction times.

Following the final trial, the experimenter revealed on the monitor screen the data collected from the subject and explained the hypothesis. Because six preference levels (1 for each color) and six mean reaction time measures were taken for each subject, it was possible to compute a correlation coefficient for each subject individually. This statistic was also displayed during the debriefing process. The data were then also saved to a disk file for later more extensive statistical analysis.

Data have now been collected independently during four semesters and each time the data have been consistent with predictions. In fact, it is rare when the expected results are not obtained even for individual subjects. Statistical analysis involved computing a coefficient of correlation between each subject's preference level for each color and the mean reaction time for choices on trials that included that color as one of the alternatives. As predicted by the hypothesis, mean reaction times were negatively correlated with the strength of the subject's preference for or against the color, $r(124) = -.337$, $p < .001$. Comparisons involving the most preferred or least preferred colors resulted in faster choices. Results highly similar to these have been obtained each semester this procedure has been used. Also, the results are consistent with those of the original investigation by Dashiell (1937). There appears to be little question of the reliability of the reported phenomenon.

I use this investigation in my research methodology course early in the semester when we consider correlational research. It introduces students to the use of microcomputers and simultaneously shows them a useful application of computers in psychological research. Having the computer present stimuli, control trial pacing, and collect data provides a vivid first-hand experience for the student in how psychological research is being carried out today. This exposure to computer-controlled research early in the semester gives the student an appreciation for how instrumentation can be used to protect against experimenter induced bias. Using computers in undergraduate research also increases students' motivation. Students get excited about the science of psychology in a way that stopwatches, paper, and pencils never allowed.

Given the reliability of the results, the investigation is a "safe" procedure to use as an early exposure to psychological research when it may not be advantageous to deal with the realities of why expected results were not obtained. In the four semesters that I have used this technique, the data have always conformed to predictions. Because the procedure requires no interfacing to the computer, our students can conduct their research at a number of microcomputer sites around the campus. This possibility sets the stage for discussing proper experimental control procedures, vis-a-vis, control over the environment during data collection.

In summary, this procedure is an effective, reliable technique for introducing microcomputer use in the undergraduate laboratory. It illustrates one way in which the laboratory experience can reflect current methodologies and increase students' interest. Designing laboratory projects to exploit the strengths of the microcomputer as a research tool appears to have great promise in the teaching of psychology.

References

Bare, J. K. (1982). Microcomputers in the introductory laboratory. *Teaching of Psychology*, 9, 236-237.

Dashiell, J. F. (1937). Affective value-distances as a determinant of aesthetic judgment-times. *American Journal of Psychology, 50,* 57-69.

Shipley, W. C ., Coffin, J. I., & Hadsell, K. C. (1945). Affective distance and other factors determining reaction time in judgments of color preference. *Journal of Experimental Psychology, 35,* 206-2 1 5.

Note

Requests for copies of the programs used in the present investigation should be sent to John R. Hovancik, Department of Psychology, Seton Hall University, South Orange, NJ 07079 Diskette copies of the program are available only for Apple II + or IIe or compatible.

Publication Bias: A Computer-Assisted Demonstration of Excluding Nonsignificant Results From Research Interpretation

Todd C. Riniolo
Department of Human Development
University of Maryland, College Park

Publication bias is an impairment to accurate interpretation of published literature. Publication bias, the increased likelihood of publication of a manuscript describing significant rather than nonsignificant findings, can arise either from researchers' failure to submit nonsignificant results for publication or journal reviewers' rejection of articles based on nonsignificant findings. Recent evidence suggests that publication bias can pose a serious impediment to accurate interpretation of research results (Berlin, Begg, & Louis, 1989; Easterbrook, Berlin, Gopalan, & Matthews, 1991; Simes, 1986) and can alter meta-analytic results designed to estimate effect sizes from published studies (Dear & Begg, 1992). Although formal studies have shown that the majority of articles published in journals are filled with positive results (Bozarth & Roberts, 1972; Sterling, 1959), introductory research methods textbooks (e.g., Graziano & Raulin, 1989; Ray, 1993) often fail to alert students that published research findings may be a biased representation of true population differences.

The cumulation of individual studies to derive an accurate interpretation of the literature is tied intimately to the Central Limit Theorem (CLT). First, the CLT states that drawing repeated samples from a given population (or differences between populations) will yield a nearly normal sampling distribution of means when the sample sizes are approximately 25 or larger for both normal and nonnormal parent populations (Hopkins & Glass, 1978). From this sampling distribution of means, the mean of the sampling distribution is an accurate estimate of the true population mean. If the full range of results from repeated sampling is not available, such as when nonsignificant findings are not published, the CLT does not accurately reflect the true population mean. Similarly, if the researcher does not have access to the full range of results because of publication bias, interpretation of the literature occurs from a biased sample. Second, the CLT states that as sample size increases, the variability (i.e., the standard error) of the sampling distribution of means decreases according to the function: $\sigma/\sqrt{N}$. A decrease in the standard error as sample size increases results in greater statistical precision to detect differences (i.e., greater statistical power) because the individual distributions being compared constrict, resulting in a smaller distributional overlap between groups.

The purpose of this article is to provide a computer-based simulation, based on tenets of the CLT, of the effects of excluding nonsignificant findings from research interpretation. The concept of publication bias may seem abstract to the student at the introductory level, and a classroom demonstration can provide a concrete and visual example to supplement class lecture and discussion.

Method

Procedure

I obtained results in this article from 10,000 trials; however, you can use 1,000 or 100 trials for the class exercise when quick processing time is essential. Processing time requires less than 5 min for 1,000 trials and less than 1 min for 100 trials on a 486-based personal computer (16MB RAM) running at 66MHz.

I performed a power analysis (desired power level as a function of effect size, significance level, and sample size) using the power function in Sigmastat 1.0 (Jandel Scientific, 1994) to approximate a 25%, 50%, and 80% chance of reaching statistical significance for two-tailed t tests ($\alpha = .05$) between Group 1 ($M = 106.36$, $SD = 10$) and Group 2 ($M = 100$, $SD = 10$). The population difference between groups corresponds to $d = .636$ (Cohen, 1988). Results used for this demonstration are as follows: (a) $1 - \beta = .245$ ($n = 9$ for each group), (b) $1 - \beta = .5$ ($n = 20$ for each group), and (c) $1 - \beta = .802$ ($n = 40$ for each group). The numbers used in this demonstration can change, but are conceptually easy to interpret and understand (e.g., differences between populations on IQ scores).

The demonstration consists of the following series of steps:

1. Provide the class with a refresher of the CLT.
2. Run the simulation with the various samples sizes starting with $1 - \beta = .50$, $1 - \beta = .245$, and $1 - \beta = .802$. Record the mean results comparing the full range of results with significant results only. Print the graph after each simulation or use the figures from

this article for illustration.
3. Lead a discussion of the results.
4. Instruct the class to browse through recent journals comparing significant versus nonsignificant findings to provide students with firsthand experience of the proportion of positive versus negative findings in the journals.

You may change the effect size difference between populations or sample sizes associated with this demonstration. For example, you may wish to compare the effects of publication bias on small, medium, and large effect size differences (Cohen, 1988) in the population while maintaining a constant sample size.

Programming

I created the program for this demonstration in Matlab 4.0 (Math Works, 1995) with Statistics Toolbox (Math Works, 1996) . The logic of the program was to use a "for" loop to draw random samples from a given population (i.e., a normal distribution) for 2 groups and to perform t tests. The random number generator is a scalar whose value changes each time it is referenced and transforms values of a uniform generator according to the algorithm described by Forsythe, Malcolm, and Moler (1977). I then labeled results as being significant or nonsignificant, allowing for easy access to compare the full distribution

Table 1. Publication Bias Program

```
SAM=input('Input number of samples to be drawn from a population:   ');
SUB=input('Input number of subjects in each group:   ');
MEAN_=input('Input the Mean for group 1:   ');
ES=input('Input the Population Mean difference between groups:   ');
STD_=input('Input the Standard Deviation for both groups:   ');
for n=1:SAM               %for loop to generate # of trials
GRP1=(randn(SUB,1)*STD_)+MEAN_;
GRP2=(randn(SUB,1)*STD_)+MEAN_+ES;
[h(n,1)]=ttest2(GRP1,GRP2);       %independent t-tests
Mean_dif(n,1)=mean(GRP2) - mean(GRP1);
   if h(n,1) == 1;           %flagging significant results
   reject_(n,1)=Mean_dif(n,1);
   else;
   reject_(n,1)= (abs(MEAN_*STD_+10000))*(-1);
   end;
end;
MIN_1=min(Mean_dif);MAX_1=max(Mean_dif);MM1=MIN_1:MAX_1;
%setting graph axis
R=sort(reject_);K=find(R(abs(MEAN_*STD_+10000))*(-1));
P=K(1,1);E=max(K);reject_2=R(P:E,1);
subplot(2,1,1); hist(Mean_dif,MM1);title('Full Distribution');ylabel('Frequency');
subplot(2,1,2); hist(reject_2,MM1);
title('Significant Results Only');ylabel('Frequency');
total_rej=sum(h);mean_diff=mean(Mean_dif);
std_diff=std(Mean_dif);reject_a=mean(reject_2);
reject_std=std(reject_2);
fprintf('Number of "Significant" Trials          =   %6.3f\n',total_rej);
fprintf('Mean Difference using the Full Distribution =  %6.3f\n',mean_diff);
fprintf('Standard Deviation of the Full Distribution  =   %6.3f\n',std_diff);
fprintf('Mean Difference of "Significant" Trials     =   %6.3f\n',reject_a);
fprintf('Standard Deviation of "Significant" Trials  =   %6.3f\n',reject_std);
clear;
```

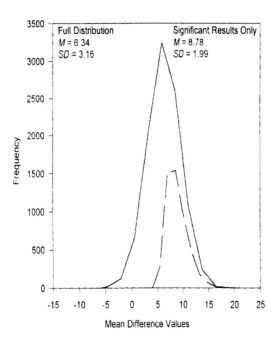

Figure 1. Frequency distributions of mean difference scores for the full distribution (solid line) and significant results only (dashed line) with $1 - \beta = .500$.

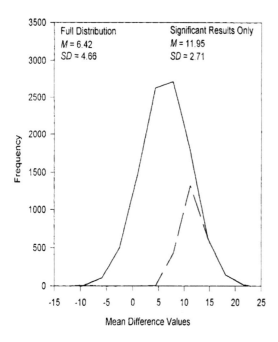

Figure 2. Frequency distributions of mean difference scores for the full distribution (solid line) and significant results only (dashed line) with $1 - \beta = .245$.

versus significant results only. The program appears in Table 1.

Results

Figure 1 (solid line) illustrates the full range of mean difference scores from Group 1 and Group 2 with power set at .5, giving an equal chance of obtaining significant or

nonsignificant results. Findings are consistent with the CLT ($M = 6.34$, $SD = 3.16$), which predicts an accurate estimation of the true difference between groups (6.36 as defined by the random number generator) from the mean of the sampling distribution. Figure 1 (dashed line) illustrates the distribution of significant results only. Of the 10,000 trials, 4,996 were significant ($M = 8.78$; $SD = 1.99$). As shown by Figure 1, exclusion of negative findings produces a positively biased distribution, which results in the biased estimation of the between groups difference.

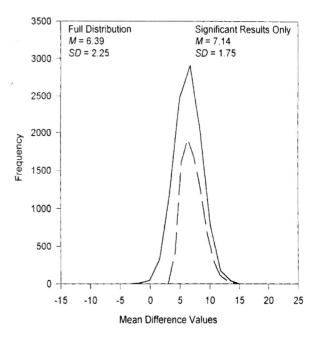

Figure 3. Frequency distributions of mean difference scores for the full distribution (solid line) and significant results only (dashed line) with $1 - \beta = .802$.

Figure 2 (solid line) shows that despite low power (.245), the full range of results still provides an accurate estimate of group differences ($M = 6.42$; $SD = 4.66$). However, when significant results only ($n = 2,532$) are examined ($M = 11.95$; $SD = 2.71$), a large overestimation of the true difference occurs from the limited distribution (Figure 2, dashed line). With power raised (.802), the full range of results (Figure 3, solid line) also provides an accurate estimate of true group differences ($M = 6.39$; $SD = 2.25$) . Although overestimating the true difference ($M = 7.14$; $SD = 1.75$; $n = 8042$), this power level provided the least biased estimate of the true difference using only significant results (Figure 3, dashed line).

Discussion

Results from this demonstration are consistent with the CLT. First, inclusion of the full range of results accurately estimates the true difference between groups (i.e., an accurate interpretation of the literature derived

248

from an unbiased sample). As shown in Figures 1, 2, and 3, exclusion of nonsignificant results biases the available distribution, impairing the interpretation by the researcher. For example, exclusion of nonsignificant results may result in a treatment (e.g., a new drug therapy for hypertension) or a group difference (e.g., gender) being represented by the literature as a greater difference than exists in the population. Second, results based on smaller samples are prone to a greater bias when nonsignificant results are excluded because of the reduction of statistical precision resulting in an increase in distributional overlap.

This demonstration provides an important lesson for psychology students that is often absent in introductory research textbooks and provides a vehicle for discussion of the more philosophical issues associated with the evolution of publication bias. Perhaps publication bias has arisen from the dichotomous nature of hypothesis testing that allows researchers to interpret only significant findings. As Hedges (1984) pointed out, when a study fails to reach statistical significance, interpretation is difficult, often resulting in unpublished manuscripts or published manuscripts with incomplete reporting of nonsignificant findings. Additionally, the ability to interpret only significant results may have contributed to the widespread overconfidence of social scientists about the probability that statistically significant findings will replicate (Cohen, 1994; Oakes, 1986; Tversky & Kahneman, 1971). Shaver (1993) recommends philosophical discussions as one method to reduce strictly mechanical application of statistics and research methodology by students and to stimulate critical analysis of research interpretation.

This computer program also works with fewer trials (e.g., 30) to simulate more realistic numbers of studies associated with a literature review of a specific research question. Additionally, this demonstration provides a transition to discuss not only philosophical issues of research methodology, but applied material such as (a) proposed methods to control and identify publication bias, (b) sample size and the probability of replication of results, and (c) the use of power analysis to determine appropriate sample sizes. By experiencing the consequences of excluding nonsignificant results from research interpretation, students will gain an invaluable lesson to aid research interpretation.

References

Berlin, J. A., Begg, C. B., & Louis, T. A. (1989). An assessment of publication bias using a sample of published clinical trials. *Journal of the American Statistical Association, 84*, 381-392.

Bozarth, J. D., & Roberts, R. R. (1972). Signifying significant significance. *American Psychologist, 27*, 774-775.

Cohen, J. (1988). *Statistical power analysis for the behavioral sciences* (2nd ed.). Hillsdale, NJ: Lawrence Erlbaum Associates, Inc.

Cohen, J. (1994).The earth is round (*p* < .05). *American Psychologist, 49*, 997-1003.

Dear, K. B. G., & Begg, C. (1992). An approach for assessing publication bias prior to performing a meta-analysis. *Statistical Science, 7*, 237-245.

Easterbrook, P. J., Berlin, S. A., Gopalan, R., & Matthews, D. R. (1991). Publication bias in clinical research. *The Lancet, 337*, 867-872.

Forsythe, G. E., Malcolm, M. A., & Moler, C. B. (1977). *Computer methods for mathematical computations.* Englewood Cliffs, NJ: Prentice Hall.

Graziano, A. M., & Raulin, M. L. (1989). *Research methods: A process of inquiry.* New York: Harper & Row.

Hedges, L. V. (1984). Estimation of effect size under nonrandom sampling: The effects of censoring studies yielding statistically insignificant mean differences. *Journal of Educational Statistics, 9*, 61-85.

Hopkins, K. D., & Glass, G. V. (1978). *Basic statistics for the behavioral sciences.* Englewood Cliffs, NJ: Prentice Hall.

Matlab 4.0 [Computer program]. (1995). Natick, MA: Math Works.

Oakes, M. (1986). *Statistical inference: A commentary for the social and behavioral sciences.* New York: Wiley.

Ray, W. J. (1993). *Methods toward a science of behavior* (4th ed.). Monterey, CA: Brooks/Cole.

Shaver, J. P. (1993). What statistical significance testing is, and what it is not. *Journal of Experimental Education, 61*, 293-316.

Sigmastat 1.0 [Computer program]. (1994). San Rafael, CA: Jandel Scientific.

Simes, R. J. (1986). Publication bias: The case for an international registry of clinical trials. *Journal of Clinical Oncology, 4*, 1529-1541.

Statistics Toolbox [Computer program]. (1996). Natick, MA: Math Works.

Sterling, T. C. (1959). Publication decisions and their possible effects on inferences drawn from tests of significance or vice versa. *Journal of the American Statistical Association, 54*, 30-34.

Tversky, A., & Kahneman, D. (1971). Belief in the law of small numbers. *Psychological Bulletin, 76*, 105-110.

Notes

1. This article is dedicated to the memory of the late Brian J. Riniolo, my brother.
2. Special thanks to John Jeka for his eloquent teaching of computer skills and to Jane Doussard-Roosevelt for her helpful suggestions in writing this manuscript.

8. USING POPULAR MEDIA AND SCHOLARILY PUBLICATIONS

Using Scholarly Journals in Undergraduate Experimental Methodology Courses

W. Newton Suter
Paula Frank
San Francisco State University

Considering the number of good undergraduate textbooks in experimental methodology, one may wonder why instructors might use supplementary instructional materials, particularly professional and scholarly journals that report original research. The answer is that judicious use of carefully chosen journal articles may provide students with insight into the application of methodological principles to realistic research endeavors and encourage students' independent exploration of original research. Reading scholarly journals is commonplace for graduate students; encouraging such activity for undergraduates may prompt their interest in pursuing graduate study in psychology. One key element for using scholarly journals in undergraduate classes is the careful selection of articles. In this article, we suggest some ways of increasing the value of using journal articles, based on 6 years of experimentation in the classroom.

Selection Criteria

Three criteria are most important for selecting journal articles to supplement standard text material. Articles must be (a) cited with high frequency in introductory psychology textbooks, (b) prime illustrations of specific Methodological principles, and (c) reasonably short and comprehensible to undergraduate students with limited backgrounds.

The criterion of frequent citation is important for several reasons. First, when students know that they are reading well-known research (not merely reading about it), their interest level increases. Second, the research findings of such classic experiments are likely to be known to the upper division major who has taken previous psychology courses (or at least an introductory course). Consequently, students can concentrate not so much on the findings of the research, but on the methods. There seems to be no better way to demonstrate that experimental outcomes are, at least in part, dependent on the way an experiment is

designed and conducted. Third, the use of noteworthy research is likely to have a positive transfer effect in other psychology courses ("Oh, yeah! I read that research in my experimental methods course"). Finally, many students experience a thrill when they uncover minor (or major!) inconsistencies between a description of an experiment in a secondary source and the documented details of the experiment itself. For example, students have proudly reported an incorrect graph of the results from the classic Festinger and Carlsmith (1959) experiment in Atkinson, Atkinson, and Hilgard (1983) and inaccurate procedural details of the same experiment in Lefrançois (1983).

The importance of the relevance criterion is fairly obvious. It makes little sense to read original research that does not relate in a methodological way to the material being covered in a standard text. The criterion of readability is also important in an obvious and not so obvious way. Students must be capable of reading original research with reasonable comprehension; otherwise, the assignment will have limited usefulness and probably will not be completed. Readability is also important because students often experience an attitudinal boost concerning the subject once they understand the major methodological principles used by the experimenters. There is also a sense of accomplishment, mastery, and confidence because the students know that they are doing what graduate students do.

Matching Classic Experiments With Core Topics

A scan of a convenient "on-the-shelf" sample of 26 major introductory psychology texts published in the years 1983-1985, representing all levels of comprehensiveness, reveals that some experimental studies are cited with such frequency that they may be termed classic. Such experiments are more likely to be remembered by students completing the introductory psychology course. Matching classic experiments with important methodological concepts in a way that maximizes the benefit for students

Table 1. Listing of Classic Experiments, Citation Frequency, Core Topics, and Recommended Use

Citation[b]	Frequency[c]	Core Topics[a]								
		A	B	C	D	E	F	G	H	I
Schachter & Singer (1962)	25		X	X			X			X
Milgram (1963)	20	X		X						X
Festinger & Carlsmith (1959)	20		X		X	X	X			
Peterson & Peterson (1959)	19	X				X			X	
Dion, Berscheid, & Walster (1972)	18				X			X		
Bandura, Ross, & Ross (1963)	15			X	X			X		
Darley & Latané (1968)	12				X				X	X
Dutton & Aron (1974)	11	X		X		X	X			
Valins (1966)	11				X		X			
Schachter & Gross (1968)	9				X	X		X	X	
Overmier & Seligman (1967)	4		X			X				X
Miller & DiCara (1967)	4		X			X			X	

Note. One appropriate schedule for the use of these journal articles is designated by an X at the intersection of the reported experiment and core topic.
[a]A = experimentation versus description; B = theory and hypotheses; C = constructs and operational definitions; D = types of variables; E = rival explanations; F = confounding; G = designs; H = graphing and analysis; I = ethical issues.
[b]Published in APA journals and ranked in order of citation frequency.
[c]Based on a sampling of 26 introductory psychology texts copyrighted 1983–1985.

poses a challenge for the instructor. Although we offer specific suggestions for concept-experiment matches (ones that have the greatest illustrative power), we must also emphasize a major advantage of this approach for teaching experimental methods: flexibility. Articles tend to come and go over the semesters and be used for specific and changing purposes. We recognize that every instructor is likely to teach an experimental psychology course somewhat differently by emphasizing different components, yet it is reasonable to conclude that there are basic or core elements common to all such courses. We refer to these basic elements as *core* topics.

With this in mind, we present some recommended journal articles and core topics in Table 1. We also indicate the citation frequency of each article (ranked), based on the sampling of 26 contemporary and widely adopted introductory psychology texts. In Table 2, we present some engaging questions that have been used successfully in the past. Because of space limitations, only a sampling of possible homework questions are included to give the flavor of questions that have stimulated interesting discussions.

The citations presented in Table 1 are found in journals published by the American Psychological Association; hence, they are widely available in college and university libraries. These articles, of course, do not exhaust the pool of pedagogically useful articles. For example, the widely cited experiment by Loftus and Palmer (1974) is a gem: It is short highly readable, enjoyed by students, and well suited for illustrating independent and dependent variables (as well as showing how simple designs may be expanded to more complex and informative factorial designs). Although not frequently cited in introductory psychology texts, Tom and Rucker (1975) catches students' attention and illustrates the partitioning of factorial designs, the presentation of descriptive and inferential (ANOVA) statistics, and the graphing of interactive factors. Additional listings of

classic articles can be found in LeUnes (1978), McCollom (1973), and Shima (1977).

We know from formal course evaluations that many original research reports are interesting to students and promote their learning about experimental methodology. We believe that classic experiments in scholarly journals, used along with traditional instructional materials, can add an important dimension to students' experience. With the proper guidance from the instructor (i.e., what to focus on

Table 2. Sampling of Questions Based on Classic Journal Articles

Citation	Question
Bandura et al. (1963)	How would you describe the experimental design?
Darley & Latané (1968)	What were the independent and dependent variables?
Dion et al. (1972)	How was jealousy operationally defined?
Dutton & Aron (1974)	Why was a double-blind procedure used?
Festinger & Carlsmith (1959)	What evidence was found in support of the theory?
Milgram (1963)	How would you evaluate this study in light of the ethical principles in the conduct of research with human participants?
Miller & DiCara (1967)	What control techniques were used and why?
Overmier & Seligman (1967)	How did these researchers rule out rival explanations, and how would you evaluate these attempts in relation to the ethics of animal experimentation?
Peterson & Peterson (1959)	What does "significant at the .01 level" mean?
Schachter & Gross (1968)	How could demand characteristics have been an artifact?
Schachter & Singer (1962)	What was the purpose of a placebo group?
Valins (1966)	What was Valins' research hypothesis?

254

and what to avoid becoming bogged down with), students are often able to differentiate the content of an article from the methodology within the first few weeks of the course. Scholarly journals help motivate students to pursue the exciting field of experimental psychology by providing the background and confidence needed to explore and understand the ever-expanding stack of published research.

References

Atkinson, R. L., Atkinson, R. C., & Hilgard, E.R. (1983). *Introduction to psychology* (8th ed.). New York: Harcourt Brace Jovanovich .

Bandura, A., Ross, D., & Ross, S. A. (1963). Imitation of film mediated aggressive models. *Journal of Abnormal and Social Psychology, 66*, 3-11.

Darley, J. M, & Latane, B. (1968). Bystander intervention in emergencies: Diffusion of responsibility. *Journal of Personality and Social Psychology, 8*, 377-383.

Dion, K., Berscheid, E., & Walster, E. (1972). What is beautiful is good. *Journal of Personality and Social Psychology, 24*, 285-290.

Dutton, D. G., & Aron, A. P. (1974). Some evidence of heightened sexual attraction under conditions of high anxiety. *Journal of Personality and Social Psychology, 30*, 510-517.

Festinger, L., & Carlsmith, S. M. (1959). Cognitive consequences of forced compliance. *Journal of Abnormal and Social Psychology, 58*, 203-210.

Lefrançois, G. R. (1983). *Psychology* (2nd ed.). Belmont, CA: Wadsworth.

LeUnes, A. D. (1978). "Classics" in abnormal psychology: A student evaluation. *Teaching of Psychology, 5*, 99-100.

Loftus,E. F., & Palmer, J. C. (1974). Reconstruction of automobile destruction: An example of the interaction between language and memory. *Journal of Verbal Learning and Verbal Behavior, 13*, 585-589.

McCollom, I. N. (1973). Psychological classics: Older journal articles frequently cited today. *American Psychologist, 28*, 363-365.

Milgram, S. (1963). Behavioral study of obedience. *Journal of Abnormal and Social Psychology, 67*, 371-378.

Miller, N. E., & DiCara, L. (1967). Instrumental learning of heart rate changes in curarized rats: Shaping, and specificity to discriminative stimulus. *Journal of Comparative and Physiological Psychology, 63*, 12-19.

Overmier, J. B., & Seligman, M. E. P. (1967). Effects of inescapable shock upon subsequent escape and avoidance responding. *Journal of Comparative and Physiological Psychology, 63*, 28-33.

Peterson, L. R., & Peterson, M. J. (1959). Short-term retention of individual verbal items. *Journal of Experimental Psychology, 58*, 193-198.

Schachter, S., & Gross, L. P. (1968). Manipulated time and eating behavior. *Journal of Personality and Social psychology, 10*, 98-106.

Schachter, S., & Singer, J. E. (1962). Cognitive, social and physiological determinants of emotional state. *Psychological Review, 69*, 379-399.

Shima, F. (1977). New classics and new classicists in psychology. *Teaching of Psychology, 4*, 46-48.

Tom, G., & Rucker, M. (1975). Fat, full, and happy: Effects of food deprivation, external cues, and obesity on preference ratings, consumption, and buying intentions. *Journal of Personality and Social Psychology, 32*, 761-766.

Valins, S. (1966). Cognitive effects of false heart-rate feedback. *Journal of Personality and Social Psychology, 4*, 400-408.

Note

We gratefully acknowledge Charles L. Brewer for his valuable assistance in the preparation of this manuscript.

Motivating Students to Read Journal Articles

David M. Carkenord
Longwood College

Exposing students to the topics and content of current journal articles is a goal of many undergraduate psychology courses. As Suter and Frank (1986) noted, by reading journal articles, students can see the application of methodological concepts in actual research settings. In addition, reading published research can help develop critical reading and thinking skills (Anisfeld, 1987; Chamberlain & Burrough, 19855. Yet, motivating students to read the articles can be difficult. Chamberlain and Burrough (1985) speculated that students skim assigned articles rather than attend carefully. Thus, it is necessary to investigate strategies aimed at increasing the frequency with which students read journal articles.

Various authors attempted to increase the motivation of students to read published literature. Buche and Glover (1980) described an experimental study in which students who were given a minicourse (instructions and guidelines on reading journal articles) read articles at a significantly higher frequency than control subjects who received no instruction. Although these results are encouraging, the authors admitted that generalizations of their findings are limited. Chamberlain and Burroughs (1985) discussed a question-based technique in which students were instructed to answer specific questions pertaining to an assigned article. The authors did not, however, report any data concerning the frequency with which the articles were read. Suter and Frank (1986) described a similar question-based approach with classic journal articles but presented no data addressing the issue of frequency of reading.

It is important to ensure that students actually read assigned articles. This article describes a technique that motivates students to read and summarize articles.

The Present Technique

Selecting the Articles

The technique was used in an industrial psychology (I/O) course and a consumer psychology course (both 200-level courses). Article selection was based on four criteria suggested in part by Poe (1990), Price (1990), and Suter and Frank (1986): (a) high correspondence between the article topic, course content, and textbook material; (b) high correspondence between the technical level of the article and students' competence (e.g., lack of excessive or advanced statistical analyses); (c) high expected student interest; and (d) generally short length ($M = 5.4$ pages, $SD = 2.0$, range = 3 to 10 pages). A complete list of the readings for both classes is available from the author.

The Assignment

One article was assigned to be read each week, except for the weeks in which a test was scheduled. Students were informed that the class would discuss the article for 10 to 15 min on the due date and that material from the article would appear on the test. In general, students were given at least 1 week to locate and read the article. Students were requested to write a summary and critique of each article on an 8 × 5 in. index card, highlighting the major points and conclusions of the article and providing their critique and opinion of the reading. The front and back of one card was usually ample space for the summaries; only one student consistently used two note cards. At the conclusion of the class discussion of the article, students who submitted their card received 1 point extra credit (cumulatively worth approximately 4% of total course points). Although the extra credit was not contingent on the quality of the summary, most students wrote thorough and accurate summaries.

In addition to earning extra credit, students were allowed to use their note cards during the subsequent test. In general, two or three articles were covered per test. The note cards were returned just before test distribution to ensure that no lecture or textbook notes were written on the cards. Both multiple-choice and short-answer/essay test items were specifically taken from the articles and referred explicitly to them (e.g., "Based on the article by...."). Inclusion of these test items encouraged students to read the articles carefully and provide accurate summaries. Because the articles had been previously discussed in class, I tried to write test questions based on information that had not come up during the discussion. My usual strategy was to touch on the articles' major points during the discussion and to write test items on more specific details from the article. In the most recent courses, test items based on the readings comprised an average of 18.2% of the test material.

Those students who did not submit a note card on the due date were encouraged to read the articles before the test. However, these students were not allowed to complete a card for extra credit or to use the card during the test. No specific penalty was enacted if students chose not to do the readings (i.e., they would not directly lose course credit).

Assessment

Objective Assessment

To evaluate students' motivation to read the articles, the total percentage of note cards submitted (which estimates the readings completed) was calculated. On average, the 34 students in both classes ($n = 21$ in I/O and $n = 13$ in consumer) submitted a summary note card for 73.7% of the readings throughout the semester. Twelve of the 34 students (35%) submitted a note card for every reading; only 1 student submitted no note cards.

The extra credit improved final course grades for 11 of the 34 students (32.4%) by one letter grade. Three students (8.8%) could have improved their final grade if they had submitted cards on all the readings.

Table 1 displays the mean percentage of correct responses on the article-based test items for students who did and did not submit note cards. For 17 of the 22 articles assigned (across both classes), students using their note cards during the tests got a higher percentage of the test items correct than students without note cards.

Student Assessment

Student attitudes concerning the technique were surveyed anonymously at the end of the term. Four items

Table 1. Mean Percentage of Correct Responses on Article-Based Test Items as a Function of Card Submission

Article	Consumer		I/O	
	Card	No Card	Card	No Card
1	84	41	71	88
2	80	33	87	43
3	84	78	94	100
4	89	75	87	80
5	100	20	86	43
6	78	50	97	90
7	99	54	90	50
8	88	80	78	33
9	97	100	98	71
10	30	67	93	100
11	—	—	100	40
12	—	—	94	60
M	83	60	90	67

Note. An 11th article was assigned in the consumer course, but no test items were developed from it.

were each rated on a 5-point scale ranging from *strongly disagree* (1) to *strongly agree* (5). Responses on these items indicated very favorable attitudes: "Receiving extra credit motivated me to read the articles" ($M = 4.2$, $SD = 1.4$); "The fact that I could use the notecards during the tests motivated me to read the articles" ($M = 4.4$, $SD = 1.3$); "Doing the additional readings increased my knowledge of the subject matter" ($M = 4.0$, $SD = 1.0$); and "Overall, reading the articles provides a good learning experience" ($M = 4.2$, $SD = 0.9$). Clearly, students recognized and responded favorably to the connection between reading the articles and the positive implications for their course grade—both on tests and for extra credit. Students also believed that reading the articles enhanced their learning.

The survey also asked students to report the percentage of articles they had read during the term. Thirty-one of the 34 students in the classes reported reading 50% or more of the articles, although only 28 students submitted note cards on 50% or more of the articles. Eighteen of the 34 students reported reading 100% of the articles, whereas 12 students submitted note cards on all articles. These discrepancies are likely the result of students reading articles after the due date in preparation for the test. This would explain why the percentage of correct responses to article-based test items is relatively high even for some students who did not submit cards (see Table 1).

Finally, the survey contained an open-ended item soliciting additional opinions about the technique. Ten students wrote additional comments, which were generally positive, about the readings in general (e.g., "I think it does help me understand research" and "I've learned a lot from [the readings] and have actually enjoyed most of them!") and the extra credit opportunity in particular (e.g., "If any teacher gives me a chance for extra credit, I take it" and "Extra credit also gives a chance to reward people who go the extra mile").

Three students did, however, express concerns. One commuter student had difficulty scheduling adequate library time. Two students expressed the opinion that the articles should be mandatory because test items covered the readings. These two responses were intriguing, but I do not know what motivated them.

Discussion

The technique outlined herein was effective in motivating most students to read assigned journal articles, and students' attitudes toward the technique were very favorable. Beyond the primary benefit of getting students to read the articles, the technique has other benefits. First, with most students having read an article, class discussion of the material can be lively and productive. Students are willing to add to the discussion not only as a result of having read the article but also because they have a summary of the article (notecard) in their possession for easy reference in answering questions or adding comments. Furthermore, at the end of the course, students have a permanent file of information that may be of future use. I strongly encourage students to maintain their note cards for later reference, and many students tell me that they have made an effort to keep the cards.

Some instructors may take slight offense at the decidedly operant "carrot-and-stick" approach of the technique—motivating students to read articles with extra course credit rather than a primary emphasis on the importance of knowledge acquisition. Admittedly, research suggests that many instructors are uncomfortable with the entire concept of extra credit (Norcross, Horrocks, & Stevenson, 1989). Practical experience, however, indicates that most students do not read textbooks or journal articles as a result of their intrinsic interest and desire to learn. The present technique attempts to integrate the importance of learning with students' desires and expectations for tangible rewards. Awarding extra credit for reading a journal article may be more constructive than awarding extra credit for nonacademic factors (i.e., attendance), and it is a form of extra credit that is equally available to all students. If an instructor holds negative views of extra credit, the approach may be modified so that students receive no extra credit but are allowed to use their note cards on tests. Such a modification may also prompt students to read the assigned articles.

This approach to motivating students has applications in any course that incorporates the reading of journal articles. Instructors are encouraged to use the technique and report their impressions of its value.

References

Anisfeld, M. (1987). A course to develop competence in critical reading of empirical research in psychology. *Teaching of Psychology, 14*, 224-227.

Buche, D. D., & Glover, S. A. (1980). Teaching students to review research as an aid for problem solving. *Teaching of Psychology, 7*, 206-209.

Chamberlain, K., & Burrough, S. (1985). Techniques for teaching critical reading. *Teaching of Psychology, 12*, 213-215.

Norcross, J. C., Horrocks, L. S., & Stevenson, J. F. (1989). Of bar fights and gadflies: Attitudes and practices concerning extra credit in college courses. *Teaching of Psychology, 16*, 199-203.

Poe, R. E. (1990). A strategy for improving literature reviews in psychology courses. *Teaching of Psychology, 17*, 54-55.

Price, D. W. W. (1990). A model for reading and writing about primary sources: The case of introductory psychology. *Teaching of Psychology, 17*, 48-53.

Suter, W. N., & Frank, P. (1986). Using scholarly journals in undergraduate experimental methodology courses. *Teaching of Psychology, 13*, 219-221.

Note

I thank Ruth L. Ault and three anonymous reviewers for their helpful comments and suggestions on an earlier version of this article.

Devising Relevant and Topical Undergraduate Laboratory Projects: The Core Article Approach

Kerry Chamberlain
Massey University

The value of research experience in the undergraduate curriculum is widely recognized (Edwards, 1981; Palladino, Carsrud, Hulicka, & Benjamin, 1982; VandeCreek & Fleischer, 1984), and various approaches can be taken to provide this experience (e.g., Carroll, 1986; Chamberlain, 1986; Kerber, 1983; Palladino et al., 1982).

The most common approach is probably the class laboratory project, which achieves several purpose, ranging from giving students research experience to developing their abilities in statistical analyses.

Several innovative procedures for laboratory assignments have been proposed. Lutsky (1986) outlined a procedure based on the analysis of data sets. Carroll (1986) described a jigsaw approach; students work in small groups and each is responsible for one aspect of the project. Suter and Frank (1986) used classical experiments from the journals as the basis for projects.

This articles outlines an approach to devising laboratory projects that are topical and relevant to the course content and meet a variety of course objectives. The approach is based on choosing a core article that provides the framework for the research project in terms of scope, method, and reporting. It differs from Suter and Frank's procedure by using recent rather than classical research articles and by having students go beyond critical reading of the article to replication of the research. Because the core article defines the research systematically, projects can be readily generated by the instructor and more easily completed by individual students.

Aims

In my second-year undergraduate course on cognition, I had several aims for my laboratory projects. First, I wanted to have the projects well integrated with the course text. Second, I wanted students to read beyond the text and to use and reference original reports in journal article format. I wanted these articles to be manageable, appropriate for the undergraduate level, and current. Third, I wanted students to function as experimenters rather than as subjects and to collect their own data from "real" subjects rather than their classmates. This data collection needed to be held to manageable proportions to ensure that it was achievable and interesting rather than tedious and time consuming. Fourth, I wanted to provide opportunities for students to develop their skills at reporting research in APA format. I also wanted to restrict the literature review and data analysis in order to sustain the students' focus on accurate and concise communication. Finally, to avoid the problems of laboratory project reports being passed on from year to year, I wanted to have projects that were easy to generate so that they could be changed annually.

Procedures

Although these aims may appear to be difficult to achieve simultaneously, in practice they were not. The central requirement was to choose a core article as the basis for each project. The core article determined the dimensions of the research and defined the scope of the reports.

Core articles were identified by scanning the course text and recent journals for possibilities, with the constraint that each had to be relevant to a central theme taught in the course, up-to-date, and suitable in length and complexity of design and analysis. Ideal core articles were typically 5 to 7 pages, reported one or two experiments, and warranted at least a brief discussion in the text. Copies of each core article, provided in conformity with current copyright legislation, were issued to students along with the materials and specific requirements for each project.

Each project was organized as a full or partial replication of an experiment in the core article. Procedural details for the research, such as list lengths, number of trials, and stimulus presentation times, were kept as close to the original as possible. Stimulus materials were taken from the core article where possible or generated under the same constraints otherwise. All students in the course completed the same projects but collected data individually. Following data collection, class meetings were held to discuss the research issues arising from each project.

Each student was required to collect data from 4 to 10 subjects, depending on how extensive the procedure was and how many conditions the research design contained. To make the analysis more viable, additional data were provided. Students added their own data and analyzed the total data set. Statistical analyses were limited to techniques already in the students' repertoires, because the course did not include teaching statistical procedures. The provision of additional data also served to ensure that students usually obtained significant results in the direction of the original research and avoided the problem of ambiguous nonsignificant results, which frequently afflicts the group laboratory class. Further, providing data meant that the success of the project did not depend entirely on the students' skills as experimenters. On the other hand, poor data collection skills could usually be identified by comparing results obtained by other class members. Sources for the additional data were either a subset taken directly from data reported in the core article or hypothetical data generated from the summary statistics given in the core article.

A report of the research in standard APA format was required. Reference sources for the report were limited to the core article and the course text, ensuring that the reports were focused and relevant.

Outcomes

I have been using this approach for 4 years and find it to have several benefits. Although the approach has not been formally evaluated, informal student feedback is positive. The use of a core article produces assignments that are focused specifically. As a result, students report being very clear about the scope of the task and what is expected of them in conducting and reporting their research. Because students are required to collect their data individually, they must rely on their own resources. They comment favorably on the opportunity to conduct research with real subjects and the freedom to complete the laboratory work in their own time. The personal responsibility associated with this approach appears to be highly valued.

From the instructor's viewpoint, the approach produces projects that are relevant to the course content. Studies described briefly in the text can be brought to life when the original material is used as a core article and for a laboratory project. Use of research literature is enhanced, as students must read and understand core articles in detail in order to conduct their projects successfully. Making copies of core articles available ensures ready access to the required material and avoids competition for library resources. Because students find assignments to have a clear and manageable scope and high relevance, compliance with requirements is high. Class laboratory times, scheduled following data collection for each project, provide useful discussion sessions on research issues arising out of the projects. Because students have conducted the research at this point, the discussions are relevant to their experience and provide pertinent learning situations. Finally, the approach allows projects to be developed and changed readily to maintain a topical content and to accommodate course changes, such as the adoption of a new text.

Projects organized on this basis do have some limitations, however. Because the background reading is quite narrowly defined, students gain only limited skills in organizing a body of literature and reporting it in an introduction section. The limited reference set also makes it difficult to develop an in-depth discussion section. Because references are readily available, students need not engage in library search or journal browsing for relevant materials. Suitable core articles are difficult to locate in some areas. Problems also arise when sophisticated equipment is required (e.g., to measure precise reaction times or to control the brief presentation of stimuli).

As with any approach to laboratory project design, this one is a compromise between an ideal and what can be achieved realistically. Certain limitations can be overcome by using other types of assignments to supplement this approach. The advantages of the core article approach outweigh its limitations and help to achieve the course aims just outlined. The approach works well, is highly accepted by students, and should be valuable for other teachers who have similar goals for the laboratory project.

Although reported here as part of a cognitive psychology course, the approach should generalize readily to other courses in which laboratory projects are required.

References

Carroll, D. W. (1986). Use of the jigsaw technique in laboratory and discussion classes. *Teaching of Psychology, 13,* 208-210.

Chamberlain, K. (1986). Teaching the practical research course. *Teaching of Psychology, 13,* 204-208.

Edwards, J. D. (1981). A conceptual framework for a core program in psychology. *Teaching of Psychology, 8,* 3-7.

Kerber, K. W. (1983). Beyond experimentation: Research projects for a laboratory course in psychology. *Teaching of Psychology 10,* 236-239.

Lutsky, N. (1986). Undergraduate research experience through the analysis of data sets in psychology courses. *Teaching of Psychology, 13,* 119-122.

Palladino, J. J., Carsrud, A. L., Hulicka, I. M., & Benjamin, L. T., Jr. (1982). Undergraduate research in psychology: Assessment and directions. *Teaching of Psychology, 9,* 71-74.

Suter, W. N., & Frank, P. (1986). Using scholarly journals in undergraduate experimental methodology courses. *Teaching of Psychology, 13,* 219-221.

VandeCreek, L., & Fleischer, M. (1984). The role of practicum in the undergraduate psychology curriculum. *Teaching of Psychology, 11,* 9-14.

Note

Requests for a list of core articles used in the course should be sent to Kerry Chamberlain, Department of Psychology, Massey University, Palmerston North, New Zealand.

Excerpts From Journal Articles as Teaching Devices

Helen Pennington
Massey University

Several psychologists have reported their use of journal articles in teaching. Suter and Frank (1986) described how their undergraduate methodology students read original reports of classic experiments. They also described techniques for promoting critical reading of research articles, as did Chamberlain and Burrough (1985) and Anisfeld (1987). Klugh (1983) reported using journal articles to promote writing and speaking skills. Ault (1991) presented a technique for teaching students about the structure of a journal article. Chamberlain (1988) used core articles as the basis for undergraduate laboratory projects. All of these activities use entire, or almost entire, journal articles. Shorter activities involving extracts can also be helpful. This article describes my use of excerpts from journal articles in introductory and advanced courses.

A Multi-Purpose Activity for an Introductory Course

In our 1st-year laboratory-tutorial program (Pennington, 1990), students read several short excerpts from journal articles and answer questions on each one while working individually or in small groups. Discussion by the whole class usually follows. The excerpts, usually either abstracts or parts of Method sections, come from journal articles cited in the chapter of the course text under consideration.

The activity has three major purposes. First, it introduces students to the general nature and function of psychology journal articles. At the start of the activity, I tell students that: (a) The journal article is the primary way in which researchers communicate their findings, (b) textbook authors obtain most of their material directly or indirectly from journals, and (c) in advanced psychology courses they will read published research and write their own original research reports. I also describe the basic structure of journal articles, tell students where to find psychology journals in the university library, and circulate recent issues of an APA journal. For students taking further psychology courses, the activity gently introduces more demanding tasks, such as reading, evaluating, and writing entire research reports.

Second, the activity reminds students about important scientific terms and concepts that they learned at the beginning of the course. For example, the activity helps students review concepts, such as independent and dependent variables, population, sample, hypothesis, operational definition, random assignment, control group, experiment versus correlational study, demand characteristics, informed consent, and significance level. Typical questions include: Was this study an experiment or a correlational study? How do you know? What were the researcher's hypotheses? How were subjects assigned to groups? What were the operational definitions of the independent and dependent variables? How do you know that inferential statistics were used? When reading an abstract, students may answer questions about the aim of the study and how to distinguish results from conclusions.

Third, the activity exposes students to details about studies cited in their text, brings the studies to life, and shows the limitations of secondary sources. Oversimplification is more common than error in some textbooks, but errors do occur (see Herzog, 1986; LeUnes, 1983; Suter & Frank, 1986). For instance, our introductory text (Kalat, 1990) says that Farmer (1983) found "the goals that high school girls set for themselves are about as high as those of high school boys" (p. 416). Farmer's abstract actually states that "A highlight among findings is that girls in high school are aspiring to higher career levels compared to boys" (p. 40). Exposing students to limitations of secondary sources helps to accomplish our department's goal of fostering critical thinking. I tell students that introductory texts often oversimplify issues, and that one must consult primary sources to obtain a true picture of the state of knowledge.

Activities for Advanced Courses

Journal article excerpts can also be used in advanced courses. For example, excerpts and activities can be tailored to help students read research reports critically and consider specific points of methodology.

Lectures and readings in our 3rd-year Developmental Psychology course teach students about methodological issues such as those concerning: cross-sectional, longitudinal, and sequential research designs; sampling; and choice of measuring instruments. Students later perform short individual or small-group activities based on journal article extracts to help consolidate their learning. These activities break up lectures and provide feedback to me and students about how much has been learned.

One activity involves questions about extracts from various sections of recent articles on aging. Students identify research designs; note any limitations in research design, sampling, or measuring instruments; and look for authors' acknowledgments of such limitations. A fringe benefit is that carefully chosen extracts expose students to topical areas of research on aging and to important journals in the field.

Another activity concerns issues of sampling. Many studies in the field of aging lack careful sampling and an adequate description of sample characteristics (Crandall, 1982). I illustrate this point by having students read a Method section extract in which the sampling procedure is inadequately described and revealed as dubious. I tell students that the sampling is fairly typical of earlier studies, and I ask them to comment on how the sample was chosen and reported.

Concluding Comments

Journal article extracts are versatile teaching tools in my classes. Activities based on journal article extracts may require only a few minutes; fit easily into lectures, tutorials, or laboratories; and serve various functions. Students seem to find the activities absorbing. I encourage instructors to devise and use similar activities for their courses.

References

Anisfeld, M. (1987). A course to develop competence in critical reading of empirical research in psychology. *Teaching of Psychology, 14*, 224-221.

Ault, R. L. (1991). What goes where? An activity to teach the organization of journal articles. *Teaching of Psychology, 18*, 45-46.

Chamberlain, K. (1988). Devising relevant and topical undergraduate laboratory projects: The core article approach. *Teaching of Psychology, 15*, 207-208.

Chamberlain, K., & Burrough, S. (1985). Techniques for teaching critical reading. *Teaching of Psychology, 12*, 213-215.

Crandall, R. C. (1982, November). *Characteristics of research appearing in gerontology journals between 1975-1980.* Paper presented at the 35th Annual Scientific Meeting of the Gerontological Society of America, Boston.

Farmer, H. (1983). Career and homemaking plans for high school youth. *Journal of Counseling Psychology, 30*, 40-45.

Herzog, H. A., Jr. (1986). The treatment of sociobiology in introductory psychology textbooks. *Teaching of Psychology, 13*, 12-15.

Kalat, J. W. (1990*). Introduction to psychology* (2nd ed.). Belmont, CA: Wadsworth.

Klugh, H. E. (1983). Writing and speaking skills can be taught in psychology classes. *Teaching of Psychology, 10*, 170-171.

LeUnes, A. (1983). Little Albert from the viewpoint of abnormal psychology textbook authors. *Teaching of Psychology, 10*, 230-231.

Pennington, H. (1990). A brief training program for graduate student teachers of laboratory-tutorial classes. *Teaching of Psychology, 17*, 120-121.

Suter, W. N., & Frank, P. (1986). Using scholarly journals in undergraduate experimental methodology courses. *Teaching of Psychology, 13*, 219-221.

Note

Requests for information about sources of useful extracts should be sent to Helen Pennington, Department of Psychology, Massey University, Palmerston North, New Zealand.

From the Laboratory to the Headlines: Teaching Critical Evaluation of Press Reports of Research

Patricia A. Connor-Greene
Clemson University

Undergraduate education in psychology should help students understand scientific methodology and improve their critical thinking. These are important skills, given the frequency with which research findings are reported in the mass media. People tend to perceive the press as an objective source of information, despite the fact that subjective decisions determine what is reported (Howitt, 1982). Constrained by space limitations, newspaper and magazine depictions of research findings often omit essential information that would permit the reader to evaluate adequately the strength of the research conclusions. News summaries often distort research findings by sensationalizing the results, minimizing discussion of the research limitations, and confusing correlation with causation (Jacobs & Eccles, 1985).

The distinction between correlation and causation is essential to understanding research methods and statistics (Boneau, 1990). Although a recent analysis indicated that correlational designs are discussed in 87% of introductory psychology textbooks (Hendricks, Marvel, & Barrington, 1990), I often hear upper level students make causal statements when describing. correlational studies. The frequency of this error highlights the need to develop teaching strategies that emphasize this important distinction.

The exercise described in this article involves a collaborative, active-learning task in which students use information about the scientific method to analyze a newspaper account of a research study. The technique is designed to increase students' awareness of the distinction between correlation and causation and to encourage them to become critical consumers of research reported in the popular press. I use this exercise in abnormal psychology classes, but it is also appropriate for introductory psychology and other courses that address research methods.

The Class Exercise

Students are given a homework assignment to study the research methods chapter in their textbook and be prepared to discuss these concepts in class. During the next class period, each student is assigned to a small group of 4 or 5 people. One member of each group serves as recorder, and each group member is expected to participate in the small group discussion. Every student is given a copy of an article from *USA TODAY* titled, "Gay Men Show Cell Distinction" (Snider, 1991; see Appendix) and the following list of questions to be addressed by the group.

1. What conclusion does this article imply? What statements in the article suggest this conclusion?
2. Is this conclusion warranted by the study described? Why or why not?
3. Is the title an accurate summary of the study described? Why or why not?
4. Can this study "prove . . . being gay or lesbian is not a matter of choice," as the task force spokesman suggests? Why or why not?
5. What questions do you have after reading this article?
6. If you had the power to create guidelines for the press's reporting of a research study, what would you recommend ?

Class Discussion

After each group addresses these questions (which takes approximately 40 min), the entire class reconvenes to discuss the group responses. At this point, I provide excerpts, via overhead projector, from the original research article published in *Science* (LeVay, 1991) that is the subject of the *USA TODAY* article. Students identify omissions and distortions in the newspaper's account of the original research study. By examining both the newspaper article and the original research report, they can now identify flaws or unanswered questions in the original study and recognize any misrepresentation of the research in the newspaper article.

Usually the small-group responses to the questions are very similar. All groups interpret the newspaper article (Snider, 1991) as implying that male homosexuality is caused by smaller brain cell nuclei. They cite the statements "The debate over the *roots* of homosexuality has been going on a long time, but this finding 'suggests a *biological phenomenon*' " (p. 1D) and "It might explain '*why* male homosexuality is present in most human populations' " (p. 1D) [all italics added] as suggesting causality.

In deciding whether this implication of causality is warranted by the research study as described, students discuss the requirements for a true experimental design. They recognize LeVay's (1991) study as a correlational design because it simply identifies a relation between size of brain cell nuclei and sexual orientation. Discussing alternative interpretations of this association (e. g., sexual orientation could affect size of brain cell nuclei, rather than the reverse; the differences may be caused by a third variable) helps to clarify the seriousness of the error of confusing correlation and causation.

Students note two problems with the title of the newspaper article. First, they think the title suggests that all cells are different in gay men, but the news article refers only to brain cell nuclei. (The difference is actually much more specific than implied in the news article; it is only one area of the anterior hypothalamus.) Second, the title suggests that gay men are the "different" ones, but the article reports gay men's brain cell nuclei to be similar in size to those of women. Consequently, the "different" ones are actually the heterosexual men. Then we discuss the political and social context in which *normal* and *deviant* are defined and how subjectivity and bias can occur in the formulation of research questions and in the interpretation and reporting of findings.

 The quote from the news article (Snider, 1991) that the study can "prove . . . being a gay or lesbian is not a matter of choice" (p. 1D) provides an excellent opportunity to discuss the nature of scientific experimentation and the inappropriateness of the term *prove* in science.

Students generate questions after reading the news article (Snider, 1991), setting the stage for discussion of the specifics of LeVay's (1991) study. After obtaining information from LeVay's article, students are able to identify limitations in the study itself. (For example, the heterosexual men were "presumed" to be heterosexual; for all but two of them, there was no available information on sexual orientation; there was no comparison of heterosexual and homosexual women; the actual cause of death can vary greatly among AIDS patients; and the brain cell nuclei differences could be a result of the disease process itself.

Students always ask "How did this study get published? How could a respectable scientist confuse correlation and causation?" At this point, I show them several quotes from LeVay's (1991) article in which he pointed out the speculative and preliminary nature of his research, identified limitations of his study, and emphasized that it is correlational and does not permit causal inferences. Then students see that the *USA TODAY* article (Snider, 1991) sensationalizes LeVay's results and

that Snider, not LeVay, confused correlation with causation.

In addition, I show the students the following excerpt from "Is Homosexuality Biological?" (1991), which appeared in the same issue of Science as LeVay's (1991) article.

> Lest eager believers jump to too many conclusions, LeVay points our that his finding *contains no direct evidence that the difference he has observed actually causes homosexuality.* He and others in the field acknowledge that the paper *needs replication*, since such studies are difficult and somewhat subjective. "Simon is very good; he's extremely well-equipped to make those observations," said one neuroscientist who is familiar with LeVay's work. *But we ought to put off big speculation until it is confirmed.* (p. 956) [all italics added]

Clearly, speculation was not put off until LeVay's (1991) findings were replicated; the study was widely reported in the print media and on the network news. Nearly all the students in my class had heard or read about this study and were surprised to learn that the research did not address causality. The extensive media coverage, contrasted with the preliminary nature of the research itself, helps students recognize that factors other than scientific merit may determine degree of media attention and that science and the reporting of science are not value-free.

Students generated recommendations for changing the press's approach to reporting scientific research. These recommendations included discussing limitations of studies, improving accuracy of headlines, distinguishing between correlational and experimental studies, providing a full reference citation to enable the reader to locate the original research article, and making the degree of media attention proportional to the scientific strength of the study.

Individual Assignment

After completing the class exercise, students were individually assigned to find a newspaper or magazine summary of research and compare it to the original journal article. Their written critiques assessed the accuracy of the popular press article and discussed important omissions or distortions in the popular press article (e. g., limitations of the study and accuracy of the title).

Because some popular press articles contain serious distortions and others are accurate summaries, this assignment helps students become critical evaluators rather than simply dismissing all popular press articles as flawed. Several weeks are needed for this assignment. Most students reported that although press summaries of research were easy to find, many of these articles failed to include a citation sufficient to locate the original article.

Evaluation and Conclusions

The day after participating in the class exercise, students ($N = 33$) anonymously completed a four-item questionnaire using a scale ranging from *very much so* (1) to *not at all* (5). The items and mean ratings are as follows: (a) This exercise gave me a clearer understanding of correlational research ($M = 1.70$), (b) this exercise will help me evaluate media reports of research more critically in the future ($M = 1.55$), (c) this exercise was interesting ($M = 1.61$), and (d) it was helpful to work in groups for the class exercise ($M = 1.61$). Students' written comments, such as "It gives me a good idea of how to look at articles critically," "newspaper articles need to be examined much more closely than I've done previously," and "this will help me remember the difference between correlational and experimental studies," suggested positive aspects of the exercise. Students were also asked for written comments after completing their individual assignment. Overall, students perceived the assignment as valuable.

The class exercise and individual assignment encourage students to apply information learned in class to their outside experiences (i.e., reading the newspaper), which makes their learning more personally relevant. The exercises help students understand why the popular press is not an appropriate source of information to be used in writing term papers. The fact that the press typically emphasizes results and not methods convinces students that they can properly evaluate the strengths and weaknesses of a study only after examining the original source. Greater awareness of the importance of precision in reporting research methods and findings should encourage students to be more critical of information they read in newspapers, journal articles, and textbooks.

References

Boneau, C. A. (1990). Psychological literacy A first approximation. *American Psychologist, 45,* 891-900.

Hendricks, B., Marvel, M. K., & Barrington, B. L. (1990). The dimensions of psychological research. *Teaching of Psychology, 17,* 76-82.

Howitt, D. (1982). *Mass media and social problems.* New York: Pergamon.

Is homosexuality biological? (1991). *Science, 253,* 956-957.

Jacobs, J., & Eccles, J. (1985). Gender differences in math ability The impact of media reports on parents. *Educational Researcher, 14*(3), 20-25.

LeVay, S. (1991). A difference in hypothalamic structure between heterosexual and homosexual men. *Science, 253,* 1034-1037.

Snider, M. (1991, August 30). Gay men show cell distinction. *USA TODAY*, p. 1D.

Note

I thank Charles L. Brewer, Ruth L. Ault, and the anonymous reviewers for their helpful comments.

Appendix

Gay Men Show Cell Distinction
By Mike Snider
USA TODAY

A new study of the brain suggests a biological difference between homosexual and heterosexual men.

The debate over the roots of homosexuality has been going on a long time, but this finding "suggests a biological phenomenon," says neurologist Dennis Landis, Case Western Reserve University, Cleveland, in comments accompanying the study in today's *Science*.

It might explain "why male homosexuality is present in most human populations, despite cultural constraints."

In a study of the brain cells from 41 people, 25 of whom had died from AIDS, certain brain cells of heterosexual men had nuclei that were more than twice as large as those in homosexual men, says researcher Simon LeVay, Salk Institute for Biological Studies.

The difference was apparently not caused by AIDS, because it was constant in a comparison of cells from heterosexual and homosexual male AIDS victims. LeVay also found homosexual men's cells similar in size to women's.

Robert Bray, spokesman for National Gay and Lesbian Task Force, called the study "fascinating."

"If used ethically, (it) can shed light on human sexuality and prove what we've always believed—being a gay or lesbian is not a matter of choice.

"Used unethically, the data could reinforce the political agenda of anti—gay groups that advocate 'curing' or 'repairing' homosexuals—the notion that gay people could be made straight be tweaking a chromosome here or readjusting a cell there."

Note

9. EXAMINING MISCELLANEOUS ISSUES

Collaborative Writing in a Statistics and Research Methods Course

Dana S. Dunn
Moravian College

Treating writing as a process skill that can be developed—not simply as an outcome-related task—is a dominant theme in contemporary pedagogy on college-level writing (e.g., Elbow & Belanoff, 1989a, 1989b; Nodine, 1990). 1 (Dunn, 1994) suggested a variety of ways that writing techniques can be incorporated into psychology classes. In this article, I apply collaborative writing and peer review in Statistics and Research Methods of Psychological Inquiry (PS 210). I also discuss student reactions to these techniques and recommend ways to refine their use in the future.

Our PS 210 is an intermediate-level, one-semester course required of all psychology majors. Two sections of the course are taught each semester, and enrollment is limited to 20 students each. The course is divided into two sections—basic descriptive and inferential statistics and elementary research methodology. The material is taught in tandem (i.e., one class is devoted to data analysis, and a subsequent class deals with methods). Students usually complete four examinations and conduct two research projects. The first project is a simple in-class exercise (e.g., survey) . The second project, the focus of this article, involves a collaborative experiment.

So that they may teach and learn from one another, pairs of students collaborate on the creation, design, data collection, analysis, and write-up of an experiment. The key to this experience is writing.

The Writing Process

Step 1: Writing a Prospectus

Students select partners and are told that they have a contractual obligation to them. All work is shared equally, and, in successful collaborations, both partners receive the same grade. Unsuccessful collaborations (i.e., one-sided pairings when one partner does most of the work) result in differential grading.

Although a polished laboratory report written in APA style is the desired product of most research methods courses, the collaborative process of creating this outcome may be more important. That is, students identify key variables, search and read relevant literature, and reason through a research idea by working closely with a partner; the process of shared writing pulls these activities together. After student pairs select a research topic and design, the process I use involves shared prewriting and freewriting (Belanoff, Elbow, & Fontaine, 1991; Wingard, Dunn, & Brown, 1993), outlining, drafting, and revising of a prospectus (essentially the Introduction, Method, and References sections of an APA manuscript). To ensure that students understand the articles they have found for the literature review in the Introduction, I provide them with a worksheet that leads them through empirical journal articles, highlighting key information that should be gleaned from them (Anselmi, Wall, & Zannoni, 1993; see also, Poe, 1990).

Step 2: Drafting the Final Project Paper

After I provide detailed comments on the prospectus (see Dunn, 1994; Elbow, 1993) and a grade, the students collect their data, conduct the appropriate statistical analyses, and begin writing the final project paper. The final paper is based on the collaborative editing and revising of the prospectus, as well as the initial writing of the Results and Discussion sections.

Peer Review

Step 3: Revising and Editing the Final Project Paper

After a draft of the final paper is completed, one entire class session is devoted to a peer review workshop. During this workshop, each pair of students shares copies of the final project draft with at least one other pair of students; thus, all student pairs act as peer reviewers. Students are instructed to make substantive evaluations of the papers they read (i.e., Why is the research interesting? What does it reveal about human behavior?) and to note grammatical errors and deviations from APA style. I coach the students on how to offer specific and constructive feedback on the papers, emphasizing that detailed comments written in the margins in addition to precise verbal comments to authors are the goals of the workshop (see Dunn, 1994; Elbow & Belanoff, 1989a, 1989b; Haaga, 1993; Wingard et al., 1993, for more specific suggestions). These reactions to the penultimate draft of the project paper aid students in making final revisions and editorial changes.

I offer to read the project papers at any stage of the writing process as long as two conditions are met: The draft (or even outline) is relatively complete, and both members of the pair are present to hear my comments. I write comments on the papers as well; experience suggests that, when students hear and later read my comments, an improved paper is likely to result.

Student Reactions to Collaboration

Process journal

Throughout their collaboration, student writers keep a process journal in which they can reflect on the quality of the effort. Is responsibility for the project being shared? Was more accomplished by two writers than one? After the project paper is complete, each student submits a separate process journal to me, thereby gaining privacy and assurance that any collaborative problems will be noted.

Survey Results

Because a collaborative project in psychology that emphasizes process writing is somewhat unusual—and in the context of an already demanding course, perhaps even stressful—I surveyed student reactions to the exercises. In spring 1994, 25 of the 43 students who comprised the two sections (22 women and 3 men) returned the survey (for a 58% response rate). Generally, their responses were highly favorable. Eighty-eight percent of the respondents indicated that the division of labor in their pair was equal. Fifty-six percent said they liked collaboration, 40% said they preferred to work alone, and 4% were neutral. These survey responses were consistent with what students wrote in their journals. However, when asked if they learned more or less about psychological research by working with another student, 96% indicated that they learned more as a result of collaboration.

Seventy-two percent of the students found the peer review exercise to be helpful. Closer examination of the responses, however, indicated a between-groups difference: On a 5-point scale ranging from *not at all helpful* (1) to *very helpful* (5), traditional-age undergraduates (those 18 to 22 years old) rated peer review as much more helpful ($M = 4.59$) than did older students from our evening program ($M = 3.25$), $t(23) = 3.22$, $p < .002$. Experience with both groups suggests that the

evening students tend to have a more mature work ethic; hence, their project papers may have been more polished at the time of the review than were those by students in the day program. Also, the concept of collaboration may be less compatible with the beliefs of older students, who were taught to rely on their own efforts. Indeed, evening students tend to be more competitive than traditional-age students, who may be more accustomed to collaborative exercises due to more recent (i.e., precollegiate) experiences with them.

In open-ended responses, several students remarked that they wished that the peer review had been done before the final draft of the prospectus was due and then again before completion of the final project paper. I will follow this suggestion next time because I believe that it will improve students' writing and make peer review more helpful.

Conclusions

Collaborative writing that focuses on process and peer review is helpful. Collaboration promotes student appreciation of the creation, presentation, and reception of ideas (see also, Dunn & Toedter, 1991). Sharing the work associated with a statistics and methods project also ensures that many details are addressed, potential errors are caught, and careful proofreading—a perennial faculty lament—actually happens. Also, material pertaining to the psychological import of the work is discussed more thoroughly than is the case for single-author papers.

References

Anselmi, D., Wall, B., & Zannoni, D. (1993, November). *Assignments that encourage critical thinking and active learning across the disciplines.* Workshop presented at the third annual conference of the Institute for the Study of Postsecondary Pedagogy: Interdisciplinary Curricula, General Education, and Liberal Learning, New Paltz, NY.

Belanoff, P., Elbow, P., & Fontaine, S. I. (Eds.). (1991). *Nothing begins with n: New investigation of freewriting.* Carbondale and Edwardsville: Southern Illinois University Press.

Dunn, D. S. (1994). Lessons learned from an interdisciplinary writing course: Implications for student writing in psychology. *Teaching of Psychology, 21,* 223-227.

Dunn, D. S., & Toedter, L. J. (1991). The collaborative honors project in psychology: Enhancing student and faculty development. *Teaching of Psychology, 18,* 178-180.

Elbow, P. (1993). Ranking, evaluating, and liking: Sorting out three forms of judgment. *College English, 55,* 187-206.

Elbow, P., & Belanoff, P. (1989a). *A community of writers: A workshop course in writing.* New York: McGraw-Hill.

Elbow, P., & Belanoff, P. (1989b). *Sharing and responding.* New York: Random House.

Haaga, D. A. F. (1993). Peer review of term papers in graduate psychology courses. *Teaching of Psychology, 20,* 28-32.

Nodine, B. F. (Ed.). (1990). Psychologists teach writing [Special issue]. *Teaching of Psychology, 17*(1).

Poe, R. E. (1990). A strategy for improving literature reviews in psychology courses. *Teaching of Psychology, 17,* 54-55.

Wingard, J., Dunn, D. S., & Brown, C. K. (1993, November). *Writing to learn: Learning to write.* Paper presented at the third annual conference of the Institute for the Study of Postsecondary Pedagogy: Interdisciplinary Curricula, General Education, and Liberal Learning, New Paltz, NY.

Notes

1. Portions of this article were presented at the First Annual American Psychological Society Teaching Institute, Washington, DC, June 1994. Preparation of this article was partially funded by the Moravian College Faculty Development and Research Committee.

2. I thank Sarah Dunn, Stacey Zaremba, the reviewers, and Charles L. Brewer for their helpful comments on a draft of this article.

3. Requests for copies of the course syllabus and hand-outs should be sent to Dana S. Dunn, Department of Psychology, Moravian College, 1200 Main Street, Bethlehem, PA 18018-6650; e-mail: dunn@ moravian.edu.

You Can't Judge a Measure by its Label: Teaching the Process of Instrumentation

Jennifer Howard Brockway
United States Air Force Academy

Fred B. Bryant
Loyola University Chicago

A difficult concept for many students to grasp is the notion that there is no one universally appropriate measure for any given psychological construct. Typically, several good (reliable and valid) instruments already exist for most constructs with which psychology students are familiar. Thus, an important skill to teach students is the ability to locate these measures and to choose the most appropriate one (Brockway &Bryant, 1997). According to Brewer et al. (1993), it is better to teach such abstract methodological issues through hands on exercises as opposed to traditional lecture format. Although instructors have suggested several excellent classroom exercises with respect to creating new psychological measures (e.g., Benjamin, 1983; Davidson, 1987), instructors have not offered exercises to teach students how to locate, evaluate, compare, and select the most appropriate measure from a database of existing measures.

The following exercise helps to familiarize students with the variety of measures that exist for any one construct and enables students to compare these different instruments to make better informed choices. The exercise includes five progressive steps: Steps 1 and 2 are part of a single assignment outside class, Steps 3 and 4 take place together during an out-of-class library session, and Step 5 takes the form of an in-class discussion or presentation.

This exercise is appropriate for use in a variety of undergraduate psychology classes, including research methods, tests and measurements, and various psychology laboratories in which students collect and analyze data. Graduate students may also benefit from this exercise by including a more rigorous analysis, critique, and comparison of existing measures. At Loyola University Chicago we have incorporated this activity into an undergraduate social psychology laboratory course and a graduate research methods course. The following example comes from the undergraduate course.

Procedure

This activity is best preceded by a review of psychological constructs and the inherent difficulty of measuring phenomena that are intangible, dynamic, and subject to multiple definitions. For this exercise to be effective, students must understand the difference between conceptual and operational definitions.

Step 1: Choose a Psychological Construct

After discussing the difficulties surrounding psychological measurement, students choose a psychological construct of interest. (Multiple students can select the same construct.) A list of constructs previously covered in the class may help to get students thinking along the right lines. Ideally, students should select a construct for which a number of available measures exist. Possibilities include altruism, aggression, perceived control, anxiety, and compliance. We use the construct guilt as an example for purposes of presentation.

Step 2: Create a Working Definition of the Construct

Next, the instructor asks students to conceptually define their construct thoroughly and carefully. Students generate their own conceptual definition of the construct, based on personal experience and intuition. Thus, one may define guilt as, "The negative emotion experienced after knowingly misbehaving" or "Feelings of distress when one's social position is better than others." The purpose of this step is to emphasize the development of a clear, precise conceptual definition before selecting an operational definition (i.e., instrument). Thus, if guilt is one's construct, it is important to distinguish it from shame, embarrassment, and regret, for example.

Step 3: Use an Instrument File to Generate List of Existing Measures

After ensuring that students have precisely defined their construct, instructors ask students to utilize their library's measurement database to generate a list of existing measures of their construct. A powerful new measurement database called the Health and Psychosocial Instrument (HaPI) File (1995) is particularly useful in this regard. HaPI provides information about thousands of behavioral and social measures through abstracted descriptions summarizing instrument characteristics (e.g., intended audience, validity and reliability information, means of obtaining copies). HaPI is available in hundreds of college libraries both in the United States and internationally.

The HaPI File has distinct advantages over traditional catalogs of instruments. First, HaPI provides a larger number of measures (more than 40,000) than other sources. HaPI also provides a more efficient means of managing the volume of measurement information that exists. We believe the HaPI File provides a more thorough and cost-effective measurement tool than other measurement volumes.

To use HaPI, students simply type in the name of their construct and generate a list of corresponding references. For instance, for the guilt construct, HaPI generated a list of 73 instruments that the originators of these measures described as assessing some form of guilt.

Step 4: Choose Two Measures With Distinct Conceptual Definitions

From the list of measures, students choose two references for distinct instruments and obtain these articles from their library. One article should define the construct in a way that resembles the students' conceptual definition. The other article should define the construct in a way that is different from the students' definition.

From the list of guilt measures, for example, we chose two articles with different theoretical orientations (Kugler & Jones, 1992; Montada & Schneider, 1989). Whereas the first article approached guilt from a macrolevel (sociological, cultural) perspective, the second article assessed guilt from a more microlevel (psychological) perspective. We chose these measures not because they are the best instruments, but because of the contrast between their conceptual and operational definitions. The greater the distinction between the two chosen measures, the easier it will be to complete the final step of the exercise. Although our students have experienced little difficulty in selecting two different instruments to compare and contrast, instructors may want to be available if students need assistance with this critical step of the exercise.

Step 5: Compare and Contrast Alternative Instruments

After ensuring that students have found distinct measures, ask students to make an in-class presentation comparing and contrasting the measures on various dimensions generated either by the instructor or by the students and the instructor. Besides each measure's overall strengths and weaknesses other dimensions could include:

1. Theoretical orientation (e.g., social justice vs. psychological conceptualizations of guilt);
2. Duration and frequency of construct manifestation (e.g., state vs. trait guilt);
3. General format of the instrument (e.g., reactive vs. unobtrusive measures of guilt, vignettes vs. self-report questions, closed- vs. open-ended items);
4. Intended audience (e.g., children, English speaking adults, etc.);
5. Number of items and scaling issues (e.g., single item vs. composite index, Likert vs. semantic differential response format).

For example, Montada and Schneider (1989) defined existential *guilt* as a prosocial emotion felt when one perceives oneself as better off than others suffering hardships. To measure guilt, Montada and Schneider embedded three guilt items within a larger questionnaire designed to tap other "prosocial emotions" such as sympathy and moral outrage. The general form of the measure is a written scenario describing the misery of a group of disadvantaged people (e.g., the unemployed). Respondents use a 6-point scale to rate the degree to which three statements reflecting guilt express their thoughts and feelings. The instrument's intended audience seems to be at least the age of young adults because it assumes respondents possess some moral awareness concerning the status of disadvantaged populations. Although the instrument appears in English, Montada and Schneider developed it using a German sample, so it is unclear whether it is applicable to other populations.

Taking a very different approach, Kugler and Jones's (1992) measure is a guilt inventory. Ninety-eight items, presented on 5-point scales, tap three specific content domains (trait guilt, state guilt, and moral standards). Both college students and adult non-students have completed this inventory.

Evidence of Pedagogical Effectiveness

To assess the effectiveness of this exercise, 10 undergraduates enrolled in a social psychology laboratory course answered open-ended questions addressing several goals of the exercise both before and after completing the exercise. Results revealed that before the exercise, only 1 student (10%) knew that the first step in measuring a construct is to carefully create a conceptual definition, whereas all 10 students (100%) gave this correct answer after the exercise (Fisher's exact $p = .00006$). Also, before the exercise, only 1 student (10%) stated that when confronted with three equally valid and reliable measures, one should choose the measure that most closely matches the conceptual definition, unlike 7 of 10 students (70%) at the posttest (Fisher's exact $p = .0099$).

As a control condition, a comparable group of 6 laboratory students completed pretest and posttest measures, but did not participate in the measurement exercise. Results revealed no significant changes in knowledge from pretest to posttest regarding the crucial first step in selecting measures (Fisher's exact $p = .50$) and how to choose from among three psychometrically equivalent measures (Fisher's exact $p = .23$). Although the size and representativeness of these samples are far from ideal, these data nevertheless support the effectiveness of the exercise.

Additional Suggestions

Instructors can simplify or expand this exercise to fit a particular time slot, lesson plan, or student population. For example, instructors can eliminate the library portion of the exercise and simply supply students with the results of the HaPI search for existing measures for a particular construct and with a copy of two preselected articles and instruments. Instructors may then ask students to compare and contrast the two measures with respect to the dimensions (or a subset of those dimensions) discussed previously.

Conversely, instructors can expand this activity to include issues more appropriate for advanced psychology students. For example, students can compare and contrast instruments with respect to the various validities (i.e., face, construct, criterion, content) and reliabilities (i.e., test-retest, parallel forms, interrater, internal consistency). Also, advanced students can locate instruments tapping similar (yet conceptually separate) constructs and highlight the subtle distinctions between the constructs (e.g., guilt vs. shame vs. embarrassment). This approach offers instructors a concrete means of teaching students about the multitrait-multimethod matrix (Campbell & Fiske, 1959) and how to implement it. Finally, and perhaps the most challenging task of all, instructors can ask students to uncover the "missing measure" after reviewing all existing instruments. By highlighting both the gaps and overlaps in current measurement options, future researchers can begin to distinguish between areas that need new instruments and areas in which new measures are unnecessary.

Conclusions

This measurement exercise teaches students several important lessons. First, it stresses the importance of having a clear conceptual definition before choosing an instrument to measure a psychological construct. Second, it teaches students that there almost always is more than one way to measure a construct and that they should compare these multiple approaches. Third, it teaches students the importance of measuring a construct in a way that best matches one's underlying definition. Finally, it introduces students to new information technologies that they can use to locate, evaluate, compare, and select the best measures. Indeed, maximizing the match between conceptual and operational definitions is the essence of construct validity (Cook & Campbell, 1979). Thus, it is important to teach students that you can't judge a book (i.e., a measure) by its cover (i.e., its label).

References

Benjamin, L. T., Jr. (1983). A class exercise in personality and psychological assessment. *Teaching of Psychology, 10,* 94-95.

Brewer, C. L., Hopkins, J. R., Kimble, G. A., Matlin, M. W., McCann, L. I., McNeil, O. V., Nodine, B. F., Quinn, V. N., & Saundra. (1993). Curriculum. In T.V. McGovern (Ed.), *Handbook for enhancing undergraduate education in psychology* (pp. 161-182). Washington, DC: American Psychological Association.

Brockway, J. H., & Bryant, F. B. (1997). *Spotlighting the second fiddle: The importance of teaching measurement.* Manuscript submitted for publication.

Campbell, D. T., & Fiske, D. W. (1959). Convergent and discriminant validation by the multitrait-multimethod matrix. *Psychological Bulletin, 56,* 81-105.

Cook, T. D., & Campbell, D. T. (1979). *Quasi-experimentation: Design & analysis issues for field settings.* Chicago: Rand McNally.

Davidson, W. B. (1987). Undergraduate lab project in personality assessment: Measurement of anal character. *Teaching of Psychology, 14,* 101-103.

Health and Psychosocial Instrument (HaPI) File (Version 4.1) [CD-ROM]. (1995). Pittsburgh, PA: Behavioral Measurement Database Services [Producer and Distributor].

Kugler, K., & Jones, W. H. (1992). On conceptualizing and assessing guilt. *Journal of Personality and Social Psychology, 62,* 318-327.

Montada, L., & Schneider, A. (1989). Justice and emotional reactions to the disadvantaged. *Social Justice Research, 3,* 313-344.

Note

An earlier version of this article was presented at the American Psychological Society Institute on the Teaching of Psychology, San Francisco, June 1996.

Research Methods Jeopardy: A Tool for Involving Students and Organizing the Study Session

Bryan Gibson
University of Utah

The research methods course is viewed by most psychology instructors as an important core course because it introduces students to the scientific method and how it is used to advance psychological knowledge. However, many students consider course completion a mere formality that is necessary for enrollment in more "interesting" courses. Thus, it is sometimes more difficult to involve students in this course as compared with upper level content courses in psychology.

One area in which students' involvement may be lacking is in the typical pretest study session. In many cases, these sessions consist of simple question-and-answer periods that are of little benefit to a majority of students. However, Aamodt (1982a, 1982b) demonstrated that study sessions do help students perform better on exams, particularly when the study session organizes the material, rather than simply giving students an opportunity to ask questions.

In an attempt to get students involved in and excited about a pretest study session and to provide a format for organizing the class material, I devised a game based on the TV game show Jeopardy. Students were assigned to one of three teams a week before the game and were told that members of the winning team would be awarded an extra point on the exam. To prepare for the game, I identified six categories that ranged from general topics, such as "the scientific method," to specific topics, such as "reliability," and devised five questions for each of the six categories. The easiest question in each category was assigned a value of 100 points, with each subsequent question increasing by 100 points.

To begin play, the teams are randomly ordered, and a member of the first team chooses a category and point value. The instructor reads the selected statement, and the student must respond with the correct question (in true Jeopardy format). For example, an item in the "ethics" category might be: "The right to be informed of all information that might influence a decision to participate in a research project." The correct response to this statement would be "What is informed consent?" If a correct response is given, the next player on that team selects a category and point value. When a student responds incorrectly, the second team has an opportunity to "steal" the points by providing the correct response. When attempting to steal, team members are allowed to discuss potential responses. If members of that team successfully steal the question, they are allowed to choose a category and point value. If they are unsuccessful, the third team may attempt to steal. If the third team is unable to answer correctly, Team 2 will then choose the next category and point value. If no one is able to provide the correct response, the instructor explains the answer and tries to stimulate discussion about the item.

A "daily double" is hidden among the items on the Jeopardy board. The student who chooses this item decides (with input from teammates) how many team points to wager. This item is presented to the student privately. If the student responds incorrectly, the wagered points are removed from that team's score, and the next team can choose an amount to wager without knowing what the item is.

After the last item on the Jeopardy board is completed, a topic for the final Jeopardy question is revealed. Team members decide how many points to wager, the final Jeopardy item is presented, and each team discusses potential re spouses and writes its response on a sheet of paper. Each team reveals its answer, and points are added or subtracted to determine the winning team.

My goal was to create an entertaining and competitive procedure that would actively involve all students and highlight the current course material. Anecdotal reports from students indicate that these goals were achieved. Several students reported that the advanced notice made them study harder than they normally would have. In addition, students displayed much team spirit through hearty congratulations for a correct response and words of encouragement for an incorrect response. Finally, when asked whether a second Jeopardy game should be planned before the next test, students were enthusiastic in their support.

The game also seemed to provide an organization of the material for students. By selecting six major topics, the instructor provided an overarching framework to help students organize their study. Students who were unable to answer questions in a given category could then focus their study on that topic. Although the nature of the game does not provide a review of the more complex theoretical concepts covered, these issues can be dealt with through writing and research critiquing assignments presented at other points in the course. In summary, research methods Jeopardy stimulated enthusiasm in the topic and helped students identify where to focus their study for the exam.

References

Aamodt, M. G. (1982a). A closer look at the study session. *Teaching of Psychology*, 9, 234-235.

Aamodt, M. G. (1982b). The effect of the study session on test performance. *Teaching of Psychology*, 9, 118-120.

Note

Requests for copies of the items used in the Jeopardy game should be sent to Bryan Gibson, 502 Behavior Sciences Building, University of Utah, Salt Lake City, UT 84112.

Reducing Fear of the Laboratory Rat: A Participant Modeling Approach

Nigel Barber

Birmingham-Southern College

The first day of attending a rat laboratory can be a harrowing experience for the student who is even slightly fearful of rats. One solution to this problem may involve preexposing students to the rat in a comparatively nonthreatening classroom situation. Hughes (1990) described a classroom demonstration of phobia treatment in which an expert and peer models handled a snake. Students enjoyed the demonstration and found it valuable, but only a small number of students participated. Because fear reduction was not measured, it is not clear that the modeling procedure was effective. This article describes a modeling procedure for fear reduction to be used with an entire class. A pretest-posttest design allowed fear reduction to be quantified and the relative effectiveness of two levels of exposure (either petting the rat or merely handling its transparent transport box) to be evaluated. Sex differences in initial fear levels and in fear reduction were also examined.

Participant modeling is a clinical procedure for treating phobias. The client is exposed directly to a phobic object in the presence of a therapist; for example, a snake phobic approaches the snake and eventually handles it. This procedure is considerably more effective than symbolic modeling in which the client merely observes an expert handling the snake apparently because direct exposure induces a sense of mastery over the situation (Bandura, Blanchard, & Ritter, 1969). Thus, I predicted that students who were exposed to the rat would show reduced fear and that those who petted the rat would show greater fear reduction than those who merely handled its transport box.

Method

Subjects

Students in two sections of an introductory psychology course served as subjects ($N = 56$, half were men).

Apparatus

The rat was an adult male Long-Evans hooded rat. It was presented in a small, transparent animal transport cage ($22 \times 14 \times 14$ cm) available from large department stores. The cage floor was covered with wood chips to a 2-cm depth. A small door in the ceiling of the cage allowed the rat to be caught. The rat was thoroughly habituated to being handled and carried in the transport cage. Band-Aids and hydrogen peroxide were available (out of sight of the students) in case the rat bit someone, but these were not needed. Plastic gloves were offered to the volunteers, but none used them. Two copies of the Fear of Rats Scale (FRS; see Table 1) were used for each subject. These were identical except that the pretest was labeled *A* and the posttest was labeled *B*.

Table 1. Items on the Fear of Rats Scale

1. Allow a lab rat to climb up your shirt.
2. Catch a lab rat with your bare hand.
3. Touch a lab rat's cage when the rat is inside it.
4. Walk up to where a lab rat's cage is in reach.
5. Walk into a room in which lab rats are housed in cages.
6. Allow a lab rat to rest on your sleeve.
7. Allow a lab rat to crawl around your bare neck.
8. Touch a lab rat with a gloved hand.
9. Open a cage and look at a lab rat.
10. Allow a lab rat to rest on your bare arm.

Note. Students rated the likelihood that they would perform each action on a 7-point scale ranging from *very likely* (1) to *very unlikely* (7).

Procedure

The entire demonstration lasted about 30 min. Subjects were informed of their right to decline participation in any of the subsequent activities. They were instructed to complete the FRS. The students scored their own FRS by summing their ratings of the 10 items; then they tuned the paper over. The rat, which had been out of sight, was then revealed in its transport cage. Instructions were as follows:

We now want to test your insight about rats. I want you to assess the age of the rat in days and write it on the back of your FRS. In order that everyone has a good chance to look at the rat, I want you to pass it around the room.

When the rat had been passed to all participants, further instructions were given:

Now I need the assistance of five volunteers to assess the friendliness of the rat. In order to do this, it is necessary to put your hand into the transport cage and pet the animal. Gloves are available for this purpose, if you wish to use them. If you wish to volunteer, please raise your hand.

Characteristics of a model, such as perceived similarity, are important in determining the model's effectiveness. Because half the subjects were women who were less likely to volunteer, any woman who volunteered was selected. The remaining volunteers were selected at random from men with raised hands. Standing behind the instructor's desk, each volunteer petted the rat in full view of the class until deciding on the animal's level of friendliness. Volunteers then returned to their own desks and wrote the word volunteer on the back of their FRS scale. They then rated the rat's friendliness on a 7-point scale ranging from *not friendly at all* (1) to *extremely friendly* (7). Students then took and scored the FRS again.

The instructor described participant modeling and informed subjects that the true purpose of the demonstration was to assess whether exposure to the rat would reduce their fear of rats. Students were asked to subtract the posttest FRS score from the pretest score. By a show of hands, most students indicated that their fear had been reduced by exposure to the rat. Data sheets were then collected so that scoring could be checked and statistical analyses conducted.

Results

Fear was significantly reduced for nonvolunteers in both class sections. One section's mean FRS score dropped from 38.76 (pretest) to 29.64 (posttest), $t(24) = 4.52$, $p < .001$. In the other section, the mean FRS dropped from 38.55 to 34.00, $t(20) = 3.64$, $p < .005$.

Volunteers had lower initial fear ($M = 29.45$) than non volunteers ($M = 38.66$), $t(54) = 1.66$, $p = .05$, one-tail test. Comparison of the difference scores (pretest - posttest) revealed that volunteers had a larger reduction in fear ($M = 13.09$) than nonvolunteers ($M = 7.09$), $t(54) = 1.89$, $p < .05$, one-tail test. This effect could have been due to the fact that volunteers had lower initial fear and were mostly men. When initial fear level and subject sex were controlled in a regression analysis, volunteer status still had a significant effect on difference scores, $t(62) = 2.69$, $p = .01$. Of the 56 subjects, 2 had a negative difference score,

12 had a difference of 0, and 42 had a positive difference score.

There was a large sex difference on pretest FRS scores: $M = 28.25$ and $M = 45.46$ for men and women, respectively, $t(54) = 4.44$, $p < .001$. The sexes did not differ, however, in the magnitude of fear reduction, $M = 6.29$ and $M = 10.25$ for men and women, respectively, $t(54) = 1.55$, $p > .05$. The posttest score for women ($M = 35.21$) was also significantly higher than for men ($M = 21.96$), $t(54) = 3.19$, $p < .01$.

Validating the FRS

I predicted that students who had almost completed a Learning class with a weekly 1.5-hr rat lab should score lower on the FRS than students without such experience. This prediction was tested by comparing 31 biology and psychology majors (9 men and 22 women) enrolled in a Learning course to the 56 Introductory Psychology students (28 men, 28 women). Using a two-way analysis of variance to control for the differing sex composition of the groups, the Learning students had significantly lower FRS scores ($M = 22.10$) than the Introductory Psychology students' pretest scores ($M = 36.86$), $F(1, 83) = 27.26$, $p < .001$; and men ($M = 25.50$) scored lower than women ($M = 36.17$), $F(1, 83) = 21.18$, $p < .001$. The interaction between sex and group was not significant.

Discussion

Even a mild level of exposure to a feared object, such as handling the container in which a rat is housed, can reduce fear in an appropriate social setting. This fact makes fear reduction a non traumatic and safe procedure for classroom demonstrations. Nevertheless, results of this study suggest that the amount of fear reduction depends on the level of exposure. Volunteers experienced significantly more fear reduction, despite their initially lower scores on the FRS, than non volunteers. Although the groups were not initially equal in FRS scores or in sexual composition, regression analysis indicated that these variables were not responsible for the difference in outcome. (However, volunteers may differ from non volunteers in other ways that may confound the result.) This demonstration can thus be varied to suit the needs of individual instructors. For example, the whole class could be exposed to the milder or to the stronger manipulation; a random half could be exposed to each condition; or, as reported here, a few peer models could handle the rat.

In addition to participant modeling, symbolic modeling was also involved in the present procedure because subjects who did not handle the rat observed others doing so. Thus, we cannot say whether the observed fear reduction was due to participation, symbolic modeling, or a combination of both.

The FRS appears to be a valid instrument because scores for students with extensive experience in handling rats were lower than for introductory psychology students. Floor and ceiling effects can occur, but these are unlikely to spoil a classroom demonstration. On the first administration, one subject (of 56) scored the maximum (70), and two scored the minimum (10).

The demonstration takes about 30 min, leaving time for extensive discussion. Good topics include the evolutionary functions of fear, volunteer biases in research, sex differences in emotional responses, and the ethical issues concerning potentially traumatic research or classroom demonstrations (Harcum & Friedman, 1991).

The demonstration could backfire and increase students' fear of rats (e.g., if a volunteer were to get bitten). However, this problem is less likely to occur in the classroom than in the early sessions of a rat lab in which frightened and inexperienced students may mishandle a rat while attempting to catch it. The benefits of this demonstration to students in a rat lab seem to outweigh its potential costs. A similar argument can be made for its use in an introductory psychology course. The data presented herein suggest that students' fear can be reduced without handling the rat, which minimizes ethical problems.

References

Bandura, A., Blanchard, E. B., & Ritter, B. (1969). Relative efficacy of demonstration and modeling approaches for inducing behavioral, affective, and attitudinal changes. *Journal of Personality and Social Psychology, 13,* 173-199.

Harcum, E. R., & Friedman, H. (1991). Students' ethics ratings of demonstrations in introductory psychology. *Teaching of Psychology, 18,* 215-218.

Hughes, D. (1990). Participant modeling as a classroom activity. *Teaching of Psychology, 17,* 238-240.

Note

I thank Ruth L. Ault and the anonymous reviewers for their helpful comments on a draft of this article.

Corporate-Sponsored Undergraduate Research as a Capstone Experience

Francis T. Durso
University of Oklahoma

Colleges and universities have introduced capstone experiences into the undergraduate curriculum. Besides classroom work, undergraduates have opportunities to engage in research, either by conducting individual projects or by participating in small teams. The value of such experiences over others (including more formal laboratories) has been extolled earlier (e.g., McGill, 1975).

This article describes the processes used to involve local businesses, industries, and government agencies in the sponsorship of capstone research projects. This sponsorship produced challenging research questions of interest to the students partly because they were of interest to the sponsor. This approach addresses the concern of preparing psychology majors for employment in business-related occupations, where many psychology alumni find positions. Some would argue that directly meeting the needs of majors entering the business world (e.g., by vocational training) is inappropriate (see Hogan, 1991), but few would contest the value of applying psychological methodology to applied problems. Finally, from a more practical perspective, sponsorship provided the research teams with resources to conduct the project, including subject matter expertise and financial support.

Psychology majors are an especially appropriate group to approach the industrial and business communities. The skills that psychology majors acquire are exactly those needed to answer many questions that exist outside of academia; furthermore, many questions can be answered without a graduate-level understanding of psychological theory. Similar attempts with students in other disciplines (e.g., physics) would be unlikely to meet these requirements and thus would be unlikely to secure sponsorship.

Securing Sponsorship

Securing sponsorship is vital to this enterprise. The goal in this case was to secure commitments from at least three sponsors. Initial contact was made early both to permit promotion of the course to undergraduates and to make clear to the sponsors exactly what they would receive in return for their largesse. Attempts to secure sponsors began before the beginning of the fall semester for the following spring semester. This phase of the project began by identifying local businesses, industries, and government agencies that might be willing to cooperate. The college's development officer and a member of our city council were contacted to help at this stage. Both of these individuals found the rationale of giving students some real-world experience and of providing local merchants with research they might otherwise not secure, a compelling reason to assist. Not only did they help identify possible sponsors using lists from the development office and the city's Chamber of Commerce, but they also contacted many of them. In addition, notifying the college's development office is wise simply to ensure that conflicts with their efforts do not occur. Thus, gaining the support of individuals with contacts outside the college will greatly aid this phase of course development.

Initial formal contact with approximately 20 potential sponsors was by letter, although many of the individuals had been introduced to the idea by the development officer or city council member. The letter contained a request for interest and described the types of research projects that might be of value to them: Opportunities for scientifically rigorous naturalistic observation, surveys, questionnaire development, field experiments, and laboratory or library research were mentioned. Examples of these methods as they might be applied were also included in the letter. The letter did not mention any particular dollar figure to qualify for sponsorship. Finally, the letter made clear that the project would be conducted by senior psychology majors, and although the sponsors would be hiring a talented group, they should understand that sponsorship would primarily be a way to supply the seniors a valuable learning experience.

The letters were followed by phone calls, meetings, or both. Discussions with the potential sponsors varied. Several had no interest. Some viewed the proposal as merely another request for limited funds. Some found the idea appealing but could not think of what a research team could do for them. Despite examples in the letter, generating some possibilities that applied directly to the particular business proved useful. Five sponsors showed sufficient interest. I spoke again with these sponsors and established approximate figures for their financial commitment, obtained a clearly phrased (although often vague) idea of what they wanted to know, and detailed to them what they should expect from the research team.

More specifically, they were told that whether or not their project was accepted would depend on the size of the class, the particular skills of the students, and the specific proposal from the sponsor. Those who were not selected were given the opportunity to be considered the following semester. None of the sponsors viewed this uncertainty as a problem.

Three projects were ultimately adopted by the class. They were not necessarily those with the larger financial commitments, although the funds offered by the sponsor did seem to be a factor in some students' decisions. One project was rejected because no one in class felt the statistical requirements were within their understanding. One project was rejected due to lack of interest. Of the three accepted, one offered a budget of less than $1,000 (the highest), one of less than $500, and one of photocopy and printing support (the lowest) . One of the projects involved analysis of flight data for the Federal Aviation Administration's (FAA) Civil Aeromedical Institute, one involved survey research for a local bank, and one involved naturalistic observation of seat belt compliance for the city's Police Department.

Each of these projects had knowledgeable and friendly contact people with whom the students could interact. These were either the sponsors or a subordinate. Although affability is not necessary, availability certainly is, and having both makes the project more appealing to the student (and the instructor) .

Teams

For the course described herein, small teams were formed based on the students' skills in statistics, methodology, computers, writing, and public speaking. The assessment of skill was a composite of previous academic performance and self report. Self-report required students to identify the skills they thought were well developed and those they thought were underdeveloped or nonexistent. Teams used this information to divide responsibilities, with an eye toward helping those who wished to develop a particular skill further. For example, one student confessed to an almost paralyzing fear of public speaking. The instructor, together with the team and other class members, slowly brought her to a point where she participated fully in the final presentation. Finally, students ranked their preference for the available projects. Skills, preferences, and prior academic performance were considered in forming the teams. Presumably instructors will have methods and techniques for forming, working with, and evaluating teams, if they choose to use teams. (See Michaelson, 1983, for one approach.)

The Class

Seniors choosing to conduct research as their capstone experience enrolled for the 3-hr Corporate-Sponsored Capstone Research class. Because the students were capstoneready seniors, they had already completed most of the departmental requirements, including a statistics and research methods (with laboratory) class. Beyond these courses, the students brought a variety of different classroom experiences to the project. In the initial offering, enrollment was intentionally kept low (maximum 15). However, a second offering is now planned, and we anticipate that enrollment will be allowed to double. The size of the class depends on the number of sponsors secured, the number of projects the instructor feels competent supervising, and the size of the teams.

The instructor's role in such a class is varied. She or he is educator, mentor, facilitator, arbitrator, and evaluator. Although less than in most classes, formal lecture and discussion were present at the beginning of the course and continued intermittently throughout. Initial lectures reviewed basic methodological and design principles. One also covered professionalism, including topics and demonstrations on dealing with sexist, preoccupied, and mercurial sponsors. Later lectures covered statistical principles, occasionally introducing more advanced concepts needed for a particular project. Finally, a few lectures near the end covered writing and public speaking.

For the most part, however, the instructor interacted as mentor and facilitator for each project. The instructor frequently met with each team, and the team often presented progress reports, ideas, and problems to the rest of the class. Class time was, in general, devoted to discussion of particular issues, exchanging and reviewing writing efforts, and presenting the work in formal and informal public-speaking settings.

Once teams were established, the class discussed each project. Vague, ambiguous, and imprecise components of the sponsor's requests were noted for an upcoming meeting. Students discussed possible methodological and statistical issues and began to think of the project as one that must be accomplished on a limited budget, within a limited time, and with limited personnel.

Approximately 2 weeks into the semester, each team met informally with the sponsor. The instructor attended this first meeting at the sponsor's place of business. Students asked questions they had formulated during the previous 2 weeks. These questions probed both the desires of the sponsors and pragmatic concerns (e.g., access to bank mailing list). Students informed the sponsor that they would present a written proposal—complete with a budget and a schedule of work and deliverable goods—within 14 days. In all cases, the deliverable goods included a written report and a formal presentation.

Development of the proposal required students to investigate the sponsor's area at a preliminary level (e.g., What do air traffic controllers actually do?). It also required that they research their methodology of choice in more detail than they had in previous courses (e.g., What size sample should we approach in the hopes of representing $N\%$ of the bank's customers?). Finally, it required them to begin investigating the relevant literature (e.g., What is the national percentage of people who wear seat belts?).

For the rest of the course, the teams developed and met goals according to their timelines. They developed surveys, created classification schemes, implemented sampling procedures, and so on. In addition, students made decisions on a variety of concerns that emerged during the semester. In one instance, a sponsor changed his mind about access to certain information. In another instance, there was a budgetary misunderstanding. In another, weather made natural observation problematic. All had to make concessions to a rapidly approaching deadline. Students adopted techniques to increase the return rate of surveys; developed unobtrusive ways to make observations; chose appropriate, sometimes complex (e.g., multiple regression) statistical procedures; and so on. In each case, with only little help from the instructor-facilitator, students reached reasonable conclusions about how to proceed. Although other solutions existed, the students, virtually on their own, made good command decisions that simultaneously satisfied constraints placed on them by the research question, the timeline, and the budget. Throughout the course, each team had access to the other teams as sounding boards, reviewers, and critics. These interactions, together with the writing and speaking workshops, prepared the students for creating the final report and delivering the formal presentation.

The Products

All teams delivered copies of their reports at the planned presentation. The sponsors had, indeed, taken these endeavors seriously. The seat belt team presented to the chief of police, members of city council, and an additional group of officers. The bank team's audience included the senior vice president and two other vice presidents. The FAA team presented to managers of the Civil Aeromedical Institute and controller instructors from the FAA Academy. The local press interviewed the teams, giving the students recognition for their efforts and making it easier to obtain sponsors' commitments for the next offering of the course.

Overall, the experience was valuable for everyone. The sponsors, who initially thought they were helping the students, were surprised by the caliber and amount of information they received. The FAA team categorized one quarter of a million flight plans, the seat belt team observed 13,000 vehicles, and the bank team surveyed over 400 residents by mail or phone. All three sponsors have agreed to finance a project during the second offering of the course. Students, who admitted they worked harder than they had in the past, rated the class highly (all ranked 4 or 5 on a 5-point scale), as indicated by formal evaluations and their recommendations to upcoming seniors. Finally, the instructor, who felt a part of each project, recognized that students had demonstrated more understanding of psychology and its methods than could ever be assessed with a classroom exam.

References

Hogan, P. M. (1991). Vocational preparation within a liberal arts framework Suggested directions for undergraduate psychology programs. *Teaching of Psychology, 18,* 148-153.

McGill, T. E. (1975). Special projects laboratory in experimental psychology. *Teaching of Psychology, 2,* 169-171.

Michaelson, L. K. (1983). Team learning in large classes. In C. Bouton & R. Y. Garth (Eds.), Learning in groups (pp. 13-22). San Francisco: Jossey-Bass.

Note

I thank Scott Gronlund and Janis Hamic for comments on an earlier draft of this article. I especially thank city council member, Tom Miller, and the college's development director, Melinda Hassebroek.

SECTION IV:
HISTORY

Promoting Active Participation

Ludy Benjamin involved both faculty and students in the development of a departmental history. The article included valuable information on topics and resources that can be used in such a project. The author advocated this activity as either a course assignment or an independent research project.

To improve the quality of student oral presentations James Goodwin had students in his History and Systems course delivered minilectures covering specific course content. Peers evaluated the lectures, and students were tested on minilecture information. In a replication, lectures were videotaped. Lecturers also wrote a paper that elaborated the content of their talks and self-evaluated their performance based on peer feedback and (in the replication) the videotape. The result was a distinct improvement over the typical oral presentation assignment.

To encourage students' active learning and critical thinking in the history of psychology course Bruce Henderson designed exercises. Students read original book and journal material and responded to questions that elicited analysis and comparisons.

Susan Rhoads and Randal Wight argued that psychology must accept responsibility for its own historiography and instill within its students an interest in and love for history. The authors describe a pedagogical assignment designed to achieve those objectives.

Charles Brooks had students in his history of psychology class portray prominent individuals. Working in teams, students developed a presentation in which they portrayed individuals from different time periods and discussed and debated psychological issues. Students also prepared bibliographies and position papers about those individuals. Brooks also described variations on this technique. Advantages of the exercise included giving students a personal appreciation for historical figures and a greater understanding about the continuity of psychological issues.

Teachers of history of psychology classes sometimes assign term papers requiring the treatment of a single major figure in the discipline. Dean Simonton created a conceptual framework for writing such "great person" essays by interpreting a psychologist's life and work according to the typical profile of an eminent scientist. Empirical research in the metasciences provided the profile, which students can use when evaluating whether an eminent psychologist fits the generic pattern.

Expanding Students' Knowledge

Joy Berrenberg and Ann Prosser instructed students to design and construct games that covered a broad range of knowledge about the history of psychology. The authors found that the procedure was a challenging, engaging, and effective supplement or alternative to traditional evaluation methods. Playing the games in class provided an excellent and enjoyable review of course material.

To expand students' knowledge about the range of contributions usually covered in a history of psychology course, Randall Wight used the social custom of toasting. Wight identified pitfalls and advantages of this technique. Who said studying history had to be stuffy?

Students in Alfred Raphelson's history of psychology class saw more than 1,000 slides illustrating biographies, concepts, and theories. The author found that scores on an unannounced, slide recognition test correlated with examination scores given throughout the semester. One conclusion was that the results indicated evidence for incidental learning.

Discovering Philosophies of Psychology

Because many psychology students have difficulty with the philosophical character of the typical history of psychology course, Brian Cox introduced students to psychology's philosophical roots by surveying their assumptions about the nature of mind, emotion, and behavior. The article describes and gives examples of a 50-item Likert-scale questionnaire concerning the positions of many philosophers, biologist, and psychologists that are typically covered in the class. The authors made suggestions for using the measure as a teaching tool.

Students in James Waller's history of psychology course began to help students begin to discover their disciplinary worldviews or philosophies of psychology by completing five pedagogical strategies. Students wrote short, in-class, contemplative essays (microthemes) on polarities of psychology (e.g., empiricism vs. rationalism). The instructor presented selected student writing samples, peers debated their positions, and students responded to their peers' microthemes. Finally, in a detailed critical analysis assignment, students intensively re-examined selected microtheme polarities.

1. PROMOTING ACTIVE PARTICIPATION

Involving Students and Faculty in Preparing a Departmental History

Ludy T. Benjamin, Jr.
Texas A&M University

Scientific psychology in the United States has entered its second century, and centennial celebrations occur each year. Some focus on the founding of psychology laboratories, for example, the University of Wisconsin (1988), University of Nebraska (1989), and Columbia University (1990); others focus on significant publications, such as James's *Principles of Psychology* (1990). These celebrations take various forms (e.g., special conferences and commemorative publications), but they have a common aim of discovering the history of notable events.

Although centennials are an important impetus, historical research can be initiated at any time. A subject of investigation and some knowledge about how to find and use relevant sources of information are required. This article presents ideas about institutional histories and describes sources for data. Such research can unite students and faculty in a cooperative learning venture as a regular course assignment or as a special independent research project. Research related to the college or university or some other local entity or event generates high student interest (Grigg, 1974; Raphelson, 1979). In addition to gaining knowledge, rediscovered or new, students enhance their library skills, learn about important resources in historical research, learn about historical research techniques and issues of interpretation, acquire some group coordination skills, and develop a better appreciation of their institution's past.

Time Requirements of the Project

A first decision concerns the time required to complete a project. If the research is part of a course, then the time frame is obviously dictated. Some projects can be continued from one class to another, but this procedure precludes the learning and satisfaction that students derive from completing the task. Institutional histories are often too complex to complete in a single term. One solution to this problem is to restrict the subject matter. By dividing it into separate units, the entire project might be completed during several school terms while allowing each group of students to experience closure on its particular unit. A second solution is to restrict the time period (e.g., look only at the first 10 years of an institution's history).

Nature of the Project

Historical research projects on institutions, such as colleges or universities, can range from preparing a departmental scrapbook to writing a comprehensive departmental history. The research can stand alone or be part of a larger institutional history project.

A comprehensive departmental history should answer a number of questions about curriculum, faculty, students, facilities, and departmental events (see Table 1). Although portions of these histories can be assigned to different groups of students, someone should serve as editor to ensure a coherent product. Publishing these extensive projects can be costly. If institutional or private financial support is unavailable, desktop publishing is an economical alternative for producing an attractive final product.

Less formal histories can take many forms. A timeline can be used to portray faculty, curriculum, or psychology major requirements as they change over time. For a faculty timeline, available photographs might be included. Timelines can be reproduced for individual distribution, but they also make excellent displays for bulletin boards. Timelines provide a "time map" on which events are placed in time locations, typically progressing from left to right. Interest in timelines for departments or institutions can be enhanced by adding external events of national or international significance.

The *chronology* is related to the timeline but uses no spatial display. Chronologies simply list items in historical order (e.g., the founding date of a laboratory, the arrival of a particular faculty member, or the introduction of a new course). Chronologies are sometimes constructed in two columns One lists events of the institution's history (internal history), and the other lists events outside the institution (external history). Sahakian (1981, pp. 445-483) provided an example of a history of psychology chronology. Sahakian's items can be used in conjunction with institutional chronologies to illustrate happenings elsewhere in the psychological world.

Table 1. Questions to Ask in a Departmental History

Curriculum

1. When were the first psychology courses offered? What were their titles? What was their content? What texts did they use?
2. How has the psychology curriculum evolved? When did particular courses first appear? Disappear? How did the catalog course descriptions change over time? What requirements have existed for the psychology major? How have those changed? What psychology courses have been required for nonmajors? What parts of the curriculum might have served other departments?
3. When did laboratory instruction begin in psychology? What was the nature of research in the laboratory? Were students involved in the research? What published research came out of the laboratory?
4. In what department(s) were psychology courses offered? When was the psychology department formally established?

Faculty

1. What faculty members have taught psychology? Where did they receive their training and in what fields? What faculty titles did they hold?
2. Can you locate former faculty members for oral histories?
3. Can you locate published research or other writing by former faculty members?

Students

1. Did student psychology clubs exist? Was there a Psi Chi chapter?
2. What careers did the early graduates of the program pursue?
3. What eminent persons did their undergraduate work in psychology?
4. What was the psychology program like from a student perspective? Can you locate former students in psychology for oral histories? Do they have class notes from their student days?

Facilities

1. What laboratory facilities existed and how long were they used? What equipment was acquired and when?
2. Were off-campus facilities used by the psychology program (e.g., for field work, training, or community service projects)?

Departmental Events

1. Did famous psychologists speak on your campus at some time? Can you locate information about those talks?
2. Were any meetings, symposia, or other special activities related to psychology held on your campus?

Another historical project is the preparation of complete *faculty genealogies* (Weigel & Gottfurcht, 1972). Each student is assigned a particular faculty member, present or past, and is asked to determine that faculty member's academic genealogy (i.e., who was the faculty member's major professor, who was the major professor's major professor, etc.) . These genealogies make nice bulletin board displays. They highlight the youth of scientific psychology and the fact that most lineages are traceable to a few psychologists, principally Wilhelm Wundt, William James, and Carl Stumpf. Hillix and Broyles (1980) provided an excellent example of a psychology department genealogy and a description of how to do the necessary research.

Other *display projects* can consist of old photos of faculty, students, buildings, and departmental apparatus; old catalog copies of the curriculum; and old newspaper clippings of departmental activities. These materials make interesting bulletin board displays, departmental scrapbooks, or even slide shows or videotapes. Old equipment can be placed in display cases along with information about the department's use of the equipment. Student or faculty articles (published or unpublished) relevant to that equipment can also be displayed. In fact, student and faculty research articles can be exhibited by themselves (perhaps just title pages) to illustrate projects of earlier years. A good source for locating authors of published articles and books in psychology from 1894 to 1958 is the *Cumulative Author Index to Psychological Index and Psychological Abstracts*, a five-volume work published by G. K. Hall in 1960. These volumes were continued in 5- or 3-year intervals until 1985 and can be found in many university libraries. Subject indexes exist from 1927 to 1985.

Consider also the possibility of *projects other that departmental histories*, such as histories of local institutions (hospitals or mental institutions), local organizations (YMCA, YWCA, Planned Parenthood, AA, or other social service agencies), or local groups (mental health advocacy groups or phrenological societies). Most communities have some psychology-related agencies, past or present. Discovering or recognizing their existence greatly expands the historical research opportunities for your classes.

Sources of Historical Information

After deciding on the time course and nature of your research project, where do you find the information you need? Sources are basically of two kinds: published and unpublished.

Published sources can be found in libraries, rare book rooms, archives, state historical societies, and newspaper publishers. They include faculty and student publications, college yearbooks and catalogs, student newspapers, notes and news listings in journals (see Benjamin et al., 1989), newsletters (e.g., faculty, alumni, and Psi Chi), and local newspapers.

Unpublished materials are more difficult to locate and, for departmental histories, include such items as class and laboratory notes, syllabi, lectures, correspondence, and oral histories. Although these materials are more scattered, the sources listed for published materials may be a good place to begin. Department and/or institutional archives usually contain correspondence, annual reports, self-study documents, alumni records, grant proposals (for instruction, research, or program development), and personal papers of former faculty and students. Locating former faculty and students provides the opportunity for collecting oral histories. If the department has had a Psi Chi chapter, contact the Psi Chi National Office, which maintains correspondence files for each chapter, some dating back to the 1930s.

The State Department of Education may have files on all state and private colleges and universities within the state. The official state archives is another source to check, and if the college or university is or was affiliated with a particular church, then check the church archives for your district.

Relevant information may exist in other archival collections (e.g., in the extensive collections of the Archives of the History of American Psychology in Akron, OH). More than 650 individuals and organizations have deposited materials at that archive (see Benjamin, 1980, Popplestone & McPherson, 1976). An annotated listing of more than 500 relevant manuscript collections in the United States was compiled by Sokal and Rafail (1982). It is an excellent source for checking the papers of a particular individual or organization .

Many archives have an index system for names of individuals and institutions that appear in their collections. They may even send you copies of pertinent documents, for a nominal sum, if the number is small and their search time short. However, if the holdings related to your project are extensive, then you will need to visit that archive. If you are researching a particular individual, then make some educated guesses about persons with whom your subject might have corresponded. If you locate relevant papers, contact the appropriate archive.

The alumni office can provide addresses of former students. Students who took classes with particular faculty members, and thus have memories of those earlier days (and perhaps even class notes), may be located by advertising for them in a local newspaper. Another way to get information on an earlier faculty member, who is perhaps deceased, is to locate that faculty member's children. Often those children attended the institution where the parent taught, and the alumni office should be able to help you find them. These children may have important materials for your research.

Some sources of information will be obvious. Others will develop from hunches pursued, exhaustive search, and serendipity. Part of the enjoyment of historical research is tracking down obscure, but often important, information.

Doing Historical Research

The projects suggested in this article do not train psychology students or faculty to be competent historians. However, those involved should learn something about the methods of "doing" history as well as the inherent pitfalls and pleasures. Should you need information on historical research methods or approaches to writing history, books by Benjamin (1981, 1988), Brozek and Pongratz (1980), and Hoopes (1979) describe techniques such as citation analysis, content analysis, oral history, and archival research, and provide examples of biographical, descriptive, quantitative, and sociopsychological approaches to writing history. These sources will help you

plan your historical research and train your students to do the project.

Before beginning, you might examine several published departmental histories (e.g., Benjamin & Bertelson, 1975; Capshew & Hearst, 1980; Freed & Roberts, 1988; Morawski, 1986; Raphelson, 1980). These will provide some models for your own research and may suggest possibilities that you had not considered. The history of psychology reference book by Viney, Wertheimer, and Wertheimer (1979) lists a number of departmental and organizational histories.

Benefits (and Costs) of Doing Historical Research

Costs for the projects described are quite modest, usually involving only photocopying, photographic work, cassette tapes, and long-distance telephone charges. Travel to archival collections can be expensive but is usually not necessary for most local history projects. Modest funds are often available from the institution for these kinds of projects.

Although costs are small, benefits can be large. Besides the benefits mentioned earlier, the final product can be added to the archival records of the institution. Indeed, at least one copy should be bound and placed in the institution's library. Information gathered in these exercises can be used in future classes, particularly in the history of psychology class. Students and faculty can better understand changes in the department over time and relate those changes to events in the broader context of the institution, national psychology, or the world at large. Finally, these projects involve students and faculty in an exercise that is as much fun as it is educational. My students report a clearer sense of purpose in this kind of written assignment, compared to some of the papers they write for other classes, and they enjoy making a real contribution to their department. Instead of waiting for a centennial, get your students involved now.

References

Benjamin, L. T., Jr. (1980). Research at the Archives of the History of American Psychology: A case history. In J. Brozek & L. J. Pongratz (Eds.), *Historiography of modern psychology* (pp. 241-51). Toronto: Hogrefe.

Benjamin, L. T., Jr. (1981). *Teaching history of psychology: A handbook*. New York: Academic.

Benjamin, L. T., Jr. (Ed.). (1988). *A history of psychology: Original sources and contemporary research*. New York: McGraw-Hill.

Benjamin, L. T., Jr., & Bertelson, A. D. (1975). The early Nebraska psychology laboratory, 1889-1930: Nursery for presidents of the American Psychological Association. *Journal of the History of the Behavioral Sciences, 11*, 142-148.

Benjamin, L. T., Jr., Pratt, R., Watlington, D., Aaron, L., Bonar, T., Fitzgerald, S., Franklin, M., Jimenez, B., & Lester, R. (1989). *A history of American psychology in notes and news, 1883-1945: An index to journal sources.* New York: Kraus International.

Brozek, J., & Pongratz, L. J. (Eds.). (1980). *Historiography of modern psychology.* Toronto: Hogrefe.

Capshew, J. H., & Hearst, E. (1980). Psychology at Indiana University from Bryan to Skinner. *Psychological Record, 30,* 319-342.

Cumulative author index to Psychological Index (1894-1935) and Psychological Abstracts (1927-1958). (1960). (5 vols.). Boston: Hall.

Freed, D. W., & Roberts, C. L. (1988). Mirror of New England: The early years of psychology at Colorado College. *Journal of the History of the Behavioral Sciences, 24,* 46-50.

Grigg, A. E. (1974). Research projects for a history of psychology. *Teaching of Psychology, 1,* 84-85.

Hillix, W. A., & Broyles, J. W. (1980). The family trees of American psychologists. In W. G. Bringmann & R. D. Tweney (Eds.), Wundt studies (pp. 422-434). Toronto: Hogrefe.

Hoopes, J. (1979). *Oral history: An introduction for students.* Chapel Hill: University of North Carolina Press.

Morawski, J. G. (1986). Organizing knowledge and behavior at Yale's Institute of Human Relations. *ISIS, 77,* 219-242.

Popplestone, J. A., & McPherson, M. W. (1976). Ten years of the Archives of the History of American Psychology. *American Psychologist, 31,* 533-534.

Raphelson, A. C. (1979). The unique role of the history of psychology in undergraduate education. *Teaching of Psychology, 6,* 12-14.

Raphelson, A. C. (1980). Psychology at Michigan: The Pillsbury years. *Journal of the History of the Behavioral Sciences, 16,* 301-312.

Sahakian, W. S. (Ed.). (1981). *History of psychology: A sourcebook in systematic psychology* (rev. ed.). Itasca, IL: Peacock.

Sokal, M. M., & Rafail, P. A. (1982). *A guide to manuscripts collections in the history of psychology and related areas.* New York: Kraus International.

Viney, W., Wertheimer, M., & Wertheimer, M. L. (1979). *History of psychology: A guide to information sources.* Detroit: Gale Research.

Weigel, R. G., & Gottfurcht, J. W. (1972). Faculty genealogies: A stimulus for student involvement in history and systems. *American Psychologist, 27,* 981-983.

Toward *Eloquentia Perfecta* in the History and Systems Course

C. James Goodwin
Wheeling Jesuit College

An objective of liberal education is to teach students to deliver an oral presentation with clarity, precision, and style. This desirable outcome is often expressed at Jesuit schools by the Latin phrase *eloquentia perfecta*—to communicate with perfect eloquence. I require some type of oral presentation in as many of my courses as possible, and I believe that students have profited from the experience to some degree. However, I never have been completely satisfied with the oral presentation assignment. The *goal of eloquentia perfecta* often seems quite elusive.

Several problems can occur with the typical oral presentation assignment. First, total class hours per semester are limited, so presentations can intrude on valuable lecture or discussion time. These time pressures might lead the instructor to omit presentations or seriously curtail them. The problem can be especially acute if student presentations are scheduled near the end of a semester (It's Thanksgiving, and we're still doing Watson!). Second, with the goal of just getting the ordeal over with as quickly as possible, some presenters go to the front of the class, read a paper at breakneck speed without removing their eyes from the page, and scurry back to the safety of their seat. Third, students listening to oral presentations are often inattentive (or rehearsing, if they are next), a behavior known to increase the anxiety of student presenters (Beatty, 1988). The strategy is understandable; students do not believe that they will be tested on the ramblings of one of their peers.

In light of these three difficulties, I developed an assignment that is effective in training students to present their ideas eloquently in public. I use it in my upper level History and Systems course, but it could work in most courses. First, to solve the lost time problem, students lecture on the same material that I would otherwise be covering. Consequently, the presentations are spread across the semester, thereby eliminating the "10 presentations on the last day of class" problem.

The problem of students rushing through a presentation and returning to anonymity as soon as possible is unsolvable for some students. To reduce some of the public-speaking anxiety, I try to make the presentations a genuine learning experience by (a) telling students their subsequent paper will include a section in which they carefully evaluate their presentation, (b) letting students know that others in the class will be helping them through a nonjudgmental (i.e., students do not grade each other) peer evaluation process, and (c) making the subsequent paper worth considerably more than the presentation. In effect, students are told that the only way to fail the presentation is to expire during it.

The problem of student inattentiveness is partially solved by testing students on the material presented in the minilectures. Listeners also pay attention because they have to evaluate each presentation, and peer evaluation seems to be an effective motivator both for student presenters and listeners (Klugh, 1983; Smith, 1990).

Method

The 21 students in my fall 1991 History and Systems course were given a list of topics on the first day of class (e. g., Galton—mental testing, Tolman—cognitive maps, and Watson—conditioned emotional reactions). The topics covered material from the 4th to the 13th week of a 15-week semester. Students were told to select a subject they would like to present in a 12- to 15-min lecture. They were encouraged to use the text as a way to make informed choices, and they listed their top four selections. Most students received their first or second choice.

In brief (5- to 10-min) meetings with each student 1 to 2 weeks before his or her talk, I discussed the information to be covered in the lecture. I also supplied students with at least one other source of information to supplement the material in the textbook by Hothersall (1990). Students knew that their presentations were to be tightly coordinated with my own lectures and that material from each minilecture would appear on exams. One or 2 days before each minilecture, I met briefly with the presenter to review the material to be covered.

Just before delivering their lectures, presenters distributed a one-page outline of their talk to the class. Immediately after the minilecture, students filled out an evaluation form (see Table 1) to provide feedback to the speaker. To encourage students to be as helpful as possible, I instructed them to give their completed evaluations directly to the lecturer; I never saw them.

Finally, within 14 calendar days after their minilectures, students turned in a five- to seven-page paper that included a thorough description of the content of their lecture and a reflection on the quality of their performance, based on the peer feedback and their analysis of the minilecture.

The procedure was replicated in the fall 1992 semester with a class of 21 students. The only significant procedural change was that I videotaped each student's performance. Students viewed their own tape to enhance the self-analysis portion of the paper. Given the option of viewing the tape in private or with me, all chose the former.

Table 1. Form Used for Peer Evaluations of Each Minilecture

Please rate the minilecture by indicating how much you agree or disagree with the statements that follow. Use the following 4-point scale:

    SD = *strongly disagree*
     D = *disagree*
     A = *agree*
    SA = *strongly agree*

The lecturer . . .

1. failed to make good eye contact with the class during the lecture.	SD	D	A	SA
2. was free of distracting mannerisms (e.g., saying "uhhh" or "like" too frequently).	SD	D	A	SA
3. appeared to be nervous during the lecture.	SD	D	A	SA
4. went at a good pace for efficient note taking—not too fast, not too slow.	SD	D	A	SA
5. did too much reading and too little lecturing.	SD	D	A	SA
6. explained things very clearly.	SD	D	A	SA
7. really understood the material being presented.	SD	D	A	SA
8. did not cover the material in the outline adequately.	SD	D	A	SA

Additional comments:

Evaluation

At the end of each semester, students evaluated the entire experience. In 1991, 18 of 21 students completed the evaluation; in 1992, 19 of 21 students evaluated the assignment. Because there were no noticeable class differences, I combined the results (except for the two video items in 1992), which are summarized in Table 2.

Students generally rated the experience positively. For example, they believed the experience helped them develop their public-speaking skills (Item 1), learned from the experience (Items 5 and 9), appreciated the quality and the confidentiality of the peer feedback (Items 3 and 4), and did not think I was avoiding my responsibility by having the students teach the class (Item 2). In the 1992 replication, students cringed when the videotape was described in the syllabus; when the experience was over, however, the evaluations about the videotape were quite positive (Items 11 and 12). As one of the 1992 students wrote, "At first I hated the assignment, but after I started in on it and actually lectured it was not as bad as I had thought. I think it is a valuable learning experience for all students."

The only item without consensus was Item 10. The fact that one half of the students believed they learned just as much from their peers as they would have from me may not be soothing to the ego, but it told me the assignment is worth continuing. Learning does not appear to suffer as the result of students carrying some of the responsibility for presenting course content.

Written comments on the evaluation form indicated two additional strengths. First, about two thirds of the students in each class were seniors who soon would be giving public presentations of their senior thesis projects. Many commented that the minilecture was valuable preparation. These comments were especially prevalent in the 1992 replication, with the merits of the videotape feedback mentioned often. Second, several students commented that the outlines prepared and distributed before each lecture were helpful in reviewing for exams.

Students' papers varied widely in the quality of self-analysis. The weaker papers simply summarized the peer feedback. Students who did the analysis well incorporated

Table 2. Student Evaluation of the Minilecture Assignment

	SA	A	D	SD
1. I believe the minilecture assignment helped me improve my ability to speak in public.	15	18	3	1
2. There were so many minilectures that it seemed like the instructor was avoiding his responsibility to teach— we taught the class for him.	0	1	10	26
3. The feedback given by my peers was helpful to me in evaluating my performance.	10	22	5	0
4. It was a good idea for the instructor not to see the results of the peer-evaluation forms.	12	17	8	0
5. In general, I don't think I learned very much from listening to the minilectures.	1	7	16	13
6. Material from the minilectures should not have been covered on exams.	1	5	18	13
7. I would encourage the instructor to continue this assignment in the future.	20	16	1	0
8. In preparing for the lecture, the supplemental material supplied by the instructor was not very helpful.	0	1	11	25
9. As a result of preparing for my minilecture, I came to know and understand the material I had to cover much better than other material encountered in the course.	23	12	2	0
10. I would have learned more if the instructor rather than the students had lectured on the material.	8	12	12	5
11. I know my lecture would have been much better if I wasn't being videotaped.	1	5	5	8
12. I would encourage the instructor to videotape these lectures in the future.	10	6	2	1

Note. The scores reported are the number of students who either strongly agreed (SA), agreed (A), disagreed (D), or strongly disagreed (SD) with each item. For Items 1–10, $n = 37$; for Items 11 and 12, $n = 19$.

the content and analysis sections of their papers. For example, one student reported presenting Galton's views on eugenics in a certain fashion, but some listeners did not connect Galton's eugenics with his mental-testing work. The student then suggested a way to reorganize the lecture to clarify the connection.

Discussion

I believe that student presentations can be effective when they cover exam-relevant material and are followed by peer evaluations and self-analysis. There are, however, some problems with these procedures. First, although the minilectures presented no scheduling problems for my small classes, they may not be feasible in a large class. At some point, class size could result in more student-lecture minutes than professor-lecture minutes, an outcome not likely to be appreciated by most academic deans. Second, some presenters may be unclear or make factual errors that could take some time for the instructor to correct. I tried to avoid these problems by providing the supplemental materials and specifying what points should be made, meeting with each student at least twice, and checking their outlines for accuracy. On five or six occasions, however, I faced the difficult task of clarifying minilecture information without publicly embarrassing a student. Third, some class time is lost (no more than 3 min) while students fill out the peer evaluation form after each minilecture. I think the advantage of the immediate feedback more than offsets the loss of time, however.

Despite the difficulties, I believe the minilecture is a distinct improvement over the typical oral presentation assignment. It can enhance the quality of student presentations, while maintaining the normal flow of course content. It engages the student listeners, who are responsible for content and will be evaluating the presenter. Ideally, it provides a means to move students toward *eloquentia perfecta.*

References

Beatty, M. J. (1988). Situational and predispositional correlates of public speaking anxiety. *Communication Education, 37,* 28-39.

Hochersall, D. (1990). *History of psychology* (2nd ed.). New York McGraw-Hill.

Klugh, H. E. (1983). Writing and speaking skills can be taught in psychology classes. *Teaching of Psychology, 10,* 170-171.

Smith, R. A. (1990). Are peer ratings of student debates valid? *Teaching of Psychology, 17,* 188-189.

Notes

This article is based on a poster presentation at the annual meeting of the American Psychological Association, Washington, DC, August 1992.

Critical-Thinking Exercises for the History of Psychology Course

Bruce B. Henderson
Western Carolina University

The history of psychology course is a common capstone course in the undergraduate psychology curriculum (Raphelson, 1982). It usually is designed to serve many objectives, including the integration of the coursework that precedes it and the provision of an overall perspective on the discipline of psychology. If the course is taught as a recounting of chronological events, an accounting of the lives of great psychologists, and descriptions of crucial experiments, it is unlikely to generate much critical thinking. However, if critical thinking is considered to be a directed response to discrepancy or uncertainty in logic, fact, opinion, or perspective, then the history of psychology course can provide many opportunities for the exercise of such thinking. Students can evaluate their ideas about the role of theory and method in psychology in light of historical developments and social context (McPherson, 1979) and the application of philosophy of science (Bohan, 1990) .

I have attempted to engage students in critical thinking in the history of psychology course with exercises in which they contrast the textbook version of the history of psychology with original source material. Class discussions of student work center on major questions designed to instigate critical thinking, such as: In what ways has the subject matter of psychology changed over the past 100 years?, What are the enduring themes in the history of psychology? Was behaviorism really the only type of psychology from 1913 to 1960?, How prominent are the major theorists when viewed in the context of the work of their own time?, and What was the role of women in the early history of psychology?

The working model of critical thinking used in the development of these exercises is one proposed by a study group of psychology instructors who met at Alverno College (Halonen, 1986). This model, although not inconsistent with the theoretical and empirical literature on critical thinking (e.g., Halpern, 1989; McMillan, 1987), was developed with the specific purpose of helping psychology teachers to teach critical thinking. The model's major premise is that critical thinking occurs when there is a perceived discrepancy between the student's personal theory (beliefs about an idea or event) and what the

environment is presenting to the student in the form of an idea, question, or event. According to the model, when a teacher leads a student to perceive a discrepancy, the student is likely to go through several steps: Seek information or collect data relevant to resolving the discrepancy, relate new and old information, and integrate and evaluate that information. Whether or not a student alters his or her personal theory will depend on many factors, including how strongly held the original belief was and the nature of the conflicting evidence or experiences the student has encountered. The process involved constitutes reflective, reasonable thinking focused on what to believe or do—critical thinking (Ennis, 1985).

Class sessions help focus students' thinking in the exercises. At the beginning of the course, two contrasting views of scientific history, those of Kuhn (1970) and Laudan (1977; also see Gholson & Barker, 1985), are presented. A Kuhnian view of the history of psychology emphasizes paradigms that dominate eras before crises and, ultimately, revolutions in which a new dominant paradigm emerges. Laudan's approach suggests that several research traditions, with their own flexible core assumptions, coexist within a discipline and compete with each other in terms of their ability to solve the problems of the discipline. Presentation of these alternative views of history and the naive views students initially hold about historic progress (Henderson, 1988) provide a framework for most of the exercises by allowing students to compare the data they collect from original sources to how they have been thinking about the historical development of psychology.

The other framework students are given at the beginning of the course deals with continuing themes that have been central to psychology throughout its history. After considerable class discussion, three themes emerge (with considerable guidance from the instructor): the mind-body relation, nature-nurture, and the problem of self-knowledge. In recent sections of the course, a philosophically oriented supplemental text by Flanagan (1991) was used to reinforce this thematic framework. Together, these philosophy of science and thematic frameworks provide a base for engaging students in critical thinking during their completion of the exercises .

Each of the major exercises I use is described briefly in the following sections. Comments about how difficult students found the exercise to do, how interesting they report it to be, and how educational they perceive it to be are based on evaluations made with a 5-point scale at the end of each exercise.

The Exercises

Finding Information on the History of Psychology

This is an introductory exercise that emphasizes the information-seeking skills important to the process of critical thinking. Students answer a series of questions that require them to find and use materials relevant to the history of psychology, including abstracts and bibliographies, journals, and books. One apparently simple task elicits considerable critical thinking. It involves identifying the oldest book on psychology in the university library (without the aid of a librarian). Students first must define psychology. Some define it broadly and identify a very old philosophical source (usually Greek). Others define it as modem psychology and identify a textbook with psychology from the late 19th or early 20th century. This exercise is rated as relatively easy (except for the old book question), low in interest value, but relatively high in educational value, perhaps because students find library resources they have never seen before.

Critical Analysis of a Journal Article

The purpose of this exercise is to introduce students to the Journal of the History of the Behavioral Sciences. It provides students with a model for critical thinking by exposing them to careful historical information gathering and analysis. The straightforward task is to select, summarize, and critique an article from any issue of the journal. Because of the generally high quality of the journal's articles, students rarely make incisive comments about the article itself. However, the articles usually model critical thinking well, and students are exposed to a resource they are unlikely to become familiar with in any other way. This exercise tends to be rated as easy to do, but it receives low ratings on interest and educational value. However, some students find an article that thoroughly interests them. In recent years, the most popular article, one chosen by many students, has been one by Benjamin, Rodgers, and Rosenbaum (1991) titled "CocaCola, Caffeine, and Mental Deficiency: Harry Hollingworth and the Chattanooga Trial of 1911."

Early Journals in Psychology

Journals covered in this exercise include American Journal of Psychology, Psychological Bulletin, and Journal of Experimental Psychology. Students look at two bound volumes, one of the first five volumes and one from 15 to 25 years later, of each of the journals published between 1887 and 1922. Students describe the types of materials included in the volumes (reports of empirical studies, literature reviews, book reviews, reports of conferences, obituaries, news items, etc.). They list the types of empirical investigations or theoretical issues addressed in each volume, and they discuss the major figures and theoretical positions they see represented in the journals.

After describing the content of the journals they have reviewed, students discuss the changes from the earlier versions to the later versions and the picture of psychology they get from these early journals compared to what is going on in the field today, particularly in terms of themes of mind-body, nature-nurture, and self-knowledge. Critical-thinking skills involved in this exercise are analysis and evaluation of the published literature and questioning assumptions about their textbook's vision of early psychology relative to what they actually see having been reported at the time.

Most students focus their responses on how similar the issues being dealt with around the turn of the century are to the major issues in current psychology. Students typically comment on the cognitive and biological nature of much of the work they see in the early journals (at least based on article titles). A common response is surprise about how little the major themes have changed over the past 80 to 100 years. For example, one student commented: "I think that we are re-embarking upon the work they started. Today's psychologists may think they are opening a totally new world, but actually we are only taking a second, much closer, look." The major differences they typically point out concern the lack of technological and statistical sophistication in the early journals and the relatively greater emphasis on philosophical issues. This exercise tends to be rated as relatively challenging to carry out, but it receives among the highest ratings for interest value and educational effect.

Psychological Bulletin: *Historical Trends*

This exercise expands on the early journals exercise by focusing students more closely on one journal over a longer period of time. The task is to select a volume of *Psychological Bulletin* from each of three periods (1905 to 1915, 1930 to 1940, and 1965 to 1985) and describe each one in terms of its structure (types and length of articles, notes, etc.) and content (types of problems and theories addressed, relative emphasis on areas of psychology, e.g., clinical, sensation and perception, physiology, developmental, social). Then, students select and briefly summarize two articles from each volume, one they think was important at the time it was published (along with an indication of why it was important) and one that still seems to be relevant. Finally, students discuss the changes they perceive to be represented in the three volumes in relation to what they know about the history of psychology. They often question their assumptions about the historical development of the discipline. If students have a Kuhnian perspective of nonoverlapping paradigms or believe the idea that the schools of psychology have represented a historical progression, they have some difficulty accommodating what they have discovered in this exercise.

Student discussions of changes over time represented in the three volumes parallel those for the early journals exercise. Students note the similarity in issues dealt with across the volumes. However, with a closer look at specific articles and articles from a longer span of time, students are more likely to report changes in the methodological sophistication of the work and an increasingly narrow focus in the articles. Student rationales for their selection of articles vary widely and correlate with their level of knowledge and their interests. Stronger students tend to link the importance of articles for the article's time to particular theoretical or historical issues or events. Some articles are selected because students recognize the author's name. Many students focus on applied issues and occasionally choose articles due to their novelty (e.g., "Much Ado About the Full Moon" and "Hallucinations and Delusions") or because of their breadth ("Memory," "Attention," "The Self," or, in early volumes, reviews of yearly progress in psychology). A common comment about the most recent period concerns the increasing emphasis on debates about purely methodological or statistical issues. For example, a student wrote the following:

> A person who knew nothing about psychology probably would conclude, after thumbing through the 1980 volume, that one of the main things psychologists do is to evaluate each other's evaluations of the importance and applicability of various statistical tests and data-interpretation methods.

This exercise tends to receive ratings of moderate difficulty and educational effect but high interest.

Textbook Comparisons

One way of tapping into historical trends is to examine the treatment of the discipline in basic introductory textbooks. This labor-intensive exercise allows students to examine how textbooks have treated the field throughout the history of psychology. This exercise involves the same critical-thinking processes as the exercises on early journals and *Psychological Bulletin* but with a different twist. Textbooks provide a clearer picture of how the discipline is structured and causes a discrepancy between the average psychology major's clinical orientation and the absence of clinical and developmental topics in much of the history of basic texts.

Students choose a textbook from two or three choices published in each of five periods separated by approximately 20 years, starting with James (1892) and Ladd (1894). The data-collecting aspect of the exercise requires that students: (a) find and record the author's definition of *psychology*, (b) use a checklist to summarize the chapter topics in the textbook (e.g., methods, physiological and biological foundations, and sensation and perception), (c) estimate the five most cited investigators in the index, and (d) estimate the relative frequency of citation of five theorists or clusters of theorists (Wundt-Titchener, Watson-Pavlov-Skinner, Wertheimer-Koffka-Köhler, Freud, and Piaget).

After gathering relevant information from the five textbooks, students discuss historical trends for each subset of data. Their response to the question about changes in the definition of psychology depends somewhat on the particular textbooks they select, but the typical trend reported is that early definitions were broad and inclusive with an emphasis on consciousness, became more focused on behavior in the middle years, and broadened somewhat to include the study of cognitive processes. Students frequently express some surprise at the breadth of the earliest definitions, often tying that breadth to psychology's links with philosophy. A common observation on changes in content is that developmental and social psychology do not appear as separate topics in most textbooks until the 1930s or 1940s. Students frequently comment on the absence of clinically oriented topics. The topic included in many of the early books that elicits the most comment from students is the will (or volition).

The question about investigators illustrates for students how little overlap there is from period to period. Their interpretation of this lack of overlap ranges from a straightforward indication of progress to evidence of paradigm change (as one student commented about the changes in names for this question, "To me, this indicates that psychology is a rapidly developing field and that investigators quickly become obsolete"). Sometimes students note the contrast between their response to this question and the one about major theorists: "Although we do learn about the few big names, the many small contributors through the years are often long forgotten." In response to the last question, students are almost always surprised by the late arrival of Freud and Piaget and the rapid and complete disappearance of Wundt and Titchener. The latter shakes their faith in the continuous, cumulative progress of the science. Sometimes students attain the insight that the history of psychology reflects the paradox of constant change and abiding sameness. As one student wrote at the bottom of her exercise: "I liked this exercise. It was beneficial to realize how, over time, psychology changes but that it always stays the same somehow." Students report that the datacollecting portion of this exercise is relatively easy to do but that the questions about changes over time are challenging. They rate it high on interest value and moderately high on educational value.

Boring's A History of Experimental Psychology

This exercise allows students to examine the changes that Boring (1929, 1950) made in his classic history of psychology textbook over a major period of growth in the discipline. Students read the prefaces of each edition, compare the tables of contents, and peruse the index looking for major changes. In the "Preface to the Second Edition," Boring outlined the changes he made and his rationale for the changes. Students look at the indexes to assess changes in who was being cited. Then, they look at the chapters on Gestalt psychology and behaviorism and discuss the changes they see. They also speculate on why the "General Survey" contained in the first edition was dropped. Finally, they read the chapter in the first edition titled "Review and Interpretation" and the chapter in the second edition titled "Retrospect," and they compare and contrast the two.

Probably because Boring (1929, 1950) was so clearly self-conscious about the changes he made, students are quite adept at describing and discussing the changes from the first to the second edition. They notice his increasing emphasis on the zeitgeist interpretation of history. The best responses to the exercises come from students who are sensitive to the change in tone in his attitude about the discipline's accomplishments from a relatively negative one to a positive, optimistic one. Student ratings indicate that they find this exercise to be one of the more challenging and educational ones, but they tend to rate it low in interest value.

A History of Psychology in Autobiography

Since 1930, eight volumes of *A History of Psychology in Autobiography* have been published. From these volumes, students select and read four individual biographies. They discuss several questions for each autobiography, including why the person would have been selected as a contributor; a summary of the stress each author put on influences from family, peers, and teachers in their intellectual development; and the student's perspective on the degree of modesty exhibited by the author. Then, students compare the backgrounds of the four psychologists they read about and discuss commonalties and differences in what seems to be important in the development of a great psychologist and great ideas.

In their textbook readings and in class discussions, students hear a good deal about the zeitgeist versus great person perspectives on the history of the field. Before doing this exercise, they also have read Boring's (1929, 1950) views on these two perspectives. Once again, questioning of assumptions frequently occurs as students deal with concrete examples of particularly influential psychologists, and they have to determine for themselves how important cultural and personal factors have been in these individual cases.

Women in Psychology

For this exercise, students first read Furumoto's (1979) article on Mary Whiton Calkins, Logan's (1980) article on Mary Cover Jones, and Gray's (1979) paper on historical treatment of female psychologists of distinction. Then, students read eight of the brief biographies of female psychologists from the two volumes published by Stevens and Gardner (1982), two each from the four periods the authors use ("pioneers," "era of acceptance," "the researchers," and "contemporary"). The questions about their readings focus on similarities and differences in the experiences of female psychologists in different eras, the problems of sexism encountered by women, the relative contributions of the women studied, and whether it is important to highlight the special contributions of women to psychology. The last question asks students to speculate on how women psychologists are likely to fare in the near future. This exercise probably causes the greatest discrepancy in relation to students' personal theories about the field. Students report that they have had little exposure to many of the early women pioneers and are often surprised there were any.

Like the autobiography exercise, this one is new. Based on initial reactions, it may be the most popular one. This exercise seems to fill a gap left by the history textbooks while encouraging students to think about the climate created for women by the discipline and its leaders and about how much, or how little, things have changed. (See Bohan, 1990, for a comprehensive approach to this topic.)

Summary

The exercises described herein have been useful in accomplishing several objectives. First, they help get students actively involved in thinking about the history of psychology. Second, the exercises put students into contact with original sources they are unlikely to see in other contexts. There seems to be something inherently educational about opening old, but important journals and books. Third, the exercises encourage directed thinking about the oversimplified histories necessarily provided in textbooks and limited class time. Many of the exercises pose questions that force students to examine their assumptions and reason carefully about the history of our discipline. Finally, compared to longer assignments like term papers, the work students do is spread across a semester with frequent opportunities for writing experiences and feedback.

References

Benjamin, L. T., Jr., Rodgers, A. M., & Rosenbaum, A. (1991). Coca-Cola, caffeine, and mental deficiency Harry Hollingworth and the Chattanooga trial of 1911.

Journal of the History of the Behavioral Sciences, 27, 42-55.

Bohan, J. S. (1990). Social constructionism and contextual history An expanded approach to the history of psychology. *Teaching of Psychology, 17,* 82-89.

Boring, E. G. (1929). *A history of experimental psychology.* New York: Appleton Century.

Boring, E. G. (1950). *A history of experimental psychology* (2nd ed.). New York: Appleton-Century-Crofts.

Ennis, R. H. (1985). A logical basis for measuring critical thinking skills. *Educational Leadership, 43,* 44-48.

Flanagan, O. (1991). *The science of the mind* (2nd ed.). Cambridge, MA: MIT Press.

Fummoto, L. (1979). Mary Whiton Calkins (1863-1930), fourteenth president of the American Psychological Association. *Journal of the History of the Behavioral Sciences, 15,* 346-356.

Gholson, B., & Barker, P. (1985). Kuhn, Lakatos, and Laudan: Applications in the history of physics and psychology. *American Psychologist, 40,* 755-769.

Gray, C. (1979, September). *Historical treatment of female psychologists of distinction.* Paper presented at the annual meeting of the American Psychological Association, New York.

Halonen, J. (Ed.). (1986). *Teaching critical thinking in psychology.* Milwaukee, WI: Alverno.

Halpern, D. F. (1989). *Thoughts and knowledge: An introduction to critical thinking* (2nd ed.). Hillsdale, NJ: Lawrence Erlbaum Associates, Inc.

Henderson, B. B. (1988). What students know about the history of psychology before taking the course. *Teaching of Psychology, 15,* 204-205.

James, W. (1892). *Psychology, briefer course.* New York: Holt.

Kuhn, T. S. (1970). *The structure of science revolutions* (2nd ed.) . Chicago: University of Chicago Press.

Ladd, G. T. (1894). *Primer of psychology.* New York: Scribner.

Laudan, L. (1977). *Progress and its problems.* Berkeley: University of California Press.

Logan, D. D. (1980). Mary Cover Jones: Feminine as asset. *Psychology of Women Quarterly, 5,* 103-115.

McMillan, J. H. (1987). Enhancing college students' critical thinking: A review of studies. *Research in Higher Education, 26,* 3-29.

McPherson, M. W. (1979). Different approaches to teaching the history of psychology: Excerpts from a 1977 APA symposium. *Psychological Record, 29,* 65-70.

Raphelson, A. C. (1982). The history course as the capstone of the psychology curriculum. *Journal of the History of the Behavioral Sciences, 18,* 279-285.

Stevens, G., & Gardner, S. (1982) . *The women of psychology* (Vols. I & 11). Cambridge, MA: Schenkman.

Of Theater, Pedagogy, and the History of Psychology: An Exploration

Susan E. Rhoads
Randall D. Wight
Ouachita Baptist University

During the American Psychological Association's 1993 meeting in Toronto, Kurt Danziger (1993) challenged the discipline to assume responsibility for its own historiography. To paraphrase Einstein (as cited in Andrews, 1987, p. 260), the art of teaching is the awakening of joy in creative expression and knowledge. A loose combination of Danziger's and Einstein's ideas suggests that psychologists who teach the discipline's history must find ways to capture their students' imaginations if psychology is to accept responsibility for its historiography.

Benjamin (1991) lamented that few—inordinately few—young psychologists are willing to meet the discipline's historiographic challenge. If, as Danziger (1993) suggested, our very subject matter requires historiographic sophistication and if, as Benjamin suggested, the upcoming generation of psychologists finds little that interests them in the discipline's historiography, then teachers of the discipline's history need to work more diligently to find and employ pedagogical techniques that awaken joy in historical scholarship and knowledge. We offer a device that, we hope, approximates this goal. We are not so naive as to believe our proposal to be a panacea, but in light of Danziger's and Benjamin's concerns, we present the device in hopes of generating a pedagogical discussion leading to the fruition of Einstein's insight in history of psychology courses.

Theater is an excellent place to explore complex concepts (e.g., Gergen, 1990) and to juxtapose disparate ideas, times, or people (e.g., Wight & Ware, 1992). Theater permits students to examine intricate concepts while exploring the humanness of the individuals from whom those concepts emerged. Our assumption is that, if students can find ways to explore the lives and times involved in the history of psychology, then these students might demonstrate a greater affinity for historical scholarship and the role it can play (no pun intended) within the discipline at large. Theater—whether performance or playwriting—is a natural tool for teaching the history of psychology.

The naturalness of historical theater is, at least, threefold. First, playwriting permits students to explore the interpersonal medium from which disciplinary achievements arise in a manner that subverts the great-minds-having-great-thoughts and-making-great-advances mythology that often passes for psychology's "history." Students need to think of humans investigating psychological matters qua human-making mistakes, experiencing false starts, being petty, arriving at new insights. Second, investigating the interpersonal dynamics of historical figures necessitates engaging in a foundational historical activity: the examination of primary source material such as letters and diaries (Cadwallader, 1975; Furumoto, 1989). Third, the performance of student-written plays provides opportunities for both performers and audience to encounter psychology's history in vibrant, memorable fashion.

Theater-as-pedagogy has at least two difficulties. First, abstractions and concepts are difficult to capture or embody on stage. We are not suggesting that doing so is impossible but that doing so might be difficult for many undergraduates. Second, instructors must remain vigilant to ensure that historical accuracy does not fall prey to creative license. This vigilance need not be without latitude. To illustrate, although the drama that follows is entirely consistent with current historical understanding both of James and Munsterberg and of their career paths, the actual voice employed is that of the late 20th century. This negative can thus become a positive if judicious license helps facilitate student empathy for the principles and concepts within the drama.

What follows is Susan E. Rhoad's response to an undergraduate history of psychology assignment in which students were to construct a stageable dialogue between figures from the discipline's history. The assignment directed students to rely as much as possible on primary sources—including direct quotations—and to find ways to bring the characters to life. The assignment's instructions suggested certain issues might prove useful in centering dramatic focus. These issues included the ontology, epistemology, and causality of psychological phenomena; the methods, data definitions, research practices, and subject-experimenter roles employed by different people at different times; and the professional, political, economic, social, and power contexts in which psychologists have worked. What follows is clearly product. Once pointed to available primary source material, students had to rely on their own devices as they struggled with the issues in the texts: Creativity was a priority.

Shhhh, the curtain is rising....

Cast of Characters

- William James, age is unimportant but must be older than Munsterberg (J)
- Hugo Munsterberg (M)
- Subtext for James, male or female, age unimportant (SJ)
- Subtext for Munsterberg, male or female, age unimport ant (SM)

Stage directions are set in italics.

The Play

Two chairs, spaced approximately 2 m apart, are on a blank stage. The stage is dark except for two pools of light illuminating the chairs. James and Munsterberg enter at the same time from opposite wings, walk directly to the chairs, and sit down. They both assume relaxed postures; no sudden movements.

J: "Is it conceivable that if you should be invited, you might agree to come and take charge of the Psychological Laboratory and the higher instruction in that subject in Harvard University for three years? This is a private question of my own and not an inquiry on the part of our University authorities. My mind is in travail with plans for regenerating our philosophical department, and the importation of you has come to figure amongst the hypothetical elements of the case. I cannot, of course, go on with the combinations till I know whether or not that particular feature is impossible. So pray tell me" (Perry, 1935, pp. 138-139).

M: "I scarcely need assure you, my dear professor, that it would be a special joy and honor to work at your side and under your protection" (Bjork, 1983, p. 48). However, I do have some reservations about leaving Germany. I had hoped to advance and work within the German university system.

The two subtext actors walk onstage from opposite wings and stand directly behind James and Munsterberg. These actors may make appropriate movements to the subtext lines they speak. They may gesticulate or approach one another and even interact with one another as necessary.

J: "We are the best university in America, and we must lead in psychology . . . [Being aged fifty years, I dislike] laboratory work and [am] accustomed to teach[ing] philosophy at large[.]... I could [, though.] ... make the laboratory run, yet [I] am certainly not the stuff to make a first-rate director thereof. ... We need a man of genius if possible" (Perry, 1935, p. 139).

SJ: [*turns toward Münsterberg*] The kind of monotonous lab work you do could only go on in a country where the people cannot be bored. I need your zeal for the work because I have to get out of the lab. It bores me. I have other interests now. If you don't come to Harvard, I'll never be free.

M: I am still hesitant about coming to Harvard and am not sure I would fare well in the United States. I have trouble with English and am afraid of being trans—planted.

SM: [*turns to James*] I'm brilliant. I should be able to advance in the German University system and want to advance here because of the prestige German universities hold over American universities. The great tradition in psychology is here and not in Boston.

J: "At your age, and with your facility, I am sure the language won't trouble you after the first year. The German brain always manages, in a couple of years, to get along with a foreign tongue" (Bjork, 1983, p. 49). Concerning your move to America, I'm sure it will be a little strange and lonely at first, but once you get involved in your work, you will become accustomed to it quite quickly.

SJ: [turns to Münsterberg] You obstinate fool. Your English is a point of concern, but you'll adjust. I'll say anything necessary to get you here, dangle any carrot in front of your nose. You're the best person for the job. You are somewhat arrogant, but you're still brilliant and I'm determined to get you to Harvard. I must get out of the lab; it's driving me mad! I want to concentrate on my philosophical studies.

Freeze momentarily to indicate a brief passage of time.

J: "A telegram arrives from you 'joyfully accepting the call.' ... I believe that this has been the best stroke I ever did for our University!... It is an enormous relief to me to see the responsibility for experimental psychology in Harvard transferred from my feeble and unworthy shoulders to those of a man as competent as you" (Perry, 1935, p. 140).

To indicate a passage of time and a different phase in their relations, the light fades to black with only floor lights behind the scrim remaining to permit the figures to be seen. Lights then rise slowly to illuminate the two principals.

J: Munsterberg, my dear colleague, you are too deterministic. Your theories concerning will leave no place for choice. Fiat is an important element in will. The consciousness does exert a force on physical processes.

M: James, I have to insist that will is nothing more than the association of acts and consequences in memory. Memory is the illusion of will. Human actions are strictly deterministic.

SJ: [*alarmed*] Your German foolishness has gone too far! You leave out all hope for free will, for choice. I've spent so many years agonizing over whether humans are strictly governed by laws or whether we have any choice in the matter of our own actions, and now you tell me unequivocally, in your snobbish German way, that it is all an illusion?

SM: [*coldly*] You are such an intelligent man to be such a simpleton. I can't tolerate your wildly unscientific outlook. You're just a philosopher trying to be a scientist; you, sir, are an imposter!

J: Why does your science have to be so schematized? Everything will not fit in a pigeon-hole. "I am satisfied with a free and wild nature" (Hale, 1980, p. 6); a fact that my pluralism makes quite evident. "You seem to me to cherish and pursue an Italian Garden, where all things are kept in separate compartments, and one must follow straight-ruled walks" (pp. 6-7). Science is not an absolute; we all come to it with basic assumptions about the world.

SJ: You pompous ass. You've been in the laboratory so long, studying your little numbers and instruments, that you've forgotten what the real world is like. The world you live in is a narrow, shallow, ordered, little world without depth and fullness.

M: "Our life's duty makes us gardeners, makes us to unweed the weeds of sin and error and ugliness and when we finally come to think over what flowers were left as valuable, and we bring together those which are similar—then we have finally indeed such an Italian garden as the world which we are seeking, as the world which has to be acknowledged as ultimate" (Hale, 1980, p. 7).

SM: Your silly, wild theories annoy me. Theory that lacks any shred of scientific order and method sickens me. You're trying to throw science back into an age of myth and fancy. If it were up to you, we would probably still believe that all is governed by fate and chance and that only God knows the future. People are deterministic; there is no room for free will, it is too unpredictable. You want to hold onto it because you are afraid. Of what are you afraid?

SJ: [*the debate is now growing heated and the two subtext actors or actresses face each other in a combative stance*] Your science would destroy my very being: Life cannot be completely measured in the laboratory; it is spontaneous and unpredictable.

SM: You speak of an aberration! Life has order, meaning! We measure and study it in the lab! [*more calmly*] If the cosmos and humanity itself were truly that chaotic, how could there be any practical applications for psychology? I've developed all sorts of uses for "our" science-for example, a lie-detector test and tests for vocational ability. My scientific rigor has been fruitful. Has yours? If all humanity were governed merely by chance, none of these developments would be of any use. In fact, why even bother at all!

SJ: [*somewhat pleading*] I never implied science has no meaning. But I object to the removal of plurality. Your science leaves no room for the individual! I . . .

SM: Shut up you babbling fool! Your "science" is not science. The future of psychology is determinism, experimentation, rigorous scientific method. There will be nothing left of your ridiculous ideas to cloud the reason of future psychologists.

The subtext actors for Munsterberg and James begin to fight. After a brief, choreographed scuffle, Munsterberg's subtext arises the winner, leaving James's subtext on the ground. James's subtext stays on stage on the ground surrounded by a red light. Munsterberg's subtext exits. James and Munsterberg arise from their chairs amicably shake hands, and exit to opposite sides of the stage.

Blackout

References

Andrews, R. (Ed.). (1987). *The concise Columbia dictionary of quotations*. New York: Columbia University Press.

Benjamin, L. T., Jr. (1991, August). *The present and future of psychology's past: History for nonhistorians*. Paper presented at the meeting of the American Psychological Association, San Francisco.

Bjork, D. W. (1983). *The compromised scientist: William James in the development of American psychology*. New York: Columbia University Press.

Cadwallader, T. C. (1975). Unique values of archival research. *Journal of the History of the Behavioral Sciences, 11*, 27-33.

Danziger, K. (1993, August). *Three challenges for the history of psychology*. Paper presented at the meeting of the American Psychological Association, Toronto, Canada.

Furumoto, L. (1989) . The new history of psychology. In I. S. Cohen (Ed.), *The G. Stanley Hall Lecture Series* (Vol. 9, pp. 5-34). Washington, DC: American Psychological Association.

Gergen, M. (1990). From mod masculinity to postmod macho: A feminist replay. *The Humanist Psychologist, 18*, 95-104.

Hale, M. H., Jr. (1980). *Human science and social order: Hugo Munsterberg and the origins of applied psychology*. Philadelphia: Temple University Press.

Perry, R. B. (1935). *The thought and character of William James*. Boston: Little, Brown.

Wight, R. D., & Ware, M. E. (1992, November). *An evening with James and Hall*. Performance presented at the Southwest Conference for Teachers of Psychology, Ft. Worth, TX.

Notes

1. The first author is presently a University of Memphis graduate student.

2. An earlier version of this article appeared in the Division 26 (the History of Psychology Division of the American Psychological Association) newsletter.

A Role-Playing Exercise for the History of Psychology Course

Charles I. Brooks
King's College

Shaklee (1957) describes an exercise for the History of Psychology course in which students portray renowned psychologists. This format allows for panel discussions and speeches among people such as Pavlov, Watson, Ebbinghaus, and Wundt. Benjamin (1981) has also suggested the possibility of using this role-playing technique as an instructional device. For the past 5 years, I have used this method in three classes that were much larger (30-40 students) than Shaklee's (12-17 students), and have experimented with some variations on the basic technique, some of which seem to work better than others.

In the standard procedure, I divide the class into sin teams of six to seven players each. The individuals to be portrayed are specified, and the students decide which role a team member will play.

The general instructions on the course syllabus are as follows:

Periodically during the semester, a class will be devoted to a team presentation. This presentation will involve each member of the team playing the role of a particular person from the history of psychology. In this way, we should generate some interesting discussions and confrontations (e.g., Skinner and Freud).

Team assignments will be made during the second class. Each team will be responsible for assigning roles and for developing a 30-minute play, scene, debate, whatever you want to call it, for presentation in class. Each team member should have an equal part in the play and will be graded separately.

The purpose of this exercise, of course, is to make some important figures in psychology come to life, and to imagine some of the things they might have discussed. Thus, it is very important to match the script to the positions, arguments, and ideas of the individuals being portrayed.

Some sample roles I have used for teams are as follows: (a) Locke, Hartley, Reid, Kant, Brown, J. S. Mill; (b) J. Muller, Gall, Broca, Fechner, Wundt, Helmholtz; (c) Wundt, Locke, Lotze, Brentano, Kulpe, Titchener; (d) Wundt, James, Pavlov, Angell, Sechenov, Titchener, Galton; (e) Thorndike, Watson, J. S. Mill, Descartes, Darwin, Morgan; (f) Köhler, Rogers, Kant, Watson,

Skinner, Freud, Locke. The presentations are scheduled only after the individuals portrayed have been covered in the course.

Students are expected to research their roles using a minimum of three sources (not including the text), one of which is a primary source. Each student also prepares a 300- to 400-word summary of the position of the individual portrayed, and a discussion of how that position compares with one other character portrayed on the team. The paper serves as a "closing argument" delivered on whatever issue was discussed by the team.

For the actual presentation, members of each team are free to coordinate the different roles in any way they wish. The only requirement is that each team member have approximately equal time in the presentation. Many of the presentations have been ingenious in the coordination of scripts and props to settings meaningful to the students. One skit re-created a local student watering hole, with Wundt the bartender patiently serving and listening to the likes of Brentano and Külpe discussing the nature of thought. Another group used the "This is Your Life" format, with psychologists from the past surprising the course professor, who was the unsuspecting guest. On another occasion, a stuffed dog was rigged with a rubber hose so that when Pavlov rang a cowbell, water literally gushed from the dog's mouth into a bucket. The effect was enhanced when Pavlov rang the bell while Titchener was making a point about the value of introspection. One particularly memorable performance was modeled after "Family Feud." Imagine Darwin as master of ceremonies asking contestants Watson and Descartes to "Give two innate ideas of the mind." (Descartes pressed the buzzer first. Watson's team, however, eventually won the grand prize: a voyage around the world on the *Beagle*).

I have tried some variations on the basic technique and have found some to work better than others. The presentations, for instance, are generally much more effective when students were allowed to form their own teams. When I randomly assigned students to teams, the "chemistry" of some of the teams was often lacking, and they gave somewhat ill prepared presentations. In the classes where the students formed their own teams, the presentations were generally much more sophisticated, lively, and informative. In these cases, the exercise was clearly social as well as academic, and the students learned much about group dynamics, cooperation, and productivity.

Originally, I required only the class presentation and the list of sources used to prepare for the session. This procedure made grading very difficult because it was hard to separate the substance of a student's role from the quality of the performance. I now base the grade (which counts 10% toward the course grade) primarily on the paper, along with how well the student represents a particular position during the class presentation. Evaluation of the latter is helped during class discussion following the team exercise. In fact, sufficient class time should be allowed for such discussion because the other students are usually eager to question the participants.

I have scheduled team sessions periodically throughout the semester, or have delayed them until close to the end of the course. The latter schedule gives more flexibility regarding team make-up. If a session is scheduled around the middle of the term, for instance, inclusion of 20th-century figures not yet covered in the course is precluded.

Students generally view the exercise as a positive experience and a worthwhile addition to the course. The mean rating on a 5-point scale (1 = *not at all worthwhile*, 5 = *extremely worthwhile*) over three classes (N = 117) was 4.63. Many students also commented informally that they thought they would remember their role and the importance of their person in the development of psychology long after other aspects of the course material were forgotten.

Overall, I view the exercise positively and plan to repeat it periodically. My experience supports those of Shaklee (1957) and of Balch (1983), who used role-playing in general psychology classes to demonstrate client-centered therapy. The students clearly get involved. Trying to be someone else, rather than merely conveying positions and principles in a term paper, makes students active and independent learners. They are forced to try to get "under the skin" of a Wundt or a Thorndike and, on the basis of their independent research, imagine how they might have responded to a critic or a supporter. The historical figures in psychology become more than words on a page.

I have also found that the exercise allows students to discover a continuity in the development of psychology. As they are forced to develop interactions among characters of different time periods, they see linkages of thought not previously apparent. Students often have difficulty in uncovering common threads and developmental trends across figures from different time periods. The role-playing exercise brings these figures together and fosters more integrative thinking.

References

Balch, W. R. (1983). The use of role-playing in a classroom demonstration of client-centered therapy. *Teaching of Psychology, 10*, 173-174.

Benjamin, L. T., Jr. (1981). *Teaching history of psychology: A handbook*. New York: Academic Press.

Shaklee, A. B. (1957). Autobiography in teaching history of psychology. *American Psychologist, 12*, 282-283.

Scientific Eminence, the History of Psychology, and Term Paper Topics: A Metascience Approach

Dean Keith Simonton
University of California, Davis

One of the essential courses in any psychology program covers the history of the discipline. History of psychology courses often require students to write a term paper on some special aspect of the subject. In this article, I describe a particular approach to term paper assignments that has proven quite successful. This approach requires the student to focus on a single "great person" in the discipline's history and to analyze that individual from a distinctive point of view. The instructions may begin as follows:

Critics of our discipline sometimes complain that psychology has yet to produce a genuine scientific genius, like a Newton or a Pasteur. For your term paper, you must evaluate this claim's validity with respect to a single major figure in our discipline's history. Through a detailed study of your subject's life and career, you must determine whether he or she fits the profile typical of an eminent scientist.

These instructions create two problems for the student. First, the student must decide whom to select as the subject of this evaluative essay. To help the student, the course syllabus includes two lists: (a) recipients of the Distinguished Scientific Contribution Award from the American Psychological Association (as updated annually in the *American Psychologist*) and (b) the 190 psychologists identified by Zusne (1987) as the figures discussed in the most textbooks on the history of psychology. In addition, students are advised to consult several biographical dictionaries, bibliographies, and autobiographical anthologies on reserve at the university library (e.g., *A History of Psychology in Autobiography*, 1930–1989, Scarborough & Furumoto, 1987, Watson, 1974-1976). These resources help to ensure that students will pick a subject for whom there is adequate information.

The second problem is more difficult: How does one gauge whether a particular psychologist manifests the generic qualities of an eminent scientist? Here the students must take advantage of the rich literature found in the metasciences (Gholson, Shadish, Neimeyer, & Houts, 1988). A *metascience* is any field of inquiry that takes science as its subject matter. The metasciences include the history, philosophy, sociology, and psychology of science. The last metascience is of special value in composing the term paper. Among the questions addressed by a psychology of science is the basis for creativity and influence in science. Classic inquiries include books by Galton (1874) and Roe (1952), and active research on this subject continues. Using this accumulated body of findings, one can compose a broad profile of the typical eminent scientist (Simonton, 1988). Hence, once students understand the key features of this profile, they can use it as a comparative benchmark for assessing the subject of their term paper.

In my course, students acquire the necessary information from three sources. First, as part of a general discussion of the metasciences, a whole lecture is devoted to the psychology of science, with special emphasis on the psychology of creators in science. Second, students are given access to books and articles that review the literature on scientific creativity (e.g., Fisch, 1977; Jackson & Rushton, 1987; Mansfield & Busse, 1981; Simonton, 1988; Taylor & Barron, 1963). These resources include studies that specifically examine eminence and creativity in psychological science (e.g., Helmreich, Spence, Beane, Lucker, & Matthews, 1980; Simonton, 1992; Wispé, 1965). Third, students get a handout titled "Tips on What to Look for in the Subject of Your Term Paper." The main portion of this handout appears in the appendix.

No psychologist will fit the profile perfectly. Even a Galileo or an Einstein will exhibit discrepancies from the overall pattern on many points. Moreover, students are warned that one may attain eminence by other than scientific means and that, even within science, luminaries may cluster into several types. The full handout closes with the following admonition:

> In making these linkages, remember that I don't expect a simple yes/no vote. Your subject may fit the typical picture according to some criteria but depart from the profile according to other criteria. For instance, some of you may be dealing with someone whose genius took an artistic turn. Others of you may be studying a scientist who attained eminence for achievements that required no genuine creativity. Even within science, we can distinguish between practitioners of "revolutionary" versus "normal" science or between classical and romantic scientists. So be flexible. The portrait of your subject will most likely be painted in diverse shades of gray rather than in black and white.

This handout may be a crucial feature of the assignment. In the first few years of teaching the history of psychology using this approach, the average rating students gave the assignment was 4.1 on a 5-point scale, with the course as a whole averaging a 4.4 rating. After I added this handout, these averages increased to 4.4 for the assignment and 4.8 for the course.

In general, this term paper assignment is highly recommended. One advantage stems from the great person approach itself. For instance, when students focus on a single individual of their choice, the chosen psychologist can serve as a role model. Many women and members of underrepresented minorities select prominent psychologists of their own gender or ethnicity. Yet, the approach has assets that go beyond those of any great person analysis. First, students cannot simply repeat what they find in biographical sources. Instead, they must weight each datum about a psychologist's life or career against the profile of an eminent scientist and judge its implications accordingly. Most students, and especially the best ones, find this intellectual challenge very stimulating and rewarding. Furthermore, the adopted analytical framework coincides with the discussion of the metasciences in many history of psychology textbooks. In particular, several standard texts discuss theories of scientific innovation and some key findings in the psychology of science. Hence, students learn how the psychology of science contributes to our understanding of great scientists, including psychologists. Students thereby acquire a twofold lesson—one in the history of psychology and the other in the psychology of science.

References

Fisch, R. (1977). Psychology of science. In I. Spiegel-Rösing & D. Price (Eds.), *Science, technology, and society: A cross-discipline perspective* (pp. 277-318). London Sage.

Galton, F. (1874). *English men of science: Their nature and nurture*. London Macmillan.

Gholson, B., Shadish, W. R., Jr., Neimeyer, R. A., & Houts, A. C. (Eds.). (1988). *The psychology of science: Contributions to metascience*. New York: Cambridge University Press.

Helmreich, R. L., Spence, J. T., Beane, W. E., Lucker, G. W., & Matthews, K. A. (1980). Making it in academic psychology: Demographic and personality correlates of attainment. *Journal of Personality and Social Psychology, 39*, 896-908.

A history of psychology in autobiography. (1930-1989). New York: Russell & Russell.

Jackson, D. N., & Rushton, J. P. (Eds.). (1987). *Scientific excellence: Origins and assessment*. Beverly Hills: Sage.

Mansfield, R. S., & Busse, T. V. (1981). *The psychology of creativity and discovery: Scientists and their work*. Chicago: Nelson-Hall.

Roe, A. (1952). *The making of a scientist*. New York: Dodd, Mead.

Scarborough, E., & Furumoto, L. (1987). *Untold lives: The first generation of American woman psychologists*. New York: Columbia University Press.

Simonton, D. K. (1988). *Scientific genius: A psychology of science*. New York: Cambridge University Press.

Simonton, D. K. (1992). Leaders of American psychology, 1879-1967: Career development, creative output, and professional achievement. *Journal of Personality and Social Psychology, 62*, 5-17.

Taylor, C. W., & Barron, F. X. (Eds.). (1963). *Scientific creativity: Its recognition and development*. New York: Wiley.

Watson, R. I. (Ed.). (1974-1976). *Eminent contributors to psychology* (Vols. 1 & 2). New York: Springer.

Wispé, L G. (1965). Some social and psychological correlates of eminence in psychology. *Journal of the History of the Behavioral Sciences, 7*, 88-98.

Zusne, L. (1987). Contributions to the history of psychology: XLIV. Coverage of contributors in histories of psychology. *Psychological Reports, 61*, 343-350

Appendix

Term Paper Handout on the Typical Profile of Eminent Scientists

To guide your biographical search, I provide some questions that you should ask yourself when pouring through the information about the subject of your paper.

You will not necessarily obtain answers to all questions, and you do not need to adhere to this particular order.

Background. What was his or her birth order? What kind of family was he or she born into in terms of socioeconomic class, professional status of parents, diversity of their backgrounds, and so on? Was the family environment stable or unstable, traumatic or bland? For example, did your subject suffer the experience of orphanhood? Were there any role models available that guided him or her in the choice of occupation and domain of achievement? Was your person popular with peers or a loner? Any disabilities? Was he or she extremely precocious or talented early in childhood? Any instances of "crystallizing experiences" that launched the individual on a scientific career?

Education. How well did your subject do in school? In college? What level of formal education did he or she attain? If a PhD or other higher degree was earned, was it received at an unusually young or old age? Were there any teachers who served a special mentor role in your person's intellectual or academic development? Was your subject's training marginal or central to the domain in which eminence was ultimately obtained? If an outsider, did that marginal background leave an impression on your subject's distinctive contribution?

Personality. Was he or she highly intelligent, perhaps even possessing a "genius-level" intellect? Independent and nonconformist? Introverted? Risk taking? Hardworking, even workaholic? Did he or she have broad intellectual interests? Any evidence of psychopathology, such as manic depression, neurosis, or mild psychosis? Any instances of psychopathology in close relatives that might help explain your subject's idiosyncrasies?

Thought processes. Was your subject an intuitive thinker? Any examples of leaps of imagination or inspiration? Or was your subject extremely analytical and logical in approaching questions? Was there a sense of purpose, of destiny underlying his or her work? Was everything, no matter how diverse, connected by some central theme or preoccupation? What role did chance play? Any examples of serendipity?

Career development. What kind of professional positions were occupied? For example, did he or she attain a professorship at a distinguished university? Did your subject establish connections with a considerable number of notable colleagues? Or was he or she professionally isolated? What about the number of students and followers? Collaborators or rivals? Did your subject receive any contemporary recognition, such as special honors or awards? In the individual's final years, did he or she become the defender of a newly established status quo, rejecting the innovative ideas that were to become important in the next generation?

Productivity. At what age did he or she first make a contribution to the field? Was this unusually young or old? At what age did your subject produce his or her single best work or "masterpiece"? Did this contribution come out at the typical age for the discipline? And at what age was the last contribution made? Was this at an exceptionally advanced age? What was the total number of works produced? How does this compare with what you would expect? Did the rate of productivity rise to some peak and then decline in a fashion you would anticipate or were there some surprises? Any instances of some "swan song"—some final work conceived shortly before death that encapsulated in a distinctive manner the entire course of a career? How influential were your subject's works in that person's own time and in later generations? Any disastrous mistakes that exerted a profound influence on the discipline?

Zeitgeist. Did your subject fit in with the mood of the times? Or was your person ahead of the zeitgeist? Were your subject's ideas rejected by contemporaries so that he or she experienced an uphill fight to fame? Or did celebrity status come easily? Can you identify any examples of *multiples*? That is, did anyone else come up with the same ideas as your subject at roughly the same time? Finally, what were the general economic, political, social, and cultural conditions in which your subject worked? Economic prosperity? Peace or war? Political or ethnic oppression? Did the general milieu help or hinder your person in achieving greatness?

Final influence. What was your subject's ultimate impact in making psychology a legitimate science? Did he or she move the field forward, placing the discipline closer to other recognized sciences? Or was your subject's effect on the field negative, lowering our discipline's status as a science? Did your subject even aspire to make psychology a science? In answering this last question, please be clear what you mean by a *science*. Do you mean a *natural* or *exact* science? Or do you mean a *human* science? If the former, what criteria do you use to define a *hard science*? Empiricism? Mathematics or quantification? Theoretical rigor? Falsifiability? If you mean a *soft science*, then by what criteria do you judge whether someone has made a scientific advance?

In addressing the foregoing questions, please remember to make explicit what your answers tell us about the fundamental theme of your essay—whether or not your individual fits the profile of a "scientific genius."

2. EXPANDING STUDENTS' KNOWLEDGE

The Create-A-Game Exam: A Method to Facilitate Student Interest and Learning

Joy L. Berrenberg
Ann Prosser
University of Colorado at Denver

Multiple-choice exams, short-answer exams, essay exams, oral exams, term papers, and class projects are traditional methods for assessing a student's mastery of course material. Although all such evaluations should engage the student in the process of reviewing and synthesizing the course material, many students, even the brightest, apply the "least effort principle" in their preparations. Often their review is cursory and involves rote memorization rather than organized analysis.

It is generally assumed that students learn and retain more when they are actively and personally involved with the course material. Although a number of class projects facilitate this type of involvement (e.g., Brožek & Schneider, 1973; Coffield, 1973; Gurman, Holliman, & Camperell, 1988; McAdam, 1987), relatively few examination procedures incorporate this active approach. One example of such an approach allows students to comment on or justify their answers on multiple-choice exams (Dodd & Leal, 1988; Nield & Wintre, 1986). This procedure encourages more thinking and less rote memorization. Another procedure involves innovative and integrative essay questions in a History of Psychology course (Berrenberg, 1990). Presumably, such questions force students to organize and synthesize the material. Benjamin (1979) described an exam "game" in which teams of students compete to identify portraits of famous figures in psychology. He suggested that the element of fun in this kind of exam helps to motivate students to learn more. Ackil (1986) and Carlson (1989) described two teacher-designed games that motivate students to learn factual material and prepare for exams. Note, however, that these last examples are not used to evaluate student performance.

To expand the options for active, personally involving evaluation procedures, we developed an examination technique in which students create a game for a particular subject area. The procedure is designed to engage students' creative talents and to encourage detailed review and synthesis of course material. Unlike assignments that require students to write their own exam questions, the create-a-game exam requires students to develop a structure (e.g., game categories) to present factual material. In many instances, it also requires students to make fine distinctions regarding the difficulty of the material (e.g., how many points to offer for a correct answer). Furthermore, the number of questions students prepare for a game usually exceeds the number requested for a write-your-own exam exercise (most students write 100 or more questions), thus requiring a more thorough review of course material. Finally, the create-a-game exam encourages students to think about and present material in creative and innovative ways that may improve understanding as well as retention.

Our approach can be readily adapted to any course in psychology and used to supplement or replace other evaluation methods. The resulting games may be played with fellow class members, thus providing additional review of course content. What follows is a description of the create-a-game technique developed in a History of Psychology course.

Procedures and Grading

We have used the create-a-game exam as part of a take home exam in a senior level History of Psychology course. Students answer one or more integrative essay questions and develop a History of Psychology game. Working individually, students have 2 weeks to complete the exam and game. Instructions for the game portion of the exam are:

Create a "History of Psychology Game." It may be a board game, word game, trivia game, or whatever. It must cover a broad range of information pertinent to the history of psychology. Include rules, game board, game pieces, or whatever is needed to play the game. Have fun and be creative!

Your game will graded on the basis of (a) the accuracy of information, (b) the breadth of coverage (e.g., game covers a variety of historical time periods, events, theories, ideas, figures in the history of psychology), (c) your understanding of course material as evidenced in meaningful organization of game material (e.g., information is grouped into appropriate categories, such as Greek Philosophers, French Positivism, Neo-Behaviorists), (d) neatness of game materials (e.g., readable instructions, game cards), and (e) originality.

We do not provide examples of games because we do not want to limit creativity. Although we have used the procedure as an individual project, it should also work well as a group assignment.

Most students satisfy the criteria so the resulting distribution of exam scores is negatively skewed. The proportion of students who do a substandard job on the game is lower than it is for other assignments. We generally make the game portion of the exam worth 25% of the course grade, which seems appropriate for the amount of time and effort involved.

The completed games, or some sample thereof, can be effective teaching techniques. We have used one full class period before an objective exam to allow students to play the games of their choice as a way of providing painless review of material.

Examples of Games

The most common games include take-offs on Jeopardy, Trivial Pursuit, and Life. Four examples of games developed by students are described next.

1. Psychological Trivia. In this game, the players compete for points by correctly answering questions from one of several categories (e.g., functionalism, psychoanalysis, the mind-body problem). The easiest questions in a category are worth 100 points (e.g., Who was the founder of psychoanalysis?); the most difficult questions are worth 500 points (e.g., What is the title and publication date of Dewey's famous "founding" paper on functionalism?).

2. Freud's Inner Circle. The object of this game is to move Freudian tokens (e.g., small cigars, toilet seats) around a game board, answer questions correctly, and accumulate enough points to move to Freud's inner circle in the middle of the game board. Once in the circle, players must demonstrate their knowledge of Freud's position or risk getting "kicked out." Variations of this basic "board and dice" game have been called The Rat Maze, The Therapeutic Couch, The Funny Farm, and Psychomania.

3. Psych-Out. This game consists of a board with photographs of famous figures in the history of psychology. Upon landing on a square associated with a particular face, players must name the figure and as many of his or her contributions to psychology as possible. The more they know, the more points they earn.

4. Psychogories. This game is similar to Gin Rummy or Go Fish; the object is to be the first to accumulate complete sets of cards. Players are dealt 10 cards, each of which states a theory, belief, or assumption (e.g.,

reinforcement plays an important role in learning, higher mental processes cannot be studied experimentally). Cards are drawn and discarded until a player's hand is full of completed sets. A set consists of three or more theoretically compatible cards (e.g., all ideas held in common by behaviorists, gestaltists). Psychogories is a conceptually challenging game because the categories are not indicated on the cards and players must determine for themselves which ideas constitute sets.

Student Response

Students are generally enthusiastic about the create-a-game exam. This enthusiasm is demonstrated by the amount of time and effort they put into their creations: one student sculpted and fired ceramic game pieces, another hand-printed 200 question cards in beautiful calligraphy, another found and copied onto the game board old photographs of Wundt's lab and other psychological memorabilia. In a recent term, 63% of the students in a class of 65 found designing the game to be an "extremely useful" method for learning course material, and 77% said using the games for review was an "extremely useful" way to spend class time. Many students spontaneously mentioned the create-a-game procedure in the comment section of the course evaluation. One student said the procedure was a "refreshing change" from traditional exams. Another said designing the game helped him to "learn history inside-out." Others described the exam as "personally involving," "lots of fun," "a really worthwhile exercise," and "a painless way to learn."

In conclusion, the create a-game technique is a method for evaluation that actively engages students in the review and organization of course material. It could easily be incorporated into a variety of courses.

References

Ackil, J. E. (1986). PhysioPursuit: A trivia-type game for the classroom. *Teaching of Psychology, 13*, 91.

Benjamin, L. T., Jr. (1979) . Instructional strategies in the history of psychology. *Teaching of Psychology, 6*, 15-17.

Berrenberg, J. L. (1990). Integrative and goal-relevant essay questions for history and systems courses. *Teaching of Psychology, 17*, 113-115.

Brožek, J., & Schneider, L. S. (1973). Second summer institute on the history of psychology. *Journal of the History of the Behavioral Sciences, 9*, 91-101.

Carlson, J. F. (1989) . Psychosexual pursuit: Enhancing learning of theoretical psychoanalytic constructs. *Teaching of Psychology, 16*, 82-84.

Coffield, K. E. (1973). Additional stimulation for students in history and systems. *American Psychologist, 28,* 624-625.

Dodd, D. K., & Leal, L. (1988). Answer justification: Removing the "trick" from multiple-choice questions. *Teaching of Psychology, 15,* 37-38.

Gurman, E. B., Holliman, W. B., & Camperell, K. (1988). Oral application questions as a teaching strategy. *Teaching of Psychology, 15,* 149-151.

McAdam, D. (1987). Bringing psychology to life. *Teaching of Psychology, 14,* 29-31.

Nield, A. F., & Wintre, M. G. (1986). Multiple-choice questions with an option to comment: Student attitudes and use. *Teaching of Psychology, 13,* 196-199.

Notes

Portions of this article were presented at the annual meeting of the American Psychological Association, Boston, MA, August 1990.

Expanding Coverage in the History Course by Toasting Significant but Often Overlooked Contributors

Randall D. Wight
Ouachita Baptist University

In teaching the history of psychology, one confronts the problem of covering much material in little time. The following activity attempts to familiarize students with a wider range of contributions to the discipline and to foster a contextual understanding of these contributions in a fashion that compresses both time and information.

I began by converting Zusne's (1984) "Appendix A: Chronological Listing by Birth Date" to a generic calendar of birth and death dates. Individuals recorded in the calendar were ones for whom Zusne recorded at least one precise date. Each week History of Psychology students (N = 8) received four to six names from the corresponding week's ensuing list of dates. "Toasting psychology," using coffee and cola, occurred during the first minutes of the following class meeting.

Participation was voluntary, and 1 extra credit point was available for each acceptable toast. An *acceptable toast* was one in which the student demonstrated a creative appreciation of a given individual's contribution; an *unacceptable toast* was one in which the student merely repeated textbook information. Students were to model Franklin Delano Roosevelt's toasting formula: "Be sincere, be brief, be seated." The campus library reserved biographical material (e.g., Gregory & Zangwill, 1987; Zusne, 1984) to help students obtain background information.

Although humorous toasts were encouraged, the guiding principle was to toast, not roast. Students were instructed to honor the accomplishments of contributors. Their toasts included: "Here's to Pinel, who lost his head saving the minds of others"; "Here's to Harlow, who had terry cloth with a monkey on its back"; "Here's to Brill, who got a thrill translating Freud." The students appeared to enjoy the exercise. Results from their semester-end evaluation of the activity confirmed this observation. On a scale ranging from *poor* (1) to *great* (10), students rated this activity as being worthwhile (M = 7.9, SD = 1.36). On a scale ranging from *ineffective* (1) to *effective* (10), students rated the technique to be efficacious in familiarizing them with the development of psychology (M = 7.0, SD = 2.14) and in facilitating their ability to verbalize information (M = 7.8, SD = 2.92).

The aforementioned salute to Brill serves to illustrate comments that an instructor may make following a student's toast. Brill came to New York in 1889 at the age of 15 to escape an intolerable homelife in his native Austria-Hungary. He struggled to put himself through New York University and the Columbia University medical school, often having to interrupt his education to earn money in order to continue that education. In 1907, Brill traveled for further medical study to Zurich where he became acquainted with the work of Freud. Intrigued with what he learned, Brill sojourned to Vienna to meet Freud.

Freud's influence changed Brill's life: Brill returned to New York and there became a principal advocate for psychoanalysis (Gay, 1988). It was Brill who first translated Freud's work into English, and therein lies an important point that an instructor may make following a toast to Brill. Brill's enthusiasm for psychoanalysis failed to prompt him to produce a careful translation of Freud's publications. Freud himself was apparently aware of Brill's inaccuracies and wrote, in 1928, to a Hungarian psychoanalyst that, "Of my *Interpretation of Dreams* there is, as far as I know, only one *English* [italics added] translation, that of Dr. Brill. It is, 1 suppose, best, if one wants to read the book at all, to read it in German" (Freud, quoted in Gay, 1988, p. 465). Students need to consider the influence of a translator on the understanding of a theory.

The technique has pitfalls. First, an instructor should provide an appropriate historical context for each individual presented. Failing to do so may perpetuate origin myths (see Samelson, 1974). Second, toasting is a social grace that is unfamiliar to most students. Some training in this custom (see Baldridge, 1978; Martin, 1983; Post, 1940) is often necessary. Third, students need prompting to generate unique toasts; otherwise, they may simply repeat what they read. Fourth, if the activity is voluntary, self-starters may benefit more than reserved students. Fifth, the exercise may be difficult to adapt to a large class.

Despite these drawbacks, there is much to commend this technique. First, and inherently countering the second stated disadvantage, students benefit from practice in public speaking. Second, students become acquainted with contributors to psychology who are often overlooked in the usual history of psychology course . Third, toasts may serve as ready-made mnemonic devices. Fourth, and perhaps more subtle, a kindling of the understanding of these historical figures as flesh-and-blood people may occur.

References

Baldridge, L. (1978). *The Amy Vanderbilt complete book of etiquette*. Garden City, NY: Doubleday.

Gay, P. (1988). *Freud: A life for our time*. New York: Doubleday.

Gregory, R. L., & Zangwill, O. L. (1987*). The Oxford companion to the mind*. Oxford: Oxford University Press.

Martin, J. (1983*). Miss Manners' guide for the turn-of-the-millennium*. New York: Pharos.

Post, E. (1940). *Etiquette: The blue book of social usage*. New York: Funk and Wagnalls.

Samelson, F. (1974). History, origin myth and ideology: "Discovery" of social psychology. *Journal for the Theory of Social Behavior, 4*, 217-231.

Zusne, L. (1984). *Biographical dictionary of psychology*. Westport, CT: Greenwood.

Notes

1. A version of this activity was presented in the Division Two Activities Exchange during the annual meeting of the American Psychological Association, New Orleans, August 1989.

2. Requests for a copy of the calendar should be sent to Randall D. Wight, Department of Psychology, Ouachita Baptist University, Arkadelphia, AR 71998-0001.

The Use of Slides in Class: A Demonstration of Incidental Learning

Alfred C. Raphelson
University of Michigan-Flint

Although considerable evidence supports the effectiveness of visual learning/teaching aids for promoting classroom learning, some controversy is still associated with their use. McKeachie (1978), for example, reviewed the research on the use of television, films, and other media and found that the evidence supports their use to achieve certain educational objectives. Their usefulness, however, depends on course objectives, characteristics of the students, and the quality of the materials.

Kulik, Kulik, and Cohen (1980) reviewed over 300 research articles on the classroom use of various types of instructional technology, including personalized, computer-based, and programmed instructions, as well as visual materials (slides, transparencies, and films). The studies they reviewed measured the effects of these technologies on learning outcomes, such as major class examinations, student ratings, and course completion. There was a general trend for such instructional technology to produce positive effects on the previously mentioned types of learning outcomes, but the outcomes varied with the type of instructional technology. Personalized systems of instruction produced the strongest results followed, in order, by computer-based instructions, programmed instruction, the auto-tutorial approach, and visual materials (slides, transparencies, and films).

The fact that visual aids appear to be the least effective of the instructional technologies is something of a surprise, given their long-standing popularity with many instructors. Benjamin (1981), for example, described ways to use slides in teaching History of Psychology that can add to the interest level and provide a change of pace. He suggested using slides in review sessions, and competitive recognition "game" situations add a dimension of "lively, friendly, fun" to the class (pp. 2-4).

Another study demonstrated that the ratings students gave the instructor and a course in Sensation and Perception increased significantly after slides were added (Beins, 1984). Students appreciated the contribution the slides made to their comprehension of the material and the break they provided from the usual lecture format.

I regularly use a large collection of slides in the History of Psychology course to illustrate biographical and historical events. These slides were made from journals, books, personal papers, as well as from visits to sites that have played a role in the lives of important psychologists and/or the history of the field. Like Benjamin, I believe that the slides add an important dimension to the class, but my evidence has always been anecdotal and intuitive. Many students have remarked that the slides are enjoyable and helped them to learn, but I had no direct evidence that they promote better learning.

An attempt was made to obtain more direct evidence that the slides promote the educational aims of the course rather than serving merely as an affective relief. The plan involved giving an unannounced Slide Recognition Test with the final examination and correlating the scores with each of the content examinations given during the course.

The slides were presented during the course as supplements to the lectures. The purpose was to make biographical, cultural, or theoretical points more concrete. The students understood that they would not be responsible for knowing any of the slides and that they would not be tested on slide recognition in any way that affected their grades. Therefore, any purposeful learning of the slides would not improve their grades.

During the semester, two essay exams were given over portions of the course; a comprehensive final exam consisted of objective questions. A total score was obtained by transforming the three exam scores into standard scores and summing them for each student. In determining the total score, the final exam was weighted 10% more than the scores on the two 1-hr exams.

When students arrived to take the 2½-hr final exam, they were told that after working on the exam for 1 hr, they would be interrupted in order to take the Slide Recognition Test. None of them appeared to be disturbed by this 5-min interruption. They were also told that, although they would be asked to put their names on the answer sheets, their names would not be seen until after their course grades were determined and recorded.

At the appropriate time, each slide was projected on the screen for 15 sec. Out of almost 1,000 slides shown during the semester, 20 were chosen as representing the content of the course and as being more unusual than the others. Eight slides were selected from material covered on the first exam, eight from the material covered on the second exam, and four from the shorter period between the second exam and the final.

The following is a description of the selected slides: S. Freud; Thorndike's Puzzle Box; Charcot in his clinic; Fechner having his "insight" on October 22, 1850 (a drawing); Clever Hans, the calculating horse; William James walking in the country; Anna O. (Bertha Pappenheim); Socrates's Death (Painting); map of Michigan highlighting Sickles, Michigan (C. Hull's boyhood home); C. Darwin; E. B. Titchener in his academic gown; Pavlov; Margaret Washburn; group picture taken during Freud's visit to Clark University in 1909; Wundt and his assistants; memorial to Pavlov's work; Jeremy Bentham icon; J. B. Watson; house in Fenton, Michigan where J. Dewey was married; urn containing Freud's ashes.

The identical procedure was followed in two different classes separated by 1 year. The first class had 27 students and the second had 50 students. Separate correlational analyses conducted for each class showed identical significant relationships. Because each exam score was transformed into a standard score, similar exams in each class were combined for the analyses reported here. Results are presented in Table 1.

Table 1. Correlations Between Examination Scores and Slide Recognition Test Scores

N = 77	Exam 2	Final Exam	Slide Recognition
Exam 1	.71*	.74*	.60*
Exam 2		.72*	.47*
Final exam			.70*

*p < .01.

All the correlations are statistically significant (Meredith, 1967). The correlation between the Slide Recognition Test and the final exam (.70) is of the same order as the correlations between the first and second exams and the final exam (.74 and .72, respectively). Therefore, the inference can be drawn that although the slides were presented during the course as incidental to the specific material to be learned, they were not perceived by the students as irrelevant. The better students recognized more slides than did the students who performed less well on the examinations.

The point may be raised that the obtained correlations between the examination scores and the Slide Recognition Scores were mediated by other variables (e.g., class attendance). That observation is probably correct. Students could not recognize a slide if they were not present when it was shown. But it is also true that class attendance plays some role in exam performance per se, especially in a lecture class like this one.

The purpose of the study was consistent with our observations. Its intent was to determine if slides presented as part of a class but labeled in presentation as only incidental to grade outcome would be related to such performance in the final analysis. If so, the inference could be drawn that slides can be considered to belong with such variables as intelligence, class attendance, previous course experience, and socioeconomic status, which have been shown to affect academic performance.

This study does not, of course, provide direct evidence that slides helped the students to learn the course material better. It does demonstrate, however, that the better students learn and recognize more of the slides even though they have been presented as only incidental to the course goals. At the very least, this result indicates that using slides does not interfere with the class learning nor is it irrelevant to it. At the very best, it is consistent with the hypothesis that these techniques contribute to learning.

References

Beins, B. (1984). The use of slides in psychology classes: Do they help or are they an invitation to sleep? *Teaching of Psychology, 11*, 229-230.

Benjamin, L. T., Jr. (1981*). Teaching history of psychology: A handbook*. New York: Academic.

Kulik, C. C., Kulik, J. A., & Cohen, P. A. (1980). Instructional technology and college teaching. *Teaching of Psychology, 7*, 199-205.

McKeachie, W. J. (1978). *Teaching tips: A guidebook for the beginning college teacher* (7th ed.). Lexington, MA: Heath.

Meredith, W. M. (1967). *Basic mathematical and statistical tables for psychology and education*. New York: McGraw-Hill.

Note

The research for this project was supported in part by a grant from the Faculty Development Fund of The University of Michigan-Flint.

3. DISCOVERING PHILOSPHIES OF PSYCHOLOGY

Students' Basic Philosophical Assumptions in History of Psychology: A Measure and Teaching Tool

Brian D. Cox
Hofstra University

A history of psychology course can be a student's first encounter with notions such as determinism, mind-body issues, positivism, philosophy of science, or even the accepted theories of evolution. Most undergraduate students take the course late in their college careers, and for many, it is difficult to recognize and discuss the organizing principles that unite the varied subfields discussed in prior classes. Moreover, good students often come to the course having learned a considerable amount of psychology, yet knows little of where it fits in the European and North American intellectual traditions.

Basic philosophical issues, of course, animated the thinking of most prominent figures in the history of psychology. Kuhn (1962) suggested that a community of scientists must take such philosophical stands early in its preparadigmatic phases, if only to position itself dialectically against other schools competing for priority in the science. As recommended by Hart (1986), my course is structured around several Kuhnian premises: (a) Science, particularly early psychology, is a social enterprise; (b) scientific revolutions occur by paradigm shifts in world view; and (c) for much of its history, psychology was a preparadigmatic science, when different schools began from different philosophical premises, accepted different data as valid, and came to different conclusions.

The Measure

How, then, does one take serious yet philosophically unso-phisticated students and introduce them to such complex notions in a way that will engage them and provide a frame. work for the semester? I administer a questionnaire during the 1st week of class that asks students to consider their own positions on these matters. This measure consists of 50 statements that characterize positions held by one or more philosophers, biologists, or psychologists covered in the course. The statements cover the paradigm shifts from supernatural causation to materialism (e.g., "A supreme being guides evolution toward a purposeful end"); creationism to evolutionism, including recapitulationist and Lamarckian variants (e.g.,

"One can see in the fetus and infants the earlier stages of evolution"); and subjective introspection to positivism and back (e.g., "Observations of the workings of one's own mental life are valid data for psychology"). In addition, the measure covers belief in various mind-body positions, determinism versus free will, the innate nature of humans, conceptions of the unconscious, and even (for comic relief) a statement of Wilhelm Fliess's nasogenital reflex hypothesis (see Sulloway, 1992). It contains one fact ("Humans are born with certain reflexes") for comparison's sake, to bring home the point that a fact is a hypothesis on which nearly everyone agrees. To discourage fence-sitting, students are asked to strongly agree, agree, disagree, or strongly disagree with each statement.

Procedure and Results

For the past three semesters, I administered this questionnaire during the 1st week of class, after introductory comments but before the lectures. The data represented here are the results of three yearly administrations, yielding 185 respondents. Most of the students were juniors or seniors, having taken five or more classes in psychology. Because the class sizes varied, the analyses used unweighted means. Items were scored from 1 (*strongly agree*) to 4 (*strongly disagree*).

A surprising feature of the data is the stability across years in the proportions of students who answered in the four response categories for each item. The simple correlations of the mean Likert scores across the three administrations are quite high (1991-1992, $r = .94$; 1992-1993, $r = .84$; 1991-1993, $r = .88$). The correlations suggest that the mean rankings of the 50 items between any 2 years remain relatively stable. Minimally, these correlations suggest that the distribution of agreements and disagreements on the questions is not an artifact of a particular class. However, more important, the use of this questionnaire makes possible a concrete illustration of Kuhn's (1962) idea that science is done by a community of practitioners who agree on certain principles. Specifically,

I suggest to my students that the stable pattern of agreements on the questions may constitute a paradigm under which Hofstra University psychology students operate, although it is impossible to know whether these responses are in any way typical of those of the national psychology undergraduate population. Of course, these correlations do not imply that there is no variability within the classes on a particular question any more than there is unanimity among members of a paradigm, but there is some commonality.

Given the high similarity of responses across years, scores were first averaged within years and then across years, to yield a single agreement score for each of the 50 items. Considering items that provoked strong agreement (low scores) or disagreement (high scores), it is no surprise that the one fact yielded the strongest agreement and lowest standard deviation ($M = 1.14$, $SD = 0.38$)—humans are agreed to have been born with reflexes. Second on the list of most agreed on notions, and thus approaching the status of a fact, is the acceptance of the "archaeological dig site" metaphor of the Freudian unconscious ($M = 1.63$, $SD = 0.62$). Students also believe that insight is important in learning ($M = 1.66$, $SD = 0.62$) but that behavior is appropriate data for psychology ($M = 1.71$, $SD = 0.59$). They agree or strongly agree with both the hierarchical and environment-specific characteristics of evolution ($M = 1.68$, $SD = 0.80$ and $M = 1.89$, $SD = 0.83$, respectively) but reject Lamarckism ($M = 3.19$, $SD = 0.92$). The students are split on their acceptance of recapitulation ($M = 2.73$, $SD = 0.95$) and also on whether evolution has a purpose or goal ($M = 2.57$, $SD = 0.98$). They accept that pleasure and pain ($M = 1.80$, $SD = 0.71$)—or innate ideas of them ($M = 1.72$, $SD = 0.82$)—motivate human behavior. They are not strictly materialists ($M = 2.79$, $SD = 0.82$); many reject atheism ($M = 3.09$, $SD = 0.91$) and some believe in a scientifically inexplicable soul ($M = 2.23$, $SD = 1.05$). Their dualism is both spiritual and psychophysical: They tend, on average, to disagree somewhat with the statement that the mind can be explained by neurochemistry ($M = 2.79$, $SD = 0.82$) and disagree that the concepts of the conscious and the unconscious mind are "useless for psychology" ($M = 3.22$, $SD = 1.06$ and $M = 3.57$, $SD = 0.66$, respectively). The students are optimistic about fundamental human nature, believing people generally to be rational and good ($M = 1.87$, $SD = 0.71$). Finally, they reject the strange nasogenital concept of Wilhelm Fliess ($M = 3.54$, $SD = 0.66$), and Broca's hypothesis that brain size is correlated with intelligence comes in dead last ($M = 3.76$, $SD = 0.50$).

Use of the Measure in an Integrated Course

Teachers of history and systems courses often face two problems. First, there is a considerable amount of information to be covered, often concerning lesser known figures and themes (Wight, 1993). Second, deeper, underlying philosophical issues must be dealt with in an engaging and rigorous fashion (Waller, 1994). This measure is helpful in addressing both of these concerns because it provides an integrative reference set for the entire course and encourages a "personalization of knowledge" (Bruner, 1965, p. 1015), linking the students' own positions to more general debates and thereby increasing awareness of them. When I present the findings to the class, students discuss the data with interest and enthusiasm. I also refer to the items throughout the course, as examples of how science develops, at least from the Kuhnian point of view. For example, we discuss the social process of accepting scientific research through peer review, as a way of emphasizing Kuhn's (1962) point that normal science is practiced by a community of scholars enforcing agreement on certain principles. We also note the importance of examining history of science from both "presentist" and "historicist" positions (Stocking, 1965), in order for the students to recognize the difference between rival paradigms as the practitioners saw them, rather than as recent sources often modify them to conform to the current paradigm. Then, through an assignment to compare textbooks on the same subject at least 20 years apart, students can see not only that data have accumulated but also that shifts can occur over time in what data are deemed important. Moreover, students discover that textbooks can distort information over time, in part because of those differences in emphasis (e.g., Harris, 1979, suggested that distortions in textbook accounts of Watson & Rayner's Little Albert experiment were possibly motivated by a desire to emphasize the positive aspects of "the science of behavior" that psychology became). I hope that these lessons enhance students' awareness that assumptions of time, place, and the values of the scientific (or nonscientific) community can easily influence what data will be gathered and how they will be interpreted.

I also randomly assign students to write papers on lesser known but important figures in philosophy, biology, or psychology (e.g., Alexander Bain, Mary Calkins, Sir Ronald Fisher). After these papers have been compiled and printed in a book, students take this and other information and place it all in "maps of psychologists" arranged by time, lineage, school, or philosophy. Some students create annotated maps of over 100 figures; others do more in-depth surveys of the history of particular schools, or focus on women (see also Diekhoff, 1982, for a similar approach). Finally, the students see the assumptions measure once again at the end of the course and are asked to name at least one figure from all of these sources who held that belief for each of the 50 items. By this time, over 90% of the students can give at least one correct name for each statement, and many students can provide several adherents for the more important statements on materialism, evolution, or consciousness. To students' credit, many do not need to find specific references to the figures' positions but can infer that theorists hold views from what they have read. Thus, students seem to have acquired a deeper knowledge of the subject and can frequently engage in surprisingly deep discussions of the underpinnings of psychology.

I do not use the assumptions questionnaire as an outcome measure—the point is not to effect a change in beliefs but to increase the awareness that all theories are based on assumptions. Those assumptions, in turn, may come from beliefs not too different from those of us in the surrounding culture and time. After all, psychology as a whole is a big tent, accepting a vast array of views, even if local orthodoxies are enforced by particular journals or organizations. In fact, students' eclectic beliefs mirror those of the field today. The centrality of behavior, thoughts, and unconscious motivation receive strong support from students, support that has remained stable over 3 years. As the science of psychology has matured, perhaps we as teachers and researchers have at least agreed to disagree about many of these issues and passed this tendency on to our students. Perhaps, following the thoughts of Kuhn (1962), ideological extremism is necessary only when the intellectual battles are being fought and extremism serves a dialectical purpose. After that, people can freely believe in both materialist evolution and the existence of a soul. Alternatively, the belief in behavior as evidence does not preclude belief in mind anymore. Although the data presented here suggest there is still strong adherence to some Freudian ideas (in a psychology department largely hostile to Freud), the psychologist that the typical student here most resembles (in belief if not in elegance of expression) appears to be William James: tolerant of religion, knowledgeable about evolution, skeptical of determinism, fundamentally dualist, and open to all information. The battles are less heated, but American functionalism appears alive and well among students.

References

Bruner, J. (1965). The growth of mind. *American Psychologist, 20,* 1007-1017.

Diekhoff, G. M. (1982). Cognitive maps as a way of presenting the dimensions of comparison within the history of psychology. *Teaching of Psychology, 9,* 115-116.

Harris, B. (1979). Whatever happened to Little Albert? *American Psychologist, 34,* 151-160.

Hart, J. J. (1986). A strategy for teaching the history and systems of psychology. *Teaching of Psychology, 13,* 67-69.

Kuhn, T. S. (1962). *The structure of scientific revolutions.* Chicago: University of Chicago Press.

Stocking, G. W. (1965). On the limits of "presentism" and "historicism" in the historiography of the behavioral sciences. *Journal of the History of the Behavioral Sciences, 1,* 211-218.

Sulloway, F. J. (1992). *Freud, biologist of the mind.* Cambridge, MA: Harvard University Press.

Waller, J. E. (1994). Philosophies of psychology: A discovery process for undergraduates. *Teaching of Psychology, 21,* 33-35.

Wight, R. D. (1993). Expanding coverage in the history course by toasting significant but often overlooked contributors. *Teaching of Psychology, 20,* 112.

Notes

1. I thank Charles Brewer, Stavros Valenti, Randolph A. Smith, and three anonymous reviewers for many helpful comments.
2. Requests for copies of the questionnaire, data, and syllabi, should be sent to Brian Cox, Department of Psychology, 127 Hofstra University, Hempstead, NY 11550; e-mail: psybdc@hofstra.edu.

Philosophies of Psychology: A Discovery Process for Undergraduates

James E. Waller
Whitworth College

Hilgard (1987) asserted that many of the distinctions among psychological theories and theorists can be discerned by oversimplifications in which one classifies, compares, and evaluates the theories and theorists by their stands on major polarities (e.g., empiricism vs. rationalism). Watson (1971) further affirmed that psychologists construct their disciplinary worldviews or personal philosophies of psychology using these polarities. This article describes five pedagogical strategies to help students begin to discover their philosophies of psychology.

During the past 5 years, these strategies have been used with notable success in a sophomore-level history of psychology course. My department places this course in the sophomore year to introduce students to the ideas and personalities they will encounter throughout the major. My aim in the course is to engage students at a level of ideas beyond the passive recording of names, dates, and events.

These pedagogical techniques require a lot from students, but they also reveal a lot to students about their reflective and philosophical capacities. I do not mean to imply that students' responses to these methods are sophisticated or mature, but I contend that they give students a vision of their cognitive potential and scholarly selves. Understood in this light, these strategies should be useful for history of psychology courses taught at any level.

Microtheme Assignments

The practice of writing to learn has received escalating attention in the undergraduate curriculum. As Zinsser (1988) suggested, writing facilitates learning by organizing and clarifying one's thoughts. By writing about a subject, one reasons one's way to what it means. This approach presupposes that writing is used to gain, not just display, learning. In other words, writing is not viewed as simply a product of learning but as part of the process of learning.

One in-class writing assignment is the contemplative essay, muse, or "I search" assignment (Walvoord, 1992). In this article, I propose short, in-class, contemplative essays (microthemes) assignments, based on the polarities of psychology, to guide students in clarifying their personal philosophies of psychology.

I present the competing viewpoints of a selected polarity in one ½ hr of the class session to focus the students on a specific thematic point. I ensure that the presented polarity corresponds, as nearly as possible, with that session's lecture focus and previously assigned readings from primary sources. Table 1 (adapted from Hilgard, 1987, and Watson, 1971), although not reflecting an exhaustive list of the course content, specifies eight prominent polarities and their corresponding lecture foci.

After having an opportunity to ask me questions, students spend 10 to 15 min writing their personal position on that polarity. Students are asked to write for an audience of their peers in psychology. This instruction alleviates the anxiety of writing for a critical instructor while giving the students a central communicative purpose of writing to a specific audience. Generally, the in-class versions of the microthemes are 2 to 3 paragraphs long.

Consistent with descriptions of similar in-class writing assignments (see Zinsser, 1988), the liabilities of grammatical errors and impulsive reactions to profound philosophical questions are offset by the increase in student involvement with the ideas. The striking pedagogical benefit of the inclass microthemes is precisely this capacity to move the student from passively recording into actively and immediately engaging the polarity.

Credit is determined by the percentage of completed microthemes. To receive full credit, students must complete seven of the eight assigned microthemes. This policy allows students to miss one assignment because of an unforeseen class absence, but excessive absences (excused or unexcused) or uncompleted microthemes result in a substantial loss of credit.

Follow-Up Strategies

Writing Samples

At the next class session, I return the microthemes and read selected writing samples. My experience concurs with Walvoord's (1992) assertion that presenting at least one writing sample, even if only a sentence or phrase, from each student over the course of the semester has striking motivational effects.

Peer Debates

Generally, four polarities generate enough diversity of opinion (see Table 1) to warrant using 10 min of the next class session for peer debates. For these debates, each student is matched with a peer who holds a contrasting opinion on this specific polarity. In these matched dyads, each student provides a brief verbal summary of his or her position. Following these summaries, students are instructed to explore possible logical inconsistencies or faulty reasoning in their partner's position.

Predictably, students initially are reluctant to engage in such open cross-examination of peers' positions. Over the semester, however, students learn that this feedback, in an informal and relatively non-threatening setting, enables them to clarify their thinking and to discover some of their implicit worldview presuppositions.

Table 1. Prominent Polarities and Corresponding Lecture Foci

Polarities	Lecture Foci
Naturalism vs. supernaturalism	Pre-Socratics
Molecular vs. molar	Democritus (Pre-Socratic)
Rationalism vs. empiricism[a]	Plato and Aristotle
Deductivism vs. inductivism	Plato and Aristotle
Mind vs. body[a]	St. Thomas Aquinas
	René Descartes
	George Berkeley
	John B. Watson
Nature vs. nurture[a]	Immanuel Kant
	John Locke
Conscious mentalism vs. unconscious mentalism	Sigmund Freud
Determinism vs. free will[a]	B. F. Skinner
	Abraham Maslow

[a]These polarities are used in peer debates.

Reader-Based Responses

After peer debates, students spend 5 min providing critical responses to their matched partner's written microtheme. Students are encouraged to be sensitive to three levels of response. At one level, the response centers on their own reading experience. For example, the reader may say: "I was confused here . . . ." A second level of response involves diagnosis: "I was confused here because. . . ." A third level of response involves suggestions for remediation: "How about trying . . . ."

Consistent with the peer debates, informal observation suggests that students initially are more comfortable focusing on the first two levels of response. Over the semester, however, students become increasingly more

willing to offer suggestions for remediation. Some of this increased willingness is simply a function of greater familiarity with peers. I believe another significant component, however, is my constant reminder of Zinsser's (1988) assertion that good writing is clear and understandable to the reader. This assertion reassures students that they are qualified to judge each other's writing. One comment from a recent class evaluation attests to the impact of this understanding "It's been good to realize that I don't have to be an English teacher to judge what good writing looks like." Peers' suggestions for remediation are not prescriptions; responsibility for corrections, due at the beginning of the next class session, still lies with the writer.

Although both of these examples of peer collaboration siphon away a significant amount of class time (15 min), Blevins-Knabe (1987) noted that a major advantage, perhaps offsetting the loss of formal instructional time, is that students get feedback about their ideas and writing from people other than the instructor. In addition, such peer collaboration creates a sense of community and shared responsibility for learning.

Critical Analysis Paper

The microthemes only partially promote the emerging awareness of one's personal philosophy of psychology. A more detailed critical analysis assignment offers an opportunity for intensive reexamination of selected microtheme polarities.

Assigned Paper

A critical analysis paper, written on a more formal level than the microthemes, involves four ideas: nature, nurture, determinism, and free will. These ideas address two of the basic questions of human nature that have concerned thinkers since the early Greeks (Hunt, 1993): (a) Is human nature the result of inborn tendencies or of acquired experience? (b) How do we explain our past, present, and future behaviors?

Baird (1988) asserted that critical analysis is the ability to differentiate three levels of an idea. The "past" of an idea refers to (a) the historical antecedents that led a particular thinker(s) to the idea and (b) the logical presuppositions that must hold for the idea to be true. The "present" of an idea refers to the nonevaluative summary of an idea as it now stands. Finally, the "future" of an idea refers to the implications that follow from a given idea. A thorough critical analysis allows one to show the connections among these levels. It also allows one to compare and contrast differing ideas at any or all of the three levels.

Initially, students address the past, present, and future of each of the four ideas. They focus on one influential thinker (preferably a psychologist) in the historical antecedents portion of the paper. In the present segment, they summarize the idea as espoused by this thinker. In the future section, they explore the implications of this idea for psychology.

In the second section of the assignment, students compare and contrast separately the two polarities of (a) nature versus nurture and (b) determinism versus free will. The comparisons focus on the logical presuppositions and implications of the ideas.

In the final section, students reexamine their individual positions on the two polarities. Their endorsement of a particular idea is not based on the historical antecedents or representatives of that idea or on the nonevaluative summary of that idea. Rather, their endorsement is specifically aimed at the logical presuppositions and/or implications of the idea. To reassure students that they do not need to agree with my position on the polarities, I emphasize that evaluation will center on the logical consistency, reliable reasoning, and coherent presentation of the stated agreement or disagreement. This assurance seems effective as the majority of student responses do not conform to my positions.

The traditional grading requirements for this paper are clearly time-intensive for the instructor. For those interested in alternative grading procedures, Madigan and Brosamer (1991) offered a helpful introduction to holistic grading of written work. In holistic grading, the grader places a writing sample in one of a small number of descriptive categories (weighted by content and writing skill) based on the grader's overall impression of the work (see White, 1985).

Student Responses

Formal evaluations from one class revealed that students judged the pedagogical strategies as equally effective in addressing the objectives of the course (see Table 2). More informal student responses have established three notable benefits. First, students enthusiastically have confirmed the importance of their emerging cognitive and philosophical self-awareness that came from their examination of these ideas. For example, one commented, "The class on a whole was extremely interesting. The critical analysis paper that was required helped me a lot in clearing up my opinions." Second,

Table 2. Mean Responses to Pedagogical Strategies

Pedagogical Strategy	Response
Lecture	1.3
Assigned readings	1.4
Microtheme assignments	1.4
Writing samples	1.5
Peer debates	1.2
Reader-based responses	1.5
Critical analysis paper	1.1

Note. Mean responses ($N = 36$) reflect reactions to the following statement: "Please evaluate the effectiveness of each of the following activities as an educational strategy in addressing the objectives of this course." Responses to this statement were rated on a 5-point scale ranging from *very effective* (1) to *very ineffective* (5).

informal comments from students who have completed the course years earlier attest to how this increased understanding facilitates the discernment of differences between theorists and theories in the remainder of their major curriculum. Finally, these assignments make it clear to students that knowledge of course content may not be divorced from style, clarity, and rationality of expression.

References

Baird, F. (1988). Critical analysis papers. *American Philosophical Association Newsletter on Teaching Philosophy, 8*, 11-13.

Blevins-Knabe, B. (1987). Writing to learn while learning to write. *Teaching of Psychology, 14*, 239-241.

Hilgard, E. R. (1987). *Psychology in America: A historical survey.* Orlando, FL: Harcourt Brace.

Hunt, M. (1993). *The story of psychology.* New York: Doubleday.

Madigan, R. J., & Brosamer, J. J. (1991). Holistic grading of written work in introductory psychology Reliability, validity, and efficiency. *Teaching of Psychology, 18*, 91 -94.

Walvoord, B. E. (1992). *Writing across the curriculum.* (Available from B. E. Walvoord, Whitworth College, Spokane, WA 99251-0706)

Watson, R. I. (1971). Prescriptions as operative in the history of psychology. *Journal of the History of the Behavioral Sciences, 7*, 311-322.

White, E. M. (1985). *Teaching and assessing writing.* San Francisco: Jossey-Bass.

Zinsser, W. (1988). *Writing to learn.* New York: Harper & Row.

Table - Volume 1

Articles	Topics												
	1	2	3	4	5	6	7	8	9	10	11	12	13
Section I: Introductory													
1. Promoting Active Learning and Discussion													
Wesp, R.	P												
Buskist, W., & Wylie, D.	P												
Osberg, T. M.	P												S
Renner, M. J., & Mackin, R. S.	P									S	S	S	S
2. Learning Psychological Terminology													
Brothen, T., & Schneider, J.	P												
Carney, R. N., & Levin, J. R.	P												
3. Introducing Research and Scientific Thinking													
Bates, J. A.	P												
Ward, R. A., & Grasha, A. F.	P												
Reinehr, R. C.	P									S			
Fish, T. A., & Fraser, I. H.	P												
Lutsky, N.	P												
Gareis, K. C.	P		S										
Carducci, B. J.	P		S									S	
Fisher, C. B., & Kuther, T. L.	P		S										
4. Using Supplemental Readings													
Appleby, D. C.	P												
Section II: Statistics													
1. Making Statistics Relevant													
Beins, B.	S	P	S										
Shatz, M. A.	S	P	S										
Weaver, K. A.		P	S										
2. Generating Data													
Thompson, W. B.		P	S										
Cake, L. J., & Hostetter, R. C.		P	S										
3. Teaching Concepts and Principles													
Dyck, J. L., & Gee, N. R.		P											
Zerbolio, D. J., Jr.		P											
Johnson, D. E.		P											
Karylowski, J.		P											
Johnson, D. E.		P											
Refinetti, R.		P											
Richardson, W. K., & Segal, D. M.		P											
Buck, J. L.		P											

Articles	1	2	3	4	5	6	7	8	9	10	11	12	13
4. Exploring Pedagogical Strategies													
Ware, M. E., & Chastain, J. D.		P											
Rogers, R. L.		P	S										
Oswald, P. A.		P	S										
Rossi, J. S.		P	S										
Low, J. M.		P											
Varnhagen, C. K., Drake, S. M, & Finley, G.	S	P	S	S	S	S	S	S	S	S	S	S	S
Section III: Research Methods													
1. Introducing Scientific Thinking													
Hatcher, J. W., Jr.	S		P										
Kohn, A.	S		P		S	S	S	S	S	S	S	S	S
Stadler, M. A.			P										
Marshall, M. J., & Linden, D. R.	S		P	S	S		S	S					
Polyson, J. A., & Blick, K. A.	S		P										
Johnson, D. E.	S		P										
Brems, C.	S		P										
McBurney, D. H.			P										
Wilson, T. L., & Hershey, D. A.			P										
2. Reviewing the Literature													
Lewis, L. K.	S		P	S	S	S	S	S	S	S	S	S	S
Baxter, P. M.	S		P	S	S	S	S	S	S	S	S	S	S
Poe, R. E.			P								S		
3. Teaching Research Ethics													
Beins, B. C.	S		P		S	S	S	S	S	S	S	S	S
Rosnow, R. L.			P										
Strohmetz, D. B., & Skleder, A. A.	S		P		S	S	S	S	S	S	S	S	S
Hubbard R. W., & Ritchie, K. L.			P										
Johnson, W. B., & Corser, R.			P										
Herzog, H. A.			P										
3. Teaching Research Design and Methods of Observation													
Vernoy, M. W.		S	P										
Zerbolio, D. J., Jr., & Walker, J. T.			P			S							
Stallings, W. M.			P										
Carr, J. E., & Austin, J.		S	P										
Herzog, H. A., Jr.			P			S	S	S	S	S				S
Krehbiel, D., & Lewis, P. T..	S		P	S	S	S	S	S	S	S	S	S	S
Zeren, A. S., & Makosky, V. P.			P								S		
Goldstein, M. D., Hopkins, J. R., & Strube, M. J.			P										S
4. Working in Groups													
Gibson, P. R, Kahn, A. S., & Mathie, V. A.			P										
Carroll, D. W.			P										
Plante, T. G.			P										
Newcomb, A. F., & Bagwell, C. L.	S		P		S	S	S	S					

Articles	Topics												
	1	2	3	4	5	6	7	8	9	10	11	12	13
5. Presenting Research Results													
Gore, P. A., Jr., & Camp, C. J.			P										
Baird, B. N.			P										
Ault, R. L.		S	P	S	S	S	S	S	S	S	S	S	S
Peden, B. F.			P	S	S	S	S	S	S	S	S	S	S
Addison, W. E.			P										
Froese, A. D., Gantz, B. S., & Henry, A. L.			P										
Marmie, W. R.			P										
Peden, B. F.	S		P	S	S	S	S	S	S	S	S	S	S
5. Using Computers													
Peden, B. F.			P										
Peden, B. F., & Steinhauer, G. D.			P										
Hovancik, J. R.			P										
Riniolo, T. C.		S	P										
6. Using Popular Media and Scholarly Publications													
Suter, W. N., & Frank, P.	S		P	S	S	S	S	S	S	S	S	S	S
Carkenord, D. M.			P										
Chamberlain, K.			P										
Pennington, H.			P	S	S	S	S	S	S	S	S	S	S
Connor-Greene, P. A.	S		P		S	S	S	S	S	S	S	S	S
7. Examining Miscellaneous Issues													
Dunn, D. S.		S	P										
Brockway, J. H., & Bryant, F. B.			P		S	S	S	S	S	S	S	S	S
Gibson, B.	S	S	P	S	S	S	S	S	S	S	S	S	S
Barber, N.			P		S		S						
Durso, F. T.			P										

Section IV: History

1. Promoting Active Participation													
Benjamin, L. T., Jr.				P									
Goodwin, C. J.	S	S	S	P	S	S	S	S	S	S	S	S	S
Henderson, B. B.	S	S	S	P	S	S	S	S	S	S	S	S	S
Rhoads, S. E., & Wight, R. D.				P									
Brooks, C. I.				P									
Simonton, D. K.				P									
2. Expanding Students' Knowledge													
Berrenberg, J. L., & Prosser, A.	S	S	S	P	S	S	S	S	S	S	S	S	S
Wight, R. D.				P									
Raphelson, A. C.	S	S	S	P	S	S	S	S	S	S	S	S	S
3. Discovering Philosophies of Psychology													
Cox, B. D.				P									
Waller, J. E.				P									

1	Introductory	8	Cognition
2	Statistics	9	Developmental
3	Research Methods	10	Personality
4	History	11	Abnormal
5	Physiological-Comparative	12	Clinical-Counseling
6	Perception	13	Social
7	Learning		

P = Primary   S = Secondary

Appendix - Volume 1

Introductory

Promoting Active Learning and Discussion
Wesp, R. (1992). *19*, 219-221.
Buskist, W., & Wylie, D. (1998). *25*, 203-205.
Osberg, T. M. (1993). *20*, 110-111.
Renner, M. J., & Mackin, R. S. (1998). *25*, 46-48.

Learning Psychological Terminology
Brothen, T., & Schneider, J. (1993). *20*, 186-187.
Carney, R. N., & Levin, J. R. (1998). *25*, 132-134.

Introducing Research and Scientific Thinking
Bates, J. A. (1991). *18*, 94-97.
Ward, R. A., & Grasha, A. F. (1986). *13*, 143-145.
Reinehr, R. C. (1991). *18*, 241-242.
Fish, T. A., & Fraser, I. H. (1993). *20*, 231-233.
Lutsky, N. (1986). *13*, 119-122.
Gareis, K. C. (1995). *22*, 233-235.
Carducci, B. J. (1996). *23*, 241-243.
Fisher, C. B., & Kuther, T. L. (1997). *24*, 172-175.

Using Supplemental Readings
Appleby, D. C. (1987). *14*, 172-174.

Statistics

Making Statistics Relevant
Beins, B. (1985). *12*, 168-169.
Shatz, M. A. (1985). *12*, 85-86.
Weaver, K. A. (1992). *19*, 178-179.

Generating Data
Thompson, W. B. (1994). *21*, 41-43.
Cake, L. J., & Hostetter, R. C. (1986). *13*, 210-212.

Teaching Concepts and Principles
Dyck, J. L., & Gee, N. R. (1998). *25*, 192-195.
Zerbolio, D. J., Jr. (1989). *16*, 207-209.
Johnson, D. E. (1986). *13*, 155-156.
Karylowski, J. (1985). *12*, 229-230.
Johnson, D. E. (1989). *16*, 67-68.
Refinetti, R. (1996). *23*, 51-54.
Richardson, W. K., & Segal, D. M. (1998). *25*, 297-299.
Buck, J. L. (1991). *18*, 46-47.

Exploring Pedagogical Strategies
Ware, M. E., & Chastain, J. D. (1991). *18*, 219-222.
Rogers, R. L. (1987). *14*, 109-111.
Oswald, P. A. (1996). *23*, 124-126.
Rossi, J. S. (1987). *14*, 98-101.
Low, J. M. (1995). *22*, 196-197.
Varnhagen, C. K., Drake, S. M, & Finley, G. (1997). *24*, 275-278.

Research Methods

Introducing Scientific Thinking
Hatcher, J. W., Jr. (1990). *17*, 123-124.
Kohn, A. (1992). *19*, 217-219.
Stadler, M. A. (1998). *25*, 205-206.
Marshall, M. J., & Linden, D. R. (1994). *21*, 230-232.
Polyson, J. A., & Blick, K. A. (1985). *12*, 52-53.
Johnson, D. E. (1996). *23*, 168-170.
Brems, C. (1994). *21*, 241-243.
McBurney, D. H. (1995). *22*, 36-38.
Wilson, T. L., & Hershey, D. A. (1996). *23*, 97-99.

Reviewing the Literature
Lewis, L. K. (1986). *13*, 38-40.
Baxter, P. M. (1986). *13*, 40-41.
Poe, R. E. (1990). *17*, 54-55.

Teaching Research Ethics
Beins, B. C. (1993). *20*, 33-35.
Rosnow, R. L. (1990). *17*, 179-181.
Strohmetz, D. B., & Skleder, A. A. (1992). *19*, 106-108.
Hubbard, R. W., & Ritchie, K. L. (1995). *22*, 64-65
Johnson, W. B., & Corser, R. (1998). *25*, 26-28.
Herzog, H. A. (1990). *17*, 90-94.

Teaching Research Design and Methods of Observation
Vernoy, M. W. (1994). *21*, 186-189.
Zerbolio, D. J., Jr., & Walker, J. T. (1989). *16*, 65-66.
Stallings, W. M. (1993). *20*, 165-167.
Carr, J. E., & Austin, J. (1997). *24*, 188-190.
Herzog, H. A., Jr. (1988). *15*, 200-202.
Krehbiel, D., & Lewis, P. T. (1994). *21*, 45-48.
Zeren, A. S., & Makosky, V. P. (1986). *13*, 80-82.
Goldstein, M. D., Hopkins, J. R., & Strube, M. J. (1994). *21*, 154-157.

327

Working in Groups

Gibson, P. R, Kahn, A. S., & Mathie, V. A. (1996). *23*, 36-38.

Carroll, D. W. (1986). *13*, 208-210.

Plante, T. G. (1998). *25*, 128-130.

Newcomb, A. F., & Bagwell, C. L. (1997). *24*, 88-95.

Presenting Research Results

Gore, P. A., Jr., & Camp, C. J. (1987). *14*, 243-244.

Baird, B. N. (1991). *18*, 27-29.

Ault, R. L. (1991). *18*, 45-46.

Peden, B. F. (1994). *21*, 38-40.

Addison, W. E. (1996). *23*, 237-238.

Froese, A. D., Gantz, B. S., & Henry, A. L. (1998). *25*, 102-105.

Marmie, W. R. (1994). *21*, 164-166.

Peden, B. F. (1991). *18*, 102-105.

Using Computers

Peden, B. F. (1987). *14*, 217-219.

Peden, B. F., & Steinhauer, G. D. (1986). *13*, 85-87.

Hovancik, J. R. (1986). *13*, 94-96.

Riniolo, T. C. (1997). *24*, 279-282.

Using Popular Media and Scholarly Publications

Suter, W. N., & Frank, P. (1986). *13*, 219-221.

Carkenord, D. M. (1994). *21*, 162-164.

Chamberlain, K. (1988). *15*, 207-208.

Pennington, H. (1992). *19*, 175-177.

Connor-Greene, P. A. (1993). *20*, 167-169.

Examining Miscellaneous Issues

Dunn, D. S. (1996). *23*, 38-40.

Brockway, J. H., & Bryant, F. B. (1998). *25*, 121-123.

Gibson, B. (1991). *18*, 176-177.

Barber, N. (1994). *21*, 228-230.

Durso, F. T. (1997). *24*, 54-56.

History

Promoting Active Participation

Benjamin, L. T., Jr. (1990). *17*, 97-100.

Goodwin, C. J. (1994). *21*, 91-93.

Henderson, B. B. (1995). *22*, 60-63.

Rhoads, S. E., & Wight, R. D. (1997). *24*, 36-38.

Brooks, C. I. (1985). *12*, 84-85.

Simonton, D. K. (1994). *21*, 169-171.

Expanding Students' Knowledge

Berrenberg, J. L., & Prosser, A. (1991). *18*, 167-169.

Wight, R. D. (1993). *20*, 112.

Raphelson, A. C. (1987). *14*, 103-105.

Discovering Philosophies of Psychology

Cox, B. D. (1997). *24*, 39-41.

Waller, J. E. (1994). *21*, 33-35.

Subject Index - Volume 1